Lecture Notes in Computer Science 2458

Edited by G. Goos, J. Hartmanis, and J. van Leeuwen

Springer
Berlin
Heidelberg
New York
Barcelona
Hong Kong
London
Milan
Paris
Tokyo

Maristella Agosti Costantino Thanos (Eds.)

Research and Advanced Technology for Digital Libraries

6th European Conference, ECDL 2002
Rome, Italy, September 16-18, 2002
Proceedings

Volume Editors

Maristella Agosti
Department of Information Engineering, University of Padua
Via Gradenigo 6/a, 35131 Padova, Italy
E-mail: maristella.agosti@unipd.it

Costantino Thanos
Istituto di Scienza e Tecnologie dell' Informazione (ISTI-CNR)
Area della Ricerca CNR di Pisa, Via G. Moruzzi 1, 56124 Pisa, Italy
E-mail: thanos@iei.pi.cnr.it

Cataloging-in-Publication Data applied for

Die Deutsche Bibliothek - CIP-Einheitsaufnahme

Research and advanced technology for digital libraries : 6th European conference ; proceedings / ECDL 2002, Rome, Italy, September 16 - 18, 2002. Maristella Agosti ; Costantino Thanos (ed.). - Berlin ; Heidelberg ; New York ; Hong Kong ; London ; Milan ; Paris ; Tokyo : Springer, 2002
(Lecture notes in computer science ; Vol. 2458)
ISBN 3-540-44178-6

CR Subject Classification (1998): H.3.7, H.2, H.3, H.4.3, H.5, J.7, J.1, I.7

ISSN 0302-9743
ISBN 3-540-44178-6 Springer-Verlag Berlin Heidelberg New York

Springer-Verlag Berlin Heidelberg New York
a member of BertelsmannSpringer Science+Business Media GmbH

http://www.springer.de

Printed in Germany

Typesetting: Camera-ready by author, data conversion by PTP-Berlin, Stefan Sossna e.K.
Printed on acid-free paper SPIN: 10871186 06/3142 5 4 3 2 1 0

Preface

ECDL 2002 was the 6th conference in the series of European Conferences on Research and Advanced Technologies for Digital Libraries. Following previous events in Pisa (1997), Heraklion (1998), Paris (1999), Lisbon (2000), and Darmstadt (2001), this year ECDL was held in Rome. ECDL 2002 contributed, together with the previous conferences, to establishing ECDL as the major European forum focusing on digital libraries and associated technical, practical, and social issues. ECDL 2002 continued the tradition already established by the previous conferences in meeting the needs of a large and diverse constituency, which includes researchers, practitioners, educators, policy makers, and users.

The focus of ECDL 2002 was on underlying principles, methods, systems, and tools to build and make available effective digital libraries to end users. Architecture, metadata, collection building, web archiving, web technologies, e-books, OAI applications, preservation, navigation, query languages, audio video retrieval, multimedia-mixed media, user studies and evaluation, humanities, and digital libraries were some of the key issues addressed.

An international Program Committee was set up composed of 61 members, with representatives from 25 countries. A total of 145 paper submissions, 15 poster submissions, and 18 proposals for demos were received. Each paper was evaluated by 3 referees and 42 full papers and 6 short papers of high quality were selected for presentation.

Besides paper presentations, the program also featured two invited talks by Hector Garcia Molina (Stanford University) and Derek Law (Strathclyde University), two panel discussions, and a poster and demo session. Moreover, tutorials and workshops conveniently arranged immediately before and after the conference extended the range of subjects and opportunities for exchange of knowledge and opinions offered by the conference.

We should like here to thank all those institutions and individuals who have made this conference possible: the organizing committee, CNR-IEI, the University of Padua and the Department of Information Engineering of the same university, the DELOS NoE, ESA, ICCU, Discoteca di Stato, Pontifical Gregorian University, the Italian Ministry for Cultural Heritage, the demo and poster chairpersons, the panel chairpersons, the workshop chairman, the tutorial chairpersons, the program committee members, the additional referees, the invited speakers, the tutorialists, the panelists, the poster presenters, the demonstrators, the sponsors, and of course all the participants.

During the preparation of the proceedings we received a great deal of help from Nicola Ferro and we thank him for this. The work for a conference like this starts at least two years before the conference happens, and during all this time Tarina Ayazi supported us. We thank her for her contribution to the success of the initiative.

July 2002 Maristella Agosti and Costantino Thanos

Organization

General Chair

Costantino Thanos (National Research Council, Italy)

Program Chair

Maristella Agosti (University of Padua, Italy)

Organization Chair

Pier Giorgio Marchetti (European Space Agency, Italy)

Organization Committee

Vittore Casarosa (National Research Council, Italy)
Marta Giorgi (Pontifical Gregorian University, Italy)
Maria Pia Mariani (Ministry for Cultural Heritage, Italy)
Giovanna Merola (Istituto Centrale per il Catalogo Unico, Italy)
M. Carla Sotgiu (Discoteca di Stato, Italy)

Demo and Poster Chairs

Edward Fox (Virginia Tech, USA)
Mike Papazoglou (University of Tilburg, The Netherlands)

Panel Chairs

Alan Smeaton (Dublin City University, Ireland)
Rachel Heery (UKOLN, UK)

Workshop Chair

Yannis Ioannidis (University of Athens, Greece)

Tutorial Chairs

Hans-Jorg Schek (ETH-Zurich, Switzerland)
Bruce Croft (University of Massachusetts, USA)

US Liaison Chair

Nick Belkin (Rutgers University, USA)

Publicity Chairs

Fillia Makedon (Dartmouth College, USA)
Simonetta Cheli (European Space Agency)

Treasurer

Ettore Ricciardi (National Research Council, Italy)

Program Committee

William Y. Arms (Cornell University, USA)
Daniel E. Atkins (University of Michigan, USA)
Paolo Atzeni (University of Roma 3, Italy)
Ricardo Baeza-Yates (University of Chile)
Thomas Baker (Fraunhofer Gesellschaft, Sankt Augustin, Germany)
Elisa Bertino (University of Milan, Italy)
Klemens Boehm (ETH Zurich, Switzerland)
Jose Borbinha (National Library of Portugal)
Stefano Ceri (Politecnico di Milano, Italy)
Ching-chih Chen (Simmons College, Boston, USA)
Hsinchun Chen (University of Arizona, USA)
Stavros Christodoulakis (University of Crete, Greece)
Panos Costantopoulos (FORTH, Crete, Greece)
Gregory Crane (Tufts University, Medford, USA)
Alberto Del Bimbo (University of Florence, Italy)
Werner A. Deutsch (Austrian Academy of Sciences)
Floriana Esposito (University of Bari, Italy)
Dieter Fellner (Technical University of Braunschweig, Germany)
Norbert Fuhr (University of Dortmund, Germany)
Wendy Hall (University of Southampton, UK)
Jane Hunter (The University of Queensland, Brisbane, Australia)
Peter Ingwersen (Royal School of Library and Information Science, Copenhagen, Denmark)
Leonid Kalinichenko (Russian Academy of Sciences)
Noriko Kando (National Institute of Informatics, Tokyo, Japan)
Judith Klavans (Columbia University, USA)
Jaana Kekalainen (University of Tampere, Finland)
Martin Kersten (National Research Institute for Mathematics and Computer Science, The Netherlands)
Traugott Koch (Lund University, Sweden)
Carl Lagoze (Cornell University, USA)

Ronald Larsen (University of Maryland, College Park, USA)
Clifford Lynch (Coalition for Networked Information, Washington, DC, USA)
Elizabeth Lyon (UKOLN, University of Bath, UK)
Gary Marchionini (University of North Carolina at Chapel Hill, USA)
Herman Maurer (University of Gratz, Austria)
Massimo Melucci (University of Padua, Italy)
Marc Nanard (LIRMM, Montpellier, France)
A. Desai Narasimhalu (National University of Singapore)
Erich Neuhold (Fraunhofer Gesellschaft - IPSI, Germany)
Bo Ohrstrom (Danish National Library Authority)
Andreas Paepcke (Stanford University, USA)
Michael Papazoglou (Tilburg University, The Netherlands)
Carol Peters (Italian National Research Council)
Berthier Ribeiro-Neto (Federal University of Minas Gerais, Brazil)
Steve Robertson (MS Research, Cambridge, UK)
Chris Rusbridge (University of Glasgow, UK)
Rudi Schmiede (Technische Universitat Darmstadt, Germany)
Fabrizio Sebastiani (Italian National Research Council)
Timos Sellis (National Technical University of Athens, Greece)
Maria Sliwinska (Nicholas Copernicus University, Poland)
Alan Smeaton (Dublin City University, Ireland)
Terrence R. Smith (University of California, Santa Barbara, USA)
Ingeborg Solvberg (Norwegian University of Science and Technology, Trondheim, Norway)
Shigeo Sugimoto (University of Library and Information Science, Tsukuba, Japan)
Elaine G. Toms (Faculty of Information Studies, University of Toronto, Canada)
Keith van Rijsbergen (University of Glasgow, UK)
Howard Wactlar (Carnegie Mellon University, USA)
Stuart Weibel (Online Computer Library Center, USA)
Robert Wilensky (University of California, Berkeley, USA)
Robin Williams (IBM Almaden Research Center, San Jose, USA)
Ian H. Witten (University of Waikato, New Zealand)
Jerome Yen (The University of Hong Kong)

Additional Referees

Gianni Amati
Michela Bacchin
Maria Bruna Baldacci
Teresa M.A. Basile
Maria Carla Cavagnis Sotgiu
Theodore Dalamagas
Marco Degemmis
Maria de Lourdes da Silveira
Nicola Di Mauro
Koji Eguchi
Nicola Fanizzi
Dieter Fellner

Stefano Ferilli
Nicola Ferro
Ingo Frommholz
Jette Hyldegaard
Gerald Jäschke
Predrag Knezevic
Marcello L'Abbate
Birger Larsen
Patrick Lehti
Oriana Licchelli
Pasquale Lops
Anne Mahoney
Pier Giorgio Marchetti
Christian Mönch
Jocelyne Nanard
Jeppe Nicolaisen
Pasquale Pagano
Luca Pretto
Thomas Risse
Piet Seiden
Luciano Romero Soares Lima
Erik Thorlund Jepsen
Marco Zens

Table of Contents

Web Archiving

e-Book

Collection Building

Web Technologies

OAI Applications

Case Studies

Navigation/Query Language

Audio/Video Retrieval

Architecture I

IR

Architecture II

Evaluation

Multimedia/Mixed Media

Preservation/Classification/User Studies

Architecture III

Humanities

Demos and Posters

A First Experience in Archiving the French Web

S. Abiteboul[1,3], G. Cobéna[1], J. Masanes[2], and G. Sedrati[3]

[1] INRIA: Serge.Abiteboul@inria.fr, Gregory.Cobena@inria.fr
[2] BnF: Julien.Masanes@bnf.fr
[3] Xyleme: Gerald.Sedrati@xyleme.com

Abstract. The web is a more and more valuable source of information and organizations are involved in archiving (portions of) it for various purposes, e.g., the Internet Archive *www.archive.org*. A new mission of the French National Library (BnF) is the "dépôt légal" (legal deposit) of the French web. We describe here some preliminary work on the topic conducted by BnF and INRIA. In particular, we consider the acquisition of the web archive. Issues are the definition of the perimeter of the French web and the choice of pages to read once or more times (to take changes into account). When several copies of the same page are kept, this leads to versioning issues that we briefly consider. Finally, we mention some first experiments.

1 Introduction

Since 1537[1], for every book edited in France, an original copy is sent to the Bibliothèque nationale de France (French National Library - BnF in short) in a process called *dépôt légal*. The BnF stores all these items and makes them available for future generations of researchers. As publication on the web increases, the BnF proposes providing a similar service for the French web, a more and more important and valuable source of information. In this paper, we study technical issues raised by the legal deposit of the French web. The main differences between the existing legal deposit and that of the web are the following:

1. the number of content providers: On the web, anyone can publish documents. One should compare, for instance, the 148.000 web sites in ".fr" (as of 2001) with the 5000 traditional publishers at the same date.
2. the quantity of information: Primarily because of the simplicity of publishing on the web, the size of content published on the French web is orders of magnitude larger than that of the existing legal deposit and with the popularity of the web, this will be more and more the case.
3. the quality: Lots of information on the web is not meaningful.
4. the relationship with the editors: With legal deposit, it is accepted (indeed enforced by law) that the editors "push" their publication to the legal deposit. This "push" model is not necessary on the web, where national libraries can themselves find relevant information to archive. Moreover, with the relative freedom of publication, a strictly push model is not applicable.

[1] This was a decision of King François the 1st.

M. Agosti and C. Thanos (Eds.): ECDL 2002, LNCS 2458, pp. 1–15, 2002.

5. updates: Editors send their new versions to the legal deposit (again in push mode), so it is their responsibility to decide when a new version occurs. On the web, changes typically occur continuously and it is not expected that web-masters will, in general, warn the legal deposit of new releases.
6. perimeter: The perimeter of the classical legal deposit is reasonably simple, roughly *the contents published in France.* Such notion of border is more delusive on the web.

For these reasons, the legal deposit of the French web should not only rely on editors "pushing" information to BnF. It should also involve (because of the volume of information) on complementing the work of librarians with automatic processing.

There are other aspects in the archiving of the web that will not be considered here. For instance, the archiving of sound and video leads to issues of streaming. Also, the physical and logical storage of large amounts of data brings issues of long term preservation. How can we guarantee that terabytes of data stored today on some storage device in some format will still be readable in 2050? Another interesting aspect is to determine which services (such as indexing and querying) should be offered to users interested in analyzing archived web content. In the present paper, we will focus on the issue of obtaining the necessary information to properly archive the web.

The paper describes preliminary works and experiments conducted by BnF and INRIA. The focus is on the construction of the web archive. This leads us to considering issues such as the definition of the perimeter of the French web and the choice of pages to read one or more times (to take changes into account). When several copies of the same page are kept, this also leads to versioning issues that we briefly consider. Finally, we mention some first experiments performed with data provided by Xyleme's crawls of the web (of close to a billion pages).

In Section 2, we detail the problem and mention existing work on similar topics. In Section 3, we consider the building of the web archive. Section 4 deals with the importance of pages and sites that turn out to play an important role in our approach. In Section 5, we discuss change representation, that is we define a notion of delta per web site that we use for efficient and consistent refresh of the warehouse. Finally we briefly present results of experiments.

2 Web Archiving

The web keeps growing at an incredible rate. We often have the feeling that it accumulates new information without any garbage collection and one may ask if the web is not self-archiving? Indeed, some sites provide access to selective archives. On the other hand, valuable information disappears very quickly as community and personal web pages are removed. Also the fact that there is no control of changes in "pseudo" archives is rather critical, because this leaves room for revision of history. This is why several projects aim at archiving the web. We present some of them in this section.

2.1 Goal and Scope

The web archive intends providing future generations with a representative archive of the cultural production (in a wide sense) of a particular period of Internet history. It may be used not only to refer to well known pieces of work (for instance scientific articles) but also to provide material for cultural, political, sociological studies, and even to provide material for studying the web itself (technical or graphical evolution of sites for instance). The mission of national libraries is to archive a wide range of material because nobody knows what will be of interest for future research. This also applies to the web. But for the web, exhaustiveness, which is required for traditional publications (books, newspapers, magazines, audio CD, video, CDROM), can't be achieved. In fact, in traditional publication, publishers are actually filtering contents and an exhaustive storage is made by national libraries from this filtered material. On the web, publishing is almost free of charge, more people are able to publish and no filtering is made by the publishing apparatus. So the issue of selection comes again but it has to be considered in the light of the mission of national libraries, which is to provide future generations with a large and representative part of the cultural production of an era.

2.2 Similar Projects

Up to now, two main approaches have been followed by national libraries regarding web archiving. The first one is to select manually a few hundred sites and choose a frequency of archiving. This approach has been taken by Australia [15] and Canada [11] for instance since 1996. A selection policy has been defined focusing on institutional and national publication.

The second approach is an automatic one. It has been chosen by Nordic countries [2] (Sweden, Finland, Norway). The use of robot crawler makes it possible to archive a much wider range of sites, a significant part of the surface web in fact (maybe 1/3 of the surface web for a country). No selection is made. Each page that is reachable from the portion of the web we know of will be harvested and archived by the robot. The crawling and indexing times are quite long and in the meantime, pages are not updated. For instance, a global snapshot of the complete national web (including national and generic domain located sites) is made twice a year by the royal library of Sweden. The two main problems with this model are: (i) the lack of updates of archived pages between two snapshots, (ii) the deep or invisible web [17,3] that can't be harvested on line.

2.3 Orientation of This Experiment

Considering the large amount of content available on the web, the BnF deems that using automatic content gathering method is necessary. But robots have to be adapted to provide a continuous archiving facility. That is why we have submitted a framework [13] that allows to focus either the crawl or the archiving, or both, on a specific subset of sites chosen in an automatic way. The robot is driven by parameters that are calculated on the fly, automatically and at a large scale. This allows us to allocate in an optimal manner the resources to crawling and archiving. The goal is twofold: (i) to cover a very large portion of the French web (perhaps "all", although all is an unreachable notion because of dynamic pages) and (ii) to have frequent versions of the sites, at least for a large number of sites, the most "important" ones.

It is quite difficult to capture the notion of importance of a site. An analogy taken from traditional publishing could be the number of in-going links to a site, which makes it a publicly-recognized resource by the rest of the web community. Links can be consider similar, to a certain extent of course, to bibliographical references. At least they give a web visibility to documents or sites, by increasing the probability of accessing to them (cf the random surfer in [5]). We believe that it is a good analogy of the public character of traditionally published material (as opposed to unpublished, private material for instance) and a good candidate to help driving the crawling and/or archiving process [13]. Some search engines already use importance to rank query results (like Google or Voila).

These techniques have to be adapted to our context, that is quite different. For instance, as we shall see, we have to move from a page-based notion of importance to a site-based one to build a coherent Web archive. (see Section 4). This also leads to exploring ways of storing and accessing temporal changes on sites (see Section 5) as we will no longer have the discrete, snapshot-type of archive but a more continuous one. To explore these difficult technical issues, a collaboration between BnF and INRIA started last year. The first results of this collaboration are presented here. Xyleme provided different sets of data needed to validate some hypothesis, using the Xyleme crawler developed jointly with INRIA. Other related issues, like the deposit and archiving of sites that can not be harvested online will not be addressed in this paper [12].

One difference between BnF's legal deposit and other archive projects is that it focuses on the French web. To conclude this section, we consider how this simple fact changes significantly the technology to be used.

2.4 The Frontier for the French Web

Given its mission and since others are doing it for other portions of the web, the BnF wants to focus on the French web. The notion of perimeter is relatively clear for the existing legal deposit (e.g, for books, the BnF requests a copy of each book edited by a French editor). On the web, national borders are blurred and many difficulties arise when trying to give a formal definition of the perimeter. The following criteria may be used:

- The French language. Although this may be determined from the contents of pages, it is not sufficient because of the other French speaking countries or regions e.g. Quebec. Also, many French sites now use English, e.g. there are more pages in English than in French in *inria.fr*.
- The domain name. Resource locators include a domain name that sometimes provides information about the country (e.g. *.fr*). However, this information is not sufficient and cannot in general be trusted. For instance

www.multimania.com is hosting a large number of French associations and French personal sites and is mostly used by French people. Moreover, the registration process for *.fr* domain names is more difficult and expensive than for others, so many French sites choose other suffixes, e.g. *.com* or *.org*.
- The *address* of the site. This can be determined using information obtainable from the web (e.g., from domain name servers) such as the physical location of the web server or that of the owner of the web site name. However, some French sites may prefer to be hosted on servers in foreign countries (e.g., for economical reasons) and conversely. Furthermore, some web site owners may prefer to provide an address in exotic countries such as Bahamas to save on local taxes on site names. (With the same provider, e.g., Gandi, the cost of a domain name varies depending on the country of the owner.)

Note that for these criteria, negative information may be as useful as positive ones, e.g., we may want to exclude the domain name *.ca* (for Canada).

The Royal library of Sweden, which has been archiving the Swedish Web for more than 6 years now, has settled on an inclusion policy based on national domain (.se and .nu), checking the physical address of generic domain name owners, and the possibility to manually add other sites. The distribution of the domain names is about 65 percent for nation domains (.se and .nu) and 25 percent for generic domains (.net, .com, .org).

Yet another difficulty in determining the perimeter is that the legal deposit is typically not very interested in commercial sites. But it is not easy to define the notion of commercial site. For instance, *amazon.fr* (note the ".fr") is commercial whereas *groups.yahoo.com/group/vertsdesevres/* (note the ".com") is a public, political forum that may typically interest the legal deposit. As in the case of the language, the nature of web sites (e.g., commercial vs. non commercial) may be better captured using the contents of pages.

No single criteria previously mentioned is sufficient to distinguish the documents that are relevant for the legal deposit from those that are not. This leads to using a multi-criteria based clustering. The clustering is designed to incorporate crucial information: the connectivity of the web. French sites are expected to be tightly connected. Note that here again, this is not a strict law. For instance, a French site on DNA may strongly reference foreign sites such as Mitomap (a popular database on the human mitochondrial genome).

Last but not least, the process should involve the BnF librarians and their knowledge of the web. They may know, for instance, that *00h00.com* is a web book editor that should be archived in the legal deposit.

Technical corner. The following technique is used. A crawl of the web is started. Note that sites specified as relevant by the BnF librarians are crawled first and the relevance of their pages is fixed as maximal. The pages that are discovered are analyzed for the various criteria to compute their *relevance* for the legal deposit. Only the pages believed to be relevant ("suspect" pages) are crawled. For the experiments, the BAO algorithm is used [1] that allows to compute page relevance on-line while crawling the web. The algorithm focuses the crawl to portions of the web that are evaluated as relevant for the legal deposit. This is in spirit of the XML-focused on-line crawling presented in [14], except that we use the multi-criteria previously described. The technique has the other advantage that it is not necessary to store the graph structure of the web and so it can be run with very limited resources. Intuitively, consider L the link matrix of the web (possibly normalized by out-degrees), and X the value vector for any page-based criteria. Then, $L * X$ represents a *depth-1* propagation of the criteria, and in general $L^n * X$ represents the propagation up to depth n. Note that the PageRank [5] is defined by the limit of $L^n * X$ when n goes to infinity. We are not exactly interested in PageRank, but only in taking into account some contribution of connectivity. Thus we define the vector value for a page as: $V = X + a_1 * L * X + a_2 * L^2 * X + a_3 * L^3 * X + ...$ Any distribution can be used for the sequence $a_1, a_2, ..., a_n$, as long as the sum converges. When the sequence decreases faster, the contribution of connectivity is reduced.

Since the same technology is used to obtain the *importance* of pages, a more detailed presentation of the technique is delayed to Section 3.

To conclude this section, we note that for the first experiments that we mention in the following sections, the perimeter was simply specified by the country domain name (*.fr*). We intend to refine it in the near future.

3 Building the Archive

In this section, we present a framework for building the archive. Previous work in this area is abundant [15,2,11], so we focus on the specificities of our proposal.

A simple strategy would be to take a snapshot of the French web regularly, say n times a year (based on available resources). This would typically mean running regularly a crawling process for a while (a few weeks). We believe that the resulting archive would certainly be considered inadequate by researchers. Consider a researcher interested in the French political campaigns in the beginning of the 21st century. The existing legal deposit would give him access to all issues of the *Le Monde* newspaper, a daily newspaper. On the other hand, the web archive would provide him only with a few snapshots of *Le Monde* web site per year. The researcher needs a more "real time" vision of the web. However, because of the size of the web, it would not be reasonable/feasible to archive each site once a day even if we use sophisticated versioning techniques (see Section 5).

So, we want some sites to be very accurately archived (almost in real-time); we want to archive a very extensive portion of the French web; and we would like to do this under limited resources. This leads to distinguishing between sites: the most important ones (to be defined) are archived frequently whereas others are archived only once in a long while (yearly or possibly never). A similar problematic is encountered when indexing the web [5]. To take full advantage of the bandwidth of the crawlers and of the storage resources, we propose a general framework for building the web archive that is based on a measure of importance for pages and of their change rate. This is achieved by adapting techniques presented in [14,1]. But first, we define intuitively the notion of importance and discuss the notion of web site.

Page importance. The notion of page importance has been used by search engines with a lot of success. In particular, Google uses an authority definition that has been widely accepted by users. The intuition is that a web page is important if it is referenced by many important web pages. For instance, Le Louvre's homepage is more important than an unknown person homepage: there are more links pointing to Le Louvre coming from other museums, tourist guides, or art magazines and many more coming from unimportant pages. An important drawback is that this notion is based strictly on the graph structure of the web and ignores important criteria such as language, location and also content.

3.1 Site vs. Page Archiving

Web crawlers typically work at the granularity of pages. They select one URL to load in the collection of URLs they know of and did not load yet. The most primitive crawlers select the "first" URL, whereas the sophisticated ones select the most "important" URL [5,14]. For an archive, it is preferable to reason at the granularity of web sites rather than just web pages. Why? If we reason at the page level, some pages in a site (more important than others) will be read more frequently. This results in very poor views of websites. The pages of a particular site would typically be crawled at different times (possibly weeks apart), leading to dangling pointers and inconsistencies. For instance, a page that is loaded may contain a reference to a page that does not exist anymore at the time we attempt to read it or to a page whose content has been updated[2].

For these reasons, it is preferable to crawl sites and not individual pages. But it is not straightforward to define a web site. The notion of web site loosely corresponds to that of editor for the classical legal deposit. The notion of site may be defined, as a first approximation, as the physical site name, e.g., *www.bnf.fr*. But it is not always appropriate to do so. For instance, *www.multimania.com* is the address of a web provider that hosts a large quantity of sites that we may want to archive separately. Conversely, a web site may be spread between several domain names: INRIA's website is on *www.inria.fr*, *www-rocq.inria.fr*, *osage.inria.fr*, *www.inrialpes.fr*, etc. There is no simple definition. For instance, people will not all agree when asked whether *www.leparisien.fr/news* and *www.leparisien.fr/shopping* are different sites or parts of the same site. To be complete, we should mention the issue of detecting mirror sites, that is very important in practice.

It should also be observed that site-based crawling contradicts compulsory crawling requirements such as the prevention of *rapid firing*. Crawlers typically

[2] To see an example, one of the authors (an educational experience) used, in the website of a course he was teaching, the URL of an HTML to XML wrapping software. A few months later, this URL was leading to a pornographic web site. (Domain names that are not renewed by owners are often bought for advertisement purposes.) This is yet another motivation for archives.

balance load over many websites to maximize bandwidth use and avoid over-flooding web servers. In contrast, we focus resources on a smaller amount of websites and try to remain at the limit of rapid firing for these sites until we have a copy of each. An advantage of this focus is that very often a small percentage of pages causes most of the problem. With site-focused crawling, it is much easier to detect server problems such as some dynamic page server is slow or some remote host is down.

3.2 Acquisition: Crawl, Discovery, and Refresh

Crawl. The crawling and acquisition are based on a technique [14] that was developed at INRIA in the Xyleme project. The web data we used for our first experiments was obtained by Xyleme [19] using that technology. It allows, using a cluster of standard PCs, to retrieve a large amount of pages with limited resources, e.g. a few million pages per day per PC on average. In the spirit of [7,8,14], pages are read based on their importance and refreshed based on their importance and change frequency rate. This results in an optimization problem that is solved with a dynamic algorithm that was presented in [14]. The algorithm has to be adapted to the context of the web legal deposit and site-based crawling.

Discovery. We first need to allocate resources between the discovery of new pages and the refreshing of already known ones. For that, we proceed as follows. The size of the French web is estimated roughly. In a first experiment using only ".fr" as criteria and a crawl of close to one billion of URLs, this was estimated to be about 1-2 % of the global web, so of the order of 20 millions URLs. Then the librarians decide the portion of the French web they intend to store, possibly all of it (with all precautions for the term "all"). It is necessary to be able to manage in parallel the discovery of new pages and the refresh of already read pages. After a stabilization period, the system is aware of the number of pages to read for the first time (known URLs that were never loaded) and of those to refresh.

It is clearly of interest to the librarians to have a precise measure of the size of the French web. At a given time, we have read a number of pages and some of them are considered to be part of the French web. We know of a much greater number of URLs, of which some of them are considered "suspects" for being part of the French web (because of the ".fr" suffix or because they are closely connected to pages known to be in the French web, or for other reasons.) This allows us to obtain a reasonably precise estimate of the size of the French web.

Refresh. Now, let us consider the selection of the next pages to refresh. The technique used in [14] is based on a cost function for each page, the penalty for the page to be stale. For each page p, $cost(p)$ is proportional to the importance of page $i(p)$ and depends on its estimated change frequency $ch(p)$. We define in the next subsection the importance $i(S)$ of a site S and we also need to define the "change rate" of a site. When a page p in site S has changed, the site has changed. The change rate is, for instance, the number of times a page changes per year. Thus, the upper bound for the change rate of S is $ch(S) = \sum_{p\ in\ S}(ch(p))$. For efficiency reasons, it is better to consider the average change rate of pages, in particular depending on the importance of pages. We propose to use a weighted average change rate of a site as:

$$\bar{ch}(S) = \frac{\sum_p ch(p) * i(p)}{\sum_p i(p)}$$

Our refreshing of web site is based on a cost function. More precisely, we choose to read next the site S with the maximum ratio:

$$\rho(S) = \frac{\theta(i(S), \bar{ch}(S), lastCrawl(S), currentTime)}{\text{number of pages in } S}$$

where θ may be, for instance, the following simple cost function:

$$\theta = i(S) * (currentTime - lastCrawl(S)) * \bar{ch}(S)$$

We divide by the number of pages to take into account the cost to read the site. A difficulty for the first loading of a site is that we do not know for new sites their number of pages. This has to be estimated based on the number of URLs we know of the site (and never read). Note that this technique forces us to compute importance at page level.

To conclude this section, we will propose a model to avoid such an expensive computation. But first we revisit the notion of importance.

3.3 Importance of Pages for the Legal Deposit

When discovering and refreshing web pages, we want to focus on those which are of interest for the legal deposit. The classical notion of importance is used. But it is biased to take into account the perimeter of the French web. Finally, the content of pages is also considered. A librarian typically would look at some documents and know whether they are interesting. We would like to perform such an evaluation automatically, to some extent. More precisely, we can use for instance the following simple criteria:

- **Frequent use of infrequent Words:** The frequency of words found in the web page is compared to the average frequency of such words in the French web[3]. For instance, for a word w and a page p, it is:

  $$I_w = \sum_{each\ word} \frac{f_{p,w}}{f_{web}} \quad \text{where} \quad f_{p,w} = n_{p,w}/N_p$$

  and $n_{p,w}$ is the number of occurrences of a word w in a page and N_p the number of words in the page. Intuitively, it aims at finding pages dedicated to a specific topic, e.g. butterflies, so pages that have some content.

[3] To guarantee that the most infrequent words are not just spelling mistake, the set of words is reduced to words from a French dictionary. Also, as standard, stemming is used to identify words such as *toy* and *toys*.

- **Text Weight:** This measure represents the proportion of text content over other content like HTML tags, product or family names, numbers or experimental data. For instance, one may use the number of bytes of French text divided by the total number of bytes of the document.

$$I_{pt} = \frac{size_{french\ words}}{size_{doc}}$$

Intuitively, it increases the importance of pages with text written by people versus data, image or other content.

A first difficulty is to evaluate the relevance of these criteria. Experiments are being performed with librarians to understand which criteria best match their expertise in evaluating sites. Another difficulty is to combine the criteria. For instance, *www.microsoft.fr* may have a high PageRank, may use frequently some infrequent words and may contain a fair proportion of text. Still, due to its commercial status, it is of little interest for the legal deposit. Note that librarians are vital in order to "correct" errors by positive action (e.g., forcing a frequent crawl of *00h00.com*) or negative one (e.g., blocking the crawl of *www.microsoft.fr*). Furthermore, librarians are also vital to correct the somewhat brutal nature of the construction of the archive. Note however that because of the size of the web, we should avoid as much as possible manual work and would like archiving to be as fully automatic as possible.

As was shown in this section, the quality of the web archive will depend on complex issues such as being able to distinguish the borders of a web site, analyze and evaluate its content. There are ongoing projects like THESU [6] which aim at analyzing thematic subsets of the web using classification, clustering techniques and the semantics of links between web pages. Further work on the topic is necessary to improve site discovery and classification

To conclude this section, we need to extend previously defined notions to the context of website. For some, it suffices to consider the site as a huge web document and aggregate the values of the pages. For instance, for *Frequent use of infrequent Words*, one can use:

$$I_w = \sum_{each\ word} \frac{f_{site}}{f_{web}} \quad \text{where } f_{S,w} = \sum_{p\ in\ S}(n_{p,w}) / \sum_{p\ in\ S}(N_p)$$

Indeed, the values on word frequency and text weight seem to be more meaningful at the site level than at the page level.

For page importance, it is difficult. This is the topic of next section.

4 Site-Based Importance

To obtain a notion of site importance from the notion of page importance, one could consider a number of alternatives:

- Consider only links between websites and ignore internal links;
- Define site importance as the sum of PageRank values for each page of the web site;

– Define site importance as the maximum value of PageRank, often corresponding to that of the site main page.

We propose in this section an analysis of site importance that will allow us to choose one notion.

First, observe that the notion of page importance is becoming less reliable as the number of dynamic pages increases on the web. A reason is that the semantics of the web graph created by dynamic pages is weaker than the previous document based approach. Indeed, dynamic pages are often the result of database queries and link to other queries on the same database. The number of incoming/outgoing links is now related to the size of the database and the number of queries, whereas it was previously a human artifact carrying stronger semantics. In this section, we present a novel definition of sites' importance that is closely related to the already known page importance. The goal is to define a site importance with stronger semantics, in that it does not depend on the site internal databases and links. We will see how we can derive such importance from this site model.

Page importance, namely PageRank in Google terminology, is defined as the fixpoint of the matrix equation $X = L * X$ [18,16], where the web-pages graph G is represented as a link matrix $L[1..n, 1..n]$. Let $out[1..n]$ be the vector of out-degrees. If there is an edge for i to j, $L[i, j] = 1/out[i]$, otherwise it is 0. We note $I_{page}[1..n]$ the importance for each page. Let us define a web-sites graph G' where each node is a web-site (e.g. *www.inria.fr*). The number of web-sites is n'. For each link from page p in web-site Y to page q in web-site Z there is an edge from Y to Z. This edges are weighted, that is if page p in site S is twice more important than page p' (in S also), then the total weight of outgoing edges from p will be twice the total weight of outgoing edges from p'. The obvious reason is that browsing the web remains page based, thus links coming from more important pages deserve to have more weight than links coming from less important ones. The intuition underlying these measures is that a web observer will visit randomly each page proportionally to its importance. Thus, the link matrix is now defined by:

$$L'[Y, Z] = \sum_{p \ in \ Y, \ q \ in \ Z} \frac{I_{page}[p]}{\sum_{p' \ in \ Y} I_{page}[p']} * L[p, q]$$

We note two things:

– If the graph G representing the web-graph is (artificially or not) strongly connected, then the graph G' derived from G is also strongly connected.
– L' is still a stochastic matrix, in that $\forall Y, \sum_Z L'[Y, Z] = 1$. (proof in appendix).

Thus, the page importance, namely PageRank, can be computed over G', L' and there is a unique fixpoint solution. We prove in appendix that the solution is given by:

$$I_{site}[Y] = \sum_{p \ in \ Y} I_{page}[p]$$

This formal relation between website based importance and page importance suggests to compute page importance for all pages, a rather costly task. However, it serves as a reference to define site-based importance, and helps understand its relation to page-based importance. One could simplify the problem by considering, for instance, that all pages in a website have the same importance. Based on this, the computation of site-importance becomes much simpler. In this case, if there is there is at least one page in Y pointing to one page in Z, we have $L'[Y, Z] = 1/out(Y)$, where $out(Y)$ is the out-degree of Y. A more precise approximation of the reference value consists in evaluating the importance of pages of a given website S on the restriction of G to S. Intuitively it means that only internal links in S will be considered. This approximation is very effective because: (i) it finds very good importance values for pages, that correspond precisely to the internal structure of the web-site (ii) it is cheaper to compute the internal page importance for all websites, one by one, than to compute the PageRank over the entire web (iii) the semantics of the result are stronger because it is based on site-to-site links.

This web-site approach enhances significantly previous work in the area, and we will see in next section how we also extend previous work in change detection, representation and querying to web sites.

5 Representing Changes

Intuitively, change control and version management are used to save storage and bandwidth resources by updating in a large data warehouse only the small parts that have changed [10]. We want to maximize the use of bandwidth, for instance, by avoiding the loading of sites that did not change (much) since the last time they were read. To maximize the use of storage, we typically use compression techniques and a clever representation of changes. We propose in this section a change representation at the level of web sites in the spirit of [9,10]. Our change representation consists of a **site-delta**, in XML, with the following features:

(i) Persistent identification of web pages using their URL, and unique identification of each document using the tuple (URL, date-of-crawl);

(ii) Information about mirror sites and their up-to-date status;

(iii) Support for temporal queries and browsing the archive

The following example is a **site-delta** for *www.inria.fr*:

```
<website url="www.inria.fr">
<page url="/index.html">
  <document date="2002-Jan-01" status="updated"
               file="543B6.html"/>
  <document date="2002-Mar-01" status="unchanged"
               file="543B6.html"/>
</page>
<page url="/news.html">
  <document date="2002-Mar-25" status="updated"
```

```
            file="543GX6.html"/>
  <document date="2002-Mar-24" status="error">
    <error httperror="404"/>
  </document>
  <document date="2002-Mar-23" status="updated"
            file="523GY6.html"/>
  ...
  <document date="1999-Jan-08" status="new"
            file="123GB8.html"/>
</page>
<mirror url="www-mirror.inria.fr" depth="nolimit">
  <exclusion path="/cgi-bin" />
</mirror>
</website>
```

Each web-site element contains a set of pages, and each page element contains a subtree for each time the page was accessed. If the page was successfully retrieved, a reference to the archive of the document is stored, as well as some metadata. If an error was encountered, the page status is updated accordingly. If the page mirrors another page on the same (or on another) web-site, the document is stored only once (if possible) and is tagged as a mirror document. Each web-site tree also contains a list of web-sites mirroring part of its content. The up-to-date status of mirror sites is stored in their respective XML file.

Other usages. The site-delta is not only used for storage. It also improves the efficiency of the legal deposit. In particular, we mentioned previously that the legal deposit works at a site level. Because our site-delta representation is designed to maintain information at page level, it serves as an intermediate layer between site-level components and page-based modules.

For instance, we explained that the acquisition module crawls sites instead of pages. The site-delta is then used to provide information about pages (last update, change frequency, file size) that will be used to reduce the number of pages to crawl by using caching strategies. Consider a news web site, e.g. *www.leparisien.fr/*. News articles are added each day and seldom modified afterwards, only the index page is updated frequently. Thus, it is not desirable to crawl the entire web site every day. The site-delta keeps track of the metadata for each pages and allows to decide which pages should be crawled. So it allows the legal deposit to virtually crawl the entire web site each day.

Browsing the archive. A standard first step consists in replacing links to the Internet (e.g. *http://www.yahoo.fr/*) by local links (e.g. to files). The process is in general easy, some difficulties are caused by pages using java-scripts (sometimes on purpose) that make links unreadable. A usual problem is the consistency of the links and the data. First, the web graph is not consistent to start; broken links, servers down, pages with out of date data are common. Furthermore, since pages are crawled very irregularly, we never have a true snapshot of the web.

The specific problem of the legal deposit is related to *temporal browsing*. Consider, for instance, a news web site that is entirely crawled every day. A user may arrive at a page, perhaps via a search engine on the archive. One would expect to provide him the means to browse through the web site of that day and also in time, move to this same page the next day. The problem becomes seriously more complex when we consider that all pages are not read at the same time. For instance, suppose a user reads a version t of page p and clicks on a link to p'. We may not have the value of page p' at that time. Should we find the latest version of p' before t, the first version after t, or the closest one? Based on an evaluation of the change frequency of p', one may compute which is the most likely to be the correct one. However, the user may be unsatisfied by this and it may be more appropriate to propose several versions of that page.

One may also want to integrate information coming from different versions of a page into a single one. For instance, consider the index of a news web site with headlines for each news article over the last few days. We would like to *automatically* group all headlines of the week into a single index page, as in Google news search engine [4]. A difficulty is to understand the structure of the document and to select the valuable links. For instance, we don't want to group all advertisements of the week!

6 Conclusion

As mentioned in the introduction, the paper describes preliminary work. Some experiments have already been conducted. A crawl of the web was performed and data is now being analyzed by BnF librarians. In particular, we analyze the relevance of page importance (i.e., PageRank in Google terminology). This notion has been to a certain extent validated by the success of search engines that use it. It was not clear whether it is adapted to web archiving. First results seem to indicate that the correlation between our automatic ranking and that of librarians is essentially as similar as the correlation between ranking by librarians.

Perhaps the most interesting aspect of this archiving work is that it leads us to reconsider notions such as web site or web importance. We believe that this is leading us to a better understanding of the web. We intend to pursue this line of study and try to see how to take advantage of techniques in classification or clustering. Conversely, we intend to use some of the technology developed here to guide the classification and clustering of web pages.

Acknowledgments. We would like to thank Laurent Mignet, Benjamin Nguyen, David Leniniven and Mihai Preda for discussions on the topic.

References

[1] S. Abiteboul, M. Preda, and G. Cobena. Computing web page importance without storing the graph of the web (extended abstract). In *IEEE Data Engineering Bulletin, Volume 25*, 2002.

[2] A. Arvidson, K. Persson, and J. Mannerheim. The kulturarw3 project - the royal swedish web archiw3e - an example of 'complete' collection of web pages. In *66th IFLA Council and General Conference*, 2000. www.ifla.org/IV/ifla66/papers/154-157e.htm.

[3] M.K. Bergman. The deep web: Surfacing hidden value. www.brightplanet.com/.

[4] Google. Google news search. http://news.google.com/.

[5] Google. www.google.com/.

[6] Maria Halkidi, Benjamin Nguyen, Iraklis Varlamis, and Mihalis Vazirgianis. Thesus: Organising web document collections based on semantics and clustering. Technical Report, 2002.

[7] T. Haveliwala. Efficient computation of pagerank. *Technical report, Stanford University*, 1999.

[8] H. Garcia-Molina J. Cho. Synchronizing a database to improve freshness. *SIGMOD*, 2000.

[9] R. Lafontaine. A delta format for XML: Identifying changes in XML and representing the changes in XML. In *XML Europe*, 2001.

[10] A. Marian, S. Abiteboul, G. Cobena, and L. Mignet. Change-centric management of versions in an XML warehouse. *VLDB*, 2001.

[11] L. Martin. Networked electronic publications policy, 1999 . www.nlc-bnc.ca/9/2/p2-9905-07-f.html.

[12] J. Masanes. Pr server les contenus du web. In *IVe journ es internationales d' tudes de l'ARSAG - La conservation l' re du num rique*, 2002.

[13] J. Masan s. The BnF's project for web archiving. In *What's next for Digital Deposit Libraries? ECDL Workshop*, 2001 . www.bnf.fr/pages/infopro/ecdl/france/sld001.htm.

[14] L. Mignet, M. Preda, S. Abiteboul, S. Ailleret, B. Amann, and A. Marian. Acquiring XML pages for a WebHouse. In *proceedings of Base de Donn es Avanc es conference*, 2000.

[15] A National Library of Australia Position Paper. National strategy for provision of access to australian electronic publications. www.nla.gov.au/policy/paep.html.

[16] Lawrence Page, Sergey Brin, Rajeev Motwani, and Terry Winograd. The pagerank citation ranking: Bringing order to the web, 1998.

[17] S. Raghavan and H. Garcia-Molina. Crawling the hidden web. In *The VLDB Journal*, 2001.

[18] L. Page S. Brin. The anatomy of a large-scale hypertextual web search engine. *WWW7 Conference, Computer Networks 30(1-7)*, 1998.

[19] Xyleme. `www.xyleme.com`.

Austrian Online Archive Processing: Analyzing Archives of the World Wide Web

Andreas Rauber*, Andreas Aschenbrenner, and Oliver Witvoet

Department of Software Technology and Interactive Systems,
Vienna University of Technology
Favoritenstr. 9 - 11 / 188, A–1040 Wien, Austria
http://www.ifs.tuwien.ac.at

Abstract. With the popularity of the World Wide Web and the recognition of its worthiness of being archived we find numerous projects aiming at creating large-scale repositories containing excerpts and snapshots of Web data. Interfaces are being created that allow users to surf through time, analyzing the evolution of Web pages, or retrieving information using search interfaces. Yet, with the timeline and metadata available in such a Web archive, additional analyzes that go beyond mere information exploration, become possible. In this paper we present the AOLAP project building a Data Warehouse of such a Web archive, allowing its analysis and exploration from different points of view using OLAP technologies. Specifically, technological aspects such as operating systems and Web servers used, geographic location, and Web technology such as the use of file types, forms or scripting languages, may be used to infer e.g. technology maturation or impact.

Keywords: Web Archiving, Data Warehouse (DWH), On-Line Analytical Processing (OLAP), Technology Evaluation, Digital Cultural Heritage

1 Introduction

In the last few years we have witnessed the initiation of numerous projects aiming at the creation of archives of the World Wide Web. Snapshots of the Web preserve an impression of what hyperspace looked like at a given point in time, what kind of information, issues, and problems people from all kinds of cultural and sociological backgrounds were interested in, the means they used to communicate their interests over the Web, characteristics styles of how Web sites were designed to attract visitors, and many other facets of this medium and society in general. Thus, these archives may well end up forming one of the most fascinating collections of popular digital cultural heritage in the future. While several initiatives are already building Web archives [1,8,11,16], several significant challenges remain to be solved, requiring models for preserving the

* Part of this work was done while the author was an ERCIM Research Fellow at IEI, Consiglio Nazionale delle Ricerche (CNR), Pisa, Italy.

M. Agosti and C. Thanos (Eds.): ECDL 2002, LNCS 2458, pp. 16–31, 2002.

digital artifacts [6], or concepts for cost-efficient distributed storage [5], to name just a few. When it comes to the usage (or prospected usage, as many of these archives currently provide limited or no access to their collections, out of legal or technical reasons), most projects focus solely on the content-aspect of their archive. Interfaces are developed that allow users to surf through time, see the evaluation of a Web page from one crawl to the next, or trace the growth of the Web space of a given site.

Yet, with such a repository of Web data, as well as the meta-data that is associated with the documents and domains, we have a powerful source of information that goes beyond the content of Web pages. The Web is not only content, it is rather, technically speaking, a medium transporting content in a variety of ways, using a variety of technical platforms as well as data representations to make its information available. The providers of information are located in different physical places on the hyperlinked world, and information is transferred via a variety of channels. Having an archive of the World Wide Web means, that not only can we see which information was available at which time, we can also trace where information was being produced and replicated, which technology was used for representing a certain kind of information, what kind of systems were used to make the information available. It also gives us the means to trace the life cycle of technology, following file formats, interaction standards, and server technology from their creation, via different degrees of acceptance to either prolonged utilization or early obsolescence. It provides a basis for tracking the technological evolution of different geographical areas, analyzing characteristics such as the "digital divide", not from a consumer's point of view, i.e. who has access to Web information, and who has not, but also from a provider's point of view, i.e. which areas in the world, as well as on a much smaller, regional scale, are able to make themselves heard, are able to participate in the exchange of information by publishing information on their own account on the Web.

The answers to these kind of questions require a different perspective of the Web and Web archives, focusing not solely on content, but on the wealth of information automatically associated with each object on the Web, such as its file format, its size and the recentness of its last update, its link structure and connectivity to other pages within the same site, domain, and externally, the language used, the operating system and Web server software running on the server side machine, the physical location of the machine, the use of specific protocols, cookies, and many more.

We address these issues in the scope of the Austrian On-Line Archive, a joint initiative by the Austrian National Library and the Vienna University of Technology, to analyze and devise ways for archiving the Austrian national Web space. In order to support these kind of analyzes in a flexible manner, we adopt a solution based on a Data Warehouse for the Austrian On-Line Archive Processing module (AOLAP), allowing interactive analysis of the accumulated data using on-line analytical processing techniques. On top of the Data Warehouse, additional Data Mining techniques may be applied to analyze and characterize specific problem domains, such as time-series prediction for technological evolution.

The remainder of this paper is organized as follows: Section 2 provides an overview of related work in the field of Web archiving, navigation and analysis. This is followed by a presentation of the Austrian On-Line Archive (AOLA) in Section 3. The principles of Data Warehouse technology and OLAP processing are briefly introduced in Section 4, followed by a description of the current AOLAP system in Section 5. Section 6 gives initial results. We finally provide an outlook on future work in Section 7.

2 Related Work

In the last years we have witnessed the creation of numerous initiatives building archives of the World Wide Web. Among the most famous of these we find, for example, the *Internet Archive* [10,11], located in the US, which, among many other collections, has the largest archive of Web pages from all over the world, donated by the search engine Alexa. Within Europe, the leading project with respect to Web archiving is the *Kulturaw3* project by the Swedish Royal National Library [1]. Its archive contains frequent snapshots of the Swedish national Web space starting in 1996, using the *Combine* harvester as their means of data acquisition. A second large initiative in this field is the archiving initiative of the *NEDLIB* project [8,18], headed by the Finish National Library and the Helsinki Center for Scientific Computing. Within the scope of the project, a special crawler specifically geared towards tasks of Web page archiving, has been developed, and is currently being used to acquire a snapshot of the Finish Web space. This tool has also been used by other national groups, e.g. in Iceland, to build collections of their respective Web space. Similar initiatives are being followed e.g. in the Czech Republic by the National Library at Brno, the National Libraries of Norway and Estonia, and others.

With respect to the usage of these Web archives, the *Nordic Web Archive* initiative [14] is currently developing an access interface, that will allow users to search and surf within such an archive. A similar interface, called the *Wayback Machine*, is already available for the *Internet Archive*, providing, for each URL entered, a timeline listing the dates when this specific URL was added to the archive, i.e. which versions of the respective file are available.

Going beyond the mere navigation within the archive as a mirror of the World Wide Web existing at the respective times, several projects take a more structured approach to storing and analyzing the Web. The *Web Archaeology* project [13] studies the content of the World Wide Web using a variety of content representations, referred to as features, including *links* capturing connectivity, *shingleprints* capturing syntactic similarities, and *term vectors* capturing semantic similarities. The *Mercator Extensible Web Crawler* is used for large-scale data acquisition, and specific database models were developed at the second layer of the system architecture for storing the feature databases. Various tools are added to the top layer of the system architecture to facilitate specific types of analysis, such as, e.g. in the *Geodesy* project trying to discover and measure the structure of the Web.

Another Web page repository is being built within the *WebBase* project at Stanford University, addressing issues such as the functional design, storage management, as well as indexing modules for Web repositories [9]. The main goal of this project is to acquire and store locally a subset of a given Web space in order to facilitate the performant execution of several types of analyzes and queries, such as page ranking, and information retrieval. However, it limits its scope to the archiving of one copy of each page at a time, thus providing no historization, and focuses on html pages only.

On a different level we find the *WHOWEDA* project, pursued by the Web Warehousing and Data Mining Group at the Nanyang Technological University in Singapore [2]. Within this project, Data Warehouse technology is used for the storage of consecutive versions of Web pages, adding a time dimension to the analysis of content and link structure. URL, size, date of last modification (and validity, with respect to subsequent visits to a given site), size, etc. are stored together with the content and structure of a document. Furthermore, link information, as well as the position of links within documents are recorded and made available for further analysis. Although a more structured approach to the analysis of Web pages is taken within the scope of this project, it primarily focuses on a detailed analysis and representation of the content of the documents.

3 AOLA: The Austrian Online Archive

The *Austrian On-Line Archive*[1] (AOLA) [16,17] is an initiative to create a permanent archive documenting the rise of the Austrian Internet, capturing the sociological and cultural aspects of the Austrian Web space. With respect to the AOLA project, the Austrian Web space covers the whole *.at* domain, but also servers located in Austria yet registered under "foreign" domains like *.com, .org, .cc,* etc. are included. The inclusion of these servers so far is determined semi-automatically by maintaining a list of allowed non-at servers. Furthermore, sites dedicated to topics of Austrian interest as well as sites about Austria (so-called "Austriaca") are considered even if they are physically located in another country. Austrian representations in a foreign country like the Austrian Cultural Institute in New York at `http://www.aci.org` are examples for such sites of interest. These sites are fed into the system using a currently manually maintained list.

Web crawlers, specifically the Combine Crawler, are used to gather the data from the Web. While the crawling process itself runs completely automatically, manual supervision and intervention is required in some cases when faulty URLs are encountered. The pages downloaded from the Web are stored together with additional metadata in a hierarchical structure defined by the Sweden's *Kulturaw3*-project, and archived in compressed format on tapes.

[1] `http://www.ifs.tuwien.ac.at/~aola`

The data and the associated metadata gathered from the crawl by the AOLA project are the basis for our analysis within the AOLAP project. The archive currently consists of about 488 GB of data from two crawls, with more than 2,8 million pages from about 45.000 sites from the first partial crawl in 2001 (118 GB in total), as well as about 370 GB (approx. 8,2 Mio URLs from more than 120.000 different servers, which amount to about 170.000 servers including alias names of servers) from the second crawl in spring 2002.

4 Data Warehousing and OLAP

When it comes to the analysis of large amounts of data in a flexible manner, Data Warehouses (DWH) have evolved into the core components of Decision Support Systems. In this section we will briefly sketch the main characteristics of DWHs in general, without being able to address issues of DWH design and different types of data models used for subsequent analytical processing in detail. We rather refer to the wealth of literature on DWH design for these issues, e.g. [12, 15].

A Data Warehouse is a subject-oriented, integrated, time-variant, non-volatile collection of data in support of decision-making processes. Rather than storing data with respect to a specific application, the information is processed for analytical purposes, allowing it to be viewed from different perspectives in an interactive manner. It furthermore integrates information from a variety of sources, thus enriching the data and broadening the context and value of the information. One of the core components of any DWH analysis is, contrary to conventional transaction-oriented database systems, the core functionality of the time dimension, facilitating analysis of the development of data across time periods. To achieve this, data, rather than being up-dated or deleted, is only added to a DWH with reference to a validity time-stamp (or rather: a range of time-stamps, depending on the concept of time used, such as valid time, revealed time, etc. See [3] for a detailed treatise of time-related aspects in DWH maintenance).

The main concept of a DWH is the separation of information into two main categories, referred to as *facts* and *dimensions*, respectively. Facts is the information that is to be analyzed, with respect to its dimensions, often reflecting business perspectives, such as a geographic location, evolution over time, product groups, merchandising campaigns, or stock maintenance. No matter whether the data is actually stored in a flat relational DBMS using a dimensional design, such as the star or snowflake models, or whether a multi-dimensional DBMS is used, the DWH may be viewed as a multi-dimensional data cube. This data cube allows us, using OLAP (on-line analytical processing) tools, to interactively drill-down, roll-up, slice and dice, to view and analyze the data from different perspectives, derive ratios and compute measures across many dimensions. The *drill-down* operation can be used for example to navigate from the top-level domains to the sub-level domains. The inverse *roll-up*, when applied to the aggregation of total links from hosts which are located, e.g., in Graz (a city) will result in an aggregation of links from hosts located in Styria (the respective county). The *slice* operation defines a sub-cube by performing a selection on, for instance, *domain = .ac.at* on the dimension *domains*, to get all information concerning the educational Internet domain in Austria. The *dice* operation defines a sub-cube by performing selections on several dimensions. For example, a sub-cube can be derived by interactively dicing the cube on three dimensions resulting in the generated clause, *county = "Vienna" and operating system = "linux" and web-server = "apache"*.

These OLAP operations assist in interactive and quick retrieval of 2D and 3D cross-tables and chart-table data from the cube which allow quick querying and analysis of a Web-linkage data storage.

5 AOLAP: Austrian Online Archive Processing

In this section we outline the various types and sources of information used in the context of the AOLAP project, comment on some feature extraction and transformation steps, as well as on the design of the DWH.

As the primary source of information we use the data gathered by the *Austrian On-Line Archive (AOLA)* project. The archive consists of Web pages, including all types of files as collected by the harvesting software, and rests on tape archives organized primarily according to domain names. In addition to the actual pages, meta-information that is provided or created during the crawling process, is collected and stored as part of the archived files. This includes information provided as part of the http protocol as well as other information provided by the server, such as the server software type and version, the operating system used by the server, date and time settings at the server, as well as last-modified dates for the respective file being downloaded. This information is stored together with each individual file, encapsulated in MIME format.

Based on this archive, a set of perl-scripts is used to extract relevant data from the files, producing intermediary files that are used for data cleansing and further preprocessing. The information extracted from the pages includes *file types* based on file extensions and the associated MIME type obtained from the Web server, *file size*, internal and external *links*, information about *frames*, *e-mail addresses* and interactive *forms* used in the case of html files, *date of last modification*, and others. With respect to the various domains we mainly concentrate on *IP addresses* and thus *network types*, *operating system* and *Web server software* information.

Furthermore, we integrate information from other sources to enrich the data provided by the harvesting system. Specifically, we use a set of WHOIS servers to provide geographic location information of Web service registrars, alias names, etc. Please note, however, that the domain name registry information obtained this way, while providing the location of the owner of a specific domain, does not necessarily reflect the actual physical location of a server. Other approaches to evaluate the geographical location may be used, such as directly using host or domain name information, or analyzing references to locations in the textual content [7]. Yet, they do not provide as detailed information, or actually address a different concept, such as in the latter case, a content-based geographic coverage of a site, rather than its location. As we will see during the discussion of the experiments, the inclusion of this kind of content-based geographical coverage, even if it is somewhat less precise, might proof beneficial for detailed analysis.

The information is further transformed and loaded into a relational DBMS using a star-model like design for the data storage. The data model basically consists of two parts. The first part arises from all tables containing data referring to the Web hosts the data derives from. The second part consists of the tables containing data about the hosts where links point to. Connecting these parts is the table where all the links are stored. This table forms the central fact table in the Data Warehouse. Below we provide a brief description of the main tables in the database.

- *domains:* This table contains the names of the Web hosts organized by sub-level domains. This allows us to drill down through the address space during analysis. We also check if the domain is reachable over the Internet at a specific time and store this information in this table. Identical hosts, i.e. hosts having the same IP address, yet reachable via different domain names, are stored multiple times in this table to reflect the actual domain name space.
- *IPs:* The IP addresses of the Web hosts, separated into the octets ranging from 0 to 255 are stored in this table. This is used to identify the different types of IP nets, i.e. class A, B and C networks. Class A addresses are reserved for very large networks such as the ARPANET and other national wide area networks. Class B addresses are allocated to organizations that operate networks likely to contain more than 255 computers and Class C addresses are allocated to all other network operators. Server reachable via multiple domain names but having the same IP address are stored only once.
- *server:* In this table server information like the type and version of the server (e.g. MS IIS, Vers 5.0) is stored, structured hierarchically by Producer, Product, and Version. Please note, that no checking of the validity of this information is performed during the download, i.e. disguised servers are not identified as such.
- *OS:* The table OS contains the reported name and the specificity of the operating system of the hosts. Again, no checking of the validity of this information is performed.
- *maintainers, netnames, and netblocks:* These tables contain information gathered from the WHOIS servers. The owner of the netblock in which the specific host is addressed can be retrieved from the maintainer table. In the table netnames, the name of the netblock is stored, and the table netblocks contains the range of the IP addresses of a specific netblock.
- *owner and address:* These two tables are filled with further data from the WHOIS server. In the first one the owner of the Web host and in the second one the address registered at the WHOIS server is stored in a hierarchical structure.
- *pages:* In this table all pages gathered from the AOLA database are stored. There is a column *page* were the name of the page is stored, a column *url*

containing the URL of the specific page. Further information includes the size of the page, crawl date, as well as the date of the last modification for the downloaded page if provided by the server.
- *link_domains:* This table stores the Web hosts which are not in the Austrian Web space (so-called foreign Web hosts) but are linked to by the Austrian hosts. The sub-level domains are stored separately as in the table domains described above.
- *link_pages:* This table contains all the so-called foreign link pages, i.e., pages referenced by pages of the AOLA database which themselves are not in the Austrian Web space, and thus not part of the AOLA archive.
- *forms:* This table stores, for pages in the AOLA archive, the number of forms per page and the total amount of fields of a specific page to facilitate analysis of interactive Web pages, types and amount of interaction encountered etc.
- *filetype:* This table contains the different file types of the pages in the archive as well as those of the foreign pages. The information is structured hierarchically by *media* (e.g., application, video, or image), followed by the *MIME type* or the *filename extension.* As basis for this structuring, both the MIME type provided with the downloaded page, as well as the file extension are used, forming two independent dimensions. This separation is necessary due to the fact that the information provided both by the MIME type as well as by the file extensions is prone to errors, and quite frequently these two dimensions do not correspond to each other. Retaining both types of information domains thus provides greater flexibility in the analysis.
- *run:* In order to be able to compare the characteristics of the Austrian Web over time, we have to compare data from different crawls. For each crawl we define a run number, start and end date, stored in the run table.
- *domain_to_domain_links:* All the links we gathered are stored in this table. In the column *type* there are the different prefixes of the URL which indicate the protocol (http, https, ftp, etc.) of the stored link. *External* is an additional column which is used to differentiate between external and internal links, i.e., if the link references a page from another Web host or from the same domain.

Based on these tables, a multi-dimensional cube is created which can further be used for interactive analysis.

6 Experimental Results

In this section we present examples of the analytical capabilities of the AOLAP system. We should emphasize, however, that the current results are based on incomplete crawls of the Austrian Web space, representing data from the first pilot crawl in spring 2001 and a second crawl started in spring 2002. Thus, the numbers provided below can only depict a trend, rather than be taken as confirmed results yet. However, the large amount of data already available at least allows us to analyze the current situation of the Austrian Web space, as well as obtain ideas of its usage, challenges with respect to its preservation, as

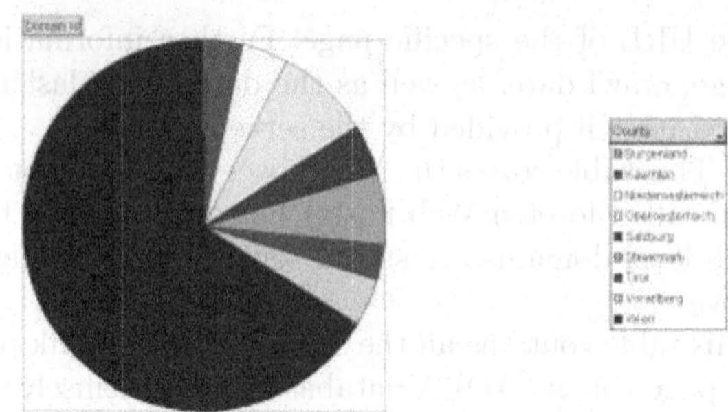

Fig. 1. Distribution of Web servers in Austria

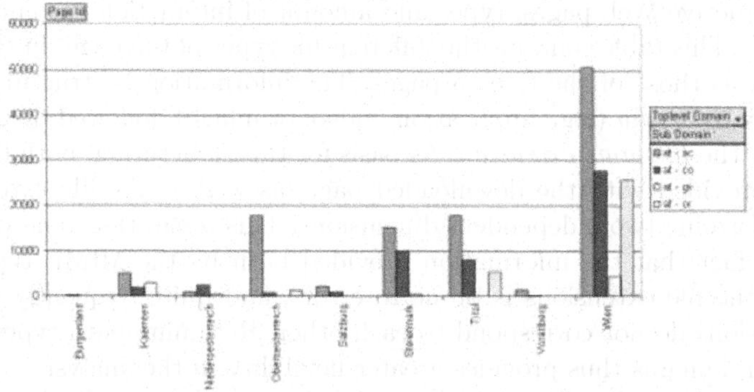

Fig. 2. Distribution of Web servers across counties and domains

well as to discover the benefits of interactive analysis provided by a DWH-based approach. In order to exploit the most important characteristic of such a Web archive, i.e. to analyze its historic perspective and use this as a basis for impact evaluation and trend analysis, a series of snapshots over several years will need to be accumulated in order to facilitate evaluation along the time dimension.

6.1 Distribution of Web-Servers over the Counties

Figure 1 represents a distribution graph of the domains in Austria, showing that most of the Web servers are located in the capital Vienna. If we make another slice by restricting the IP addresses to class A IPs only, the difference is even more obvious. Although this fact is not really surprising, the magnitude of the difference between the metropolis and the rest of Austria still is astounding, especially when we consider that just less then a quarter of the population lives in Vienna. More precisely, our analysis reveals that 66% of the Web-hosts are registered in Vienna, followed by Upper Austria with 9% and Styria with 6%. The distribution of the Web hosts in these other counties are comparable to the distribution of the population. This points towards the much-discussed issue of the "metropolitan media Internet".

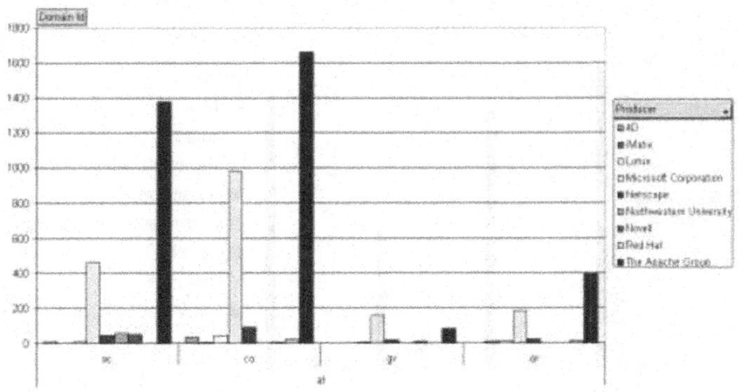

Fig. 3. Distribution of Web servers across domains

However, care must be taken with respect to the information represented by the geographical domain, which reflects the location of the owner of a certain IP segment, rather than the actual location and area serviced by a specific server. As many nation-wide operating ISPs are based in Vienna, and thus have their address block registered there, the actual saturation and distribution of Internet services differs from the impression provided by this analysis. A combination with other means of location or geographical coverage determination should be incorporated to cover these issues, such as content-based coverage identification mentioned in Section 5.

A drill-down onto the sub-domains provides a different view of the national distribution, where, for example, the academic and commercial nets are at least somewhat more evenly dispersed among the counties, whereas governmental Web sites as well as organizational sites are less wide-spread. Furthermore, we may not forget to take into account the "foreign" hosts, i.e. hosts registered in Austria, but registered under foreign domains, which currently amount to more than 6.500 individual domains (or close to 9.000 if alias names of servers are considered independently). These are not assigned to any of the *.at* sub-domains. such as e.g., some Austrian University Institutes that have their Web space located directly under the top-level *.edu* domain.

6.2 Distribution of Web Servers across Domains

While the distribution of the different Web servers used on the Web is one of the most frequently analyzed facts, and thus in itself does not reveal any surprising results, the application of DWH technology allows us to more flexibly view the various facets of this subject. We came across 35 different types of servers or server producers, in a total of about 300 different versions, but the most common ones are the APACHE and the IIS server, followed by the Netscape-Enterprise server. For a selection of the various types encountered, see Table 1.

By drilling-down we can take a look at the distribution of Web servers at the first sub-domain level. Figure 3 depicts the resulting distribution focusing on

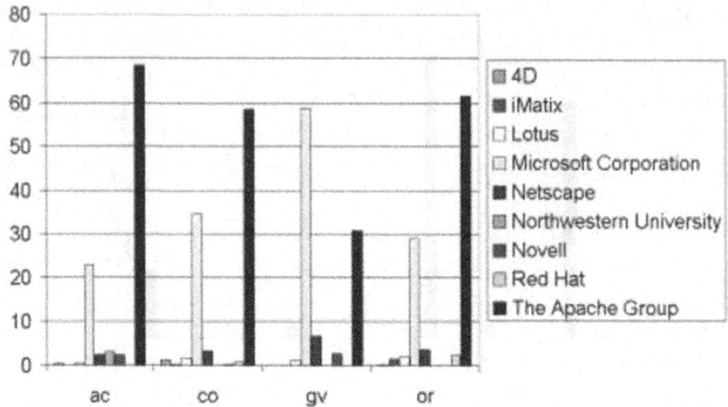

Fig. 4. Relative distribution of Web servers across domains

Table 1. Selection of server types and versions encountered

Producer	# Versions	# Ocurrences
4D	13	361
Able Solutions	1	10
Apple ShareIP	5	24
Caucho	5	19
DIMAX Hyperwave-Info-Server	4	68
IBM	14	78
Lotus Lotus-Domino	2	506
Microsoft IIS	7	20947
NCSA	4	48
Netscape	26	1509
Northwestern Univ.	1	63
Novell	3	138
RapidSite	2	438
Red Hat Stronghold	6	297
Roxen	2	102
The Apache Group	52	47383

the most prominent types of Web servers. The general trends in market shares remain more or less unchanged, with probably a slightly stronger dominance of the Apache Web server in the academic domain. However, an interesting characteristic is represented by the presence of the WN Web server from Northwestern University, an open-source Web server that basically is used exclusively in the academic domain. This difference becomes even more obvious when we take a look at the relative distributions, depicted in Figure 4. Here the dominance of Apache in all but the governmental domains is clearly visible.

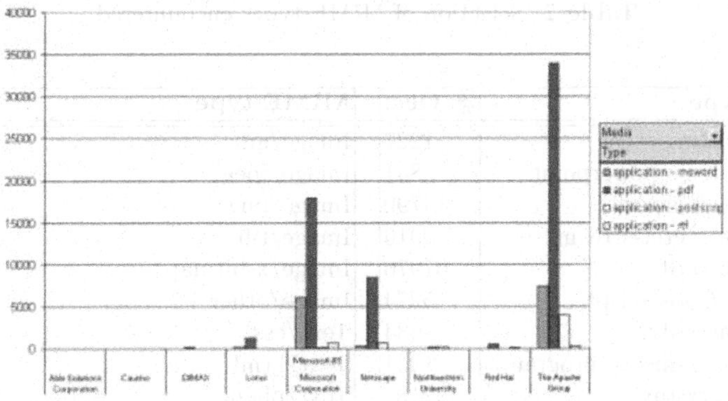

Fig. 5. Distribution of document file types across Web servers

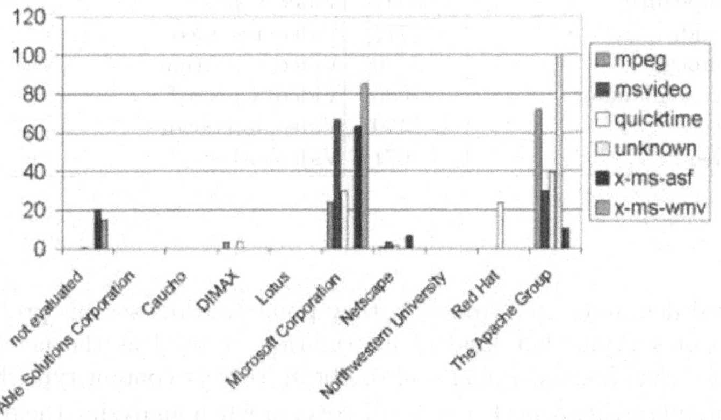

Fig. 6. Distribution of video file types across Web servers

6.3 Distribution of File-Types over Different Web Servers

The number of file types encountered in the Web archive is of high relevance with respect to the preservation of the archive, in order to keep the pages viewable in the near and far future. It also represents a good mirror of the diversity of the Web with respect to the technologies employed for conveying information. All over we encountered more than 200.000 different types of files based on their extensions, and more than 200 different types of information representation when we use the MIME type as the indicative criterium. However, we should stress, that the quality of the information provided this way is very low, as a large number of both file extensions as well as MIME types are actually invalid, such as files with extensions *.htmo*, *.chtml* or *.median, .documentation.* A listing of some of the most important types of files found in the archive is provided in Table 2. For a comprehensive overview of almost 7.000 different file extensions and their associated applications, see [4]. While the major part of file extensions

Table 2. Selection of MIME types encountered

MIME type	# Occ.	MIME type	# Occ.
Application/ms-excel	1227	Image/gif	35144
Application/ms-powerpoint	841	Image/jpeg	145200
Application/msword	14799	Image/png	349
Application/octet-stream	9916	Image/tiff	1025
Application/pdf	67976	Image/x-bitmap	426
Application/postscript	5274	Image/other	123
Application/x-dvi	634	Text/css	713
Application/x-msdos-program	1231	Text/html	7401473
Application/x-tar	2189	Text/plain	32549
Application/x-zip-compressed	15314	Text/rtf	2783
Application/other	6985	Text/vnd.wap.wml	2961
Audio/basic	246	Text/other	753
Audio/x-mpegurl	3947	Video/mpeg	983
Audio/x-midi	1777	Video/msvideo	596
Audio/x-mpeg3	3240	Video/quicktime	768
Audio/x-pn-realaudio	5006	Video/x-ms-asf	646
Audio/x-wav	1430	Video/unknown	4
Audio/other	671	Video/other	20

encountered definitely are erroneous, they point towards serious problems with respect to preserving that kind of information, as well as the need to define solutions for cleaning this dimension to obtain correct content type descriptors.

Several interesting aspects can be discovered when analyzing the distribution of file types across the different types of Web servers. General known tendencies, like the dominance of the PDF format over the previously very important Postscript file format for document exchange can be verified this way, as depicted in Figure 5.

Figure 6 depicts the distribution of various types of video file formats across Web servers. Here we find significant differences the way video information is provided with respect to the type of Web server employed. *Mpeg* is by far the dominant format on Apache Web servers, followed by *Quick-time*, which is less than half as popular, but still ahead of various other video formats identified by their MIME type as flavors of *ms-video*. (We also find a video format identified as MIME type *video/unknown* on Apache servers. By viewing the associated file extension dimension these files were identified to be *.swi* and *.raw* files, the former, for example, being a *swish* data file used in connection with *Flash* animations).

This is sharply contrasted by the situation encountered at Web sites running the MS IIS Web server, where the family of *ms-video* and *ms-asf* formats by far dominate the type of video files provided. When we take a look at the Netscape Web server we again find a slight dominance of *ms-video* file formats. Another interesting characteristic is exhibited by the Stronghold Web server, the Red-Hat

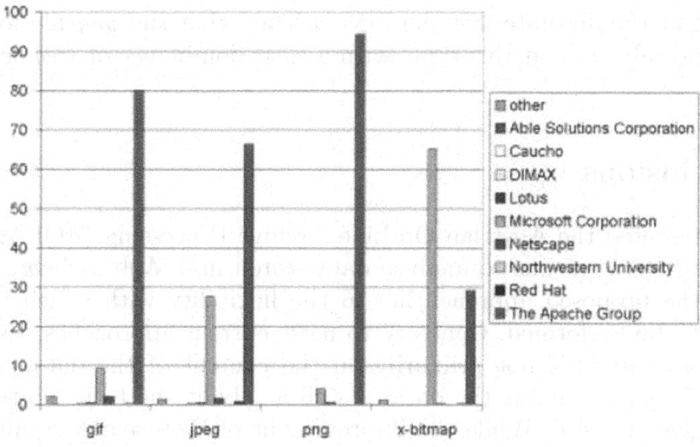

Fig. 7. Relative distribution of image file types across Web servers

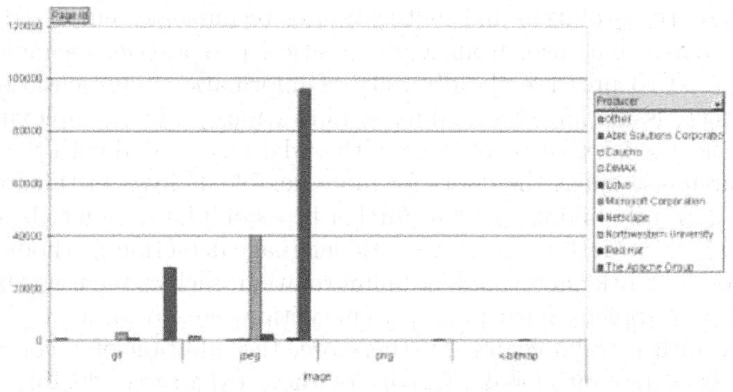

Fig. 8. Absolute distribution of image file types across Web servers

Secure Web server for Linux operating systems, which, when it comes to video files, provides only *Quick-time* movies. Untypical distributions like this may quite frequently be attributed to artifacts such as a single Web server running a specific system and providing a large amount of files as part of a collection. The Data Warehouse allows us to interactively drill-down on this section and reveals, that in this case the distribution can be attributed to a sub-group of 10 domains out of several hundred sites using the Stronghold server. Of these 10 sites, however, 9 are closely related to each other and are part of one larger organization providing identical information, thus actually being a kind of mirror of one site. Due to the flexibility of the interactive analysis facilitated by the DWH, these artifacts can easily be identified.

Similar characteristics can be detected when analyzing image file type distributions across different server types as depicted in Figure 7. Here we find an almost exclusive presence of the *png* file type on Apache servers, whereas more than 60% of all *bmp* files are to be found on MS IIS servers. However, when we take a look at the absolute distributions, we find that the *png* file format still plays a neglectable role at this time, with a clear dominance of *jpeg*, followed by *gif* images.

7 Conclusions

We have presented the Austrian On-Line Archive Processing (AOLAP) system providing a flexible means to analyze data stored in a Web archive. The main benefit of the proposed approach lies in the flexibility with which interactive analysis may be performed. Contrary to most current approaches, the focus of this type of analysis is not primarily on the content of the data, but rather on meta-information about the data as well as about the technologies used to provide a given service. While the improvement of Web search results may be facilitated by the collection and integration of additional information such as link structure analysis, by far more fascinating insights into the Web and its evolution will become possible, providing a basis for crucial technology decision. These include the evolution and maturation of technologies employed, analysis of market shares, but also, from a preservation perspective, technologies and efforts required to preserve the diversity of information representation. While several of these issues have been addressed in various projects employing special purpose tools, the integration of the wealth of data associated with the Web into a Data Warehouse opens the doors for more flexible analysis of this medium.

We are currently taking a look at further types of information to be extracted from the pages, integrating e.g. automatic language detection methods, covering in larger detail additional technological information, such as the usage of cookies, embedded java applets, flash plug-ins, encryption, etc., in order to be able to incorporate future technologies. Furthermore, the addition of a content-based dimension is being considered. As part of these expansions flexible interfaces to modify/increase the number and type of technologies to be scanned for in the data, will be analyzed. Furthermore, the application of specific data mining techniques for specific problem domains, especially with respect to time-line analysis will be studied in greater detail.

References

1. A. Arvidson, K. Persson, and J. Mannerheim. The Kulturarw3 project - The Royal Swedish Web Archiw3e - An example of "complete" collection of web pages. In *Proceedings of the 66th IFLA Council and General Conference*, Jerusalem, Israel, August 13-18 2000. `http://www.ifla.org/IV/ifla66/papers/154-157e.htm`.
2. S. Bhowmick, N. Keong, and S. Madria. Web schemas in WHOWEDA. In *Proceedings of the ACM 3rd International Workshop on Data Warehousing and OLAP*, Washington, DC, November 10 2000. ACM.
3. R. Bruckner and A. Tjoa. Managing time consistency for active data warehouse environments. In *Proceedings of the Third International Conference on Data Warehousing and Knowledge Discovery (DaWaK 2001)*, LNCS 2114, pages 254–263, Munich, Germany, September 2001. Springer. `http://link.springer.de/link/service/series/0558/papers/2114/21140219.pdf`.

4. Computer Knowledge (CKNOW). FILExt: The file extension source. Webpage, June 2002. `http://filext.com/`.
5. A. Crespo and H. Garcia-Molin. Cost-driven design for archival repositories. In E. Fox and C. Borgman, editors, *Proceedings of the First ACM/IEEE Joint Conference on Digital Libraries (JCDL'01)*, pages 363–372, Roanoke, VA, June 24-28 2001. ACM. http://www.acm.org/dl.
6. M. Day. Metadata for digital preservation: A review of recent developments. In *Proceedings of the 5. European Conference on Research and Advanced Technology for Digital Libraries (ECDL 2001)*, Springer Lecture Notes in Computer Science, Darmstadt, Germany, Sept. 4-8 2001. Springer.
7. J. Ding, L. Gravano, and N. Shivakumar. Computing geographical scopes of web resources. In *Proceedings of the 26th International Conference on Very Large Databases, VLDB 2000*, pages 545–556, Cairo, Egypt, September 10-14 2000.
8. J. Hakala. Collecting and preserving the web: Developing and testing the NEDLIB harvester. *RLG DigiNews*, 5(2), April 15 2001. `http://www.rlg.org/preserv/diginews/diginews5-2.html`.
9. J. Hirai, S. Raghavan, H. Garcia-Molina, and A. Paepcke. Webbase: A repositoru of web pages. In *Proceedings of the 9th International World Wide Web Conference (WWW9)*, Amsterdam, The Netherlands, May 15-19 2000. Elsevir Science. `http://www9.org/w9cdrom/296/296.html`.
10. The Internet Archive. Website. `http://www.archive.org`.
11. B. Kahle. Preserving the internet. *Scientific American*, March 1997. `http://www.sciam.com/0397issue/0397kahle.html`.
12. R. Kimball. *The Data Warehouse Toolkit: The Complete Guide to Dimensional Modeling*. John Wiley & Sons, 2 edition, 2002.
13. S. Leung, S. Perl, R. Stata, and J. Wiener. Towards web-scale web archeology. Research Report 174, Compaq Systems Research Center, Palo Alto, CA, September 10 2001. `http://gatekeeper.dec.com/pub/DEC/SRC/research-reports/SRC-174.pdf`.
14. Nordic web archive. Website. `http://nwa.nb.no`.
15. T. Pedersen and C. Jensen. Multidimensional database technology. *IEEE Computer*, 34(12):40–46, December 2001.
16. A. Rauber. Austrian on-line archive: Current status and next steps. Presentation given at the ECDL Workshop on Digital Deposit Libraries (ECDL 2001) Darmstadt, Germany, September 8 2001.
17. A. Rauber and A. Aschenbrenner. Part of our culture is born digital - On efforts to preserve it for future generations. *TRANS. On-line Journal for Cultural Studies (Internet-Zeitschrift für Kulturwissenschaften)*, 10, July 2001. `http://www.inst.at/trans/10Nr/inhalt10.htm`.
18. T. Werf-Davelaar. Long-term preservation of electronic publications: The NEDLIB project. *D-Lib Magazine*, 5(9), September 1999. `http://www.dlib.org/dlib/september99/vanderwerf/09vanderwerf.html`.

Conversion of eBook Documents Based on Mapping Relations

Seung-Kyu Ko[1], Myoung-Soo Kang[1], Won-Sung Sohn[1],
Soon-Bum Lim[2], and Yoon-Chul Choy[1]

[1]Department of Computer Science, Yonsei University,
Seodaemun-gu Shinchon-dong 134, Seoul, 120-749, South Korea
{pitta, soo, sohn, ycchoy}@rainbow.yonsei.ac.kr
[2]Department of Multimedia Science, SookMyung Women's University,
Seoul, 140-742, South Korea
sblim@sookmyung.ac.kr

Abstract. An electronic book means a digital form of a paper book. Currently, to promote an eBook market, many countries have established eBook content standards. But, the publication of different caused exchanging problems due to mismatch of content forms. Therefore, to exchange eBook conforming each standard, the content has to be converted according to document structure and its semantic information. But existing conversion methods are almost based on syntax information. Even, using semantic information they are not reflected eBook characteristics. So, to precise and correct eBook conversion, we analyze each standard and define mapping relations considering semantic information and eBook characteristics. To generalize the mapping relations, we classify mapping relations into ten conversion classes, and provide conversion scripts examples for each class. With defined mapping relations and conversion classes, we write up conversion scripts for EBKS to OEB PS/JepaX, and experiment with them. We believe defined conversion classes can be applied to normal document conversions.

1. Introduction

An electronic book(eBook) means a digital form of a paper book. Currently, to promote an eBook market, many countries have established standards for eBook content. In USA, OEBF(Open eBook Forum) has announced OEB PS(Open eBook Publication Structure Specification)[7] in 1999 for publishing and displaying the eBook. In Japan, Jepa(Japanese Electronic Publishing Association) announced JepaX 0.9[6] in 1999 for storing and exchanging of eBook. In Korea, the Korean eBook Consortium (EBK: Electronic Book of Korea) sponsored by the Ministry of Culture & Tourism, announced a draft of EBKS(EBK Standard) 1.0[20] in 2001 for clear exchanging of eBook contents. But, the publication of different standards in many countries caused an exchanging problem due to mismatch of content forms.
Two methods can be considered to solve this problem. First is to define an intermediary model, which can describe all of the contents, and convert source content to an intermediary model and convert the intermediary model to a target

M. Agosti and C. Thanos (Eds.): ECDL 2002, LNCS 2458, pp. 32-46, 2002.

content form. This method is flexible for a new content form due to an intermediary model, but because defining methods of each content structure are too different, it is difficult to represent all three content forms in one. And there is a problem of expressing the semantic information of contents in an intermediary model. Second is to define mapping relations among eBook contents by analyzing them, and converting them using defined relations. This method makes clear exchange possible by defining mapping relations, which reflect semantic. But as content standards increased, so does the number of mapping relations.

Most of existing conversion methods are for general purposes. So, they only consider relational schema, XML and Object Oriented classes but not the specific domain structure. Moreover most of them[3][4][12] are based on syntax information and not semantic information, so the components of content structure are not properly mapped often. So user validation is a must. Even the conversion methods using semantic information[8][9][10] also need user validation. This means, to properly convert logical structures, the manual work is inevitably necessary, and mapping relations defined by user are most accurate information. In other words, the second method is better than the first for clear exchanging.

Hence, we use the second method. And we not only define mapping relationships, but also define general conversion classes by classifying them. And to show that each conversion is possible, we offer conversion scripts for each class. So when new content standard is published and mapping relations between the new one and other contents are in defined conversion classes, then the conversion is possible and the conversion scripts can be easily defined using existing ones. Moreover, we believe that defined conversion classes include all general XML document mapping relations.

The paper is organized as follows. In Section 2, we describe eBook content standards. In Section 3, the mapping relations of eBook standards based on EBKS are explained, and in Section 4, each conversion classes and experiments are presented. Finally, we conclude the paper in Section 5.

2. Introduction to eBook Contents Standards

In this section, we briefly look at EBKS, OEB PS, and JepaX, which are respectively the eBook standards of Korea, USA, and Japan.

2.1 EBKS

EBKS[20] is established for clear exchange of contents, and is composed of three parts; content, metadata, and style. For clear exchange of contents, it defines a logical document structure such as shown in Fig. 1. The structure of EBKS is made up of “metainfo” and “books”. And “books” is composed of “cover”, “front”, “book”, and “back”. “books” describes the collection of books, and “book” describes the content of an eBook. “book” is composed of “cover”, “front”, “body”, and “back”. The structure of a “body”, which has the actual content is composed of “part”, “chapter”, and “section”, as shown in Fig. 1. In Fig. 1, ‘+’ indicates one or more than one, ‘*’ means zero or more than zero, and ‘?’ means zero or one. And EBKS offers an extension mechanism similar to that of SGML[5].

Metadata of EBKS is based on Dublin Core[2] like OEB PS, and does not use qualifiers. By not using qualifiers, the public can easily create metadata. For style, XSL-FO(eXtensible Stylesheet Language)[18] is recommended but not specified, so arbitrary style is possible.

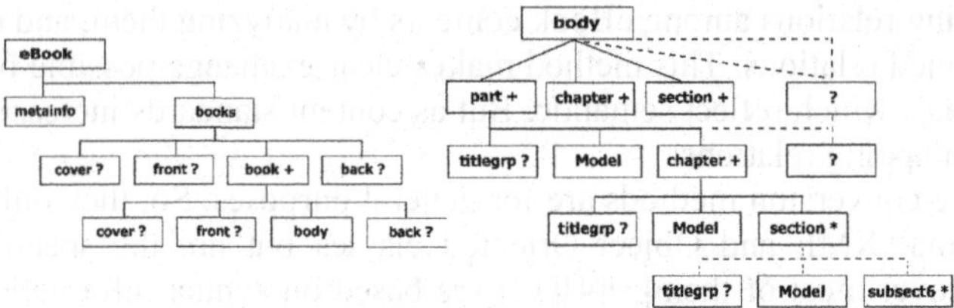

Fig. 1. Overview of EBKS

2.2 OEB PS

The objectivity of OEB PS[7] is making an eBook success in marketplaces. So, to support existing documents, OEB PS is based on XHTML 1.0[16], which is based on HTML 4.0[15]. OEB PS is composed of OEB document and package, as shown in Fig. 2. OEB document is classified into a basic document and an extended document. A basic document conforms to OEB specification based on XHTML 1.0, and the logical structure is not defined. An extended document is an XML document, which can describe any document structure. In other words, any XML document can be an OEB extended document. OEB PS defines package for distribution of a publication. Package describes the structure of an OEB publication but not contents. It is made up of a package identifier; metadata that contains publication information based on Dublin Core[2]; a manifest that expresses document file, image and style sheet that makes up a publication; a spine; tours, and a guide that describes extra information such as a table of contents, references, and indexes. OEB PS also defines style information based mostly on CSS1(Cascading Style Sheet)[13], and partially on CSS2[14].

2.3 JepaX

The goal of JepaX[6] is being used as the means for storing and exchanging contents of an eBook. The structure of JepaX is made up of a whole structure, metadata, logical elements, list elements, block elements, inline element, and logical style elements. The whole structure information is composed of "jepainfo" describing extended structure, "bookinfo" describing matatada and constitution of book like "cover", "front", "body" and "back". This structure is shown in Fig. 3. JepaX defines a high level structure of a book and does not define the structures below "front", "body", and "back". Instead, it defines the constitution of the structure. So, to express the structure, attributes such as "type" of "div" element are used, as TEI[11] or DocBook[1] does. For example, if lower structure of "body" is "section" and "subsect1", then the structure can be represented as shown in Fig. 3. And it defines user-defined extension mechanism by offering "xtype", similar to "type" of "div" element. JepaX defines its own nine metadata. Logical elements mean "div", "head", "title", and "author". Block and inline elements are analogous to HTML. To allow companies to use style information most appropriate to their needs, style information is not defined.

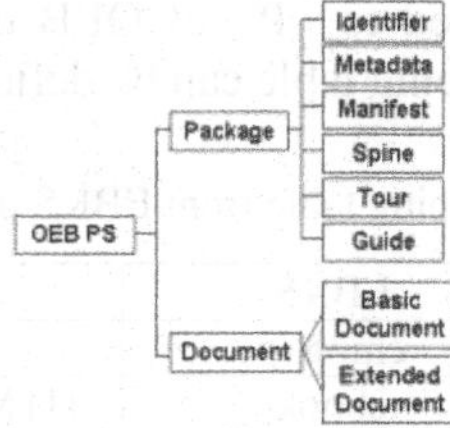

Fig. 2. Overview of OEB PS

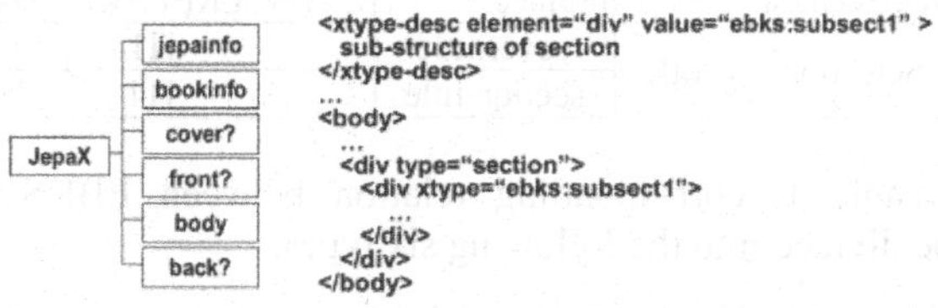

Fig. 3. Overview of JepaX and an example of using "div"

3 Mapping Relations between EBKS and OEB PS/JepaX

All three standards are based on XML[17], so how to map the structure information is important when converting. Because EBKS defines only the contents and metadata, and style is recommended, we mainly focus on contents and metadata aspects of conversion.

3.1 EBKS and OEB PS

OEB document can be an extended or a basic document, so there are two conversion cases. Because extended document is an arbitrary XML document, EBKS document can be an OEB extended document. But reverse is not true, for EBKS has a fixed document structure. Moreover, because the structures of extended documents vary, consistent conversion scripts cannot be defined. Therefore, in this paper, only the basic document is considered when converting between EBKS and OEB document.

3.1.1 EBKS to OEB PS

① Content

OEB basic document is based on HTML, so its content components are related to output rather than structure. So converting EBKS to OEB document is similar to applying style to EBKS document. And applying style to a document is different from a person to person, which is the case when converting EBKS to OEB. For example, title of a chapter in EBKS document can be mapped to <H3> of OEB document and title of a section can be mapped to <H4>, and in extreme cases, every elements in EBKS document can be mapped to <P> of OEB document. But by reflecting the logical structure of EBKS, mapping table can be defined like Table 1.

Table 1. A mapping table from EBKS to OEB document

<table>
<tr><td>Relations</td><td colspan="2">EBKS</td><td>OEB PS</td></tr>
<tr><td>Exactness</td><td colspan="2">emph, p</td><td>EM, P</td></tr>
<tr><td>Extension</td><td colspan="2">ebook</td><td>HTML, HEAD, BODY</td></tr>
<tr><td>Reduction</td><td colspan="2">artwork, fig</td><td>IMG</td></tr>
<tr><td>Omission</td><td colspan="2">ebks</td><td>-</td></tr>
<tr><td>Replacement</td><td colspan="2">preface</td><td><H4>PREFACE</H4></td></tr>
<tr><td rowspan="2">Selection</td><td rowspan="2">title</td><td>cover.title</td><td>H1</td></tr>
<tr><td>section.title</td><td>H4</td></tr>
</table>

As shown in Table 1, corresponding relation between EBKS and OEB basic document can be divided into the following six types.

- □ Exactness: This relation means that there is exactly one target element related to a source element.
- □ Extension: This means that more than two elements are needed to express one source element. This relation can be classified into "Dilation" and "Template". "Dilation" is continuous elements, and "Template" is not.
- □ Reduction: This means that a concept is expressed in many elements in source document, but it is described in one element in target document.
- □ Omission: This means that a source element does not need to be expressed in target document.
- □ Replacement: This means that a source element cannot be expressed in target document. So to describe the element, new element should be generated. But OEB document does not have extension mechanism. So a source element is converted into a content of a special element. This relation corresponds to the "Creation" of EBKS and JepaX mapping relation.
- □ Selection: This means a source element can be mapped to many target elements. In Table 1, "title" can be mapped to one of <H1>~<H6>. In this case, user selects an appropriate mapping element according to his/her purpose.

Out of six corresponding relations, top four can be automatically mapped but for "Selection", user has to decide to which element it should be mapped. Also, for "Replacement", modification should be allowed depending on the needs of user.

When defining mapping table, the fact that the meaning of an element can be different depending on locations should be considered. For example, in case of "title", it can be either a book title or a chapter title. So, to solve this problem, document structure is analyzed in detail in semantic level, and to describe such elements path notation should be used, as shown in Table 1.

② *Metadata*

Both OEB PS and EBKS metadata are based on Dublin Core. And extension mechanisms of metadata are almost the same. Therefore the relation of metadata is "Exactness".

③ *Style*

EBKS recommends XSL-FO and OEB defines style information based on CSS. Compared to CSS, XSL-FO has more abundant functionalities such as multi-column, vertical writing and page support. Hence, some style information cannot be expressed when converted to CSS. However, style expressed in CSS can also be expressed in XSL-FO. Currently, because style is a recommended factor of EBKS, both XSL-FO and CSS can be used.

3.1.2 OEB PS to EBKS

① *Content*

Generation of structure information is needed when converting OEB document to EBKS document. But structure information cannot be easily extracted in flat document, such as OEB document. For example, in OEB document, one element may be used for expressing more than one concept(title, author, …), or one element may have more than one concept(<H2>title, author</H2>). So, automatic conversion is not possible. And each part of actual document has to be converted case by case.

② *Metadata*

Conversion of metadata converting is the same as the conversion from EBKS to OEB document.

③ *Style*

EBKS recommends XSL-FO for style and, currently, what style is used does not matter. CSS can be used but since, then, the structure of document is changed, appropriate style change is necessary. There are two ways to express style. First is defining CSS or XSL-FO on corresponding part of converted document. Second is defining a common style that can be applied to normal EBKS documents.

3.2 EBKS and JepaX

JepaX does not specify style information, so we investigate on content and metadata.

3.2.1 EBKS to JepaX

① *Content*

Unlike EBKS, JepaX only defines the upper level of a document structure and lower level structure is defined by "div". With this in consideration, mapping table for converting EBKS document to JepaX document is as shown in Table 2.

Table 2. A mapping table from JepaX to EBKS document

Relations	EBKS	JepaX
Exactness	ebks, emph vita	jepax, em <div type="vita">
Omission	titlegrp	-
Extension	title	head, head.title.
Creation	subsect1	<div xtype="ebks:subsect1">
	othersect1	<div xtype="ebks:othersect1">

When looking at Table 2, corresponding relation between EBKS and JepaX can be classified into the following four types.

- □ Exactness
- □ Omission
- □ Extension: In this case, extension is "Dilation".
- □ Creation: This means that a source element cannot be expressed in target document. So to describe the element, new element should be generated using extension mechanism. In jepaX, extension mechanism is offered by attribute "xtype" of element "div", as shown in Fig. 3.

Automatic conversion is possible in the four mapping relations mentioned above and fixed mapping table can be defined. Normally, since EBKS has more detailed structure than JepaX, out of the four mappings, "Creation" occurs more frequently than others.

② Metadata

EBKS use Dublin Core for defining metadata, but JepaX defines its own metadata. Among them, five are identical to EBKS and the rest are different. Therefore, for the metadata not expressed in JepaX, extension mechanism of JepaX is used as contents do. So, there are two mapping relation in metadata conversion, "Exactness" and "Creation". Table 3 is a mapping table for metadata between JepaX and EBKS.

Table 3. A metadata mapping table from EBKS to JepaX

Relationships	EBKS	JepaX
Exactness	metadata	bookinfo
	dcLidentifier	isbn
	dc:title	book-title
	dc:creator	book-author
	dc:date	pub-date
	dc:publisher	publisher
Creation	dc:subject	<div xtype="dc:subject">
	dc:contributor	<div xtype="dc:contributor">

In "Creation", to identify the originator of the structure, namespace should be used as in Table 3. It makes a consistent interpretation of converted document.

3.2.2 JepaX to EBKS

① Content

JepaX defines document structure as upper structure, logical structure, list, block elements and inline elements. With consideration for element kinds, and arranging them according to the relations, mapping table can be defined like Table 4.
As shown in Table 4, corresponding relation between JepaX and EBKS can be classified into the following six types.

- □ Exactness
- □ Extension: In this case, extension is dilation.
- □ Reduction
- □ Selection
- □ Omission
- □ Creation: In this case, extension mechanism of EBKS is used.

Table 4. A mapping table from JepaX to EBKS document

<table>
<tr><th>Relations</th><th>JepaX</th><th>EBKS</th></tr>
<tr><td>Exactness</td><td>jepax,front
p, pre, em</td><td>ebks, front
p, prestr, emph</td></tr>
<tr><td>Extension</td><td>title</td><td>titlegrp.title</td></tr>
<tr><td>Reduction</td><td>float, res</td><td>uri</td></tr>
<tr><td>Selection</td><td>author
key</td><td>author|(authorgrp.(author|corpauth))
keyword | keyphrase</td></tr>
<tr><td>Omission</td><td>head</td><td>-</td></tr>
<tr><td>Creation</td><td>ruby, rb</td><td>Extension mechnism</td></tr>
</table>

Out of the six mapping relations, “Exactness”, “Extension”, “Reduction”, and “Omission” allow automatic conversion, but “Selection” needs a preference of a user. And, for “Creation”, JepaX document should be scanned as preprocess to determine which structure of EBKS should be extended.

Mapping information for “div”, an element for defining the logical structure of JepaX, can be classified into the two types, exist in both or exist in JepaX. So possible relationships are “Exactness” or “Creation”.

② Metadata

JepaX defines its own nine metadata. Out of them, five is the same as metadata of EBKS as shown in Table 3, and remains are only in JepaX. So for these metadata, metadata extension mechanism of EBKS should be used which is similar to that of OEB PS. So possible relations are “Exactness” and “Creation”.

4 Conversion of eBook Documents

To convert standard eBook, conversion scripts are needed. For writing conversion scripts, we define conversion classes from mapping relation, and offer conversion scripts for each class using XSLT[19]. So, with the conversion classes and corresponding XSLT, anyone can easily generate conversion scripts. We believe this conversion classes are not only used between eBook content standards, but also general XML documents.

4.1 Conversion Classes

For general content conversion, we classify defined mapping relations into following ten conversion classes.

Table 5. Conversion classes

<table>
<tr><th colspan="2">Conversion classes</th><th>Mappng relations</th><th>Conversion</th></tr>
<tr><td colspan="2">Zero-to-one
Zero-to-many</td><td>Creation</td><td>ebks2jepax, jepax2ebks</td></tr>
<tr><td colspan="2">One-to-zero</td><td>Omission</td><td>ebks2oeb, ebks2jepax, jepax2ebks</td></tr>
<tr><td rowspan="3">One-to-one</td><td>One-to-one</td><td>Exactness</td><td>ebks2oeb, ebks2jepax, jepax2ebks</td></tr>
<tr><td>One-to-value</td><td>Replacement</td><td>ebks2oeb</td></tr>
<tr><td>One-to-adaptive-one</td><td>Selection</td><td>ebks2oeb, jepax2ebks</td></tr>
<tr><td colspan="2">One-to-many</td><td>Extension</td><td>ebks2oeb, ebks2jepax, jepax2ebks</td></tr>
<tr><td colspan="2">Many-to-zero</td><td>Omission</td><td>ebks2oeb, ebks2jepax, jepax2ebks</td></tr>
<tr><td colspan="2">Many-to-one</td><td>Reduction</td><td>ebks2oeb, jepax2ebks</td></tr>
<tr><td colspan="2">Many-to-many</td><td>Selection</td><td>-</td></tr>
</table>

Because one source element is converted to one target element, “One-to-one”, “One-to-value”, and “One-to-adaptive-one” can be viewed as the class of “One-to-one”. But in conversion scripts side, each class is different, so subdivide “One-to-one” to three classes. In defining conversion classes, “Many-to-many” is not occurred in mapping relations, but from defined conversion classes, it can be inferred naturally. And it may include “Selection” relation. “Zero-to-one” or “Zero-to-many” requires a manual work, and “One-to-adaptive-one” and “Many-to-many” needs a user selection. Because user selection can be decided precedently, we regard it as semi-automatic work. And remains can be processed automatically.

In each class, the following scripts are possible. We explain each conversion classes with examples.

i) Zero-to-one, Zero-to-many

This is when source component exists but there is no corresponding target component. So extension mechanism of target should be used. If target does not support extension mechanism, other mechanism like “One-to-value” may be used. The following example uses JepaX’s extension mechanism.

```
Ex) from <subsect1> of EBKS to JepaX
   <xsl:template match="subsect1">
         <xtype-desc element="div" value="ebks:subsect1">
            first sub-structure level of section (EBKS)
         </xtype-sesc>
```

```
•       <div xtype="ebks:subsect1">
          <xsl:apply-templates />
        </div>
    </xsl:template>
```

ii) One-to-zero

This is when a source component does not need to be expressed in target document. So, this is ignored in conversion scripts.

iii) One-to-one

a. One-to-one

This class is when a component information in source document has an exact corresponding element in target.

Ex) from <cover> of EBKS to JepaX

```
<xsl:template match="cover">
   <cover>
      <xsl:apply-templates />
   </cover>
</xsl:template>
```

b. One-to-value

This is when the component information in source has no exact corresponding element in target but, there is other element that can express the information through its value. And its content is expressed by target content element.

Ex) from <preface> of EBKS to OEB PS

```
<xsl:template match="preface">
  <h4> Preface</h4>
  <p> <xsl:value-of select="preface"/> </p>
  <xsl:apply-templates />
</xsl:template>
```

c. One-to-adaptive-one

Similar to “One-to-one” but user designation is needed.

iv) One-to-many

This is when the information expressed by an element in source can be described by more than one element. This class includes “Template” and “Dilation”. Each example is as follows.

Ex) from <ebks> of EBKS to OEB PS

```
<xsl:template match="ebks">
  <html>
    <head>
        <xsl:apply-templates select="title"/>
    </head>
    <body>
        <xsl:apply-templates />
```

- *</body>*
  </html>
  </xsl:template>

  Ex) from <title> of JepaX to EBKS

```
<xsl:template match="title">
    <titlegrp>
        <title>
            <xsl:apply-templates/>
        </title>
    </titlegrp>
</xsl:template>
```

v) Many-to-zero

This class is similar to "One-to-zero".

vi) Many-to-one

This class means that a concept is described by many elements in source document but in target document, it is expressed by one element. Conversion scripts of this are similar to "One-to-one".

vii) Many-to-many

The conversion scripts for this class can be established by the composition of scripts used in "One-to-adaptive-one".

4.2 Experiments

Using defined conversion classes, conversion flow is like Fig. 4, and conversion process is as follows.

i) Extract content structures by analyzing source document.
ii) Generate target structure by analyzing target content form.
iii) Define mapping relations between the source structure and the target structure.
iv) Classify mapping relations to defined conversion classes.
v) With examples of conversion scripts of each conversion class, write up conversion scripts.

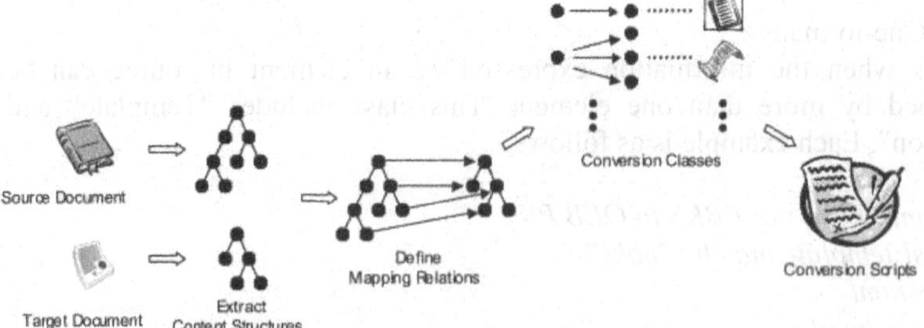

Fig. 4. Conversion flow

The conversion process shown above is a normal flow, and a little bit of customization is necessary to be applied in real conversions. In this section, we adapted it to the real conversion of eBooks. We illustrate two cases of real conversion, EBKS to OEB PS, and JepaX to EBKS.

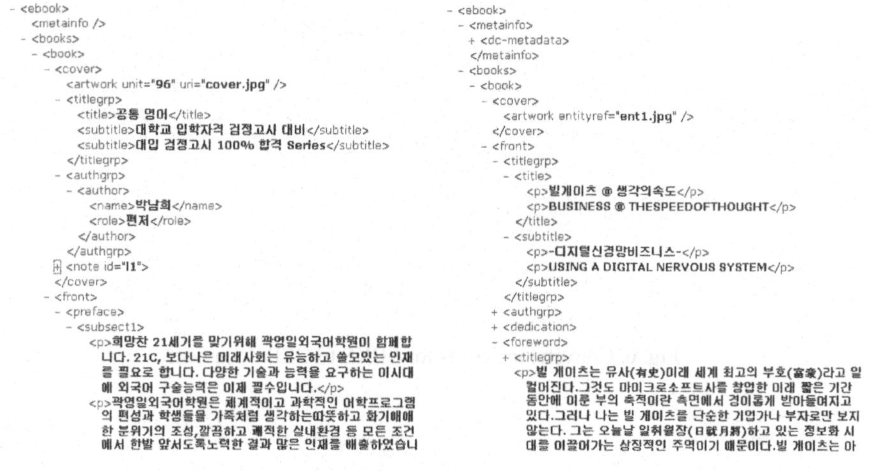

```
- <ebook>
    <metainfo />
  - <books>
    - <book>
      - <cover>
          <artwork unit="96" uri="cover.jpg" />
        - <titlegrp>
            <title>공통 영어</title>
            <subtitle>대학교 입학자격 검정고시 대비</subtitle>
            <subtitle>대입 검정고시 100% 합격 Series</subtitle>
          </titlegrp>
        - <authgrp>
          - <author>
              <name>박남희</name>
              <role>편저</role>
            </author>
          </authgrp>
        + <note id="l1">
        </cover>
      - <front>
        - <preface>
          - <subsect1>
              <p>희망찬 21세기를 맞기위해 곽영일외국어학원이 함께합
                니다. 21C, 보다나은 미래사회는 유능하고 쓸모있는 인재
                를 필요로 합니다. 다양한 기술과 능력을 요구하는 이시대
                에 외국어 구술능력은 이제 필수입니다.</p>
              <p>곽영일외국어학원은 체계적이고 과학적인 어학프로그램
                의 편성과 학생들을 가족처럼 생각하는따뜻하고 화기애애
                한 분위기의 조성,깔끔하고 쾌적한 실내환경 등 모든 조건
                에서 한발 앞서도록노력한 결과 많은 인재를 배출하였습니
```

```
- <ebook>
  - <metainfo>
    + <dc-metadata>
    </metainfo>
  - <books>
    - <book>
      - <cover>
          <artwork entityref="ent1.jpg" />
        </cover>
      - <front>
        - <titlegrp>
          - <title>
              <p>빌게이츠 @ 생각의속도</p>
              <p>BUSINESS @ THESPEEDOFTHOUGHT</p>
            </title>
          - <subtitle>
              <p>-디지털신경망비즈니스-</p>
              <p>USING A DIGITAL NERVOUS SYSTEM</p>
            </subtitle>
          </titlegrp>
        + <authgrp>
        + <dedication>
        - <foreword>
          + <titlegrp>
            <p>빌 게이츠는 유사(有史)이래 세계 최고의 부호(富豪)라고 일
              컬어진다.그것도 마이크로소프트사를 창업한 이래 짧은 기간
              동안에 이룬 부의 축적이란 측면에서 경이롭게 받아들여지고
              있다.그러나 나는 빌 게이츠를 단순한 기업가나 부자로만 보지
              않는다. 그는 오늘날 일취월장(日就月將)하고 있는 정보화 시
              대를 이끌어가는 상징적인 주역이기 때문이다.빌 게이츠는 아
```

Fig. 5. Source EBKS documents

4.2.1 Converting EBKS to OEB PS

The difference between OEB PS and other content standards is that OEB PS has a package. The package contains information for composing a publication with contents. The information of package is processed as follows. First, extractable information of package is used in conversion. Second, a part of package information is mapped to other content with "Exactness" relation. And third, remaining package information is omitted with "Omission" relation.

We have written conversion scripts based on XSLT using the defined mapping table and conversion classes, and it is shown in Fig. 6. Figure 5 is source EBKS documents, and Fig. 7 is converted OEB documents. Conversion scripts are used with Microsoft's XML Parser, MSXML 3.0. In Fig. 7, EBKS document is properly converted to OEB document according to the mapping table.

4.2.2 Converting EBKS to JepaX

In JepaX case, to process "Zero-to-one" or "Zero-to-many" classes, extension mechanism of JepaX should be used. To extend in JepaX, first, component of structure should be defined in "xtype-desc", and it is used in "div", as shown in Fig. 3. At the same time, to describe the originality of extended structure, namespace should be used.

With the defined mapping relation and conversion classes, we write and apply conversion scripts. Figure 5 is source EBKS documents, and Fig. 8 is converted JepaX documents. Conversion scripts' environments are the same as that of EBKS to OEB document. In Fig. 8, EBKS document is properly converted to JepaX document according to the mapping table.

```
- <xsl:stylesheet xmlns:xsl="http://www.w3.org/TR/WD-xsl">
  - <xsl:template match="/">
      <xsl:apply-templates select="ebook" />
    </xsl:templates>
  - <xsl:template match="ebook">
    - <HTML>
      - <head>
        - <TITLE>
            <xsl:value-of select="books/book/cover/titlegrp/title" />
          </TITLE>
        </head>
      - <body>
          <xsl:apply-templates />
        </body>
      </HTML>
    </xsl:template>
  + <xsl:template match="metainfo">
  + <xsl:template match="books">
  - <xsl:template match="book">
      <xsl:apply-templates select="cover" />
      <xsl:apply-templates select="front" />
      <xsl:apply-templates select="body" />
      <xsl:apply-templates select="back" />
    </xsl:template>
  + <xsl:template match="cover">
  + <xsl:template match="cover/artwork">
  - <xsl:template match="cover/titlegrp">
      <xsl:apply-templates select="./title" />
      <xsl:apply-templates select="./subtitle" />
    </xsl:template>
```

Fig. 6. Conversion scripts for EBKS to OEB document

```
- <HTML>
  - <head>
      <TITLE>공통 영어</TITLE>
    </head>
  - <body>
      <hr />
    - <center>
        <img src="cover.jpg" />
      </center>
      <h1 align="center" color="blue">공통 영어</h1>
      <br />
      <h5 align="center">대학교 입학자격 검정고시 대비</h5>
      <h5 align="center">대입 검정고시 100% 합격 Series</h5>
      <h5 align="right">박남희 : 편저</h5>
      <blockquote>개편된 교과 내용을 쉽고 간결하게 정리 각 단원마다 예상 문제
        엄선 수록 문제 에 따른 상세한 해설 기출문제 완전 분석</blockquote>
      <hr />
      <br />
      <h1 align="center">머리말</h1>
      <br />
      <p style="text-indent:12pt">희망찬 21세기를 맞기위해 락영일외국어학원
        이 함께합니다. 21C, 보다나은 미래사회는 유능하고 쓸모있는 인재를 필요
        로 합니다. 다양한 기술과 능력을 요구하는 이시대에 외국어 구술능력은 이
        제 필수입니다.</p>
      <p style="text-indent:12pt">락영일외국어학원은 체계적이고 과학적인 어
        학프로그램의 편성과 학생들을 가족처럼 생각하는따뜻하고 화기애애한 분
        위기의 조성,깔끔하고 쾌적한 실내환경 등 모든 조건에서 한발 앞서도록노
        력한 결과 많은 인재를 배출하였습니다.</p>
      <p style="text-indent:12pt">앞으로도 저희 락영일외국어학원은 최상의
        어학프로그램을 위한 다양한 연구와 개발을 통해어학전문기관으로서의 역
```

```
- <html>
  - <head>
      <title>빌게이츠 @ 생각의속도</title>
    </head>
    <!-- metadata is in package -->
  - <body>
    - <center>
        <img src="ent1.jpg" />
      </center>
      <h1 align="center" color="blue">빌게이츠 @ 생각의속도</h1>
      <br />
      <h2 align="center">-디지털신경망비즈니스-</h2>
      <h5 align="center">USING A DIGITAL NERVOUS SYSTEM</h5>
      <h5 align="right">빌게이츠 지음</h5>
      <h5 align="right">이규행 감역</h5>
      <h5 align="right">안진환 역</h5>
      <hr />
    - <centger>
      - <blockquote>
          <h3>헌사(Dedication)</h3>
        + <p>
        </blockquote>
      </centger>
      <hr />
      <h3>서문(Foreward)</h3>
      <h5 align="right">감역자의 말</h5>
      <p>빌 게이츠는 유사(有史)이래 세계 최고의 부호(富豪)라고 알려어진다.그
        것도 마이크로소프트사를 창업한 이래 짧은 기간 동안에 이룬 부의 축적이
        란 측면에서 경이롭게 받아들여지고 있다.그러나 나는 빌 게이츠를 단순한
        기업가나 부자로만 보지 않는다. 그는 오늘날 일취월장(日就月將)하고 있는
```

Fig. 7. Converted OEB documents

```
- <jepax>
  - <jepainfo>
      <char-exp type="general" />
      <pref-layout flow="both" />
      <xtype-desc element="div" value="ebks:preface" />
      foreword from EBKS
      <xtype-desc />
      <xtype-desc element="div" value="ebks:subsect1" />
      foreword from EBKS
      <xtype-desc />
      ...
    </jepainfo>
  - <bookinfo>
      <pub-date>1999-02-23</pub-date>
    </bookinfo>
  - <cover>
    - <div type="表紙">
      - <head>
          <img src="cover.jpg" />
        </head>
      </div>
    - <title>
        공통 영어
      + <subtitle>
      </title>
      <author>박남희</author>
    </cover>
  - <front>
    - <div xtype="ebks:preface">
      - <div xtype="ebks:subsect1">
```

```
- <jepax>
  - <jepainfo>
      <char-exp type="general" />
      <pref-layout flow="both" />
      <xtype-desc element="div" value="ebks:foreword" />
      foreword from EBKS
      <xtype-desc />
      ...
    </jepainfo>
  + <bookinfo>
  - <cover>
    - <div type="表紙">
      - <head>
          <img src="ent1.jpg" />
        </head>
      </div>
    </cover>
  - <front>
      <title />
      빌게이츠 @ 생각의속도 BUSINESS @ THESPEEDOFTHOUGHT
    + <subtitle>
      <author>빌게이츠 지음</author>
      <author>이규행 감역</author>
      <author>안진환 역</author>
    - <div xtype="ebks:dedication">
      - <head>
          <p>이 책을 나의 아내 멜린다와 딸 제니퍼에게 바칩니다.</p>
        </head>
      </div>
    + <div xtype="ebks:foreword">
      . . .
```

Fig. 8. Converted JepaX documents

5 Conclusions and Future Directions

In the aspect of structure information, conversions of eBook contents are divided into up, down, and equal conversion. Generally, in a down conversion, consistent conversion scripts can be easily defined because this involves only the removal of structures. In an up conversion, because generating structure information is not easy, a consistent conversion script cannot be defined, and each document should be converted one by one.

To find out whether automatic conversion is possible or not, conversion classes can be classified as in Table 6. In Table 6, "One-to-value" and "One-to-adaptive-one" need user decision, and "Zero-to-one(many)" requires manual works when using extension mechanism. Remaining does not need user intervention.

Table 6. Conversion classes operation classification

Conversion classes		Operation
Zero-to-one Zero-to-many		Manual
One-to-zero		Automatic
One-to-one	One-to-one	Automatic
	One-to-value	Semi-automatic
	One-to-adaptive-one	Semi-automatic
One-to-many		Automatic
Many-to-zero		Automatic
Many-to-one		Automatic
Many-to-many		Semi-automatic

With Table 6 and structure information as references, eBook conversions are classified as shown in Table 7.

Table 7. Classification of eBook conversion methods

Classification	Domain	Methods
Down	EBKS to OEB PS	Automatic
Equal	EBKS and JepaX	Semi-automatic
Up	OEB PS to EBKS	Manual

Down conversion in Table 7 can be done automatically when user selection is performed in advance. And because equal conversion has "Zero-to-one(many)" class, it can be semi-automatic.

In summary, we analyzed each standard for eBook contents, defined mapping relations based on EBKS with regard for semantic information, classified mapping relations into eight conversion classes, and provided conversion scripts examples for each class. With defined mapping relations and conversion classes, we wrote up conversion scripts for EBKS to OEB PS/JepaX, and experimented with them. We believe the defined conversion classes can be applied to normal document conversions and we plan to pursue out study in this direction.

In a document conversion, it is possible for the structure constitution to have different meanings depending on the location of the structure. So, it is recommended to use a path to specify a structure element. And in "zero-to-one(many)" class, new element is generated. To maintain consistent meaning of elements, namespace should be used.

References

1. DocBook 2.0.2, http://www.dockbook.org, 2001.
2. *Dublin Core Metadata Element Set, Version 1.1*: Reference Description, Internet RFC 2413, http://purl.org/dc/elements/1.1, 2001.
3. Erhard Rahm, Philip A. Bernstein, *A survey of approaches to automatic schema matching.* The VLDB Journal, *10:334-350, 2001*
4. Hong Su, Harumi A. Kuno, and Elke A. Rundensteiner, *Automating the transformation of XML documents*. Proc. of WIDM, pp. 68-75, 2001.
5. *Information Processing – Text and Office System - Standard Generalized Markup Language (SGML),* ISO 8879:1986, 1986.
6. Japanese Electronic Publishing Association (JEPA), http://www.jepa.or.jp, 2001.
7. Open eBook Forum, Open eBook Publication Structure 1.0, http://www.openebook.org, 1999.
8. Ronaldo dos Santos Mello, Carlos A. Heuser, *A Rule-Based Conversion of a DTD to a Conceptual Schema,*. Proc. of ER 2001, Yokohama, Japan, pp. 27-30, 2001, LNCS 2224 Springer 2001.
9. Ronaldo dos Santos Mello, Carlos A. Heuser, *A Bottom-Up Approach for Integration of XML Sources*. Proc. of workshop on Information Integration on the Web, pp. 118-124, 2001.
10. Sonia Bergamaschi, Silvana Castano, Maurizio Vincini, Domenico Beneventano, *Semantic integration of heterogeneous information sources*, Data & Knowledge Engineering, Volume 36, pp. 215-249, 2001.
11. The Text Encoding Initiative Home Page, http://www.uic.edu/orgs/tei, 1999.
12. Tova Milo, Sagit Zohar, *Using Schema Matching to Simplify Heterogeneous Data Translation,* Proc. of VLDB, pp. 122-133, 1998
13. W3C Consortium, *Cascading Style Sheets (CSS) level 1.0*, http://www.w3.org/TR/ REC-CSS1-961217, 1996.
14. W3C Consortium, *Cascading Style Sheets level 2 CSS2*, http://www.w3.org/TR/ 1998/REC-CSS2-19980512, 1998.
15. W3C Consortium, *Hypertext Markup Language (HTML) 4.0*, http://www.w3.org/ TR/REChtml40 -971218, 1997.
16. W3C Consortium, *Extensible Hypertext Language (XHTML)*, http://www.w3.org/ TR/ 2000 /REC-xhtml1-20000126, 2000.
17. W3C Consortium, *Extensible Markup Language (XML) 1.0*, http://www.x3c.org/ TR/1998 /RECxml-19980210, 1998.
18. W3C Consortium, *Extensible Stylesheet Language (XSL)*, http://www.w3.org/ TR/2000/CR-xsl-20001121, 2000.
19. W3C Consortium, *XSL Transformations (XSLT)*, http://www.w3.org/TR/ 1999/REC-xslt-19991116, 1999.
20. Won-Sung Sohn, Seung-Kyu Ko, Kyong-Ho Lee, Sung-Hyuk Kim, Soon-Bum Lim, and Yoon-Chul Choy, *Standardization of eBook documents in Korean Industry*. Computer Science & Interface, 24:45-60, 2002.

Guidelines for Designing Electronic Books

Ruth Wilson, Monica Landoni, and Forbes Gibb

Department of Computer and Information Sciences, University of Strathclyde
ruth.wilson@cis.strath.ac.uk,
monica.landoni@cis.strath.ac.uk,
forbes.gibb@cis.strath.ac.uk

Abstract. This paper presents the guidelines emerging from the EBONI (Electronic Books ON-screen Interface) Project's evaluations of electronic textbooks [1], which describe how e-learning content can be made usable for the UK Higher Education community. The project's on-screen design guidelines are described, including recommendations as to which features of the paper book metaphor should be retained, and how the electronic medium can best be exploited. Advice on hardware design is also provided. Finally, accessibility issues are examined and practical considerations for the creators of digital educational content are discussed.

1 Introduction

In line with the growth of the Internet and the increasing availability of electronic resources, an abundance of literature encouraging the good design of such resources has emerged. For instance, Jakob Nielsen's *Designing Web Usability* expounds simplicity as the key to usable web site design [2]; Ben Schneiderman's *Designing the User Interface* discusses strategies for effective human-computer interaction including speech input-output and anthropomorphic design [3]; and several guides to effective hypertext design have been written [4, 5].

The EBONI (Electronic Books ON-screen Interface) Project has added to this corpus by developing a set of guidelines for the design of electronic textbooks [6]. However, by responding to the specific requirements of academics and students in Higher Education, the guidelines occupy a unique and important place within the profusion of recommendations. At a time when digital learning and teaching material is growing in availability, they describe how to design electronic resources so that they can be used most effectively as learning tools.

In the Visual Book [7] and the WEB Book experiments [8], two central themes emerged as fundamental to the usability of ebooks in terms of their on-screen design:

- The legacy of the paper book metaphor, and the wisdom of adhering to this, where appropriate, in the construction of the electronic book.
- The different set of requirements arising from when the reader interacts with the new medium; in particular, the needs that arise from an e-learning environment where bite-sized teaching or learning objects are needed to break down the learning process into manageable chunks.

M. Agosti and C. Thanos (Eds.): ECDL 2002, LNCS 2458, pp. 47-60, 2002.

These themes, as well as aspects of hardware design, were explored in detail by the EBONI Project in a series of ebook evaluations, with the findings forming a set of *Electronic Textbook Design Guidelines*.

2 Summary of Methods

The ebook evaluations which informed the *Electronic Textbook Design Guidelines* involved around 100 students, lecturers and researchers from a range of disciplines in UK Higher Education. Evaluations included:

- An evaluation of three textbooks in psychology, all of which have been published on the Internet by their authors and differ markedly in their appearance.
- A comparison of three electronic encyclopaedias: *Encyclopaedia Britannica* [9], *The Columbia Encyclopaedia* [10] and *Encarta* [11].
- A comparison of a title in geography which is available in three commercial formats: MobiPocket Reader [12], Adobe Acrobat Ebook Reader [13] and Microsoft Reader [14].
- A study into usability issues surrounding portable electronic books.

A specially developed "Ebook Evaluation Model" was implemented by each of these experiments, ensuring that all results could be compared at some level. This methodology comprised various options for selecting material and participants and described the different tasks and evaluation techniques which can be employed in an experiment. The methodology, presented in full at the European Conference on Research and Advanced Technologies for Digital Libraries in 2001 [15], comprised four stages:

1. Selection of material. Texts could be selection for evaluation according to three parameters: format/appearance, content and medium.
2. Selection of actors. Four possible actors in an experiment can be distinguished: the participants, the evaluators, the task developers and the task assessors.
3. Selection of tasks. The following task-types were proposed to gather quantitative feedback from participants about the material:
   a. Scavenger hunts, which involved participants in hunting through the material selected for evaluation in search of specific facts.
   b. Exams, which involved the participant reading a chapter or a chunk of text for a short period of time, learning as much as possible in preparation for a short exam.
4. Selection of evaluation techniques. The following evaluation procedures were used:
   a. Subjective satisfaction questionnaires.
   b. Think-aloud sessions.
   c. Interviews.

3 Adhering to the Book Metaphor

The Visual Book study concluded that readers approach texts in electronic format with expectations inherited from their experience with paper books [16]. EBONI's studies have confirmed that the structure and appearance of paper books are at the forefront of readers' minds when negotiating electronic texts, as summed up in the words of one participant: "It didn't feel like I was reading a book. The fact that it was an electronic device rather than a traditional book with a cover and pages somehow seemed to me to take something away from the experience" [17]. Moreover, EBONI's evaluations have highlighted particular aspects of paper books that were regarded as important and should be retained in the electronic medium.

3.1 Cover Your Book

Although of no practical value in an electronic environment, the inclusion of a textbook "cover" adds to the enjoyment of the reading experience, reinforcing the user's perception that he or she is reading a unique set of pages which form a cohesive unit, and providing a point of recognition on return visits to the book. If the textbook has a paper counterpart, the cover should resemble the cover of the paper book. If the textbook does not have a paper counterpart, a colour illustration should be used, together with the title and author's name. In both cases, a prominent link should be provided to the table of contents. The cover should comprise one page and fit in one screen; scrolling should not be required.

As well as providing a point of recognition for an individual book, covers may also be used to provide a unifying identity across several texts and other learning resources within the same course or subject area. By "branding" a cover with a logo, font or colour scheme belonging to a particular series of resources, students will be able to recognise a relevant text immediately.

3.2 Include a Table of Contents

Tables of contents are an essential feature in both print and electronic media, used by readers to skim the contents of an unfamiliar book to gain an idea of what can be found inside. They also provide the reader with a sense of structure, which can easily be lost in the electronic medium, and can be an important navigation tool where hypertext is used to link from the table of contents to individual chapters.

When using the table of contents as a browsing tool, the more meaningful the chapter headings and the more detail that is provided under each heading, the more informed the reader will be about the relevance of the chapter to his or her requirements.

In the evaluation of psychology texts, *The Joy of Visual Perception* had the option to view the table of contents in a frame on the left side of the screen, throughout the entire book [18]. Users liked having it always present as it performed the function of a navigation bar, enabling them to jump quickly to other sections and to view the contents and structure of the book without having to return to a "contents page".

3.3 Include an Index

An index helps readers to find information on a specific topic within a book. By including hyperlinks from each index item to the relevant section in the book, it can become an important navigation tool.

Because it is more difficult to "flick" through the pages of an electronic book when searching for information, the index may be more heavily relied upon than in the paper medium, and its availability should be made prominent and clear to the user. In printed books, readers know to look towards the back for the index. In an electronic book, it should be just as easy to find.

A dynamic index, which links index items to the relevant pages of the book automatically, no matter how the book is divided, would be a valuable tool, and further research is required to define and develop this technology.

3.4 Treat the Book in Terms of the Individual User's Learning Style

Users' learning styles differ and, while some prefer to focus exclusively on one book at a time, others prefer to consult several texts simultaneously. Therefore, it should be made possible to treat the book as a closed environment, containing no links to external sources unless clearly labeled as such (for example in a reference section or bibliography). This assists the user in understanding the book as a single unit, avoids confusion about which pages are part of the book, and which are part of another resource, and, in the case of texts available via the Web, prevents readers from becoming "lost" in cyberspace.

For those who would rather look at several books at once, a more open learning environment should be made possible, with links to external sources and the ability to open and view several books on a screen at any one time.

3.5 Design Typographical Aspects Carefully

The positioning of textual and other elements on screen was heavily commented on by users, particularly in the comparison of psychology texts, and has an important impact on their ability to learn.

Therefore, readers expect typographical sophistication, and pagination has to be designed carefully to enhance readability. Line lengths similar to that of the printed page (10 to 15 words) are preferred, punctuated with plenty of "white space" to give each page a clean, uncluttered appearance. Paragraphs should be left-justified, providing a uniform starting point for each line and enabling the reader to scan the text effectively. Finally, the typographical style should be consistent throughout the book.

3.6 Use Short Pages

Very long pages (for example, containing an entire chapter) are difficult to scan, and scrolling up and down to refer to different sections of text can be frustrating. Rather, dividing chapters into several pages can increase users' intake of information. However, very short pages with little content which require the reader always to be continually "turning" pages can also be annoying and readers easily become lost. Therefore, the typical page length of a print textbook should be considered as an approximate model for the length of pages in an electronic book, and the amount of scrolling required should be minimised, especially for smaller screen sizes.

In terms of logical structure, chapters should be divided according to natural breaks in the text (for example, one sub-section per page), and hypertext should be used to provide links between the pages. Readers are able to comprehend up to two levels of sub-division (e.g. a chapter, and a section within a chapter), and such a breakdown enhances the clarity of the structure; however, three or more levels of subdivision may result in confusion about the interrelationship of the sections and hinder retrieval.

3.7 Provide Orientation Clues

Readers gain a sense of their place in a printed book via the page numbers and by comparing the thickness and weight of the pages read against the thickness and weight of the pages still to be read. It is important for this "sense of place" also to be present in the electronic medium, via page numbers, chapter and section headings, or navigation bars which highlight the current position. These indications of a reader's progress through the book should be accurate and visible.

It is also important to be able to move around the book quickly and easily, jumping several pages at a time or from one chapter to another. Adobe Acrobat Ebook Reader's navigation bar, which enables movement from any page to any other page, was praised in this respect.

3.8 Use Non-text Items with Care

Readers expect images, diagrams and formulae to be included and to look as visually sophisticated as they do on the printed page. As one participant in EBONI's evaluations said, "I like these pictures; they're just like you get in a paper book!" If possible, and where appropriate, pictures should be in colour.

The advantages of dividing long streams of text using colours and graphics are outlined in section 4.6 below, and it is suggested that diagrams therefore be included in the main body of the text to add colour and interest.

However, in scientific and mathematical disciplines, it is often necessary to study diagrams and formulae closely and to make comparisons, and this should be taken into account when positioning these items in the text. In such cases, it is advisable not only to insert images, diagrams and formulae within the main body of the text, but also to allow the user to view enlarged versions in a separate window. Images should be of a sufficient resolution to remain clear when viewed in either size.

3.9 Provide Bookmarking and Annotating Functions

Advanced functionalities such as bookmarking, highlighting and annotating were not heavily used by participants, but several commented that they liked the inclusion of these facilities and would use them on a future occasion. "I didn't think you'd be able to make notes on the computer - I think that's quite good. I'd definitely be willing to give this a try", said one user.

Such facilities, often supplied by commercial ebook reader software products, can be awkward, difficult or time-consuming to use. If they are provided, they should be as powerful, straightforward and quick to use as possible. Users would also like to perform advanced functions using these features, such as searching across annotations, or generating lists of annotations for use in other applications.

4 Adapting to the Electronic Medium

In his Alertbox for July 26, 1998 Jakob Nielsen suggested that, in order to be a success, an electronic text should not simply mimic its paper counterpart [21]. He believes that the new medium inevitably involves the reader in a different way and that much more powerful user experiences can be achieved by deviating from a linear flow of text. In particular, increasing the "scannability" of a text through use of extra headings, large type, bold text, highlighted text, bulleted lists, graphics and captions, can have a direct influence on its usability.

This theory was applied in the WEB Book experiment, and again in EBONI's evaluations. In addition to the above guidelines, which focus on maintaining features of the paper book, the following interface design considerations emerge.

4.1 Provide a Search Tool

Tables of contents and indexes both offer access points for browsing. These can be supplemented by search tools which provide another method of finding information in an electronic text, and are appreciated by readers (especially readers of reference material such as encyclopaedias, where specific information is sought). They should not replace tables of contents and indexes, and should be intelligent enough to simulate and enhance the way readers search in paper books. Frequent Internet users want to apply the same information seeking techniques they use online when searching for information in an electronic textbook. They like to use search tools, and expect them to be powerful and easy to use. A choice between simple searches (searching the whole book, a chapter or a page for a keyword), and advanced searches should be offered to suit different levels of reader, and search tips should be provided.

4.2 Use Hypertext to Enhance Navigation and Facilitate Cross-Referencing

Cross-referencing between the pages of a book, between the main text and table of contents, index, footnotes, glossary or references, and between two or more books is considered an important property of the printed medium. Readers strongly value the ability to achieve these cross-referencing tasks in an electronic environment. This can be difficult to achieve with the same simplicity and effectiveness as flicking through paper pages, but can be made more possible in an electronic book by adopting a strong structure and a clear and simple navigation system.

Separating the glossary and references from the main body of text is considered an advantage; they do not interrupt the text but are just a click away. However, a straightforward means of returning from the glossary/references to the correct place in the text is also important. An expectation inherited from the paper medium is that it will be possible to look up the meaning of a term and then return to the relevant place in the book, quickly and easily.

The functionality provided by browsers (e.g. "Back", "Forward") is very basic and should not be relied on. Standard link colours such as those used in Web browsers should be used where possible, and the functions of any navigation icons should be explicit.

4.3 Provide Content Clues

Section headings, keywords or abstracts under chapter headings in the main table of contents will inform the reader's understanding of the contents of each chapter at a glance. By the same token, the inclusion of abstracts, keywords or tables of contents (linking to headings in the text) at the top of a page help readers to decide on the relevance of the contents of that page quickly.

4.4 Choose a Readable Font

Fonts should be large enough to read comfortably for long periods of time. If possible, readers would like to choose a font style and size to suit their individual preferences, thereby satisfying the needs of those with perfect vision and those with low vision or reading difficulties. Nielsen recommends sans-serif typefaces such as Verdana for small text, 9 points or less, since the low resolution of many monitors means that the detail of a serif font cannot be rendered fully [22]. Fonts which include specific special characters such as italics should be used, and a colour that contrasts sufficiently with the background should be chosen.

4.5 Use Colour to Create a Consistent Style and Aid Scannability

Careful use of a few colours throughout can create a consistent style and increase the likeability and attractiveness of the book. Use of too many colours, however, can be distracting, and plain backgrounds should be used. Pure white backgrounds can "dazzle" readers, causing eye-strain, and should be avoided. Several students commented that white page backgrounds increased glare from the computer screen, making it difficult to read the text.

Microsoft Reader, one of the commercial formats tested, has white "pages" of the book set against a black background, which was found to reduce glare.

4.6 Break Text into Short Chunks

Within each page, breaking the text into short chunks improves the scannability of the page. This can be achieved by, for example, interspersing text with images and diagrams and keeping paragraphs short, and by using meaningful sub-headings, indented, bulleted lists, and colour to break the uniformity of the text.

4.7 Use Multimedia and Interactive Elements to Engage Users

Readers perceive one of the main advantages of presenting educational material in the electronic medium as being the ability to exploit multimedia elements such as video and audio, and interactive elements in the form of experiments and quizzes, methods of communication which are not possible in the paper medium. Interaction in an e-learning environment might include:

- **Reflection** on the information being presented;
- **Action**, for example clicking on a link to another source, conducting a search or participating in an experiment;
- **Assessment**, either by the student or the tutor, of what he or she has learnt; and
- **Integration** of new information, concepts and ideas into the student's understanding of the subject as a whole.

Facilitating interactivity can increase a reader's sense of engagement with the book and enhance the material's likeability. It also increases readers' ability to remember the information being conveyed. In the study of e-encyclopaedias, for example, it was found that the encyclopaedias with greater interactivity and added value content (such as video or audio) contributed to greater memorability.

With many students disliking the experience of reading large amounts of text from a computer screen, multimedia demonstrations and interactive quizzes provide an incentive to study using a computer, and can create an effective alternative learning environment. However, multimedia and interactive elements can make it more difficult to scan material in search of specific facts; therefore, textual equivalents for all information conveyed via these means should be provided (this is also good practice in terms of accessibility) and multimedia and interactive elements should be used to supplement and enhance, rather than replace, text.

4.8 Enable Customization

Readers appreciate the ability to customise a book according to their individual preferences. Aspects such as font style, size and colour should, where possible, be manipulable by the reader (although conforming by default to best practice). It should be possible for readers to save their preferred settings for continued use. Such functionalities are sometimes provided by commercial ebook products; for example, with Adobe Acrobat Ebook Reader, it is possible to zoom in and out of the book, thereby effectively increasing or decreasing the size of the text.

The above on-screen design guidelines are primarily intended to be applied to books published on the Web, but the principles will be relevant to ebooks of all descriptions and, in certain cases, it is possible that only commercial ebook software companies will have the resources to comply at their disposal. They simply reflect the results of EBONI's user evaluations, and it is recognised that they will be implemented at different levels by different content developers.

5 Hardware Design Guidelines

During Summer 2001, EBONI researched the second factor affecting ebook usability: the hardware surrounding the content, which enables the user to interact with the book. Five portable devices were evaluated by lecturers and researchers at the University of Strathclyde: a Hewlett-Packard Jornada [23] with Microsoft Reader, Franklin's eBookMan [24], a Palm Vx [25] with Palm Reader [26], a Rocket eBook [27] and a Softbook [28] (now superseded by the REB 1100 and the REB 1200 respectively). Feedback indicated several design elements that can enhance or detract from the experience of reading or consulting an electronic book. These are outlined in the following five guidelines:

5.1 Employ High Quality Display Technology

Display technology should be high resolution, with high contrast and minimal glare; lower resolution monitors can cause eye-strain with prolonged use. Backlighting can increase portability, in that it enables text to be read in poor lighting conditions. In EBONI's hardware evaluations, users preferred the device with a colour screen and expressed desire for a colour screen where this was not available.

5.2 Balance Lightness and Portability against Legibility

Finding the optimum size of ebook hardware is a question of balancing weight, portability and ergonomics against legibility and quantity of text on screen. Small, slim, lightweight devices are easier to hold and more attractive than large and heavy ones; however, users dislike very small screens which restrict the amount of text displayed in any one "page", as they have to turn pages very frequently.

A host of limitations when reading a textbook from a small screen was uncovered, and this issue deserves a more dedicated, detailed study than this experiment afforded. Palm Reader on the Palm Vx, the smallest of the devices, was found to be less usable on nearly every count. All users found it difficult to discover the information they were looking for and it was reported to be more frustrating and confusing and less clearly structured than the other electronic formats. All users scored 0% in memory tasks and, when asked what he particularly liked about reading the book, one user responded, "Nothing. It just made me frustrated".

5.3 Design Devices for Comfort

Ebook hardware should be designed for comfort (large, heavy devices can be difficult to hold), and the ability to hold a device easily in one hand is considered an advantage. The necessity to use a stylus should be kept to a minimum; they are awkward to handle, and users worry about losing them.

5.4 Use Buttons and Dials to Improve Page Turning

Careful design of buttons or dials for turning pages can improve the page turning aspect of the paper book metaphor, leading to a smoother, faster transition from one page to the next. In EBONI's evaluations, users of the devices which employ dials commented that they felt they could read faster using this method of page turning. Simple "page forward/page back" buttons are felt to be intuitive, but buttons should be large, as opposed to small and fiddly.

All the commercial formats were praised for the ease with which pages of books can be turned (both forward and backward). In each format, this can be achieved by simply hitting a key or clicking on an icon.

5.5 Make Devices Robust

The number and diversity of situations in which ebooks can be read can be constrained when devices are delicate, fragile or costly. Most devices used in EBONI's evaluations were criticised for being too fragile and thereby restricting usage. Rubber edges and hard covers can help with this aspect of ebook design.

6 Accessibility Considerations

The above guidelines outline the findings of EBONI's studies. However, investigations into accessibility issues by the World Wide Web Consortium's Web Accessibility Initiative are also relevant to the design of electronic textbooks, and have been incorporated into EBONI's guidelines where appropriate.

The W3C's Web Content Accessibility Guidelines [29] identify the following issues to consider when designing for accessibility:

- Users may not be able to see, hear, move, or may not be able to process some types of information easily or at all.
- Users may have difficulty reading or comprehending text.
- Users may not have or be able to use a keyboard or mouse.
- Users may have a text-only screen, a small screen, or a slow Internet connection.
- Users may not speak or understand fluently the language in which the document is written.
- Users may be in a situation where their eyes, ears, or hands are busy or interfered with (e.g. driving to work, working in a loud environment, etc.).
- Users may have an early version of a browser, a different browser entirely, a voice browser, or a different operating system.

Electronic books have the potential to address all of these issues and to overcome many of the barriers to accessibility presented by paper books [30]. In the electronic medium, font sizes can be adjusted to suit the eyes of the visually impaired reader, multimedia capabilities can be exploited so that blind users can listen to text being read aloud, or to present information in a choice of media to those with cognitive disabilities, and reading devices can be designed for use by readers with limited dexterity.

However, the wealth of opportunities presented by the digital medium is accompanied by a set of potential dangers. Kerscher notes that the evolution of electronic publishing is now well underway and that there are powerful forces at work to shape future advances in IT which may not have the interests of the whole population at heart [31]. Despite the capability of technology to present information to readers of all abilities, there is a chance that, unless a proactive and coordinated approach is adopted by technologists, bodies of electronically published material may not be accessible to those with disabilities.

EBONI believes that the wants and needs of the widest possible audience should be represented, and that, in any case, good design for students and teachers with disabilities will be good design for all. As such, in addition to incorporating the results of its series of studies into various aspects of ebook usability, the guidelines also integrate recommendations from the W3C specifications and refer users to the DAISY Digital Talking Book standard, which has emerged in response to the concerns outlined above [32].

7 Practical Considerations for Content Creators

Further, in order that the guidelines would reflect the requirements of students and lecturers from different disciplines and backgrounds, a survey of the use of e-resources in Higher Education was carried out in November 2001. This was in accordance with a core objective of the project, to "identify and report on the individual requirements of academics and students in learning and teaching on the Web". The intention was to understand any differences in needs from, use of and attitudes to technology between lecturers in different academic disciplines, as well as between those teaching undergraduate, postgraduate and evening classes. The identification of such differences would inform EBONI's best practice guidelines for e-textbook design, in order that they reflect requirements at a more individual level.

Over 100 lecturers from Glasgow's three universities (Strathclyde, Glasgow and Glasgow Caledonian) responded to an online questionnaire, asking about which course(s) they teach, whether any course material is delivered electronically, and whether electronic material forms part of the list of recommended reading for their courses.

The following conclusions are of note:

- Undergraduate teachers were more likely than postgraduate or evening class tutors to deliver electronic course material and to recommend electronic material to students.

- Respondents in the Humanities were least keen to use e-course material or to recommend electronic reading to students in the future.
- Electronic books were not used at all by respondents in Computer and Information Science, Engineering, Mathematics and Statistics, or Medicine. They were used most heavily as course material in Business, but also in English, Languages, Law and Science. They featured most heavily on recommended reading lists in the Social Sciences and the Humanities, but also in Business, Education, English, Geography, Languages, Law and Science.
- Multimedia resources were not used at all by respondents in Computer and Information Science, and very little in Business, the Humanities and Law. They were used most heavily in Medicine, English, Engineering, Geography, and Mathematics and Statistics.
- Several resource types emerged as unique or especially important to particular disciplines. For example, software was used in Computer and Information Science, electronic case reports and statutes in Law, and online theorem proofs in the Humanities.

Responses to open questions revealed teachers' views on the advantages offered by electronic learning and teaching material, as well as the obstacles to its current or future use.

A lack of resources was the most frequently cited obstacle to the use of electronic teaching material, with insufficient time and overstretched IT support services inhibiting development in all disciplines. Several lecturers extolled the use of electronic material in enabling students to access resources from anywhere at any time, and in potentially including previously excluded students. However, some feared that increasing the quantity of course material delivered electronically could actually inhibit access: students' technical skills vary, and less competent computer users could be disadvantaged. Evening class tutors were keen to incorporate electronic course material, but said that provision of equipment would have to increase so that all students have access to a PC and printer.

The quality of educational material currently available online was a concern for lecturers in some disciplines. It was acknowledged that some excellent, authentic and up-to-date material is provided on the Web, and that quality international unpublished papers and resources are freely available. However, large quantities of unreliable, incorrect and out-of-date material are also accessible, and finding resources of a suitable quality can be an onerous task.

The most enthusiastic proponents of electronic educational material felt that it increased the learning opportunities offered to students. In particular, the interactive and multimedia elements provided by the electronic medium can:

- enable a greater variety of learning experiences than those offered by text on paper;
- provide instant feedback to students; and
- offer alternative explanations, facilitating students' ability to visualise concepts.

Lecturers who expressed the least enthusiasm for electronic teaching, on the other hand, felt that the digital medium alone does not provide a pedagogically enhancing environment. They prefer face-to-face teaching and believe that this enables the most effective learning. This view was most commonly expressed by lecturers in

Education and the Humanities, but also by Social Science, Geography, Engineering, and Medicine lecturers on undergraduate, postgraduate and evening courses.

8 Conclusions

Therefore, while many lecturers are keen to explore the potential of electronic teaching material and to offer new learning channels to students, in many cases a lack of time and resources remains an obstacle to the implementation of their ideas.

Although support is required from several directions in order for greater quantities of educational material to be delivered to students electronically, EBONI's guidelines provide support on developing resources of a high quality, in terms of their design. They are not intended to establish a strict uniformity of interface for all electronic textbooks, but rather to encourage use of those styles and techniques which have been shown to be successful in a Higher Education learning environment. As such, they are of use to all creators of digital educational content, including:

- Writers and publishers of scholarly digital information
- Lecturers in HE
- Information Professionals
- Agencies which invest in the creation of scholarly digital resources
- Electronic book hardware and software developers
- Projects and services involved in the digitisation of learning and teaching resources

The development of an ebook authoring package based on the guidelines would further assist authors in creating usable content, and the feasibility of this is being considered by the Project Team. Further, it will be important to obtain feedback from students and lecturers regarding their experiences with electronic resources on an ongoing basis. Over time, their familiarity with new technologies will increase and new metaphors will influence their expectations; observing and recording their interactions with ebooks will reveal such changes, and ensure that the guidelines continue to reflect current needs, demands and expectations.

References

1. EBONI (Electronic Books ON-screen Interface), http://eboni.cdlr.strath.ac.uk/
2. Nielsen, J.: Designing web usability. Indiana: New Riders, 2000.
3. Schneiderman, B.: Designing the user interface. Massachusetts: Addison-Wesley, 1997.
4. Horton, W.: Designing and writing online documentation: hypermedia for self-supporting products. Wiley, 1994.
5. Horn, R.: Mapping hypertext : the analysis, organization, and display of knowledge for the next generation of on-line text and graphics. Lexington Institute, 1990.
6. EBONI Electronic textbook design guidelines, http://ebooks.strath.ac.uk/eboni/guidelines/
7. Landoni, M.: The Visual Book system: a study of the use of visual rhetoric in the design of electronic books, Glasgow: Department of Information Science, University of Strathclyde (PhD Thesis) (1997).

8. Wilson, R.: The importance of appearance in the design of WEB books, Glasgow: Department of Information Science of the University of Strathclyde (MSc Dissertation) (1999).
9. Encyclopaedia Britannica. Available: http://www.eb.com/ (Last visited 29/04/02).
10. Columbia Encyclopaedia. Available: http://www.bartleby.com/65/ (Last visited 29/04/02).
11. Encarta Encyclopaedia. Available: http://encarta.msn.com/reference/ (Last visited 29/04/02).
12. MobiPocket Reader. Available: http://www.mobipocket.com/ (Last visited 29/04/02).
13. Adobe Acrobat Ebook Reader. Available: http://www.adobe.com/products/ebookreader/ (Last visited 29/04/02).
14. Microsoft Reader. Available: http://www.microsoft.com/reader/ (Last visited 29/04/02).
15. Wilson, R. and Landoni, M.: Evaluating electronic textbooks: a methodology. Proceedings of the Fifth European Conference on Research and Advanced technology for Digital Libraries (ECDL 2001), Darmstadt, Germany, 4-9 September 2001.
16. Landoni, M., and Gibb, F.: The role of visual rhetoric in the design and production of electronic books: the visual book. The Electronic Library. 18 (3), 190-201, 2000.
17. Wilson, R.: The 'look and feel' of an ebook: considerations in interface design. Proceedings of the 17th ACM Symposium on Applied Computing (SAC 2002), Universidad Carlos III de Madrid, Spain, March 10-14, 2002.
18. Kaiser, Peter. The joy of visual perception. Available: http://www.yorku.ca/eye/thejoy1.htm (Last visited 29/04/02).
19. Timmons, C. and Hamilton, L. Drugs, brains and behaviour. Available: http://www.rci.rutgers.edu/~lwh/drugs/ (Last visited 29/04/02).
20. Chudler, Eric. Neuroscience for kids. Available: http://faculty.washington.edu/chudler/neurok.html (Last visited 29/04/02).
21. Nielsen, J.: Electronic books – a bad idea. Alertbox, 26 July 1998. Available: URL http://www.useit.com/alertbox/980726.html (Last visited 8/4/02).
22. Nielsen, J. (2000). *op. cit.*
22. Hewlett-Packard Jornada. Available: http://h30027.www3.hp.com/gatewayPages/handhelds.htm (Last visited 29/04/02)
24. Franklin's eBookMan. Available: http://www.franklin.com/ebookman/ (Last visited 29/04/02)
25. Palm Vx. Available: http://www.palm.com/products/palmvx/ (Last visited 29/04/02)
26. Peanut Reader. Available: http://www.peanutpress.com/ (Last visited 29/04/02)
27. Rocket eBook. Available: http://www.planetebook.com/mainpage.asp?webpageid=15&TBToolID=1115 (Last visited 29/04/02).
28 SoftBook Reader. Available: http://www.planetebook.com/mainpage.asp?webpageid=15&TBToolID=1116 (Last visited 29/04/02)
29. W3C Web Accessibility Initiative. Web Content Accessibility Guidelines 1.0, 5 May 1999. Available: http://www.w3.org/TR/WCAG10/ (Last visited 29/04/02).
30. Wilson, R. "Electronic books for everyone: designing for accessibility", *Vine*. 125, December 2001.
31. George Kerscher.: A forecast of information technology. Hong Kong Society for the Blind Keynote Address. 2 December 1996.
32. DAISY Consortium. DAISY 2.02 Specification. Recommendation, 28 February 2001. Available: http://www.daisy.org/dtbook/spec/2/final/d202/daisy_202.html

Personalized Classification for Keyword-Based Category Profiles*

Aixin Sun, Ee-Peng Lim, and Wee-Keong Ng

Centre for Advanced Information Systems
School of Computer Engineering
Nanyang Technological University, Singapore
{p140971904, aseplim, awkng}@ntu.edu.sg

Abstract. Personalized classification refers to allowing users to define their own categories and automating the assignment of documents to these categories. In this paper, we examine the use of keywords to define personalized categories and propose the use of Support Vector Machine (SVM) to perform personalized classification. Two scenarios have been investigated. The first assumes that the personalized categories are defined in a flat category space. The second assumes that each personalized category is defined within a pre-defined general category that provides a more specific context for the personalized category. The training documents for personalized categories are obtained from a training document pool using a search engine and a set of keywords. Our experiments have delivered better classification results using the second scenario. We also conclude that the number of keywords used can be very small and increasing them does not always lead to better classification performance.

1 Introduction

Text classification refers to the process of assigning documents to suitable predefined categories. In the context of World Wide Web, the text classification problem becomes much more difficult due to several reasons. Firstly, in terms of problem size, classification of text documents on the web has to deal with huge number of documents and users. Efficient classification methods are therefore necessary. Secondly, text classification methods have to deal with documents with diverse content and users with diverse interests. The traditional assumption of fixed pre-defined categories clearly cannot cater for all user interests. In this paper, we therefore focus on classifying documents according to diverse user interests by introducing *personalized classification*. In other words, we would like the users create their own personalized categories and the classifiers for these categories will be automatically constructed for classifying documents under such categories. Personalized classification is clearly useful in many applications such as online news classification, new book recommendation, and others.

To develop a personalized classification method, we have to answer the following questions:

* The work is partially supported by the SingAREN 21 research grant M48020004.

M. Agosti and C. Thanos (Eds.): ECDL 2002, LNCS 2458, pp. 61–74, 2002.

- *How is a personalized category defined?*
  In the traditional text classification problem, a category is defined with a set of training documents. This assumption can no longer hold for personalized classification as it is not possible for users to painstakingly select adequate number of training documents for their personalized categories. If training documents cannot be directly given, what are the other alternatives for users to define personalized categories? In this work, we will study the possibility of defining personalized categories using keywords since it is much simpler for users to select keywords for their personalized categories.

- *How can the classifier for a personalized category be constructed?*
  Since training documents are not available at the point a personalized category is defined, it is therefore necessary to obtain a set of good training documents for the construction of classifier based on the earlier user input (or keywords). Once the training documents are derived, one can apply different techniques to construct the classifier for the personalized category.

- *How can a personalized classification method be evaluated?*
  The effectiveness of classification methods can be determined by experiments. For the evaluation of personalized classification, it is necessary to determine the appropriate experimental setup and performance measures for comparing the different classification methods.

- *How can the changes to the user interest affect a personalized category and its classifier?*
  As a user changes his or her interest domain, the corresponding personalized category will be affected. In this case, feedback from users will be critical as they allow the personalized classifiers to be revised. The amount of feedback and their frequency are important issues to be addressed. Furthermore, the evaluation of such personalized classification methods with feedback mechanism will require different kinds of experiments.

Among the above research issues, we have chosen to address mainly the first, second and third in this paper. We have also divided the personalized classification process into 4 distinct steps, namely:

1. Definition of personalized category profile, where the profile refers to the information supplied by a user to create the category.
2. Selection of training documents.
3. Construction of classifiers.
4. Classification of documents.

These steps are similar to *non-adaptive batch filtering task* as defined by the TREC competition [14]. We will elaborate further on this in Section 2.

Our work is unique in the use of keywords to define personalized category profiles. In most previous classification work, a category profile is often defined by a set of training documents provided by the user. To minimize user efforts, we have instead chosen keyword-based category profiles. Personalized classification using keyword-based category profiles has several distinct advantages. Apart from little user efforts, the keywords give some opportunity to derive a larger set of training documents for the construction of classifiers, instead of being restricted by the small number of training documents given by the user.

In this paper, two approaches of personalized classification for keyword-based category profiles are introduced, namely *flat* and *hierarchical* personalized classification. The former assumes each personalized category is defined independently while the latter explores the possibility of having the personalized categories defined under some pre-defined general categories. The classification methods using SVM classifiers for the two approaches have also been developed. Our experiments on the two approaches have shown that the hierarchical personalized classification outperforms the flat one significantly. We also found out the number of keywords used can be very small and increasing them does not always lead to better classification performance.

This paper is organized as follows. In Section 2, research related to personalized classification are discussed. Our proposed personalized classification processes are described in Section 3. The experimental are described in Section 4 and our results are reported in Section 5. Finally, in Section 6, we conclude our paper and give some pointers to our future research.

2 Related Work

Personalized classification based on document content is considered as a type of *text filtering*, an information seeking process in which documents are selected from a dynamic text stream to satisfy a relatively stable and specific information need [10,11]. In text filtering, one or more set of features each representing a different user interest domain is first derived. Text documents are then retrieved based on their semantic similarity with each set of features. Text filtering techniques have been well-studied in the Text REtrieval Conference (TREC) [14].

TREC classifies filtering task into three types, namely, *adaptive filtering*, *batch filtering* and *routing* [12]. In adaptive filtering, a user supplies a small set (e.g. 2 or 3) of training documents relevant to his/her interest. The decisions of whether the newly coming documents are relevant to the user will be determined immediately upon the documents' arrival. For each retrieved document, the category profile is updated with the feedback given by the user. In this way, filtering decisions can be improved over time. In batch filtering and routing, the system may start with a large set of training documents to construct the category profile. For each newly arrived document, batch filtering involves deciding if the document is relevant or not. In the case of routing, the given document is ranked among other newly arrived documents. When a batch filtering method can update its category profile by collecting user feedback, it is known to be *adaptive.* Much work in text filtering has been reported in TREC [12]. The classifiers involved include k-Nearest-Neighbor (kNN) classifier [1], incremental Rocchio classifier [17] and SVM classifier [7].

Ault and Yang applied the multi-class kNN algorithm to batch and adaptive filtering tasks in TREC-9 [1]. The kNN classifier represented each document x as a vector $\boldsymbol{x}$, and computed the relevance to a category C, $s(C, \boldsymbol{x})$. In their work, different approaches to transform relevance score into a binary decision on assigning that document to the category were discussed in detail. The main difficulty in applying kNN classifier to filtering was the determination of the k value.

Lee *et al.* proposed a batch filtering method combining query zone (QZ), SVM, and Rocchio techniques [7]. The Rocchio's algorithm was used to construct category profiles, while the query zone technique was used to provide negative training documents to the SVM classifier. The final decision of whether a document was relevant or not is dependent on the voting results between SVM output and the profile-document similarity with thresholds. However, the performance of this hybrid filtering method was not promising compared to that based on SVM classifiers only.

At present, our personalized classification problem is similar to batch filtering as they both require a set of training documents for constructing their classifiers. However, our personalized classification methods simplify the user efforts by adopting keyword-based category profiles. The main challenge in our method is in the derivation of appropriate training documents for any personalized categories. To our best knowledge, there has not been research conducted to evaluate personalized classification (or batch filtering) using keyword-based categories. On the other hand, our proposed methods have not considered the possibility of user feedback. Our proposed methods can therefore be treated as non-adaptive batch filtering. In our experiments, we have therefore adopted the performance measures used in the TREC's filtering track. User feedback is a powerful mechanism to improve the accuracy of classification. The extension of our proposed methods to handle user feedback will be part of our future work.

3 Personalized Classification Processes

3.1 Flat Personalized Classification

Personalized classification using keyword-based category profiles requires users to provide a few keywords for each personalized category profile. When the personalized categories are defined independently of one another, the category space is said to be *flat* (i.e., there is no structural relationship defined among the categories), and the corresponding classification method is known as *flat personalized classification method (FPC)*.

Our proposed flat personalized classification process is shown in Figure 1. For each personalized category to be defined, a category profile needs to be created based on the user supplied keywords. Using these keywords, a search engine ranks all the documents from a training document pool according to their relevance to the category profile. Here, we assume that a fairly large pool of training documents is available and from it we are able to find some training documents for the personalized classifiers. Although this assumption may not

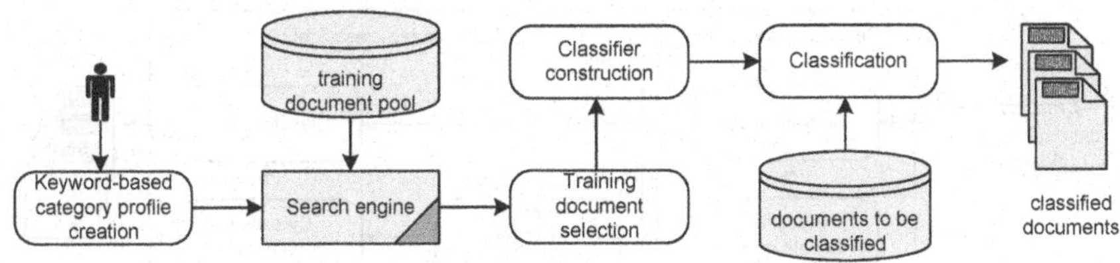

Fig. 1. Flat personalized classification process

be applicable in some situations, it is nevertheless a reasonable assumption for many real-life applications, e.g. personalized classification for online news, technical reports, etc.. Using the ranks (and scores) provided by the search engine, training documents are further selected and used in the construction of personalized classifiers, i.e. the classifiers for personalized categories. Each personalized category will be associated with a personalized classifier that determines if new documents should be assigned to the category.

3.2 Hierarchical Personalized Classification

As the number of keywords provided for each personalized category is usually very small, they may not always be able to characterize the category very well. A straightforward extension is to allow the personalized categories to be defined within some pre-existing general categories that provide the broad context. For example, within the *computing* general category, one may be able to define a personalized category for documents related to mobile devices. In this way, documents that are related to non-computing mobile devices will be excluded from the personalized category. The general categories are pre-defined and and therefore, good sets of training documents can be easily obtained for them. When each personalized category is defined within some general category, we say that the corresponding classification method a *hierarchical personalized classification method (HPC)*.

Our proposed hierarchical personalized classification process is shown in Figure 2. In this process, there are two kinds of classifiers to be constructed, one for the general categories and another for the personalized categories. We call them the *general classifiers* and *personalized classifiers* respectively. Hence, each general and personalized category will be associated with a general classifier and personalized classifier respectively. We currently assume that the training documents of the general categories are determined manually. On the other hand, the training documents of the personalized categories will be obtained from the training documents of the corresponding general categories with the search engine using the user-provided keywords.

Given a document to be classified, it is first classified by the general classifiers. Only when the document is assigned to a general category, it will be further classified by the personalized classifiers associated with the personalized categories under the general category.

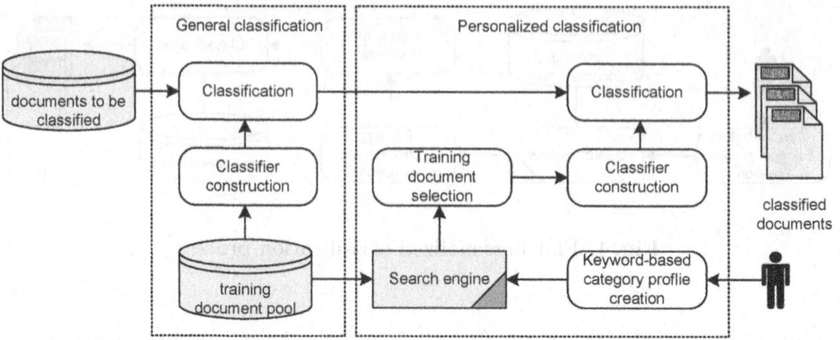

Fig. 2. Hierarchical personalized classification Process

4 Experimental Setup

4.1 Data Set

In our experiment, Reuters-21578 news collection[1] was used. The Reuters corpus is one of the most popular data sets used in text classification [15]. The 21578 documents in this collection are organized into 135 categories. Each document may have zero, one or more categories labelled to it. Since the Reuters' categories are not organized in a hierarchical manner, we manually derived 3 hierarchies from the 135 categories similar to the ones used by Kohler and Sahami [6] (see Figure 3). The 10 personalized categories are grouped under the 3 general categories (i.e., *crude group*, *grain group*, and *veg-oil group*).

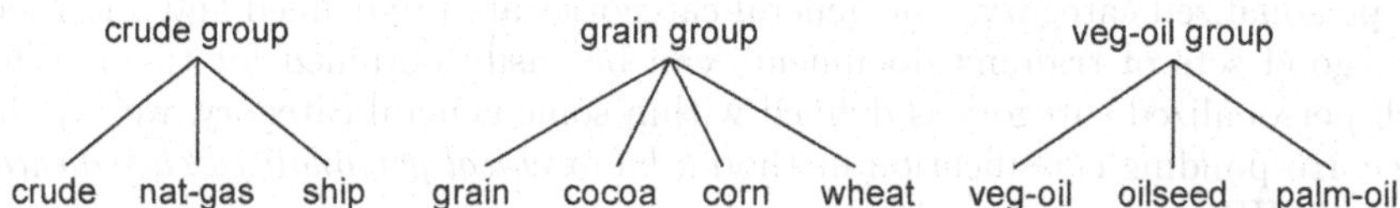

Fig. 3. The general and personalized categories used in the experiments

We used *Lewis Split* provided by the Reuters collection to obtain training documents and test documents. The pool of training documents included all training documents (i.e., LEWISSPLIT="TRAIN") of the 10 personalized categories. In addition, equal number of documents not belonging to the any of the 10 categories were also added to the pool to serve as the "noises" to the search engine. A total of 2314 training documents were included in the pool. The test document set in our experiments included all the test documents (i.e., LEWISSPLIT="TEST") belonging to any of the 10 personalized categories and same number of test documents not belonging to the 10 personalized categories.

[1] http://www.research.att.com/˜lewis/reuters21578.html.

There were in total 910 test documents used in our experiments. After stopword removal and stemming, a feature vector was obtained for each document without applying any other feature selection. The feature vector recorded the words that appear in the document and their frequencies. The stopword list and the stemming algorithm were taken directly from the BOW library [8].

4.2 Search Engine for Training Document Pool

Given the keyword-based category profiles, positive and negative training documents are selected from the training document pool for the construction of the personalized classifiers. In our work, a small-scale search engine is implemented to search the training documents in the pool.

The search engine computes for each training document its *tfidf* rank based on the keywords provided. The *tfidf* weight of a index term w_k in a document d_j is computed from the term frequency $Freq(w_k, d_j)$ and the inverse document frequency.

$$tfidf(w_k, d_j) = Freq(w_k, d_j) \times \log_2 \frac{N}{DF(w_k)} \tag{1}$$

where N is the number of documents in the given document collection, $DF(w_k)$ is the number of documents in the given document collection with the word w_k occurs at least once. The rank of a document is defined by the sum of the *tfidf* weights of all the keywords in the personalized category profile denoted by *cp*.

$$rank(d_j) = \sum_{w_k \in cp} tfidf(w_k, d_j) \tag{2}$$

4.3 Flat Personalized Classification

In flat personalized classification, our experiments simulated the user-provided keywords for each of the 10 personalized categories in Figure 3 by using some feature selection techniques. In the following, we will describe the generation of keywords for personalized categories and the selection of training documents for the construction of personalized classifiers.

Generation of Keyword-based Category Profiles. In our work, we would like a keyword-based category profile to consist of a small set of keywords that can describe or represent the content of the personalized category to be constructed. Intuitively, personalized classification will work optimally when the keywords provided by the user have high discriminatory power in distinguishing documents under a personalized category from those under the other categories. We assume that users are in a good position to define the appropriate keywords for their category profiles. This assumption is important as it was adopted by our experiments to *simulate* the user-chosen keywords generation using *feature selection* techniques.

A number of feature selection techniques have been described in the survey by Sebastiani [13]. Among them, document frequency and information gain (IG)

are most commonly used. However, when a user wishes to construct a personalized category, he will most likely choose the ones that appear in the personalized category with the highest probability while lowest probability in the other categories. We therefore adopted *Odds Ratio* (OR) feature selection technique to generate the keywords for each personalized category. There are several variants of Odds Ratio. In our experiment, we use the exponential form due to its simplicity and excellent performance [9].

$$OR(w_k, C_i) = e^{P(w_k|C_i) - P(w_k|\overline{C_i})} \tag{3}$$

where $OR(w_k, C_i)$ is the Odds Ratio value (between e^{-1} and e) for the word w_k in category C_i, $P(w_k|C_i)$ is the conditional probability of w_k occurring in C_i and $P(w_k|\overline{C_i})$ is the conditional probability of w_k occurs in other categories (i.e., not in C_i). $P(w_k|C_i)$ can be easily calculated using word frequency as shown in Equation 4, where $Freq(w_k, C_i)$ is the times of occurrences of w_k in C_i. $P(w_k|\overline{C_i})$ can be calculated similarly by replacing C_i with $\overline{C_i}$ in Equation 4.

$$P(w_k|C_i) = \frac{Freq(w_k, C_i)}{\sum_{w_j \in C_i} Freq(w_j, C_i)} \tag{4}$$

In the case of flat personalized classification, each personalized category C_p consists of all training documents that belong to the category, and $\overline{C_p}$ consists of all training documents (see Section 4.1) that do not belong to the category. By selecting the words with the highest OR values, the keyword-based category profile of a personalized category is obtained. In our experiments, we evaluated the performance of personalized classification using top 1, 2, 3, 4, 5, 10 and 20 keywords.

Construction of Personalized Category Classifiers. In our experiments, *Support Vector Machine (SVM)* classifiers were chosen for the classification tasks. SVM is good at finding the best surface that separates the positive and negative training examples at the widest margin, and has been successfully applied to text classification problems [3,5]. Since SVM classifiers are binary classifiers, they need to be trained with both positive and negative examples. Our experiments used the SVM^{light} Version 3.50 package implemented by Joachims to construct the SVM classifiers [4].

To construct the personalized SVM classifier for a personalized category in Figure 3, we selected the top-ranked 50 training documents returned by the search engine (using the category keywords) as positive training documents and the bottom-ranked 50 documents as negative training documents. Unlike the document features used by the search engine in document ranking, the SVM classifiers were trained using the binary feature vectors of the training documents.

4.4 Hierarchical Personalized Classification

In hierarchical personalized classification, each personalized category is defined under some pre-defined general category and the choice of keywords for the personalized category profile will therefore be related to the context provided by the general category. Each general category has a well-defined set of training documents which are used in the construction of a general classifier. On the other hand, each personalized classifier is constructed using the training documents selected from the training documents of its general category. In the following, we will describe the generation of keyword-based category profiles, and the construction of general and personalized classifiers in detail.

Generation of Keyword-based Category Profiles. In hierarchical personalized classification, the keywords of a personalized category must be chosen carefully so that they can discriminate documents relevant to the personalized category from the rest in the same general category. Similar to flat personalized classification, we simulated the user-provided keywords based on Odds Ratio.

Given a personalized category C_l, C_l contains the training documents under the category, and $\overline{C_l}$ consists of training document of its parent general category that are not under the C_l. For instance, the training documents of $\overline{corn}$ are the documents that belong to *grain group* but not *corn*. The Odds Ratio values can be easily computed using Equation 3.

Construction of General Classifiers. In our experiments, the general classifiers are also based on SVM. For each general category, we chose all the training documents that belong to its child categories as the positive training documents and all the other training documents from the training document pool to be the negative training documents. Again, the training documents were represented in binary feature vectors when they were used in the construction of the general classifiers. Altogether 3 general classifiers were constructed for the three general categories *crude group*, *grain group* and *veg-oil group*. Each general classifier would determine whether a test document should be classified into the corresponding general category.

Construction of Personalized Classifiers. A personalized classifier is built for each personalized category to determine whether a test document should be assigned to it. However, before that could happen, such a test document must be first accepted by the general classifier of the parent general category.

Hence, in the construction of a personalized classifier for HPC, the positive training documents are chosen from the training documents of the parent general category. We use the search engine to rank the training documents of the parent general category. The top-ranked 50 documents are selected as positive training documents and the bottom-ranked 50 documents are selected as negative training documents for the construction of the personalized classifier.

4.5 Performance Measurement

Most of the classification and filtering tasks have been measured using the classical information retrieval notations of *precision* and *recall* [12,13,15] denoted by *Pr* and *Re* respectively. In TREC-9, two other measures have been used, namely *linear utility measure* and *precision-oriented measure*. These two measures are denoted by $T9U$ and $T9P$ respectively. Let TP be the number of relevant retrieved documents; FP be the number of irrelevant retrieved documents; FN be the number of relevant but not retrieved documents.

$$Pr = \frac{TP}{TP + FP} \tag{5}$$

$$Re = \frac{TP}{TP + FN} \tag{6}$$

$$T9P = \frac{TP}{\max(Target, TP + FP)} \tag{7}$$

$$T9U = \max(2 \times TP - FP, MinU) \tag{8}$$

$T9P$ is the ratio between the relevant retrieved documents over all the retrieved documents. The $Target$ is set to 50 in TREC-9, that is, a target of 50 documents are retrieved over the period of simulation for each category by controlling the classifier (or filter engine) threshold. The actual number of retrieved document may be slightly less or greater than the target. Note that only if the number of retrieved documents is less than the target, Pr will be different from $T9P$. $T9U$ is an utility measure where each relevant retrieved document is given a credit of 2 and each irrelevant retrieved document is given a credit of -1. The lower bound is defined by $MinU$. The $MinU$ is -100 for OHSU topics and -400 for MeSH topics in TREC-9. As for the Reuters collection, we used -100 for $MinU$ in our experiments.

To measure the overall classification performance, the category based average of the measures were computed. For example, given n categories, $C_1, C_2, \cdots, C_n$, $MacPr$ refers to the mean precision over $C_1, C_2, \cdots, C_n$. In this work, only the macro-averages of the performance measures, i.e., $MacPr$, $MacRe$, $MnT9U$ and $MnT9P$, are reported.

5 Experimental Results

5.1 Flat Personalized Classification

For each personalized category, category profiles containing 1 to 5, 10 and 20 keywords were tested. The classification results with the test documents were presented in Table 1.

Similar to most of experiments in TREC-9, our experiments were optimized to the $T9P$ measure. That is, $MnT9U$, $MacPr$ and $MacRe$ were computed when 50 was the target number of documents to be retrieved for each category. As the number of target retrieved documents was controlled by a threshold upon outputs of the classifiers for each category, 50 documents can be easily retrieved for each category. This is the reason that our $MacPr$ values were equal to $MnT9P$.

As shown in Table 1, the macro-precision and recall values were within the range 0.36 and 0.49, while $MnT9U$ values were between 10 and 23. These results were comparable to the ones reported for non-adaptive batch filtering in the

Table 1. Overall results of FPC

Keywords	*MacPr*	*MacRe*	*MnT9P*	*MnT9U*
1	0.49	0.47	0.49	23
2	0.47	0.43	0.47	20
3	0.45	0.40	0.45	18
4	0.47	0.41	0.47	20
5	0.44	0.40	0.44	17
10	0.45	0.40	0.45	17
20	0.40	0.36	0.40	10

Table 2. Detailed results of FPC (with 4 keywords)

Category	*Pr*	*Re*	*T9P*	*T9U*
crude	0.88	0.23	0.88	82
grain	0.82	0.28	0.82	73
veg-oil	0.40	0.54	0.40	10
nat-gas	0.28	0.47	0.28	-8
ship	0.76	0.43	0.76	64
cocoa	0.20	0.56	0.20	-20
corn	0.44	0.39	0.44	16
wheat	0.44	0.31	0.44	16
oilseed	0.32	0.34	0.32	-2
palm-oil	0.12	0.60	0.12	-32

TREC-9 final report [12] despite different data sets were used. On the whole, the performance of FPC was poor. As SVM had been shown to deliver good classification results [3], we believe that the performance had not been good enough due to the quality of the training documents. As the training documents were selected from a pool of documents using only keywords, it would not be always possible to get exactly 50 correct *positive* training documents from the top 50 documents returned by the search engine, especially for personalized categories that do not have large number of training documents. An example of such personalized categories is *palm-oil* which has only 10 training documents.

Another conclusion that can be drawn from the results is that the number of keywords supplied was not the key factor that affects the performance of flat personalized classification. If very few keywords, for example only one or two, were used, the information carried by the keywords would have been too limited to fully describe the category. Hence, it would be difficult to obtain the correct set of training documents. As the number of keywords increased, more "noise" was added into the category profile. The noise would prevent the correct training documents from being highly ranked by the search engine. From the experimental results, we noticed that about 4 keywords were good enough to describe each personalized category. On the other hand, the 4 keywords must be carefully selected. The detailed results for each personalized category using 4-keyword category profiles are shown in Table 2. It can be noticed that some of the categories received high precision while low recall, for instance, *crude* and *grain*. The reason behind is the number of training documents. It is always easier for the search engine to get 50 high-quality positive training documents for the categories with large number of training documents, e.g., more than 100. If one category has less than 50 positive training documents in the training document pool, even if the search engine ranks all these documents in the top 50, some noise documents will be included as positive training documents for the classifier. In Reuters collection, categories have large number of training documents may have large number of test documents too. Since we only retrieve 50 documents (as our target), a large proportion of test documents for these categories can not be included, and that results the low recall values, e.g., *crude* and *grain*. However, for the categories that have fewer test documents, the recall values could be quite high, e.g., *cocoa* and *palm-oil*.

5.2 Hierarchical Personalized Classification

Similarly, we conducted experiments on hierarchical personalized classification with category profiles containing 1 to 5, 10 and 20 keywords. The results are shown in Table 3.

Table 3. Overall results of HPC

Keywords	*MacPr*	*MacRe*	*MnT9P*	*MnT9U*
1	0.63	0.62	0.63	45
2	0.62	0.60	0.62	42
3	0.61	0.60	0.61	42
4	0.61	0.60	0.61	42
5	0.59	0.57	0.59	39
10	0.57	0.56	0.57	36
20	0.55	0.54	0.55	32

The hierarchical personalized classification method performed much better than flat classification method. The improvements were consistent across all numbers of keywords and performance measures. The reason was that some of the classification efforts had been done by the well-trained general classifiers. For the personalized classifiers, the classification space was limited to the documents accepted by their general classifiers. Consistent with the conclusion given by Dumais and Chen, our experiments confirmed that the performance of hierarchical classification for category tree is better than that for the flat categories [2].

Once again, the experiment showed that by increasing the number of keywords did not help much in the classification performance. Table 4 presents the results when the number of keywords was 4 for each category profile. Macro sign test (S-test) [16] comparing the detailed results of HPC and FPC showed that in all measures, *Pr*, *Re*, *T9P* and *T9U*, the P-value, $P(Z \geq 10) = 0.000976$. This indicates that the improvement of HPC over FPC was significant.

Table 4. Detailed results of HPC (with 4 keywords)

Category	*Pr*	*Re*	*T9P*	*T9U*
crude	0.96	0.25	0.96	94
grain	0.94	0.32	0.94	91
veg-oil	0.64	0.86	0.64	46
nat-gas	0.44	0.73	0.44	16
ship	0.98	0.55	0.98	97
cocoa	0.26	0.72	0.26	-11
corn	0.54	0.48	0.54	31
wheat	0.58	0.41	0.58	37
oilseed	0.60	0.64	0.60	40
palm-oil	0.20	1.00	0.20	-20

6 Conclusion

In this paper, we have designed, implemented and evaluated two personalized classification methods known as the flat and hierarchial personalized classification methods. The former allows personalized categories to be defined within a flat category space. The latter requires each personalized category to be defined under some pre-existing general category. Both methods allow users to specify their personalized category profiles by a few keywords.

Our experimental results showed that the hierarchical personalized classification method yielded better performance as the classifiers of the general categories were able to filter away irrelevant documents that could not be effectively recognized by the personalized classifiers built upon only a few user-specified keywords. Nevertheless, compared to the classification systems built upon purely training documents, there are still rooms for performance improvement in our keyword-based personalized classification methods. In particular, our experiments had been conducted on a rather small document collection. A more comprehensive set of experiments could be conducted on a large document collection to examine if the same observations in this paper still hold in a different setting. In the current work, we have also implicitly assumed that the personalized categories are fairly static. In real-life, users may have their interest changed over time. To cope with such evolution and also to improve the accuracy of personalized classification, it is necessary to consider user feedback in the future research.

References

1. T. Ault and Y. Yang. kNN at TREC-9. In *Proc. of the 9th Text REtrieval Conference (TREC-9)*, Gaithersburg, Maryland, 2000.
2. S. T. Dumais and H. Chen. Hierarchical classification of Web content. In *Proc. of the 23rd ACM Int. Conf. on Research and Development in Information Retrieval (SIGIR)*, pages 256–263, Athens, GR, 2000.

3. S. T. Dumais, J. Platt, D. Heckerman, and M. Sahami. Inductive learning algorithms and representations for text categorization. In *Proc. of the 7th Int. Conf. on Information and Knowledge Management*, pages 148–155, 1998.
4. T. Joachims. SVM^{light}, An implementation of Support Vector Machines (SVMs) in C. http://svmlight.joachims.org/.
5. T. Joachims. Text categorization with support vector machines: learning with many relevant features. In *Proc. of the 10th European Conf. on Machine Learning*, pages 137–142, Chemnitz, DE, 1998.
6. D. Koller and M. Sahami. Hierarchically classifying documents using very few words. In *Proc. of the 14th Int. Conf. on Machine Learning*, pages 170–178, Nashville, US, 1997.
7. K.-S. Lee, J.-H. Oh, J. Huang, J.-H. Kim, and K.-S. Choi. TREC-9 experiments at KAIST: QA, CLIR and batch filtering. In *Proc. of the 9th Text REtrieval Conference (TREC-9)*, Gaithersburg, Maryland, 2000.
8. A. K. McCallum. BOW: A toolkit for statistical language modeling, text retrieval, classification and clustering. http://www.cs.cmu.edu/~mccallum/bow, 1996.
9. D. Mladenic. Feature subset selection in text-learning. In *Proc. of the 10th European Conf. on Machine Learning*, pages 95–100, 1998.
10. D. W. Oard. The state of the art in text filtering. *User Modeling and User-Adapted Interactions: An International Journal*, 7(3):141–178, 1997.
11. M. J. Pazzani and D. Billsus. Learning and revising user profiles: The identification of interesting web sites. *Machine Learning*, 27(3):313–331, 1997.
12. S. Robertson and D. A. Hull. The TREC-9 filtering track final report. In *Proc. of the 9th Text REtrieval Conference (TREC-9)*, Gaithersburg, Maryland, 2000.
13. F. Sebastiani. Machine learning in automated text categorization. *ACM Computing Surveys*, 34(1):1–47, 2002.
14. TREC. Text REtrieval Conference. http://trec.nist.gov/.
15. Y. Yang. An evaluation of statistical approaches to text categorization. *Information Retrieval*, 1(1-2):69–90, 1999.
16. Y. Yang and X. Liu. A re-examination of text categorization methods. In *Proc. of the 22nd ACM Int. Conf. on Research and Development in Information Retrieval*, pages 42–49, Berkeley, USA, Aug 1999.
17. Y. Zhang and J. Callan. YFilter at TREC-9. In *Proc. of the 9th Text REtrieval Conference (TREC-9)*, Gaithersburg, Maryland, 2000.

Statistical Analysis of Bibliographic Strings for Constructing an Integrated Document Space

Atsuhiro Takasu

National Institute of Informatics
2-1-2 Hitotsubashi, Chiyoda-ku
Tokyo 101-8430, Japan
takasu@nii.ac.jp

Abstract. It is important to utilize retrospective documents when constructing a large digital library. This paper proposes a method for analyzing recognized bibliographic strings using an extended hidden Markov model. The proposed method enables analysis of erroneous bibliographic strings and integrates many documents accumulated as printed articles in a citation index. The proposed method has the advantage of providing a robust bibliographic matching function using the statistical description of the syntax of bibliographic strings, a language model and an Optical Character Recognition (OCR) error model. The method also has the advantage of reducing the cost of preparing training data for parameter estimation, using records in the bibliographic database.

1 Introduction

It is an important task to construct integrated document spaces in digital libraries. The citation index is one key technique for document space integration. It enhances integration in two ways. First, it enables linkage of articles, and provides users with a highly connected document space. For example, CrossRef, the central source for reference linking [4], constructs such a document space consisting of articles published by several publishers. Second, it widens document space access methods. Citation index construction is a traditional problem in library and information science and it has been used for research trend analysis, authoritative article detection, etc. CiteSeer [5,11] successfully made a citation index of articles on the World Wide Web (WWW) and provides an attractive, and effective, information access method on the WWW using the resulting citation analysis.

The article identification facility of a citation index is very important when constructing an integrated document space. The citation index becomes more useful when extended by two aspects. First, current citation indices concentrate on identification at the article level. By identifying objects with a finer granularity, such as author and institution as well as article, we can access the document space by person and institution, as well as by article. The Digital Object Identifier (DOI) [8] aims to identify objects at any level of granularity. Second, many printed articles should be utilized in the digital document space. This problem

M. Agosti and C. Thanos (Eds.): ECDL 2002, LNCS 2458, pp. 75–90, 2002.

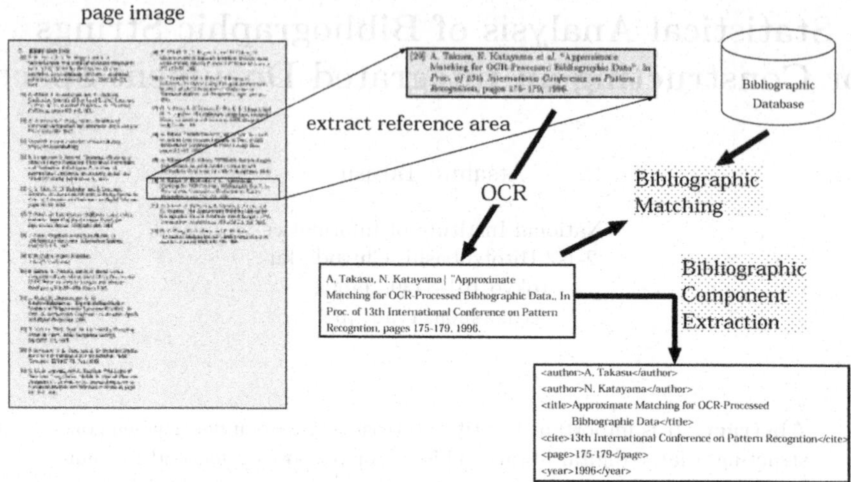

Fig. 1. Outline of bibliographic string analysis

was addressed at the early stages of digital library study and in early document image recognition technologies, such as OCR and document layout analysis [3]. These have been applied to extract textual information from scanned document images. Wong's document layout analysis system [19] is an early one that extracts document components such as article title, author's name, sections, paragraphs, etc. Rightpages [15] is an early digital library system based on document images, and which realized various basic functions of digital libraries, such as delivering articles according to the user's preferences.

In this paper, we propose an analysis method of recognizing bibliographic strings and apply it to bibliographic matching and bibliographic component extraction problems. Figure 1 depicts an outline of the recognized bibliographic string analysis. First, document page layout analysis is applied to a scanned document image, to extract reference areas from the page image. Then OCR is applied to produce bibliographic strings. During this phase, we obtain strings, which may contain some recognition errors. The bibliographic string analysis proposed in this paper is applied to these erroneous strings for bibliographic matching and extraction of bibliographic components. The bibliographic matching extracts the record that is most similar to the given bibliographic string, from a bibliographic database.

In this way, references in document images are identified and integrated into a citation index. On the other hand, bibliographic component extraction extracts bibliographic components such as author's name, article title, etc., from recognized bibliographic strings. In this way, various bibliographic components in document images are identified.

Bibliographic matching has been studied extensively. Its main use is to detect and remove duplicate records in bibliographic databases [6,7,1,13], but it is also used in citation index construction [5,11]. In some studies, matching was performed with data where bibliographic components had been separated previously, e.g., a record in a bibliographic database, and in others, bibliographic components were extracted from clean strings by applying syntactical analysis. For syntactical analysis, delimiters separating bibliographic components play an important role. In the case of recognized bibliographic strings, syntactical analysis becomes much more difficult because delimiters may not be recognized correctly. That is, we must handle strings that have syntactical ambiguity caused by both syntactical variation of the bibliographic strings and by incorrect OCR.

Only a few studies [2,14] were performed by bibliographic matching of recognized strings. These studies used various types of dictionaries to analyze erroneous bibliographic strings. However, bibliographic components in the objective string are not always registered in dictionaries. Therefore, we also require an analysis method without a dictionary. We proposed a statistical model called Dual Variable length output Hidden Markov Model (DVHMM) that can represent the recognizer's error patterns probabilistically, and developed a parameter estimation algorithm [17]. In this paper, we propose a recognized bibliographic string analysis method. In this method, both syntactical variety of the bibliographic strings and OCR error patterns are represented integrally with DVHMM. Since DVHMM can be derived from training data, it functions without a dictionary. In Section 2 we first overview DVHMM and derive a model for analyzing recognized bibliographic strings. Then in Section 3 we present algorithms for the bibliographic matching and bibliographic component extraction. Section 4 gives experimental results of the method using scanned academic articles published in Japanese societies, and Section 5 presents the conclusions of the study.

2 DVHMM

Recognition errors of OCR are usually categorized into substitution, deletion, insertion and framing errors [10]. Substitution error means one character is incorrectly recognized as another character. This type of error happens most frequently. A deletion error means that one character is deleted and an insertion error means that one character is inserted. A framing error means that a sequence of characters is incorrectly recognized as another sequence of characters. For example, "fi" is recognized incorrectly as "h".

Several OCR error models have been proposed. The most typical OCR error model is the confusion matrix, which maps a character c to a set of characters that an OCR possibly incorrectly recognizes as c. For each entry of the confusion matrix, we can assign the probability that an OCR incorrectly recognizes the character [9]. However, the confusion matrix and its probabilistic companion cannot handle framing errors. Li and Lopresti proposed an OCR error model where error patterns were categorized from the viewpoint of string lengths [12]. In this model, a pair (i, j) of original and recognized string lengths is used as an error pattern of OCR and weight, or a penalty of incorrect recognition is assigned to each pattern to calculate the similarity of two strings by dynamic programming matching. This model can represent insertion, deletion and framing errors as well as substitution errors. However, in order to apply the model to a

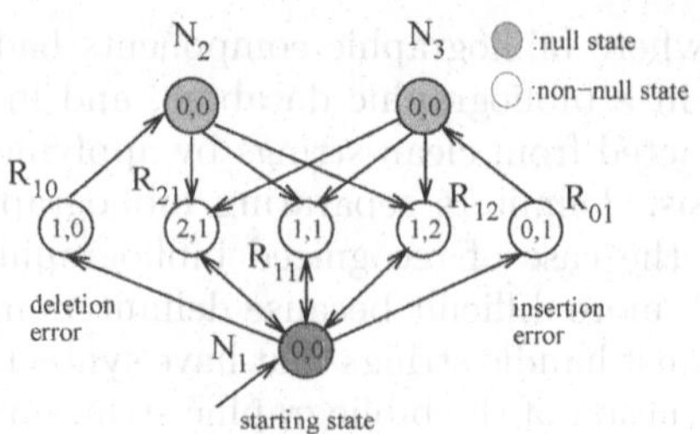

Fig. 2. An example of DVHMM

matching problem, we must determine the weight for every pattern. Furthermore, the weight is the same if an error pattern is the same.

DVHMM categorizes OCR errors from the viewpoint of output string length, similar to Li and Lopresti's model, and uses a Hidden Markov Model (HMM) to

- define the weights in a more detailed manner, and
- calculate the weights systematically.

A DVHMM is a form of HMM. Instead of producing a string, it produces a pair of strings, each of which represents an original string and a corresponding recognized string. States of the DVHMM correspond to recognition error patterns from the viewpoint of output string length, and they are characterized by a pair of lengths of the original and recognized output strings. For example, a pair (2,1) of output string lengths means that an OCR recognizes two consecutive characters as one unit and transforms it to one character. As an output symbol, the state corresponding to a pair (i, j) produces a pair of original and recognized strings whose lengths are i and j, respectively. States are categorized into two groups:

- *non-null* state that produces a pair of original and recognized strings, and
- *null* state that produces null output and controls state transitions.

A state (1,0) means that the length of the original (resp. recognized) output string is 1 (resp. 0), i.e., deletion error, whereas a state (0,1) corresponds to a insertion error. A state (1,1) corresponds to both a substitution error and a correct recognition.

Figure 2 shows an example of DVHMM that represents five OCR error patterns, i.e., (1,0),(0,1),(1,1),(2,1) and (1,2). In this example, three null states are used. One functions as a pivot (N_1 in Figure 2) and has transitions to all non-null states with certain probabilities. The other two states are used to prohibit consecutive insertion and/or deletion errors, which allows recognition of a null string as an infinitely long string, and vice versa. Non-null states other than deletion and insertion have a transition to the pivot with a probability of 1.0. Two null states are counterparts of the deletion (N_2 in Figure 2) and insertion (N_3 in Figure 2), and have transitions to non-null states except for insertion and deletion states with certain probability. On the other hand, deletion and insertion states have a transition to their counterpart with probability 1.0. There is

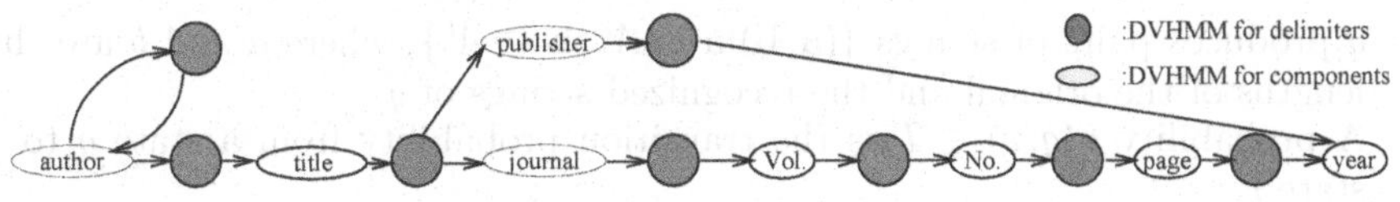

Fig. 3. An example of the syntactical structure of a bibliographic string

no transition among null states, nor transition among non-null states. Therefore, any sequence of transitions visits null states and non-null states alternately. In this way, consecutive insertion and/or deletion errors are prohibited. This is a typical usage of null states to control state transitions.

In Figure 2, output symbols are omitted due to space restrictions. Suppose the alphabet is {a,b}. Then, the output symbols of the state (2, 1) are {(aa,a),(aa,b),(ab,a),(ab,b),(ba,a), (ba,b),(bb,a),(bb,b)}.

DVHMM defines joint probability distribution of a pair of original and recognized strings.

[**Example 1**] Suppose that a string "aba" is recognized "ab". Then, the DVHMM in Figure 2 produces a pair (aba,ab) of strings by the following five sequences of state transitions.

$$N_1R_{10}N_2R_{21}N_1R_{01}$$
$$N_1R_{10}N_2R_{11}N_1R_{11}$$
$$N_1R_{10}N_2R_{12}N_1R_{10}$$
$$N_1R_{21}N_2R_{11}$$
$$N_1R_{11}N_2R_{21}$$

Since the probability that DVHMM produces a pair of strings with a sequence of state transitions is calculated by multiplying corresponding state transition probabilities and output probabilities; the joint probability of (abaa,aba) is obtained by summing the probabilities of all the five sequences of transitions.

Before defining DVHMM formally, we define the notation used in the following discussion. Generally, an uppercase letter denotes a set, a bold face letter denotes a sequence and a string, and a Greek and calligraphic letters denote a function symbol. For a set S, S^l denotes the set of sequences of length l consisting of elements in S. $|S|$ denotes the cardinality of a set S. For a sequence $\mathbf{x}$, $|\mathbf{x}|$ denotes the length of $\mathbf{x}$, $\mathbf{x}[i]$ denotes the i-th component of $\mathbf{x}$, and $\mathbf{x}[i:j]$ denotes a partial sequence of $\mathbf{x}$ starting at the i-th character and ending at the j-th character of $\mathbf{x}$. A partial sequence, $\mathbf{x}[:i]$ and $\mathbf{x}[i:]$, denotes a prefix ending at the i-th component and a suffix starting at the i-th component of $\mathbf{x}$, respectively. DVHMM is denoted as a four-tuple $M \equiv (A, Q, T, O)$:

- A set A is an alphabet. Although we use the same alphabet for both original and recognized characters, we could use different alphabets.
- A set Q comprises states consisting of non-null states Q_x and null states Q_0, i.e., $Q = Q_x \cup Q_0$. Q_0 contains a starting state. On the other hand, Q_x consists of states corresponding to the pairs of lengths. Each non-null state

q produces pairs of strings $\{(\mathbf{a}, \mathbf{b}) | \mathbf{a} \in A^a, \mathbf{b} \in A^b\}$, where a and b are the lengths of the original and the recognized strings of q.
- A probability $\tau(q, r) \in T$ is the transition probability from a state q to a state r.
- A probability $o(q, \mathbf{a}, \mathbf{b}) \in O$ is the output probability that a state q produces $\mathbf{a}$ and $\mathbf{b}$ as an original and a recognized string, respectively.

In DVHMM, we use a starting state (N_1 in Figure 2) instead of an initial probability distribution, i.e., any sequence of state transitions is started from the starting state with a probability of 1.0.

DVHMM differs from ordinary HMMs in the following two aspects:

- DVHMM produces a pair of strings as output, and
- the length of the output symbols is variable.

3 Statistical Model for Erroneous Bibliographic String Analysis

DVHMM has the nature of HMM and can represent syntactical structure in the class of regular grammar. In this section we construct a statistical model for erroneous bibliographic string analysis by combining OCR error models and syntactical structure represented by DVHMM, using the following steps:

1. constructing a syntactical structure of bibliographic strings consisting of bibliographic components and delimiters,
2. replacing each bibliographic component with a DVHMM that produces a pair comprising the component string and its recognized string, and
3. replacing each delimiter with a DVHMM in the same way as for a bibliographic component.

Bibliographic components are located in a specific order, separated by delimiters in references. The form of reference may differ depending on the type of article referenced. For example, a reference to an article in a journal may be represented with a regular expression

$$\text{author}(,\text{author},)^* : \text{“title”}, \text{journal}, \text{vol}, \text{no}, \text{page}, \text{year}.$$

whereas a reference to a book may be represented

$$\text{author}(,\text{author},)^* : \text{“title”}, \text{publisher}, \text{year}.$$

This syntactical variety of references is represented using an *or* operator in the regular expression. Figure 3 depicts an example of a finite automaton for both references to an article in a journal and a book. Notice that a regular expression has an equivalent automaton. Possible patterns of references are enumerated manually and combined into a finite automaton.

OCR error models are constructed for each bibliographic component using a DVHMM similar to that in Figure 2. In order to handle various errors let us consider a DVHMM consisting of non-null states that correspond to pairs

$$\{(i, i+1), (i+1, i) \mid 0 \le i < m\} \cup \{(1, 1)\} \tag{1}$$

of output string lengths for a maximum number m. Figure 2 is a DVHMM for $m = 2$. Generally, a larger m enables more precise modeling of OCR errors. However, since the number of parameters for the output probability distribution is $O(|Q| \times |A|^{2m})$, we cannot estimate the parameters accurately for large m from a limited quantity of training data. This problem becomes serious, particularly for languages using a large set of characters, such as Chinese and Japanese, among others. Therefore, we need to find appropriate m depending on the language used. We discuss this point later in the section on experimental results.

In order to handle bibliographic strings appearing in references, we modified the DVHMM of Figure 2 in two ways. First, bibliographic components are sometimes omitted in the reference. In order to handle this situation, we allow a string of any length to be recognized as a null string, that is, we remove two null states for insertion and deletion errors, i.e., N_2 and N_3, and non-null states for insertion and deletion errors have transition to N_1 with a probability of 1.0 as shown in Figure 4 (a). Second, in order to embed component DVHMMs into the automaton representing the syntactical structure of a bibliographic string, the final states are assigned to the DVHMM. The inbound arcs of a bibliographic component in the automaton are connected to the starting state of the corresponding DVHMM, and outbound arcs are started from the final states of the corresponding DVHMM. In the DVHMM for bibliographic components all non-null states are final states.

A DVHMM for a delimiter is similar to that for a bibliographic component. It has a set of starting states and a set of final states. Various types of delimiters are used in references. For example, volume and number of an article may be described as "Vol.24, No.3" in some references, whereas they may be described as "24(3)" in others. In the former case, the delimiter for number is ", No.", whereas it is "(" in the latter case. In order to handle variation of these delimiters, we use states

$$\{(1, i) \mid 0 \leq i < m\}$$

where m is large enough to express delimiters, including its incorrect recognition. We separate bibliographic components in the original strings with a special character that does not appear in the alphabet. Therefore, the length of the original string is fixed to 1. Furthermore, the original string of output symbols is fixed to the special character. Figure 4(b) depicts a DVHMM for the delimiter of a number. In Figure 4(b), states R_{10}, R_{11} and R_{12} mainly correspond to a delimiter consisting of one character such as ",", whereas states R_{13} and R_{14} correspond to a delimiter such as ", No.".

Training data are given as a pair of an original bibliographic string and a recognized string. The following string is an example of an original bibliographic string for the article [18] in the references of this paper:

> Atsuhiro Takasu †Norio Katayama ‡Approximate Matching for OCR-Processed Bibliographic Data §Proceedings of 13th International Conference on Pattern Recognition ¶175-179 †1996

where † is used to separate authors, ‡ separates author and article titles, etc. On the other hand, the following string is the recognized string of the reference described above:

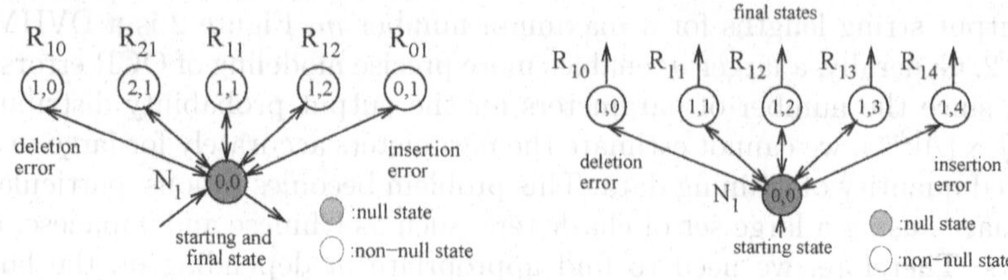

(a) DVHMM for a bibliographic component (b) DVHMM for a delimiter

Fig. 4. DVHMMs for components and delimiters

> A, Takasu, N. Karayama— “Approximate Matching for OCR-Processed Bibhographic Data,, In Proc. of 13th International Conference on Pattern Recognition, pp. 175-179, 1996.

where the underlined strings are incorrectly recognized strings. For this pair of strings, the state transition and output probabilities are estimated using a parameter estimation algorithm of the DVHMM [17]. Note that the integration of a finite automaton for syntactical structure of a bibliographic string and DVHMMs for bibliographic components and delimiters produces a DVHMM; therefore, the parameter estimation algorithm can be applied without any modification.

4 Algorithms for Bibliographic String Analysis

In order to define bibliographic component extraction and bibliographic matching problems based on DVHMMs, we first define the notation and functions employed. For a pair $\mathbf{z} \equiv (\mathbf{x}, \mathbf{y})$ of an original string $\mathbf{x}$ and a recognized string $\mathbf{y}$, $P(\mathbf{z}|M)$ denotes the probability that a DVHMM M produces $\mathbf{z}$. For a sequence $\mathbf{q} \equiv q_1 q_2 \cdots q_l$ ($q_i \in Q$) of state transitions, $P(\mathbf{q}|\mathbf{z}, M)$ denotes the conditional probability that a sequence of transitions producing $\mathbf{z}$ is $\mathbf{q}$. Note that a sequence of state transitions uniquely determines the partial strings of $\mathbf{z}$ produced by each state in $\mathbf{q}$. For example, for a pair $\mathbf{z} = (aba, ab)$, let us consider the sequence $N_1 R_{10} N_2 R_{21} N_1 R_{01}$ of state transitions in Figure 2. Then, non-null states R_{10}, R_{21} and R_{01} produce the pairs (a, λ), (ba, a) and (λ, b), respectively, where λ represents a null string. $P(\mathbf{q}|\mathbf{y}, M)$ denotes the conditional probability that a sequence of transitions producing a recognized string $\mathbf{y}$ is $\mathbf{q}$.

4.1 An Algorithm for Bibliographic Component Extraction

Syntactical structure is represented with a sequence of state transitions in the DVHMM. For a given recognized bibliographic string $\mathbf{y}$, the bibliographic component extraction problem is solved by finding the most likely sequence $\mathbf{q}$ of transitions that produces $\mathbf{y}$ as a recognized string. Note that the most likely sequence $\mathbf{q} \equiv q_1 q_2 \cdots q_l$ produces a pair $(\mathbf{x}, \mathbf{y})$ and separates them into $((\mathbf{x}_1, \mathbf{y}_1), (\mathbf{x}_2, \mathbf{y}_2), \cdots, (\mathbf{x}_l, \mathbf{y}_l))$. Since a DVHMM contains information of the syntactical structure of a bibliographic string, the most likely sequence of state transitions can be decomposed into fragments that correspond to the bibliographic components, such as author's name, article title, etc. For a bibliographic component, let the corresponding fragment of the sequence be $\mathbf{q}[i : j]$. Then a substring $\mathbf{y}_i\mathbf{y}_{i+1}\cdots\mathbf{y}_j$ is the most likely portion of the given recognized string to the bibliographic component, and a substring $\mathbf{x}_i\mathbf{x}_{i+1}\cdots\mathbf{x}_j$ is the most likely portion of the original string. If a dictionary for the bibliographic component is available, we can search the dictionary instead of generating the original string $\mathbf{x}_i\mathbf{x}_{i+1}\cdots\mathbf{x}_j$.

The key to the bibliographic component extraction problem is to find the most likely sequence $\mathbf{q}$ of state transitions. Let $Q(\mathbf{y})$ be a set of sequences of state transitions that produces $\mathbf{y}$. Then, the most likely sequence is given by

$$\operatorname*{argmax}_{\mathbf{q}\in Q(\mathbf{y})} P(\mathbf{q}|\mathbf{y}, M) \ . \tag{2}$$

This optimization problem can be solved by dynamic programming. For a state q and a partial string $\mathbf{y}[: i]$ of the given recognized string, let $\mathcal{V}_i(\mathbf{y}, q)$ be the maximum probability that a DVHMM reaches the state q after producing $(\mathbf{x}, \mathbf{y}[: i])$ along a sequence of state transitions. Then the probability is represented by the following recursive form:

$$\mathcal{V}_0(\mathbf{y}, q) = \begin{cases} 1.0 & q \text{ is a starting state} \\ 0.0 & \text{otherwise} \end{cases} \tag{3}$$

$$\mathcal{V}_i(\mathbf{y}, q) = \max_{r\in Q} \max_{\mathbf{a}} \{\mathcal{V}_{i-g}(\mathbf{y}, r)\ \tau(r, q)\ o(r, \mathbf{a}, \mathbf{y}[i-g+1 : j])\} \tag{4}$$

where g is the length of the recognized output symbol of a state r, and $\mathbf{a}$ is an original output symbol of a state r. In calculating the probability $\mathcal{V}$, we must take account of any null state. If a null state q has a transition to a state r, then $\mathcal{V}_i(\mathbf{y}, q)$ must be calculated before $\mathcal{V}_i(\mathbf{y}, r)$. By this constraint, DVHMM is not allowed to have a loop consisting of only null states. Let $\mathbf{N}$ be an ordered set of states in Q that satisfies the following conditions:

- any null state is located before any non-null state, and
- for any pair of null states q and r, if $q <_N r$ holds, then there is no direct transition from a state r to a state q.

Here, $q <_N r$ means that q is located before r in $\mathbf{N}$. For each position i of $\mathbf{y}$, we can calculate the probability $\mathcal{V}$ correctly by applying the recursive form (4) to states in the order of $\mathbf{N}$.

Figure 5 depicts an algorithm to solve the optimization problem (2) using the recursive forms (3) and (4). This algorithm is a DVHMM version of the Viterbi algorithm used in HMM. The procedure takes a DVHMM M and a recognized string $\mathbf{y}$ as input and produces the sequence of state transitions satisfying (2). In Figure 5, g at line 2 stands for the length of the recognized output string at state q_l. It is clear that $\max_k W[k][|\mathbf{y}|]$ is the maximum probability of $P(\mathbf{q}|\mathbf{y}, M)$, and the sequence of state transitions from a starting state to q_{max} is the sequence satisfying (2). This sequence is obtained by tracing backward the transitions in T from the q_{max}.

```
bibExtract(M, y)
begin
  foreach state q_k in N do
    set initial probability of q_k to W[k][0] by (3)
  end
  for(i = 1; i ≤ |y|; i++) do
    foreach state q_k in N in this order do
1     find a state q_l that satisfies (4)
      set the maximum probability to W[k][i]
2     set (l, i − g) to T[k][i]
    end
    set q_k maximizing W[k][i] for i to q_max
  end
  return the sequence ended at q_max in T
end
```

Fig. 5. Algorithm for bibliographic component extraction

At line 1 in the algorithm of Figure 5, we need to find the state and the output pair of symbols that satisfy (4). Each state q_l requires $O(m \log |A|)$ calculations to find an output pair of symbols that matches $\mathbf{y}[i-g+1:i]$, because the size of recognized output symbols is at most $O(|A|^m)$ and a binary search is applicable. On the other hand, $\mathbf{a}$ satisfying (4) is obtained in $O(1)$ by ordering original output symbols according to the output probability for each recognized symbol in advance. Therefore, the calculation of line 2 requires $O(m|Q| \log |A|)$, and the time complexity of *bibExtract* is $O(m\ |Q|^2\ |\mathbf{y}| \log |A|)$.

The area $W[k][i]$ is used to keep the probability $\mathcal{V}_i(\mathbf{y}, q_k)$ for each state q_k and position i in $\mathbf{y}$. The area $T[k][i]$ is used to keep a sequence of state transitions to a state q_k that has the probability $\mathcal{V}_i(q_k)$. Therefore, the space required for solving a bibliographic component extraction is $\max\{O(|Q|\ |\mathbf{y}|), O(|M|)\}$. Usually, the size $|M|$ of DVHMM is much larger than $|Q|\ |\mathbf{y}|$, and therefore the required space is the size of the DVHMM.

4.2 Algorithm for Bibliographic Matching

Suppose a record in a database D is represented by a string similar to an original string in the training data in Section 3. Then, for a given recognized bibliographic string $\mathbf{y}$, the bibliographic matching problem is to find the most likely record defined as

$$\operatorname*{argmax}_{\mathbf{x} \in D} P(\mathbf{x}|\mathbf{y}, M) = \operatorname*{argmax}_{\mathbf{x} \in D} \frac{P(\mathbf{x}, \mathbf{y}|M)}{P(\mathbf{y}|M)} = \operatorname*{argmax}_{\mathbf{x} \in D} P(\mathbf{z}|M) \tag{5}$$

where $\mathbf{z} \equiv (\mathbf{x}, \mathbf{y})$.

This optimization problem can be solved by introducing a forward probability. For a partial pair $(\mathbf{x}[:i], \mathbf{y}[:j])$ of strings and a state q, a forward probability of a DVHMM, denoted as $\mathcal{F}_{i,j}(\mathbf{z}, q)$, is defined as the probability that the state

q is reached after producing $(\mathbf{x}[:i], \mathbf{y}[:j])$. The forward probability is calculated inductively in the following manner:

$$\mathcal{F}_{0,0}(\mathbf{z}, q) = \begin{cases} 1.0 & q \text{ is a starting state} \\ 0.0 & \text{otherwise} \end{cases} \tag{6}$$

$$\mathcal{F}_{i,j}(\mathbf{z}, q) = \sum_{r \in Q} \{\mathcal{F}_{i-g,j-h}(\mathbf{z}, r) \;\; \tau(r, q) \tag{7}$$

$$o(r, \mathbf{x}[i-g+1:i], \mathbf{y}[j-h+1:j])\}$$

where g (resp. h) is the length of the original (resp. recognized) output symbol at state r. Then, the probability $P(\mathbf{z}|M)$ is represented by

$$P(\mathbf{z}|M) = \sum_{q \in Q_x} \mathcal{F}_{|\mathbf{x}|,|\mathbf{y}|}(\mathbf{z}, q) \; . \tag{8}$$

We can solve the optimization problem (5) by calculating the probability $P(\mathbf{z}|M)$ by (8) for each record in a database, and thus finding the record maximizing the probability. Usually, there are millions of records in a bibliographic database. Therefore, it is not feasible to calculate (8) for all records, and a record filtering method such as [18] should be applied to select a small set of candidate records before bibliographic matching.

In calculating the forward probability $\mathcal{F}$, we must deal with a null state in the same way as in the calculation of $\mathcal{V}$ for bibliographic component extraction. If a null state q has a transition to a state r, then $\mathcal{F}_{i,j}(\mathbf{z}, q)$ must be calculated before $\mathcal{F}_{i,j}(\mathbf{z}, r)$. Therefore, the ordered set $\mathbf{N}$ of states is also used for the forward probability calculation. Figure 6 shows an algorithm for calculating the forward probabilities. It takes a DVHMM M and a pair $\mathbf{x}$ and $\mathbf{y}$ of strings. A procedure, *forward*, calculates the forward probabilities of all states for a position i of $\mathbf{x}$ and a position j of $\mathbf{y}$. In order to calculate forward probabilities of (8), we must calculate the forward probability $\mathcal{F}_{i,j}(\mathbf{z}, q)$ before $\mathcal{F}_{k,l}(\mathbf{z}, q)$ for any q, if $i < k$ or $j < k$ holds. The procedure *forwardProbability* controls the order of probability calculations to satisfy this constraint. In order to simplify the description of the algorithm, we assume $|\mathbf{x}| \le |\mathbf{y}|$. With a little modification we can handle the case of $|\mathbf{x}| > |\mathbf{y}|$.

The calculation of the forward probabilities at line 1 in the procedure *forward* in Figure 6 requires $O(m|Q|^2 \log |A|)$ time, because the number of output symbols at each state is at most $|A|^{2m}$ and a binary search is applicable to find the pair of output symbols for $\mathbf{z}$ at positions i and j. In the algorithm, the procedure forward is called $O(|\mathbf{x}| \; |\mathbf{y}|)$ times. Therefore, the calculation required for forward probabilities is $O(m|Q|^2 \; |\mathbf{x}| \; |\mathbf{y}| \; log|A|)$.

Area $F[k][i][j]$ is used to keep the forward probability $\mathcal{F}_{i,j}(\mathbf{z}, q_k)$, and therefore the size of the area F is $O(|Q| \; |\mathbf{x}| \; |\mathbf{y}|)$. The size $|M|$ of a DVHMM is usually much larger than the area F, and therefore the required space is the size of the DVHMM.

```
forwardProbabilities(M, x, y)
begin
  foreach state q_k in N do
    set initial probability of q_k to F[k][0][0] by (6)
  end
  for(i = 1; i ≤ |x|; i++) do
    for(j = 0; j < i; j++) do
      forward(M, x, y, i, j, F)
    end
    forward(M, x, y, i, i, F)
  end
  for(j = |x| + 1; j ≤ |y|; j++) do
    forward(M, x, y, |x|, j);
  end
  return F
end

forward(M, x, y, i, j, F)
begin
  foreach state q_k in N in this order do
1   set F_{i,j}((x, y), q_k) to F[k][i][j]
  end
end
```

Fig. 6. Algorithm for forward probabilities

5 Experimental Results

5.1 Experiment Setting

We carried out experiments extracting bibliographic components, and performing bibliographic matching using the DVHMM. In these experiments, we used three sets of data:

- bibliographic strings obtained from scanned document images,
- a bibliographic database, and
- text in an encyclopedia.

Bibliographic strings were obtained from scanned images of papers in journals and transactions published in 1995 by three major Japanese academic societies, all on the subject of computer science. Most of these were written in Japanese. The total number of references used in the experiments was 1,575. In order to obtain bibliographic strings, we first applied page layout analysis [16] to scanned reference pages to extract reference image areas, then corrected the extracted areas manually, and finally applied a commercial OCR (Toshiba Co.'s Express-Reader 70J) to each reference area of the papers as shown in Figure 1.

We used a set of bibliographic databases that has been compiled and is stored at the National Institute of Informatics, Japan. These bibliographic databases

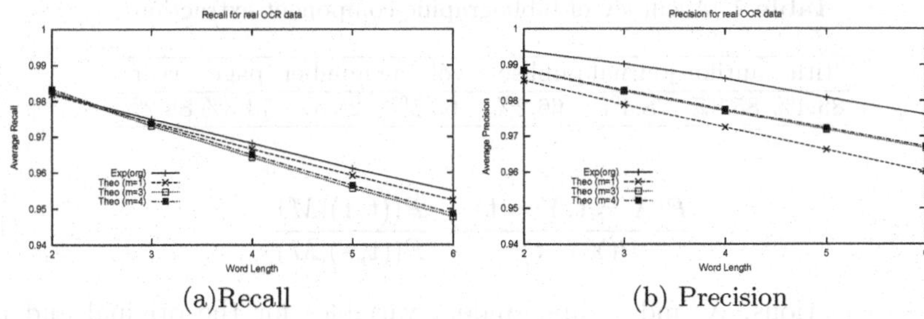

(a)Recall (b) Precision

Fig. 7. Characteristics of DVHMM

contained a total of 2,121,707 bibliographic records of books and academic articles. Most of them are written in Japanese.

Since the number of characters contained in the articles used in this experiment was not large enough to measure the characteristics of the DVHMM, we used an encyclopedia text written in Japanese that was available. This encyclopedia contains characters of 46.14 Mbyte (15,876,308 characters). We scanned the encyclopedia with 150 DPI resolution and applied the OCR. For this data set the error rate of the OCR was 0.943 %.

5.2 DVHMM Parameter Setting

As described in Section 3, for a maximum length m of the output string, the number of parameters of a DVHMM is $O(|Q| \times |A|^{2m})$. Therefore, we need a large quantity of training data for the parameter estimation of a DVHMM with large m. In order to determine the appropriate length m, we first experimented with the characteristics of the DVHMM. In this experiment, we used the text of an encyclopedia.

In order to measure the basic characteristics of the DVHMM we used recall and precision, which are two of the most basic metrics for searching and matching problems. For a query term $\mathbf{t}$, the full text search problem is enumerating places where $\mathbf{t}$ appears in a database. Suppose D is an original collection of text and D' is a recognized collection of the text of D. Then recall and precision of a query $\mathbf{t}$ to a database D are represented by (9) and (10), respectively.

$$\frac{\text{number of correctly detected positions of } \mathbf{t} \text{ in } D'}{\text{number of occurrences of } \mathbf{t} \text{ in } D} \tag{9}$$

$$\frac{\text{number of correctly detected positions of } \mathbf{t} \text{ in } D'}{\text{number of occurrences of } \mathbf{t} \text{ in } D'} \tag{10}$$

On the other hand, we can derive recall and precision from a DVHMM M by (11) and (12), respectively.

$$\frac{P(X = \mathbf{t}, Y = \mathbf{t})}{P(X = \mathbf{t})} = \frac{P((\mathbf{t}, \mathbf{t})|M)}{P((*, \mathbf{t})|M)} \tag{11}$$

Table 1. Accuracy of bibliographic component extraction

title	author	journal	publisher	volume	number	page	year
86.4%	85.8%	78.4%	66.2%	64.5%	28.5%	74.3%	88.2%

$$\frac{P(X = \mathbf{t}, Y = \mathbf{t})}{P(Y = \mathbf{t})} = \frac{P((\mathbf{t}, \mathbf{t})|M)}{P((\mathbf{t}, *)|M)} \tag{12}$$

In these equations, X and Y are random variables for the original and the recognized strings, respectively. $P((*, \mathbf{t})|M)$ is a probability that M produces a recognized string $\mathbf{t}$ with any original string.

By comparing the metrics measured by (9) and (10) with those derived from (11) and (12), we can measure the accuracy of the DVHMM. We carried out the experiment using five-fold validation. We first decomposed the text data of the encyclopedia into five sections. Four sections were used as training data for the DVHMM parameter estimation, and the remaining section was used as test data. DVHMMs with a maximum length m from one to four were learned from the training data. On the other hand, 10,000 query terms of lengths ranging from 2 to 6 were randomly chosen from the test data. Then, for each query term, recall and precision were measured using the test data by (9) and (10). Similarly, for each query term, the estimated recall and precision were derived from the trained DVHMMs. These experiments were carried out for any combination of training data and test data. Then, the metrics were averaged over 10,000 query terms and over combinations of training and test data.

Figure 7 shows the experimental results. In the figure, "Exp(org)" represents the measured metrics by (9) and (10), whereas "Theo(m=k)" represents the derived metrics from the DVHMMs whose maximum output length is k by (11) and (12). The graphs show that a DVHMM tends to underestimate metrics for any length k, and a DVHMM with larger k seems to estimate precision more precisely, but estimates recall less precisely. As a whole, a DVHMM with $m = 4$ estimates metrics most accurately, and therefore we used $m = 4$ in the following experiments.

5.3 Bibliographic Component Extraction

In the experiment of bibliographic component extraction, five-fold validation was applied. We first decomposed 1,575 pairs of recognized bibliographic strings and corresponding records in the bibliographic database into five groups. Then we estimated the parameters of the DVHMM as described in Section 3 using four groups of bibliographic data. Finally, we extracted bibliographic components from recognized bibliographic strings in the remaining group. This experiment was repeated five times for each combination of training and test data.

We extracted the bibliographic components listed in Table 1. This table shows the accuracy of bibliographic component extraction for each component, where the accuracy is measured as the ratio of the number of correctly detected bibliographic components over the total number of components in the test data. As shown in the table, the accuracies for author and title are high, whereas the accuracies for volume and number are low. These results seem to mainly come from the syntactical ambiguity of bibliographic strings. For example, the bibliographic components such as volume and number are usually separated by a comma, and this delimiter sometimes appears within a string of bibliographic components; this causes syntactical ambiguity. For the purpose of object identification, authors and titles are more important than other bibliographic components. Therefore, this experimental result is preferable for object identification.

6 Conclusion

This paper proposes a method for analyzing a recognized bibliographic string using an extended HMM called DVHMM. The feature of this problem is in handling erroneous bibliographic strings, and the proposed method enables integration of a large quantity of documents accumulated as printed articles into the citation index. The advantages of the proposed method are:

– providing a robust bibliographic matching function by using a statistical description of the syntax of bibliographic strings, a language model and an OCR error model, and
– reducing the cost of preparing training data for parameter estimation using records in a bibliographic database.

A DVHMM requires a large memory, especially for languages that have a large set of characters, such as Japanese. This is one of the disadvantages of the proposed method. By introducing a class of characters, i.e., hashing the characters, we will be able to reduce the memory required drastically. One future problem is to develop a hash function that reduces characters, but causes little decrease in the accuracy of string analysis. Character reduction will also reduce the required training data.

The DVHMM can reduce the cost of preparing training data using records in bibliographic databases. However, we may obtain a more effective model by using training data that are decomposed into components and delimiters. We plan to experiment to clarify the relationship between the type of training data and the performance of the string analysis of the proposed method.

References

1. F. H. Ayres, J. A. W. Huggill, and E. J. Yannakoudakis. The universal standard bibligraphic code (usbc): its use for clearing, merging and controlling large databases. *Program - Automated Library and Information Systems*, 22(2):117–132, 1988.
2. A. Belaid, J. C. Anigbogu, and Y. Chenevoy. Qualitative Analysis of Low-Level Logical Structures. In *Proc. of International Conference on Electronic Publishing*, pages 435–446, 1994.
3. H. Bunke and P.S.P. Wang, editors. *Handbook of Character Recoginition and Document Image Analysis.* World Scientific, 1997.
4. CrossRef The central source for reference linking:. http://www.crossref.org/. In *Proc. of International Conference on Digital Libraries*, pages 89–98, 1998.

5. C. L. Giles, K. D. Bollacker, and S. Lawrence. CiteSeer: An Automatic Citation Indexing System. In *Proc. of International Conference on Digital Libraries*, pages 89–98, 1998.
6. P. Goyal. An investigation of different string coding methods. *Journal of the American Society for Information Science*, 35(4):248–252, 1984.
7. P. Goyal. Duplicate record identification in bibiliographic databases. *Information Systems*, 12(3):239–242, 1987.
8. The Digital Object Identifier:. http://www.doi.org/. In *Proc. of International Conference on Digital Libraries*, pages 89–98, 1998.
9. S. Kahan, T. Pavlidis, and H. S. Baird. On the recognition of printed characters of any font and size. *IEEE Trans. on Pattern Analysis and Machine Intelligence*, 9(2):274–288, March 1987.
10. Karen Kukich. "Techniques for Automtically Correcting Words in Text". *ACM Computing Surveys*, 24(4):377–439, 1992.
11. S. Lawrence, C. L. Giles, and K. D. Bollacker. Digital libraries and autonmous citation indexing. *IEEE Computer*, 32(6):67–71, June 1999.
12. Y. Li, D. Lopresti, and A. Tomkins. "Validation of Document Image Defect Models for Optical Character Recognition". In *Proc. of 3rd Annual Symposium on Document Analysis and Information Retrieval*, pages 137–150, 1994.
13. T. O'Neill, E., A. Rogers, S., and M. Oskins, W. Characteristics of duplicate records in OCLC's online union catalog. *Library Resources & Technical Services*, 37(1):59–71, 1992.
14. F. Parmentier and A. Belaid. "Bibliography References Validation Using Emergent Architecture". In *Proc. of IAPR International Conference on Document Analysis and Recognition*, pages 532–535, 1995.
15. G. A. Story, L. O'Gorman, D. Fox, L. L. Schaper, and H. V. Jagadish. The right-pages image-based electronic library for alerting and browsing. *IEEE Computer.*, 25(9):17–26, 1992.
16. A. Takasu. Probabilistic interpage analysis for article extraction from document images. In *Proc. of 14th International Conference on Pattern Recognition*, pages 932–935. IAPR, 1998.
17. A. Takasu and K. Aihara. "DVHMM: Variable Length Text Recognition Error Model". In *submit to 15th Internationa Conference on Pattern Recognition*, pages xx–xx, 2002.
18. A. Takasu, N. Katayama, and et. al. "Approximate Matching for OCR-Processed Bibliographic Data". In *Proc. of 13th Internationa Conference on Pattern Recognition*, pages 175–179, 1996.
19. K. Y. Wong, R. G. Casey, and F. M. Wahl. "Document Analysis System". *IBM journal Research and Development*, 26(6):647–656, 1982.

Focused Crawls, Tunneling, and Digital Libraries

Donna Bergmark, Carl Lagoze, and Alex Sbityakov

Cornell Digital Library Research Group

Abstract. Crawling the Web to build collections of documents related to pre-specified topics became an active area of research during the late 1990's, crawler technology having been developed for use by search engines. Now, Web crawling is being seriously considered as an important strategy for building large scale digital libraries. This paper covers some of the crawl technologies that might be exploited for collection building. For example, to make such collection-building crawls more effective, focused crawling was developed, in which the goal was to make a "best-first" crawl of the Web. We are using powerful crawler software to implement a focused crawl but use tunneling to overcome some of the limitations of a pure best-first approach. Tunneling has been described by others as not only prioritizing links from pages according to the page's relevance score, but also estimating the value of each link and prioritizing them as well. We add to this mix by devising a tunneling focused crawling strategy which evaluates the current crawl direction on the fly to determine when to terminate a tunneling activity. Results indicate that a combination of focused crawling and tunneling could be an effective tool for building digital libraries.

1 Introduction

What are the tools and techniques to build truly large scale digital libraries? Answering this question is crucial to the success of the National Science Digital Library (NSDL) project [1,2]. Our goal in NSDL is to build what will quite possibly be the largest and most diverse digital library to date. To accomplish this goal, we will not only include resources from partner NSF projects, but incorporate much of the wealth of scientific and mathematical information available on the open Web. Building a digital library of this breadth and scale requires innovative techniques. While many of the tasks could undoubtedly be undertaken with ample and expert human labor, the scale of such labor is also prohibitively expensive. As noted by Arms [3] the key to moving digital libraries from dependency on expensive human labor lies in the combination relatively inexpensive raw computing power and smart algorithms.

This paper describes one aspect of our work in this area; techniques to automatically build online collections of topic specific resources. This task is critical to finding and organizing the many needles in the vast Web haystack. In an earlier paper [4] we described initial results from our attempts to use focused Web crawling to build collections from an established topic hierarchy. In this paper we focus on techniques to make that process more efficient, which becomes

M. Agosti and C. Thanos (Eds.): ECDL 2002, LNCS 2458, pp. 91–106, 2002.

increasingly important with the increasing size of the Web (while computers do get faster, the scale of the problems always seem to increase at a greater rate!). We describe a technique called *tunneling* as a means of determining what are the best links to follow from a source page during a selective crawl to build collections. Our hypothesis is that by examining the patterns of document-to-collection correlations along Web link paths we can devise more efficient selective crawling techniques.

The paper is structured as follows. Part 2 provides background on our work on automated collection building. Part 3 describes general issues in focused Web crawling. Part 4, the heart of the paper, describes tunneling as a technique to improve the efficiency of focused Web crawls. Part 5 provides results of our Web characterization work to develop better tunneling techniques. We close with Part 6 that describes how our results might be applied and Part 7 with some related work.

2 Automated Collection Building

We start with a set of *centroids* which are constructed from the subjects in the given topic hierarchy, by a process described below. Each centroid is a weighted term vector describing a topic. During the crawl, each down-loaded document is tentatively classed with the nearest subject vector, with the correlation being the degree to which the document is considered to be in that collection. If the correlation is sufficiently high, then links from that HTML page are also followed.[1] Once the collections have been built, each of the items in a collection is represented by its URL and a figure of merit indicating the degree to which the item belongs to this collection.

The *quality* of the collection depends on the initial input (the topic hierarchy and centroids) and on the metric used to assign downloaded documents to collections. The *efficiency* of collection building depends on being able to do a *focused crawl* [5]. Focused crawling is discussed in the next section.

We build a number of collections at once for a particular subfield of technology (e.g. mathematics, nano-physics). We start with a topic hierarchy or subject index, and then leverage Google to return a few good documents on each subject, and construct a centroid from those. (The hits from Google are used *only* to build centroids; crawl seeds are independently selected, and include such hubs as `yahoo.com`.) Specifically, for each topic query to Google, the centroid is constructed from the first k hits returned in the search results. (This is done automatically, by using a program to submit the query to Google and then scraping the resulting response page for the hit URLs. We are considering replacing this ad hoc approach with the more formal SOAP API, recently announced by Google.) We limit k to the range of 4 through 7. In other words, topics for which Google finds fewer than four documents are discarded; search result hits after the first 7 are ignored.

[1] If the link is to a .pdf or .ps file, those are also added to the same collection, with their parental correlation values.

Then the concatenated k pages are turned into term vectors. The term weights are basically the frequency of the word in the set of k pages, divided by the frequency of the word in pages downloaded for all the queries. This is the TF-IDF weighting from standard information retrieval [6,7]. (One advantage to building many collections simultaneously is that a term's document frequency can be estimated from term occurrence in the other query sets. However, the centroids can be weighted by term frequency alone if the centroids are being built in parallel [8].)

The general success of our implementation of focused crawling depends heavily on the initial subject descriptors. We found that using the index term list from the Math Forum[2] worked well as a source of math subject descriptors, but that a curriculum outline for 1st and 2nd grade science failed because it contained too many broad and general terms. Finding the proper term specificity and helpful subject hierarchies will be crucial for automatic NSDL collection synthesis.

3 About Focused Crawling

The selective harvesting of interesting URLs from the Web became an intense research topic in the late 1990's, although there was some early work on topic-directed web crawling at Xerox Parc by Pirolli and Pitkow [9]. Chakrabarti *et al.*'s seminal paper [5] introduced focused crawling for collecting topic-specific web pages, and described its advantages over search engines. Both produce collections of topic-specific pages, but search engines must be prepared to answer any query and therefore use Web crawlers which do not distinguish between which pages to analyze or which links to follow. Rather, any and all newly discovered links are placed onto the *crawl frontier* to be downloaded when their turn comes. Focused crawling, on the other hand, attempts to order the URLs that have been discovered to do a "best first" crawl, rather than the search engine's "breadth-first" crawl.

"Best" has been defined in a couple of ways. Kleinberg's hub and authorities [10] and Brin and Page's Page rank [11] define "best" in terms of being often linked to. The other definition – the one on which we concentrate – is relevance to a particular topic. These definitions can be combined of course; link analysis can be used to not only find pages on a specific topic, but also authorities on that topic.

Focused crawling grew out of mid-90's text categorization work, assigning documents to categories. Then the HITS algorithm did focused searching by staying within certain communities to extract their topics of interest[12].

Since then, a number of focused crawlers have been developed and used for Web experimentation. Chakrabarti *et al.* implemented a focused crawler using off-the-shelf database and storage managers [13]. Rennie and McCallum [14] designed a focused crawler that attempted to crawl pages only of a certain type

[2] `www.mathforum.org`.

by using feedback during the crawl. Menczer *et al.* [15,16] have done work since 1999 on designing and evaluating focused crawlers. Mukherjee's WTMS [17] reports being able to build a topic-based collection with high precision. [18] is a good summarization of results in focused crawling as of the end of 1999. An interesting technique for focusing crawls by using Context Graphs was introduced by [19] in 2000.

We have continued this work by experimenting with a focused crawler based on the powerful Atrax/Mercator crawler software [20,21]. This crawler is written in Java, uses a configuration file in which many options for a crawl can be specified, and has base classes which are extensible. The extensibility supports many different flavors of crawling, including focused crawling. Our extensions have led to a focused crawler which builds a number of collections simultaneously and automatically, starting only with a set of topic descriptions.

Several assumptions lie behind the idea of focused crawling. One is that by following links from a page which is relevant to the topic, one is more likely to get to another relevant page. That is, the assumption is made that if two pages are linked to each other, they are likely to be on the same topic. One study [22] actually found that the likelihood of linked pages having similar textual content was high, if one considered random pairs of pages on the Web.

Another assumption is that anchor text describes the content of the page being pointed to. The problem is that anchor text is often too brief to contain much content. (Common anchor texts include "here", "this", "top", etc.)

Another assumption is that it is possible through page analysis (say, using TF-IDF) to determine whether that page relates to the topic of the collection being assembled.

The final assumption is that the link itself, the URL, contains information that can help focus the crawl. Some studies [23] found that the text in the URL string can contain important information. For example, if one is collecting physics documents about lasers, a URL that contains "sailing" is less likely to be relevant than a URL that contains the word "optical". Stop lists can be applied to URLs as well, such as not following "contents.html" pages. This is supported directly via Mercator's configuration file, which includes an optional filter on URL strings. Similarly, if the crawl has encountered many low-scoring pages from a particular server, URLs to this server could be marked as less desirable. It should also be noted that there is a Semantic Web initiative to type links [24]. Such additional information attached to the links could help focused crawlers be more effective.

In summary, the trick to focused crawling has so far been to order the crawl frontier so that links to probably relevant pages are followed before links to probably off-topic pages. This requires estimating the relevance of the page pointed to by the link, based on some of the assumptions listed above. Reasonably enough, this estimation can be fraught with error.

Prioritizing the frontier is computationally intensive and is thus opposed to our goal of increased crawling efficiency. Although Mercator does support prioritized queues, we chose instead to focus our crawl by using two knobs, *threshold* and *cutoff*.

The threshold is a number between zero and one which determines the correlation level above which we consider a document to be on-topic with respect to some centroid. The correlation score for a downloaded normalized document d is

$$\text{score} \;=\; \begin{matrix}\text{argmax}\\ \{c\}\end{matrix} \left\{ \sqrt{\frac{\sum_i d_i^2 \cdot c_i^2}{||c_i||}} \right\} \qquad (1)$$

where c is a centroid. Argmax says choose the cluster whose centroid maximizes the score. Weights of term i are d_i, c_i. This is the standard *cosine correlation.*

The cutoff is how far to crawl from a page whose value is above the threshold. Since Mercator can keep track of the number of pages in a path, it is possible to keep incrementing a counter on a particular crawl path until it exceeds the cutoff, at which point we terminate the crawl going in this direction.

Setting the threshold high encourages high precision collections. Setting the cutoff low limits the amount of irrelevant material one has to crawl through. Our experience has been that good settings for a focused crawl are threshold=0.35 and cutoff=0.

While this gets you collections that have a better-than-average chance of being relevant [4], threshold and cutoff are rather crude ways of focusing the crawl. Essentially we are saying that the "best links" are those from an on-topic page and from pages not too far from that last on-topic page. While this does help minimize the size of the crawl frontier, it might be too limiting in scope. Tunneling is one way to extend the scope of a focused crawl.

4 Adding Tunneling to Focused Crawling

Focused crawling, while quite efficient and effective does have some drawbacks. One is that it is not necessarily optimal to simply follow a "best-first" search, because it is sometimes necessary to go through several off-topic pages to get to the next relevant one. With some probability, the crawl should be allowed to follow a series of bad pages in order to get to a good one.

It is important here to recall our objective: to build collections of 25–50 URLs of expository pages on given subjects. Thus precision is not defined in terms of number of crawled pages, but in terms of rank. In other words, downloading and inspecting what amounts to trash does not hurt precision or impede effectiveness; the only impact is on efficiency. The need is to obtain a high-precision result within a reasonable timeframe.

Another application for tunneling is right at the start of the crawl. One does not necessarily start with on-topic seeds. In our case where we build several dozen collections at a time, the starting seed will certainly not apply equally well to all collections. In this case, tunneling is useful for getting to desirable parts of the Web.

Clearly, tunneling can improve the effectiveness of focused crawling by expanding its reach, and its efficiency by pruning paths which look hopeless. So, the main challenge now becomes how to decide when to stop tunneling, i.e. terminate the direction in which the crawl is proceeding.

To be more precise about tunneling, we propose the following definitions. A *nugget* is a Web document whose cosine correlation with at least one of the collection centroids is higher than some given threshold. Thus the "nugget-ness" of a document is represented by its correlation score. A *dud*, on the other hand, is a document that does not match any of the centroids very highly. A *path* is

Table 1. Tunneling definitions and path notation

Notation	Definition
0	A nugget, i.e. correlation $\geq .5$
X	A dud
0-0	A path of length 2
0-X-X-X-X-0	A path of length 6
0-X-X-0-X-0	Two paths linked by a common relative, one path being length 4, the other path length 3
	Partial Paths
X-...-0	X is a seed but not a nugget; we treat the seed as a "pseudo" nugget
0-X...$X_{>c}$	Terminated path because final dud's distance from some nugget is greater than or equal to the cutoff
0-X...$X_{<c}$	Incomplete path due to crawl's time being up
0 / \ 0 X	A very brief crawl, consisting of two paths, one incomplete The crawl begins at the root of the tree and proceeds downward

the sequence of pages and links going from one nugget to the next. The path *length* is 2 minus the number of duds in the path. A *crawl* is the tree consisting of all the paths, linked together in the obvious way. Table 1 illustrates these definitions and introduces some notation.

Our experimental setup was a collection of 26 topics in the area of Mathematics. An example topic is `basic linear algebra graphing equations`. An 8 hour crawl was performed to collect the 50 best documents on each topic. But in order to collect experimental data about tunneling, we set the threshold to 0.50 and the cutoff to 20 (to maximize the tunneling). The data we saved for each downloaded URL included:

- the downloaded URL
- the correlation of that URL's page with the nearest centroid
- the URL of the parent (the document which contained a link to this URL; only the seeds of the crawl had no parent)
- the "distance" of the downloaded URL from its nearest nugget ancestor

The *distance* is an integer saying how far from the most immediate nugget ancestor this node is. It is thus a function of a page's cosine correlation value and the parent's distance. The simplest distance metric is related to path-length:

$$\text{distance} = \begin{cases} 0 & \text{if this node is a nugget} \\ 1 + \text{parent's distance} & \text{otherwise} \end{cases} \quad (2)$$

Related to distance is *level*, which is simply 1 plus the parent's distance.

To more precisely characterize the benefits of tunneling, a tunneling crawl can be performed and then the results can be statistically analyzed. With this data in hand, we can gain insight into the structure of the crawled portion of the Web. Our path data has many properties: path length, sequence of correlation values, trends, signal to noise ratios, etc. By statistically analyzing the collected data, we stand a chance of empirically being able to answer the following questions:

- How far might you have to go from one nugget to get to the next? (The diameter of the Web would be the maximum.)
- Given that a page is downloaded with correlation X, how well does that predict that one of its links is a nugget? Or does it instead depend on what led up to this dud (i.e. are we in a bad part of the Web and will never get to a nugget even though the correlation is as high as X)?
- How good is the correlation score for predicting whether it will lead to a nugget?
- What is the shape of the paths like? If they are purely white noise, then we cannot use information as we crawl along a path to determine whether we should abandon the path.
- What, if anything, can be inferred from path length? Intuitively, it seems that the longer a path becomes, the more likely it is that the crawl is in an irrelevant part of the Web.

The answers to these questions could lead to finding ways to make tunneling effective. In other words, the evidence could be used to estimate, dynamically, whether tunneling in a particular instance is going to pay off. The next section reports on some statistical results of this empirical study.

5 Experimental Results

With the experimental setup, almost 500,000 unique documents were downloaded and analyzed. While this is only a very small portion of the Web, it is a sufficiently large sample from which to make some statistical observations. No paths were terminated due to the cutoff (which was set very high), so the results approximate a maximally tunneling crawl. We hope to find some information in the statistics that would allow us to design a good tunneling strategy.

5.1 It Can Be a Long Way from One Nugget to the Next

In this run there were 6620 completed paths; the most common length of a completed path was between 7 and 8. This corresponds rather well with the figures in Table 2 which shows the distribution of distance from the closest ancestor nugget for the general population. Note also that at every length from an ancestor nugget, it is possible to find another nugget (column 4 has high values at all levels). These figures suggest that tunneling does have merit, although at some point it may not be worthwhile to go that far for a nugget.

Table 2. Correlation vs. path length. Column 1 is the distance from the closest ancestor nugget. Column 2 is the number of nodes at that level, including nuggets. Average correlation over all levels is 0.153. Seeds are not included

Level	Number	avg. corr.	max corr.
1	16422	0.1520	0.877
2	18106	0.2008	0.894
3	12699	0.1740	0.828
4	26356	0.1536	0.798
5	49018	0.1460	0.857
6	62728	0.1559	0.826
7	82287	0.1547	0.853
8	109297	0.1383	0.855
9	59370	0.1427	0.859
10	36672	0.1336	0.828
11	12390	0.1479	0.801
12	5981	0.0926	0.627
13	6604	0.1536	0.627
14	1485	0.1913	0.706

5.2 Better Parents Have Better Children

In Table 3, we consider the distribution of correlations across the general population and compare it with distribution of the children of high-scoring nodes. The distribution is approximated by dividing the data into buckets of .05 correlation each. The second column indicates the likelihood of falling into any particular bracket; the third column shows the distribution of children of parents who scored in the .45 to .5 range (i.e. high-scoring, but not a nugget). We then look at the distribution of their children, and note that they are more likely to be nuggets than on average.

The opposite is not true. If you look at the children of nuggets (Table 4), you see that their correlation bracket predicts nothing (high standard deviation). This means that making a big effort to estimate the relevance of link targets is perhaps misguided.

5.3 Path History Matters

If the score of an individual node is a poor predictor, what about the history of a path? Should the crawl strategy be dynamically altered according to the shape

Table 3. Better parents have better children: here we consider parent nodes in the .45-.50 range and look at the distribution of their children. These parents have higher-scoring children than the general population

Correlation Bracket	General Population No. Nodes (%)	Nodes with corr (.45-.5] No. Nodes (%)
.05	149188 (21)	1102 (12)
.10	99479 (14)	422 (4.5)
.15	147185 (21)	892 (10)
.20	115576 (17)	897 (10)
.25	66530 (10)	1134 (12)
.30	42529 (6)	1022 (11)
.35	27710 (4)	944 (10)
.40	16549 (2)	740 (7.9)
.45	11787 (2)	768 (8.2)
.50	8126 (1)	614 (6.6)
.55	4613 (.6)	310 (3.3)
.60	3444 (.5)	224 (2.3)
.65	1971 (.3)	148 (1.6)
.70	1166 (.2)	78 (.83)
.75	656 (.1)	38 (.41)
.80	310 (.04)	11 (.12)
.85	96 (.01)	2 (.02)
.90	29 (.004)	1 (.02)
Total	696944 (100)	9347 (100)

Table 4. Average path length for children of nuggets according to their correlation score. Path length is 0 if the child contains a link to a nugget

Correlation Bracket	Number of Nodes	Average Path Length to Nugget	Standard Deviation
0.05	3380	4.64	2.19
0.10	3152	3.52	1.52
0.15	4702	3.64	2.07
0.20	3008	2.61	1.58
0.25	2345	2.28	1.14
0.30	5479	4.00	1.93
0.35	2973	3.08	1.83
0.40	2102	2.84	1.63
0.45	2727	4.03	2.88
0.50	1077	0.67	1.36

of the path? The question is should we treat paths *path1*: `0.45 0.25 0.30 0.35` and *path2:* `0.10 0.05 0.09 0.35` equivalently, or should we prioritize path1? Intuitively, path1 appears better because it is in a relevant area of the Web. Path2 may not be.

We chose to analyze this by comparing paths like ...X-X-0 (sequences ending in a nugget) with paths like ...X-X-X (sequences ending in a dud) to see if the penultimate two documents would predict the "nuggetness" of the final document. Figure 1 shows the results. This is the clearest indication that it might be good to pay attention to path history since the last nugget. The display is divided into two graphs - one for low-scoring dud parents (0 to .25) and one for high-scoring dud parents (scores between .25 and .5). Then we look at the distribution of the grandparents' scores in each case. For low-scoring parents, the score of the parent hardly matters. The probability of reaching a nugget matches that of the general population. On the other hand, for high-scoring parents, highly scoring grandparents do make a difference; the curve shifts distinctly to the right. A path of "almost-nuggets" is a significant predictor of future success.

5.4 Frontier Grows Rapidly

This has been discovered by many researchers, and again by us and is worth keeping in mind: after a few minutes of a breadth-first crawl, there will be a million URLs on the frontier. In this experiment, there were 4 million after 3 hours. A large frontier makes prioritizing computationally expensive.

Focused crawling is very helpful in weeding out URLs before they land on the frontier and slow down the run. Typically a full breadth-first crawl with Mercator will during the first 3 hours drop from an initial speed of 400 pages per second to about 50 pages per second, as the data structures grow larger and larger. If the threshold is dropped from .5 to .4, the crawl will drop even further, to 40 documents/second largely because the crawl runs into an increasing amount of the same material. Focusing the crawl is crucial to efficiency, provided it does not impact precision. Allowing tunneling, but knowing when to stop will help achieve both.

6 Putting the Findings to Practical Use

We have been focusing our crawls via threshold and cutoff values. But the statistical path data indicate that path history should also be taken into account in a way more complex than giving each node a fixed number of edges to go before the crawl is cut off. We take the path into account by replacing distance metric (2) with the following adaptive one:

$$\text{distance} = \begin{cases} 0 & \text{if this is a nugget} \\ min(1,\ (1-c)e^{2d_p/C}) & \text{otherwise} \end{cases} \quad (3)$$

where c is the correlation score for the current node, d_p is the parent's distance, and C is the cutoff, which remains constant for the crawl. Thus a node's distance metric grows exponentially as the parent's distance approaches the cutoff, and the lower the correlation score of a node, the greater its distance.

We used this adaptive cutoff in a 3.3 hour crawl with threshold 0.5 and cutoff 20. The results are shown in Figure 2 and Table 5. In Figure 2 the adaptive crawl

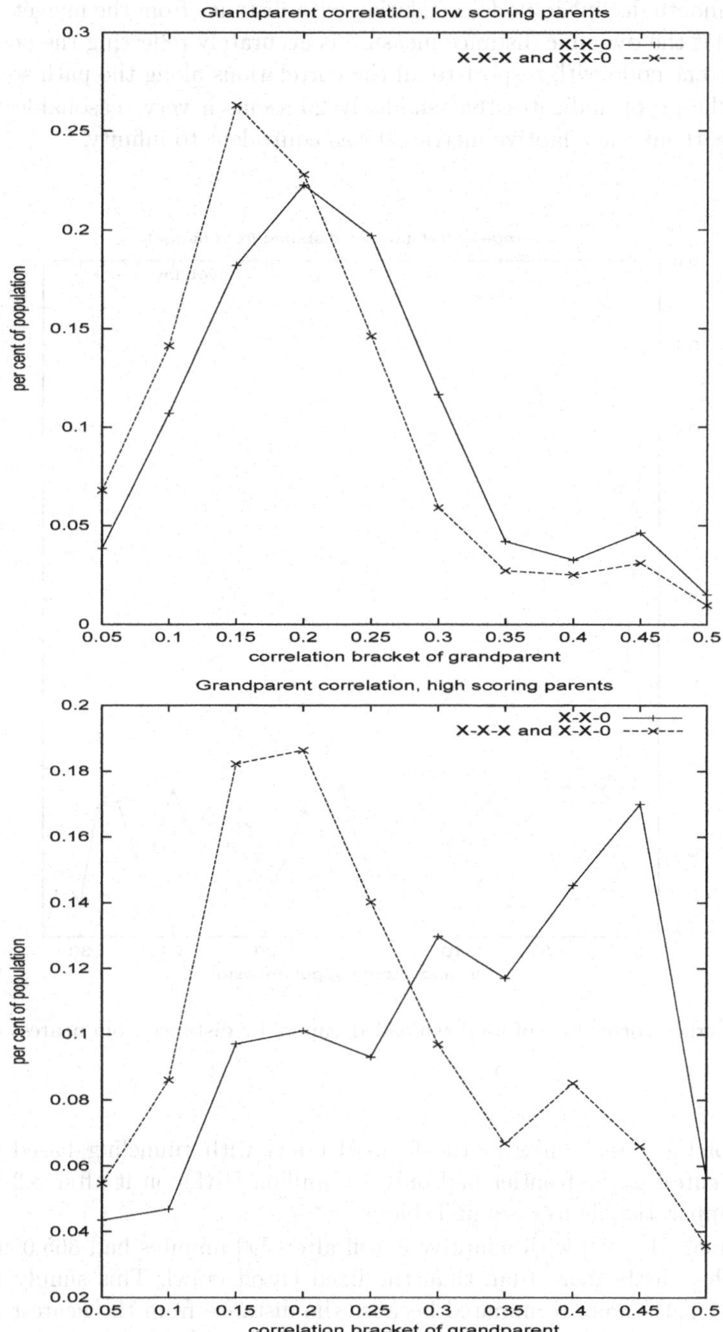

Fig. 1. Path shape does matter. Here we look at the two ancestors of a nugget vs. the population at large. The combination of high-scoring parents and high-scoring grandparents is likely to lead to a nugget.

shows a smooth decline in node correlation with distance from the nugget, which implies that the dynamic distance measure is accurately reflecting the goodness of the current node with respect to all the correlations along the path so far.

Also the graph indicates that suddenly 20 seems a very reasonable cutoff, whereas without the adaptive metric 20 was equivalent to infinity.

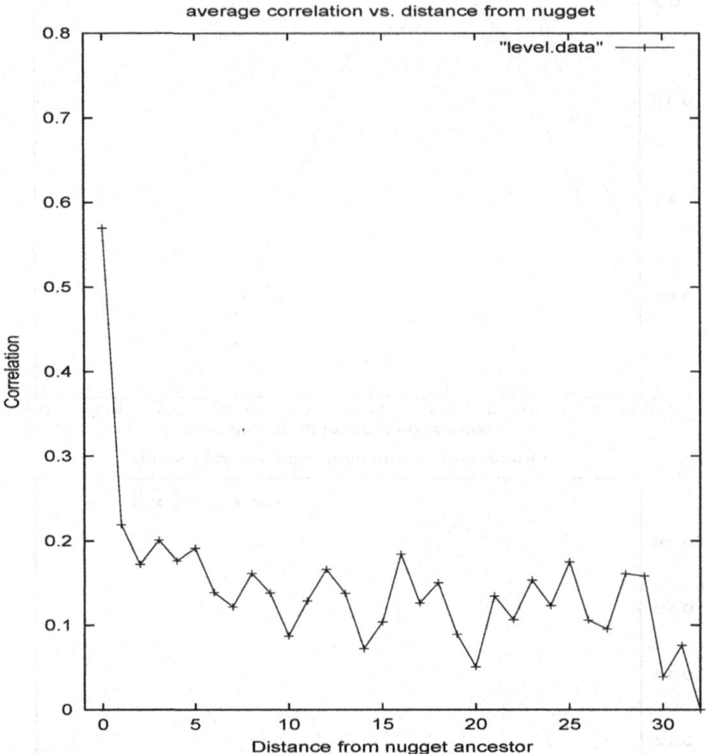

Fig. 2. Average correlation of all downloaded papers by distance from nearest nugget ancestor.

One of the best results of the focused crawl with tunneling based on an adaptive cutoff is the frontier had only 1.6 million URLs on it after 3.3 hours. Other comparative figures are in Table 5.

The focused crawl with adaptive cutoff after 200 minutes had 365,050 complete paths, vastly more than than the fixed cutoff crawl. This simply means that many paths were terminated because the distance from the nearest ancestor nugget exceeded the cutoff. The results in the table show the benefits that accrued. In the first part of the table, we see various statistics related to the crawl. The most surprising is the difference in the terminal documents/second being downloaded. Even though the adaptive cutoff has a larger frontier than

Table 5. Comparison of 100 minutes of regular focused crawl vs. 200 minutes of focused crawl with adaptive cutoff. In the second part of the table, percentages are of the number of documents ≥ 0.25

	Regular Crawl	Adaptive Cutoff
Threshold	.5	.5
Cutoff	20	20
Length	100 min	200 min
Final docs/sec	15.1	43.8
Urls on frontier	1M	1.6M
unique docs	91,859	541,205
$\geq$ 0.25	13,265	48,196
[.5–.6)	1195 (1.94%)	4497 (4.22 %)
[.6–.7)	461 (.75 %)	1094 (2.27%)
[.7–.8)	125 (.20%)	285 (.59%)
[.8–.9)	27 (.04%)	39 (.08%)
[.9–1.)	0	0

the first 100 minutes of the regular crawl, and thus a larger data structure, the download rate is much faster. Why?

The crawls were performed at comparable times during the day, so network congestion is unlikely to be the answer. More likely is that without the cutoff going into effect, the first crawl was staying much longer in already well-crawled territory and spending time figuring out that URLs and/or documents had already been seen. This is reflected in the unique documents downloaded figure as well. The adaptive focus has clearly gained us a lot of efficiency.

The second part of the table talks about the quality of the downloaded documents. First, anything with a correlation of < 0.25 is just ignored. Of the documents above that, what percentage are higher ranking? Again, the adaptive cutoff wins hands down. A much larger proportion of the downloaded documents are actually nuggets.

7 Related Research

Our work is similar to other work in focused crawling, e.g. Kluev [25]. Kluev's work is conceptually similar to ours but executes differently. He starts with a hand-picked set of documents, runs only one thread, and builds only one collection at a time. He reports on two collections, both broad in scope. We on the other hand exploit parallelism and automatic processing insofar as possible. Han and Karypis [26] use exactly the same vector space model as we do, but like Kluev and others, starts with a given set of documents, from which the centroid is constructed. We require no such hand seeding. Topic distillation [27,13] is a technique that locates topic-related pages on the Web, but lets the topics emerge from what is intrinsically there. We start with a given taxonomy. But the question is, how do we know that the taxonomy is current? In future, topic distillation work may well become crucial to automating digital libraries, by determining the current topic structure of the Web.

Another aspect of collection building is its relationship to clustering in the field of artificial intelligence. Many recommend the application of AI clustering techniques such as Support Vector Machines to text classification, which is close in spirit to collection building. [26], for example, used a set of 23 existing document collections and constructed a centroid for each collection by making a term vector out of 80% of the collection. Then the remaining 20% of the documents were classified with the nearest centroid. The classification was good if that document was classified into the collection from which it originated. What is really interesting about this work is that centroid-based classification was compared with classification algorithms more typical in artificial intelligence: naive Bayesian, C4.5 Decision Trees, and k-nearest neighbor algorithms. The experiment concluded that the centroid-based document classification was the most accurate. If these results can be extended to Web documents, then we feel justified in using the centroid-based approach.

8 Conclusion

In this paper we described several technologies for using a Web crawler to help build collections for large scale digital libraries. We build on technologies introduced by other researchers: from information retrieval we take centroids, term vector space, and the cosine correlation; from the Web community we take crawling, focused crawling, and tunneling. We introduce the terms nugget and dud, and the concept of paths from one nugget to the next. We then performed a large crawl to gain statistical insight into the nature of the paths. This indicated that path history was relevant. Using this information we designed an adaptive cutoff that reflects path history, and expanded on the tunneling concept to achieve highly efficient and effective focused crawling. We expect to apply this strategy to future work in topic-specific digital collection synthesis.

Acknowledgments. This work was funded in part by the NSF grant on Project Prism, IIS 9817416. Thanks are due to Bill Arms for suggesting this particular research focus on automated collection building. We also acknowledge the considerable technical help received from the Systems Research Center at Compaq, especially from Raymie Stata, Marc Najork, and Richard Schedler. Chris Wilper implemented the Mercator extensions to capture path data. Thanks to Vicky Weissman for suggesting the term, "nugget". Sbityakov came up with the term "dud".

References

1. Lagoze (ed.), C., Arms, W., Gan, S., Hillmann, D., Ingram, C., Krafft, D., Marisa, R., Phipps, J., Saylor, J., Terrizzi, C.: Core services in the architecture of the National Digital Library for science education NSDL). In: Proceedings of the Second ACM/IEEE-CS Joint Conference on Digital Libraries, Portland, OR (2002)
2. Zia, L.L.: The NSF national science, technology, engineering, and mathematics education digital library (NSDL) program: New projects and a project report. D-Lib Magazine: The Magazine of Digital Library Research **7** (2001)
3. Arms, W.: Automated digital libraries: How effectively can computers be used for the skill tasks of professional librarianship. D-Lib Magazine: The Magazine of Digital Library Research (2000) `<http://www.dlib.org/dlib/july00/arms/07arms.html>`.
4. Bergmark, D.: Collection synthesis. In: Proceedings of the Second ACM/IEEE-CS Joint Conference on Digital Libraries, Portland OR (2002) Available: `<http://mercator.comm.nsdlib.org/CollectionBuilding/bergmark-paper.pdf>`.
5. Chakrabarti, S., van den Berg, M., Dom, B.: Focused crawling: a new approach to topic-specific Web resource discovery. In: Proceedings of the Eighth International World-Wide Web Conference., Toronto, Canada (1999) 545–562 Available: `<http://www8.org/w8-papers/5a-search-query/crawling/index.html>` and `<http://www.cs.berkeley.edu/~soumen/doc/www99focus/>` Current as of August 2001.
6. Belew, R.K.: Finding Out About. Cambridge Press (2001)
7. Salton, G.: Automatic Information Organization and Retrieval. McGraw-Hill, New York (1968)
8. Bergmark, D.: Using high performance systems to build collections for a digital library. In: Proceedings of the 2002 International Conference on Parallel Processing Workshops (ICPP 2002 Workshops), Vancouver, Canada (2002) Preprint available at `<http://mercator.comm.nsdlib.org/CollectionBuilding/DCADL_bergmark.ps>`.
9. Pirolli, P., Pitkow, J., Rao, R.: Silk from a sow's ear: Extracting usable structures from the Web. (1996) Available: `<http://www.acm.org/pubs/articles/proceedings/chi/238286/p118-pirolli/p118-pirolli.html>`.
10. Kleinberg, J.: Authoritative sources in a hyperlinked environment. Journal of the ACM **46** (1999) 604–632
11. Brin, S., Page, L.: The anatomy of a large-scale hypertextual Web search engine. In: Proceedings of the 7th International World Wide Web Conference (WWW7), Brisbane, Australia (1998) Available online at `<http://www7.scu.edu.au/programme/fullpapers/1921/com1921.htm>`, (current as of 28 Feb. 2001).
12. Gibson, D., Kleinberg, J., Raghavan, P.: Inferring Web communities from link topology. In: Proceedings of the 9th ACM Conference on Hypertext and Hypermedia: Links, Objects, Time and Space – Structure in Hypermedia Systems (HYPERTEXT'98, Pittsburg, PA). (1998) 225–234
13. Chakrabarti, S., van den Berg, M., Dom, B.: Distributed hypertext resource discovery through examples. In: Proceedings of the 25th VLDB Conference, Edinburgh, Scotland, Morgan-Kaufman (1999) 375–386
14. Rennie, J., McCallum, A.: Using reinforcement learning to spider the Web efficiently. In: Proceedings of the International Conference on Machine Learning (ICML). (1999)

15. Menczer, F., Belew, R.K. In: Adaptive Retrieval Agents: Internalizing Local Context and Scaling up to the Web. (1999) 1–45 Republished in Machine Learning, 39(2/3) pp. 203–242, 2000.
16. Menczer, F., Pant, G., Srinivasan, P.: Evaluating topic-driven Web crawlers. In: SIGIR '01, September 9–12, New Orleans, La. USA (2001)
17. Mukherjea, S.: WTMS: A system for collecting and analyzing topic-specific Web information. In: Proceedings of the 9th International World Wide Web Conference: The Web: The Next Generation, Amsterdam, Elsevier (2000) Available: `<http://www9.org/w9cdrom/293/293.html>` (current as of August 2001).
18. Chakrabarti, S.: Recent results in automatic Web resource discovery. ACM Computing Surveys (1999) Available: `<http://www.acm.org/pubs/articles/journals/surveys/1999-31-43es/a17-chakrabarti/a17-chakrabarti.pdf>`.
19. Diligenti, M., Coetzee, F., Lawrence, S., Giles, C., Gori, M.: Focused crawling using context graphs. In: Proceedings of the 26th International Conference on Very Large Databases. (2000)
20. Heydon, A., Najork, M.: Mercator: A scalable, extensible Web crawler. World Wide Web **2** (1999)
21. Najork, M., Heydon, A.: High-performance Web crawling. Technical Report Research Report 173, Compaq SRC (2001) Available at `<http://gatekeeper.research.compaq.com/pub/DEC/SRC/research-reports/abstracts/src-rr-173.html>`.
22. Davison, B.D.: Topical locality in the Web. In: Proceedings of the 23rd Annual International Conference on Research and Development in Information Retrieval (SIGIR 2000), Athens, Greece, ACM (2000)
23. Joachimes, T.: A support vector method for learning ranking functions in information retrieval (2002) Cornell University Colloqium.
24. Parsia, B.: A simple, prima facie argument in favor of the semantic web. MonkyFist (2002) Available: `<http://monkeyfist.com/articles/815>`.
25. Kluev, V.: Compiling document collections from the Internet. SIGIR Forum **34** (2000) Available at `<http://www.acm.org/sigir/forum/F2000/Kluev00.pdf>`.
26. Han, E.H.S., Karypis, G.: Centroid-based document classification: Analysis & experimental results. Technical Report 00-017, Computer Science, University of Minnesota (2000)
27. Katz, V., Li, W.S.: Topic distillation on hierarchically categorized Web documents. In: Proceedings of the 1999 Workshop on Knowledge and Data Engineering Exchange, IEEE (1999)

Goal-Oriented Requirements Specification for Digital Libraries

Davide Bolchini and Paolo Paolini

[1] University of Lugano, Faculty of Communication Sciences, TEC-lab,
via G.Buffi 13 - 6900 Lugano – CH
davide.bolchini@lu.unisi.ch, www.lu.unisi.ch/tec-lab
[2] Politecnico di Milano, Dipartimento di Elettronica e Informazione,
Via Ponzio, 34/5- 20133 Milano
paolo.paolini@polimi.it, http://hoc.elet.polimi.it

Abstract. This paper presents a model for systematically organizing the activity of requirements analysis for web-based hypermedia digital libraries and for tying it up with design in a coherent fashion. In order to accomplish this goal, three conceptual tools are proposed: a goal-oriented requirements analysis model based on existing practices and concepts in requirements engineering; a lightweight notation and a taxonomy for requirement specifications. The approach presented in this paper has been developed and validated within the EU-funded UWA project (Ubiquitous Web Applications, IST-2000-25131).

1 Introduction

Modern digital libraries can be seen as complex interactive communication means between the company or the institution offering a set of services and the end users.

It has been acknowledged that, in order to be successful and accepted by the target audience, such applications should be user-centred: they have to be shaped so as to meet the needs and goals of the end users. On the other hand, digital libraries – similarly to general web-based and traditional hypermedia applications - have also to fulfil the goals of the stakeholders who are to build the application.

Thus, requirements should derive from two main worlds of interests:

a) *The world of the end users*: the set of heterogeneous interests, expectations, needs and goals of the various people who might have an interaction experience with the application.

b) *The world of the client*: the set of heterogeneous interests, expectations, needs and goals of the various people who provide financial support to the application and have a stake in achieving and maintaining the success of the application (e.g. the institution promoting the applications, the application managers, i.e. the librarian [17, 18]). The activity of requirements analysis should allow passing from the business and communication goals (gathered through proper elicitation techniques) to the requirement specifications the application should actually meet. So far, within the hypermedia community and in related fields, valuable research effort has been put in conceiving hypermedia techniques and methodologies for web-based applications that could well support the design activity of a digital library [19, 20]. Unfortunately,

M. Agosti and C. Thanos (Eds.): ECDL 2002, LNCS 2458, pp. 107-117, 2002.

comprehensive models and specific conceptual tools for the requirement analysis of digital library applications represents a research field far to be fully explored. Currently, little attention is paid to the definition of goals and requirement specifications, although this is usually acknowledged as the activity where the most crucial decisions about the strategic features of the application are taken.

In general, two aspects have been often underestimated:

1. *Organization of requirements*

This activity addresses the following issue: What are the steps leading from the high-level goals of the digital library to the requirement specifications? Needed research actions to be undertaken are:

1a) The systematic investigation of the refinement activity from business and communication goals to requirements specifications. The reasons why certain requirements specifications have been defined have to be questioned.

1b) The definition of heuristics principles for the refinement process should be defined for improving the outcome of the requirement analysis.

2. *The connection between requirements specifications and design*

The following issue has to be addressed: What are the reasons behind design decisions [21]? Needed research actions to be undertaken are:

2a) Define a hypermedia-specific traceability model from design solutions to requirement specification. As far as now, no guidance is given to understand why a piece of design is there, whether it fulfils a requirement, or even what the correspondent requirement is. On the other hand, even if requirements are specified, no insight is provided to see why that specific design solution has been implemented instead of other reasonable alternatives.

2b) Requirements should clearly reflect on all the design dimensions of a digital library (e.g. content, access paths to content, information architecture, navigation, functionality, and visual presentation). Requirements analysis should quest for the purpose of the navigation structure (e.g., Why is this list of retrieved items ordered by author's name? Which user's need does it fulfil? Why are the features of a new item organized in a guided-tour way? Which was the goal of the „librarian" who designed it?); of a piece of information (e.g., To which stakeholder is this information useful? Which goal does this service try to fulfil?); or of a functionality (e.g., Could it be relevant for this kind of user to subscribe to the mailing list? Why has a forum been designed?).

Taking into account aspects 1) and 2) above, the overall research question to be explored is: How do the stakeholders' goals reflect on the actual design of a digital library?

The complexity of the issue calls for an ad-hoc solution that both helps understanding the relationship between high-level goals and requirements and bridges the gap between requirement specifications and design.

The paper introduces a model based on goal-oriented requirements engineering practices for defining specific conceptual tools for supporting the requirements analysis of web-based and hypermedia digital libraries. Namely, basic concepts are drawn from the GBRAM model, developed for aiding the activity of requirements definition for generic software systems.

This approach to requirements engineering specific for interactive communication means as hypermedia applications is an integral part of the EU-funded UWA project (Ubiquitous Web Applications, IST-2000-25131), whose goal is to define a coherent set of methodologies, notations and tools for this purpose.

2 Background

2.1 Goal-Oriented Requirements Analysis

The approach described in this paper is based on goal-oriented requirements engineering. The key achievement of this approach, first introduced by Yue [16] and van Lamsweerde [4], is that it makes explicit the why of requirements [15].

van Lamsweerde's goal-oriented requirements engineering copes with requirements specification from a formal perspectives, adopting proper algorithms and formal languages to refine the goals of the system into requirements. This approach is often referred to in the literature as KAOS. Though being a reference point in requirements engineering for mission-critical systems, KAOS does not provide enough conceptual tools for the requirements analysis of highly-interactive hypermedia applications, as digital libraries are. Moreover, formal approaches to requirements risk to turn out to be not understandable to analyst and designers which are either less-experienced or without a software engineering background.

A more flexible and comprehensive approach to goal-oriented requirements engineering is GBRAM [22]. This goal-based method addresses the issues of requirements analysis providing common concepts like Goal, Scenario, Requirements, and a Taxonomy for requirements. We claim that the combined employment of these concepts captures most of the complexity of the requirements analysis activity and offers useful guidelines also to non-experienced designers. The approach presented in this paper is based on GBRAM and extends some of its concepts in order to tailor it to the specific features of digital library requirements process.

2.2 Requirements Analysis for Web Applications

In the hypermedia and web design community it was recently acknowledged [8] that there is an actual gap between the requirements definition and the actual design of the content, of the navigation and of the functionalities of the application.

In the last ten years, a lot of effort has been put in conceiving conceptual design models that could cover the whole spectrum of the hypermedia design dimensions (among the most relevant: HDM [7], OOHDM [13], RMM [9], WSDM [4], WebML [3], UHDM [1]). Good insights and concepts have been provided for describing the navigation architecture of a web application, the functionalities and services offered to the user, the design of the interface and the way the content pieces are structured. Guidelines, golden rules and design patterns have been defined for capturing the design experience ad improving the outcome of the design activity [12].

Current approaches seem to ignore the fact that from requirements does not always necessarily descend one design solution [8]. Requirement definition rather identifies a space of possible design solutions. The designers will then discern and detail the most adequate (according to his/her knowledge, skills and experience) to fulfil the requirements. Moreover, as far as now, no systematic investigation was carried out to see how requirements impose constraints to design (in all its several dimensions) and to point out the reasons behind design decisions.

What is actually missing is a systematic approach to requirement analysis for hypermedia digital libraries that could help in a step-by-step refinement from high-level goals to application requirement specifications.

In particular, the problem of requirement *traceability* is an open issue in web engineering and has to be coped systematically. An approach based on goal-oriented requirements engineering can help maintain proper traces between the high-level goals, the requirements specifications and the actual design artifacts.

One of the most crucial issues in the refinement process from communication and business goals to requirements specifications is the proper level of detail in which such requirement specifications are defined. Requirements should be defined in a sufficiently high-level fashion so as not to give premature design solutions; on the other hand, they should be expressed in a sufficiently low-level manner so as to be understood by the designers. A proper level of abstraction for the definition of requirement specifications is needed. Analysts and web designers should be helped in agreeing on the proper level of detail of requirements. Therefore, a solution in this concern could help both designers and analysts to do their own job effectively.

3 From Goals to Requirements through Scenarios

Figure 1 shows the main elements composing the goal-oriented requirements analysis model for hypermedia digital libraries. The concepts involved in the proposed goal oriented model are: Stakeholder, Goal (and Sub-goal), Scenario, Requirement, Design dimension. All the various elements that appear in the model will be covered in some detail in the rest of this section.

A *stakeholder* is someone or something that has an interest in the system. This definition is purposely very vague because a stakeholder is an extremely generic concept. Examples include end-users, developers, opinion makers, content provider, sponsors, buyers, managers (i.e., people who will not use the system but who manage people who do), but also a company or an institution. These stakeholders are very important but too often neglected in the requirements engineering process.

Note that a stakeholder is not the same as an actor in UML terms. An UML actor models someone or something interacting with the system. A stakeholder, on the contrary, does not necessarily interact with the system but s/he has an interest in it. Thus, the very essence of a stakeholder, far from being anything that has an interaction with the application (as UML proposes), is much more analogue to the concept of *persona* [24], i.e. an archetype subject (in our case a person or an institution) which has a stake in the existence of the application.

A *goal* is a high-level, long-term objective that one or more stakeholders own. Adopting a stakeholder-centered perspective, every goal can be traced back to its owners. A stakeholder may own an arbitrary number of goals, but must own at least one. On the other hand, a goal may be owned by an arbitrary number of stakeholders but must be owned by at least one. In fact, a goal that interests no-one is a non-goal, and should therefore be removed. Examples of goals are: *Attract more users to the application* (owned by the sponsor); *Maintain all resources updated* (owned by content managers); *Drive the user to the new acquisitions* (owned by the communication manager); *Access suggested publications* (owned by a frequent end-user).

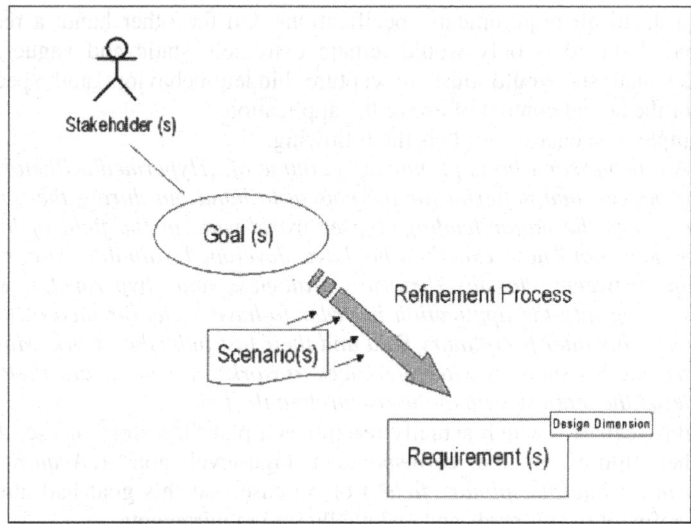

Fig. 1. The synopsis of the goal-oriented model

High-level goals represent the ultimate desires and expectations of stakeholders. However, for them to be of use, they have to be refined into lower-level goals. This refinement process is extremely useful because a high-level goal per se does not say much to the designer. It is too abstract, too high-level and too long-term to be fed directly to hypermedia designers.

In addition, refining the goals into sub-goals is invaluable for eliciting new requirements, and assessing existing ones. According to our experience, it is often very hard to understand what the real goal of the customer is. Therefore, quite often during the refinement process one realizes that a goal they had previously stated is actually not a goal of theirs, but probably of some other stakeholder, or probably that's not a goal at all, in that nobody is interested in that.

For the acquisition and the refinement of goals, *scenarios* [2] can help the analyst figure out concrete behaviors of the system. A scenario can be defined as the description of a concrete episode of use of the application. A scenario helps identify stakeholders performing goals in an everyday context of use; under this respect scenarios and goal refinement are mutually supportive for the requirements analysis [23]. While goals appear quite abstract and context-independent (since they are valid for many situation of use), scenarios add to goals useful details to understand the implications of a real situation of use and to uncover hidden goals.

Iterating from goals to requirements through scenarios allows the analyst and the designers to share a detail view of the reasons behind requirements. Since the activity of requirements analysis is commonly considered as highly critical for the success of the application and, at the same time, highly complex to manage, the iterative interplay between goals, scenarios and requirements should be considered flexible and recursive throughout the process rather than fixed and ruled by a strict sequence of steps.

If analysts rely upon scenarios only, requirements specifications risk to be incomplete; in real projects, it is unfeasible to define all possible scenarios necessary to cover in detail all requirements specifications. On the other hand, a requirement analysis based on goals only would remain extremely static and vague, and less-experienced analysts would miss to capture hidden behaviors and specifications deriving for the actual context of use of the application.

An example of scenario (Sc_1) is the following:

James is a professor who is preparing a course of „Hypermedia Rhetoric". He is looking for background material for the course to hand out during the introductory lesson. He knows the major leading figures world-wide in the field of hypermedia design but does not know exactly who have developed valuable research on the relationship between classic rhetoric strategies and hypermedia structures. Therefore, he log into the application in order to have a clearer idea of well-known researchers in this interdisciplinary field and their last published work. Moreover, he wants to provide his students with references to works in hypermedia rhetoric which are considered the main stream of the research in the field.

Given this scenario, which actually resembles a plausible story of use, the analyst could either figure out the correspondent high-level goal („*Acquire valuable references in an interdisciplinary field*") or, in case that this goal had already been identified, refine it in sub-goals and eventually into requirements.

Figure 2 shows in a schema a possible refinement process for this goal. From the high-level goal (the top circle), three sub-goals (the derived circles) are defined thanks to the detailed information captured by the scenario. The letters „Sc_1" in the figure points out the refinement processes that have been facilitated by the employment of the scenario described above. The scenario is rich of those details that can greatly help the analyst to figure out clearly which sub-goals can be properly derived for the high-level goal.

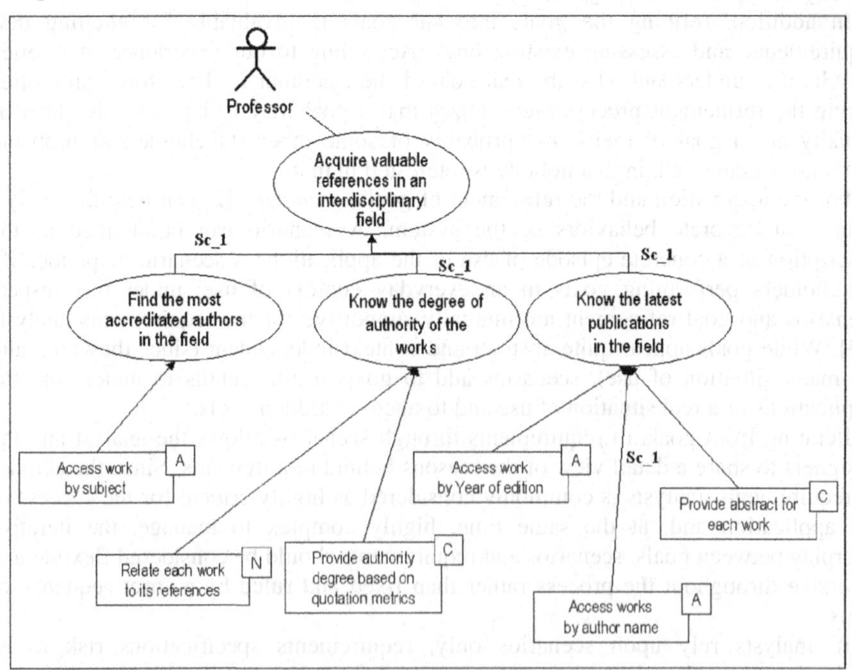

Fig. 2. An example of the derivation graph

The leaves of the derivation graph (the bold rectangles) are the *requirements*. A requirement represents the operationalisation of a goal. In other words, a requirement is a possible mean to fulfill one or more goals. This means that a requirement turns one or more goals into a concrete specification that a designer can read and apply. We should note that the proposed derivation example shows only one of the possible requirements that could derive from the high-level goal. For achieving the result of each refinement step (being it a sub-goal or a requirement), the analyst cannot apply any algorithm but has to make strategic decisions about the features that the application will meet. Actually, the derivation process is not a mechanical activity but a highly creative one. However, it has been acknowledged that it is difficult to define in absolute terms „the" proper level of abstraction by which requirements should be defined [14]. Since requirements are the result of an on-going negotiation between the analyst, the domain expert and the designer, the level of detail of requirements is strongly dependent on at least three variable factors:

1. *Shared domain knowledge*

The requirements resulting from the negotiation process are strongly dependent on the degree of implicit and shared domain knowledge between the analyst and the web designer. The more is the shared domain knowledge between the analyst and the designer, the less information should be explicated and specified during the requirement negotiation.

2. *The degree of design experience of the designer*

If the designer of the hypermedia digital library has long-standing experience, s/he can easily figure out how to transform ill-defined and generic requirements into effective design solutions. On the contrary, less-experienced designers should be helped in achieving a proper solution by very detailed requirement specifications. Thus, personal experience, intuition and ingenuity play a key role throughout the process.

3. *The conceptual design tools mastered by the designer*

The more a designer masters comprehensive design models, proven design methods and effective design patterns, the less the requirements should be detailed. Proper conceptual tools can actually help the designer to conceive and document a set of possible design solutions from a given requirement specification.

Whatever the combination of the mentioned factors will be, a number of assumptions about the environment and the application requirements are unavoidable. For this reason, it is often very difficult to make explicit the assumptions that the requirements engineer took into account, and therefore it will be often the case that they will not be made explicit. In addition, some assumptions need not be made explicit because they are entirely obvious.

However, given the necessary assumptions, the level of abstraction of requirements should be defined in such a way to avoid taking premature and ill-grounded design decision and to state specifications that can be understood by the designers.

4 A Taxonomy for Requirements

Requirements are categorized into *dimensions*. As shown in Figure 2, each requirement is labeled according to the design dimensions it gives indications about.

Categorizing requirements is a fairly standard activity within a requirements engineering methodology, and common categories are described in many general-purpose frameworks, including GBRAM and KAOS. In order to tailor the requirements process to the specific features of hypermedia digital library and, more in general, to web-applications we propose a novel categorization scheme for requirements. Figure 3 shows the different categories that were devised.

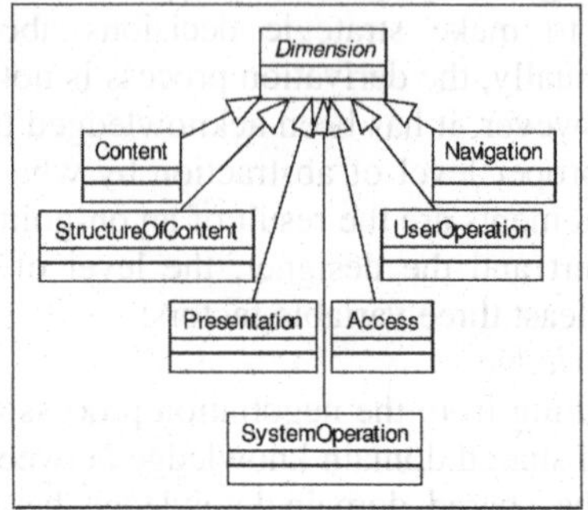

Fig. 3. Hypermedia and Web-specific requirements dimensions.

The dimensions presently comprised in the taxonomy are:

1. Content. It is the core value of any hypermedia applications. It refers to that set of ideas and messages that the site communicates to its users. Ideas and messages are mainly specified in terms of the core information objects available. Designing such information objects means designing „what" the user will actually consume and interpret along the session. In the requirements specifications of our example, a requirement concerning this dimension is *„Provide abstract for each work"*. In the proposed notation, requirements belonging to this dimension are labeled with „C" (see Figure 2).

2. Structure of content. Requirements can also give coarse-grain insight about how the information objects identified are structured. By „structure" we mean the organization of content within the same information object. Giving indications about the structure of content may mean basically two things: *a)* defining pieces of content that are part of a given information object; *b)* highlighting pieces of content as opposed to others within the same information object. For example, in case that a work had been structured into several information component, a requirement falling into this category could be: *„highlight title and abstract"*. In the proposed notation, requirements belonging to this dimension are labeled with „S".

3. Access. This dimension refers to the navigational paths available to the user in order to reach the needed content. The user should be allowed to access the needed information or be guided in the exploration of the offered content following the navigational access paths best corresponding to their expectations and goals. This design dimension captures the hypermedia artifacts exploited by the user to start the navigation, to locate and reach the interested content. Examples include: *„access published works by author, by paper title, and by theme"*. In the proposed notation, requirements belonging to this dimension are labeled with „A" (see Figure 2).

4. Navigation. Requirements can suggest to connect different information objects allowing the user to navigate from one piece of content to another. Semantic relationships among pieces of information can be relevant for navigation i.e., they can be exploited by the user to traverse the path connecting one object to one or more others in order to complete their cognitive or operational task. This design dimension captures the hypermedia artifacts exploited by the user to navigate, after having accessed a given information object, from that object to one or more other semantically related artifacts. For example: *„relate a work to all its references,“ „relate a work to the details of its authors“*, *„allow to navigate from an author to all the works written by that author“*. In the proposed notation, requirements belonging to this dimension are labeled with „N“ (see Figure 2).

5. Presentation. Requirements can also give guidelines for defining the visual communication strategies for presenting content, navigational capabilities, and operation to the user. Presentation implies two main aspects: graphics and layout. Graphics are concerned with the visual elements composing the user interface (buttons, icons, images, font proportions, titles, etc.). Layout is concerned with the physical positioning of these objects on the page. In the proposed notation, requirements belonging to this dimension are labeled with „P“.

6. User operation. User operations are those operations that are visible to users. They are the only operations the users must be aware of. Roughly, these operations are all the operations that users can enable by interacting with the application. For example: *„download paper,“ „post review,“ „submit comment,“ „post personal data,“* etc. In the proposed notation, requirements belonging to this dimension are labeled with „U“.

7. System operation. System operations are those operations that are not visible to users, but are performed for system's purposes or become mandatory to „build“ user operations. For example: *„force authentication“*, *„Induce user preferences from recurrent navigational paths“*. In the proposed notation, requirements belonging to this dimension are labeled with „O“.

A requirement belongs to exactly one dimension. Actually, this restriction can also be seen as a necessary (although certainly not sufficient) condition for a requirement to be considered such: if a requirement cannot be easily and clearly assigned to exactly one dimension, then it is too general to be called a requirement (and is therefore still a goal). Again, the number and nature of dimensions is not fixed a priori, but new ones can be added at will and at any time.

5 Future Work

Within the UWA project, the methodology for requirements engineering discussed in this paper has been applied and tested for the developing of advanced multi-channel applications and one-to-one e-banking services. A set of 43 analysts, developers and designers have been provided with the conceptual tools of the framework (model and notations). The effectiveness and the perceived quality for the methodology has been appreciated by practitioners. Designers found the model effective and useful for their job; they also provided valuable suggestions for improvements. A lot of future work will then be devoted to the refinement and assessment of the model.

Besides being a part of an innovative project, the proposed approach represents also a challenging and fruitful research direction in the requirements process for web-based digital libraries. We are also testing the model on a number of web applications in the domain of cultural heritage applications (mainly museums web sites). More case studies have to be analyzed so as to assess the taxonomy for the requirements. A set of refinement principles based on heuristics capturing the designer's experience are currently under development. These guidelines should help the analyst to define requirements at a proper level of abstraction. The presented approach for the definition of requirements is turning out to be effective also for the evaluation early in the requirements analysis. Thanks to the traceability allowed, design documentation and requirements specifications could be validated even before design. For example, the soundness and the consistency of a set of requirements could be validated against the related goals.

6 Conclusions

We have presented an approach based on goal-oriented requirements engineering specific for the development of hypermedia and web-based digital libraries. A model, a notation and a taxonomy for requirements have been defined for granting a step-by-step refinement from the goals of the stakeholders and the constraints of the systems to the requirements specifications. In particular, the model – which proposed a tailored version of GBRAM - aimed at taking into account the high level of interactivity and the various navigational aspects that a modern web application provides. The rationality of the requirements has been investigated paying particular attention to the proper level of detail in which requirements should be expressed in order to be understood by the designer without introducing premature design solutions. The creativity of the requirements analysts can be in this way disciplined during the interpretation of the needs and goals of the stakeholders.

Acknowledgements. The work was partially funded by UWA project (Ubiquitous Web Applications, IST-2000-25131, www.uwaproject.org). The authors express their sincere thanks all the partners of the UWA consortium for their support and collaboration to conceive and bring forth this work.

References

1. Baumeister, H., Koch, N., Mandel, L., Towards A UML Extension For Hypermedia Design, in Proceedings of UML'99 The Unified Modeling Language - Beyond the Standard, LNCS 1723, Fort Collins, USA, October 1999.
2. Carrol, J.M., Scenario-based Design: Envisioning Work and Technology in System development, John Wiley & Sons, 1995.
3. Ceri, S., Fraternali, P., Bongio, A., Web Modeling Language (Webml): A Modeling Language For Designing Web Sites, Proc. Int. Conf. WWW9, Amsterdam, May 5, 2000. See also: www.webml.org.
4. Dardenne, A. van Lamsweerde, and S. Fickas. Goal-directed Requirements Acquisition. Science of Computer Programming, 20:3–50, 1993.

5. De Troyer, O.M.F., Leune, C.J., WSDM: A User-Centered Design Method For Web Site, in Proc. of Int. World Wide Conf. WWW7.
6. Garzotto, F., Baresi, L., Paolini, P., From Web Sites To Web Applications: New Issues For Conceptual Modelling, Proceedings of the World Wide Web and Conceptual Modeling'00 Workshop, ER'00 Conference, Salt Lake City, 2000, Springer.
7. Garzotto, F., Paolini, P., Schwabe, D., HDM - A Model-Based Approach to Hypertext Application Design, TOIS, 1993.
8. Güell, N., Schwabe, D., Vilain, P., Modeling Interactions and Navigation in Web Applications, Proceedings of the World Wide Web and Conceptual Modeling'00 Workshop, ER'00 Conference, Springer, Salt Lake City, 2000.
9. Isakowitz, T., Stohr, E., Balasubramanian, P., RMM: A Methodology for Structured Hypermedia Design, CACM, 1995.
10. Jackson, M. The World and the Machine. In Proceedings of the 17th International Conference on Software Engineering, pages 283 – 292, Seattle, Washington, USA, April 24 – 28, 1995.
11. Jacobson, I., Booch, G., Rumbaugh, J. The Unified Software Development Process. Addison-Wesley, 1999.
12. Paolini, P., Garzotto, F., Bolchini, D., Valenti, S., Modelling by Pattern of Web Applications, in Proc. of International Workshop on World Wide Web and Conceptual Modeling, (WWWCM '99), Paris, 1999.
13. Schwabe, D., Rossi, G., An Object Oriented Approach to Web-Based Application Design, Theory and Practice of Object Systems, J. Wiley, 1998.
14. Sommerville, I., Sawyer, P., Requirements engineering. A good practice guide, Wiley, 1997.
15. A. van Lamsweerde. Requirements Engineering in the Year 00: A Research Perspective. In Proceedings of ICSE'2000 – 22nd International Conference on Software Engineering, Limerick, 2000. ACM Press. Invited Paper.
16. K. Yue. What Does It Mean to Say that a Specification is Complete? In Proceedings of IWSSD-4 – the Fourth International Workshop on Software Specification and Design, Monterey, CA, USA, 1987.
17. Fox, E. A. Akscyn, R. M., Furuta, R. K., and Legget, J. J. 1995. Introduction to special issues on digital libraries. Communication of the ACM, 38, 4, (Apr), 23-28.
18. Borgman, C., 2001. Where is the librarian in the digital library. Communication of the ACM, 44, 5, (May), 66-67.
19. Nürnberg, P. J., Wiil, U. K., and Leggett, J.J. Structuring facilities in digital libraries, in Proceedings of the Second European Conference on Digital Libraries (ECDL'98), Crete, Greece, 1998.
20. Wiil, U. K., Hicks, D. L., Requirements for development of hypermedia technology for a digital library supporting scholarly work, in Proceedings of SAC'00, Como, Italy, March 19-21, 2000.
21. Potts, C., Bruns, G., Recording the reasons for design decisions, Proceedings of the 10th international conference on Software engineering, 1988 , Singapore.
22. Antòn A. I., Potts, C., The use of goals to surface requirements for evolving systems, in Proceedings of the 20th international conference on Software engineering, 1998, Kyoto, Japan.
23. Potts C., Using schematic scenarios to understand user needs, Conference proceedings on Designing interactive systems: processes, practices, methods, & techniques, August 1995.
24. Cooper Interactive Design, Perfecting your personas, www.cooper.com/newsletters/2001_07/perfecting_your_personas.htm, 2002.

OntoLog: Temporal Annotation Using Ad Hoc Ontologies and Application Profiles

Jon Heggland

Department of Computer and Information Science, Norwegian University of Science and Technology, NO-7491 Trondheim, Norway
jon.heggland@idi.ntnu.no

Abstract. This paper describes OntoLog, a prototype annotation system for temporal media. It is a Java application built to explore the issues and benefits of using ontologies, application profiles and RDF for temporal annotation. It uses an annotation scheme based on hierarchical ontologies, and an RDF-based data model that may be adapted and extended through the use of RDF Schema. Dublin Core is used as a default description scheme. The paper also describes an ontology-based logging interface and annotation visualisation, and a web-based searching and browsing system.

1 Introduction

The use of temporal, rich media such as video and audio in research, documentation and education benefits significantly from systems providing temporal annotations. High-level, semantic temporal annotations augment the information in the media, adding comments, explanations, references and links. They also act as indices and tables of content, providing access points and summaries.

Though research in the multimedia database field is focussed primarily on efficient storage and delivery of video and audio data, and less on the description mechanisms needed to handle the enormous amounts of information the data provides, several annotation systems have been proposed and implemented e.g. [1], [2], [3]. Likewise, the digital library community and HCI researchers have produced some fine examples of annotation tools ([4], [5], [6], [7], [8]). However, many such systems are tailored to a specific domain and purpose, which means they excel in their area of expertise, but are cumbersome to adapt for different uses. Others are so generic or minimalist that they may be found lacking in preciseness in complex, specialised domains.

I believe there is merit in exploring the issues of creating a lightweight, extensible and adaptable annotation framework. It should be usable without modification for non-demanding applications, but also permit modification and extension of its data model – by the users, for the users. For interoperability and user-friendliness, it should use widely-accepted technologies and metadata standards to achieve this. Since the creation of semantic annotations is potentially very time-consuming, it should also aim to simplify this process.

In this paper, I describe OntoLog, my attempt at creating such a system. It utilises the Resource Description Framework (RDF, [9]) to provide a basic annotation data model that may be extended using RDF Schemas [10]. It provides a fast and simple

M. Agosti and C. Thanos (Eds.): ECDL 2002, LNCS 2458, pp. 118-128, 2002.

interface for logging video, based on the use of ontologies, which is also RDF-based and extensible.

In the next section, I summarise the most important background technologies OntoLog builds upon. Section 3 describes the OntoLog system – its basic data model, its extensibility and adaptability mechanisms, and its user interface. Section 0 discusses preliminary experiences with the system, and section 5 concludes the paper.

2 Background

In this section, I describe the most fundamental issues concerning the annotation of temporal media. This is followed by a brief overview of the metadata standards OntoLog uses, and a short discussion of application profiles.

2.1 Annotating Temporal Media

Temporal media are media with a time extent – for instance video, animation, speech and music. Annotations are, according to [11], "notes added by way of comment or explanation". Due to the length of temporal media objects (e.g. motion pictures are typically around two hours), and the fact that they may cover many different topics in this time, annotations need to be temporal as well. They must be connected to specific time intervals in the annotated medium.

There are two main temporal annotation schemes: segmented and stratified. The segmented scheme is the oldest and simplest. The idea is to partition the media object into temporal segments, and describe each segment. A common extension of this scheme is to group related, consecutive segments together, creating a multilevel, hierarchical segmentation. This corresponds to the structure of shots, scenes and sequences in television and film production [12]. A problem with this scheme is that it may be hard to determine the most suitable granularity of the segmentation. If a segment is too large, its description will not be completely valid throughout its whole extent. If the segments are too small, descriptions will need to be repeated across consecutive segments, causing duplication of effort. Another problem is that the concepts described in the media object may partially overlap in various ways, again leading to either partially invalid descriptions, or duplication of effort due to fine granularity. All in all, segmented annotations are better suited to describe the structure of a temporal media object than its semantics.

The stratified approach [3] creates layers of descriptions called strata, where each strata describes the temporal occurrences of some concept like a person, place or topic. The intervals in different strata may overlap, so the description of the media object at any given time can be modelled as the union or projection of the strata present at that time. This is a more flexible scheme, but also more complex to implement and create user interfaces for.

Temporal annotations can be created in several ways. Doing it manually is very time-consuming, so much research has been done on algorithms and techniques for producing them automatically. Systems for segmenting video based on editing points or scene analysis are common (e.g. [13], [14], [3]); likewise, audio may be segmented by silence detection or speaker recognition ([15], [16], [17]). Face and speech recognition has been successfully implemented, as has recognition and interpretation of on-screen text. However, this is still rather low-level information, and is to some degree dependent on domain information (notice the ubiquity of the well-structured news broadcast domain). The extraction of high-level semantics still requires human intervention, as does the augmenting process of adding comments, explanations and references.

2.2 RDF and Dublin Core

The Resource Description Framework (RDF, [9]) is a World Wide Web Consortium recommendation; a domain-neutral standard for machine-readable metadata. Its basic data model consists of three object types: resources, properties and statements. A *resource* is anything addressable by a URI [18]. All things described by RDF are resources. A *property* is an attribute or characteristic used to describe a resource. A specific resource together with a property and the value of that property for that resource is a *statement*. These three parts of a statement are called the *subject*, the *predicate* and the *object*, respectively. The object may be a resource or a literal (a simple string or some other primitive datatype).

The RDF Schema recommendation [10] provides a type system for RDF. Among other things, it specifies a mechanism for defining classes of resources and properties, including subclass relationships, and for creating restrictions on what classes of resources each property may be applied to. The typing system is specified in terms of the basic RDF data model, using resources for concepts such as Class and properties for relationships like subClassOf.

The Dublin Core (DC) Element Set ([19], [20]) is a set of fifteen properties designed to cover the most common needs for describing document-like objects. The standard includes attributes such as title, author and date, and specifies their semantics and how they should be used for maximum interoperability. Though Dublin Core it is not related to RDF, the DC schema can be specified in RDF Schema, and metadata using DC may be encoded using RDF syntax.

2.3 Application Profiles

Application profiles as a type of metadata schema was first introduced by Heery and Patel in [21]. The background is that when you design a digital library, database or metadata system, there are many different metadata standards to choose from. Typically, however, none fits your need perfectly – they might be too big, too small, to restrictive or too general. Therefore, usual practise is to adapt the standards – select the most relevant elements and ignore the rest, to impose additional restrictions on cardinality and data types and to combine complementing standards.

Application profiles is the formalisation of this adaptation practise. An application profile is defined as a schema that reuse elements from other schemas without introducing new data elements. They may specify permitted values and schemes, and can refine the standard definitions. An application profile might for instance say that the Dublin Core Identifier property must have an ISBN as its value, or that the Coverage property shall only be used to denote a geographical location. Thus, you end up with a schema designed specifically for the task at hand, while still maintaining a fair degree of interoperability. How to specify, use and disseminate such application profiles is an interesting research topic – see e.g. [22] and [23].

3 The OntoLog System

OntoLog is a media annotation tool that uses ontologies or classification schemes to create and access stratified temporal annotations, and provides application profile functionality through integration of different metadata schemas. The main objectives during the development of OntoLog were:

- To explore the issues of enabling flexible, user-defined description schemes and application profiles.
- To simplify production, access and understanding of semantic, temporal annotations by using user-defined ontologies and vocabularies.
- To experiment with a novel visualisation of temporal annotations.

In this section, I first discuss OntoLog's ontology-based annotation scheme, followed by a description of its basic data model. Then, I discuss how OntoLog takes advantage of various metadata standards, before I conclude describing the user interface – the logging interface, the annotation visualisation, and the ontology-enabled, web-based search and browsing system.

3.1 Ontology-Based Annotation

Many video indexing systems, e.g. [4], [6], [24], segment the video according to topics, scenes or editing points, and annotate the segments with free-text transcripts, descriptions or keywords. OntoLog uses a different approach. It creates intervals that are unconstrained in that they may overlap freely with each other, like the stratified model presented in section 2.1. Each interval is connected to a concept or term in an ontology, vocabulary or classification scheme. Additionally, the intervals (and the concepts) may be described with properties according to various user-specified description schemas. This approach is arguably more powerful, since it may be used to implement the more restricted schemes – the intervals may be created so as to segment the media object, and annotated using various properties. Even a hierarchical segmentation scheme may be implemented by relating each layer of intervals to a shot, scene or sequence concept, and connecting the intervals between layers using a "part of" property.

Basing the indexing around a structured set of terms has many advantages, as noted by Weinstein [25]. It allows for easy and exact analysis and statistics on the length, occurrences and frequency of each term, within and among media clips. This is useful for domains such as ethnography, anthropology or other application where analysis of behaviour documented on video or audio is common. It also facilitates browsing and searching, since the ontology may be used as an index or catalogue. Compared to using free text descriptions and keywords, it is less prone to uncertainty due to misspellings and use of slightly different words to express the same concept. With support for equivalence relations and "similar term"-relations, ontologies become even more powerful. Additionally, having a standard set of terms to use makes it easier for a group of indexers to produce consistent and interoperable descriptions, and speeds up the annotating process.

OntoLog organises the concepts in hierarchical ontologies, which is also an important point. Using categories for logging video typically produces a lot of categories – the experimental project described in [7] used about 80. A flat list of this size is quite unwieldy, but arranged in a hierarchy, it is far easier to use. It also allows for easy aggregation of annotations and customisable level of detail during both logging and browsing.

3.2 Basic Data Model

Fig. 1 is an UML diagram showing the basic skeleton of OntoLog's data model. The Media Resource element represents the digital media objects, e.g. MPEG files. Each Media Resource contains an unbounded number of Intervals, with start time and end time. By default, no restrictions are put upon the temporal ordering of the intervals, so they may freely overlap.

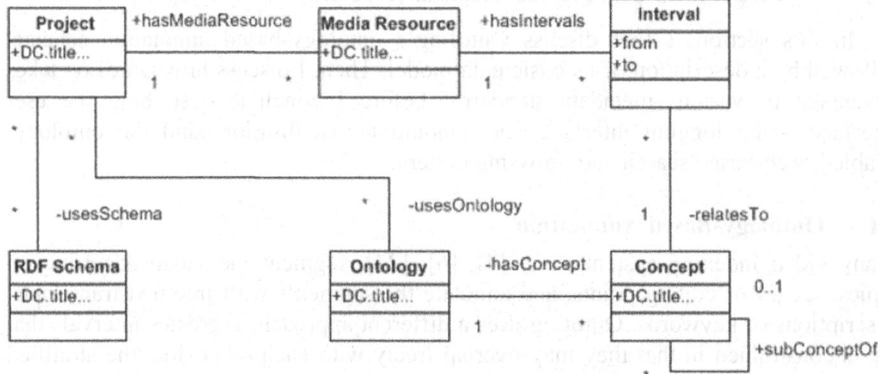

Fig. 1. OntoLog's Basic Data Model

There are two principal annotation methods in OntoLog. The main intended annotation mechanism is based on that each of the intervals is connected to a Concept. Concepts may represent terms, topics, persons, places, events – anything that it is desirable to mark the presence of in the media object. Concepts are organised into hierarchical Ontologies, using a relation with subclass or subset semantics. This creates a stratified annotation scheme, augmented by the hierarchical organisation of the strata.

Another complementing annotation mechanism – suggested by the "DC.title..." attributes in the diagram – is that the intervals and concepts (and indeed any data element in OntoLog) may be described with arbitrary properties, selected or defined by the user. The RDF Schema objects determine what properties are available, what classes of resources they may be applied to, and what types of values each property may have.

The Project class has several roles in the data model. It groups a set of media resources, and also manages the set of ontologies used to describe them. Ontologies are shared between projects, to enable reuse, consistency and interoperability. The perhaps most interesting use of the Project class, is its role as application profile. It manages a set of RDF Schemas, which determine how the rest of the data in the project may be described. The project may also adapt the schemas for the purpose at hand, by adding titles and descriptions, and possibly restricting the domains and ranges of the properties. Naturally, RDF Schemas may also be shared between projects.

3.3 Application of Metadata Standards

The data model described above is built on the RDF data model, where information is represented as statements consisting of subject, predicate and object. In the diagram, the classes act as subjects and objects, while the associations and attributes are predicates. OntoLog uses the Jena framework [26] to manipulate RDF data, storing the data in a generic relational database. Indeed, all the data in OntoLog, including the schema defining its basic data model, is expressed in RDF. This makes it easy to incorporate other standards and mechanisms that are RDF compatible, and it enables OntoLog to be indexed by RDF search engines and augmented with other RDF tools.

OntoLog is able to import and interpret RDF Schemas. The resources and properties specified in the schemas are integrated into OntoLog's user interface for adding and editing properties, thus creating a simple yet fairly powerful mechanism for extending and adapting OntoLog's capabilities. The needs of different domains and purposes are accommodated through use of different schemas. As OntoLog supports an unlimited number of schemas per project, there is no need for a single schema to encompass all possible metadata requirements.

As a default, OntoLog uses the Dublin Core Element Set 1.1 [20] as its description schema. Dublin Core was chosen because it is a widely accepted standard, and its set of attributes is by design applicable in most domains and suitable for various purposes. As Dublin Core by default puts no constraints on what kinds of resources its elements may be applied to, all kinds of entities in OntoLog – projects, media resources, ontologies, concepts – may be described with DC properties. The DC title property is used (if available) to represent the resources visually in the user interface. For RDF Schema classes and instances of the RDF Property class, the RDF Schema label property (taken from the schemas in which the classes and properties are defined) is used instead.

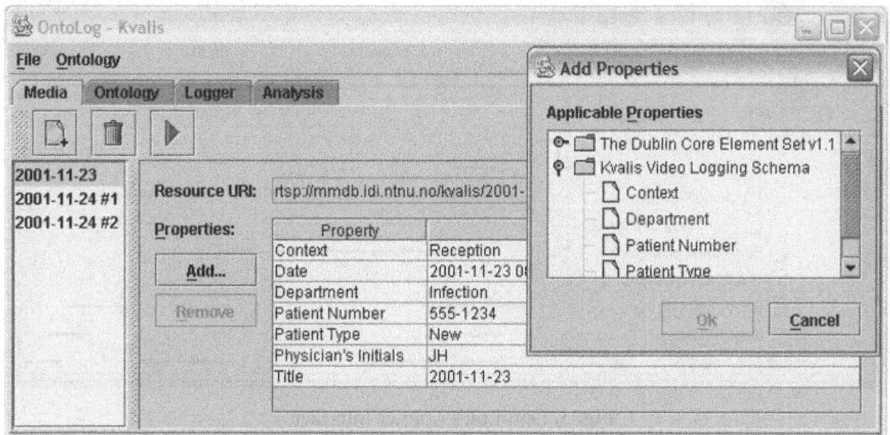

Fig. 2. Media Resources with Properties

Fig. 2 shows an example of how a media resource may be annotated with properties drawn from different schemas. This is taken from a project evaluating the use of electronic journals in hospitals through analysing video recordings of medical consultations. The properties of the selected video (titled "2001-11-23") is shown; the

Date and Title properties are from Dublin Core, while the rest of the properties are from a schema designed for the project. The "Add Properties" dialog shows how applicable properties are presented: as a two-level tree structure, the roots being the names of the schema the properties are defined in.

3.4 The User Interface

OntoLog's user interface is designed to be simple and fast to use. Due to its use of the RDF data model, describing and managing projects, media resources and ontologies is consistent and straightforward. Importing and using other RDF Schemas is transparent and seamless, since OntoLog already uses RDF Schema for its basic data model and its default description schema, Dublin Core.

Real-Time Logging Interface. In logging mode, each concept in the ontologies can be clicked on and off during playback, thus creating intervals linked to the concepts. A keyboard shortcut can be defined for each concept, further simplifying the process. Informal studies of users logging video with OntoLog have shown that with a reasonably small number of relevant concepts, only one or a few passes through the clip is necessary for an adequate set of annotations.

Fig. 3 shows the logger interface logging a video from the video analysis project mentioned in section 3.3. The tree on the left shows the ontology used to annotate the video; the underlined characters in the concept titles indicate the keyboard shortcuts. The timeline display on the right shows the annotations connected to each concept.

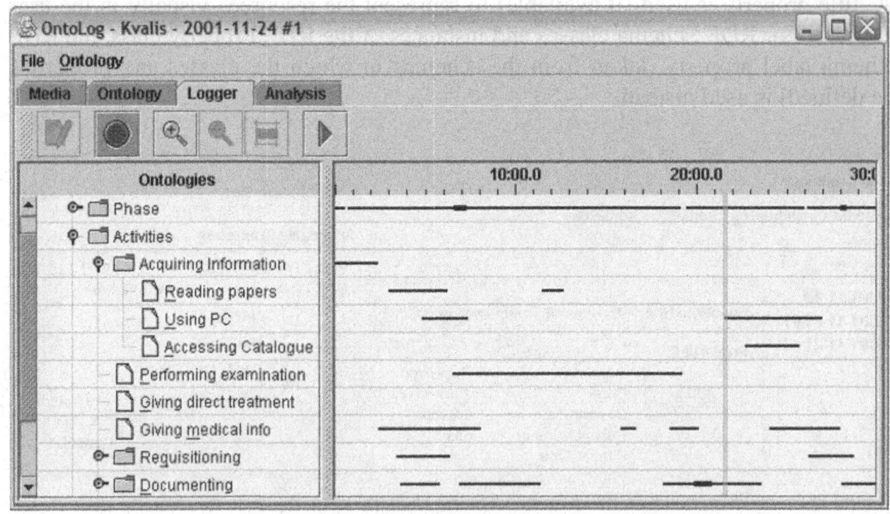

Fig. 3. OntoLog's Logger Interface

Once created, the annotations may be edited by direct manipulation. The start and end times of the intervals can be modified by click-and-drag, and intervals can be reclassified to other concepts by dragging them. Properties can be added, edited and removed through a pop-up dialog box.

Visualisation of Stratified, Hierarchical Annotations. OntoLog exploits the hierarchical organisation of the ontologies in its visualisation of the annotation intervals. The ontologies are displayed in a collapsible tree structure, while the corresponding annotations are shown as horizontal lines next to each concept in a timeline display. If a concept is collapsed – that is, hiding its descendants – the corresponding set of lines representing annotations is similarly collapsed, displaying the union of all the annotations linked to the concept and its descendants, thickening the line according to how many intervals overlap at any given time. This provides a nice visual summary of the annotations – with most or all of the concepts collapsed, the display shows how thickly the media is annotated, and which concept subtrees are most important. By expanding and collapsing subtrees, users can concentrate on the concepts that are most relevant to the task at hand, and hide non-relevant information.

Fig. 3 illustrates this hierarchical aggregation in some of the collapsed concepts, but in Fig. 4 the visualisation of all the intervals connected to the Activities concept and its subconcepts shows it better. Here, it is plain to see that some activity is "active" throughout the video (as there are no gaps in the line), and that a lot of different activities take place near the start of the video, where the line is very thick.

Fig. 4. Collapsed Concept with Lots of Annotations

Web-Based Searching and Browsing Interface. As part of a project on streaming digital media, a web-based searching and browsing system called OntoLog Crawler has been developed. It takes advantage of the simplicity and uniformity of the RDF subject-predicate-object data model to provide a simple and consistent browsing interface to the data in OntoLog. It dynamically creates web pages describing RDF resources by listing the RDF statements they are used in, both as subject, predicate and object. Each of the terms in each statement are hyperlinks leading to pages describing them and their statements in the same way. Fig. 5 shows the page describing the MediaResource resource, one of the classes in OntoLog's basic data model (cf. Fig. 1).

OntoLog Crawler also takes advantage of the semantics provided by OntoLog's fundamental RDF Schema. The pages describing media resources and intervals contain a media player configured to play the relevant media clip, and the ontology and concept pages shows the structural organisation of the concepts.

The browsing system requires some familiarity with the RDF data model. The search system does not have this drawback. Given a search term, it searches the properties describing media resources, concepts and intervals, and presents the results as lists of hyperlinks leading to media clips. It can also join the set of clips produced by a search, combining them into a seamless presentation using SMIL [27]. The search system also utilises the semantics of the data model: If a concept is considered a "hit", the concepts in the subtree below it are also considered "hits", and all the intervals related to them are included in the search result.

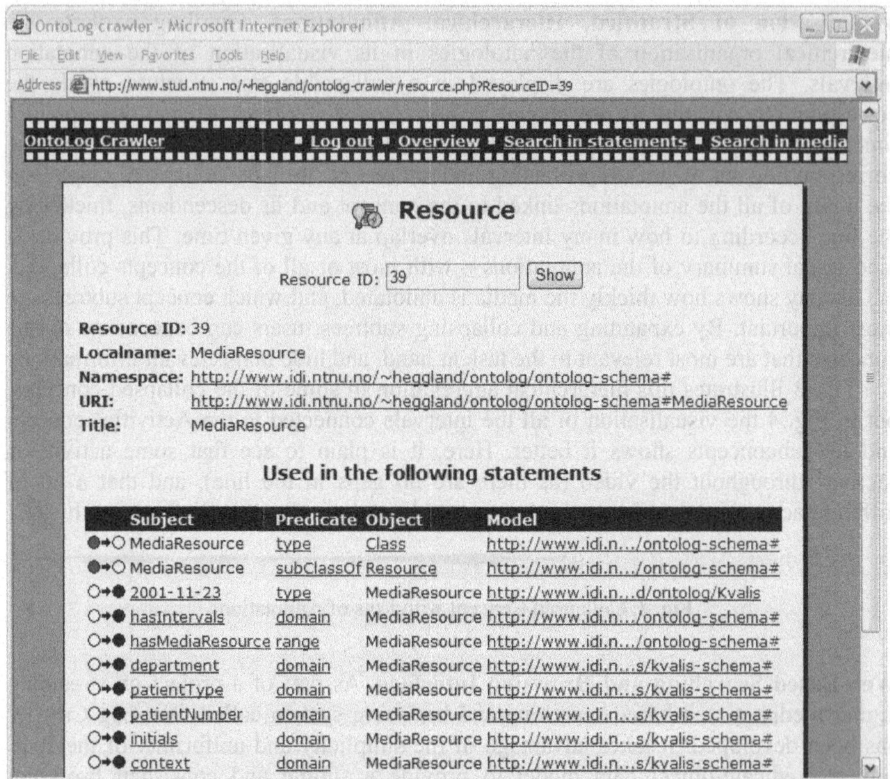

Fig. 5. Browsing OntoLog RDF Data

4 Experiences

OntoLog has during development been informally evaluated as a possible replacement for Qualitative Media Analyzer (QMA [28]) in a project analysing video recordings of medical consultations. This evaluation has mainly been concerned with the user interface, which was found to be better than QMA's in several ways. Particularly the editing and rearrangement of annotation intervals is easy and intuitive in OntoLog. The logging interface was also considered good, especially the complementary methods of keyboard shortcuts and mouseclicks for turning concepts on and off during logging. On the other hand, the use of Java for media playback makes rapid navigation through video somewhat sluggish.

The extensibility and adaptability functions in OntoLog were evaluated to a lesser degree, due to the small scale of the project. A small RDF Schema for describing the videos was constructed (cf. Fig. 2). The integration of this into OntoLog was very smooth, but it is a drawback that OntoLog as yet does not provide a graphical user interface for creating such schemas – they have to be written by hand in RDF/XML. This is not a problem if standard schemas are used, as they already exist in RDF/XML form, but OntoLog should cater to the needs of projects needing or wanting to create their own schemas without much RDF knowledge as well.

5 Conclusion and Further Work

OntoLog is a system for logging and annotating video and audio swiftly and accurately, using user-modifiable combinations of ontologies, RDF schemas and metadata standards. Its purpose is to function as a testbed for exploring the issues concerning the use of application profiles, ontologies and RDF for temporal annotations. In its current incarnation, OntoLog's extensibility and adaptability mechanisms are simple yet powerful, its use of RDF enables it to interoperate with the semantic web, search engines and other RDF-enabled tools with ease, and its user interface is clean, fast and friendly.

However, OntoLog is by no means a finished tool; the version of OntoLog described in this paper is merely a first increment. For instance, its support for RDF Schemas is a bit rudimentary, and its ability to adapt them for a specific application leaves something to be desired. Similarly, the ontology handling can be extended to handle more advanced models, e.g. DAML+OIL [29]. There is also work in progress to apply the SESAM searching approach [30] to OntoLog.

Acknowledgements. I would like to thank Hallvard Lærum for ideas and input on the capabilities of OntoLog, particularly the ontology-based logging interface and the visualisation of the intervals, and for evaluating the system. Also, thanks to my advisor Roger Midtstraum and my colleague Jon Olav Hauglid, for feedback on OntoLog and critical reviews of this paper; and to Per Håkon Meland and Jørgen Austvik for their work on OntoLog Crawler. This work is supported by Accenture.

References

1. Correia, N. and T. Chambel. *Active Video Watching using Annotation.* in *The seventh ACN international conference on Multimedia*. 1999. Orlando, FL USA.
2. Mele, F. and G. Minei, *Digital Video Management for Heterogeneous and Distributed Resources.* IEEE Multimedia, 2001. **8**(3): p. 30-38.
3. Chua, T.-S., L. Chen, and J. Wang, *Stratification Approach to Modeling Video.* Multimedia Tools and Applications, 2002. **16**(1/2): p. 79-97.
4. Weher, K. and A. Poon. *Marquee: A Tool For Real-Time Video Logging.* in *Human factors in computing systems: "celebrating interdependence"*. 1994. Boston, MA USA.
5. Carrer, M., *et al.*, *An Annotation Engine for Supporting Video Database Population*, . 1996, Multimedia Communications Laboratory, Boston University: Boston.
6. Hunter, J. and R. Iannella. *The Application of Metadata Standards to Video Indexing.* in *European Conference on Digital Libraries*. 1998. Crete.
7. Cohen, J., M. Withgott, and P. Piernot. *Logjam: a tangible multi-person interface for video logging.* in *CHI 99 conference on human factors in computing systems*. 1999. Pittsburgh, Pennsylvania: ACM Press.
8. Hunter, J. and D. James. *The Application of an Event-Aware Metadata Model to an Oral History Project.* in *European Conference on Digital Libraries*. 2000. Lisbon, Portugal.
9. Lassila, O. and R.R. Swick, *Resource Description Framework (RDF) Model and Syntax Specification,* http://www.w3.org/TR/1999/REC-rdf-syntax-19990222/. The World Wide Web Consortium 1999.
10. Brickley, D. and R.V. Guha, *Resource Description Framework (RDF) Schema Specification 1.0,* http://www.w3.org/TR/2000/CR-rdf-schema-20000327/. The World Wide Web Consortium 2000.

11. Merriam-Webster, *Merriam-Webster's Online Collegiate Dictionary,* http://www.m-w.com/dictionary.htm. 1998.
12. Monaco, J., *How to Read a Film.* 1981: Oxford University Press.
13. Arman, F., *et al. Content-based Browsing of Video Sequences.* in *ACM Multimedia.* 1994. San Francisco, USA: ACM Press.
14. Foote, J., *et al. An intelligent media browser using automatic multimodal analysis.* in *ACM Multimedia.* 1998. Bristol, UK: ACM Press.
15. Hindus, D., C. Schmandt, and C. Horner, *Capturing, Structuring and Representing Ubiquitous Audio.* ACM Transactions on Information Systems, 1993. **11**(4): p. 376-400.
16. Arons, B., *SpeechSkimmer: A System for Interactively Skimming Recorded Speech.* ACM Transactions on Computer-Human Interaction, 1997. **4**(1): p. 3-38.
17. Whittaker, S., *et al., Jotmail: a voicemail interface that enables you to see what was said,* in *CHI Letters.* 2000. p. 89-96.
18. Berners-Lee, T., *et al., Uniform Resource Identifiers (URI): Generic Syntax,* http://www.ietf.org/rfc/rfc2396.txt. 1998.
19. Weibel, S., *Metadata: The Foundations of Resource Description,* in *D-Lib Magazine.* 1995.
20. DCMI, *Dublin Core Element Set, Version 1.1 - Reference Description,* http://www.dublincore.org/documents/dces/. 1999.
21. Heery, R. and M. Patel, *Application profiles: mixing and matching metadata schemas,* in *Ariadne.* 2000.
22. Baker, T., *et al., What terms does your metadata use? Application profiles as machine-understandable narratives.* Journal of Digital Information, 2001. **2**(2).
23. Hunter, J. and C. Lagoze. *Combining RDF and XML Schemas to Enhance Interoperability Between Metadata Application Profiles.* in *WWW10.* 2001. Hong Kong.
24. Hunter, J. and J. Newmarch. *An Indexing, Browsing, Search and Retrieval System for Audiovisual Libraries.* in *European Conference on Digital Libraries.* 1999. Paris, France.
25. Weinstein, P.C. *Ontology-Based Metadata: Transforming the MARC Legacy.* in *ACM Digital Libraries.* 1998. Pittsburgh, USA.
26. McBride, B., *Jena: Implementing the RDF Model and Syntax Specification,* http://www-uk.hpl.hp.com/people/bwm/papers/20001221-paper/. 2000.
27. Ayars, J., *et al., Synchronized Multimedia Integration Language (SMIL 2.0),* http://www.w3.org/TR/smil20/. The World Wide Web Consortium 2001.
28. Skou, C.V., *Qualitative Media Analyzer,* http://www.cvs.dk/qma.htm. 2002.
29. Harmelen, F.v., P.F. Patel-Schneider, and I. Horrocks, *Reference Description of the DAML+OIL (March 2001) Ontology Markup Language,* 2001.
30. Hauglid, J.O. and R. Midtstraum. *SESAM - Searching Supported by Analysis of Metadata.* in *ACM Symposium on Applied Computing.* 2002. Madrid, Spain.

An XML Log Standard and Tool for Digital Library Logging Analysis

Marcos André Gonçalves, Ming Luo, Rao Shen, Mir Farooq Ali, and Edward A. Fox

Virginia Tech, Blacksburg VA 24061, USA
{mgoncalv,fox}@vt.edu

Abstract. Log analysis can be a primary source of knowledge about how digital library patrons actually use DL systems and services and how systems behave while trying to support user information seeking activities. Log recording and analysis allow evaluation assessment, and open opportunities to improvements and enhanced new services. In this paper, we propose an XML-based digital library log format standard that captures a rich, detailed set of system and user behaviors supported by current digital library services. The format is implemented in a generic log component tool, which can be plugged into any digital library system. The focus of the work is on interoperability, reusability, and completeness. Specifications, implementation details, and examples of use within the MARIAN digital library system are described.

1 Introduction

Log analysis is a primary source of knowledge about how digital library patrons actually use DL systems and services and how systems behave while trying to support user information seeking activities. Log recording and analysis allows evaluation assessment and opens opportunities to improvements and enhanced new services. Indeed, the benefits of logging are numerous, including improving performance by recording effective evaluation data [13], helping in designing and testing of user interfaces [7], and better allocation of resources [17].

Conventional libraries have a long history of concern for privacy [10]. While circulation statistics are widely available, storage of patron-related information is rare in such libraries. The introduction of On-Line Public Access Catalogs (OPACs) has changed the picture and allowed some degree of log recording and analysis to improve library services [1,16,17,15]. More recently, web servers and proxy caching servers have made web log analysis become common place, recording each and every access to their documents. These, along with the advance of techniques in web log mining, have made possible a number of new and enhanced services such as customization and personalization [14].

Digital libraries differ from the Web in many ways. Firstly, digital library collections are explicitly organized, managed, described, and preserved. Secondly, web sites and web search engines assume very little about the users, tasks, and data they deal with. Digital libraries normally have much more knowledge of

M. Agosti and C. Thanos (Eds.): ECDL 2002, LNCS 2458, pp. 129–143, 2002.

their users and tasks since they are built to satisfy specific needs of interested communities. And thirdly, the digital objects in DL collections tend to be much more structured than the information presented in the Web. Therefore, digital library logging should offer much richer information and opportunities. Despite the fact that many current DL systems do some kind of logging, they tremendously differ in the format in which they record the information and even the sort of information that is recorded. Interoperability, reuse of log analysis tools, and comparability of log analysis results are major problems.

In this paper, we propose an XML-based standard digital library log format that captures a rich, detailed set of system and user behaviors supported by current digital library services. The proposed standard is implemented in a generic log component tool, which can be plugged into any digital library system to produce the specified format. The focus of this work is on interoperability, reusability, and completeness. Specifications, implementation details, and examples of use within the MARIAN digital library system are described.

This paper is organized as follows. Section 2 covers related work and analyzes associated problems. Section 3 describes the DL log format and motivation for design. Section 4 presents the log tool, its implementation and some examples. Section 5 outlines future work and concludes the paper.

2 Related Work

Most current Web servers store log files in the Common Log Format (CLF)- a simplistic format which reflects the stateless nature of the HTTP protocol by recording just individual server events. Apache, perhaps the most used web server, uses an extension of CLF called Combined Log Format, which tries to keep some state information by recording the links between resources.

A sample of CLF is given below. The fields are host; rfc931, i.e., information returned regarding identity of the person, otherwise '-'; authuser, if a userid is sent for authentication, otherwise '-'; day; month; year; hour; minutes; seconds; request; the first line of the HTTP request as sent by the client; ddd, status code returned by the server, otherwise '-'; and bbb, the number of bytes sent (not including the HTTP/1.0 header), otherwise '-'.

```
bbn-cache-3.cisco.com - - [22/Oct/1998:00:20:21 -0400] "GET
/~harley/courses.html HTTP/1.0" 200 1734
bbn-cache-3.cisco.com - - [22/Oct/1998:00:20:22 -0400] "GET
/~harley/clip_art/word_icon.gif HTTP/1.0" 200 1050
www4.e-softinc.com - - [22/Oct/1998:00:20:27 -0400] "HEAD
/ HTTP/1.0" 200 0
user-38ldbam.dialup.mindspring.com - - [22/Oct/1998:00:20:48 -0400] "GET
/~lhuang/junior/capehatteras.html HTTP/1.0" 200 328
user-38ldbam.dialup.mindspring.com - - [22/Oct/1998:00:20:48 -0400] "GET
/~lhuang/junior/PB2panforringed.mirror.gif HTTP/1.0" 200 20222
eger-dl01.agria.hu - - [22/Oct/1998:00:20:51 -0400] "GET
/~tjohnson/pinouts/ HTTP/1.0" 200 26994
```

Distinct from simple web servers, which focus primarily on browsing behavior, web search engines and digital libraries also record data about search and other information seeking behaviors. The following is a sample of a query transaction submitted through the OpenText search engine. It shows the search terms and operations, but also records a good deal of internal cryptic information about how the system operates internally.

```
Mon Sep 28 17:48:42 1998
----- Starting Search -----
Mon Sep 28 17:48:42 1998
{Transaction Begin}
Mon Sep 28 17:48:42 1998
{RankMode Relevance1}
Mon Sep 28 17:48:42 1998
"Bacillus thuringiensis "
Mon Sep 28 17:48:42 1998
P0 = "Bacillus thuringiensis "
Mon Sep 28 17:48:42 1998
R = (*D including (*P0))
Mon Sep 28 17:48:42 1998
R = (((*R rankedby *P0)))
Mon Sep 28 17:48:42 1998
S = (subset.1.10 (*R))
Mon Sep 28 17:48:42 1998
SL0 = (region "OTSummary" within.1 (*S))
Mon Sep 28 17:48:42 1998
(*SL0 within.1 ( subset.1.1 *S ))
Mon Sep 28 17:48:42 1998
(*SL0 within.1 ( subset.2.1 *S ))
Mon Sep 28 17:48:42 1998
{Transaction End}
Mon Sep 28 17:48:42 1998
----- Ending Search -----
```

Digital library systems, most probably for historical reasons, usually implement logs that resemble web log formats or utilize proprietary formats. As an example, below is an annotated sample of a portion of the log of the Greenstone digital library system [23]. Greenstone is a comprehensive, open-source digital library system, which enables logging by setting a specific flag in the configuration file. Each line in the sample user log contains: (a) the IP address of the user's computer; (b) a timestamp in square brackets; (c) the CGI arguments in parentheses; and, (d) the name of the user's browser (Netscape is called "Mozilla").

```
ADMINISTRATION 37
/fast-cgi-bin/niupepalibrary
(a) its-www1.massey.ac.nz
(b) [Thu Dec 07 23:47:00 NZDT 2000]
(c) (a=p, b=0, bcp=, beu=, c=niupepa, cc=, ccp=0, ccs=0, cl=, cm=,
```

```
cq2=, d=, e=, er=, f=0, fc=1, gc=0, gg=text, gt=0, h=, h2=, hl=1,
hp=, il=1, j=, j2=, k=1, ky=, l=en, m=50, n=, n2=, o=20, p=home,
pw=, q=, q2=, r=1, s=0, sp=frameset, t=1, ua=, uan=, ug=,
uma=listusers, umc=, umnpw1=, umnpw2=, umpw=, umug=, umun=, umus=,
un=, us=invalid, v=0, w=w, x=0, z=130.123.128.4-950647871)
(d) "Mozilla/4.08 [en] (Win95; I ;Nav)"
```

The last CGI argument, "z", is an identification code or "cookie" generated by the user's browser: it comprises the user's IP address followed by the timestamp when they first accessed the digital library. The log file usage.txt is placed in the /etc directory in the Greenstone file structure.

Other digital library log formats that we analyzed include those associated with the Dienst protocol (used by the old NCSTRL-Networked Computer Science Technical Reference Library), and the EMERGE, Phronesis, and MARIAN digital library systems.

2.1 Problems with Existing DL Logs

A careful analysis of the logs of the web and DL systems discussed above reveals a common set of problems. These include:

1. **Disorganization:** Barring a few, most of the system logs were very poorly organized and structured.
2. **Complexity of analysis:** Lack of proper thought in recording the log information makes log analysis a hard problem. Indeed, complex data mining techniques are currently needed to extract some useful information from web and similar types of logs [19,20].
3. **Incompleteness:** Important information that would be necessary for analysis was omitted from some logs. As an example, most of the logs failed to record the client postal and email address, information that is essential in any user-based study of the system.
4. **Incompatibility:** Each of the systems had their own log formats, making it difficult to use the same tools to analyze logs from different systems for the same kind of study.
5. **Ambiguity:** Many of the log entries and their semantics were not properly and precisely specified in the log format itself, which could lead to ambiguity in analyzing them.
6. **Inflexibility:** The logs recorded a good deal of system specific information which would not be applicable to other systems. This information was recorded in conjunction with other information that was system independent.
7. **Verboseness:** Many of the logs looked just like code dumps used for debugging by the implementers of the system, rather than containing clear and precise information about system usage and behavior.

The above problems were found across the whole set of logs that we analyzed. In the next section, we present our standardized digital library log format design, which attempts to solve many of those problems.

3 The Digital Library Standardized Log Format

As per the previous analysis, current web and digital library logging has a number of problems. Our solution is to propose an XML-based DL standard format which is comprehensive, reflective of the actual DL system behavior, easily readable, precise, flexible to accommodate in varying systems, and succinct enough to be easily implemented.

3.1 DL Log Standard Design

As a first step in creating the DL log format, we collected an extensive, flat set of attributes that we felt were necessary to be recorded in the DL log. The next step was to organize these attributes in a fashion that was logical and structured and could be easily represented and implemented. We chose to produce an XML Schema [21] to formally describe the syntax and semantics of our DL log format. XML provides a standard syntax for the log format; different XML element tags represent different semantic attributes to be registered in the log. As a matter of fact, a similar use of XML to guarantee structural quality of web logs is reported in [24]. XML Schema provides an equivalent to a grammar in XML syntax to specify the structure of the log format. Also, XML log files produced by our tool can be validated against the schema for correctness. Besides that, XML Schema has a rich set of basic types, such as those for numbers, dates, and times, which further contribute to standardization. And finally, the abundance of XML parsers and other related software helps in the construction of analysis tools.

The DL log format had to be reflective of how a generic DL system behaves. We achieve this goal in two ways:

1. By using the 5S digital library theory of Streams, Structures, Spaces, Scenarios and Societies [22] as guidance for how to organize the log structure and define the semantics of the DL components whose behavior would be logged.
   The 5S theory formally defines a standard nomenclature and the semantics of the most common DL components using compositions of mathematical objects. Informally, using the 5S concepts, we summarize that a digital library involves managed *collections* of digital information, accessible over a network, and with associated *services* to support the needs of its communities. Information is manifest in terms of *digital objects*, which contain structured textual or multimedia streams (e.g., images, audio, video). *Metadata* describes different properties of digital objects, and is commonly structured into records. *Collections* and *Catalogs*, i.e., organized sets of metadata records, are stored in persistent, probably distributed *repositories*. In many cases, structures of digital objects and metadata are explicitly represented and explored to improve the quality of services. Basic DL services include indexing, searching, and browsing, and their behaviors are described by means of sets of *scenarios*, which correspond to sequences of user and/or system events and associated actions.

2. By having the notion of a "transaction" as the basic unifying entity of the log format.
   Basically everything that occurs in a DL system could be broken down to the level of a transaction, either as interaction between users and the system or among the system components themselves. Simple examples of a transaction in our format would be a search query submitted by a user, the registering of a new user, or the recording of some system failure. This may be an isolated transaction in a system that does not have the notion of an explicit "session", or it might be a part of a bunch of transactions that define a session. However, most of the current DL log formats, such as CLF, record just one or a few kinds of events or transactions. All or most of the entries in those log files have similar semantics. Our log format is designed to record a number of different kinds of transactions. Examples of distinct transactions are search, browse, session start, etc.

3.2 DL Log Format Structure

Figure 1 shows the higher-level organization of the DL log format. Each DL log file consists of a number of log entries, each entry representing a type of transaction. Transactions could be categorized as being related to session creation, user registration, user and system events associated with the use of DL services, administration activities, errors, and user-responses. An important and essential feature of the format should be to identify each transaction precisely. To achieve this, we record the timestamp at which it occurred and also associate a unique ID with each transaction. This ID should ideally be monotonically increasing across one server to provide a logical representation of successive transactions. Additionally, in case we're dealing with a non-session based system, we need a way to identify the user. One way to do this is to associate the location (IP address) from which the user is interacting with the system. Each transaction is then associated with a specific statement. A partial XML Schema of the high level organization is shown below.

```
<xsd:complexType name="LogType">
  <xsd:element name="LogEntry" minOccurs="0" maxOccurs="unbounded">
  <xsd:complexType>
    <xsd:sequence>
      <xsd:element name="Transaction"/>
        <xsd:complexType>
          <xsd:attribute name="ID" type="xsd:int/>
        </xsd:complexType>
      </xsd:element>
      <xsd:element name="TimeStamp" type="xsd:dateTime"/>
      <xsd:element name="MachineInfo">
        <xsd:complexType>
          <xsd:sequence>
            <xsd:element name="IPAddress" type="xsd:string"/>
            <xsd:element name="Port" type="xsd:int" minOccurs="0"/>
```

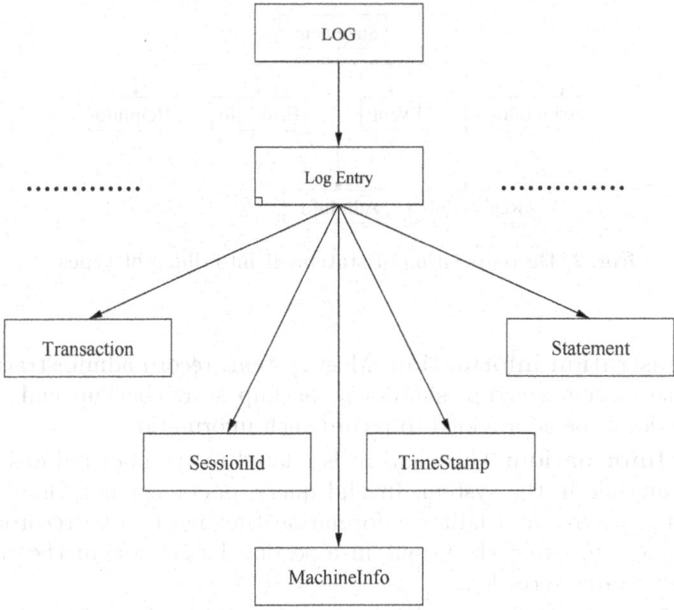

Fig. 1. Top level Hierarchy.

```
        </xsd:sequence>
      </xsd:complexType>
    </xsd:element>
    <xsd:element name="SessionId" type="xsd:string" minOccurs="0"/>
    <xsd:element name="Statement" type="StatementType"/>
  </xsd:sequence>
 </xsd:element>
</xsd:complexType>
```

There are basically two kinds of statements: 1) those related to specific user and system events associated to DL services; and 2) general statements related to administrative and other general activities. In more detail (Figure 2), the following types of statements are defined:

- **SessionInfo:** In the case of an explicit session based system, the session start and end times, as well as the user's and associated information, need to be recorded. We also assign a globally unique ID to each session. Using this ID, it is very easy to group together all the transactions that occur within this session.
- **Registration info:** In many session-based systems, users have to register themselves with the system when they use it for the first time. They usually have to select a user-ID, password, and possibly provide their identifying and demographic information.

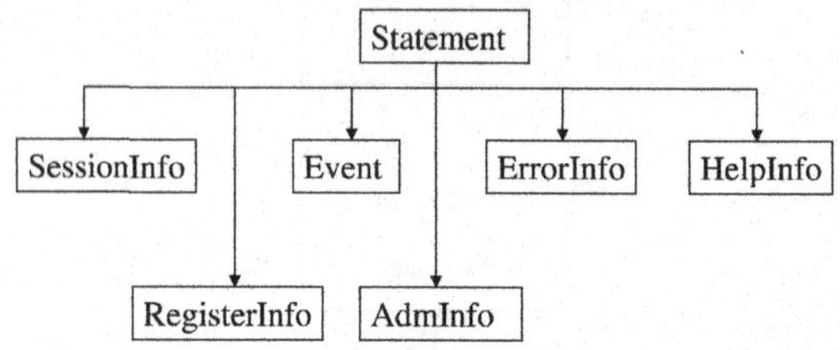

Fig. 2. Decomposition of statement into different types.

- **Administration information:** Most systems record administration activities like system startup, shutdown, backup start, backup end, etc. This transaction type is provided to record such information.
- **Error Information:** This element is related to errors or failures that may occur anytime in the system. Invalid query, document not found, etc., are examples of error and failure information that need to be recorded. If the user forgets to explicitly logout in a session based system the connection time out can be recorded.
- **Help Information:** Some DL systems provide help facilities to aid the user. Use of this feature should be considered to be separate from the other actions described above. Our log format considers this to be another type of transaction. It can be an interesting investigation to find out which kinds of help are frequently used by a user.
- **Event:** We consider this to be the heart of the DL log format. User or system events occur as a result of users performing information seeking activities and using digital library services, or as a system response to those activities. Each event is associated with an action, which encompasses the main operations associated with DL services such as searching, browsing, updating, and recording of system information related to these three operations. Each of those actions is performed over a collection of digital objects or a catalog of metadata. User events also have a status code that is based on the outcome of the action (e.g., success, failure, etc.). Four different kinds of actions are currently defined (Figure 3):

  1. **Search:** Searching is a basic DL service. Different systems implement a number of different query languages and search schemes based on the underlying retrieval model they use. Two of the common models are boolean and ranked retrieval [5,4]. Each of these systems also can provide additional features like selection of collection(s), structure related information such as which field the search concerns (author, title, subject, ...), the duration of activities, and some way to indicate whether this search operation is to be performed in the context of a previous, larger search. Systems also can provide options to the users to select how they want to view the results from their queries, including sort option and maximum number of results to be presented. The details of the search element are presented in the portion of the Log Schema below.

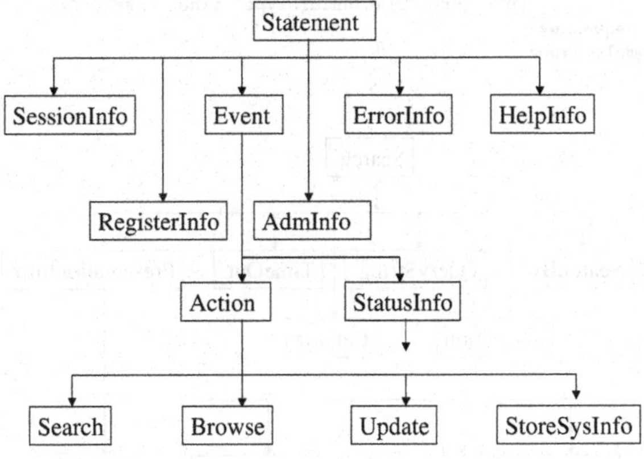

Fig. 3. Decomposition of an event into different types.

```
<xsd:complexType name="SearchType">
  <xsd:sequence>
    <xsd:element name="Collection"
              type= "xsd:string" minOccurs="0"/>
    <xsd:element name="MetadataCatalog" type= "xsd:string" minOccurs="0"/>
    <xsd:element name="ObjectType">
       <xsd:complexType>
        <xsd:element name="DigitalObject"
                type="xsd:string" minOccurs="0"/>
        <xsd:element name="MetadataRecord"
                type="xsd:string" minOccurs="0"/>
        <xsd:element name="HoldingsRecords"
                type="xsd:string" minOccurs="0"/>
        <xsd:element name="CommunityRecords"
                type="xsd:string" minOccurs="0"/>
       </xsd:complexType>
    </element>
    <xsd:element name="SearchBy"
              type= "xsd:string" minOccurs="0"/>
    <xsd:element name="SearchType">
       <xsd:complexType>
        <xsd:element name="persistent"
                type="xsd:string" minOccurs="0"/>
        <xsd:element name="non-persistent"
                type="xsd:string" minOccurs="0"/>
       </xsd:complexType>
    <xsd:element>
    <xsd:element name="QueryString"
              type= "xsd:string" minOccurs="0"/>
    <xsd:element name="TimeOut"
              type= "xsd:string" minOccurs="0">
      <xsd:complexType>
        <xsd:sequence>
          <xsd:element name="StartDate" type="xsd:date"/>
          <xsd:element name="EndDate" type="xsd:date"/>
        </xsd:sequence>
      </xsd:complexType>
```

```
    </element>
    <xsd:element name="PresentationInfo"
                 type= "PresentationInfoType" minOccurs="0"/>
  </xsd:sequence>
</xsd:complexType>
```

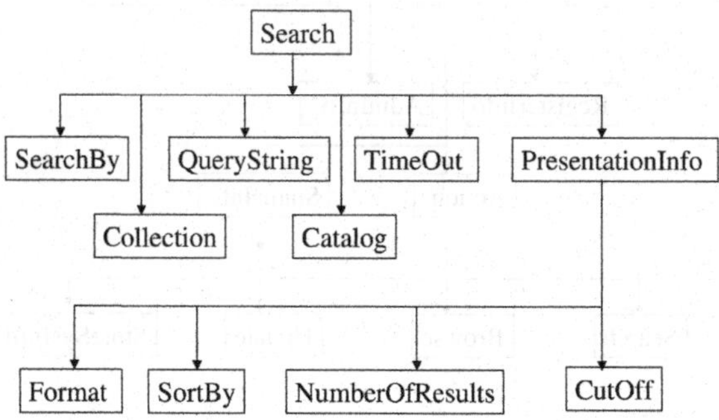

Fig. 4. Search Attributes.

Specific types of objects can be searched including generic digital objects, metadata records, holding records (which keep holding information for real objects in a library system), and community records (non-bibliographic resources that fulfill some information need of a community). SearchBy is used in structured queries and covers specific fields under which the query will be performed. The value of SearchType is set to persistent if the search is to be performed over the result of a previous search. Since query syntax is heavily dependent on the specific DL system and underlying retrieval model, we only record the exact query string used. Log analysts will consider this information in the context of the particular system for their studies. The PresentationInfo includes presentation format (e.g., list, threaded, tabular), which type of sort to apply (e.g., by confidence, by a specific field), number of results, and cut off threshold.

2. **Browse:** Browsing services can be performed by navigation through lists of search results, indexes organized by specific fields, and generic hypertexts. In the browse section we include identifiers of nodes and links navigated, and presentation information.
3. **Update:** Some systems also provide facilities to allow an administrator or user to add, modify or edit some part(s) of collections and/or catalogs resident in a repository.
4. **Store information:** This action allows us to record the data associated with the search and browse actions from the point of view of the system. So, basically actions 1, 2 and 3 above record the user's data, while this action records the system's response data. After any action the system needs to record some information like number of bytes transferred, response time of the action, highest and lowest ranked item, etc.

4 DL Log Tool and Its Implementation

The DL XML Log Tool is implemented using generic Java classes and can be used by any digital library or analysis system. There are mainly two classes in the log tool implementation, XMLLogData.java, used for storing data, and XMLLogManager.java, which provides methods to write and read log information according to our DL log format. XMLLogData.java basically provides a structure to hold private data with Set and Get methods to set and get values. For example it has one attribute String SessionInfo for session-based systems and it has SetSessionInfo() and GetSessionInfo() methods to set and get the value of SessionInfo. All the read and write methods are synchronized to avoid conflicts and inconsistences. The most difficult part is how to plug-in the tool into the target system. That should be done by calling specific methods of the XMLLogManager wherever a specific type of transaction occurs. Since this is heavily dependent on the target system architecture and implementation, that should be done by developers or administrators.

First tests were performed on the MARIAN digital library system [12]. MARIAN is a session-based digital library software designed to store, search, and browse large numbers of objects in a distributed environment. MARIAN was originally developed at Virginia Tech in C++ and recently evolved to a pure Java version. MARIAN has a resource management mechanism, which administers and allocates all the system resources such as class managers and searchers. In the MARIAN system, we only have one XMLLogManager Java object in memory, created as an attribute of the ResourceClassManager. Whenever information needs to be logged the client calls the corresponding method of the XMLLogManager instance of the ResourceManager.

4.1 Examples

We have included examples of some log transactions in MARIAN captured from real use of the system. In the examples, we use the Dirline collection, a U.S. National Library of Medicine's online digital library containing location and descriptive information about a wide variety of information resources including organizations and projects concerned with health and biomedicine.

1. Login to the System:

```
<Transaction ID = "3452">
   <SessionId > 987654usr3 </SessionId>
   <SessionInfo>
      <SessionStart> Start </SessionStart>
      <LoginInfo>
         <UserId> mhabib <UserId>
      </LoginInfo>
   </SessionInfo>
   <TimeStamp> 2002-05-31T20:10:55.000-05:00 </TimeStamp>
   <MachineInfo>
      <IPAddress> 128.173.244.56 <IPAddress>
```

```
    <Port> 8000 </Port>
  </MachineInfo>
</TransId>
```

2. Query on all Dirline records enties about "low back pain" in any part of the record.

```
<Transaction ID = "3455">
  <SessionId > 987654usr3 </SessionId>
  <TimeStamp> 2002-05-31T20:11:07.000-05:00 </TimeStamp>
  <MachineInfo>
    <IPAddress> 128.173.244.56 <IPAddress>
    <Port> 8000 </Port>
  </MachineInfo>
  <Statement>
    <Event>
      <Action>
        <Search>
          <Collection>Dirline</Collection>
          <ObjectType>CommunityRecord</ObjectType>
          <SearchBy>SearchByAnyParts</SearchBy>
          <SearchType>NonPersistant</SearchType>
          <QueryString>low back pain</QueryString>
          <TimeFrame>
            <StartTime>2002-05-31T20:11:07.000-05:00</StartTime>
            <EndTime>2002-05-31T20:11:09.000-05:00</EndTime>
          </TimeFrame>
          <PresentationInfo>
            <Format>List</Format>
            <SortBy>ByRank</SortBy>
            <NumberOfResults>217</NumberOfResults>
            <Cutoff>20</Cutoff>
          </PresentationInfo>
        </Search>
      </Action>
      <StatusInfo>successful</StatusInfo>
    </Event>
  </Statement>
</Transaction>
```

3. Browse an item of the ranked list returned as a answer for the previous search.

```
<Transaction ID = "3456">
  <SessionId > 987654usr3 </SessionId>
  <TimeStamp> 2002-05-31T20:11:15.000-05:00 </TimeStamp>
  <MachineInfo>
    <IPAddress> 128.173.244.56 <IPAddress>
    <Port> 8000 </Port>
  </MachineInfo>
  <Statement>
```

```
      <Event>
        <Action>
          <Browse>
            <DocID> 5114 </DocID>
            <DocName>University of Washington School of
             Medicine Multidisciplinary Pain Center ( UWPC )
            </DocName>
          </Browse>
        </Action>
      </Event>
    </Statement>
  </Transaction>
```

5 Conclusions and Future Work

We propose an XML-based digital library log format standard that captures a rich, detailed set of system and user behaviors supported by current digital library services. The format is implemented in a generic log component tool, which can be plugged into any digital library system. Specifications, implementation details, and examples of use within the MARIAN digital library system were described.

Future work will proceed on several fronts. We will be using our log format to allow evaluations of several of our projects, collections and systems, including those in the context of the Networked Digital Library of Theses and Dissertations (NDLTD, www.ndltd.org) and the Computing and Information Technology Interactive Digital Educational Library (CITIDEL, www.citidel.org). Since CITIDEL is a part of the National STEM (Science, technology, engineering, and mathematics) education Digital Library (NSDL, www.nsdl.org), we will advocate use of the log format and tools throughout NSDL. We will test the log tool with other DL systems. A major concern of any comprehensive log format such as ours should be user privacy. We should allow users to choose the level of detail they want the system to log about their activities. Ideally, user information should be logged and maintained at the client side [11] so that users can use that information as they desire, for example, to provide portions of the data to personalization tools in order to get personalization services. We will be investigating extensions in the MARIAN Webgate module to allow such a view.

The current XML format can be very verbose. We will investigate efficient compression techniques to allow scalable analysis of our DL logs. Also, we will consider the application and possible extension of our XML format and tools to support alternative DL architectures, e.g., that of the NCSTRL+ digital library which uses buckets (object-oriented digital objects that contain data, metadata, and the methods for accessing both [9]). Finally, our log proposal needs to be discussed and related to standards and framework activities like OAIS [28].

Acknowledgements. Thanks also are given for the support of NSF through its grants: IIS-9986089, IIS-0002935, IIS-0080748, IIS-0086227, DUE-0121679, DUE-0121741, and DUE-0136690. The first author also is supported by CAPES, process 1702/98-0.

References

1. Borgman, Christine L., Hirsh, Sandra G., and Hiller, John, *Rethinking Online Monitoring Methods for Information Retrieval Systems: From Search Product to Search Process,* Journal of the American Society of Information Science, 47(7) 568-583, 1996.
2. Borgman, Christine L., Personal communication, 1998.
3. Bishop, Ann P., *Digital Libraries and Knowledge Disaggregation: The Use of Journal Article Components,* Proceedings ACM Digital Libraries '98, Pittsburgh, 29-39, 1998
4. Sparck Jones, Karen and Peter Willett, editors, *Readings in Information Retrieval,* San Francisco, CA: Morgan Kaufmann Publishers, Inc., 1997, xv, 589.
5. Frakes, William B. and Ricardo Baeza-Yates, editors, *Information Retrieval: Data Structures & Algorithms,* Englewood Cliffs, NJ: Prentice-Hall, 1992, viii, 504.
6. Marchionini, Gary, *Information seeking in electronic environments,* Boston: Cambridge University Press, 1995.
7. Marchionini, Gary, *Advanced Interface Designs for the BLS Website: Final Report to the Bureau of Labor Statistics,* http://ils.unc.edu/~march/blsreport98/final_report.html
8. Jones, Steve, Cunningham, Sally Jo, and McNab, Rodger, *Usage Analysis of a Digital Library,* Proceedings ACM Digital Libraries '98, Pittsburgh, 293-294, 1998.
9. Nelson, Michael L., Maly, Kurty, Shen, Stewart N. T., Zubair, Mohammad, *NC-STRL+: Adding Multi-Discipline and Multi-Genre Support to the Dienst Protocol Using Clusters and Buckets,* Proceedings of the IEEE Forum on Research and Technology Advances in Digital Libraries, IEEE ADL '98, April 22-24, 1998, Santa Barbara, California, USA, 128-136
10. Lynch, Clifford. *Personalization and Recommender Systems in the Larger Context: New Directions and Research Questions (Keynote Speech),* Proceedings of the DELOS Workshop: Personalisation and Recommender Systems in Digital Libraries, Dublin, Ireland, 18-20, June, 2001.
11. Cassel, Lillian N., Wolz, Ursula, *Client Side Personalization,* Proceedings of the DELOS Workshop: Personalisation and Recommender Systems in Digital Libraries, Dublin, Ireland, 18-20, June, 2001
12. Gonçalves, Marcos A., France, Robert K., and Fox, Edward A., *MARIAN: Flexible Interoperability for Federated Digital Libraries,* Proceedings of the 5th European Conference on Research and Advanced Technology for Digital Libraries, Darmstadt, Germany, September 4-9, 173-186, 2001.
13. Barclay, Jean, *Assessing the benefits of learning logs,* Education and Training, Vol.38 No.2, 1996.
14. Riecken, Douglas, *Introduction: personalized views of personalization,* Communications of the ACM, 43(8): 26-28, 2000.
15. Peters, Thomas A., *The history and development of Transaction Log Analysis,* Library Hi Tech, 11(2): 41-66, 1993.
16. Sandore, Beth, *Applying the Results of Transaction Log Analysis,* Library Hi Tech, 11(2): 87-97, 1993.
17. Kaske, Neil K., *Research Methodologies and Transaction Log Analysis: Issues, Questions and a Proposed Model,* Library Hi Tech, 11(2): 79-86, 1993.
18. Gladney, H. M. and Lotspiech, J. B., *Safeguarding digital library contents and users. Assuring convenient security and data quality,* D-Lib Magazine, May 1997.

19. Spiliopoulou, Myra, *Web usage mining for Web site evaluation,* Communications of the ACM, 43(8): 127-134, 2000.
20. Mobasher, Bamshad, Cooley, Robert, Srivastava, Jaideep, *Automatic Personalization Based on Usage Mining,* Communications of the ACM, 43(8): 142-151, 2000.
21. H. S. Thompson, D. Beech, M. Maloney, and N. Mendelsohn (Eds). "XML Schema Part 1: Structures". W3C Recommendation, May 2001. http://www.w3.org/TR/xmlschema-1/.
22. M. A. Gonçalves, E. A. Fox, L. T. Watson, and N. A. Kipp. Streams, structures, spaces, scenarios and societies (5S): A formal model for digital libraries. Technical Report TR-01-12, Virginia Tech, Blacksburg, VA, 2001.
23. Witten, Ian H., Bainbridge, David, Boddie, Stefan J., *Greenstone: open-source digital library software with end-user collection building,"* Online Information Review, 25(5), 2001
24. Suleman, Hussein, Fox, Edward A., Abrams, Marc, *Building quality into a digital library,.* the Proceedings of the Fifth ACM Conference on Digital Libraries, June 2-7, San Antonio, TX, USA, 228-229, 2001.
25. Davis, Lagoze, Krafft, *Dienst: Building a production technical report server,* Advances in Digital Libraries '95, Springer Verlag, 1995.
26. *Networked Computer Science Technical Reference Library,* http://www.ncstrl.org/
27. *Dienst Protocol,* http://www.cs.cornell.edu/NCSTRL/protocol.html
28. *Open Archival Information System Recommendation,* http://www.ccsds.org/documents/p2/CCSDS-650.0-R-1.pdf
29. *OpenText Search Engine,* http://www.opentext.com

Notes from the Interoperability Front: A Progress Report on the Open Archives Initiative

Herbert Van de Sompel[1] and Carl Lagoze[2]

[1]Research Library, Los Alamos National Laboratory,
Los Alamos, NM
herbertv@lanl.gov
[2]Computing and Information Science, Cornell University
Ithaca, NY USA 14850
lagoze@cs.cornell.edu

Abstract. The Open Archives Initiative Protocol for Metadata Harvesting (OAI-PMH) was first released in January 2001. Since that time, the protocol has been adopted by a broad community and become the focus of a number of research and implementation projects. We describe the various activities building on the OAI-PMH since its first release. We then describe the activities and decisions leading up to the release of a stable Version 2 of the OAI-PMH. Finally, we describe the key features of OAI-PMH Version 2.

1 Introduction

Over a year has passed since the first release of the Open Archives Initiative Protocol for Metadata harvesting (OAI-PMH) in January 2001. During that period, the OAI-PMH has emerged as a practical foundation for digital library interoperability. The OAI-PMH supports interoperability via a relatively simple two-party model. At one end, *data providers* employ the OAI-PMH to expose structured data, *metadata*, in various forms. At the other end, *service providers* use the OAI-PMH to harvest the metadata from data providers and then subsequently automatically process it and add value in the form of services. While resource discovery is often mentioned as the exemplar service, other service possibilities include longevity and risk management [19], personalization [16], and current awareness.

The general acceptance of the OAI-PMH is based on a number of factors. It is intentionally low-barrier, exploiting widely deployed Web technologies such as HTTP and XML. It builds on many years of metadata practice, leveraging the development of a lingua franca metadata vocabulary in the Dublin Core Metadata Initiative [4]. It accommodates a number of community and domain-specific extensions such as the co-existence of multiple domain-specific metadata vocabularies, collection descriptions, and resource organization schemes.

The first sixteen months after the Version 1 release of the OAI-PMH were purposefully experimental. The intention during that time was to provide a reasonably stable platform for early adopters to test the concepts of metadata harvesting and build a number of fundamental services. Indeed, that intended

M. Agosti and C. Thanos (Eds.): ECDL 2002, LNCS 2458, pp. 144-157, 2002.

stability was accomplished, with only one change in the protocol occurring over the sixteen months due to a change in the XML Schema specification [17].

This paper reports on the results of that approximately year and a half of experimentation and the follow-on activity leading up to a stable Version 2 release of the OAI-PMH. This paper serves as a direct follow-on to an earlier paper [21] that provides background information on the initial development of the OAI-PMH. That historical material is not repeated in this paper and readers new to the OAI are invited to first read that paper.

This paper is organized as follows. The next section of the paper, Section 2, describes the communities of implementers, service providers, and researchers that have developed since the release of the OAI-PMH. Section 3 then describes the process of developing Version 2 of the OAI-PMH and enumerates the changes incorporated into that new version. The paper closes with Section 4 that describes possible next steps and the general future of the OAI.

2 Measures of Success

Measuring the success of the OAI-PMH is problematic. Unlike user-oriented technologies (e.g. word processors, spreadsheets), there are no immediate or direct benefits from individual adoptions. Therefore, while a simple count of protocol implementations is indeed useful as a metric, other factors should be considered.

Using terms presented by Shapiro and Varian [25], technologies such as the OAI-PMH exhibit *network effects*, in which initial adoption may be slow and steady and positive feedback then dramatically increases the adoption rate. In the context of the OAI-PMH, positive feedback occurs at two levels. First, it comes from the establishment of communities and/or research projects that collectively agree to adopt the protocol as a basis for information federation. Second, positive feedback comes from the growth of service providers who encourage data provider implementations by adding value to the metadata that they provide.

The past sixteen months indicate that the bases of this positive feedback loop are indeed being established. The remainder of this section describes the activities that contribute to this. First, we give a summary of some notable research grants and projects that provide a context for individual implementations. We then describe a number of service provider implementations. In the next section, we describe a number of the tools that make it easier for, and thus encourage, data providers to undertake repository implementations. We close with a summary of the growth of data providers that has been encouraged by these other developments.

2.1 Funded Research Projects and Programs

Over the past year a number of US and European research initiatives and projects have been established that apply the metadata harvesting model provided by the OAI-PMH. Collectively these projects provide a strong incentive for data providers to reveal their metadata via the OAI-PMH. The following list includes some of the more notable ones.

National Science Digital Library (NSDL). The NSDL is a National Science Foundation funded project to build what will probably be the largest and most diverse digital library to date. Over the next five years the library is expected to serve millions of users and provide access to tens of millions of digital resources. Complete details on the NSDL are provided in a set of earlier papers [10, 20, 31].

The OAI-PMH plays a fundamental role in the NSDL architecture, and the expected size of the NSDL will make it one of the primary deployment contexts for the protocol. A core component of the NSDL architecture is a Metadata Repository (MR) that provides robust, central storage of metadata in multiple formats related to resources and collections in the NSDL. Figure 1 illustrates the role of OAI-PMH in relation to the NSDL MR. On the ingest side (the bottom of the figure) OAI-PMH is the preferred mechanism for retrieval of collection and resource level metadata from participating data providers. A "front porch" then normalizes and crosswalks (to other preferred formats) this metadata and metadata collected via other means (gathering and direct entry). The processed metadata is then transferred via OAI-PMH to the MR. Finally, the MR exposes its multiple format metadata via OAI-PMH for harvesting by services that provide the bulk of NSDL functionality (e.g., search and discovery, preservation).

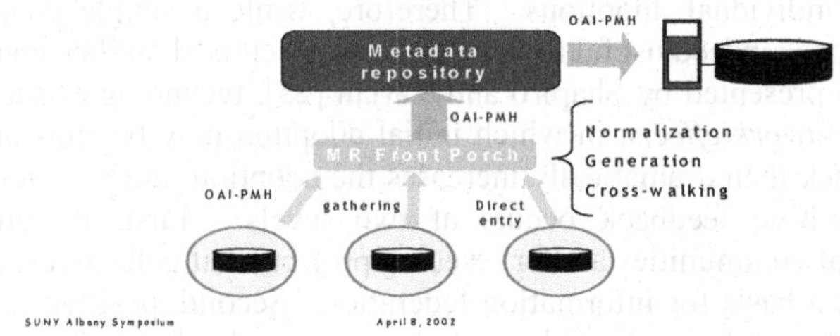

Fig. 1. Role of OAI-PMH in the NSDL Metadata Repository

The first production release of the NSDL is scheduled for 3rd quarter 2002 with subsequent releases over the next four years. We expect that this will be reflected in a dramatic increase in the number of OAI-PMH compliant data providers.

Metadata Harvesting Initiative of the Mellon Foundation. In August, 2001 the Andrew W. Mellon Foundation awarded seven grants totaling $1.5M to fund development of services on top of the OAI-PMH infrastructure [29]. The awarded projects address a variety of scenarios including:

- designing portal services based on metadata from multi-disciplinary and multi-instutitional domains.
- harvesting metadata from archives and special collections.
- harvesting metadata related to materials in a specific topic area, but which are in a variety of formats.

The awardees are Research Libraries Group, University of Michigan, University of Illinois at Urbana-Champaign, Emory University, Woodrow Wilson International

Center for Scholars, University of Virginia, and Southeastern Library Network. At the time of writing this paper (May, 2002), many of these projects are still in the start-up phase although preliminary results are available from some [15]. We expect that these projects will help develop guidelines for future service providers and help clarify the relationship between metadata quality and service functionality.

Open Language Archives Community (OLAC). OLAC is a distributed, federated archive of language resources [12]. There are currently fourteen repositories that support an extended version of the Dublin Core metadata set and a compatible but profiled version of the OAI-PMH [11]. While interesting from a technical standpoint, the most intriguing aspect of OLAC is the rich scholarly community that the technical infrastructure has engendered. In a real sense this is what infrastructure like the OAI-PMH is about – not as an object of attention in itself, but as an almost invisible catalyst for far more interesting activities.

eprints.org. The eprints.org self-archiving software has been developed by the Electronics and Computer Science Department at the University of Southampton (UK) [5]. The software has been built as basic infrastructure in support of a general model of "author self-archiving". This model is proposed by Steven Harnad [18] as a means of reforming the scholarly publishing framework. eprints is available for free under an open source license to individuals, institutions, and learned societies who wish to set up an archive for submission, storage, and dissemination of scholarly publications. The software is fully OAI-PMH-conformant, thus enabling the open federation of scholarly eprint archives that inspired the origination of the OAI [27, 28]. eprints is currently installed at approximately thirty institutions and the recent release of Version 2 of the software (February 2002), featuring significantly easier installation, promises to ensure the rapid growth of these OAI-PMH-conformant repositories.

European OIA-PMH Funding Programs. During the past year a number of programs providing funding for OAI implementations and services have been announced in Europe. These include:

- *JISC FAIR* - In January, 2002 the Joint Information Systems Committee in the UK announced the Focus on Access to Institutional Resources Programme (FAIR) [6]. This program will provide considerable funding for projects to explore dissemination of institutional assets or create services via the OAI-PMH.
- *DINI* - Die Deutsche Initiative für NetzwerkInformation (DINI) (German) is funding projects that implement and use the OAI-PMH [3].
- *Open Archives Forum* – OAF is an EU-funded accompanying measure involving the University of Bath – UKOLN (UK), Istituto di Elaborazione della Informazione-CNR (Italy) and Computing Center of Humboldt University (Germany) [8]. The goal of the project is to facilitate the creation of an OAI community in Europe through workshops and support activities. The first workshop of the OAF is being held in Pisa in July, 2002.

Museum Community Projects. The CIMI Consortium [2] has been working with members to support the deployment of the OAI-PMH in the museum community [24].

As part of this process CIMI has developed a number of OAI-PMH tools for the museum community and run workshops at major museum conferences. At present, the most active area of deployment is in Australia led by Australian Museums OnLine, which is building a search and discovery system over the collections of member museums [1].

2.2 OAI-PMH-Related Tools

A key factor in the growth of implementations of the OAI-PMH has been the availability of tools to build OAI-PMH-conformant repositories and harvesters. In this section, we enumerate some of the available toolsets.

Repository Explorer. The Repository Explorer [26] is an easy-to-use interactive tool that allows repositories to test conformance of their implementation of the OAI-PMH. The interface available on the Web at http://purl.org/net/oai_explorer allows implementers to enter the base-URL of their OAI repository and then test responses to each verb with varying arguments. The availability of the Repository Explorer has proven to be extremely valuable for new implementers.

ALCME. The Advanced Library Collection Management Environment (ACLME) is a set of OAI-related tools developed by OCLC. The tools include OAICAT, an open source metadata server that can be placed on top of existing databases to turn them into OAI repositories with minimal coding effort, an OAI harvester, and a MARC to DC translator. The toolset is available at http://alcme.oclc.org/index.html.

OAIB. The Open Archives In a Box is an application for exporting metadata from a relational database system via the OAI-PMH. OAIB was developed as part of the University of Illinois at Urbana-Champaign Metadata Harvesting Project. The toolset is available at http://emerge.ncsa.uiuc.edu/documentation_oaib.html.

DP9. This is a tool that allows exposure of the metadata in OAI-PMH-conformant repositories to conventional web-search engines [23]. The concept behind DP9 is deceptively simple but ingenious. The data provider exposes metadata via OAI-PMH, DP9 harvests it and creates a static HTML page with hard links, which actually are OAI-PMH GetRecord requests, to metadata records in the harvested repository. Web-crawlers then encounter this page in normal crawling activity, follow the links provided in the page and as such obtain the metadata from the repository for indexing. As a significant portion of the Web is invisible to search engines due to robots.txt exclusions or the lack of fixed URLs for resources that are dynamically served via database queries [22], DP9 allows a content provider hidden in such a manner to make metadata about content visible to search engines (e.g., Google), and thus searchable by users. DP9 description and tools are available at http://arc.cs.odu.edu:8080/dp9/about.jsp.

2.3 Service Providers

In addition to the funded projects described earlier, there have been a number of individual efforts to develop services that process metadata harvested via the OAI-PMH.

SCIRUS. This is an Internet search tool, developed by Elsevier Science that focuses on scientific content. Its corpus includes both web and journal content. The SCIRUS engine also indexes metadata of all180,000 articles in arxiv.org which is harvested via OAI-PMH. Harvesting other OAI-PMH-conformant repositories is planned.

CDL eScholarship Repository. This a project by the California Digital Library to provide faculty with a mechanism to support pre-publication scholarship. The repository supports OAI-PMH and thus can be federated with similar repositories at partner institutions.

my.OAI. This a search engine that harvests metadata from selected repositories and offers the user options to personalize the service and create alerting profiles. my.OAI is at http://www.myOAI.com.

2.4 Data Providers

Beginning the first release of the protocol in January 2001, the OAI has maintained a registration service both for tracking implementations and as a convenience for data and service providers. Registration is not required (there would be no way to enforce it anyway!). Sites that request registration must first pass a conformance test. All sites that successfully complete this test are then listed in browsable form at http://www.openarchives.org/Register/BrowseSites.pl and in an XML formatted list at http://www.openarchives.org/Register/ListFriends.pl. This XML list is used by a number of the service providers described above.

Figure 2 shows the steady growth of registered data providers since the introduction of the protocol. Historical statistics on the growth of the number of metadata records harvestable via OAI-PMH are not available. However, the current (May 2002) count is approximately 6 million.

It is obvious that the "network effects" described earlier have not yet occurred, and there is no evidence to predict it will. We note two issues. First, a number of service provider projects have just recently gotten up-to-speed or have not yet reached implementation level (the NSDL project is a notable example). Second, the protocol is actively being used in environments where metadata is being shared amongst a restricted amount of nodes, and where public advertisement of the metadata collection is considered inappropriate. Anecdotal evidence indicates that the number of registered sites represent less than half of the actual implementers of the OAI-PMH.

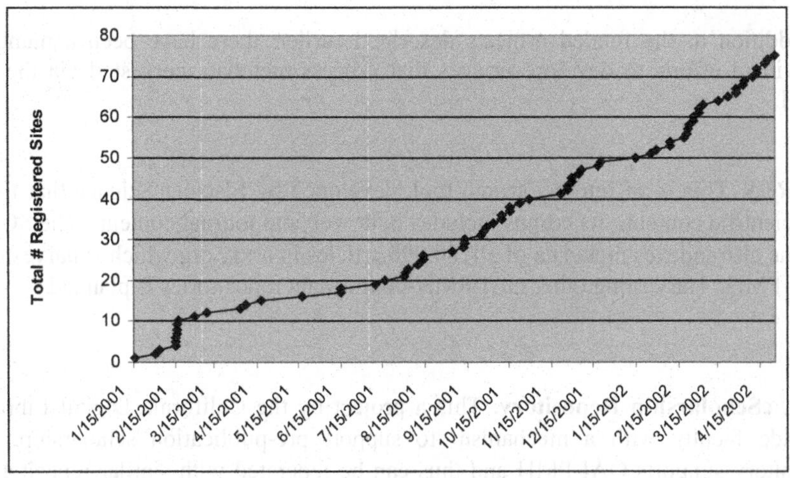

Fig. 2. Growth of data providers in the OAI registry

3 OAI Protocol for Metadata Harvesting Version 2

As noted earlier, Version 1.x[1] of the protocol was explicitly experimental. Results over the past sixteen months, described in Section 2, indicate that the underlying technical scope of the OAI-PMH was properly defined. As described in [21], this scope was motivated by the belief that widespread adoption of the protocol (and any technical infrastructure) depends on ease of understanding and implementation. As such the original protocol specification left controversial issues such as access management out-of-scope and when possible chose simple approaches rather than more functional, but complex approaches.

The decision process for Version 2.0 of the protocol (described in Section 3.1), and the results of that decision process (described in Section 3.2), reflect the results of that experimental period. Major functional changes were determined to be out-of-scope and the focus was directed toward fine-tuning existing functionality and improving the general clarity and overall consistency of the protocol document.

---

[1] Version 1.0 was released in January, 2001. A subsequent update release Version 1.1, required due to changes in the W3C XML Schema specification, was released in June 2001.

3.1 Protocol Review and Definition Process

An important information tool during the length of the Version 1.x experimental process was the OAI-implementers [7] list that was activated at the time of the initial release. The list and its archive quickly became a valuable source of information for newcomers to the protocol, as well an active forum for detailed discussion of protocol related issues by expert implementers. Those discussions had a considerable influence on the process of reviewing the protocol uncovering missing functionality or parts of the protocol that were confusing.

The first step in the process of officially defining Version 2 of the OAI-PMH was the creation, in June 2001, of a new OAI Technical Committee[2], OAI-tech. The Committee is a group of expert implementers many of whom had been involved in the creation and/or alpha testing of v.1.0 of the OAI-PMH. The group has twelve representatives from US institutions and four from European institutions. The charge for OAI-tech was:

- To review the details of v.1.x of the protocol and determine whether its functionality and nature was correct;
- To compile a stabilized version of the Metadata Harvesting Protocol by mid-2002.

The entire OAI-tech process has been conducted online or via telephone. It began in September 2001, when OAI-tech members were invited to submit brief descriptions of issues they felt required discussion. These issues were motivated by their own implementation experience and from discussions in the OAI-implementers list. The initial issues list was then discussed in a conference call during which advocates for each issue, willing to submit a white paper, were solicited. Those issues for which no one volunteered to write a white paper about were dropped. Then followed a process of detailed discussion per white paper, and a proposal for resolution by the OAI Executive[3], which itself was again commented upon by the group.

By February 2002, most issues had been resolved through this process. A few issues remained unresolved and these were taken offline for review and resolution by the OAI Executive who worked with an appointed writing sub-committee of OAI-tech – Michael Nelson and Simeon Warner – to draft a first alpha version of the revised protocol. That version was released to OAI-tech early March 1st 2002, at which point the group was extended with a relatively diverse group of alpha-testers. In-depth on-list discussion of the protocol document was conducted throughout March and April 2002, which led to a number of significant changes both in text and in function[4]. On May 1st 2002, the OAI-PMH 2.0beta was released to OAI-implementers. On June 1st 2002, Version 2.0 was officially released, 1 month behind schedule.

---

[2] An earlier incarnation of the OAI technical committee was instrumental in the creation of OAI-PMH Version 1.0.

[3] The OAI-Executive is Herbert Van de Sompel and Carl Lagoze (the authors of this paper).

[4] One example of a protocol notion requiring extensive review during the alpha process related to idempotency of resumption tokens, described later in this document.

3.2 Features and Changes in OAI-PMH Version 2

Clarifications and Specification Cleanups. In general the major changes introduced in Version 2 of the protocol are of the nature of clarifications to ambiguities or better means of expressing existing functionality. The following list summarizes these changes.

Core Protocol versus Extensible Notions. A clear boundary has been established in Version 2 between the core OAI-PMH protocol and peripheral notions. This has been achieved by the creation of Implementation Guidelines documents, which covers issues such as the XML Schema for domain-specific profiling of the OAI-PMH through the usage of container structures provided by the core protocol. Such information had previously been part of the protocol document.

Clarified Data Model. Version 2 of the protocol builds on a well-defined "resource – item – metadata-record" data model, correcting a level of ambiguity that existed with this respect in v.1.x. This correction is a consequence of extending the applicability of the OAI-PMH beyond the exchange of metadata about document-like objects, for which the previously established notions about the nature of full content in repositories were meaningful. It is also a consequence of the increasing prevalence of metadata aggregators, such as the NSDL Metadata Repository described in Section 2.1, that have a distant relationship to actual full content.

Metadata in the OAI-PMH is now about resources in general. As a result an item is now defined as a constituent of a repository from which metadata about a resource can be disseminated. The notion of an item now plays an important role in the OAI-PMH, as it has become the logical point of entry to physical metadata records.

Error Reporting. Version 2 establishes a clear separation between errors occurring at the HTTP transport layer used by the OAI-PMH and errors at the OAI-PMH level. This is achieved by introducing a set of OAI-PMH error and exception conditions, which can be reported in a dedicated element in the XML responses to OAI-PMH requests.

Dublin Core Metadata Definition. In a successful and trend-setting collaboration with the Dublin Core Metadata Initiative (DCMI) **[4]**, an XML Schema for unqualified Dublin Core has been created, which is hosted by the DCMI and used in the delivery of metadata in the mandatory DC format in the OAI-PMH. This Schema replaces the one previously created and maintained by the OAI.

Single XML Schema for OAI-PMH Responses. OAI-PMH now defines a single XML Schema to validate responses to all OAI-PMH requests. This single schema has a number of advantages relative to the schema per verb strategy in Version 1: it eliminates redundancy in type definitions, allows for clean handling of OAI-PMH errors, and simplifies protocol implementations.

Language Cleanup. The OAI-PMH now uses the notions *must*, *must not*, *may*, *should*, etc. as in RFC2119 [14], allowing for a better understanding of protocol conformance.

Error Corrections. In addition to the clarifications listed above, a number of other changes are introduced in OAI-PMH v.2.0 that correct flaws exposed during the period of experimentation with v.1.x.

Uniform Date and Time Encoding. Dates and times are now uniformly encoded using ISO8601 [30] and are expressed in UTC throughout the protocol. When time is included, the special UTC designator (" Z") must be used. This change corrects the fact that v.1.x required repositories to express the date/time of responses in *local* time, encoded in ISO8601. However, the time zone of the datestamp, which is crucial for harvesting, was left undefined. This caused synchronization problems between harvesters and repositories.

Flow Control Idempotency. The experimentation period revealed a number of problems harvesting large result sets in the face of transaction failures. In the OAI-PMH, large lists are typically broken up into several incomplete lists. At the end of each incomplete list, a harvester receives a resumptionToken, which it can issue to receive the next incomplete list. When, as a result of some error, a harvester does not receive a response to a request with a resumptionToken, v.1.x does not provide any guarantees that re-issuing the request with the resumptionToken returns the response that had failed. In order to fix this, Version 2 clearly defines and mandates the idempotent nature of resumptionTokens, providing deterministic behavior in the face of transmission errors.

New Functionality. In a number of areas new functionality has been introduced in OAI-PMH Version 2.

Multiple Time Granularity. In response to requests originating mainly from the union-catalogue realm, the OAI-PMH now supports harvesting at different levels of time-granularity: support of year, month and day granularities is mandatory, while support for hour, minutes and seconds granularity is optional.

Enhanced Identify Semantics. The response to the Identify request is more expressive than in Version 1.x, providing more information to harvesters and supporting multiple harvesting strategies. The response now includes information on the earliest datestamp used in a repository, HTTP-level compression schemes supported by a repository, an indication of the finest granularity with which a repository can be harvested, and information about the support that the repository has for deleted items.

Item Set Membership. For repositories that support set-structures, it is now mandatory to list set membership of items in the responses to the GetRecord, ListRecords and ListIdentifiers requests. This allows harvesters to gather set-membership information for an item in a single request.

Related Changes and Activities. Version 2 introduces a number of interesting additions or changes ancillary to the core protocol.

Implementation Guidelines. Implementation Guidelines documents are provided to support interpretation of the protocol document by implementers of repositories, harvesters, aggregators, mirrors, caches, etc.

Provenance Schema. Version 2 provides a recommended provenance XML Schema that is useful in situations where harvested records are aggregated and subsequently made available for re-harvesting. When re-exposing a record, a provenance container can be attached to it, which unambiguously identifies the origin record. The provenance schema allows listing multiple origins for a given record. The schema is designed to be useful for de-duplicating harvested datasets.

Friends Schema. A "friends" XML Schema is recommended to help establish a dynamic approach to the process of discovering repositories. In the response to the Identify request, repositories can use the friends schema to list the BASE-URLs of other repositories they know about. If successful, this approach would allow harvesters to assemble a comprehensive list of harvestable targets by jumping from repository to repository. This may provide a sustainable alternative to a central registration service as currently operated by the OAI.

Mini-Archive Specification. Version 2 provides an XML Schema that defines an XML document format containing all the information required to respond to OAI-PMH requests. The so-called mini-archives specification comes with an accompanying PHP-tool accepting OAI-PMH requests as input, processing the XML document according to the request, and returning a valid OAI-PMH response. Usage of this approach is recommended for data providers exposing metadata collections, the size of which does not justify the usage of a database.

Proposed but rejected changes. In a determined attempt to keep Version 2 of the protocol conceptually and functionally as close to Version 1.x as possible, many proposals for changes made by OAI-tech members were rejected after in-depth deliberations. Two are listed here.

Machine Readable Rights. Beginning with the first release of the OAI-PMH, there has been considerable discussion on the OAI-general list about intellectual property rights for the metadata harvested through the OAI-PMH. Because a fundamental concept in the OAI-PMH is the physical exchange of metadata, this seemed an issue that could not be ignored. Thus, the addition of machine-readable statements identifying the boundaries of acceptable use of harvested metadata was considered during the Version 2.0 process.

The decision was made not to deal with this matter at the protocol level, but rather to motivate communities to investigate it in detail and to propose solutions that could be made part of Implementation Guidelines. It was determined that emerging DRM vocabularies have not reached a required level of maturity and that acceptance of solutions in this area would very much depend on individual communities. By means of the extensible container structures, the protocol does provide locations where such information can eventually be stored.

Search functionality. A proposal to extend the functionality of the protocol by allowing simple Boolean queries using Dublin Core elements as arguments was rejected. The general perception was that such functionality clearly crossed the borders of a harvesting protocol, as well as the boundaries with other standardization efforts such as ZING SRW and SRU [9].

4 Prospects for the Future

The release of v.2.0 of the OAI-PMH in June 2002, marks the end of a 17 month experimentation period that was announced with the release of v.1.0 of the protocol in January 2001. Version 2.0 of the OAI-PMH is released as a protocol ready for prime time. In order to motivate migration of existing repositories to Version 2.0, the OAI registration service will no longer accept registration of v.1.x repositories starting September 1st 2002; repositories not conformant to v.2.0 will be removed from the registry on December 1st 2002.

Interest has been expressed in the creation of a SOAP [13] version of the OAI-PMH. This path will most likely be explored in the upcoming months. The current thinking with this respect is that the SOAP version should provide the same functionality as v.2.0 of the OAI-PMH, making it a parallel rather than a new version. As a matter of fact, care has already been taken to prepare protocol responses in OAI-PMH v.2.0 for usage in a SOAP version.

It is expected that the OAI-PMH will become part of the basic infrastructure for work in digital libraries. Early indications of this trend have become visible during the past months, as communities have moved from talking about the protocol to talking about projects in which the protocol is used, to talking about projects and failing to mention usage of the protocol. As a result, the emergence of community-specific implementations of the protocol is anticipated, with innovations expected especially in the realm of XML Schema for metadata formats, for collection and set-level description, shared set-structures and machine-readable digital rights.

A fundamental question faced by the authors, in their roles of OAI Executives, is concerned with the future of the OAI, its protocol and its registration service. The generous funding in support of OAI activities provided by the Digital Library Federation and the Coalition of Networked Information will terminate by the end of 2002. It is not in the authors' nature to run an organization for the its own sake. However, both authors share a sense of responsibility for what they have helped create, and as such they see it as their task to find an alternative strategy that provides adequate guarantees regarding the successful maintenance of the OAI-PMH and its evolution. At the time of writing of this paper, the details on how to do this are being developed.

Acknowledgements. Support for Open Archives Initiative activities comes from the Digital Library Federation, the Coalition for Networked Information, and from

National Science Foundation Grant No. IIS-9817416. The authors acknowledge the fantastic support this work has gotten from the OAI Steering Committee, OAI Technical Committee, and the OAI community as a whole.

References

1. *AMOL OAI-PMH Service Demonstration*, 2002 http://amol.org.au/oai/service/.
2. *CIMI Consortium*, 2001 http://www.cimi.org.
3. *DINI und die Open Archives Initiative*, 2001 http://www.dini.de/dinioai/dinioai.php.
4. *Dublin Core Metadata Initiative*, http://dublincore.org.
5. *eprints.org*, 2002 http://www.eprints.org.
6. *FAIR Programme (Focus on Access to Institutional Assets)*, 2002 http://www.jisc.ac.uk/events/02/fair.html.
7. *OAI-implementers list and archive*, http://www.openarchives.org/mailman/listinfo/OAI-implementers.
8. *Open Archives Forum*, 2002 http://www.oaforum.org/.
9. *ZING: Z29.50 International: Next Generation*, 2002 http://www.loc.gov/z3950/agency/zing/.
10. Arms, W. Y., Hillmann, D., Lagoze, C., Krafft, D., Marisa, R., Saylor, J., Terrizzi, C., and Van de Sompel, H., "A Spectrum of Interoperability: The Site for Science Prototype for the NSDL," *D-Lib Magazine*, 8 (1), 2002.
11. Bird, S. and Simons, G., *OLAC Protocol for Metadata Harvesting*, 2001 http://www.language-archives.org/OLAC/protocol.html.
12. Bird, S., Simons, G., and Huang, C. R., "The Open Language Archives Community and Asian Language Resources," presented at Workshop on Language Resources in Asia, 6th Natural Language Processing Pacific Rim Symposium (NLPRS), Tokyo, 2001.
13. Box, D., Ehnebuske, D., Kakivaya, G., Layman, A., Mendelsohn, N., Nielsen, H. F., Thatte, S., and Winer, D., "Simple Object Access Protocol (SOAP) 1.1," World Wide Web Consortium, W3C Note May 08 2000. http://www.w3.org/TR/SOAP.
14. Bradner, S., "Key words for use in RFCs to Indicate Requirement Levels," IETF, RFC 2119, March 1997. http://www.ietf.org/rfc/rfc2119.txt.
15. Cole, T. W., Kaczmarek, J., Marty, P. F., Prom, C. J., Sandore, B., and Shreeves, S., "Now That We've Found the Hidden Web, What Can We Do With It? The Illinois Open Archives Initiative Metadata Harvesting Experience," presented at Museums and the Web, Boston, 2002.
16. Dushay, N., "Localizing Experience of Digital Content via Structural Metadata," presented at submission to Joint Conference on Digital Libraries, Portland, Oregon, 2002.
17. Fallside (ed.), D. C., "XML Schema Part 0: Primer," World Wide Web Consortium, W3C Candidate Recommendation CR-xmlschema-0-20001024, 24 October 2000. http://www.w3.org/TR/xmlschema-0/.
18. Harnad, S., "Free at Last: The Future of Peer-Reviewed Journals," *D-Lib Magazine*, 5 (12), 1999.
19. Kenney, A., McGovern, N., Boticelli, P., Entlich, R., Lagoze, C., and Payette, S., "Preservation Risk Management for Web Resources," *D-Lib Magazine*, 8 (1), 2002.
20. Lagoze, C., Arms, W., Gan, S., Hillmann, D., Ingram, C., Krafft, D., Marisa, R., Phipps, J., Saylor, J., Terrizzi, C., Hoehn, W., Millman, D., Allan, J., Guzman-Lara, S., and Kalt, T., "Core Services in the Architecture of the National Digital Library for Science Education (NSDL)," Cornell University, Ithaca, arXiv Report cs.DL/0201025, January 29 2002. http://arxiv.org/abs/cs.DL/0201025.

21. Lagoze, C. and Van de Sompel, H., "The Open Archives Initiative: Building a low-barrier interoperability framework," presented at Joint Conference on Digital Libraries, Roanoke, VA, 2001.
22. Lawrence, S. and Giles, C. G., "Search Engines Fall Short," *Science*, 285 (5426), pp. 295, 1999.
23. Liu, X., "DP9 Service Provider for Web Crawlers," *D-Lib Magazine*, 7 (12), 2001.
24. Perkins, J., "A New Way of Making Cultural Information Resources Visible on the Web: Museums and the Open Archives Initiative," presented at Museums and the Web, Seattle, 2001.
25. Shapiro, C. and Varian, H. R., *Information rules : a strategic guide to the network economy*. Boston, Mass.: Harvard Business School Press, 1999.
26. Suleman, H., "Enforcing Interoperability with the Open Archives Initiative Repository Explorer," presented at Joint Conference on Digital Libraries, Roanoke, 2001.
27. Van de Sompel, H., Krichel, T., and Nelson, M. L., "The UPS Prototype: an experimental end-user service across e-print archives," *D-Lib Magazine*, 6 (2), February, 2000.
28. Van de Sompel, H. and Lagoze, C., "The Santa Fe Convention of the Open Archives Initiative," *D-Lib Magazine*, 6 (2), 2000.
29. Waters, D. J., "The Metadata Harvesting Initiative of the Mellon Foundation," ARL, Washington DC, ARL Bimonthly Report 271, August 2001.
30. Wolf, M. and Wicksteed, C., "Date and Time Formats," World Wide Web Consortium, W3C Note 15, 15 September 1997. http://www.w3.org/TR/NOTE-datetime.
31. Zia, L. L., "Growing a National Learning Environments and Resources Network for Science, Mathematics, Engineering and Technology Education," *D-Lib Magazine*, 7 (3), 2001.

Dynamic Generation of Intelligent Multimedia Presentations through Semantic Inferencing

Suzanne Little[1], Joost Geurts[2], and Jane Hunter[3]

[1] ITEE Dept. University of Queensland little@itee.uq.edu.au
[2] CWI, Amsterdam joost.geurts@cwi.nl
[3] DSTC, Brisbane jane@dstc.edu.au

Abstract. This paper first proposes a high-level architecture for semi-automatically generating multimedia presentations by combining semantic inferencing with multimedia presentation generation tools. It then describes a system, based on this architecture, which was developed as a service to run over OAI archives - but is applicable to any repositories containing mixed-media resources described using Dublin Core. By applying an iterative sequence of searches across the Dublin Core metadata, published by the OAI data providers, semantic relationships can be inferred between the mixed-media objects which are retrieved. Using predefined mapping rules, these semantic relationships are then mapped to spatial and temporal relationships between the objects. The spatial and temporal relationships are expressed within SMIL files which can be replayed as multimedia presentations. Our underlying hypothesis is that by using automated computer processing of metadata to organize and combine semantically-related objects within multimedia presentations, the system may be able to generate new knowledge by exposing previously unrecognized connections. In addition, the use of multilayered information-rich multimedia to present the results, enables faster and easier information browsing, analysis, interpretation and deduction by the end-user.

1 Introduction and Objectives

Information about a particular person or topic can be created by multiple users, served by various services and dispersed across multiple sites over the Internet. Adoption of standardized metadata vocabularies and ontologies, expressed in standardized machine-processable languages such as the Resource Description Framework [26] or DAML+OIL [23] are contributing to the realization of the next generation Web - the Semantic Web. One of the key promises of the Semantic Web [1] is that it will provide the necessary infrastructure for enabling services and applications on the Web to automatically aggregate and integrate information into a sum which is greater than the individual parts.

The current Web technology is at the 'hunter-gatherer' stage. The result of a typical search is a sequential list of URL's, referring to the HTML pages which match the metadata search field, displayed according to rank. The fact that

M. Agosti and C. Thanos (Eds.): ECDL 2002, LNCS 2458, pp. 158–175, 2002.

there are semantic relations between the retrieved objects or that many more semantically related information objects exist, is ignored in the final presentation of results.

In parallel with advancements in the development of the Semantic Web, is a rapid increase in the size and range of multimedia resources being added to the Web. Archives, museums and libraries are making enormous contributions to the amount of multimedia on the Internet through the digitization and online publication of their photographic, audio, film and video collections.

Within this paper we attempt to exploit all of these developments - the rapid growth in multimedia content, the standardization of content description and the semantic web infrastructure - to develop a system which will automatically retrieve and aggregate semantically related multimedia objects and generate intelligent multimedia presentations on a particular topic.

Using the Open Archives Initiative (OAI) [4] as a testbed, we have developed a service which uses the Dublin Core metadata published by the OAI data providers, to infer semantic relations between mixed-media objects distributed across the archives. Using predefined mapping rules, these semantic relationships are then mapped to spatial and temporal relationships between the objects. The spatial and temporal relationships are expressed within SMIL files which can be replayed as multimedia presentations.

Our premise is that by using automated computer processing of metadata to organize and combine semantically-related objects within multimedia presentations, the system may be able to generate new knowledge, not explicitly recorded, by inferring and exposing previously unrecognized connections. In addition, the use of multilayered information-rich multimedia to present the results, enables faster and easier information browsing, analysis, interpretation and deduction by the end-user.

The remainder of the paper is structured as follows. The next section describes related initiatives and projects and outlines how the work described here differs or builds on these. Section 3 describes the high-level system architecture, followed by details of the components and processes which make up our actual implementation. Section 4 provides the results of running a real example query and Section 5 concludes with a discussion of problem issues and future work.

2 Background

2.1 OAI

The Open Archives Initiative (OAI) [4] is a community that has defined an interoperability framework, the Open Archives Metadata Harvesting Protocol [3], to facilitate the sharing of metadata. Using this protocol, *data providers* are able to make metadata about their collections available for harvesting through an HTTP-based protocol. *Service providers* then use this metadata to create value added services.

To facilitate interoperability, data providers are required to supply metadata which complies to a common schema, the unqualified Dublin Core Metadata Element Set [2]. Additional schemas are also allowed and are distinguished through the use of a metadata prefix.

To date, OAI service providers have mostly developed simple search and retrieval services [5]. These include *Arc*, *citebaseSearch* and *my.OAI.* One of the more interesting services is *DP9*, a gateway service which allows traditional web search engines (e.g., Google) to index otherwise hidden information from OAI archives. Although originating in the E-Print community, OAI data providers now include multimedia collections such as the Library of Congress: American Memory collection [15], OpenVideo [17] and University of Illinois historical images [16]. Our goal is to exploit this increasing availability of multimedia resources and associated metadata to develop more interesting search, retrieval and aggregation services.

2.2 The Semantic Web

The Semantic Web [25] is an activity of the W3C which aims to extend the current Web by providing tools that enable resources on the web to be defined and semantically linked in a way that facilitates automated discovery, aggregation and re-use across various applications.

One of the cornerstones of the Semantic Web is the Resource Description Framework (RDF) [26]. RDF provides a common underlying framework for supporting semantically-rich descriptions, or metadata which enables interoperable XML data exchange. The Web Ontology Working Group are currently developing a Web Ontology Language (OWL), based on RDF Schema [28] (and its extension, DAML+OIL [23]) for defining structured, Web-based ontologies which will provide richer integration and interoperability of data among descriptive communities.

As the Semantic Web expands and more communities use RDF Schema or DAML+OIL to describe and annotate their data and build ontologies, the need for RDF-enabled storage and querying mechanisms to support large-scale Semantic Web applications, has grown. Research groups have been developing new query languages such as RQL [7] and SquishQL [14] which enable the storing and querying of web-based ontology/metadata standards, such as Dublin Core, RDF, RDFS, Topic Maps, DAML+OIL and the forthcoming Web Ontology Language (OWL).

A few of these RDF-enabled query languages (those based on logic models) also provide support for inferencing - in the form of either arbitrary deduction rules or user-defined inference rules. These rules enable new associations and knowledge, not explicitly recorded, to be inferred. Both Intellidimension's RDFQL [11] and TRIPLE [20] provide support for user-defined inference rules of the form *if A is the case then so is B*, to infer new knowledge and enable powerful deductive searches. A number of RDF and Topic Map inference engines (such as Cerebra and Empolis K2) exist, which also allow the automatic inferencing of new associations based on pre-defined rules.

A number of research groups are working on the next stage beyond semantic inferencing - the aggregation of semantically related data sources. Intellidimension's *RDF Gateway* [11] uses the new associations deduced from the RDFQL inferencing capabilities, to compile multiple data sources into a single knowledge base. *WebScripter* [10] is a tool that enables users to assemble reports by extracting and fusing information from multiple, heterogeneous DAMLized Web sources. A number of research groups have used RST (Rhetorical Structure Theory) relations to link mixed-media resources into tree structures which can be translated into a coherent multimedia presentations [6], [24]. However, the idea of semantically inferring relationships between mixed-media resources on the fly, and then translating these relationships to generate multimedia presentations, is a relatively new idea and, will provide better user interfaces to integrated information sources.

2.3 SMIL, Cuypers

Synchronized Multimedia Integration Language (SMIL) [27] is a W3C Recommendation designed for choreographing web-based multimedia presentations which combine audio, video, text and graphics in real-time. It uses a simple XML-based markup language, similar to HTML, which enables an author to describe the temporal behavior of a multimedia presentation, associate hyperlinks with media objects and describe the layout of the presentation on a screen. Its advantages include platform independence, network and client adaptability and the simplicity of XML for generation.

Cuypers [24] is a research prototype system, developed to experiment with the generation of Web-based presentations as an interface to semi-structured multimedia databases. Given a rhetorical structure (which models the intended message of the presentation) and a set of rules (which map rhetorical structures to spatio-temporal relations). Cuypers generates a presentation that adheres to the limitations of the target platform (system capabilities) and supports the user's preferences. Further details of Cuypers are provided in Section 3.5.

2.4 Other Related Work

Some earlier research has focussed on using hyperlinks to link semantically related information objects [22] within hypertext documents. A certain amount of work has also been done on formalising semantic relationships between media items. Both the MAVIS-2 [21] project, and MPEG-7 Semantic Description tools [12] propose a separation of the semantic layer from the actual media content. The MAVIS-2 project expresses the semantics of the multimedia content in an ontology which has links from concept definitions to the media that represent them. Semantic relations between seperate media objects can be inferred if they are all described using the same ontology. Similarly, the MPEG-7 Semantic Description Tools define XML Schemas for describing the semantics of multimedia through a number of top level semantic entities such as Objects, Agents, Events,

Concepts, State, Place, Time and SemanticRelation. As with MAVIS-2, the semantic descriptions are linked to the corresponding media segments through temporal and spatial media locators.

In addition to the need to formalize the semantic descriptions of multimedia, is the need to formally describe the segmentation metadata and low level audio and visual features/descriptors and formatting metadata. MPEG-7 has been designed specifically to standardize such multimedia content descriptors. In the future, as larger collections of multimedia described using MPEG-7 are developed, then we anticipate developing systems which can infer much richer semantic relationships through the MPEG-7 metadata and the associated MPEG-7 Ontology [9], but for the moment and in the context of this paper, we are limited to semantic inferencing using simple Dublin Core.

3 Implementation

3.1 Architecture

Figure 1 shows the high-level system architecture and the processes which transform the data models at each stage of the system. There are five stages in the overall presentation generation process. These are described in more detail in the following subsections:

- Iterative Search Process - users are able to interactively search and navigate the content of selected OAI archives, interpreting the retrieved results, selecting the pertinent resources and directing the subsequent search focus;
- Semantic Inferencing - the Dublin Core metadata is used to infer semantic relationships between the retrieved media objects;

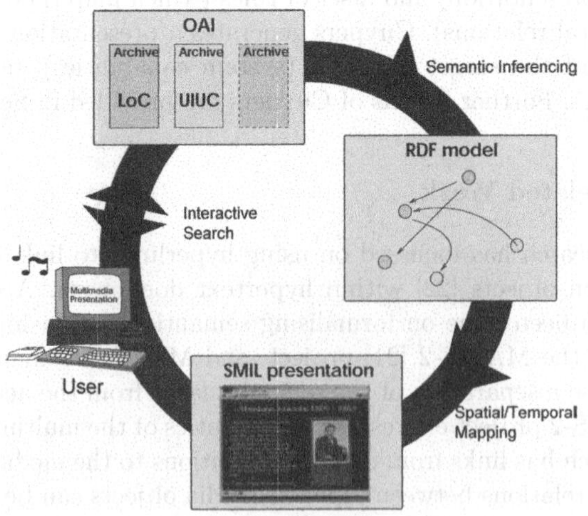

Fig. 1. Architecture overview

- Mapping - the inferred semantic relationships are then mapped to spatial and temporal relationships or multimedia formatting objects[1](MFO)
- Presentation Generation - a multimedia presentation is generated from the input media objects, semantic relations, mappings to MFO's and other constraints;
- User-directed Presentation Regenerator - a user can change the focus of the current presentation and generate a new presentation by clicking on a media item of interest in the current presentation.

3.2 Interactive Search Process

Performing a simple keyword search on the metadata from the OAI archives is likely to return a large set of items, including much irrelevant information. For example, a search for *Lincoln* will return information about both the American President and the town in Nebraska. The result set is also limited, in that there are often many other interesting related resources which are missed by a traditional keyword search e.g., information about Stephen A. Douglas who argued against Lincoln in the slavery debate, would not be retrieved.

To overcome these restrictions and fully exploit the resources in the OAI, an iterative search process has been developed. This process manipulates the Dublin Core elements and values at each search stage to enable the discovery of semantically linked media items. The user first enters a keyword which describes their topic of interest. The system then performs a search across the *dc.title* and *dc.subject* elements of the archives' metadata to find occurrences of that keyword and presents the results to the user in a traditional list format. The user then has the option to direct the search by selecting those media items which are most pertinent to their area of interest. Based on these choices the system applies the semantic inference rules described in Section 3.3 to generate new searches based on the metadata of the chosen resources. For example, the system may take a *dc.contributor* value for a chosen resource and search for resources which have *dc.subject* equivalent to this value, in order to find out more about the colleagues of the creator of the original resource. Through such iterative processing, semantic relationships between resources related to the user's topic can be inferred. The user has the opportunity to direct the search after each retrieval of media therefore ensuring that the presentation maintains its focus and relevance to the user. An outline of the overall process is shown in figure 2.

Consider, for example, the two media items and their corresponding metadata, displayed in Figure 3. A simple keyword search for *Lincoln* will return item 1 but not item 2, a portrait of Stephen Douglas, because the key term *Lincoln* doesn't appear in the metadata of item 2. Douglas was a contemporary and influential figure of Lincoln's and therefore item 2 is highly relevant to the topic *Lincoln*.

[1] MFO's are called communicative devices in Cuypers.

1. User selects archive(s) and enters keywords
2. System searches for media whose dc.title or dc.subject elements contain the keyword
3. System presents results to the User
4. User selects relevant media items from the list (optional)
5. System manipulates metadata and retrieves new results
6. User tells system to generate presentation
7. System applies inference rules
8. System generates presentation
9. User watches presentation
10. User finds media item of interest in presentation
11. User redirects focus by selecting media item

Fig. 2. Iterative Search Process

```
<title>Lincoln-Douglas
debate</title>
<subject>Abraham Lincoln</subject>

<subject>Stephen Douglas</subject>
<description>poster advertising
re-enactment of the Lincoln-Douglas
Debate</description>

<date>Aug 27 1858</date>
<contributer>Abraham
Lincoln</contributor>
<contributer>Stephen
Douglas</contributor>
<type>image</type>
```

```
<title>Stephen Arnold
Douglas, portrait</title>
<subject>Stephen
Douglas</subject>

<description>Stephen Arnold
Douglas, head-and-shoulders
portrait, slightly to left,
facing light</description>
<date>1844-1860</date>

<type>image</type>
```

Fig. 3. Media items with selected metadata.

Using the iterative search process described here, the system takes the *dc.contributor* value associated with the first item, the advertisement for the 'Lincoln-Douglas' debate, and searches for occurrences of 'Douglas, Stephen' in the *dc.title* or *dc.subject* fields of resources. This retrieves the portrait of Douglas and, if selected by the user, it will be included in the final presentation.

Through such manipulation of the contents of the DC elements, it is possible to retrieve interesting, related media items that would otherwise be lost and hence build up a network of rich semantic relationships through a semantic inferencing process which is described in the next section.

3.3 Semantic Inferencing Using Dublin Core

A set of pre-defined rules is applied to the Dublin Core metadata associated with the acquired set of media objects, to determine the semantic relationships between them. An example of such a relation is the *created* relation which can be inferred between two resources if, for example the *dc.creator* value of one resource equals the *dc.subject* value of a second image resource[2].

In order to define consistent mappings from semantic relations to spatial/temporal relations, we require a fixed set of semantic relations. In the context of our application, the MPEG-7 Semantic Relations Description Scheme specified in the MPEG-7 Multimedia Description Schemes specification [12] provides a good base set. Rather than restrict the allowed semantic relations to this set, we have chosen instead to define an object-oriented semantic relation ontology, which has the MPEG-7 semantic relations at the top level. This allows low-level domain-specific semantic relations to be inferred and assuming that they are a sub-property of a higher level MPEG-7 relation/property, which has a corresponding presentation construct, then we will be able to determine a spatial-temporal mapping (e.g., *translationOf* is a subPropertyOf *mpeg7:versionOf* and hence has the same spatial-temporal mapping).

Table 1 shows a list of inferencing rules which we have applied to the metadata of retrieved, selected resources - both to determine new searches and to infer specific semantic relations between resources retrieved at each stage. To date our work has mainly focussed on searches on people, the objects they have created and the influences on them, e.g., Lincoln, Picasso, Ellington. This has been both because of the nature of the multimedia content in the OAI archives and because of the nature of Dublin Core metadata.

The definition of equality in the inference rules(table reftbl:infrules is rather loose since the DC element values may not be exactly equal but may include substrings or perhaps eventually synonyms. By comparing combinations of element values more interesting semantic relationships (eg: *shareContext*, *versionOf*) can be inferred. Sequences or groups of media items, related to a common item by the same relation, are ordered through *precedes* and *follows* relations, two examples of which have been provided here.

[2] This rule does not work in all cases and one of our goals is to determine the specific circumstances in which semantic inferencing works

Table 1. Example Inferencing Rules

1. IF (obj1[dc.creator] = obj2[dc.subject] AND (obj1[dc.creator] = obj2[dc.title] AND obj2[dc.type] = 'image') → created(obj2,obj1)
2. IF (obj1[dc.title] = obj2[dc.subject] AND obj2[dc.type] = 'text') → describes(obj2, obj1)
3. IF (obj1[dc.title] = obj2[dc.subject] AND obj2[dc.type] = 'image') → depicts(obj2, obj1)
4. IF (obj1[dc.source] = obj2[dc.identifier]) → sourceOf(obj2, obj1)
5. IF (obj1[dc.source] = obj2[dc.source] → shareSource(obj1, obj2)
6. IF (obj1[dc.title,dc.creator,dc.subject] = obj2[dc.title,dc.creator,dc.subject]) → versionOf(obj1, obj2)
7. IF ((obj1[dc.subject] = obj2[dc.subject]) AND (obj1[dc.date] = obj2[dc.date] OR obj1[dc.coverage] = obj2[dc.coverage] OR obj1[dc.contributor] = obj2[dc.contributor])) → shareContext(obj1, obj2)
8. IF (obj1[dc.creator] = obj2[dc.subject] AND obj2[dc.type] = 'image' AND obj1[dc.contributor] = obj3[dc.subject] AND obj3[dc.type] = 'image') → colleagueOf(obj2,obj3) AND colleagueOf(obj3,obj2)[3]
9. IF (versionOf(obj1, obj2) AND obj1[dc.date] < obj2[dc.date]) → precedes(obj1, obj2) AND follows(obj2, obj1)
10. IF (created(obj1,obj2) AND created(obj1,obj3) AND obj2[dc.date] < obj3[dc.date]) → precedes(obj2,obj3) AND follows(obj3,obj2)

Rule 1 states that if an object's creator is the subject of another object which is also an image then the second subject is the 'creator' of the first. Figure 5 in Section 4 provides an example of the application of this rule. The photograph on the left shows Lincoln who is the creator of the speech which is represented by the image on the right. Because the *created* relationship is inferred for a number of portraits of Lincoln, a *group* relation is then inferred over the portraits.

The rules provided here are a relatively simple set of inferences based on binary relations and which focus primarily on 'people' searches. This has, to a certain extent, been because we are limited to simple Dublin Core metadata. Richer semantic relationships could be inferred through n-ary relations or more complex metadata, such as MPEG-7. This higher level of complexity would best be addressed using more powerful inference engines, such as RDFGateway [11], TRIPLE [20] or Cerebra. However, for simple, unqualified Dublin Core the rules listed here are adequate and can produce a structured, ordered results set suitable for translating into a presentation.

3.4 Mapping from Semantic Relationships to Temporal and Spatial Relationships

As the number of possible semantic relations is infinite, while the number of possible spatial and temporal relations are limited, we use a semantic relationship ontology/hierarchy in which all semantic relationships are derived from the top-level MPEG-7 semantic relationships. Table 2 shows the mapping from our inferred semantic relationships to the top-level MPEG-7 semantic relationships. If more complex domain-specific semantic relationships can be inferred then their mapping to MPEG-7 semantic relationships will need to be added to this table. Table 3 illustrates the corresponding mapping from the MPEG-7 semantic relationships to Cuypers MFO's, desribed here as logical spatial and temporal relationships. For example, the fact that there is an order between created works can be illustrated by presenting them in chronological order. Similarly, a way of conveying 'grouping' between media items is to align them together spatially.

Table 2. Semantic Relations Mapping Table

Semantic	MPEG7/Parent
X created Y	X result Y
X colleagueOf Y	X accompanier Y
X depicts Y	X depicts Y
X describes Y	X annotates Y
X shareContext Y	X similar Y
X sourceOf Y	X component Y
X versionOf Y	X identifier Y
X precedes Y	X before Y
X follows Y	X after Y

Table 3. Mapping from MPEG-7 Semantic Relations to Spatio-temporal Relations

MPEG7/Parent	Examples of Temporal/Spatial Relations
X result Y	spatialLeft(X,Y)
X accompanier Y	spatialLeft(X,Y), spatialSmaller(X,Y)
X depicts Y	spatialRight(X,Y
X annotates B	spatialBelow(X,Y), spatialAlign(X, Y)
X similar Y	spatialLeft(X,Y), spatialEqualSize(X,Y), spatialAlign(X,Y)
X component Y	spatialLeft(X,Y), spatialSmaller(X,Y)
X identifier B	spatialLeft(X,Y), spatialSmaller(Y,X
X precedes Y	temporalBefore(X, Y), spatialAlign(X, Y)

Although we have defined a single mapping from semantic relations to spatio-temporal relations in Table 3, the mapping from semantic to spatio-temporal relations is not always so straightforward. For example, when grouping media items, such as a group of works by the same artist, the actual number of media items, and their physical sizes are initially unknown. Unlike an HTML document, which is in principle, unbounded by page size, multimedia documents are generally less flexible.[4]. Although one approach to overcoming physical limitations is to display media items one after the other, this can be problematic. From a user's perspective, it is inadvisable to generate an over-repetitive presentation (e.g., slide show) which doesn't display new information or modify the layout.

[4] Scrollbars besides and below the document allow a viewer to navigate to any point in a HTML document

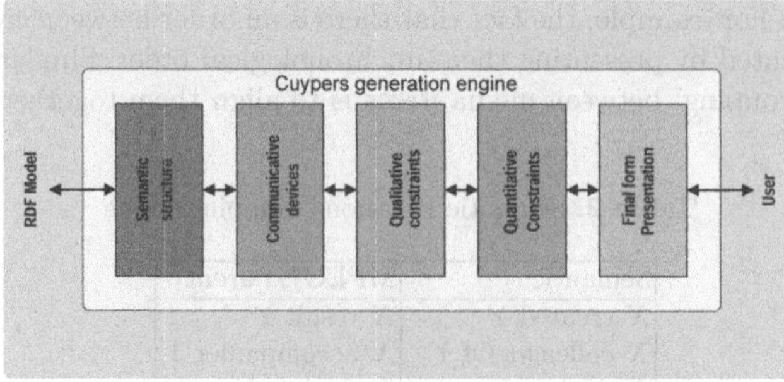

Fig. 4. Processing layers in Cuypers

Moreover certain semantic relationships, such as *created*, might be better presented ordered spatially to illustrate the development in the works, rather than as a sequential slide show. In order to convey a grouping or ordering between media items, it would be better if a number of alternative spatiotemporal mappings were defined, in order of priority, if they cannot all physically fit on the screen at once. This problem is addressed by the *overflow stategies* of Rutledge et al. [19] and implemented within the Cuypers presentation engine, described in the next section. These strategies ensure that the intended semantics associated with the spatial-temporal relations, are respected and retained for an arbitrary number of media items of arbitrary sizes.

3.5 Cuypers Presentation Generator

The Cuypers presentation generation system [24] implements *overflow strategies* by applying constraint-solving mechanisms. It provides an abstract layer on top of the spatio-temporal relations found in multimedia document specification languages, such as SMIL [27]. Besides overflow strategies, the abstract layer allows Cuypers to adapt the presentation to other external factors such hardware constraints e.g., is the client using a multimedia PC or a mobile phone. Figure 4 illustrates the different processing layers within the Cuypers Presentation engine, which are described in more detail below.

1. **Semantic structure level.** This level completely abstracts from the presentation's layout and hyperlink navigation structure and describes the presentation purely in terms of higher-level, 'semantic' relationships or rhetorical structure. This level within Cuypers is extended within our system by the semantic inferencing and semantic to spatio-temporal mapping processes described in the previous two sections which translate semantic relationships to the communicative devices of the next layer.
2. **Communicative device level.** The highest level of abstraction describing the presentation's layout makes use of *communicative devices*[5] [19]. These

[5] MFO's are called communicative devices in Cuypers.

are similar to the patterns of multimedia and hypermedia interface design described by [18] in that they describe the presentation in terms of well known spatial, temporal and hyperlink presentation constructs. An example of a communicative device is the *bookshelf.* This device can be effectively used in multimedia presentations to present a sequence of media items, especially when it is important to communicate the *order* of the media items in the sequence. How the bookshelf determines the precise layout of a given presentation in terms of lower level constraints can depend on a number of issues. For example, depending on the cultural background of the user, it may order a sequence of images from left to right, top to bottom or *vice versa.* Also its *overflow strategy,* that is, what to do if there are too many images to fit on the screen, may depend on the preferences of the user and/or author of the document. It may decide to add a 'More info' hyperlink to the remaining content in HTML, alternatively, it could split the presentation up into multiple scenes that are sequentially scheduled over time in SMIL.

3. **Qualitative constraints level.** An example of a qualitative constraint is "caption X is positioned below picture Y", and backtracking to produce alternatives might involve trying right or above, etc. Some final-form formats allow specification of the document on this level. In these cases, the Cuypers system only generates and solves the associated numeric constraints to check whether the presentation can be realized at all, it subsequently discards the solution of the constraint solver and uses the qualitative constraints directly to generate the final form output.
4. **Quantitative constraints level.** To generate presentations of the same information using different document formats, we need to abstract from the final-form presentation. On this level of abstraction, the desired temporal and spatial layout of the presentation is specified by a set of format-independent constraints, from which the final-form layout can be derived automatically.
5. **Final-form presentation level.** At the lowest level of abstraction, is the final-form presentation, which encodes the presentation in a document format that is readily playable by the end user's Web browser or media player. Examples of such formats include, HTML, SVG, and — the focus of our prototype — SMIL. This level is needed to make sure that the end-user's Web-client remains independent of the abstractions used internally in the Cuypers system, and to make sure that the end-user can use off-the-shelf Web clients to view the presentations generated by Cuypers.

3.6 User-Directed Hypermedia Browsing

Currently the scope of a dynamically-generated presentation is limited to a single concept. A concept being, for example 'President Lincoln' or 'the Eiffel Tower'. However, each concept has a number of related concepts, such as speeches Lincoln has written or 'Gustav Eiffel' - these related concepts can be further explored by the user through hyperlinks from individual media objects within the current presentation.

Users are able to redirect a presentation's focus by clicking on particular individual media objects within the presentation to trigger a new iterative search process, using the metadata of the selected resource as the starting point. In this way, new presentations, focussing on a related concept can be dynamically generated. This step in the overall system is represented by the arrow from the presentation to OAI in figure 1.

4 Example

A user interested in the life of former American president *Abraham Lincoln* searches for the term 'Lincoln' across the OAI archives. The results include (apart from a certain amount of irrelevant material) a number of portraits, images of documents written by him, a news article reporting his assassination, an article about his life and images of the Lincoln Memorial. Two of the objects and their associated metadata are shown in Figure 5 below.

Because the 'subject' of the object on the left, is equivalent to the 'creator' of the object on the right, and the object on the left is of type 'image', it is possible to infer that the object on the left is a photograph of the creator of the object on the right. Further comparison of the dates associated with the objects indicates that the photo is of the creator at around the time the document was written.

Translating these inferred semantic relationships into spatial and temporal relationships generates a SMIL presentation which displays a chronological sequence of portraits on the left, with spatially beside them, playing in parallel, the display of the biography, images of documents he has created and concluding with the news paper article reporting his death. Figure 6 shows the user interface for the dynamically generated SMIL presentation.

5 Discussion, Conclusions, and Future Work

5.1 OAI

The OAI repositories and the OAI protocol offered many advantages as a testbed for this work. In particular, the availability of interesting content and associated metadata, ease of use and the simplicity of the protocol will undoubtedly ensure the OAI's long-term sustainability and potential for useful service provision. However a number of issues limited the OAI's effectiveness in the context of the work descibed here.

Firstly, it was difficult to find topics within the OAI archives, which are useful, interesting and have sufficient number and variety of related media objects to generate interesting presentations. Although existing OAI data providers make a relatively large number of items available, many of them are e-prints and hence of only limited suitability for creating multimedia presentations. Others, such as the Library of Congress, have multimedia but only on limited or generic topics.

<title>Abraham Lincoln</title>	<title>Draft of the Emancipation Proclamation</title>
<creator>Gardner</creator>	<creator>Abraham Lincoln</creator>
<subject>Abraham Lincoln</subject>	<subject>Emancipation Proclamation</subject>
<subject>President</subject>	
<description>Photograph of Abraham Lincoln taken in Washington</description>	<description>Draft of the Emancipation Proclamation by President Abraham Lincoln, July 22, 1862</description>
<date>1862</date>	<date>22/7/1862</date>
<type>photograph</type>	<type>hand written document</type>
<type>image</type>	<type>image</type>

Fig. 5. Media items with associated metadata.

For example, pictures of a 'boat' or a 'park' are useless in this context without more specific metadata.

Secondly, the existing metadata is highly inconsistent, sometimes inaccurate and created with simple resource discovery in mind. Use of different thesauri and widely variable levels of detail and structure within the metadata make it difficult to effectively compare. Cole et. al. [8] encountered similar problems and suggest the use of metadata normalization for searching across OAI archives..

Finally, there is often either no link from the metadata record in OAI to the actual content or the link is broken. In many cases, the *dc.identifier* value points to the data provider's web page which may or may not contain the media

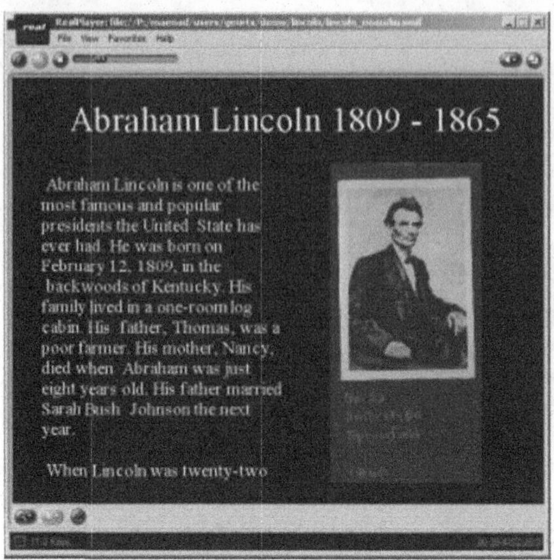

Fig. 6. Final form presentation

item or a link to it. For automatic processing of metadata and generation of presentations, a direct link to the actual media item is essential.

5.2 Dublin Core

The unqualified Dublin Core metadata schema was chosen by OAI to maximize the chance of interoperablilty between data providers and because many of the participating institutions already have metadata in this format. It is also a simple yet flexible schema, suitable for many different subject areas. However we found that, in the context of the work described here, Dublin Core has some serious limitations.

Firstly unqualified Dublin Core is too simplistic to infer many rich or interesting semantic relationships. Disallowing qualifiers removes a level of detail from the metadata which is essential for anything other than fairly simplistic semantic inferencing. The extent to which this effects the quality of the final presentation is uncertain, since it is possible to produce a complete presentation with only a few relationships.

Secondly, the application of inferencing rules is further hampered either by unstructured metadata values or the use of incompatible schemas for many of the element values. For example, some data providers use textual values for the *dc.relation*, *dc.identifier* and *dc.source* elements, while others use URIs. This makes comparisons between values problematic. On the other hand, if particular controlled vocabularies or schemes are used for certain DC elements, it may not be applicable to migrate these values to other DC elements in order to infer semantically-related resources.

Thirdly, there is significant ambiguity over the purpose and content of many of the DC element's values. This is exacerbated by the use of unqualified Dublin Core. For example, in some cases the 'creator' is the creator of the digital surrogate. In other cases, the 'creator' is the person who created the object depicted in the digital surrogate. In some organisations, the 'creator' of a musical recording is the composer, while in others, the 'creator' is the primary musician. Likewise the *dc.date* value may be the date of creation of the original source item, the digital surrogate or the date of publishing in the OAI archive.

Finally, Dublin Core is not designed for describing multimedia resources. It is inadequate, in particular, for describing the fine-grained details such as segmentation, formatting and low-level audiovisual feature metadata which would be most useful for inferring interesting semantic relationships between multimedia objects.

None of these problems are new but their implications in the context of this work are accentuated and debilitating to the overall goal.

5.3 Conclusions and Future Work

Our first conclusion is that even given the limited range of multimedia resources available through OAI and the simple semantic relationships we have been able to infer from their metadata, we have been able to generate quite interesting and intelligent multimedia presentations. The advantage of our approach is that it can present previously unrecognized connections between related, distributed mixed-media resources in an easily interpreted, interesting and multi-layered display. Because the system is dynamic, new online resources with semantic relations to the search topic will be picked up and included automatically.

Our next conclusion is that much more interesting semantic inferencing would be possible if either qualified Dublin Core, or a richer model such as the ABC model [13] or MPEG-7 (where applicable), were used as the metadata model. The recent development of an MPEG-7 ontology [9], opens the way for richer semantic inferencing between resources described using MPEG-7 and resources described using other domain-specific ontologies.

However if we were to use more complex metadata schemas, such as ABC or MPEG-7, then we would need to replace the current iterative search and inferencing process with a more powerful and automated inferencing engine such as RDFGateway [11].

Although we have focussed on searches for information about 'people', specific semantic inferencing rules could be defined for searches on 'events', 'places' or 'physical objects'. Expanding the types of searches and associated inference rules would expand the potential applications for the system e.g., automatic generation of multimedia news articles, obituaries, genealogies, museum presentations.

Our final conclusion is that in the next few years we will see the emergence of a new generation of search engines based on approaches similar to the one proposed in this paper. As the amount of multimedia on the internet expands, as the semantic web infrastructure develops and as more resources and ontologies are described using standards such as MPEG-7 and RDF, search engines are going to start delivering results in the form of automatically aggregated, knowledge-enhanced multimedia presentations.

Acknowledgements. The work described in this paper has been funded by the Cooperative Research Centre for Enterprise Distributed Systems Technology (DSTC) through the Australian Federal Government's CRC Programme (Department of Industry, Science and Resources). Thanks also to CWI, Lynda Hardman and Frank Nack for lending us Joost, paying his travel expenses and providing us with feedback and a copy of Cuypers for research purposes.

References

1. Tim Berners-Lee, James Hendler, and Ora Lassila. The Semantic Web. *Scientific American*, May 2001.
2. Dublin Core Community. Dublin Core Element Set, Version 1.1. See `http://www.dublincore.org/documents/dces/`, 07/02 1999.
3. OAI Community. OAI Protocol for Metadata Harvesting 2.0. See `http://www.openarchives.org/OAI/openarchivesprotocol.html`.
4. OAI Community. Open Archives Initiative. See `http://www.openarchives.org/`.
5. OAI Community. Open Archives Initiative Registered Service Providers. See `http://www.openarchives.org/service/listproviders.html`.
6. T. Rist E. Andr. Generating Coherent Presentations Employing Textual and Visual Material. In *Artificial Intelligente Review, Special Volume on the Integration of Natura1 Language and Vision Processing*, 9(2–3):147–165, 1995.
7. Gregory Karvounarakis et al. RQL: A Declarative Query Language for RDF. In *WWW2002 Conference*, Honolulu, May 2002.
8. T. Cole et al. Now That We've Found the 'Hidden Web' What Can We DO With It? The Illinois Open Archives Initiative Metadata Harvesting Experience. In *Museums on the Web Conference 2002*, Boston, April 2002.
9. Jane Hunter. Adding Multimedia to the Semantic Web - Building an Mpeg-7 Ontology. In *International Semantic Web Working Symposium (SWWS)*, Stanford, July 2001.
10. USC Information Science Institute. Webscripter Project Overview. See `http://www.isi.edu/webscripter/`.
11. Intellidimension. Intellidimension's RDF Gateway. See `http:// www.intellidimension.com/RDFGateway/`.
12. ISO IEC. *15938-5 FDIS Information Technology - Multimedia Content Description Interface - Part 5: Multimedia Description Schemes*, March 2002.
13. Carl Lagoze and Jane Hunter. The ABC Ontology and Model. *Journal of Digital Information*, 2(2), 2001.
14. Alberto Reggiori Libby Miller, Andy Seaborne. Three Implernentations of SquishQL, a Simple RDF Query Language. In *1st International Semantic Web Conference ISWC2002*, Sardinia, June 9–12 2002.
15. Library of Congress. Library of Congress: American Memory Collection. See `http://memory.loc.gov/`.

16. University of Illinois Library. University of Illinois Open Archives Collection. See `http://bolder.grainger.uiuc.edu/uiLibOAIProvider/OAI.asp`.
17. OpenVideo Organisation. OpenVideo. See `http://www.open-video.org/oai/`.
18. Gustavo Rossi, Daniel Schwabe, and Alejandra Garrido. Design Reuse in Hypermedia Applications Development. In *The Proceedings of the Eighth ACM Conference on Hypertext und Hypermedia*, pages 57–66, Southampton, UK, April 1997. ACM, ACM Press.
19. Lloyd Rutledge, Jim Davis, Jacco van Ossenbruggen, and Lynda Hardman. Interdimensional Hypermedia Communicative Devices for Rhetorical Structure. In *Proceedings of the International Conference on Multimedia Modeling 2000 (MMM00)*, pages 89–105, Nagano, Japan, November 13–15, 2000.
20. Michael Sintek and Stefan Decker. TRIPLE – A Query, Inference, and Transformation Language for the Semantic Web. In *1st International Semantic Web Conference ISWC2002*, Sardinia, June 9–12 2002.
21. Robert Tansley. *The Multimedia Thesaurus: Adding a Semantic Layer to Multimedia Information.* PhD thesis, Dept. of Electronics and Computer Science, Uni. of Southhampton, August 2000.
22. Douglas Tudhope and Daniel Cunliffe. Semantically Indexed Hypermedia: Linking Information Disciplines. *ACM Computing Surveys*, 31(4es), December 1999.
23. Frank van Harmelen, Peter F. Patel-Schneider, and Ian Herrocks. Reference description of the DAML+OIL (March 2001) ontology markup language. `http://www.daml.org/2001/03/reference.html`. Contributors: Tim Berners-Lee, Dan Brickley, Dan Connolly, Mike Dean, Stefan Decker, Pat Hayes, Jeff Heflin, Jim Hendler, Ora Lassila, Deb McGuinness, Lynn Andrea Stein, . . .
24. Jacco van Ossenbruggen, Joost Geurts, Frank Cornelissen, Lloyd Rutledge, and Lynda Hardman. Towards Second and Third Generation Web-Based Multimedia. In *The Tenth International World Wide Web Conference*, pages 479–488, Hong Kong, May 1–5, 2001. IW3C2.
25. W3C. Semantic Web Activity. See `http://www.w3.org/2001/sw/`.
26. W3C. Resource Description Framework (RDF) Model and Syntax Specification. W3C Recommendations are available at `http://www.w3.org/TR`, February, 22, 1999. Editied by Ora Lassila and Ralph R. Swick.
27. W3C. Synchronized Multimedia Integration Language (SMIL 2.0) Specification. W3C Recommendations are available at `http:// www.wS.org/TR/`, August 7, 2001. Edited by Aaron Cohen.
28. W3C. RDF Vocabulary Description Language 1.0: RDF Schema. W3C Candidate Recommendations are available at `http://www.w3.org/TR`, 30 April 2002. Edited by Dan Brickley and R.V. Guha.

Technical Report Interchange through Synchronized OAI Caches

Xiaoming Liu[1], Kurt Maly[1], Mohammad Zubair[1], Rong Tang[1], Mohammed Imran Padshah[1], George Roncaglia[2], JoAnne Rocker[2], Michael Nelson[2], William von Ofenheim[2], Richard Luce[3], Jacqueline Stack[3], Frances Knudson[3], Beth Goldsmith[3], Irma Holtkamp[3], Miriam Blake[3], Jack Carter[3], Mariella Di Giacomo[3], Major Jerome Nutter[4], Susan Brown[4], Ron Montbrand[4], Sally Landenberger[5], Kathy Pierson[5], Vince Duran[5], and Beth Moser[5]

[1] Old Dominion University.
Norfolk, Virginia, USA
[2] NASA Langley Research Center,
Hampton, Virginia, USA
[3] Los Alamos National Laboratory,
Los Alamos, New Mexico, USA
[4] Air Force Research Laboratory / Phillips Research Site, Kirtland AFB,
New Mexico, USA
[5] Sandia National Laboratory,
Albuquerque, New Mexico, USA

Abstract. The Technical Report Interchange project is a cooperative experimental effort between NASA Langley Research Center, Los Alamos National Laboratory, Air Force Research Laboratory, Sandia National Laboratory and Old Dominion University to allow for the integration of technical reports. This is accomplished using the Open Archives Initiative Protocol for Metadata Harvesting (OAI-PMH) and having each site cache the metadata from the other participating sites. Each site also implements additional software to ingest the OAI-PMH harvested metadata into their native digital library (DL). This allows the users at each site to see an increased technical report collection through the familiar DL interfaces and take advantage of whatever valued added services are provided by the native DL.

1 Introduction

We present the Technical Report Interchange (TRI) project, which allows integration of technical report digital libraries at NASA Langley Research Center (LaRC), Los Alamos National Laboratory (LANL), Air Force Research Laboratory (AFRL), and Sandia National Laboratory. LaRC, LANL, Sandia and AFRL all have thousands of "unclassified, unlimited" technical reports that have been scanned from paper documents or "born digital". Although these reports frequently cover complementary or collaborative research areas, it has

M. Agosti and C. Thanos (Eds.): ECDL 2002, LNCS 2458, pp. 176–189, 2002.

not always been easy for one laboratory to have full access to another laboratory's reports. The laboratories would like to share access to metadata with links to full text document initially, and eventually replicate the document collections. Each laboratory has its own report publication tracking, management and search/retrieval systems, with varying levels of interoperability with each other. Since the libraries at these laboratories have evolved independently, they differ in the syntax and semantics of the metadata they use. In addition, the database management systems used to implement these libraries are different (Table 1).

Table 1. Native Metadata Formats and Library Systems

Laboratory	Native Metadata Format	Native Library System - Source	Native Library System - Destination
LaRC	MARC	BASIS+	TBD
LANL	USMARC+ Local Fields	Geac ADVANCE	Science Server
AFRL	COSATI	Sirsi STILAS	Sirsi STILAS
Sandia	MARC	Horizon	Verity

One major effort that addresses interoperability started with the Santa Fe Convention [11]. The objective of the Santa Fe Convention, now the Open Archive Initiative (OAI) [4] is to develop a framework to facilitate the discovery of content stored in distributed archives. OAI is becoming widely accepted and many archives are currently or soon-to-be OAI-compliant. While DL interoperability has been well studied in NCSTRL [1], STARTS [2] and other systems, OAI is significantly different in several aspects. Most significantly, OAI promotes interoperability through the concept of metadata harvesting. The OAI framework supports Data Providers (archives or repositories) and Service Providers (harvesters). A typical data provider would be a digital library without any constraints on how it implemented its services with its own set of publishing tools and policies. However, to be part of the OAI framework, a data provider needs to be 'open' in as far as it needs to support the OAI protocol for metadata harvesting (OAI-PMH). Service providers develop value-added services based on the information collected from cooperating archives. These value-added services can take the form of cross-archive search engines, linking systems, and peer-review systems.

OAI-PMH provides a very powerful framework for building union-catalog-type databases for collections of resources by automating and standardizing the collection of contributions from the participating sites, which has traditionally been an operational headache in building and managing union catalogs [7]. By implementing the OAI-PMH, the TRI system enables the sharing of documents housed in disparate digital libraries that have unique interfaces and search capabilities designed for their user communities. This allows a native digital library to export and ingest information from other digital libraries in a manner transpar-

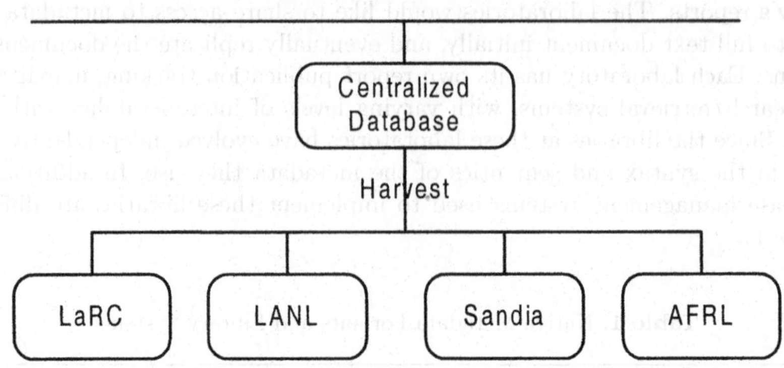

Fig. 1. Centralized Approach

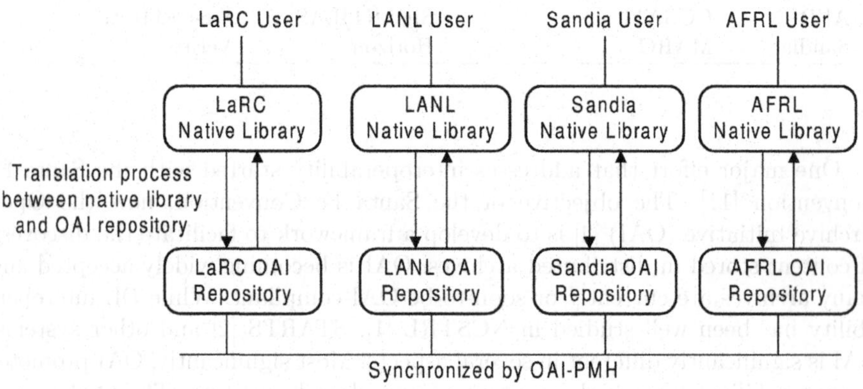

Fig. 2. Replicated Approach

ent to its user community. That is, the users access information from other digital libraries through the same native library interface the users are accustomed to using. The importance of this approach is that it not only allows for one-time historical sharing of a corpus amongst participating libraries, it also provides for continuous updating of a native library's collection with new documents when other OAI-compliant repositories add to their collections. Additionally, all libraries will always (with some tunable time delay) be consistent in having the totality of all holdings available within their own library.

Based on OAI-PMH, there are two approaches to build a federated digital library that allow users to access reports in all the libraries through a single interface: centralized and replicated. We had to determine which of these approaches would work better for the TRI project. In the centralized approach (Fig. 1), a federation service harvests metadata from the four OAI enabled libraries and provides a unified interface to search all the collections. This approach has been adopted by Arc [5], the first OAI service provider prototype, and other OAI service providers [8] [3] [10]. However, a centralized search service is not a suitable approach for the TRI project given that the primary object of the project is for participating laboratories to provide access to technical reports using their existing library interfaces. Besides this limitation, the centralized approach suffers from the organizational logistics of maintaining a centralized federation service, and having a single point of failure. The TRI system is based on a replicated approach, which addresses these problems (Fig. 2). This approach can be viewed as mirrored OAI repositories, where every laboratory has its own federation service. The consistency between these services is maintained using OAI-PMH. As a federation service is locally available, it becomes easy to push other laboratory's metadata into the native library. In addition, this approach supports several levels of redundancy, thereby improving the availability of the whole system. For example, a failure of a TRI system at one laboratory would not severely impact users at other laboratories. In fact, users at the affected laboratory will continue to search and discover reports from other laboratories, though they may not be able to see reports that are added to the system at other laboratories during the down time.

A single node in the TRI system is based on Arc (http://arc.cs.odu.edu) [5], the first OAI service provider that has been in use for nearly two years. While Arc has a built-in infrastructure for OAI harvesting, there are many new challenges in TRI:

Integration with native DL: Since each laboratory has its own DL management system and native search interface, the TRI must be seamlessly integrated into native DL system.

Metadata translation: Because each DL uses different native metadata format, to enable interoperability, we need use a standard metadata format and there must be translation between the native and standard metadata formats.

Seamlessly support new participants: The system must support new participants with limited effort, and any new participant should not adversely impact the existing installations.

Changes progagation: Metadata is duplicated in each DL, so when add, update and delete operations occur in one native library, the changes must be propagated to other libraries.

The rest of the paper is organized as follows. Section 2 presents the architecture of TRI system. In Section 3 we discuss the OAI implementation and common modules across all participating laboratories. Section 4 discusses the issues of integrating TRI system with native library. In Section 5 we discuss records update, deletion and duplicate detection. In Section 6 we analyze the experiences to date and outline future work.

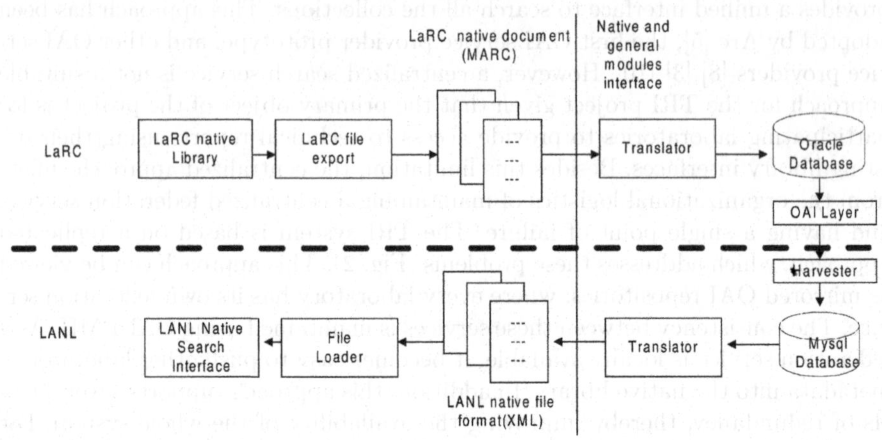

Fig. 3. A Typical Workflow- LANL shares documents from LaRC

2 System Architecture

In the TRI system, each participant has its own user community and a local search interface allowing users to retrieve data from other library systems. A translation process in each DL is responsible for translating native metadata format to a standard metadata format and vice versa, i.e., MARC tags are converted into Dublin Core (DC) [12] and DC into MARC. The standard metadata format is saved in an OAI compliant repository, which can selectively serve metadata when an external OAI harvesting request arrives. A harvester located at each DL periodically harvests metadata from other DLs (Fig. 3).

Since each library has its data format and management system that is maintained by local librarians/information specialists, a file-system based solution is a simple and flexible way for each library to import/export native metadata. The last modification time of records provides a basic mechanism to detect newly added or changed metadata. The exported native metadata is translated into unqualified DC format, which is the default used by OAI to support minimal interoperability. Although richer metadata formats such as MARC or Qualified DC would provide richer semantics and support greater "precision" in search results, the variation in technical report metadata formats (including many unique to a given laboratory) suggested that unqualified DC would be the best metadata format for the initial phase of TRI. As Figure 3 illustrates, the native metadata is converted into OAI-compliant DC, and DC metadata is harvested by other libraries. Once harvested, metadata is converted from DC into local metadata format and stored in an import directory. The local libraries then integrate the newly harvested metadata into their local systems.

The developed software is highly modularized and can easily support new participants with minimal effort. The software modules are:

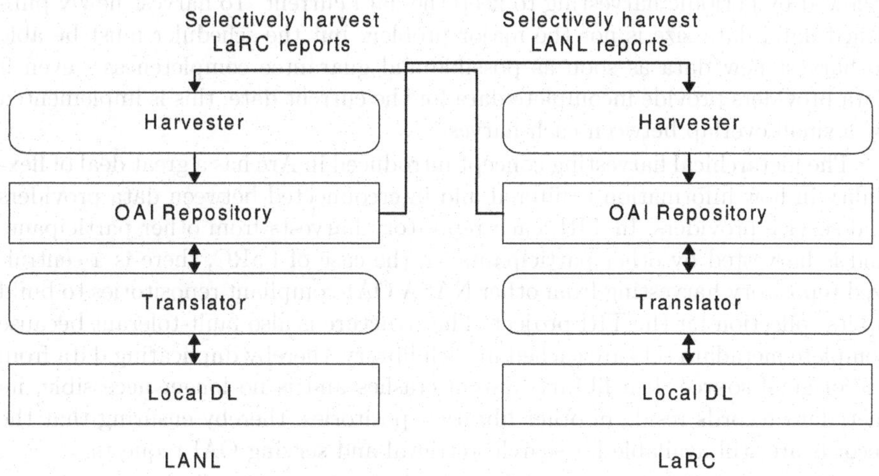

Fig. 4. OAI Repository and Harvester

Scheduler: A tool manages and schedules various tasks in TRI system.
OAI repository: A database-based system makes each library OAI-compliant.
Harvester: An application issues OAI request and collects metadata.
Translation tool: Translates native metadata format in each library to a standard metadata and vice versa.

These modules are the same for all repositories. The translation tool requires some customization for a particular library because its local metadata format will need to be mapped into a standard format. This can be accomplished by creating a mapping table between the metadata and the standard.

3 Harvester and OAI Repository

The harvester and OAI repository designs and configurations are based on Arc's implementation design. Arc uses an OAI layer over harvested metadata, making hierarchical harvesting possible. Figure 4 outlines the major components of the system and how they interact with each other.

3.1 Harvester

Similar to a Web crawler, the TRI harvester traverses the data providers automatically and extracts metadata, but it exploits the incremental, selective harvesting defined by the OAI-PMH. Historical and newly published data harvesting have different requirements. When a service provider harvests a data provider for the first time, all past data (historical data) needs to be harvested, followed by periodic harvesting to keep the data current. To harvest newly published data, data size is not the major problem but the scheduler must be able to harvest new data as soon as possible and guarantee completeness - even if data providers provide incomplete data for the current date, this is implemented by a small overlap between each harvest.

The hierarchical harvesting concept introduced in Arc has a great deal of flexibility in how information is filtered and interconnected between data providers and service providers. In TRI, each repository harvests from other participants and is harvested by other participants. In the case of LaRC, there is a centralized repository harvesting from other NASA OAI-compliant repositories to build up its collection for the TRI project. The structure is also fault-tolerant because complete metadata sets are cached in each library, thereby duplicating data from the original source. If a library system crashes and is no longer accessible, its metadata records reside in other library repositories, thereby ensuring that the records are still available for search, retrieval and serving OAI requests.

3.2 Scheduler and Task Management

The scheduler manages various tasks in the TRI repositories. In each library, there are several typical tasks:

Local read: It makes native DL OAI-compliant and harvestable by other partners;
Remote harvest: It issues requests to OAI compliant repositories;
Local write: It writes harvested records into its local library system.

The scheduler's functions include: automatically launching these tasks, monitoring current status, and addressing network and other system errors. If the harvesting is successful, the scheduler tracks the last harvest time so that the next harvest will start from the most recent harvest.

Each task has its configurable parameters so that the participating laboratories have the flexibility in controlling the system. Tasks can be set up as a historical or fresh process and it allows combining multiple repositories to one single virtual repository (in the case of LaRC). The interval between harvesting is also configurable allowing system administrators to customize how often the data will be harvested: more frequent harvests require additional system resources but provide more current data. However, the whole system works in a coordinated way. For example, a typical working sequence is local read, remote harvest and local write.

The TRI scheduler can be configured as a daemon with its own timer or be controlled by a system timer (e.g. crontab files in Unix). At the initialization stage, it reads the system configuration file, which includes properties such as user-agent name, interval between harvests, data provider URL, and harvesting method. The scheduler periodically checks and starts the appropriate task based on configuration file.

4 Local Repository

While each site shares similar repository and harvester modules, they also have specific DL management systems and native metadata formats. We follow several guidelines in designing the local repository management in TRI system: Each library should maintain its own management system, an identical one is not feasible or possible; Considering the different software/hardware environment in each library, the interface between the native library and TRI system should be portable across platforms and should be simple; The effort to add a new participant should be minimal.

Based on these requirements we defined a file system based interface between native library and TRI general modules (Fig. 3). Each library exports its native format to a configurable directory, and the changed/added document is automatically marked by last modified time. The TRI local reader periodically polls this directory and any file whose modified date is newer than last harvesting time is translated into unqualified DC format and inserted into the OAI repository. Additionally, there is also an import directory in each library; the TRI local writer periodically checks whether any new/changed metadata is harvested from remote repository, translates it into local format and writes it to import directory. Each site may have its own program that exports metadata from local library system, and a loader that reads the import directory. Such a mechanism is highly integrated with a given local repository so its implementation is out of the control of the TRI common modules.

For historical reasons, each digital library may use different metadata formats. While it is possible to implement a one-to-one mapping for each metadata pair, the mapping complexity dramatically increases with the number of participants (n laboratories would require $n(n-1)$ mappings). With a common intermediate metadata format, only $2n$ mappings are necessary. So we chose unqualified DC as the common intermediate metadata format, and mapped each native metadata format to unqualified DC. However, with a common metadata format, the rich metadata element in each library may be lost as the common metadata format is the minimal subset of all libraries. This problem can be alleviated if we adopt a richer common metadata format in the future.

4.1 Mapping Metadata Formats

LANL, LaRC and Sandia use MARC in their local libraries, but each library has its own extensions or profiles. AFRL supports its own metadata format. Each library exports its metadata in its convenient way and also defines a bi-directional mapping table (See samples in Table 2 & 3).

In Table 2, the mapping table follows the structure of Library of Congress's MARC to DC crosswalk [6] with additional features from LaRC. In the MARC to DC mapping, the MARC file is parsed and corresponding fields are mapped to DC; some information may be lost, for example, the identifier field may be an ISSN number, technical report number or URL. Information like ISSN and URL

Table 2. LaRC MARC to DC Mapping(excerpt)

LaRC MARC Metadata Set	Dublin Core
D245a, D245d, D245e, D245n, D245p, D245s	title
D513a, D513b	coverage
D520b	description
D072a,D072b(001), D650a,D659a	subject
D090a(000), D013a, D020a, D088a, D856q, 856w	identifier

Table 3. DC to Sandia Mapping

Dublin Core element	Sandia Metadata Field
identifier	report numbers
identifier – URI	URL
subject	subject category codes
title	title
subject	keywords
creator	personal names
creator	corporate names
date	date
format – extent	extent
description	notes
rights	classification & dissemination

is clearly defined in MARC, but it will map to the undistinguished "identifier" field in unqualified DC, losing the distinctions between metadata fields.

4.2 Subject Mapping

Each library may use a different subject thesaurus and/or classification scheme. For example, LANL uses a combination of Library of Congress Subject Headings (LCSH) and subject terms from other relevant thesauri (including *International Energy: Subject Thesaurus (ETDE/PUB-2)* and its revisions). The metadata for a given LANL technical report may also include numerical subject categories or alpha-numerical report distribution codes representing a broad subject concept. Subject category code sources used by LANL include: *Energy Data Base: Subject Categories and Scope (DOE/TIC-4584-R#)* and its succeeding publication and revisions, *International Energy: Subject Categories and Scope (ETDE/PUB-1)*. Report distribution category code sources include various revisions of *Program Distribution for Unclassified Scientific and Technical Reports: Instructions and Category Scope Notes (DOE/OSTI-4500)*.

LaRC uses its own subject thesaurus and the NASA-SCAN system. The local library may organize the information by subject classification and it is necessary to do a subject classification mapping, for example, mapping NASA subject code (77 Physics of Elementary Particles) to LANL report distribution code (UC-414) (Table 4). Subject metadata is an area where the generically grouping

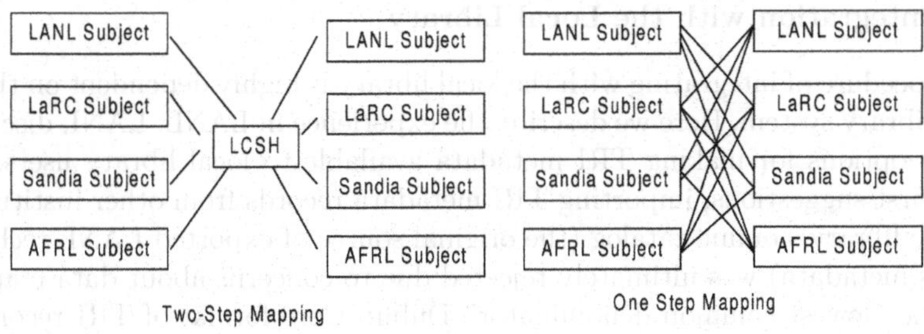

Fig. 5. Subject Mapping (Assume the unique subject schema is LCSH)

Table 4. Subject Mapping: LANL UC-414 maps to NASA SCAN 77

Digital Library	Subject Schema	Sample Subject Format
LANL	UC Report Distro Category	UC-414 sddoeur
	ETDE Subject Category	430100 edbsc
	INIS Subject Category (old)	E1610 inissc
	INIS Subject Category (new)	S43 inissc
	Text (LCSH)	Controlled formatted text
	Text (other thesauri)	Controlled formatted text
	Text (local subject heading)	Locally controlled text
NASA	SCAN	77
	Text	PHYSICS ELEMENTARY PARTICLES AND FIELDS

the various subject related metadata into a single unqualified DC data element results in loss of the source information for a given thesaurus or classification scheme thereby complicating the subject metadata mapping.

There are several approaches to address the lack of unified subject access. One way is to use a standard terminology and map each library's controlled metadata to the standard [9]. However, the granularity of subjects/keywords is significantly different among participating libraries; a unified standard is difficult to define and two-step mapping may cause more inconsistencies. Another way is to perform an individual mapping for each subject category pair. This alternative approach is more accurate because only one-step mapping is used. However, both approaches may introduce significant human effort to maintain the relationships (Fig. 5). A third approach is to use an automatic classification algorithm, however, the precision of this mapping is low as we are dealing with limited metadata. The easiest approach is to map all numeric subject codes into text strings using the mapping provided by the contributing organization. We have implemented all the methods except the unified subjects, and we are currently evaluating the different approaches in terms of validity and cost.

4.3 Integration with the Local Library

The procedure of integrating with the local library is highly dependent on the existing library system. Here we describe the experience in LANL. LANL discussed various options for making TRI metadata available to local library users. One of the first suggestions, importing TRI metadata records from other institutions into the library's online catalog (the original source of exported LANL technical reports metadata) was ultimately rejected due to concerns about data mapping from the "lowest common denominator" Dublin Core format of TRI records to the MARC format required for the online catalog. It was decided to make TRI metadata records available through the library's Science Server software as a proof-of-concept test.

Science Server, a locally modified version of software provided by Science Server LLC, enables simple content management while delivering electronic journals and IEEE Conference and Standards records directly to the desktop. At LANL, Science Server was ultimately selected for integration of and access to TRI records for the following reasons:

1. Provides a unified, familiar search interface to library users;
2. Offers robust indexing and searching capabilities with support for full text links (hyperlinks to technical reports);
3. Permits the definition of "collections" for each harvested site, with appropriate access restrictions for the collections as needed. Since the Science Server product was originally designed for access to journal literature, the "journal paradigm" was adapted for technical reports - with the TRI database becoming one collection within Science Server, each TRI archive institution treated as a "title", individual report years handled as volumes/issues, and the individual reports handled as "articles".

With the above paradigm in mind, it was a simple matter to design a loader for Science Server that mapped the TRI Dublin Core fields into Science Server fields. TRI's configuration tables were updated to perform "local writes", exporting the records from each archive to Dublin Core XML flat-file format. These records were then copied to test version of the Science Server system, converted from DC (loaded) and indexed. At this point, approximately 72000 TRI metadata records are locally searchable through the test Science Server system.

4.4 Security

There are four types of interactions in an OAI based data/service provider framework.

User - Search Service: a user interacts with a service provider, for example an interaction of a search user with a cross-archive search service.

Data Provider - Service Provider: a service provider interacts with a data provider using the OAI-PMH, for example, when a service provider harvests metadata from a data provider.

Publisher - Data Provider: an author publishes a digital object in a data provider, for example, when a researcher submits her pre-print in a pre-print collection.

User - Data Provider: a search user has found metadata record and wants to retrieve an associated object.

One approach to make these interactions secure is the use of Secure Socket Layer (SSL), and the other approach is based on IP address-based restrictions. In the current TRI system, we take the latter approach since it is simpler and is sufficient for the security needs of all partners. Thus, clear text is used for all four types of operations and authentication is provided by checking that a user (or program) comes only from a pre-defined set of acceptable machines. SSL can be adopted in the future if the TRI members wish to exchange more sensitive metadata.

5 Deletion, Update, and Duplication Detection

The TRI system is a fully distributed system with redundant data in each participating library; thus changes in one library need be propagated to other libraries. Furthermore, each library integrates data from many different sources, inside or outside of TRI project, which sometimes may lead to the existence of more than one legitimate copies of an article. Therefore we need to consider the duplication detection problem.

5.1 Deletion

Since the local library repository is not controlled by TRI system, the deletion is done in an advisory way. The deletion is initiated by the originating DL, the target TRI database deletes the records during the propagation of the information of action taken, finally an alert mechanism is provided to libraries that have imported the data to their local databases, and the deletion in a local DL is dealt with by its own management system.

The OAI-PMH defines a basic mechanism in dealing with deleted records: a record that is deleted can be indicated by a status of “deleted” in its header. This status means that an item has been deleted and therefore no record can be disseminated from it. This mechanism is integrated with local database management in our implementation. To initiate the document deletion, the local administrators mark a record as “deleted” in their administrative page. This information is kept in local TRI repository and when a remote site starts to harvest from this repository, it notices the “deleted” status based on the mechanism defined by OAI-PMH, and delete the record from its local TRI repository. At the same time the deleted records is marked in its local admin system. The system administrator can find deleted records in local admin page and apply the appropriate operations.

5.2 New and Updated Records

In OAI-PMH, updated or newly added records are identified by a "datestamp", which is defined as the date of creation, deletion, or latest date of modification. Similar to deleted records, updated records need to be integrated with local database management. When a file is changed or added to local export directory, the last modification date of this file is changed too. During each operation, the date of the last harvesting is saved, and it is compared with the date of each file under local export directory. Any file whose last modification time is newer than the last harvested time is imported into the local OAI repository and its datestamp is also changed. Later when a remote repository issues a fresh harvesting request, only the updated and new metadata is returned. This data is written into the import directory and later could be integrated into local search interface.

5.3 Duplication Detection

There are many cases in which duplication may occur. For example, one paper may be co-authored by authors at multiple TRI sites and the report indexed by the respective DLs. Especially in LaRC, there are multiple OAI repositories with overlapping collections. To accommodate each library's policy about duplicate records, the TRI system provides a mechanism that detects possible duplicates by similarity of key metadata fields like title and author. It then alerts the local system administrator of possible duplicate records to verify and delete.

6 Conclusions

In the first stage of the TRI project, LaRC and LANL installed TRI systems and each site has shared approximately 30K technical reports with each other. Both were able to automatically harvest newly published metadata from other site on a daily basis. LANL also loaded the harvested records into its native library, the Science Server, a system external to the TRI project repositories. ODU has finished the AFRL and Sandia translation modules and they will be deployed soon. We are also working on implementation of a user-friendly administrator page for deletion and other system management work.

During the implementation, one of the most significant problems is that unqualified DC does not match well with the sophisticated metadata formats used by the participants. The mappings, especially the subject mapping, is also difficult, and in many circumstances the semantics of original data is lost. This could be partially solved by defining a qualified DC profile for technical reports; however, the standard definition itself is time-consuming and is outside the scope of TRI. We intend to solicit additional participants for TRI after the current round of testing concludes. The initial result of using OAI-PMH as a mechanism for sharing data indicates that OAI-PMH is a flexible and powerful way to automate and standardize metadata exchange.

References

1. Davis, R., and Lagoze, C. (2000)"NCSTRL: Design and Deployment of a Globally Distributed Digital Library". Journal of American Society for Information Science, 51, 273-280.
2. Gravano, L., Chang, K., Garcia-Molina, H., Lagoze, C. and Paepcke, A. (1997)"STARTS:Stanford proposal for internet meta-searching". In Proceedings of the ACM SIGMOD International Conference on Management of Data, pp. 207-218
3. Harnad, S. and Carr, L. (2000) "Integrating, Navigating and Analyzing Eprint Archives Through Open Citation Linking (the OpCit Project)". Current Science (special issue honour of Eugene Garfield) 79, 629-638. http://cogprints.soton.ac.uk/documents/disk0/00/00/16/97/
4. Lagoze, C. and Van de Sompel, H. (2001) "The Open Archives Initiative: Building a low-barrier interoperability framework". In Proceedings of the ACM/IEEE Joint Conference on Digital Libraries, Roanoke VA, June 24-28, 2001, pp. 54-62.
5. Liu, X., Maly, K., Zubair, M. and Nelson, M. L. (2001) "Arc - An OAI Service Provider for Digital Library Federation". D-Lib Magazine, 7(4). http://www.dlib.org/dlib/april01/liu/04liu.html
6. LOC (2001) "MARC to Dublin Core Crosswalk". Network Development and MARC Standards Office, Library of Congress. http://www.loc.gov/marc/marc2dc.html
7. Lynch, C. (2001) "Metadata Harvesting and the Open Archives Initiative". ARL Monthly Report 217, August 2001. http://www.arl.org/newsltr/217/mhp.html
8. McClelland, M., McArthur, D., Giersch, S. and Geisler G. (2002) "Challenges for Service Providers When Importing Metadata in Digital Libraries". D-Lib Magazine, 8(4). http://www.dlib.org/dlib/april02/mcclelland/04mcclelland.html
9. Koch, T., Neuroth, H. and Day, M. (2001) "Renardus: Cross-browsing European subject gateways via a common classification system (DDC)". IFLA satellite meeting: Subject Retrieval in a Networked Environment, OCLC, Dublin, Ohio, USA
10. Suleman, H. and Fox, E. A. (2001) "A Framework for Building Open Digital Libraries". D-Lib Magazine, 7(12). http://www.dlib.org/dlib/december01/suleman/12suleman.html
11. Van de Sompel, H. and Lagoze, C. (2000) "The Santa Fe Convention of the Open Archives Initiative". D-Lib Magazine, 6(2). http://www.dlib.org/dlib/february00/vandesompel-oai/02vandesompel-oai.html
12. Weibel, S., Kunze, J., Lagoze, C. and Wolfe, M. (1998) "Dublin Core metadata for resource discovery". Internet RFC-2413, ftp://ftp.isi.edu/in-notes/rfc2413.txt

Functional Requirements for Online Tools to Support Community-Led Collections Building

Michael Khoo[1], Holly Devaul[3], and Tamara Sumner[2]

[1] Department of Communication UCB 270
[2] Department of Computer Science UCB 470
University of Colorado, Boulder, CO 80309 U.S.A.
{michael.khoo, tamara.sumner}@colorado.edu
[3] DLESE (Digital Library for Earth System Education) Program Center
University Corporation for Atmospheric Research
P.O. Box 3000, Boulder, CO 80307-3000, U.S.A.
devaul@ucar.edu

Abstract. The Digital Water Education Library collection (DWEL) is being generated by primary and secondary school teachers in the United States. This complex process involves both individual research and team design, and the use of a variety of online tools, such as an online cataloguing tool. Interactions amongst DWEL members are being ethnographically analysed in order to identify requirements for further development of these tools. The analysis suggests that many DWEL members envision their work as occurring in an integrated environment with stable documents, a situation which is not supported by the current configuration of DWEL tools. The design implications of these findings are reviewed.

1 Introduction: DWEL and Community-Led Collections Building

The Digital Water Education Library (DWEL) is a two-year National Science Foundation funded project to provide catalogued records of five hundred online resources related to water and the earth system. The project is collaborating with the Digital Library for Earth System Education (DLESE) and is using their recently-released catalog management tool. This tool facilitates individual contributions of resources as well as coordinated group development of sub-collections. DWEL is experimenting with, and implementing a community-led collections development process that we shall refer to in this article as 'CLCD.' In CLCD, disciplinary and special interest groups can design and create collections tailored to their own specific needs.

The DWEL collection is being designed by a distributed group of approximately thirty individuals, predominantly primary and secondary school teachers, who share an interest in water-related education topics. This group is sub-divided into four separate working groups, covering kindergarten to year four, years five to eight, years nine to twelve, and informal education. Each of these groups is responsible for selecting, reviewing and cataloguing appropriate online educational resources for their age range. Members are also responsible for designing a series of evaluation and review rubrics for assessing and accessioning resources into the collection, and are thus also engaged in a process of 'meta-design,' 'activities, processes, and objectives to create new media and environments that allow users to act as designers and be creative' [6].

M. Agosti and C. Thanos (Eds.): ECDL 2002, LNCS 2458, pp. 190-203, 2002.

In anticipating rapid development of digital library infrastructure in the United States, it is thought that CLCD models such as DWEL's offer the possibility of a scalable growth model with economic and administrative advantages over more centralised systems. In CLCD, many of the tasks required for collections development can be decentralised to user communities, rather than being incrementally accumulated at a centralised facility. As DWEL is a prototype for these suppositions, it has a built-in component of ethnographic-based independent project evaluation to study the efficacy of CLCD as a design process. This article presents ethnographic data from this research that has studied DWEL members' perceptions of CLCD, and their expectations of a close structural integration between the various tools they use to carry out their tasks.

2 Theoretical Background: The Social Context of Technology Adoption

In investigating the implementation of CLCD in DWEL, we assume a complex and non-linear relationship between a technology and its context of use [12] in which the introduction of a technology into a social context involves mutual processes of social and technological co-evolution [e.g. 2, 3, 4]. From this point of view, technology can be seen as eliciting unpredicted responses in users, responses that can in turn affect the way a technology is restructured and redesigned. Early groupware, for instance, with its potential for reducing the general messiness of human interaction, was thought suitable for supporting and managing focused organisational tasks [5, 15, 17, 22]. The overall benefits of groupware adoption have however proved unpredictable [7], particularly 'in the wild,' where the technological rubber hits the social and organisational road [e.g., 9, 11, 18].

Two examples help to illustrate this assertion. In the first one, Harper and Sellen studied why a new computer intranet at the International Monetary Fund was infrequently used [9]. The network was designed to facilitate sharing of the economic data files used to compile economic reports, and should have made the process of report generation easier. The authors found however that each report's genesis lay in individual economists focusing on his/her own particular area of expertise, compiling the statistics that would underpin the final report, work Harper and Sellen characterise as 'judgment.' Only at a later stage in the workflow, characterised as 'collaboration' and at which the reports are drafted, were these data deemed 'solid' enough to be included in the IMF's database. Knowledge generation at the IMF therefore consisted of at least two distinct processes. First, there was an initial division of labour amongst team members, in which economists worked on their own data, and second, an emergent stage, termed collaboration, in which team members communicated with each other to produce the final report. Harper and Sellen found that the new IMF intranet was not supportive of the first task. As will be described below, this conclusion bears some similarity to our analysis of the DWEL workflow.

A second example of unpredictable adoption is drawn from Weatherley et al.'s [23] analysis of an HTML-based anchored discussion forum, the Digital Document Discourse Environment (D3E). In D3E, an electronic document is provided with embedded anchors that link specific elements of that document to discussion threads. The D3E user can see both the parsed document, and the threaded discussions, either in overlapping windows or in side-by-side frames. The authors examined two cases of

D3E use in which a number of reviewers under the guidance of an editor reviewed complex electronic educational resources. One initial design supposition was that D3E would permit reviewers to pursue collaborative, threaded, asynchronous discussions of each component of the resource before coming to a conclusion regarding its validity. What was found to occur in practice, however, was cooperative behaviours: rather than initiating threaded discussions with their colleagues, each reviewer posted comments to threads that no other reviewers had posted to. This appeared to be done with reference to the shared visual outline of the review process afforded by the GUI, which showed who was reviewing each unit of the resource, and what units had yet to be reviewed. Thus while the intended technological affordance of D3E was to support collaboration in task construction, an emergent social affordance appeared to be that of cooperation in task allocation so as to minimise duplication of effort.

We have presented these two examples to suggest the complexity of the interaction between technology design and technology use. In the next section, it will be argued that implementing CLCD in DWEL involves similarly complex processes. To investigate these processes, we describe how DWEL members talk about their work and DWEL, and how they see CLCD as working. Particular attention will be paid to comments that indicate that DWEL members envision their online work as occurring in a seamless and integrated environment. In the pursuant discussion, this talk will be treated as evidence of the design requirements that DWEL members feel necessary to support their work in CLCD.

3 The Case Study: DWEL and Community-Led Collections Development

The DWEL project is the subject of ethnographic research that involves iterative cycles of data collection, analysis, and heuristic generation [18]. This research is aimed at supporting project evaluation for project management, and it therefore strives to generate recommendations for practical interventions as much as theoretical models. As presented in this discussion however, some general theoretical approaches are also emerging from the analysis. Close examination is being paid to the discourse and communication of DWEL members, which is being treated as an activity that constitutes the symbolic worlds in which DWEL members operate [e.g. 1, 10, 27]. From this perspective, everyday conversation becomes a rich repository of individually and collectively held notions of what CLCD, as a technology-supported social process, means to the people involved. The data analysed for this paper therefore include: transcriptions of video tapes of three days of DWEL meetings held in January, 2002; analysis of one year of DWEL documentation; and interviews with DLESE staff responsible for overseeing various aspects of DWEL project workflow. Note that in the following section, transcriptions from video have been redacted to reduce length, and where necessary pseudonyms have been used.

3.1 DWEL Workflow as a Complex Task

Before describing how DWEL members talk about their work, a brief description of that work itself will be provided.

DWEL members are engaged in a number of different tasks, and work with a variety of online tools that are distributed in both time and space. As such they are engaged in asynchronous distributed interaction. Two main tools are involved. First, intragroup communication is carried out in WebCT, a proprietary distributed groupware environment designed to support online classrooms and distance learning, that runs in frames in a web browser window [24]. WebCT claims to facilitate and 'transform' the learning process both for students (for instance by allowing on-demand access to course materials and assignments) and for course administrators (for instance by allowing remote uploading and downloading of course materials, and monitoring of student participation and progress). WebCT allows DWEL members to take part in discussion threads, post documents, and to message each other. The messages stay within the WebCT environment and cannot be broadcast to outside accounts.

Second, DWEL catalogue records are created through the DLESE Catalog System (the 'cataloguing tool'), a tool accessed on a server at the DLESE Program Center. The cataloguing tool permits DWEL members to enter bibliometric data as they apply to an online resource, such as title, URL, date and author (if they can be found!). The tool also requires users to complete a large number of sub-fields, either with free text or with choices from controlled vocabularies. These subfields permit the precise indexing (and therefore search and retrieval) of a resource according to a wide range of custom terms such as resource type (lab activity, curriculum, visualization, dataset etc.), scientific and educational content, audience or grade range, technical requirements, and so on. It is important to note that while catalogue record generation, and also catalogue record viewing, takes place within a web browser interface, catalogue records themselves are not static web pages in the common 'HTML' sense, but are generated dynamically from an underlying database.

In some cases, WebCT and the cataloguing tool have conflicting browser version requirements. For instance, the cataloguing tool is optimized for Netscape 6.0, but WebCT does not support 6.0 at all. If using Internet Explorer, version 5.5 or higher is necessary to use the cataloging tool, 5.5 however has a file download bug when running WebCT. Further, the cataloguing tool is in development and requires scheduled and unscheduled maintenance, and it is recommended that anyone using it should also keep open an e-mail window to be alerted of impending shut downs, to avoid losing work in progress. Finally, word processors may be used to draft text portions of catalogue records before they are entered into a record.

DWEL cataloguing workflow typically proceeds as follows. First, a browser is used to log on to the WebCT environment, to check for current tasks and instructions (Figure 1a). Second, a browser is then used to look for a suitable online resource (if a PDF is found, a PDF reader will be launched) (Figure 1b). Third, after the resource is located, a browser is used to access the cataloguing tool; and after checking that the resource is not already catalogued, cataloguing may proceed (Figure 1c). Fourth, cataloguing may also involve use of an e-mail utility (to be warned of shutdowns in the cataloguing tool) and a word processor (to compose the longer pieces of text that have to be entered into the cataloguing tool). In Figure 1d, there are five windows open: three browser windows (WebCT, the cataloguing tool, and the resource), an e-mail window (Telnet), and a word processor window (Microsoft Word). There are also five applications open (dial-up software, Adobe Acrobat, Microsoft Word, Telnet, Netscape Navigator), requiring, in addition to the OS, approximately 174 MB of RAM.

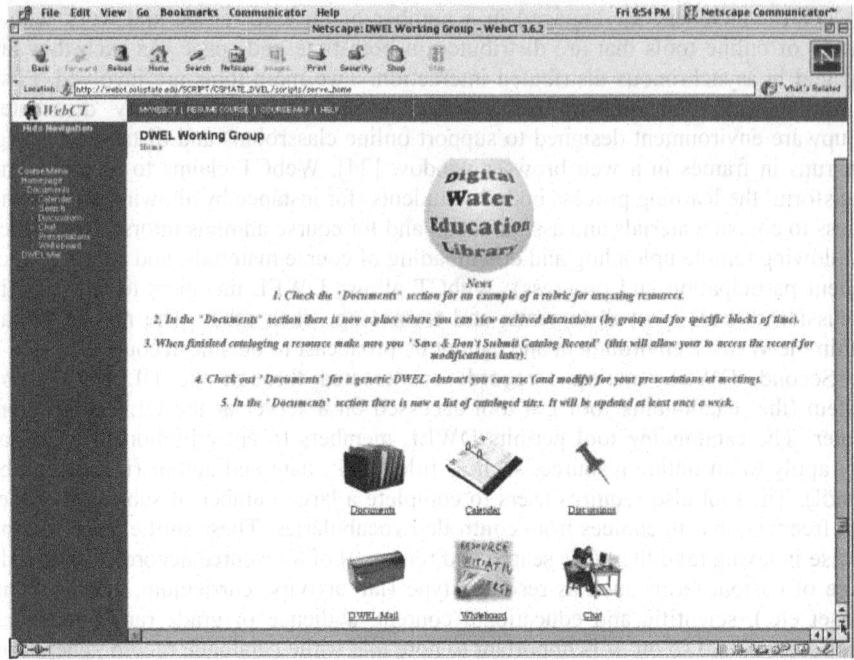

Fig. 1a. Checking workflow: The WebCT interface

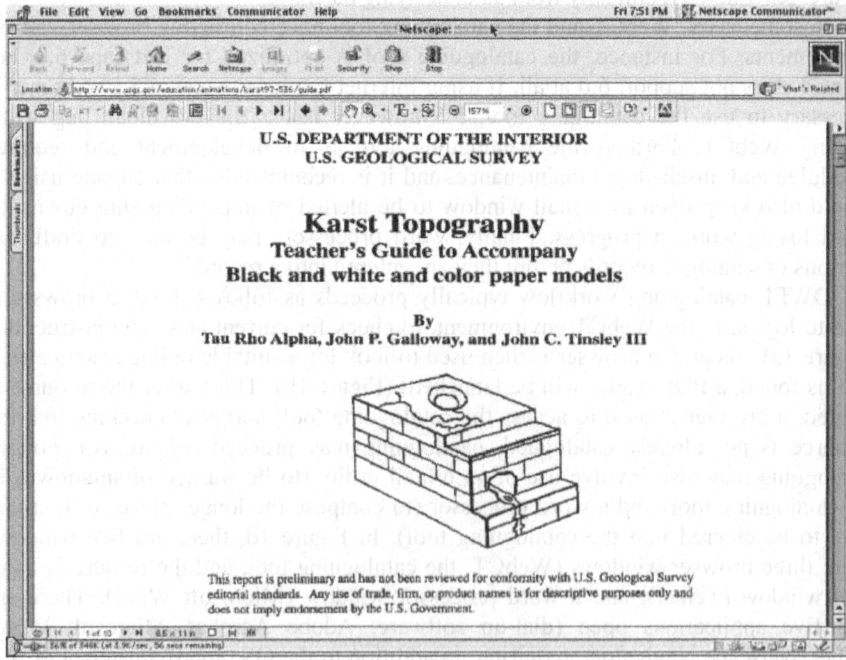

Fig. 1b. Locating a resource

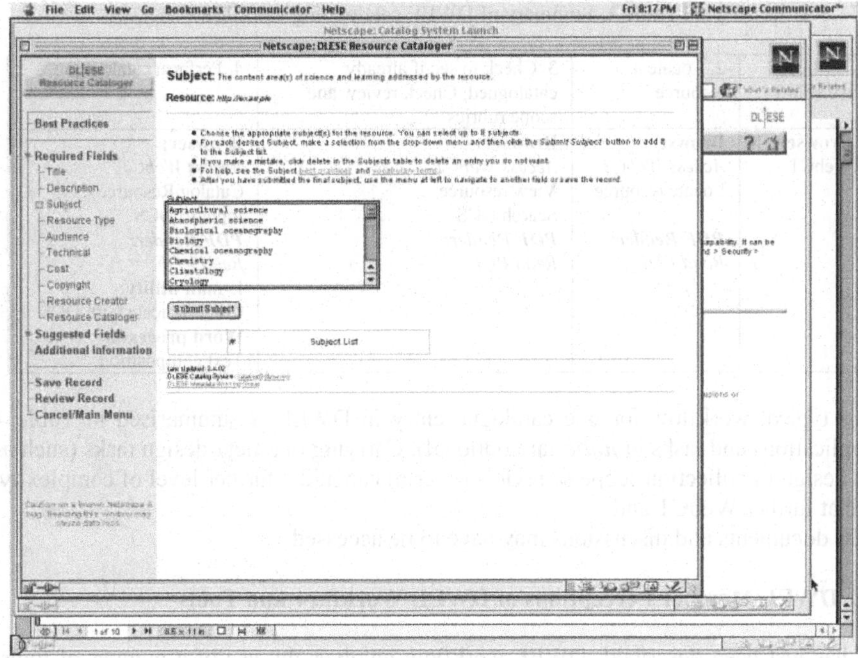

Fig. 1c. The cataloguing tool

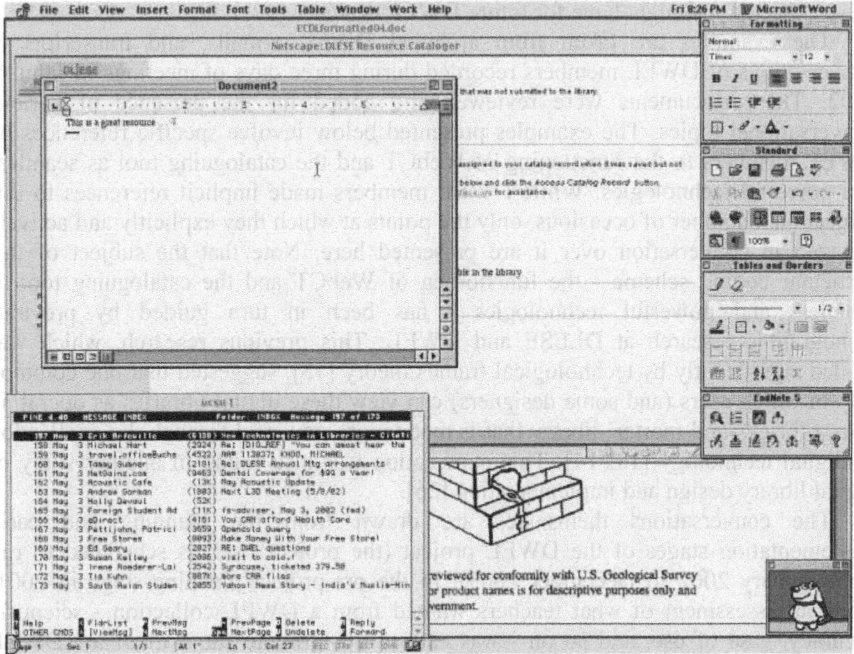

Fig. 1d. Cataloguing a resource

Table 1. Summary of DWEL cataloguing workflow

1. Check workflow	2. Locate a resource	3. Check to see if already catalogued; Check review and scope rubrics	4. Perform cataloguing
Browser: WebCT	**Browser:** *Access WebCT* Locate resource ***PDF Reader:*** *Read PDF*	**Browser:** *Access WebCT* View resource Search DCS ***PDF Reader:*** *Read PDF*	**Browser:** *Access WebCT* Catalog Resource Input to DCS ***PDF Reader:*** *Read PDF* **E-mail utility:** Communicate with DCS **Word processor:** Text composition

This typical workflow for one catalogue entry in DWEL is summarised in Table 1 (applications and tasks in *italics* are optional). Carrying out meta-design tasks (such as the design of collection scope or review criteria) can add a further level of complexity, in that further WebCT and
DCS documents and discussions may have to be accessed.

3.2 DWEL Member Perceptions of DWEL Workflow and Tools

As has just been described, DWEL workflow involves the use of a number of tools. We will now provide examples of how DWEL members talk about the functions of, and the relationships between these tools. We will then discuss what implications these expectations might have for future DWEL design.

The examples are taken from archived DWEL e-mails, and transcripts of conversations of DWEL members recorded during three days of meetings in January 2002. These documents were reviewed and coded for the presence of various conversational topics. The examples presented below involve specific references by DWEL members to the functioning of WebCT and the cataloguing tool as seamless and powerful technologies. While DWEL members made implicit references to this subject on a number of occasions, only the points at which they explicitly and actively engaged in conversation over it are presented here. Note that the subject of this particular coding scheme - the functioning of WebCT and the cataloguing tool as seamless and powerful technologies - has been in turn guided by previous ethnographic research at DLESE and DWEL. This previous research, which was guided significantly by technological frames theory [18], suggested that one common way in which users (and some designers) can view these digital libraries as operating is as a 'bricks-and-mortar' library that is made more powerful through the application of digital technology [13, 14]. This expectation was also found in another study of digital library design and implementation [26].

The conversations themselves are drawn from the planning and early implementation stages of the DWEL project (the project itself is scheduled to run from January 2002 to December 2003). In the pre-project planning stage in 2001, while an assessment of what teachers wanted from a DWEL collection - scientific accuracy, ease of use, and so on - was carried out prior to the start of the DWEL project, the operational interaction between DWEL tools was not explicitly defined (this is not surprising, given that designing and evaluating the CLCD process was part of the proposed DWEL research agenda). Some high level expectations of what the tools might offer were however apparent. Project e-mails sent in 2001 referred to the need to '*[d]evelop good communications structures within and between working groups*' (e-mail, 18/7/01), and to '*setting up our WebCT page (if we decide that is the best way to communicate and share resources)*' (e-mail, 19/9/01). The groupware-like features of WebCT were described in the latter e-mail, which asked:

> *Would you like to communicate with your group via the DLESE list serves set up for K-4, 5-8, 9-12, and informal* [groups] *or would you like us to set up a Project WebCT page with space for each working group to have threaded discussions, post resources, and have access to the discussions from the other working groups* (e-mail, 19/9/01).

During January 2002, these expectations – that WebCT could be used to share both communication and resources - were expressed in three days of DWEL face-to-face meetings. (The following comments, which have been rendered anonymous, are taken from transcripts of video tape recordings of these meetings). According to 'Andy,' for instance:

> Andy: [Talking of working group members] *What we want them is to be able to use WebCT, share the information, get feedback, so they're actually using all the tools that we think are going to be vital for communicating throughout the next two years ...*

> Andy: *Each of the teams will be responsible for the work being done in their group, for helping to make sure that it's organised, that people are on task, they're producing different things, and they're also sharing resources with each other, for example through the WebCT site and through the DLESE tools ...*

While Andy's second statement indicates an expectation that WebCT would enable the sharing of resources between DWEL members, the definition of what resources could be shared was unclear. It seems to assume that a resource in the cataloguing system (i.e. a catalogue record) would also be accessible and perhaps manipulable in the WebCT environment. Thus Chris, a DWEL designer, also assumed that DWEL catalogue records created on the cataloguing tool would be accessible in WebCT for discussion and critique by DWEL members. This is not in fact possible, as records in the cataloguing tool do not exist in a format easily accessible to browser software, and he was corrected by another member (Beth) in the following exchange:

> Beth: *I think that the most problematic aspect will be the fact that* [WebCT] *is a separate tool, a separate system from the cataloguing.*

> Chris: *So we could put a link to the cataloguing system in WebCT?*

> Beth: *The problem is, what you want is not a link to the cataloguing system, you want a link to that record, which is not a URL you can just point to.*

Another discussion debated whether WebCT archives were searchable in the same way that records are searchable in the cataloguing tool. This was raised because it was thought useful to be able to keep track of what DWEL members were talking about in WebCT. However, while records in the cataloguing tool are searchable across a range of controlled vocabularies, WebCT discussions exist only as text files with no controlled vocabularies attached, searchable only in terms of the text they contain. This realisation prompted a discussion regarding making sure that when WebCT users post to discussion threads, abbreviations are not used, and spellings are correct.

> Dave: *And Chris may correct me if I'm wrong – but I think with the WebCT you can run a search on text in any of the uh, letters or -*
>
> Chris: *- threaded discussions -*
>
> Dave: *- discussions that are put in there, so let's say if you're interested in assessment, you can type in the key word 'assessment,' and it allows you to just kind of lurk through the archives to see what these guys are talking about ... so if you want to put in things like a science standard, or a particular content topic or whatever, you have that ability just to see what they're doing ...*
>
> Chris: *So we should make sure that people don't use abbreviations for words.*
>
> Andy: *Right.*
>
> Chris: *So that the searches work.*
>
> Evelyn: *Right, that's a good point.*
>
> Beth: *And spelled correctly, good luck.*

This perception - that WebCT embodied at least some functions that were similar to the cataloguing tool, that would allow its use in managing catalogue records at various stages in the workflow - was also observed in a meeting of the thirty or so people who would form the various working groups within DWEL:

> Chris: [On the WebCT site we have a place] *where the working groups can post documents, web pages, anything they want, so if one person wants to upload a document for the rest of the group to download, this is where you have that capability ... and so I was thinking okay, put up web sites that you are considering, and you can put a little description so your co-workers can understand why you posted it there ...*
>
> Andy: *This is an area where you can share resources, look at different types of resources under consideration. One of the queries that we need to look at is what happens once you've reviewed something, where does it go, does it go into a file labeled 'reject,' or perhaps we need to look at this later on and make sure it gets into DLESE at some point, or it maybe suitable for DWEL but not for your age range, so we need to set up a series of bins here where resources could be kept, along with notes as to why they might be good for a particular group.*

Here, WebCT is seen as a repository for resources that 'might come in useful later,' a sort of 'holding tank' for DLESE. Chris notes that such a holding tank might be organised by posting lists of resources to WebCT. However, as a teacher in the group pointed out, given that there the project's goal was to generate five hundred resources, plus a large number of 'also rans' that might be of interest to other collections:

> Teacher: ... *if we're all doing this, we're going to have tons of sites. In that search thing [i.e. the WebCT search tool] will we be able to search and see whether somebody else has looked at a site?*

Chris replied, '*As long as we have it in HTML format, then it's searchable,*' but this assertion was then modified by Beth:

> Beth: *Wait a minute, I think that it's very important to realise that there's two tools that you're going to have to use in this process. One is WebCT, which is really your communication, collaboration, and hopefully coordination tool. Another one is the DLESE catalogue system, and this is not only where you enter the metadata for the resource that you're considering, but there are certain facilities within that to tell you that someone's already grabbed this resource.*

As a DLESE project member put it, at least the DLESE catalogue system had been designed to try and catch duplicate catalogue records; '*I would not,*' she told the audience, '*recommend you trying to do that [i.e. track duplicate records] just within the confines of WebCT, you'll step all over one another and duplicate the work.*'

3.3 Summary of Observations

We suggest that these examples of conversation illustrate that DWEL members often do not distinguish between the functionalities of WebCT and the cataloguing tool, even though these are separate tools. Both are perceived to enable somewhat similar functions. WebCT in particular is seen as providing, in integrated fashion, both communication, and also the means to manage cataloguing workflow. Further, the potential of the cataloguing tool to manage and track workflow was overlooked.

4 Discussion

The preceding section presented excerpts from DWEL members' conversations that evidenced an expectation of integration across various DWEL tools. In practice, as has also been described, the DWEL workflow is complex, and involves the use of a number of separate tools. It was therefore concluded that DWEL members' expectations of tool integration were not being fully realised (or even possible) in practice. A related conclusion also suggested itself: that if DWEL members had high expectations of the tools that were at least partly unfounded, they might also find the tools harder to use than they expected. (These initial conclusions gained in significance when monitoring of the DWEL members' use of WebCT and the cataloguing tool showed that members were participating unevenly, and some hardly at all. A subsequent questionnaire, partly informed by the research described here, suggested that many DWEL members were experiencing difficulties in using the tools (either separately or in combination), especially in pursuit of the task of cataloguing described in Section 3 (above). This research will be reported at a later stage.)

In this section we address therefore (a) short-term strategies for integrating WebCT and the cataloguing tool as they are currently configured, and (b) the longer term development of a groupware layer that will sit on top of a future releases of the cataloguing tool.

4.1 Short-Term Support Measures for DWEL

One strategy involves generating paper documentation to simplify the workflow for participants. A number of studies have found paper to provide significant support for complex individual and group tasks [e.g., 16, 19, 20]. Following the initial analysis presented above, and a series of telephone conferences and small meetings involving DWEL designers, concept maps of workflow and task allocation have been produced, and will be further developed. A more explicit calendar of deliverables has also been drafted. Supplementary support documentation for the cataloguing tool, such as structured worksheets for making notes while cataloguing, and a step-by-step outline with screen shots, is being considered. It is hoped that these and other measures will help participants to develop their understanding of CLCD workflow. Providing paper documentation for some of the tasks that require accessing and scrolling through long documents can lessen the electronic access load.

Additional training in the capabilities of the cataloguing tool is also suggested, as it has many features that have the potential to fulfill the requirements DWEL members have been talking about. For instance, participants have expressed the desire to view other participants' work, and to have a way to sort and organize catalog records into a variety of groups. Since viewing catalogue records in WebCT is not possible, participants will be informed of and encouraged to use features of the cataloguing tool that allow all members to view the entire collection in addition to their own work. Individuals will thus be able to work independently in selecting and cataloging their own resources, but also to view (but not edit) the work of others. Sorting on a particular concept (e.g. a working group name) can be done if participants insert their working group name into their original catalogue record, and there are other search strategies available in the DCS that could facilitate discussions about scope and content. Finally, the idea of a 'holding tank' - that is, of a storage place for records not suitable for one working group but possibly suitable for another group, or for DLESE - is also possible in the tool, where records whose fate is as yet unknown can be stored indefinitely away from the workflow in one searchable location.

4.2 Long Term Design Considerations for the Cataloguing Tool

This analysis also provides input for future development of the cataloguing tool, which was designed to help coordinate distributed collections development by community members working independently, rather than collaboratively. While the web-based nature of the tool fully accommodates distributed cataloging and collection building, social and community interaction needs were not part of the original design. This case study has revealed a number of requirements for possible expansions of the tool. A new module could be built to support the communication functions that collection building requires. This module would interact with member's regular email accounts using email groups that also archive as threaded discussions accessible from the tool (an HTML page). Participants would be aware of new messages via their usual email and could choose to store messages locally, or rely on the archive. Hot links to the email group addresses, individual members and support personnel would also be available. Document sharing, so that files can be attached, viewed and downloaded from the module would be enabled. The DLESE website already supports a posting tool; expanding this to handle document files and images may be a reasonable extension of this tool. The cataloging tool would be much improved by adding a spell-checking and character count enforcement to the free-text fields in the cataloging tool. A „smart" alert feature is envisioned, such that any users currently in the system could be sent an alert message at any time by the DLESE Program Center, to warn them of unscheduled shutdowns of the cataloguing tool.

Over time, integrating these features into the cataloguing tool will reduce the number of applications that must be run simultaneously, eliminate version conflicts between tools, and minimize the number of new environments necessary to perform the cataloging and communication tasks of collection building. While the degree of integration envisioned by DWEL members is perhaps not technologically feasible, at the same time CLCD involves complex tasks and new skills, and is important that DWEL, and other projects that rely on volunteer educators, provide the workspace and support that makes meeting CLCD work commitments as easy as possible.

In summary, drawing upon the observation, recording, and analysis of communication within the DWEL project, the research presented in this article has generated a number of implemented and potential suggestions for managing the CLCD efforts in DWEL, as well as more general design guidelines for tools to support distributed community-based collection development in digital libraries.

5 Conclusion

This paper has described the perceptions of the tools involved in community-led collections (CLCD) design amongst members and designers in the DWEL project. We noted how before the project commenced, there was little formal discussion of the precise structure of project architecture. DWEL staff considered communication needs, while DLESE Program Center staff considered record creation and management needs. We described how in practice DWEL workflow emerged as a series of tasks that must be accomplished with a range of different tools.

In contrast to this heterogeneous CLCD architecture, we described how on occasions DWEL members talk about CLCD as being managed in a relatively integrated fashion, often within just one tool (WebCT). This description was based on an analysis of how DWEL members talk amongst themselves about the tools they are using for CLCD. The findings from this analysis were used in turn to generate requirements for the future development of these tools, that address other emergent findings from DWEL that indicate that some users are finding the prototype CLCD architecture complex or difficult to use.

What implications do these findings have for the wider digital library community? One important outcome lies in its description of CLCD itself. DLESE is a major actor in the development of digital libraries in the United States, and as the focus of building DLESE expands from the contributions of individual records to include the support of numerous sub-collections for wholesale accessioning, it is becoming increasingly important to understand how to technologically support these new communities. As has been emphasised, as the process of CLCD is prototypical, design and management issues will only emerge in implementation and interaction. As the foundation of DWEL and DLESE growth is based on users as contributors, understanding how to facilitate the development of user-developed thematic sub-collections via CLCD is central to other digital library communities engaged in similar processes.

A second important outcome lies in reporting the desirability of providing ongoing monitoring and analysis of large scale digital library implementations, in this case CLCD. While the analysis has drawn upon theoretical roots (such as technological frames theory), and has been implemented through inductive ethnographic methodologies that are also theoretically informed, its fundamental aim has been to generate practical recommendations for implementation. Its utility lies therefore as much in interventions in messy local practice, as in the generation of tidy theory.

Acknowledgements. The authors thank Ed Geary, Bryan Aivazian, and other DWEL members for cooperating with this research. This research made possible by NSF Grant # DUE-0121724.

References

1. Anderson, R.: Work, ethnography and system design. Rank Xerox Research Centre, Cambridge (1996)
2. Barley, S.: Technology as an occasion for structuring. Admin. Sci. Quarterly **31** (1986) 78-108
3. Bijker, W.: Of bicycles, bakelites, and bulbs. Toward a theory of sociotechnical change. Cambridge, MA: The MIT Press (1995)
4. DeSanctis, G., Poole, M.: Capturing the complexity in advanced technology use: Adaptive structuration theory. Organization Science **5** (1994) 121-147
5. Ellis, C. Gibbs, S., Rein, G.: Groupware. Some issues and experiences. Communications of the ACM **34** (1991) 38-58
6. Fischer, G., and Scharff, E.: Meta-design: Design for beginners. Presented at DIS 2000, New York, 2000
7. Fjermestad J., Hiltz, S.: An assessment of Group Support Systems experimental research. Jnl Management Info. Systems **15** (1998-99) 7-149
8. Grudin, J.: CSCW: History and focus. IEEE Computer **27** (1994) 19-26
9. Harper, R., Sellen, A.: Collaborative tools and the practicalities of professional work at the IMF. Procs CHI,1995 122-129
10. Harper, R.: The ethnographic turn. Why is has come about and how to do it. Rank Xerox Research Centre, Cambridge (1996)
11. Heraclous, L., Barrett, M. Organizational change as discourse: Communicative actions and deep structures in the context of IT implementation. Academy of Management Jnl. (2001) **44** 755-778
12. Jackson, M.: The meaning of „communication technology“: The technology-context scheme. Communication Yearbook **19** 1996 229-268
13. Khoo, M.: Community Design of DLESE's Collections Review Policy: A Technological Frames Analysis. In Procs. ACM/IEEE JCDL (2001) 157-164.

14. Khoo, M.: Ethnography, evaluation, and design as integrated strategies. In: Constantopoulos, P., & I. Sølvberg (eds.)., Procs. ECDL 2001, LNCS **2163** Springer-Verlag, Berlin (2001) 263-274
15. Kling, R.: Social analyses of computing. Computing surveys **12** (1980) 61-110
16. Malone, T.: How do people organise their desks? Implications for design of office information systems. ACM Trans. Office Info Systems **1** (1983) 99-112
17. Mandviwalla, M., Olfman, L.: What do groups need? A proposed set of generic groupware requirements. ACM Trans. Office Info Systems **1** (1994) 245-268
18. Orlikowski, W., Gash, D.: Technological frames: Making sense of information technology in organizations. ACM Trans Info Systems **12** (1994) 174-207
19. Sellen, A., Harper, R.: Paper as an analytic resource for the design of new technologies. Procs CHI 1997 319-326
20. Star, S., Griesmer, J.: Institutional ecology, 'translations' and boundary objects. Social Studies of Science. **19** (1989) 387-420
21. Star, S., Ruhleder, K.: Steps towards an ecology of infrastructure. Presented at CSCW 94, Chapel Hill, NC
22. Walther, J.: Computer-mediated communication: impersonal, interpersonal, and hyper-personal interaction. Communication Research **23** (1996) 3-43
23. Weatherley, J. Sumner, T., Khoo, M., Wright, M., Hoffman, M.: Partnership reviewing. In Procs. ACM/IEEE JCDL (2002). In press.
24. WebCT. Corporate website: http://www.webct.com
25. WebCT. Leveraging technology to transform the educational experience. White paper. (2001)
26. Weedman, J.: The Structure of Incentive: Design and Client Roles in Application-Oriented Research. Science, Technology, and Human Values **23(3)** (1998) 315–345

A Study on the Evaluation Model for University Libraries in Digital Environments

Byeong Heui Kwak[1], Woochun Jun[2], Le Gruenwald[3], and Suk-Ki Hong[4]

[1] University library, Seoul National University of Education, Korea
kwak@ns.snue.ac.kr

[2] Dept. of Computer Education, Seoul National University of Education, Seoul, Korea
wocjun@ns.snue.ac.kr

[3] School of Computer Science, University of Oklahoma, Norman, OK 73069, USA
ggruenwald@ou.edu

[4] Dept. of Business Administration, KonKuk University, Chungju, Korea
skhong01@kku.ac.kr

Abstract. Advanced information technology has changed our society in various aspects. University libraries are also changing with the adoption of advanced information technology. Specifically, digital technology including the Internet has changed traditional university libraries in their operations as well as infrastructures. Traditional university libraries have stored and distributed scholarly information in printed media. However, most of current university libraries are hybrid libraries, which are dependent on digital media as well as printed media, and are based on both network facilities and physical facilities. The evaluation metrics developed for traditional university libraries are no longer adequate to evaluate current university libraries. This paper presents an evaluation of hybrid libraries. Based on the opinions of library experts and the previous works on the evaluation of both traditional and digital libraries, an initial evaluation model was developed, which consists of 8 categories, 33 items, and 84 indicators. The Delphi method was then applied to develop a valid evaluation model for university libraries. A survey was conducted 3 times for 50 balanced subjects among library-related professors, researchers, and senior university librarians. Based on the surveys' results, the categories, items, and indicators were modified to derive the new evaluation model, which consists of 7 evaluation categories, 35 items, and 92 indicators. The content validity of this model was confirmed through the survey results of 184 university librarians.

Keywords: Hybrid Library, Digital Library, Delphi Method

1 Introduction

Digital technology has changed the way in which scholarly information is distributed. Traditional university libraries are changing to networked hybrid libraries which collect, process, and distribute information in the form of digital media as well as printed media. As advanced information technologies are adopted, traditional university libraries require many changes in their facilities, management, and

M. Agosti and C. Thanos (Eds.): ECDL 2002, LNCS 2458, pp. 204-217, 2002.

services. Subsequently, they also require a new evaluation model that reflects these changes.

This research aims to develop an evaluation model of hybrid university libraries. To achieve the objective, in the first phase of the research, an initial evaluation model was developed based on the previous research on the evaluation measurements of both traditional and digital libraries. Through the survey results by the Delphi method [1], the final evaluation model was determined, which includes evaluation categories, items, and indicators. The rationales of this evaluation model are as follows. First, it should include indicators applicable to university libraries in digital environments. Second, it should include input, output, and effectiveness indicators to evaluate the effectiveness of the operations of university libraries. Third, it should consist of qualitative indicators as well as quantitative indicators to evaluate the service quality of university libraries. And fourth, it should encompass indicators to evaluate social responsibilities and functions of university libraries.

The organization of the rest of the paper is as follows. Environmental changes in university libraries are examined and discussed in Section 2. Previous works on evaluation models for digital libraries as well as traditional libraries are examined in Section 3. The initial and final evaluation models are presented in Sections 4 and 5, respectively. Finally conclusions and future research are provided in Section 6.

2 Research Background

2.1 Changing Environments of University Libraries

External environmental changes that university libraries confront can be largely divided into 3 parts: changes in information technology environment, changes in educational environment, and changes in social environment. The detailed factors of the changes in each part are shown in Table 1.

Table 1. External environmental changes and their factors

External Environmental Changes	Changing Factors
Changes in information technology	· Changes in accessing and using information · Accumulation, distribution, and recreation of information in cyber space · New ways of information services by information technology
Changes in educational environment	· Introduction of Cyber Campus, on-line education, and home school · Changes to more students-oriented education philosophy · Increased demand for continuing education and various educational programs
Changes in social environment	· Introduction to the knowledge-based society · Increase in diverse information needs · Competition with the differentiation of information services · Outsourcing of facilities management and other works

As the external environment of university libraries changes, it also affects the internal environment of university libraries. Internal environmental changes can be classified into 3 categories: changes in collection media, changes in working environment, and changes in service environment as shown in Table 2.

Table 2. Internal environmental changes and their factors

Internal Environmental Changes	Changing Factors
Changes in storing media	· Digitalization of storing media · Diversification of media · Multimedia
Changes in working environment	· On-line acquisition through networks · Technical processing by copy cataloging and shared cataloging · Automation systems (self-checkout and check-in) · OPAC (Online Public Access Catalog) and on-line search environment · Providing full text and multimedia information
Changes in service environment	· Changes in library service from just-in-case approach to just-in-time approach · Introduction of web-based digital information service · Introduction of remote on-line information service · Specialization, diversification, and customization of information

2.2 The Necessity of a New Evaluation Model for Digital Environments

The evaluation of traditional university libraries is focused on quantitative indicators and input-related indicators. However, these traditional measurements cannot reasonably evaluate the overall operations of university libraries in digital environments because of the significant gap between the evaluation indicators and the actual operations of university libraries. Today, most of the university libraries are in the type of hybrid, in which both printed media and digital media coexist. Also, both physical and networked facilities are utilized for the operations of university libraries. Therefore, a new evaluation model for hybrid libraries is required. It should reflect the changes in internal and external environments presented earlier in Section 2.1.

S. Sutton presented four types of libraries, traditional libraries, automated libraries, hybrid libraries, and digital libraries. In addition, it was expected that a library as a physical place would be changed to a logical entity [2]. Hybrid libraries can overcome the limitation of physical location by accessing digital information in other libraries through the network connectivity [3]. In addition, hybrid libraries should provide an integrated access approach, which can accommodate diverse media and technologies [4]. In most of the current university libraries, information exists in diverse forms and places. In addition to diverse media such as printed and digital media, information is in electronic networks as well as in physical libraries. Accordingly, library services and operations also become diverse [5].

The main purpose of this research is to develop an evaluation model for hybrid libraries. It consists of several measuring categories, items, and indicators, which are designed to accommodate external and internal environmental changes.

3 Previous Works

J. T. Jung introduced a comprehensive tool measuring user's satisfaction of libraries in digital environment. He developed two models providing objective and subjective measurements [6]. F. W. Lancaster explained the differences between the evaluation systems of traditional libraries and those of digital libraries and suggested indicators for the evaluation of digital libraries [7].

One Japanese Library Science and Information Department, in its research report, described the evaluation items for the web-based electronic information services [8]. Gary Marchionini, as the results of the PDL (Perseus Digital Library) Project, introduced 5 types of digital libraries, and suggested the necessity of diverse measurements and a long-range study on the evaluation of libraries [9].

Tefko Saracevic provides a conceptual evaluation model for digital libraries, and emphasized both the researcher's and librarian's perspectives [10]. Christine L. Borgman described digital libraries as an educational environment, and tried to identify the effectiveness of digital libraries based on the relationship between digital libraries and students' creativity [11].

B. Butternfield introduced the strategies evaluating the usability of digital libraries [12]. June P. Mead and Gary Geri, as a part of MoA (The Making of America) Project, introduced a conceptual mapping method to evaluate digital libraries [13]. Andrew Dillion suggested an evaluation method focusing on user interface [14]. However, all these new evaluation methods suggested by Mead, Geri and Dillion are conceptual, and cannot provide specific evaluation indicators. Erica B. Lilly presented three evaluation levels, intellectual, physical, and technological levels, for information resources in virtual libraries [15].

Even though abundant research on library evaluation has been conducted, a comprehensive library evaluation model in a digital environment, consisting of specific evaluation indicators, has not been developed.

4 Establishing an Initial Evaluation Model

For the development of an initial evaluation model, the evaluation measurements for both traditional and digital libraries were examined. The following are the sources that describe evaluation measurements of traditional libraries.

(1) International Federation of Library Associations (IFLA) [1]
(2) International Organization for Standardization (ISO) [16]
(3) American Library Association (ALA) [17, 18]
(4) Japan Association of National University Libraries [19]
(5) Japan Association of Private University Libraries [20]

The following sources describe evaluation measurements of digital libraries.

(1) MIEL2 Project [21]
(2) EQUINOX Project [22]
(3) Tefko Saracevic [23]
(4) John Crawford [24]

The evaluation measurements in the 9 references above were thoroughly examined to develop an initial evaluation model. The indicators of the references above were compared with one another. Through the review of theoretical validity, the initial evaluation model was derived as shown in Table 3. It consists of 8 evaluation categories, 33 items, and 84 indicators.

Table 3. The initial evaluation model

Categories	Items	Indicators
Library Plan	Goal Setting	• Validity of Library's Goal • Clearness of goal statement
	Library Plan	• Concreteness and appropriateness of establishing plan • Accomplishment of plan
Library Specialization	Objectives for Specialization	• Validity of specialization goal and strategy • Accomplishment of specialization objectives
	Specialized Collections	• Specialization level of books • Specialization level of non-books • Specialization level of library's DB
	Special Service Systems	• Management of special service
	Special Facilities	• Management of special facilities
Information Resources	Collecting Level of Books	• Number of monographs per student • Number of journal subscriptions per academic dept.
	Utilization of Books	• Number of borrowed books per student • Collection turnover (Annual borrowed books/total collections)
	Collecting Level of Non-Books	• Number of non-books • Number of Web DB
	Utilization of Non-Books	• Number of borrowing non-books per student • Utilization of Web DB
	Quality of Collections	• Increasing number of average information resources per student in the last 3 years • Average unit cost of purchasing information resources in the last 3 years • The ratio of discarded collection to increasing collection in the last 3 years
Information Usability Environment	Library Facilities	• Appropriateness of building and using information processing system • Appropriateness of digital information facilities • Appropriateness of user-oriented facilities
	Appropriateness of Reading Desks	• Number of students per reading desk • The ratio of open-shelf reading desks to total reading desks
	Access to Information Systems	• Convenience of using information systems • Convenience of accessing in-house info. resources • Convenience of accessing remote information • resources • Waiting time for using Internet • Number of computer terminals for information retrieval
	Network in Library (LAN Speed)	• Performance of backbone • Appropriateness of network structure • Number of nodes per student
	Network outside Library (Internet Speed)	• Capacity (speed) of exclusive line

	Information Systems Security	• Establishment of in-house firewall • Appropriateness of system backup • Stability of systems
	D/B Security	• Identification and authentication • Control of access • Application of DB protection technology
	Copyright Management	• Operations of copyright management systems • Management of library's own literary work and copyrights
Information Sharing	Participation in Info. Sharing Systems	• Number of uploading union catalog bibliographic data • Number of document delivery using inter library loan • Number of providing full-text (academic journals, dissertations) • Participation of cooperative buying foreign DB
	OPAC	• Number of OPAC users • Quality of OPAC data • Performance (response time, convenience) of • OPAC
	Library Homepage	• Quality of contents • Easiness and appropriateness of links and navigation • Connection of curriculum
	Interoperability	• Interoperability of print materials and digital materials • Interoperability of different DBs • Interoperability of different digital libraries • Level of integrated search
	Openness of Library	• Extent of library facility's openness • Openness of information resources to the community • Contribution rate to the community
Information Services	Information Providing Services	• Number of providing information (full-text, content, abstracts, index, SDI) • Timeliness of providing information • Accuracy of Providing information • User satisfaction with information
	Information Retrieval Services	• Number of information retrieval (OPAC, On-line, Internet) • Timeliness of information retrieval • Accuracy of Information retrieval • User satisfaction with information retrieval
	Electronic Reference Services	• Guidance of web-based electronic info. resources • Providing Web-based electronic reference services
	Utilization of Electronic Information Services	• Number of sessions per service (monthly) • Number of downloads per service (monthly) • Number of hits per service (monthly)
	User Education	• Number of implementing user educations • Evaluating of user education • Operating we-based user education program
Human Resources	Current Librarian	• Number of special librarians (by qualification) • Number of users per librarian
	Continuing Education for Employees	• Implementing continuing education in the last 3 years • The ratio of educated employees to total library employees

Budget	Library Budget	• The ratio of library budget to total university budget in the last 3 years • Appropriateness of budget for information-oriented projects in the last 3 years
	Information Material Purchasing expense	• Purchasing expense for information materials per student in the last 3 years

5 Developing a Final Evaluation Model

5.1 Research Process

The Delphi method [1] was applied to verify the content validity of the initial evaluation model. The objective of most Delphi applications is the reliable and creative exploration of ideas or the production of suitable information for decision making. The Delphi method is based on a structured process for collecting and distilling knowledge from a group of experts by means of a series of questionnaires interspersed with controlled opinion feedback. For the application of the Delphi method, a survey was conducted 3 times. Each survey questionnaire consists of detailed evaluation indicators. The relative importance of each indicator is measured by 5 items Likert scale [1].

5.2 Subjects

The Delphi method was applied to 50 subjects from the three different expert groups that have abundance experience and knowledge about university libraries: library-related professors, researchers, and senior university librarians. The detailed information on subjects and response rates is shown in Table 4.

Table 4. Survey subjects and return rates of questionnaire responses

Subjects	Size	Survey			Return Rates (%)		
		1st	2nd	3rd	1st	2nd	3rd
Digital library-related professors	8	8	7	6	100.00	87.85	75.00
Digital library-related researchers	12	12	10	10	100.00	83.30	83.30
Public university librarians (senior)	15	14	14	13	93.30	86.60	86.60
Private university librarians(senior)	15	12	11	10	80.00	66.60	66.60
Total	50	46	42	39	92.00	84.00	78.00

5.3 Analysis Results

The survey was conducted 3 times. However, in the second and third survey, the information on median and quartile range of each indicator was provided to the subjects in order to help them make decisions. Through the analyses of each survey's results, some items, and indicators were deleted, added, and combined as shown in Table 5.

Table 5. Modified contents in Delphi method

Survey	Contents	
	Deleted	**Added**
1st	• Appropriateness of reading desk • Number of students per reading desk • The ratio of open-shelf reading desks to total reading desks	• Metadata management • Preservation of digital resources • Providing web-based user help
2nd	The ratio of discarded collections to increasing collections in the last 3 years	• User convenience • Providing information service application forms thru online
		• Changing item title: goal setting & vision • Combing categories: human resources & budget

5.3.1 The First Survey's Results

The first survey's results are summarized by each group of subjects as shown in Table 6. The mean of each category is greater than 3 (the median of 5 items in Likert scale), and grand mean is 4. The results imply that the evaluation categories are valid [25]. The standard deviation of each category ranges from 0.48 to 0.62. It implies that the opinions among the subject groups are not significantly different.

As explained in the previous section, some item and indicators were deleted because their mean values were less than 3 (less important). Based on the first survey's results, some items and indicators were also modified. Several implications can be derived from the information in Table 6. For instance, all of the 4 groups provided high scores in the category of library budget. It implies that the library budget is considered more important than other categories.

Table 6. Results analysis of the 1st survey

Group \ Category		Plan	Special	Info. Res.	Info. Use.	Info. Shar.	Info. Serv.	Human Res.	Budget
Professors	Mean	4.17	4.04	3.66	4.08	4.07	4.22	4.41	4.35
	Std. d.	0.33	0.51	0.50	0.37	0.32	0.44	0.73	0.57
Researchers	Mean	3.83	3.75	3.14	3.80	3.62	3.75	3.77	3.93
	Std. d.	0.71	0.62	0.71	0.50	0.54	0.77	0.62	0.61
Librarians (Public U.)	Mean	4.19	4.00	3.70	4.05	4.13	4.21	4.31	4.51
	Std. d.	0.58	0.68	0.40	0.51	0.34	0.25	0.54	0.48
Librarians (Private U.)	Mean	4.46	3.90	3.69	3.84	3.95	4.10	4.19	4.22
	Std. d.	.037	0.58	0.54	0.58	0.53	0.59	0.49	0.45
Total (4.00, 0.56)	Mean	4.17	3.92	3.55	3.94	3.94	4.07	4.16	4.00
	Std. d.	0.57	0.61	0.59	0.51	0.48	0.57	0.62	0.56

5.3.2 The Second Survey's Results

According to the Delphi method, the second survey was conducted. The analysis results of the second survey are shown in Table 7. The mean of each category is greater than 3 (the median of 5 items in Likert scale), and grand mean is 4.03. It implies that the evaluation categories are valid. In addition, the standard deviation of each category ranges from 0.44 to 0.58. The range of standard deviations at this time is smaller than that of the first survey. The opinions among the subject groups were converging.

In addition, based on the analysis results, some evaluation categories, items, and indicators were modified as shown earlier in Table 5. For instance, the category of *library plan* was replaced with *Goal setting and Vision*, the term that many subjects suggested for the open question of the survey. Also, according to the subjects' opinions, the categories of *human resource* and *budget* were combined together.

Table 7. Analysis results of the 2nd survey

Group \ Category		Plan	Special	Info. Res.	Info. Use.	Info. Shar.	Info. Serv.	Human Res.	Budget
Professors	Mean	4.22	4.02	4.03	4.11	4.08	4.32	4.38	4.33
	Std. d.	0.21	0.29	0.33	0.16	0.28	0.35	0.43	0.46
Researchers	Mean	3.78	3.71	3.28	3.96	3.72	3.79	3.81	4.07
	Std. d.	0.77	0.70	0.69	0.48	0.46	0.74	0.62	0.55
Librarians (Public U.)	Mean	4.27	4.05	3.73	4.06	4.04	4.16	4.35	4.44
	Std. d.	0.44	0.59	0.35	0.51	0.47	0.32	0.48	0.56
Librarians (Private U.)	Mean	4.32	3.96	3.64	3.97	3.88	3.95	4.18	4.28
	Std. d.	0.43	0.57	0.57	0.45	0.52	0.65	0.59	0.46
Total (4.03, 0.53)	Mean	4.16	3.95	3.65	4.03	3.93	4.05	4.18	4.29
	Std. d.	0.54	0.58	0.55	0.44	0.47	0.56	0.57	0.52

5.3.3 The Third Survey's Results

The analysis results of the third survey are shown in Table 8. The mean of each category is greater than 3, and grand mean is 4.04. It implies that the evaluation categories are valid. In addition, the standard deviation of each category ranges from 0.40 to 0.55. As the three surveys continued, the standard deviations of the data set were reduced from 0.56, 0.53 to 0.49, and also the ranges of the standard deviations were shrinking, from 0.48~0.62 to 0.44~0.58, and 0.40~0.55.

Table 8. Analysis results of the 3rd survey

Group \ Category		Plan	Special	Info. Res.	Info. Use.	Info. Shar.	Info. Serv.	Human Res.& Budget
Professors	Mean	4.21	4.05	4.06	4.22	4.22	4.46	4.51
	Std. d.	0.21	0.15	0.13	0.10	0.16	0.14	0.17
Researchers	Mean	3.78	3.81	3.44	3.95	3.66	3.77	3.83
	Std. d.	0.68	0.60	0.56	0.49	0.56	0.67	0.42
Librarians (Public U.)	Mean	4.32	4.02	3.82	4.12	4.12	4.26	4.37
	Std. d.	0.32	0.60	0.28	0.40	0.31	0.21	0.44
Librarians (Private U.)	Mean	4.52	3.89	3.73	4.10	3.97	4.12	4.29
	Std. d.	0.21	0.62	0.55	0.38	0.50	0.67	0.50
Total (4.04, 0.49)	Mean	4.21	3.93	3.73	4.08	3.97	4.11	4.22
	Std. d.	0.51	0.55	0.48	0.40	0.47	0.55	0.48

In addition to the survey results, a further analysis was conducted to identify the highest ranked indicators. The analysis results of the highest ranked indicators also supported the content validities of the evaluation categories, items, and indicators developed by Delphi method.

5.3.4 A Final Evaluation Model

According to the analysis results of the 3 surveys, a final evaluation model was developed. The evaluation model consists of 7 evaluation categories, 35 items, and 92 indicators as shown in Table 9. The weight of each category comes from the relative mean values of each category in the third survey. This new evaluation model can be utilized to evaluate hybrid libraries. Its content validity was confirmed through the survey results of 184 university librarians. The detailed results are shown in [25]

Table 9. The final evaluation model developed by the Delphi method

Categories (Weight)	Items	Indicators
Goal Setting and Vision (13.12%)	Goal Setting & Vision	• Validity of library's goals • Appropriateness of middle and long-term development plan
	Library Plan	• Concreteness and appropriateness of establishing library plan • Accomplishment of library plan
Library Specialization (13.38%)	Objectives and Strategies for Spec.	• Validity of specialization objectives and strategy • Scheme and feasibility of specialization plan
	Specialized Collections	• Specialization level of information resources (book, non-book, web resources) • Utilization of specialized resources • Specialization level of library's DB
	Special Service Systems	• Management of special service • Utilization of special service
	Special Facilities	• Management of special facilities • Utilization of special facilities
Information Resources (15.61%)	Collecting Level of Books	• Number of monographs per student • Number of journal subscriptions per academic dept.
	Utilization of Books	• Number of borrowing books per student • Collection turnover (Annual borrowing books/ total collection)
	Collecting Level of Non-Books	• Number of non-books • Number of Web DB • Number of e-journals
	Utilization of Non-Books	• Number of borrowing non-books per student • Utilization of Web DB • Utilization of e-journals
	Quality of Information Resources	• Growth of average information resources per student in the last 3 years • Average unit cost of purchasing information resources in the last 3 years • Accuracy, completeness and consistency of DB quality
	Metadata Management	• Propriety of metadata management system • Application of metadata standards

	Preservation of Digital Resources	• Propriety of digital resource preservation • Maintaining permanency of digital resources
Information Usability Environment (12.83%)	Library Facilities	• Appropriateness of building and using information processing systems • Appropriateness of digital information facilities • Appropriateness of user-oriented facilities
	Access to Information Systems	• Convenience of using information systems • Convenience of accessing in-house information resources • Convenience of accessing remote information resources • Waiting time for using the Internet • Number of computer terminals for information retrieval
	Network in Library (LAN Speed)	• Performance of backbone • Appropriateness of network structure • Number of nodes per student
	Network outside Library (Internet Speed)	• Capacity (speed) of exclusive line
	Information Systems Security	• Establishment of in-house firewall • Appropriateness of system backup • Stability of system
	D/B Security	• Identification and authentication • Control of access • Application of DB protection technology
	Copyright Management	• Operations of copyright management systems • Management of library's own literary work and copyrights
Information Sharing (12.90%)	Participation in Info. Sharing Systems	• Number of uploading union catalog bibliographic data • Number of document delivery using inter library loan • Number of providing full-text (academic journals, dissertations) • Participation of cooperative buying foreign DB
	OPAC	• Number of OPAC users • Quality of OPAC data • Performance (response time, convenience) of OPAC
	Library Homepage	• Quality of contents • User-friendliness and appropriateness of links & navigation • Connection of curriculum
	Interoperability	• Interoperability of print materials and digital materials • Interoperability of different DBs • Interoperability of different digital libraries • Level of integrated search
	Openness of Library	• Extent of library facility's openness • Openness of information resources to the community • Contribution rate to the community
Information Services (16.66%)	Information Providing Services	• Number of providing information (full-text, content, abstracts, index, SDI) • Timeliness of providing information • Accuracy of providing information • User satisfaction with information

	Information Retrieval Services	• Number of information retrieval (OPAC, On-line, Internet) • Timeliness of information retrieval • Accuracy of Information retrieval • User satisfaction with information retrieval
	Electronic Reference Services	• Guidance of web-based electronic information resources • Providing Web-based electronic reference services
	Utilization of Electronic Information Services	• Number of sessions per service (monthly) • Number of downloads per service (monthly) • Number of hits per service (monthly)
	User Education	• Number of implementing user educations • Evaluating of user education • Operating web-based user education program
	User Convenience	• Providing web-based user help • Providing information service application forms online
Human Resources & Budget (15.48%)	Current Librarian	• Number of special librarians (subject specialists, computer managing librarian) • Number of users per librarian
	Continuing Education for Employees	• Implementing continuing education in the last 3 years • The ratio of educated employees to total library employees in the last 3 years
	Library Budget	• The ratio of library budget to total university budget in the last 3 years • Appropriateness of budget for information-oriented projects in the last 3 years
	Information Material Purchasing expense	• Purchasing expenses for information materials per student in the last 3 years

6 Conclusions and Further Research Issues

With the rapid development of information technology, education and research environments in universities have been changed. One of the phenomena is the advent of information technology-oriented libraries. Traditional university libraries have adopted information technology to overcome the limitations of library services that were based on printed media and physical facilities. Through the adoption of digital media and network facilities, traditional university libraries are being transformed to digital libraries. However, most of the current university libraries are in the type of the hybrid library, in which the characteristics of both libraries coexist.

In spite of the rapid change of university library environments, research on the evaluation metrics for the hybrid library has not been sufficiently conducted. Therefore, the paucity of the research on this area is a growing concern. This research was conducted to develop an evaluation model of university libraries in digital environments. Based on the opinions of library experts and the previous works on the evaluation of both traditional and digital libraries, an initial evaluation model was developed which consists of 8 categories, 33 items, and 84 indicators.

The Delphi method was applied to develop a valid evaluation model for university libraries. A survey was conducted 3 times for 50 balanced subjects among library-related professors, researchers, and senior university librarians. During the first and second survey processes, some categories, items, and indicators were modified.

During the third survey, the opinions among subjects were converged. The new evaluation model that consists of 7 evaluation categories, 35 items, and 92 indicators was finally developed. The content validity of this model was confirmed through the survey results of 184 university librarians.

Our immediate research issue is to extend our evaluation model to various types of libraries such as public library, etc. Also, for those types of libraries, it is interesting to develop or investigate validation methodologies for evaluation models other than the Delphi method.

References

[1] Ziglio, E. (1996) The Delphi Method and Its Contribution to Decision-Making, In M. Adler and E. Ziglio (Eds.), Grazing into the Oracle: The Delphi Method and Its Application to Social Policy and Public Health. London: Jessica Kingsley Pub.

[2] Sutton, Stuart A. (1996), Future Service Models and the Convergence of Functions: The Reference Librarian as Technician, Author and Consultant, In Kathleen Low [ed.]. Roles of Reference Librarians: Today and Tomorrow. New York: The Haworth Press.

[3] Oppenheim, Charles and Smithson, Daniel (1999), What is the hybrid library?, Journal of Information Science, 25(2), 99.

[4] Rusbridge, Chris (1998), Towards the Hybrid Library, D-Lib Magazine, http://www.dlib.org/dlib/july98/rusbridge/07rusbridge.html

[5] Ojiro, K. (2000) Designing and Building TDL (Titech Digital Library): Seeking a Digital Library, Journal of College and University Libraries, No.58, 1-15.

[6] Jung, Jin Taek (1997), Measuring User Success in the Digital Library Environment, Ph. D. Dissertation, Drexel University, USA.

[7] Lancaster F. W. (1997), Evaluation in the Context of the Digital Library, In Toward a World Library: 19th International Essen Symposium. ed. by Ahmed H. Helal, Joachim W. Weiss. Essen: Essen Univ. Library.

[8] Graduate School of Library and Information Science Keio Univ., (1999) Electronic Information Services and Their Evaluation Frames in University Libraries. School of Library and Information Science Keio Univ.

[9] Marchionini, Gary (2000), Evaluating Digital Libraries: A Longitudinal and Multifaceted View, Library Trends, 49(2), 304~333.

[10] Saracevic, Tefko (2000), Digital Library Evaluation: Toward an Evaluation of Concept, Library Trends, 49(2), 350~369.

[11] Borgman, Christine L. et al. (2000), Evaluating Digital Libraries for Teaching and Learning in Undergraduate Education: A Case Study of the Alexandria Digital Earth Prototype (ADEPT), Library Trends, 49(2), 228~250.

[12] Buttenfield, B. (1999), Usability Evaluation of Digital Libraries, In Digital Libraries: Philosophies, Technical Design Considerations, and Example Scenarios. ed. by David Stern. New York: Haworth Press.

[13] Mead, June P. and Gay, Geri. Concept Mapping: An Innovative Approach to Digital Library Design and Evaluation. http://edfu.lis.uiuc.edu/allerton/95/s2/mead/mead.html

[14] Dillon, Andrew. Evaluating on Time: A Framework for the Expert Evaluation of Digital Library Interface Usability. http://www.slis.indiana.edu/adillon/web/IJHCI99.html

[15] Lilly, Erica B (2001). Evaluation the Virtual Library Collection, In Library Evaluation: A Casebook and Can-Do Guide. ed. by Danny P. Wallace, Connie Van Fleet. Englewood: Libraries Unlimited, Inc., 165~182.

[16] International Organization for Standardization, ISO 11620 (1998): Information and Documentation - Library Performance Indicators, Geneve: ISO.
[17] Association of College & Research Libraries (1989), Standards for University Libraries: Evaluation of Performance, College and Research Libraries News, 50(8), 679-691.
[18] Association of College & Research Libraries, Standards for College Libraries 2000 Edition, http://www.ala.org/acrl/guides/college.html
[19] Fujiwara Hideyuki et al., (1993), Self-Evaluation of Library Services and Practices at Japanese University Libraries, Journal of College and University Libraries, No. 42, 66-73.
[20] Japan Association of Private University Libraries (1999), A Guideline to Self-Inspection Evaluation Method, Tokyo: JAPUL.
[21] Brophy, P. and Wynne, P. M. (1997), Management Information System and Performance Measurement for the Electronic Library: eLib Supporting Study (MIEL2) Final Report. Preston: Univ. of Central Lancashire.
[22] Brophy, Peter et al. (2000), EQUINOX: Library Performance Measurement and Quality Management System: Performance Indicators for Electronic Library Services. http://equinox.dcu.ie/reports/pilist.html
[23] Saracevic, Tefko (2000), Digital Library Evaluation: Toward an Evaluation of Concept, Library Trends, 49(2), 350~369.
[24] Crawford, John (2000), Evaluation of Library and Information. London: Aslib.
[25] Kwak, Byeong Heui (2002), A Study on Developing Evaluation Indicators of University Libraries in Digital Environment, Ph.D. Dissertation, Chung-ang University, Seoul, Korea.

Renardus: Following the Fox from Project to Service

Lesly Huxley

Institute for Learning and Research Technology, University of Bristol,
8-10 Berkeley Square, Bristol BS8 4JR, UK
lesly.Huxley@bristol.ac.uk

Abstract. The Renardus academic subject gateway service in Europe was launched in April 2002. The author first presented the challenges facing this pan-European collaborative project at ECDL 2000. This paper identifies the progress made in information, technical and organisational developments and deployment since Lisbon 2000, presents the results of evaluation activities and outlines the challenges, setbacks and successes for Renardus transition—in June 2002—from project to service.

1 Introduction: The Renardus Project

The Renardus academic subject gateway service in Europe[1] originated as a project under the European Union's IST 5th framework programme[2]. Its name determined the fox logo and other branding that have helped to maintain a high project profile. The author outlined the challenges facing partners from seven European countries, and the immediate workplan for this collaborative pan-European project, at the European Conference on Digital Libraries 2000 in Lisbon[3]. In April 2002, following several months of testing, pilot operation and evaluation, partners formally launched the Renardus broker service. As planned, it provides a single, multilingual user interface for cross-searching and cross-browsing distributed metadata collections held by twelve participating subject gateways across Europe, which currently serve Renardus with over 65,000 records. Based largely on existing technologies and standards, the Renardus project has nevertheless demonstrated some forward-thinking work in the areas of classification cross-mapping and cross-browse navigation and, through evaluation, provided some useful insight into users' perspectives on design and use of complex information systems.

As project funding draws to a close, this paper reviews the progress made by partners against information, technical and organisational aims and highlights key findings from the evaluation programme. The new opportunities, challenges and potential solutions for members of the Renardus Consortium during the transition period from project to service operation are also indicated. Together these experiences provide a rich source of information that may be used to underpin future research and development in key interoperability areas as well as to start to learn from practice in developing similar projects into services.

M. Agosti and C. Thanos (Eds.): ECDL 2002, LNCS 2458, pp. 218-229, 2002.

1.1 Renardus Context and Aims

The Renardus project built on late 1990s trends towards greater collaboration, standardization and interoperability between existing quality-controlled subject gateway services across Europe. Renardus' rationale was very simple: none of those individual services—whether at local, national or regional levels—could hope to discover, evaluate, describe and organise the ever-growing numbers of Internet resources to support their target communities in higher education learning and research. A move was foreseen from individual and potentially isolationist project approaches towards collaborative service models. For Renardus, this was manifest in development of a collaborative framework at European level that anticipated benefits for both service providers and end users alike. It recognised the importance of ensuring consideration of local and national cultural and linguistic requirements in international services and the need to strengthen, through collaboration, gateways' ability to maintain and sustain their services in future. Users would be able to benefit from a single interface to discover and connect to broader collections with greater provision for multi-lingual access and subject coverage than their local subject gateways.

With the twin imperatives of potential benefits for both users and participating gateway services, the Renardus project aimed to build the 'Renardus broker service'. The service was to develop and/or deploy technical and information interoperability tools and standards to (1) Provide cross-search and cross-browse functionality in a single Web interface; (2) Offer integrated views of metadata drawn from existing distributed European subject gateways and collections of other Internet-accessible resources; (3) Undertake experiments in metadata sharing and provision of multilingual access and (4) Develop a sustainable organisational and business model for an operational pan-European broker service.

The practical challenges of the collaborative framework became clear very early in the project, when two key decisions were made that would have significant impact on subsequent progress towards the aims listed above. As the author has described elsewhere[4], partners agreed firstly that the original concept of collaboration only between 'national initiatives' grounded in national libraries would not be viable in the evolving information landscape and secondly that a distributed architectural model was preferable to one of a centralised metadata repository. The first decision allowed for participation of single cross-disciplinary gateways such as DutchESS[5] from the National Library of the Netherlands; individual subject services based in universities such as Germany's Special Subject Guides[6] and national collaborative broker services from both university and library organisations, such as the Finnish Virtual Library[7], the UK's Resource Discovery Network[8] and, most recently, the Danish Subject Portal gateways[9]. Contributions from research organisations such as NetLab[10] in Sweden and ILRT[11] and UKOLN[12] in the UK were as valued as they were varied. The second—grounded in the need to allow gateways to maintain full control over their content and intellectual property rights—provided impetus to research and develop new ways of sharing and integrating metadata from distributed, heterogeneous services and presenting them in a coherent way to users (challenges still facing portal developers today).

1.2 Evaluation: A Quantitative Overview

Project partners had to ensure that evaluation and feedback played a key part in service development and enhancement to demonstrate both that it meets its planned aims and is also appropriate for target audience's needs. A discrete element of the project's workplan was dedicated to evaluation and testing, both from a user and service provider perspective. Project partners at Jyväskylä University in Finland took the lead in developing and implementing the evaluation plan, although the majority of other project partners were also involved. The evaluation plan covered three main deliverables for the final months of the project: (1) An end user evaluation programme (2) A review of the project's functional and technical specifications and (3) An evaluation of management, maintenance and availability procedures for the service. The latter two reports and recommendations have yet to be finalised at the time of writing, but their findings will inform the future running of the service.

The end user evaluation programme was undertaken in Autumn 2001 (September-November). Details of the programme methodology, and findings (including statistical tables and diagrams) have been published as a project deliverable report[13] and are briefly referred to at relevant points throughout this paper. The programme was based on a survey of potential end users (researchers, librarians, information scientists, academic staff) across Europe, delivered via the Web in five languages. Evaluators were invited, via announcements on the project Web site, the project's email newsletter and relevant mailing lists across Europe, to apply for a username and password to access the beta version of the service, undertake some specific research tasks and then complete the online survey. Project partners in five countries also hosted 17 structured evaluation workshops where, in addition to completing the survey in the same way as individual evaluators, participants were invited to discuss their experience of using Renardus in open forum.

A total of 296 questionnaires were completed, in 22 countries. Most responses were obtained in Finland (n = 84), Germany (n = 65), France (n = 50), The Netherlands (n = 31) and the UK (n = 27). Two thirds (68%) of the evaluators described themselves as librarians or information specialists; 11 % as researchers, lecturers or other academic staff; 10% students; 3 % computing staff; and 8% others. Almost half, 45% (n = 133) completed the questionnaire in workshops. The low numbers of academic and research users was disappointing and perhaps indicated a failing in the promotion of the evaluation programme. However, librarians and information specialists are also an important group of target users of the fully operational Renardus service, and their expert input was valuable. The majority of evaluators described themselves as regular Internet users. Of the 296 people who evaluated the Renardus beta system, about 80% said they would want to use Renardus again.

All quantitative evaluation questions asked evaluators to rate their answers on a four-point-scale: 'very clear'; 'clear' (or easy, or informative, depending on the question); 'unclear' and 'very unclear' (or difficult, or uninformative, again depending on the question). The distributions of responses were very similar in most of the evaluation questions, with a majority of responses at the positive end of the scale. For example, 10-40% of responses fell into the very clear/very easy/very informative category; 50-70% in the clear/easy/informative category. 10-20% of responses were in the unclear/difficult/uninformative group and 1-10% in very unclear/very difficult/very uninformative.

These distribution patterns were evident in questions relating to: the clarity of the Renardus service concept (presented in the *About Renardus* text); the correspondence of search results with search terms and the informative value of search results; the value of online help; ease of use of the advanced search function; terminology and language used throughout, visual clarity of the service and ease of navigation. The distribution was different for questions relating to the ease of use of the browsing functionality (very easy – 15%, easy – 44%, difficult – 35%, very difficult – 7%), which indicates that browsing was, for several respondents, a difficult feature to use. On the other hand, browsing was considered interesting and innovative and several evaluators commented positively on the graphical features offered to support browsing.

So to what extent has the Renardus project been able to meet the challenges set by its information, technical and organisational aims, and what did evaluators really think of the service? The remainder of this paper considers each of these challenges in turn with reference, where appropriate, to the quantitative and particularly qualitative evaluation findings and project partners' future plans.

2 The Project: Meeting the Information Challenges

Project work was scheduled to allow for parallel technical and information developments once an initial data gathering phase was complete. There were two key challenges for achieving coherent integration and presentation of metadata from distributed and heterogeneous collections: (1) Development of—and ability to comply with—a common metadata set for participating gateways, and (2) Deployment of a consistently-applied classification scheme specifically to meet the demands of cross-browsing. Subsidiary but no less challenging issues prevailed in notions of metadata sharing and multilingual information access.

2.1 Towards a Common Metadata Model

As other project partners have described in detail [14], a simple, eight-element common metadata model was developed for the pilot service, based on seven Dublin Core elements and one other. Mandatory elements were DC.Title, DC.Description, DC.Identifier, DC.Subject, whilst the remaining four elements DC.Creator, DC.Language, DC.Type and Country were strongly recommended. These content elements were supplemented by two administrative elements providing information about participating gateways and the original metadata records that formed the basis for the metadata served to Renardus: Subject Based Information Gateway (SBIG) ID and Full Record URL. The same model has been retained in the launched service. However, some participating gateways still struggle to provide content in all eight fields, leading to gaps in the information displayed to the user in anything other than the brief format of search or browse results. Provision of the full record URL and a dynamically-linked icon for the originating gateway are offered to users in the brief display and go some way to filling the gaps when viewing the full Renardus record, allowing users to connect from Renardus' results pages to the locally-held record where other, richer data may be discovered.

The end user evaluation survey asked about the quality and adequacy of information provided by the metadata presented in search and browse results: the majority of respondents reported that it *was* possible to assess the relevance of a resource from a reading of the metadata supplied, and that the metadata were informative or very informative, precluding the need to connect to the resource itself to decide. Even in the beta system, with a minimum common metadata set where not all elements were supported by all gateways, respondents' comments indicated general satisfaction with the results:

Remark 1: "The descriptions were particularly helpful as they give much more detailed information than search engines such as Google."

Remark 2: "I was quickly able to tell that some of my results … were irrelevant, thanks to the information about the record that was supplied"

There were, however, comments about the extent of information provided and the difficulty, particularly for users outside the world of library and information science, in identifying the relevance of some of the metadata elements. Some reordering of the way in which the elements were presented (eg placing of those most likely to be understood by any user, such as title, description and URL) was suggested to enhance users' understanding and assessment decisions.

2.2 Towards a Common Classification

Individual participating gateways have deployed and in some cases developed from scratch classification schemes that suit their target audiences. Indeed, some services use a number of subject-specific classification schemes within a single gateway where that service covers several subject areas. There are valid reasons for gateways to retain these, given that they can often provide richer and more meaningful representation and navigation of metadata records. However, in order to achieve one of the key innovative elements of functionality planned for Renardus, project partners needed to identify a mechanism that would allow a common classification scheme to be presented to end users for cross-browsing purposes, whilst minimising re-classification effort required of participating gateways.

The challenge of cross-browsing was met by a process of mapping participating gateways' classification schemes to a general scheme: the Dewey Decimal Classification (DDC)[15]. The DDC was selected for a number of reasons, including its ready availability (through WebDewey), regular maintenance, widespread use worldwide and multilingual versions. OCLC supported Renardus' use of the DDC in the Renardus research context, and expressed interest in its development for similar services.

Agreement on the classification scheme was an important but relatively small first step towards meeting the demands of implementing the cross-browsing functionality. Participating gateways would need to contribute more or less effort in mapping their own schemes to DDC, depending on the number, status and format of their existing records. To facilitate the process, Renardus partners adapted a mapping tool developed initially by the Carmen[16] project. Called CarmenX, the Renardus cross-mapping tool is Web-based, with a relational database 'backend'—the open source software mySQL—and a range of Web server applications and scripts. Staff from participating gateways use two windows in the CarmenX interface to display and navigate machine-readable versions of their local scheme and of the DDC, and a third window to enter mapping relationships and notes. Relationships can be specified at five levels of detail (eg broader, narrower, fully equivalent, minor overlap, major overlap) and are used to create mapping links in the user interface and to generate a DDC mapping for each resource in the local gateways' normalised Renardus database. Project partners have described our research into and development of cross-mapping mechanisms (eg Neuroth, 2001)[17] so I will not repeat those findings here. The cross-mapping processes underpinned the cross-browsing functionality identified as a key innovative feature of the planned Renardus service – but how did end user evaluators react when using the resulting beta cross-browse pages to locate resources?

The cross-browse functionality received most comments and suggestions in the evaluations, positive and negative. Some found it difficult to use, largely because of the layout of results presented as the user clicks through the vertical subject browsing tree. On the other hand the innovative graphical browsing feature, although slow to use in the beta system, was seen to be interesting and useful:

Remark 3: "The "Graphical Navigation Overview" is brilliant! I've never seen this type of presentation used in a www search engine before."

Some users recognised that the graphical overview could have limitations when viewing larger subject areas, but on the whole reported positively on this feature. The option to alternate between graphical and text-based views of the browsing structure were also appreciated, although there was some criticism of the use of DDC and its lack of relevant captions and structures for some subjects.

2.3 Towards an Extended Collaborative Framework: Metadata Sharing

Although not part of the original project workplan, some experiments with metadata sharing were scheduled after the first year, to explore enhancements and extensions to the collaborative framework beyond the project lifetime. If the Renardus service were to become popular, and the current trends in the information landscape continue to 'squeeze' the capacity and sustainability of individual gateways whilst moving towards greater interoperability, then post-project there may be a case for development of metadata sharing agreements amongst some or all of the participating gateways. The time available for metadata sharing experimentation was limited: the work therefore focused on sharing metadata focused on geographical subject headings. These were chosen as being of importance in a broad range of disciplines and also because the geographical entity (lake, river, mountain, region, etc) is always the same, regardless of how it may be described in different metadata schemes.

As with the classification cross-mapping, the decision on *what* metadata to share was only a first step: the challenge was in the method deployed to achieve metadata sharing. Once again, Renardus partners were able to adapt an existing tool—first developed to support work in the German SSG-FI (Special Subject Guides) —for the purpose. The full results of these experiments and the part they may play in any future service organisation will not be known until the project ends in June 2002, when the subset of participating partners report.

2.4 Towards a Multilingual Interface

Original project plans highlighted the potential for multilingual developments in a single user interface designed to access metadata records from gateways across Europe. However, after an initial project review, plans for multilingual developments were scaled down to what was realistically achievable within the project timespan. The user interface is currently available in five languages: English (default), French, German, Dutch and Finnish. 'Interface' includes all the help text, the instructions and explanations which appear on each page relating, for example, to search and browse functionality and the menu options.

A simple tagging mechanism has been developed to allow partners to translate text elements of the user interface, which is now available in five languages: The effort required to maintain these interfaces, including help and descriptive texts, graphical icons and dynamically created user feedback messages is not inconsiderable, and probably not sustainable in the longer term without specific support. To avoid user confusion, the option to select user interface language is available only from the home page: switching between languages in other sections of the service is not currently on offer.

At the time of writing, the DDC subject headings displayed in the browse pages are only available in English, regardless of user interface language selected. This will change shortly following agreement from OCLC that Renardus can have access to versions of the DDC in several different languages although not, unfortunately, each of those offered as options for the general user interface. Decisions are now being made on how best to implement the multilingual versions of the browsing structure balancing, on the one hand, added value for users with, on the other, the potential for user confusion and frustration because of the range of languages supported by DDC.

The evaluation questionnaire was offered in the same number of languages as the user interface. Respondents were asked to indicate languages they generally prefer to use on the Internet: the majority reported a preferred use of English (85.1%), with French, German and Finnish also being popular choices. Not surprisingly there was a strong correlation between preferred languages and the main languages of evaluation respondents, the majority of whom originated from the countries of project partner organisations. In the majority of these countries, English is also widely spoken. But there was also quite a lot of evidence in the evaluation responses for support for a multilingual service, given that other languages such as Spanish and Italian were also chosen, and these may be supported by the DDC.

Unfortunately, project partners' available effort for translation is limited. Whilst the tagging mechanism was used to develop the initial pilot interface, some parts of the broker service formally launched in April 2002 are currently available in English only. This includes a new About Us section which provides background details and access to the project document archive.

3 The Project: Meeting the Technical Challenge

In parallel with developments in Renardus' information infrastructure, project partners brought their technical expertise and experience to bear on meeting the challenge of developing an appropriate and sustainable system architecture, usable interface and supporting tools. An early review of broker models[18] showed that the majority of other similar aggregating services were using either HTML or Z39.50 protocols. In solving the problem of creating a distributed system architecture, both were deployed by the Renardus development team, led by NetLab in Sweden and DTV[19] in Denmark.

3.1 An Appropriate System Architecture

Participating gateways must set up and maintain a Renardus server with content and administrative data fields as described above. Z39.50 is the search and retrieval protocol used to perform queries against normalised, interoperable sets of highly structured data provided by each participating gateway in accordance with the common metadata model. A Renardus server comprises a content database and administrative data, and may be implemented in a number of ways: (1) Single server (services make their content available directly through a Z39.50 interface conforming to the Renardus profile); (2) Server with protocol conversion* (a Renardus-compliant Z39.50 front-end is directly interfaced to a native database server); (3) Joint server* (involving several services using a common joint server) or (4) Server to a broker with protocol conversion* (combining 2 and 3 above). Those marked * were not implemented in the pilot.

Given the collaborative aspects of the project organisation, a number of tools have been developed to support participating gateways in normalisation and quality control processes. For example, normalisation is achieved through use of a set of programs designed to import original gateway records and their subject mappings and export records from these in the required format (profile) for Renardus.

Participating services must also assure the quality of their normalised records and response times. The former requires some human effort in checking and simulating the user experience of following links from Renardus to the local gateway and taking remedial action to improve record quality, local browsing structures or their own user interfaces. An automated system also simulates the user experience and analyses it in a quantitative way, by submitting a range of simple and complex queries to each gateway's server and displaying the number of records returned and response times. A simple system and network monitoring package (Spong) is also available so that system administrators at local and Renardus level can check availability and quality of Renardus servers.

A full technical specification for the Renardus pilot system was published early in the project (available from the Renardus Project Archive[20], alongside details of technical requirements for participating gateways). An internal document detailing installation and maintenance procedures is available for current participating gateways and those that may join in future.

3.2 An Appropriate User Interface

User interface design and usability are key to the user experience of any electronic service and especially so in presenting a coherent and consistent view on distributed and heterogeneous resources. The pilot service interface design adapted some of the design elements of the original project Web site (eg the logo and stylesheet of font sizes and colours). It is worth noting that the design has not entirely successfully taken account of the different design needs of an information and news site (the original project Web site) and of an information discovery and retrieval service based on distributed components.

Nevertheless, evaluation programme feedback from users on the beta Renardus interface was in general positive and constructive. Some suggestions for improvement were made, some of which will be implemented before the project end. These included minor criticisms of spelling and translation mistakes, particularly of the help text, and the need for more clarity in descriptive text and instructions. Conversely, some found the texts and layout easy to understand and very useful:

Remark 4: "Presentation very clear due to the fact that the little part "About Renardus" presents simply and clearly the process of search used within this gateway. We know where we go!"

The distributed architecture does place some specific requirements for clarity on the service. Some evaluation respondents were confused about what the service offered and how they could best search and browse. Terminology (and particularly what was seen as library jargon) was also a problem reported by many evaluators, even though the majority of respondents were library or information specialists. Some also found the advanced search options confusing, again often as the result of the screen layout and descriptive text rather than the concepts themselves. The end user evaluation report details a list of suggested interface improvements which will be prioritised by project partners. Top priority changes are likely to be implemented in the current service before the end of the project lifetime, although some more complex enhancements may be deferred until further developments can be fully supported by a new organisational and business model.

4 A Service: Meeting Organisation and Business Challenges

In development of an academic subject gateway service in Europe, Renardus partners have found that the major challenges lie not in the information and technical aspects of the service (although it should not be understood by that that these were trivial). One of the biggest challenges has been development of an appropriate organisational structure and business model to sustain the service beyond the project lifetime. Exploitation plans are high on the European Commission's agenda in reviewing projects such as Renardus, and although very positive on most aspects of the project, reviewers have been at pains to point out the need to develop an adequate exit strategy for Renardus.

A successful workshop for potential participant gateways was held in Copenhagen in November 2001[21] to present requirements and procedures for participation. The Danish subject portal gateways subsequently joined Renardus and their records are currently accessible via the Renardus service. Several other gateways expressed an interest in future participation and an interest in the models and standards developed and deployed by project partners. However, most gateways not already participating in the project understandably raised questions about the service's sustainability and likely future organisational and business models.

Work on the organisational infrastructure focused initially on a description of tasks to be carried out by some kind of central Renardus organisation and by participating gateways in a not-for-profit Consortium arrangement. Associated costs were also estimated, and risks and alternative strategies explored. An interim Management Group has been working to develop proposals for further funding with a number of international organisations, as well as securing commitment from existing partners to continue to participate and serve their data to the service. There is a considerable issue that pan-European initiatives in the public sector face: the lack of any coherent organisation or network at European level that can take strategic decisions on service provision, collaboration and development funding for information services. There are networks such as Terena that support collaborative projects in areas of infrastructure, but their members are not in the business of directly supporting content provision. Each of the countries involved in the Renardus project has a distinct model of public funding for educational content projects and services, either through national libraries, research or education funding councils, education ministries or even individual educational institutions. It has therefore been difficult for Renardus partners to identify any one organisation that can be seen as representative of the interests of the varied 'players' across Europe.

The fragility of this particular part of the information landscape—one of the main drivers for the development of the Renardus project—has been demonstrated by the review of support for one or two participating gateways by their current funding organisations. National and other initiatives and organisations are being impelled to reconsider the decisions made in the 1990s, when subject gateways appeared to be the way forward. National libraries, in particular, are reviewing the way that they dispose of their limited resources and prioritise the services they provide. It is therefore as important now as at the beginning of the project that the Renardus Consortium is able to develop and sustain a robust organisational structure and business model.

Commitment from current partners is vital, and has been largely obtained, both for a 'lightweight' service model including server maintenance at SUB Gottingen and a CVS repository at NetLab; the time and effort of Management Group members in licence, partnership, coordination and dissemination activities, and data provision. Interest in the collaborative tools and cross-classification developments in the project has been demonstrated by commercial and not-for-profit organisations alike. The project will therefore undergo transition from project to service in June 2002 with a continuing collaborative model that is expected to evolve over the next twelve months from lightweight maintenance activity to further enhancement and development through a more robust and internationally-supported Consortium of educational and commercial organisations.

The project concludes with a new Management Group in place to take further funding negotiations forward. A Consortium Agreement is being drawn up for signature by all those interested in participation in this next phase of Renardus' maintenance and development. A Data Provider Agreement has also been drafted, for signature by those Consortium members that also provide data from their subject gateways or other services to Renardus. In the first instance, and for the foreseeable future, no membership fee will be levied for participation in the Consortium. Participating data providers will be expected to continue to maintain their Z39.50 servers, normalization and quality routines and any additional cross-mapping effort with their own resources (staff and funding). Support for maintenance of the central Renardus server and for assisting new gateways to join Renardus in future is being provided by one of the original project partners, SUB in Göttingen, Germany. Other partners have undertaken to provide effort and limited travel funding to support management and dissemination tasks for a further year. In the meantime, the Management Group and other Consortium members will be actively pursuing sponsorship or collaborative models to support continuing maintenance and development of Renardus.

The Project Archive, with links to all public deliverables, articles and reports, is available from the About Us[22] section of the new service. Service news will also be posted there so that interested parties in the research and user communities can 'follow the fox' as progression from project to service is achieved.

References

1 Renardus academic subject gateway service in Europe. Renardus Consortium. <URL http://www.renardus.org/>

2 Information Society Technologies (IST) 5th framework programme. European Commission. <URL http://www.cordis.lu/ist/home.html >

3 Huxley, Lesly (2000). Follow the Fox to Renardus: An Academic Subject Gateway Service for Europe. In J Borbinha and T Baker (Eds), ECDL 2000, LNCS 1923, pp395-298, 2000. Springer-Verlag Berlin Heidelberg

4 Huxley, L, Carpenter, L and Peereboom, M (forthcoming). The Renardus broker service: Collaborative Frameworks and Tools. *The Electronic Library*.

5 DutchESS. Dutch Electronic Subject Service. The National Library of the Netherlands. <URL http://www.kb.nl/dutchess/>

6 University of Göttingen. SSG-FI special subject guides Web site. <URL http://www.SUB.Uni-Goettingen.de/ssgfi/>

7 The Finnish Virtual Library. Web site (English version). <URL http://www.jyu.fi/library/virtuaalikirjasto/engvirli.htm>

8 Resource Discovery Network. RDN Web site. <URL http://www.rdn.ac.uk/>

9 Deff.dk. Danmarks Elektroniske Forskningsbibliotek. Deff Subject Portals Web site (English version). <URL http://deff.dk/?lang=eng>

10 Lund University. NetLab Web site. <URL: http://www.lub.lu.se/netlab/>

11 Institute for Learning and Research Technology (ILRT). University of Bristol. <URL http://www.ilrt.bristol.ac.uk/

12 University of Bath. UKOLN Web site. <URL http://www.ukoln.ac.uk/>

13 Renardus Consortium. Project Deliverable D5.2 User Evaluation report (March 2002<URL: http://www.renardus.org/about_us/deliverables/d5_2/D5_2_final.pdf>

14 Neuroth, Heike and Koch, Traugott (2001). Cross-browsing and cross-searching in a distributed network of subject gateways: architecture, data model and classification. Proceedings of the ELAG2001 Conference, June 2001. <URL: http://www.stk.cz/elag2001/Papers/HeikeNeuroth/HeikeNeuroth.html>

15 OCLC Forest Press. Dewey Decimal Classification home page. <URL: http://www.oclc.org/dewey/>

16 University of Regensburg Library. Carmen project Web site. <URL http://www.bibliothek.uni-regensburg.de/projects/carmen12/>

17 Neuroth, Heike (2001). Metadata mapping and Application Profile. Approaches to Provide for Cross-searching of Heterogeneous Resources in the EU Project Renardus. Proceedings of the DC-2001 International Conference on Dublin Core and Metadata Applications. <URL: http://www.nii.ac.jp/dc2001/>

18 Renardus Consortium. Project Deliverable D1.1 Evaluation Report of Existing Broker Models in Related Projects (April 2000). <URL: http://www.renardus.org/about_us/deliverables/d1_1/D1_1_final.pdf>

19 Technical and Knowledge Center and Library of Denmark (DTV). Web page (English version). <URL: http://www.dtv.dk/index_e.htm>

20 Renardus Consortium Project Archive. <URL: http://www.renardus.org/about_us/project_archive.html>

21 Renardus Consortium. Project Deliverable D9.6 Workshop (November 2001). <URL http://www.renardus.org/about_us/deliverables/workshop/index.html>

22 Renardus Consortium About Us pages. <URL http://www.renardus.org/about_us/>

From Digital Archive to Digital Library – A Middleware for Earth-Observation Data Management

Stephan Kiemle

German Aerospace Center (DLR)
German Remote Sensing Data Center (DFD)
Oberpfaffenhofen, D-82234 Weßling, Germany
Stephan.Kiemle@dlr.de
http://www.dfd.dlr.de

Abstract. The German Remote Sensing Data Center (DFD) has developed a digital library for the long-term management of earth observation data products. This Product Library is a central part of DFD's multi-mission ground segment Data Information and Management System (DIMS) and is successfully in operation since 2000. Its data model is regularly extended to support products of upcoming earth observation missions. The Product Library implements a middleware filling the gap between application-level object data models and physical storage structures such as a digital robot archive with hierarchical storage management. This paper presents the principles of the Product Library middleware and its application in the specific earth observation context.

1 Introduction

Digital libraries are generally based on powerful catalogue and archive systems for the management of metadata and primary data. The semantic gap between high-level information modeling, search and retrieval requirements on one side and existing data storage systems on the other side requires keen solutions to overcome nonsatisfying compromises with respect to the sustainability of the library system.

In the context of earth observation where hundreds of terabytes have to be kept accessible for long term, the sustainability of a digital library is a key issue. The library has not only to cope with a permanently growing amount of data, diversity of data and evolving physical storage technology, it has also to integrate existing digital archives and provide application-level interfaces for other services in order to jointly cover all earth observation ground system tasks of product processing, monitoring, storage, ordering and delivery [1].

The basic requirement of sustainability led to two main concepts followed by the Product Library: first the separation of metadata characterizing a product and the original primary data of the product, and second a middleware decoupling the application interface from the internal storage solution. Both ideas are principally applicable to other digital libraries handling large data objects such as image, audio and video data.

M. Agosti and C. Thanos (Eds.): ECDL 2002, LNCS 2458, pp. 230-237, 2002.

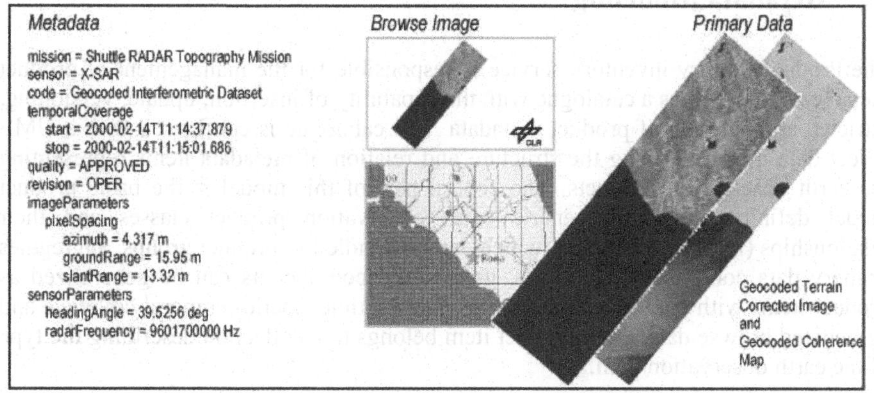

Fig. 1. Earth observation product example with metadata, browse and primary components. The scene shows a geocoded RADAR amplitude image of the tyrrhenian coast north of Roma

A typical earth observation data product consists of different components like the original primary data (e.g. hierarchical data format files), browse images reduced in resolution and auxiliary data useful e.g. for data interpretation (Fig. 1). In addition, each product is described by metadata, parameters describing the product like geo-temporal coverage information, sensor adjustments and feature vectors. Metadata is typically used to search, identify, retrieve and analyze products. The separation of metadata and primary data is motivated by the huge difference in size. Whereas metadata usually takes several Kbytes, the primary data can have up to a GByte of size, depending on the geographic extension, resolution and dimension (e.g. number of channels) of the data.

The Product Library manages products as a whole but internally separates metadata and primary data to store it in an inventory and an archive service [2] (Fig. 2). The inventory service is optimized for search and retrieval of geo-referenced metadata and based on an object-relational database management system. The archive service provides management of primary product files based on a hierarchical storage management system with extensible capacity[1].

The consistency between archive and inventory part is guaranteed by a transaction mechanism spanning both parts controlled by the Product Library itself. The internal Product Library inventory and archive services are implemented in Java and interact through CORBA [3], like all other services of the Data Information and Management System (DIMS).

Fig. 2. Product Library Structure

[1] Currently the DFD Product Library instance manages more than half a million product items and the archive hosts 25 TByte, numbers which are expected to multiply by ten until 2005.

2 Metadata Modeling

The Product Library inventory service is responsible for the management of product metadata and provides a catalogue with the capability of insertion, update, versioning, retrieval and deletion of product metadata. The catalogue is configured with a UML object data model defining the structure and relation of metadata items representing the earth observation products. The central part of this model is the basic product model defining the main generic earth observation product classes and their relationships (Fig. 3). A product, which can be bundled in product groups, aggregates primary data components. Products, groups and components can be generalized as product items with common features like creation time, spatio-temporal coverage and aggregated browse data. Each product item belongs to a collection describing the type of the earth observation item.

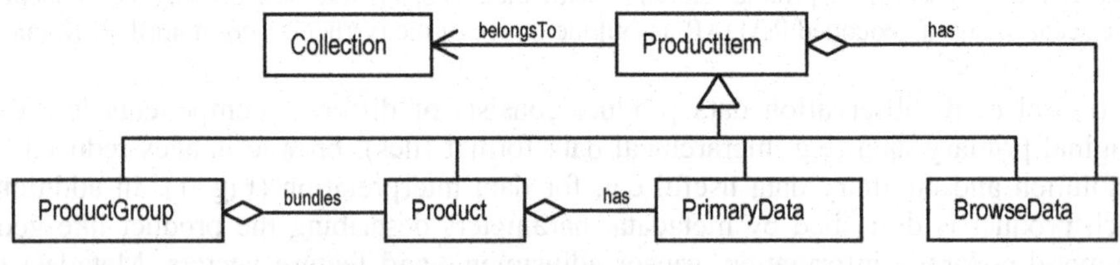

Fig. 3. Basic product model (extract)

Each time new products have to be supported, the product model configuration is extended by new specific definitions like product types, product component types and product parameters. Therefore the generic classes *ProductGroup*, *Product*, *PrimaryData* and *BrowseData*, or other previously defined classes are extended by new specific classes. Specific parameters can be added by defining new attributes. Attributes that have already been defined for other types can be reused in the definition of new types. This is possible because the inventory service stores all modeling elements (classes, types, attributes, methods, references) ever defined in a meta object repository[2].

The Product Library provides a configuration tool for the definition of metadata model extensions. This tool has direct access to the meta object repository so that the administrator is able to browse the modeling elements that have already been defined. The administrator is encouraged to reuse definitions as much as possible to avoid an uncontrolled growth of modeling elements with similar semantics. After configuration of a UML metadata model extension, the inventory service automatically deduces mapping rules that map the different modeling elements to relational structures. The metadata model extension requires no software updates and can be performed during Product Library operation.

By applying the generated mapping rules, the inventory middleware decouples the application metadata view from the relational storage organization. Tables can be renamed, fragmented, split, indexed and merged for performance or other internal

[2] The modeling elements and their relationships are defined in the so-called MetaItemModel, a UML data model describing the modeling capabilities which is itself defined in the meta object repository. The meta object repository is therefore self-contained.

reasons without effect on the metadata model presented at the Product Library interface. In addition new metadata views can be defined in parallel upon the same underlying relational structures e.g. to respond to specific catalogue protocol requirements of a certain application client. This feature becomes more and more important in the context of interoperable library systems and integration with geographical information systems.

At the external Product Library interface, the product structure and metadata is represented in an XML document, the so-called item information file. This document has to be provided if a product shall be inserted and it is newly generated by the Product Library each time a product is extracted. For each product item, i.e. the product itself and each component, the item information file specifies

- the type of the item,
- its logical identifier, a list of specific attributes uniquely identifying the item,
- the aggregated components,
- the location (name, path, host) of the data files,
- the basic product item metadata (applicable to all product items) and
- the specific product item metadata.

The following paragraph shows an extract of the XML document type definition (DTD) of the item information file. Aggregated components and other associated items can either be referenced locally within the item information file or reference existing items in the Product Library by indicating their identifier. All structures within the item information file are well defined except the specific product item metadata. Here, the DTD allows any structured, list and set parameters because the specific metadata structure changes from one product type to another. (Element nodes not further detailed are text nodes mapping to #PCDATA.)

```
<!ELEMENT IIF (item*)>
<!ELEMENT item (admin,components,fileInformation,
                parameters,specificParameters)>
  <!ELEMENT admin (type,keys)>
    <!ELEMENT keys (basicFeature*)>
      <!ATTLIST basicFeature name CDATA #REQUIRED>
  <!ELEMENT components (component*)>
    <!ELEMENT component (role,ref)>
      <!ELEMENT ref (localId|remoteId)>
  <!ELEMENT fileInformation (file*)>
    <!ELEMENT file (host,path,name)>
  <!ELEMENT parameters (availability,quality,creation,
            spatialCoverage,tempCoverage,predecessor)
    <!ELEMENT creation (time,creator)>
      <!ELEMENT creator (remoteId)>
    <!ELEMENT spatialCoverage (point|box|circle|
                               string|polygon)>
      <!ELEMENT point (latitude,longitude)>
      <!ELEMENT box (east,north,west,south)>
      <!ELEMENT circle (point,radius)>
      <!ELEMENT string (point*)>
      <!ELEMENT polygon (point*)>
```

```
    <!ELEMENT tempCoverage (start,stop)>
    <!ELEMENT predecessor (remoteId)>
  <!ELEMENT specificParameters (feature*)>
    <!ELEMENT feature (#PCDATA|feature*)>
    <!ATTLIST feature name CDATA #REQUIRED>
```

3 Archive Management

The primary data of earth observation products usually consists of a couple of files per product component, the smallest logical unit managed by the Product Library. In order to decouple and hide internal storage issues, all product files have to be managed by the archive middleware such that

- the internal archive location is hidden to the external user
- the internal archive location is comprehensive to the internal archive operator (concise root points, balanced directory trees etc.)
- the internal archive location fulfils the requirements of the underlying archive system for storage/access optimization (e.g. files spread over different media types)
- the files can be extracted again given the identification of the product component previously retrieved from the inventory service.

The archive service of the Product Library is structured in archive area sub-services, one area per file system. The archive area service is responsible for the file I/O (via FTP) to and from its archive file system which can be a standard UNIX file system or a hierarchical storage file system [6] where certain file I/O activities are optimized to avoid unnecessary media reload and positioning procedures. The underlying robot library is able to handle different types of media, for example magneto-optical discs and tapes from different vendors. Several media drives fed by the robot operate in parallel. When new data is copied on the cache, the robot library automatically generates a first and a second copy on media. For safety reasons the second copy is not stored in one of the library towers but off-line in a separate location and is used only for disaster recovery.

The middleware implemented by the archive service maps primary product file requests like insertion, retrieval and deletion to the corresponding archive area and directory path. Therefore, the archive service is configured with the archive mapping rules consisting of

- the product component type for which this mapping is applicable
- the archive area responsible to store data of this type
- the path rule defining how the directory path within the archive area's file system has to be built up.

The path rule takes metadata of the product component to generate an individual directory path for the component files. However, the path needs not to be unique because the internal file names contain the unique identifier of the product component to avoid collisions and enable version management. For means of directory path balance, path rules are configured individually using comprehensive metadata parameters of the specific product component.

Table 1. The path rule configured at DFD's operational Product Library for the product component type "MODIS.L0-RAW", the primary data of the level 0 product acquired from the optical sensor Moderate-Resolution Imaging Spectroradiometer

Parameter	Type	Append	*Example Value*
mission	String	_	`TERRA`
sensor	String	_	`MODIS`
code	String	/	`L0`
startTime	date, format: y_m/d		`2002-05-13T16:09:12.281`

Assuming a parameter value assignment with the example values in the table, the resulting directory path will be `TERRA_MODIS_L0/y2002_m05/d13` and the component files will be transferred into this directory relative to the archive area root location, usually the file system mount point. As shown with the mapping of the *startTime* parameter, the archive service uses the configured format definition and performs certain modifications to guarantee results usable for directory names (e.g. elimination of special characters).

For all earth observation product components inserted in the Product Library, the internal archive location is determined in this way. For consistency purpose this internal location is additionally stored in a special space within the inventory service, the file information catalogue. This catalogue is exclusively accessible for internal use and not part of the Product Library application interface. The archive operator can browse the file information catalogue e.g. to get an overview about the internal archive structure or to search for specific files.

Products that are already stored in an existing archive file system can be registered whereby the library takes over their management, adding their file locations to the file information catalogue.

The Product Library uses itself the file information catalogue when products have to be delivered. The external user or system specifies a product identifier and the archive service middleware takes this identifier to look up the internal file location in the file information catalogue. With this information it can request the file delivery from the responsible archive area.

By applying archiving rules, the archive middleware of the Product Library hides internal storage structures. Advantages are e.g. internal migration of data to future media generations, reorganization of archive hosts, file systems and directory paths without effect on external Product Library client systems.

4 Query Interface

In general the query requirements of operators and client services like processing systems are not predictable. Therefore, the Product Library provides an ad-hoc query interface and an object query language which is a subset of the Object Data Management Group OQL standard [5] extended by special features for the earth observation context such as search methods like intersect, inside, outside, within and beyond for spatio-temporal specifications.

In the Operating Tool, the graphical operator client of DIMS, the operator can textually enter any OQL query and submit the query to the Product Library. The inventory service maps the query to SQL queries processed by the underlying database system. The Operating Tool visualizes query results in a result table, a detailed metadata view (on demand) and on the map.

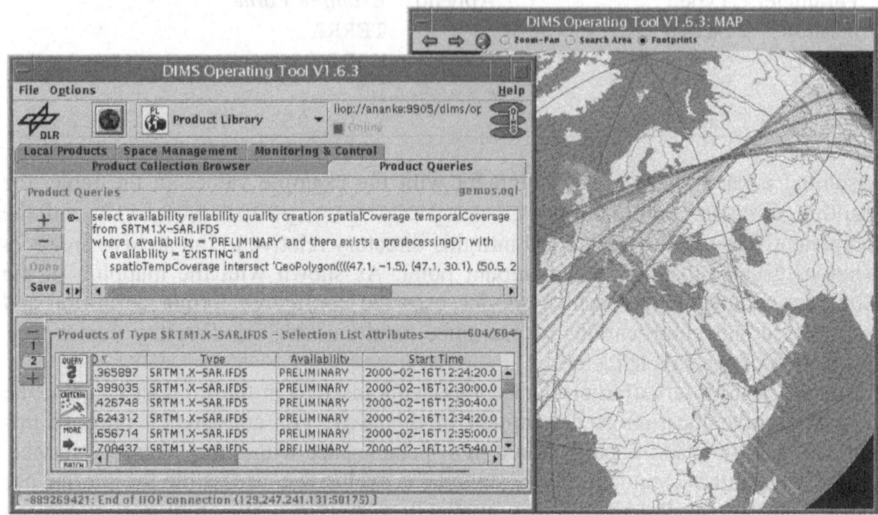

Fig. 4. Ad-hoc product query interface in the DIMS Operating Tool

The example in Fig. 4 shows an object query that searches all preliminary interferometric data sets whose associated predecessing data take is existing and intersects a certain region over central Europe. The footprints of the resulting products are shown on the map (in pink). For additional information all data takes intersecting the same region have been queried before (displayed in green).

The Product Library query interface is not only used by operators but also by processing systems e.g. to find the correct input products required for the processing of certain output products. Processing systems can also subscribe for specific product events, specifying the action (e.g. product insertion) and a query condition that must be fulfilled by the corresponding product. This triggering mechanism is used to build up self-controlled processing chains where value-added products are automatically generated when the required low-level input products become available.

5 Conclusion

The Product Library is a live example that a transition from existing digital archives to digital library systems is feasible and brings comprehensive data management functionality and finally increases the value of the archived data e.g. by adding sophisticated search and retrieval capabilities. The library middleware decouples the application oriented external interface from internal storage concerns and therefore guarantees stable interfaces and reduces administration efforts – precondition for sustainable long-term management of earth observation data products.

The archive service middleware determines where and how primary data files have to be inserted in/extracted from the archive system. Therefore, an external application system does not need any knowledge about the physical archive structure like file systems and directory paths. Existing archive file systems can be integrated and reorganized e.g. for migration purpose without impact on the application interface.

The inventory service middleware allows easy and flexible application object data modeling and maps object models to relational structures. Based on this mapping, the inventory automatically translates catalogue search queries specified in the expressive application-level object query language. Again the physical storage can internally be optimized without impact on the library interface, easily overcoming the minimal performance impact of the mapping process.

The Product Library middleware is implemented in Java and uses state-of-the-art technologies and common standards like CORBA, XML and JDBC [4]. It is one of the services of the Data Information and Management System (DIMS) and operational since 2000, hosting more than half a million product items (25 TByte data) of various airborne, shuttle and satellite missions.

References

1. Mikusch, E., Diedrich, E., Göhmann, M., Kiemle, S., Reck, C., Reißig, R., Schmidt, K., Wildegger, W., Wolfmüller, M.: Data Information and Management System for the Production, Archiving and Distribution of Earth Observation Products. Data Systems in Aerospace 2000, EUROSPACE. ESA Publications Division, SP-457, Noordwijk (2000)
2. Kiemle, S., Mikusch, E., Göhmann, M.: The Product Library – A Scalable Long-Term Storage Repository for Earth Observation Products. Data Systems in Aerospace 2001, EUROSPACE. ESA Publications Division, SP-483, Noordwijk (2001)
3. Object Management Group and X/Open: The Common Object Request Broker 2.3: Architecture and Specification. John Wiley & Sons Inc., New York (1999)
4. Kiemle, S., Mikusch, E., Reck, C., Reißig, R., Wildegger, W., Wolfmüller, M.: Data Information and Management System for Earth Observation Products based on CORBA and Java. EOGEO 2000, http://webtech.jrc.it/eogeo2000. JRC, Ispra (2000)
5. Object Data Management Group ODMG: The Object Data Standard: ODMG 3.0. Morgan Kaufmann (2000)
6. Kampa, R.A., Bell, L.V.: UNIX Storage Management. Springer-Verlag, Berlin Heidelberg New York (2002)

Navigating in Bibliographic Catalogues

Trond Aalberg

Norwegian University of Science and Technology,
Department of Computer and Information Science
Trond.Aalberg@idi.ntnu.no

Abstract. The FRBR-model provided by the *IFLA Study group on the Functional Requirements for Bibliographic Records* addresses the need for a more thorough model of bibliographic information. This paper describes a solution for applying the FRBR model to existing bibliographic catalogues. This is accomplished by augmenting the catalogue with an externally stored map that contains relationships and entities according to the model. The core of the system is the *Digital Library LinkService* developed at the Norwegian University of Science and Technology – a flexible and general purpose link service developed to support the structuring of information objects in digital libraries. A client application is developed to visualize the map and to enable users to interact with the map by navigating along the available paths.

1 Introduction

Information about books, journals, and other knowledge carrying items, are today made available to the public by a large number of Web Based Public Access Catalogs (WEBPACs). When using these systems, however, we often discover that it is not as easy and intuitive to locate relevant information as we would like it to be. This can be exemplified by searching for the works of Henrik Ibsen in one of the Norwegian bibliographic catalogues, like BIBSYS[1] or the National Bibliography of Norway[2]. A search using the author's name will produce a listing of thousands of publications. The only way to narrow the scope is often to formulate a more specific query, like additionally specifying a title. Even in this case, the list of publications may be longer than the common user is able to deal with. An even more specific query is the next alternative, but at this stage the user may be lost. The ability to specify a precise query is depending on a thorough understanding of the information and behavior of the system – an understanding most users do not have. Another reason for failure is when the user has a vaguely defined information need and rather needs to explore which publications are available by browsing the catalogue using meaningful navigational paths. Finally, we often find that WEBPACs do not support the queries we would like to submit, like querying for specific translations of a play or a video recording of a performance.

[1] http://www.bibsys.no
[2] http://www.nb.no/baser/norbok/

M. Agosti and C. Thanos (Eds.): ECDL 2002, LNCS 2458, pp. 238–250, 2002.

A fundamental issue when addressing any of the problems in the above example, is the need for a conceptual model that captures the entities and the relationships of main concern when users search for information. Such models have been explored, e.g. in [7,10,11], but a major contribution has been provided by the *IFLA Study group on the Functional Requirements for Bibliographic Records*, by the definition of an entity-relationship based model commonly referred to as the *FRBR model* [6].

The FRBR model is, however, only an initial step towards the "next generation" of bibliographic systems. The next question we have to ask is; how can this model be implemented in current and future catalogues and WEBPAC systems?

In this paper we describe a solution for applying the FRBR model to existing bibliographic catalogues. This is accomplished by augmenting existing catalogues with an externally stored map that contains relationships and entities according to the model. The core of the system is the *Digital Library LinkService* developed at the Norwegian University of Science and Technology – a flexible and general purpose link service developed to support the structuring of information objects in digital libraries [1].

The FRBR map is constructed by extracting and processing existing bibliographic information, and storing this information externally to the catalogue. The map can be visualized and integrated with the catalogue in various ways; in this paper we describe a solution using a web browser plugin. This allows a user to interact with the WEBPAC in an ordinary way to search, retrieve and view bibliographic records. In addition the user can inspect and interact with the catalogue using the map.

2 The FRBR Model

The main objective of the FRBR model is to provide a "clearly defined, structured framework for relating the data that are recorded in bibliographic records to the needs of the users of those records" (p. 2 in [6]). To achieve this, the FRBR defines a model of the entities, attributes and relationships needed to support the generic tasks that are performed when searching and making use of national bibliographies and library catalogues.

The entities of the model reifies the main concepts or objects of interest to users. The core of the model is a group of entities representing the products of artistic or intellectual endeavor; the *work*, *expression*, *manifestation* and *item* entities (entitled Group 1 Entities). Another group of entities is representing those responsible for the content, and a third group contains entities that serves as the subject of the works. The focus in this paper is limited to the Group 1 entities; work, expression, manifestation and item.

The *work* is an abstract entity representing a distinct intellectual or artistic product. The *expression* entity is a specific intellectual or artistic form a work takes when it is realized. A *manifestation* entity is a physical embodiment of an expression, and the *item* is a single exemplar of the manifestation.

When we refer to the play by Ibsen entitled "A dolls house", in a generic sense without considering a specific translation, edition or performance, we are dealing with the play as a conceptual *work* entity. This work can be realized in a various intellectual or artistic shapes – as *expression* entities. The original Norwegian text is one realization of this work, the English translation by Henrietta Frances Lord in the 1880s is another realization. The latter English translation was published by different publishers in England and in America, and should be considered different *manifestations* of this particular realization of the work. A specific copy of the American publication, available in the shelves of a library, is an *item* entity.

In addition to the entities, and the attributes that identify and characterize the entities, the FRBR model emphasizes bibliographic relationships (p. 56 in [6]):

> In the context of the model, relationships serve as the vehicle for depicting the link between one entity and another, and thus as the means of assisting the user to "navigate" the universe that is represented in a bibliography, catalogue, or bibliographic database.

The work, expression, manifestation and item entities are associated to each other by a set of possible relationships. A work *is realized through* one or more expressions. An expression *is embodied in* one or more manifestation and a manifestation *is exemplified by* one or more items. In addition to these basic relationships, the FRBR-model also defines relationships that may exist between the various entities orthogonal or parallel to the basic relationships. One expression can be the *translation* of another expression, or the relationship between expressions may be that one is the *adaptation* of the other.

So what does the FRBR model contribute in terms of the example described in the beginning of this paper? In the case of Ibsen, his plays have been translated to numerous languages and published in a variety of editions throughout the years. In this example, the FRBR model contributes several dimensions for organizing these publications. Organizing along the dimension of works would enable the user to view the set of unique works by Ibsen (a reasonable number) and select the relevant one without being distracted by the numerous translations and editions that exist. Organizing along the dimension of expressions would allow users to select a specific translation, a specific adaptation, a video or sound recording of a theater performance of a specific play etc. Further more, if the relationships between entities are instantiated as typed links, a user would be able to navigate his way using the relationship types of the FRBR-model as meaningful road signs.

3 Extending Current WEBPACS

A library catalogue can be defined as a set of bibliographic records – usually based on the MARC format. A record acts as a surrogate for the publication, and contains information describing many aspects of the publication.

To some extent the bibliographic record also captures some of the aspects of the FRBR model. When comparing a MARC based catalogue with the FRBR model, we generally find a 1:1 association between the record and the manifestation entity of the FRBR model. In a specific catalogue there will be one record for each manifestation, and each manifestation will be described by one record. This does not imply that manifestations are the only entities present in the catalogue, but rather that the descriptions of other entities are distributed in a different way. Multiple item entities can be listed in one record and information related to the expression and work entities can be found in multiple records. One example is the MARC field "uniform title" – which is comparable to the work title of the FRBR model. The same work title can be found in many records if there are many publications containing this work, but the work is not present as a distinct and identifiable entity in the catalogue.

Since the catalogue already contains aspects of the FRBR model, it is possible to process the data in the catalogue and generate some of the entities and relationships of the model. The resulting information will constitute an FRBR map over the entities contained within the bibliographic catalogue as illustrated in figure 1. The above interpretation of a bibliographic record as mainly a manifestation surrogate, is a pragmatic but convenient way to align the map with the catalogue. The manifestation corresponds to one identifiable record in the catalogue, and the record corresponds to one identifiable manifestation entity on the map.

This map can then be integrated with catalogues in different ways. The map can be tightly integrated and more or less be a part of the records in the catalogue, or the map can be a distinct separate source of information to be applied dynamically at runtime. The most reasonable solution at the moment is to rely on the latter approach. The FRBR model is still a theoretical work and is yet not reflected in current cataloguing rules and standards. By using external storage of a map, the FRBR model can be imposed on the catalogue at runtime, and the user can take advantage of the pathways of this model without any further consequences for the catalogue.

4 A Prototype Application

The map-based approach introduced in the previous section is implemented in a prototype system. As a case study we are using BIBSYS – the Norwegian bibliographic database for university and college libraries. The map was constructed by extracting and processing a set of bibliographic records from this database. The resulting map is stored and managed using the Digital Library LinkService. At runtime the map is dynamically integrated with the WEBPAC by using a plugin developed for Internet Explorer. The plugin implements a standard tree view control to visualize the relationships and entities of the map.

When a user views a record from the BIBSYS system, a complementary window in the Internet Explorer browser shows a map of the existing relationships and the entities participating in these relationships. The map can be navigated

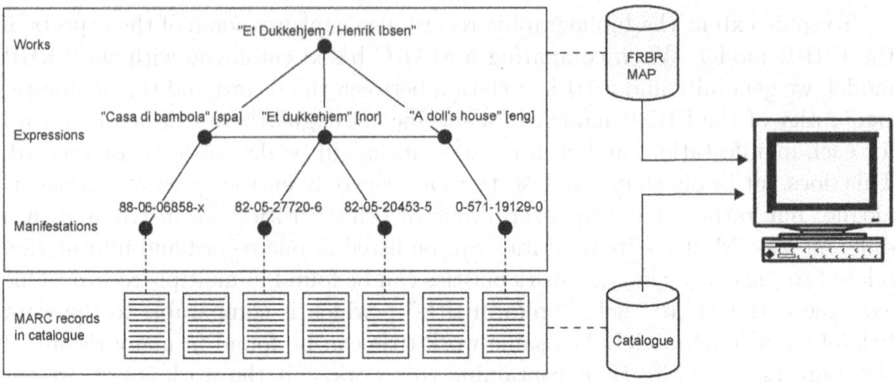

Fig. 1. FRBR map aligned with MARC records.

by selecting any of the available entities, causing the focus to shift to the selected entity. If a manifestation is selected, the corresponding record is additionally retrieved from the BIBSYS WEBPAC.

The various components of the prototype, the extraction and the representation of the FRBR map are further discussed in the following sections.

4.1 The DL-LinkService

The Digital Library LinkService is a general purpose link service developed at the Norwegian University of Science and Technology (NTNU). The purpose of this service is to support the structuring of information objects in digital libraries by enabling relationships to be defined and processed. The service combines aspects of the link services of hypermedia with relationship mechanisms of relational and object oriented databases. Details of the service can be found in [1].

Using the Digital Library LinkService terminology, a link is interpreted as the instance of a relationship, and for this reason links and relationships are used as interchangeable terms. The link term is used to indicate an instance of the data structure that implements a relationship.

The data model of the service is based on node, role and link objects. A node object represents an entity and this entity can be an existing resource like a record in a library catalogue, or it can be an abstract concept like a specific work or expression. The only requirement is that an entity must be identified by an URI or another unique string. Nodes participate in relationships on behalf of the entities they represent. The actual relationships are instantiated using a compound structure of role and link objects.

The Digital Library LinkService is fully capable to represent the entities and the relationships of the FRBR model. The relationship structure can easily be navigated by calling methods on the various objects and relationships are bidirectional. In essence this means that from a node object all the relationships

Table 1. The FRBR entities and relationships used in the prototype.

Node	Role	Link	Role	Node
Work	Is realized through	Realization	Is a realization of	Expression
Expression	Is embodied in	Embodiment	Is an embodiment of	Manifestation
Expression	Has a translation	Translation	Is a translation of	Expression
Expression	Has adaptation	Adaptation	Is an adaptation of	Expression
Manifestation	Is part of	Whole/part	Has part	Manifestation

and opposite nodes are accessible. The service is implemented using the CORBA distributed object middleware which essentially means that it is accessible over the network and easy to use in any kind of development environment.

4.2 Defining a Link Typology for the FRBR-Model

The relationships and the nodes allowed in a particular usage of the Digital Library LinkService service are constrained by the use of a typology. A typology is mainly a definition of the relationships and the nodes that are allowed and how they can be used. The semantics of a relationship is captured using both a general typename and role typenames as illustrated in table 1.

For the purpose of this prototype we translated the entities and relationships defined in the FRBR model into the format used by the Digital Library LinkService. Work, expression and manifestation entities are defined as node types. Item entities are not considered in our system since information about items usually are present as a part of a the bibliographic record, and thus require no further support. Table 1 exemplifies the typology used. The actual typology is implemented as a XML file according to a specific XML schema. In addition to the type names listed in the table, additional details were captured as well. All relationships are defined as binary, meaning that only two entities may participate in a relationship. The cardinality is captured by defining cardinality ratios – like the rule that a work node may participate in several *realization* relationship while an expression may only participate in one *realization* relationship. This captures the rule of the FRBR model that a work can be realized by different expressions, while an expression can only be the realization of one work.

In addition to the formal typenames, the various objects can be assigned a title value at creation time, to further indicate the semantics of the various parts. A work node representing the play "A doll's house" is given the proper work title as well as the author name to facilitate easy interpretation of the FRBR map.

4.3 Extracting Entities and Relationship

The BIBSYS database uses the BIBSYS-MARC format which is based on NORMARC – the standard Norwegian MARC format – with the exception of some

Table 2. BIBSYS-MARC fields occurring in more than 10% of the records.

Field	Subfield	Data	Count(*)
008	c	General information - language code	2339
020	a	ISBN	448
100	a	Main entry - personal name	2535
240	a	Uniform title	1118
240	l	Uniform title - language	907
241	a	Original title	340
245	a	Title statement - title	2535
245	b	Title statement - remainder of title	1242
245	c	Title statement - responsibility	2295
250	a	Edition statement - edition	367
260	a	Publication - place	2513
260	b	Publication - publisher name	2285
260	c	Publication - date	2527
440	a	Series statement	737
500	a	General note	894
700	a	Added entry - personal name	1404
740	a	Added entry - uncontrolled title	498

historically related deviations. The database also contains some records converted from other systems and the records are for that reason of varying quality.

A test case was constructed based on records having "Ibsen, Henrik" as the main entry - personal name. The size of the test case was 2535 records[3] and the purpose of this selection was to create a manageable test case that was likely to contain a large set of entities and relationships. Information regarding the most relevant BIBSYS-MARC fields is presented in table 2. The column on the right is showing in how many test case records a specific field occurs.

A relational database was used to store and process the test case, and after extraction of the entities and the relationships, the constructed information was inserted into the Digital Library LinkService to make the information accessible for further use.

The mapping between the MARC format and the FRBR model is a fairly new area, but there is some guidance available on how to do this. Our solution is partly guided by [3,4] and partly based on inspection of the test case records to uncover other alternative ways. Some fields/subfields in the MARC format can be mapped directly to the FRBR model, like the 240$a and 241$a which correspond to the title of the work entity. In such cases the identification of the FRBR entities and the relationships can be straight forward. Other fields in the MARC format only indicate FRBR entities or relationships. In such cases the identification of entities and relationships can be complicated and unreliable.

[3] The BIBSYS database holds a total number of 3.3 million records.

Table 3. Work entities found.

	240$a/241$a	740$a	245$a	Total
Records containing this field	1447	498	2535	
Extracted possible work titles	64	296	289	
Extracted Norwegian work titles	64	94	132	
After manual error corrections	41	61	38	
Incrementally unique work titles	41	43	38	122

In the selected test case the work entities can be sufficiently identified by the title of the work. To single out a set of unique work titles, a sequence of queries was performed. First a set of titles was extracted from the 240/241 entries, then additional titles were extracted from the 740 field – but only in the subset of records without entries in the 240/241 fields. Finally, titles were extracted from the 245 field but only from the records that had neither 240/241 nor 740 entries. The result was a set that contained a large number of erroneous work titles. In particular the titles from 740 and 245 entries contained errors like titles in foreign languages as well as comparable titles with spelling variations. The set was further reduced by only including titles from records having a Norwegian language code entry in field 008, to exclude titles that were likely to be translations. The set was finally inspected manually and corrected to improve the results. Table 3 shows some statistics from the extraction of work titles. The first row shows the number of records having an entry in this field. The next rows show how a set of work titles was constructed according to the procedure described above.

A number of expressions may exist for a specific work. From the test case we extracted expressions to represent the original text, translations of the original text into foreign languages, and adaptations of the work like sound or video recordings of a performance. The identification of expressions is highly problematic because relevant information is distributed over several fields, including 008 (language and form codes), parts of the title statement in 245 (subfield b and c), possible translators name in 700, etc. Much of the information needed to identify expressions is, additionally, often present in an inconsistent way. Information telling that this is a translation may be found in the fields 700, 245, or

Table 4. Expression entities found.

Kind of expression	No. of expressions
Original expression	122
Translations	452
Adaptations	183

Table 5. The number of relationships found.

From entity	To entity	Relationship type	Unique relationships
Work	⇔ Expression	Realization	757
Expression	⇔ Manifestation	Embodiment	2469
Expression	⇔ Expression	Translation	1533
Expression	⇔ Expression	Adaptations	183
Manifestation	⇔ Manifestation	Whole/part	453

500 – often expressed using an uncontrolled syntax and vocabulary. The number of expressions found in the test case is shown in table 4.

The original expressions are easily captured in this test case, because there will always be an original expression for each of Ibsen's works. Translations can be identified by having a foreign language code combined with an original title that exists as a work title. Further identification of translations – like several different translation into the same language – is possible by using additional information like the translators name. In our test case it was, however, difficult to identify the translator or other information that could distinguish between different translations into the same language. For this reason we considered different translations into the same language to be one and the same expression. Finally, adaptations can be identified by using title and form code, personal names - added entries etc, but this only caused a small number to be found. Searching for words like video, sound, radio, and manuscript, did however uncover additional adaptations that were included in the result set.

A particular problem occurred when trying to create titles for the translations. The works of Ibsen are often published as several plays together in one volume. When catalogued, the original Norwegian titles and the translated titles are listed as multiple entries in the 740 field. There is, however, no way of telling which translated title corresponds to which original title. Due to this problem all expressions had to be entitled using the title of the work entity.

Manifestations may be identified by various attributes, either using a single field value like the ISBN found in 020, or several field values in combination like the title statement combined with the author name and publication statement etc. Since this case study only included records from one catalogue, and each record corresponds to a manifestation, we could rely on the unique record identifier as the manifestation identifier. This means that the number of manifestations found is equal to the total number of records in the test case.

Once entities are defined it is possible to capture the relationships. The number of relationships found is summarized in table 5. Most relationships include an expression, and in many cases the identity of an expression is determined by a variable set of attributes. The task of capturing relationships is for that reason not as easy as it might appear, and must be conducted in a stepwise fashion.

Missing work titles in the records was a major problem for detecting relationships – in particular between translations and their corresponding work entities.

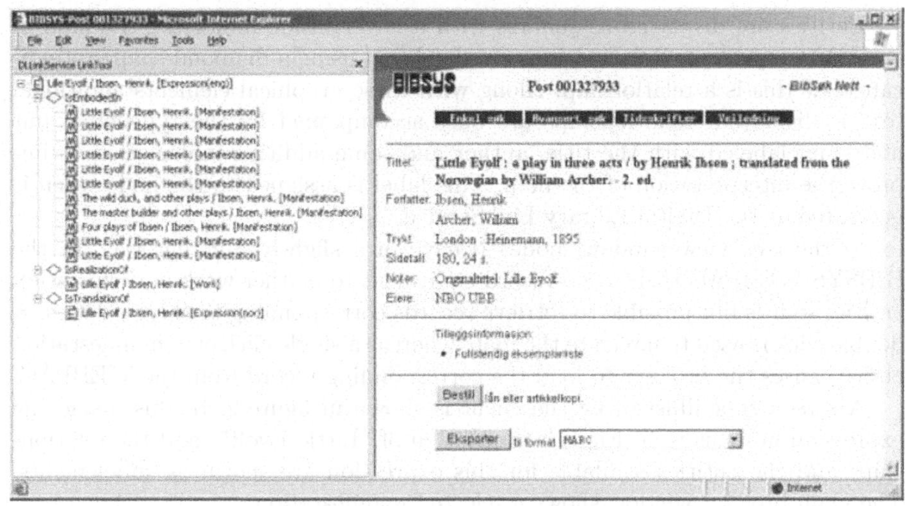

Fig. 2. Screenshot of the client.

This problem was partly solved by the use of a translation table based on the combinations of known manifestation titles and work titles that existed in other records. If one record contains the English title "A doll's house" in 245$a and the original title "Et dukkehjem" in 240/241 or 740, this information can be applied on comparable records where the work title is missing.

4.4 The Client Application

The client for viewing and navigating the map is developed as a plugin application for Internet Explorer. The client is tightly integrated into the browsing environment as an Explorer bar – using the same window that otherwise is used for presenting favorites lists and browsing history. The actual view of the map is implemented using the tree view control with available relationships and nodes shown as a tree structure. Only a subpart of the graph is shown at one time, using the node in focus as the root and directly connected nodes as leaf nodes.

The plugin communicates with the main window by sinking the events of the explorer and sending events to the main application to initiate specific actions. When a bibliographic record is loaded, the plugin is notified and can update the view according to the record in focus. In this application we rely on the URL of a bibliographic record in the WEBPAC to link the manifestation of the map and the record displayed in the WEBPAC.

The plugin application implements a CORBA client for talking to the Digital Library LinkService. When a web page is loaded the client looks up the link server for the node corresponding to this URL, and retrieves the relationships and nodes. This information is then displayed in the tree view control.

Entities are displayed as squares with a letter inside indicating the kind of node they represent. Relationships are displayed using a diamond shape to indicate that this is a relationship. Along with these graphical elements additional text is displayed. Relationships are only accompanied by the typename, but nodes are labeled with the title, author and some addition information to improve the interpretation of the map. This label is assigned to the node when it is created at the Digital Library LinkService.

In the tree view window, nodes behave in a slightly different way. In the BIBSYS WEBPAC there is no record equivalent to neither work nor expression entities so it is not possible to retrieve records corresponding to these entities. A double click is used to navigate the map, whereas a single click on a manifestation entity causes the browser to load the corresponding record from the WEBPAC.

A screen shot illustrating the client is shown in figure 2. In this image the expression in focus is an English translation of "Little Eyolf", and the relationships and the entities available for this expression are shown as subelements. The main browser window shows a selected manifestation.

5 Discussion

The main contribution of this paper is a framework for adding the FRBR model to current bibliographic catalogues based on the use of an external map. The system implemented shows that this is an adequate solution to the problem of adding structure to existing catalogues. The Digital Library LinkService is specifically designed to support this kind of structuring, and has proven to be an applicable solution.

Extraction of the entities and the relationships is in this project conducted using a variety of queries on the test case data. In addition, the focus has been on a specific subset of records describing works by Henrik Ibsen. Some entities and relationships can directly be identified and similar techniques can be applied on the whole BIBSYS database. Other entities and relationships are identified using more pragmatic ad-hoc solutions that only are valid for the specific subset of records having "Ibsen, Henrik" as main entry. In general we found that the guidelines suggested in [3] are valid, but a major problem is the significant difference between the indication of an entity and the proper identification of an entity. In particular we found that expressions are hard to identify, and this is a problem that will apply to the whole catalogue.

In the client that is developed, the node in focus and its directly connected nodes are presented using the Microsoft tree view control. This is, however, a limited solution because the tree only presents a simplified subpart of the underlying graph of the stored map. A better presentation of the map may be achieved by using other graph presentation and interaction techniques. Another problem with the user interface is how to label nodes and relationships in such a way that users easily can interpret the map. The entities have to be presented using selected metadata elements, and a suitable balance has to be made between the need for a compact and still informative presentation.

The test case of this project is based on the use of a single bibliographic database. This is, however, not a limitation. The Digital Library LinkService supports linking of distributed content, and the service itself may also be distributed. A map that implements relationships between distributed entities can easily be constructed, e.g. with paths to digital facsimiles of the original manuscripts stored elsewhere on the Internet.

The solutions described in this paper can be related to the works of other in different areas. Solutions for more powerfully and/or more user friendly OPACs and WEBPACs are too numerous to be mentioned. A main element of our solution is that it is based on the FRBR model, and thus implies a more sharable and interoperable solution.

Display techniques for the FRBR model are discussed in [4,9]. The display solution presented in this paper is slightly different due to the focus on an interactive map that allows convenient navigation. The complexity of the FRBR model calls for a user interface that provides an overview of the larger structure in which an entity participates.

Another related area is the use of link services in advanced hypermedia systems [2,8], and in particular to the use of such systems in digital library applications, e.g. solutions for citation linking like the Open Journal Project [5]. The Digital Library LinkService serves the same purpose as these kinds of systems, but it also differs significantly by its focus on a more formal representation of relationships.

This project opens for further work in different directions. In particular, this solution is applicable as a testbed environment for further development and research related to the FRBR model. The use of navigation along the FRBR model – as an information discovery strategy – is one relevant area for future work. The FRBR model defines a specific set of road signs that can be applied on a catalogue, but what pathways real users will follow in a real setting, is yet to be discovered.

References

1. Aalberg, T. Linking Information with Distributed Objects. In *Proc. 5th European Conference on Research and Advanced Technology for Digital Libraries (ECDL2001)*, volume 2163 of *Lecture Notes in Computer Science*, pages 149–160, Darmstadt, Germany, September 2001. Springer.
2. Carr, L., Hall, W., Roure, D.D. The Evolution of Hypertext Link Services. *ACM Computing Surveys*, 31(4es), Dec. 1999.
3. Delsey, T. Functional Analysis of the MARC 21 Bibliographic and Holdings Format. Technical report, 2002. Prepared for the Network Development and MARC Standards Office , Library of Congress. URL: `http://www.loc.gov/marc/marc-functional-analysis/home.html` [last visited 2002-06-26].
4. Hegna, K., Murtomaa, E. Data mining MARC to Find: FRBR? Technical report, BIBSYS/HUL, 2002. URL: `http://folk.uio.no/knuthe/dok/frbr/datamining.pdf` [last visited 2002-06-26].

5. Hitchcock, S., Carr, L., Hall, W., Harris, S., Evans, D., Brailsford, D. Linking Electronic Journals : Lessons from the Open Journal project. *D-Lib Magazine*, December 1998.
6. IFLA study group on the functional requirements for bibliographic records. Functional Requirements for Bibliographic Records : Final Report. Technical report, IFLA, 1998. URL: `http://www.ifla.org/VII/s13/frbr/frbr.pdf` [last visited 2002-06-26].
7. Leazer, G.H., Smiraglia, R.P. Toward the Bibliographic Control of Works: Derivative Bibliographic Relationships in an Online Union Catalog. In *Proceedings of the 1st ACM International Conference on Digital Libraries*, pages 36–43, Bethesda, MD USA, March 1996. ACM.
8. Lewis, P.H., Hall, W., Carr, L.A., Roure, D.D. The Significance of Linking. *ACM Computing Surveys*, 31(4es), Dec. 1999.
9. Library of Congress. Displays for Multiple Versions from MARC 21 and FRBR. Technical report, Network Development and MARC Standards Office, Library of Congress, 2002. URL: `http://www.loc.gov/marc/marc-functional-analysis/multiple-versions.html` [last visited 2002-06-26].
10. Tillett, B.B. A Taxonomy of Bibliographic Relationships. *Library Resources & Technical Services*,, 35(2):150–158, April 1991.
11. Weinstein, P. Ontology-Based Metadata: Transforming the MARC Legacy. In *Proceedings of the Third International ACM Digital Library Conference*, pages 254–263, Pittsburgh, PA, USA, June 1998. ACM.

Foundations of a Multidimensional Query Language for Digital Libraries

Donatella Castelli, Carlo Meghini, and Pasquale Pagano

Istituto delle Tecnologie e Scienze dell'Informazione
Consiglio Nazionale delle Ricerche
Area della Ricerca di Pisa, Pisa, Italy
{castelli,meghini,pagano}@iei.pi.cnr.it

Abstract. A query language for Digital Libraries is presented, which offers access to documents by structure and sophisticated usage of metadata. The language is based on a mathematical model of digital library documents, centered around a multilevel representation of documents as versions, views and manifestations. The core of the model is the notion of document view, which is recursive, and captures the content and structure of a document. The metadata representation distinguishes between formats and specifications, so being able to accommodate different metadata formats, even for the same document. A query is a logical formula, and its result are the digital library documents satisfying the user query.

1 Introduction

Current Digital Libraries (DLs) strongly resemble traditional libraries based on on-line public access catalogs: the only added value offered by DLs is the on-line availability also of documents [2,4,3]. As a consequence, the information retrieval service offered to DL users boils down to queries expressing very simple conditions on descriptive metadata. From an information system point of view, this kind of functionality equates current DLs to pre-database information systems and, what is worse, prevents the full exploitation of DL contents, defeating the huge investments that are necessary to create such contents in the first place.

Emerging standards and well-consolidated technologies can contribute to overcome the present state of affair, permitting the realization of DLs offering information access services that are adequate to user expectations. Three aspects on which progress is possible are:

– more sophisticated usage of metadata[1]. A wide range of metadata formats exist and are actually employed for describing DL content [1,13,16]. Potentially, a DL could store information about the metadata models themselves, thus supporting in a principled way the co-existence of more standards in the same system, and even the exploitation of the metamodel in querying. For instance: "What are the fields available in the metadata format x?", or "What different formats are supported for a certain attribute value?".

[1] throughout the paper, we use the term "metadata" as a synonym of "descriptive metadata".

M. Agosti and C. Thanos (Eds.): ECDL 2002, LNCS 2458, pp. 251–265, 2002.

- structure-based access. Digital formats highlighting document structure are available nowadays (*e.g.* Postscript, PDF), which means that, potentially, all the results obtained for querying structured (*e.g.* XML) or semi-structured data, could be put at work in a DL system. For instance: "What documents have a section titled x?", or "What documents have a reference to x in the bibliography?".
- content-based access. Typically, a DL stores its documents in digital format, which means that, potentially, all the results obtained in content-based multimedia information retrieval, could be put at work in a DL system.

The objective of the present work is to advance the state of the art in DL systems, by introducing a query language that addresses the first two aspects introduced above, while being amenable to be extended to the third one. This query language, which we call "multi-dimensional" as it addresses various dimensions of existence of a document, is to be intended as a foundation for DL systems, in the same sense that first-order predicate calculus is a foundation for relational database systems. Thus, we are not aiming at user-friendliness or efficient processing, but rather *expressivity.* Despite its theoretical nature, this work is carried out in the context of a project aiming at the implementation of a DL system [10,5], as a feasibility study of a novel information access service that the project will eventually realize.

The paper is structured as follows. The semantic universe of the query language is introduced in 3 stages: the document model (Section 2), the metadata model (Section 3) and the DL model (Section 4). The query language itself is given in Sections 5 and 6. Finally, Section 7 concludes.

As notational conventions, we will let $\mathbf{N}$ stand for the set of natural numbers and $\mathbf{N}_+$ for $\mathbf{N} - \{0\}$. The set of the first i natural numbers, *i.e.* $\{0, 1, \ldots, i-1\}$, will be denoted $[i]$ for short. Given any set A, $A^\star$ denotes the set of finite sequences of A's elements, while $|A|$ stands for the cardinality of set A.

2 The Document Model

The document model is inspired to the IFLA-FRBR model [16]. It distinguishes four aspects of a document:

(1) *documents,* which model the more general aspect of a document, seen as a distinct intellectual creation. For example, the article "The SOMLib Digital Library System" by Andreas Rauber and Dieter Mekl, the book "Digital Libraries and Electronic Publishing" by William Arms, the lesson "A dynamic Warehouse for XML Data of the Web" by Serge Abiteboul, the proceeding of the conference ECDL'99, are all modeled as documents.

(2) *document instances,* also referred to as *versions,* which are specific editions of documents. In fact, a document is recognized through its individual instances along the time dimension. The preliminary version of the paper "The SOMLib Digital Library System", the version submitted to the conference ECDL'99, the version published on the ECDL'99 proceeding, are examples of successive editions of the same document.

(3) *views,* which are specific intellectual expressions of document instances. A view is one specific intellectual expression of the version of a document. A view excludes physical aspects that are not integral to the intellectual perception of a document. A document version is perceived through one or more views. For example, the original version of the ECDL'99 proceedings might be disseminated in three different views: (a) a "structured textual view" containing a "Preface" created by the conference Chair, and the list of papers presented to the conference, b) a "textual view structured into thematic sessions", where each session contains the documents presented during that session, and c) the "presentation view", containing the list of the slides presented at the conference.

(4) *manifestations,* which model the physical formats under which a document is disseminated. Example of manifestations are: the MPEG file which maintains the video recording of the presentation made by Andreas Rauber at the ECDL '99 Conference, the AVI file of the same video, the Postscript file of the paper presented by Andreas Rauber at the ECDL '99, etc.

2.1 Documents

Each document is modelled, according to the above requirements, mainly as a sequence of versions, which are drawn from a set $\mathcal{V}$, to be defined next. Formally, the set of documents, $\mathcal{D}$, is the countable set:

$$\mathcal{D} = \{\langle n, h, V, v\rangle \in (\mathbf{N}_+ \times \mathcal{H} \times 2^{\mathcal{V}} \times (\mathbf{N} \to \mathcal{V})) \mid v \text{ is a bijection from } [n] \text{ to } V\}$$

where, for each document $d = \langle n_d, h_d, V_d, v_d\rangle$: (a) n_d is the document *order;* (b) h_d is the document *publishing authority,* which is the entity responsible for the document; as authorities play a major role in the definition of document collections, they are explicitly considered by the model, unlike the (rather large) number of attributes of documents that the model ignores for reasons of relevance; authorities are drawn form a countable set $\mathcal{H}$; (c) V_d are the document *versions;* (d) v_d is the document *version function,* which indexes the document versions with the first n_d natural numbers; v_d is required to be total (to make sure that all indexes have a version), injective and surjective (to make sure that each version is indexed exactly once).

2.2 Versions

As a document version is just a finite set of views, we can use the same style adopted for documents to model the set $\mathcal{V}$,*i.e.*:

$$\mathcal{V} = \{\langle n, W\rangle \in (\mathbf{N}_+ \times 2^{\mathcal{W}}) \mid |W| = n\}.$$

2.3 Views

The definition of views is more complex, thus it will be developed in stages: in the first one, we will describe how views are analyzed; in the second stage, we will provide an informal definition of views, based on the previous analysis; finally, in the third stage we will give the mathematical definition of the set $\mathcal{W}$.

View analysis. Let us consider the view shown in Figure 1.(a), which is a section titled "Views", has an opening text and a couple of subsections, titled "High Views" and "Low Views". Regularity can be imposed on this view by analyzing it as shown in Figure 1.(b), in which the view is seen as an object (the outer box), divided into two pieces: one, the inner top box, holds content, *i.e.* the section opening text; the other, depicted as an oval, holds the section structure, and consisting in the example of two parts: the section title and the section body (for better readability these two parts are separated in Figure 1.(b) by a dashed line). These parts can be analyzed (Figure 1.(c)) in the same way: the title part has content (the title itself) and no sub-parts; the body part, on the other hand, has no content but two sub-parts: the two subsections. The same pattern can finally be applied (Figure 1.(d)) to each subsection.

This example shows that the notion of view is inherently recursive: the basic elements of the recursion, technically the *atomic views,* have just content and no sub-elements, hence no structure (the title part of the previous example is one such element). All the other views are built by aggregating these elements into hierarchical structures, and endowing with content each so created view (*e.g.* the section in Figure 1).

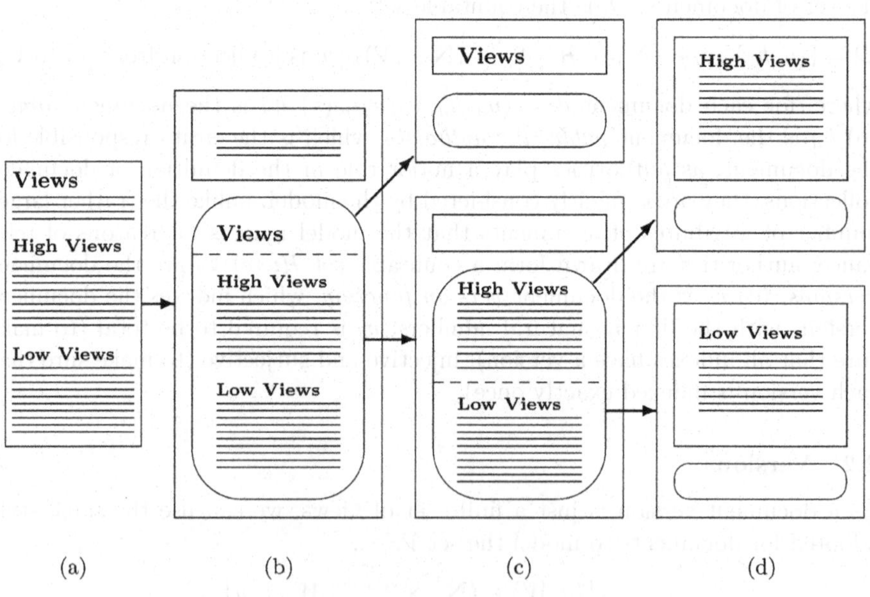

Fig. 1. View analysis.

For simplicity, our model will only consider contents of type text, even though the extension to other types is possible [14]. As far as structure is concerned, we consider ordered sets and sequences. The former kind is useful to model views whose elements are, albeit ordered for formal reasons, to be regarded as likewise; this could be the case of a list of references in a paper, which are in fact order even though their order does not really matter. Sequences are useful when structure implies order, as for instance amongst the chapters of a book.

Both structure and content can be enriched. As for the former, we add labels to views, in order to embody structural information that may be very useful in querying. Labels can be envisioned in Figures 1.(b)-(d) as tags attached to ovals; these labels could be *SECTION* for the oval in Figure 1.(b), *TITLE* and *BODY* for the ovals in Figure 1.(c) (from the top down), and *SUBSECTION* for both the ovals in Figure 1.(d). As for content, in the context of a digital library, content implies metadata, that is descriptions of content in standard formats. As there are many metadata formats, it is better to assume that each view may have several descriptions, in different formats, for its content.

Informal definition of views. Let $\mathcal{L}$ be a countable set of *labels,* and $\mathcal{T}$ a disjoint, countable set of *content elements*, *i.e.* text. Also, we will need one more object e, not belonging to any of the sets introduced so far, to represent the basic structure for building complex views, *i.e.* the *empty view.* Informally, views are defined as follows:

1. the empty view e is a view;
2. if $w_1, \ldots, w_k$, for $k \geq 1$, are views, $l \in \mathcal{L}$ and $t \in \mathcal{T}$, then:
   (i) the object having l as label, t as content and the ordered set $\{w_1, \ldots, w_k\}$ as structure, is a view;
   (ii) the object having l as label, t as content and the sequence $\langle w_1, \ldots, w_k \rangle$ as structure, is a view;
3. nothing else is a view.

For instance, the view shown in Figure 1.(a) is represented by the object $w \in \mathcal{W}$, defined as follows, letting t be the opening text of the section, t_1 and t_2 the contents of the two subsections (title included), and using parentheses to enclose all the elements of a view (*i.e.* label, content and structure):

$$
\begin{aligned}
w \ = \ (\mathit{SECTION},\ t,\ \{&(\mathit{TITLE},\ \text{“}\mathit{Views}\text{”},\ e),\\
&(\mathit{BODY},\ \lambda,\ \langle(\mathit{SUBSECTION},\ t_1,\ e\ ),\\
&\qquad(\mathit{SUBSECTION},\ t_2,\ e\ )\ \rangle\ )\ \}\ ).
\end{aligned}
$$

Figure 2 shows an XML serialization of w, consisting of a DTD followed by the actual data. As in XML it is not possible to differentiate sequences and ordered sets, no bijective mapping between our model and XML exists: different views may result in the same XML data, thus in translating from XML back to our model, only views entirely structured as either sequences or ordered sets can be generated.

Formal definition of views. In order to make the above definition of view precise, we rely on the notions of constructors and closed sets [11]. Let U be any

```
<?xml version="1.0" standalone="yes"?> <!DOCTYPE SECTION [
   <!ELEMENT SECTION (TITLE, BODY)>
   <!ELEMENT TITLE (#PCDATA)>
   <!ELEMENT BODY (SUBSECTION+)>
   <!ELEMENT SUBSECTION (#PCDATA)>
]> <SECTION>
    <TITLE> Views </TITLE>
    <BODY>
      <SUBSECTION> t1 </SUBSECTION>
      <SUBSECTION> t2 </SUBSECTION>
    </BODY>
  </SECTION>
```

Fig. 2. XML serialization of a view.

non-empty set. The *view constructors* on U are any two families of functions defined as follows:

$$A_U = \{\alpha_i : \mathcal{L} \times \mathcal{T} \times U^i \to U \mid i \in \mathbf{N}_+\}$$
$$B_U = \{\beta_i : \mathcal{L} \times \mathcal{T} \times U^i \to U \mid i \in \mathbf{N}_+\}$$

and satisfying the following conditions, for all $i, j \in \mathbf{N}_+$, $i \neq j$: (1) $ran(\alpha_i) \cap ran(\alpha_j) = \emptyset$, where $ran(\alpha_i) = \{u \in U \mid u = \alpha_i(\mathbf{u})$ for some $\mathbf{u} \in U^i\}$; (2) $ran(\beta_i) \cap ran(\beta_j) = \emptyset$; (3) $ran(\alpha_i) \cap ran(\beta_i) = \emptyset$; (4) α_i is injective, that is for all $\mathbf{u}, \mathbf{u}' \in \mathcal{U}^i$ $\alpha_i(\mathbf{u}) = \alpha_i(\mathbf{u}')$ implies $\mathbf{u} = \mathbf{u}'$; (5)β_i is injective. Taken all together, these conditions amount to say that the functions in $(A_U \cup B_U)$ are injective; this guarantees unique readability of views.

Let $\mathcal{U}$ be a countably infinite and let $\mathcal{B} = \{e\}$ be a subset of $\mathcal{U}$. The set $\mathcal{W}$ of views is the closure of $\mathcal{B}$ under $A_\mathcal{U}$ and $B_\mathcal{U}$, that is:

1. $\mathcal{W}$ contains $\mathcal{B}$;
2. $\mathcal{W}$ is closed under $A_\mathcal{U} \cup B_\mathcal{U}$;
3. if $\mathcal{W}'$ is a subset of $\mathcal{U}$ that is closed under $A_\mathcal{U} \cup B_\mathcal{U}$, then $\mathcal{W} \subseteq \mathcal{W}'$.

It can be shown [11] that $\mathcal{W}$ exists, is unique, and is given by:

$$\mathcal{W} = \mathcal{B} \cup \bigcup_{R \in (A_\mathcal{U} \cup B_\mathcal{U})} R(\mathcal{W}^{n_R})$$

where for each $R \in (A_\mathcal{U} \cup B_\mathcal{U})$, R is n_R-ary. $\mathcal{W}$ is said to be *freely generated* by $(A_\mathcal{U} \cup B_\mathcal{U})$ over $\mathcal{B}$, which guarantees uniqueness and existence of the recursive functions on $\mathcal{W}$ to be defined next.

View selectors. For ordered sets, we want to be able to denote the association between a view and the members of the ordered set in which the view is structured. Accordingly, we define the relation among views $\epsilon \subseteq \mathcal{W} \times \mathcal{W}$ as follows:

$$\epsilon = \{(w, w') \in \mathcal{W}^2 \mid \text{for some } l \in \mathcal{L},\, t \in \mathcal{T}, \text{ and } i, j \in \mathbf{N}_+,\\ w' = \alpha_i(l, t, w_1, \ldots, w_{j-1}, w, w_{j+1}, \ldots, w_i)\}$$

For sequences, we want to be able to select the k-th element of the sequence that makes up a view structure. Accordingly, we define the function $\sigma : (\mathbf{N}_+ \times \mathcal{W}) \to \mathcal{W}$ as follows:

$$\sigma(k, w) = \begin{cases} w' \text{ if for some } l \in \mathcal{L},\, t \in \mathcal{T}, \text{ and } i \in \mathbf{N}_+, \\ \quad w = \beta_i(l, t, w_1, \ldots, w_{k-1}, w', w_{k+1}, \ldots, w_i) \\ e \quad \text{otherwise} \end{cases}$$

Finally, we make available a relation that captures view composition regardless of the constructor. This is the relation among views $\pi \subseteq \mathcal{W} \times \mathcal{W}$:

$$\pi = \epsilon \cup \{(w, w') \in \mathcal{W} \times \mathcal{W} \mid \text{for some } k \in \mathbf{N}_+,\, w = \sigma(k, w')\}.$$

3 The Metadata Model

In order to develop a model of metadata able to incorporate as many metadata formats as possible, we look at the area of conceptual modeling [8], and specifically at that of semantic data modeling. The model we are going to propose next is inspired to a class of models known as object-oriented semantic data models [12,15]. The model is divided in two parts: one addressing metadata formats and the other addressing metadata specifications.

Let us be given two countable sets: $\mathcal{S}$, the *classes*, and $\mathcal{P}$, the *properties*. Informally, a *metadata format* (MF) is a 4-tuple $\langle S, P, def, \Rightarrow \rangle$, where:

- $S \subseteq \mathcal{S}$ is the finite set of the MF classes;
- $P \subseteq \mathcal{P}$ is the finite set of the MF properties;
- def: $(S \times P) \to S$ is the *property definition function;*
- $\Rightarrow \subseteq S \times S$ is the MF *subclass* relation.

Classes group objects of the same kind, *i.e.* having the same properties, or attributes. These properties are defined by the partial function *def*, which assigns to a class and a property at most one domain, that is the class from which the property may assume values. The subclass relation models an intuitive generalization/specialization criterion. Formally, the set of metadata format $\mathcal{F}$ is defined to be:

$$\mathcal{F} \subseteq 2^{\mathcal{S}} \times 2^{\mathcal{P}} \times ((\mathcal{S} \times \mathcal{P}) \to \mathcal{S}) \times 2^{\mathcal{S} \times \mathcal{S}}$$

such that, for all $\langle S, P, def, \Rightarrow \rangle \in \mathcal{F}$: (a) def: $(S \times P) \to S$; (b) $(S, \Rightarrow)$ is a partial order; (c) (structural inheritance) for all $c, c', d \in S$ and $p \in P$, if $def(c, p) = d$ and $\Rightarrow (c', c)$ then there exists $d' \in S$ such that $def(c', p) = d'$ and $\Rightarrow (d', d)$.

Tables 1 and 2 show a formulation of the Dublin Core as a metadata format $m_{DC} = \langle S_{DC}, P_{DC}, def_{DC}, \Rightarrow_{DC} \rangle$, where: S_{DC} is given by the class `DublinCore`

Table 1. Properties and their definitions for the Dublin Core format

	$def(C,P) = D$	
Property	(C,P)	D
Title	(DublinCore, Title)	String
Creator	(DublinCore, Creator)	String
Subject	(DublinCore, Subject)	SubjectScheme
Description	(DublinCore, Description)	String
Publisher	(DublinCore, Publisher)	String
Contributor	(DublinCore, Contributor)	String
Date	(DublinCore, Date)	DateScheme
Type	(DublinCore, Type)	DCMITypeVoc
Format	(DublinCore, Format)	String
Identifier	(DublinCore, Identifier)	URI
Source	(DublinCore, Source)	URI
Language	(DublinCore, Language)	LanguageScheme
Relation	(DublinCore, Relation)	URI
Coverage	(DublinCore, Coverage)	CoverageScheme
Rights	(DublinCore, Rights)	String

and the classes shown in the third column of Table 1; P_{DC} consists of the properties listed in the first column of Table 1; def_{DC} is defined in the second and third column of Table 1; $\Rightarrow_{DC}$ is shown in Table 2.

For metadata specifications (MS) we will need a countable set of *objects* $\mathcal{O}$. Given a MF $m = \langle S, P, def, \Rightarrow \rangle$, a *metadata specification for m,* is a triple $\langle O, \rightarrow, prop \rangle$, where:

- $O \subseteq \mathcal{O}$ is the finite set of MS objects;
- $\rightarrow \subseteq O \times S$ is the MS *instance* relation;
- *prop*: $(O \times P) \rightarrow O$ is the *property* function.

The objects in O are the entities that are used to represents metadata values. An object may be a simple value such as a string or a number, or may be complex, that is endowed with properties, such as dates or any other user-defined object. The *prop* function assigns to each object the properties which it is entitled to, in accordance to the property definitions in *def.*

There are three conditions that we require on a MS: *instantiation,* that is each object must be instance of at least one class; *property induction,* that is each property of an object must be induced by an appropriate definition; and *extensional inheritance,* that is if an object is an instance of a class, then it is also instance of all the superclasses of that class. Formally, we will capture these conditions in two stages. In the first one, the set of metadata specifications $\mathcal{E}$ is defined to be: $\mathcal{E} \subseteq 2^{\mathcal{O}} \times 2^{\mathcal{O} \times \mathcal{S}} \times ((\mathcal{O} \times \mathcal{P}) \rightarrow \mathcal{O})$ such that, for all $\langle O, \rightarrow, prop \rangle \in \mathcal{E}$ (instantiation): $dom(\rightarrow) = O$. In the second stage, the set of *metadata values,* $\mathcal{M}$, is defined to be $\mathcal{M} \subseteq \mathcal{F} \times \mathcal{E}$ such that, for all $(\langle S, P, def, \Rightarrow \rangle, \langle O, \rightarrow, prop \rangle) \in \mathcal{M}$, the following hold:

Table 2. The specialization relation of the DC metadata format

$\Rightarrow (C, D)$		$\Rightarrow (C, D)$	
C	D	C	D
LCSH	SubjectScheme	ISO639-2	LanguageScheme
MeSH	SubjectScheme	RFC1766	LanguageScheme
DDC	SubjectScheme	DCMIPoint	CoverageScheme
LCC	SubjectScheme	ISO3166	CoverageScheme
UDC	SubjectScheme	DCMIBox	CoverageScheme
DCMIPeriod	DateScheme	TGN	CoverageScheme
W3C-DTF	DateScheme	DCMIPeriod	CoverageScheme
		W3C-DTF	CoverageScheme

- $range(\rightarrow) \subseteq S$;
- (property induction) for all $o, o' \in O$ and $p \in P$, $prop(o,p) = o'$ implies that there exists classes $c, c' \in S$ such that: $\rightarrow (o,c)$, $def(c,p) = c'$ and $\rightarrow (o',c')$,
- (extensional inheritance) for all $o \in O$ and $c, c' \in S$, $\rightarrow (o,c)$ and $\Rightarrow (c,c')$ imply $\rightarrow (o,c')$.

A metadata value is thus a pair whose first member is a MF giving the "type" of the second member, a MS. For instance, a Dublin Core metadata value of the Joyce's *Ulysses* could be the pair (m_{DC}, s_{DC}) where m_{DC} is as given in the previous Section and s_{DC} includes one object, `ulysses`, representing the whole specification; `ulysses` is an instance of the class `DublinCore` (*i.e.* , the pair (`ulysses`,`DublinCore`) is in $\rightarrow$) and as such specifies a value for each of the 15 properties of the `DublinCore` class, as desired. As mandated by the property induction principle, each such value must be an instance of the class that the function *def* assigns as range of the property.

4 Digital Libraries Information Space

A digital library information space (DLIS) consists of two main things: the documents and the metadata. Technically, a DLIS δ is a pair $\delta = (\Delta, \Lambda)$ where Δ is a *document base* and Λ is a *metadata base*.

A document base Δ is given by $\Delta = \langle D, A, r\rangle$ where:

- $D \subseteq \mathcal{D}$ is a set of documents satisfying two constraints: (1) no two documents can share the same version, and (2) no two authorities can have the same document;
- $A \subseteq \mathcal{A}$ is a set of manifestations, where $\mathcal{A}$ stands for the set of all manifestations;
- r is a relation that associates the views in D with the manifestations in A. Formally, letting:

$$V_D = \cup_{d \in D} V_d \quad \text{and} \quad W_D = \cup_{v \in V_d} W_v,$$

$r \subseteq W_D \times A$. We further require r to be injective, so that the same manifestation cannot be associated to two different views.

Unlike documents, metadata are not independent entities, in that they exist in order to describe something else. Accordingly, given a document base Δ, a metadata base Λ for $\Delta = \langle D, A, r\rangle$ is given by $\Lambda = \langle F, E, g\rangle$ where:

- $F \subseteq \mathcal{F}$ is a set of metadata formats;
- $E \subseteq \mathcal{E}$ is a set of metadata specifications;
- g is a function that assigns metadata specifications in E to document entities in D, according to the metadata formats in F. Formally, letting $\Omega_D = D \cup V_D \cup W_D \cup A$, $g : (\Omega_D \times F) \to E$ such that, for all $x \in \Omega_D$, $f \in F$, $g(x, f) = e$ implies $(f, e) \in \mathcal{M}$.

Ω_D collects all the entities to which metadata can be attached: documents (in D), their versions (in V_D), the views of these versions (in W_D) and the manifestations in the DLIS. $g(x, f)$ gives the metadata specification, e, assigned to an element x in Ω_D for a given metadata format $f \in F$. The condition that (f, e) be in $\mathcal{M}$ guarantees that e is a specification in the appropriate format f.

Table 3. Syntax and semantics of document predicate symbols

Predicate sym.	Semantics
`Document`	$(\delta, \varphi) \models$ `Document(d)` iff $d \in D$
`Version`	$(\delta, \varphi) \models$ `Version(v)` iff $v \in V_D$
`View`	$(\delta, \varphi) \models$ `View(w)` iff $w \in W_D$
`Manifestation`	$(\delta, \varphi) \models$ `Manifestation(a)` iff $a \in A$
`HasAuthority`	$(\delta, \varphi) \models$ `HasAuthority(d,h)` iff $d = \langle n, h, V, v\rangle \in D$
`HasVersion`	$(\delta, \varphi) \models$ `HasVersion(d,v)` iff $d = \langle n, h, V, v\rangle \in D$ and $v \in V$
`HasView`	$(\delta, \varphi) \models$ `HasView(v,w)` iff $v = \langle m, W\rangle \in V_D$ and $w \in W$
`HasManifest`	$(\delta, \varphi) \models$ `HasManifest(w,a)` iff $w \in W_D$ and $(w, a) \in r$

5 The Query Language

This section presents a language for querying digital libraries. For reasons of space, familiarity with first-order syntax is assumed.

5.1 Sorts and Semantic Structure

A many-sorted logic is the most appropriate tool to take advantage at the syntactic level of the structure of the semantic universe. Thus, our sorts are the sets which have been defined in the previous part of the paper. For each of these sort, we will have in the language: (a) a countable set of constants, which are intended to be names for the objects in the sort; (b) a countable set of variables, which are intended to range over the objects in the sort; and (c) an existential quantifier, which will be denoted by subscripting the symbol $\exists$ by the sort name; thus, for instance, the existential quantifier for metadata formats will be $\exists_{\mathcal{F}}$. The intuitive reading of $(\exists_{\mathcal{F}} x)$, where x is a variable of sort $\mathcal{F}$, is "there exists a metadata format x".

Table 4. Syntax and semantics of structure predicate symbols

Predicate s.	Semantics
`In`	$(\delta, \varphi) \models$ `In(w,w')` iff $w, w' \in W_D$ and $(w, w') \in \epsilon$
`Of`	$(\delta, \varphi) \models$ `Of(w,n,w')` iff $w, w' \in W_D$ and $w = \sigma(n, w')$
`PartOf`	$(\delta, \varphi) \models$ `PartOf(w,w')` iff $w, w' \in W_D$ and $(w, w') \in \pi$
`Root`	`Root(w)` iff `View(w)` $\wedge \neg(\exists_{\mathcal{W}} x)$`PartOf(w,`$x$`)`
`Leaf`	`Leaf(w)` iff `View(w)` $\wedge \neg(\exists_{\mathcal{W}} x)$`PartOf(`$x$`,w)`
`HasParent`	`HasParent(w,w')` iff `PartOf(w,w')`
`HasChild`	`HasChild(w,w')` iff `PartOf(w',w)`
`HasAncestor`	$(\delta, \varphi) \models$ `HasAncestor(w,w')` iff $w, w' \in W_D$ and $(w, w') \in \pi^*$
`HasDescendant`	$(\delta, \varphi) \models$ `HasDescendant(w,w')` iff $w, w' \in W_D$ and $(w', w) \in \pi^*$
`IsLabelled`	$(\delta, \varphi) \models$ `IsLabelled(w,l)` iff $w \in W_D$ and for some $i \in \mathbf{N}_+$, $w = \alpha_i(l, t, w_1, \ldots, w_i)$ or $w = \beta_i(l, t, w_1, \ldots, w_i)$

The language has no function symbols, and several predicate symbols, which are illustrated below, categorized by the dimension of DLIS objects they refer to. In order to introduce these symbols and their semantics we fix the semantic structure of the language, that is the class of mathematical objects which will be used to assign meaning to queries. A *denotation function* is a bijection, mapping each constant symbol of each sort to an object of the corresponding set. On keeping with simplicity, amongst the denotation functions, we chose as *the* denotation function φ of our semantics, the one which equates the query language and the metalanguage ; so, since we have used throughout the paper the (meta)symbol d to denote a generic document, we will use the constant `d` to denote the same document in queries, *i.e.* $\varphi($`d`$) = d$. A *DLIS structure* is a pair (δ, φ), where δ is a DLIS. Notice that the function φ does not change from structure to structure.

5.2 Predicate Symbols

Table 3 shows syntax and semantics of the predicate symbols for querying the various entities of a document and their relationships. The first column of the table gives the symbol, while the second gives its semantics. Semantics is defined relatively to a DLIS structure, and is given by the conditions that make an assertion involving the predicate symbol *true* in the DLIS structure. For instance, the assertion `Document(d)` turns out to be true in a DLIS structure (δ, φ) just in case the document d, which is the object denoted by the name `d`, is in the set of documents D, which is part of the document base Δ, which is in turn part of the DLIS δ. By the same semantics, the assertion $(\exists_{\mathcal{D}} x)$`Document`$(x)$ reads as "there exists an object of sort $\mathcal{D}$ that is a document" and is true in a DLIS structure just in case the set D is not empty. If we remove the existential quantifier, we obtain the open formula `Document`(x) so called because in it the variable x is free, *i.e.* not bound to any quantifier. The last formula denotes all the objects u in the domain of interpretation whose names would make the formula true, if used in place of x. More simply, we say that the object u (a document, in the present case), *satisfies* the query. Thus, the above formula is satisfied by all the documents in the DLIS.

Table 5. Syntax and semantics of metadata predicate symbols

Predicate s.	Semantics
`HasMetadata`	$(\delta,\varphi) \models$ `HasMetadata(b,f,e)` iff $g(b,f) = e$
`HasClass`	$(\delta,\varphi) \models$ `HasClass(f,c)` iff $f = \langle S, P, def, \Rightarrow\rangle \in F$ and $c \in S$
`HasProperty`	$(\delta,\varphi) \models$ `HasProperty(f,p)` iff $f = \langle S, P, def, \Rightarrow\rangle \in F$ and $p \in P$
`HasDef`	$(\delta,\varphi) \models$ `HasDef(f,c,p,d)` iff $f = \langle S, P, def, \Rightarrow\rangle \in F$ and $def(c,p) = d$
`IsA`	$(\delta,\varphi) \models$ `IsA(f,c,d)` iff $f = \langle S, P, def, \Rightarrow\rangle \in F$ and $(c,d) \in\Rightarrow$
`HasObject`	$(\delta,\varphi) \models$ `HasObject(e,o)` iff $e = \langle O, \rightarrow, prop\rangle \in E$ and $o \in O$
`Instance`	$(\delta,\varphi) \models$ `Instance(e,o,c)` iff $e = \langle O, \rightarrow, prop\rangle \in E$ and $(o,c) \in\rightarrow$
`Prop`	$(\delta,\varphi) \models$ `Prop(e,o,p,o')` iff $e = \langle O, \rightarrow, prop\rangle \in E$ and $prop(o,p) = o'$

The usage of free variables is essential for querying. Since each free variable "returns" an object, one uses one free variable for each object desired in the answer to a query. Thus, in oder to retrieve all the documents *and* their versions, the following formula must be used `HasVersion`(x, y).

5.3 Structural Predicate Symbols

Table 4 shows the set of predicate symbols for specifying conditions on view structure. These symbols are divided into three sets. From the top down, we have:

- The predicate symbols addressing the structure of a view; thus, in order to state that the desired view is the 3rd component of a known view `w`, one uses the formula `Of`$(x, 3, $`w`$)$.
- The symbols allowing to "navigate" a view structure on the basis of the parent-child relationship. Notice that the ancestor and descendant relationships are the transitive closure of the parent and child relationships, respectively, and this fact is captured semantically by using the transitive closure of the relation π, denoted π^*.

- A special symbol to exploit labels as node markers. For instance, by combining the last two sets of symbols, one can request a chapter with a figure by means of the formula

$$\texttt{IsLabelled}(x, \texttt{Chapter}) \wedge ((\exists_{\mathcal{W}} y)\texttt{HasAncestor}(y, x) \wedge \texttt{IsLabelled}(y, \texttt{Figure}))$$

It has already been pointed out that there exists a strong relation between views and XML data. At query level, this relation can be exploited in two ways: one would be to serialize views as shown in Section 2.3 and query them by using any of the several languages that are being studied for XML, such as XQUery [7]. The other way would be to import in our query language significant portions of XML query languages, making them specialized sub-languages; a good candidate for this role would be [6], a language for addressing parts of an XML document which could be cast in the model ontology.

5.4 Metadata Predicate Symbols

Table 5 illustrates the predicate symbols for querying metadata. These can be divided in 3 sets:

- the symbol HasMetadata, which links a document entity in Ω to its metadata values;
- the symbols for querying metadata formats, which are: (a) HasClass, which is true of a format and a class if the latter is part of the former; (b) HasProperty, which does the same for properties; (c) HasDef, which mirrors property definitions; and (d) IsA, which permits to query the subclass hierarchy of a given format:
- the symbols for querying metadata specifications, which are the remaining symbols in the Table, and whose role is perfectly analogous to those of the previous set of symbols.

Thus, in order to know the fields available in the metadata format f one uses the formula:

$$(\exists_{\mathcal{C}} x_c)(\exists_{\mathcal{C}} x_d)\texttt{HasDef}(f, x_c, x, x_d),$$

while for the classes that are in the metadata formats associated to a certain known document d, one uses the formula:

$$(\exists_{\mathcal{F}} x_f)(\exists_{\mathcal{E}} x_e)\texttt{HasMetadata}(\texttt{d}, x_f, x_e) \wedge \texttt{HasClass}(x_f, x).$$

For the range of the property date in the same metadata formats of the previous formula:

$$(\exists_{\mathcal{F}} x_f)(\exists_{\mathcal{E}} x_e)(\exists_{\mathcal{C}} x_c)\texttt{HasMetadata}(\texttt{d}, x_f, x_e) \wedge \texttt{HasDef}(x_f, x_c, \texttt{date}, x).$$

In the same context, the specializations of the class author can be found by:

$$(\exists_{\mathcal{F}} x_f)(\exists_{\mathcal{E}} x_e)\texttt{HasMetadata}(\texttt{d}, x_f, x_e) \wedge \texttt{IsA}(x_f, x, \texttt{author}).$$

As far as querying metadata specifications, the following formula returns the views that have the field Creator of the Dublin Core metadata format equal to "John Doe":

$$(\exists_{\mathcal{F}} x_f)(\exists_{\mathcal{E}} x_e)(\exists_{\mathcal{O}} x_o)\texttt{View}(x) \wedge \texttt{HasMetadata}(x, x_f, x_e) \wedge \texttt{HasClass}(x_f, \texttt{DublinCore}) \wedge \texttt{Prop}(x_e, x_o, \texttt{Creator}, \texttt{JohnDoe}).$$

6 Querying Digital Libraries

For organizational reasons, the documents in a DLIS are organized in *collections,* which are virtual subsets of the document base, collecting documents on the basis of their authorities. Collections are defined via a special kind of queries, called *collection definition predicates* (CDPs). A CDP is a formula of the query language, having the form:

$$(\texttt{HasAuthority}(x, \mathtt{a}_1) \vee \ldots \vee \texttt{HasAuthority}(x, \mathtt{a}_n)) \wedge \phi(x)$$

for $n \geq 1$, where $\phi(x)$ is a query having x as only free variable and including only metadata predicate symbols. In practice, a CDP denotes a set of documents in the document base, namely those having as authority one of $a_1, \ldots, a_n$, and satisfying the query $\phi(x)$.

An *extended DLIS* is a tuple $\Gamma = (\delta, \Phi_1(x), \ldots, \Phi_k(x))$ where δ is a DLIS and $\Phi_1(x), \ldots, \Phi_k(x)$ are CDPs, for $k \geq 0$. A *query* to an extended DLIS Γ is given by $(\Upsilon, \Psi(x_1, \ldots, x_m))$, where Υ is a (possibly empty) subset of the collections in Γ, the *target* of the query, and $\Psi(x_1, \ldots, x_m)$ is a formula of the previously introduced language whose only free variables are $x_1, \ldots, x_m$, for $m \geq 1$. The *predicate* of a query $(\Upsilon, \Psi(x_1, \ldots, x_m))$ is the formula $\Xi(x, x_1, \ldots, x_m)$ given by

$$(\bigvee_{\psi(x) \in \Upsilon} \psi(x)) \wedge \Psi(x_1, \ldots, x_m).$$

In practice, the predicate of the query is the formula that denotes all the documents x belonging to anyone of the target collections (as required by the first disjunction of the above formula), *and* satisfying $\Psi(x_1, \ldots, x_m)$. In case Υ is empty, the semantics of the language guarantees that all the documents in the document bases are considered.

The *result set* of a query $(\Upsilon, \Psi(x_1, \ldots, x_m))$ to the extended DLIS $\Gamma = (\delta, \Phi_1, \ldots, \Phi_k)$, is the set of $(m+1)$-tuples $\langle u_0, u_1, \ldots, u_m \rangle$ that satisfy the query predicate $\Xi(x, x_1, \ldots, x_m)$, that is:

$$(\delta, \varphi) \models \Xi(\mathtt{u}, \mathtt{u}_1, \ldots, \mathtt{u}_m).$$

7 Conclusions and Future Work

The presented query facility permits structure- and sophisticate metadata-based document retrieval, and as such advances current DL models. In order to arrive at a precise definition of this query facility, a mathematical model of Digital Libraries has been developed, and used to assign meaning to user queries. This level of precision makes the language universally available, implementable and, also important, extensible with more capability, notably content-based access.

As already pointed out, this work, albeit of a foundational nature, is carried out within a project, aiming at the development of a DL system. We plan to implement a significant fragment of the language presented. Specifically, our work programme is to cut down the expressivity of the language down to a subset of first-order logic, which is powerful enough to express all significant queries but also simpler from the computational point of view. The idea is to partition the language presented here into a set of sub-languages, each addressing a different dimension of documents, and use the general framework of logic for combining these sub-languages. In this respect, the inclusion of content-based retrieval in the language presents no conceptual problem, as a logical framework supporting this kind of functionality has already been developed [14]. An architecture for implementing the language is described in [9].

References

1. Dublin core metadata element set, version 1.1: Reference description. http://dublincore.org/documents/dces/.
2. NCSTRL: Networked computer science technical reference library. http://www.ncstrl.org.
3. Networked digital library of theses and dissertations. http://www.theses.org.
4. The new zealand digital library. http://www.nzdl.org.
5. SCHOLNET: A digital library testbed to support networked scholarly communities. http://www.ercim.org/scholnet.
6. XML path language (XPath) 2.0. http://www.w3.org/TR/xpath20.
7. XQuery 1.0: An XML query language. http://www.w3.org/TR/xquery.
8. M. Brodie, J Mylopoulos, and J. Schmidt, editors. *On Conceptual Modelling.* Springer Verlag, 1984.
9. D. Castelli and P. Pagano. OpenDLib: a digital library service system. In *Proc. of ECDL2002, 6th European Conf. on Research and Advanced Technology for Digital Libraries*, Rome, I, 2002.
10. D. Castelli and P. Pagano. Global system architecture report. Technical Report D2.2.1, Scholnet Project Deliverable, 2001. http://www.ercim.org/scholnet/results.html.
11. P. Fejer and D. Simovici. *Mathematical Foundations of Computer Science. Volume 1.* Springer-Verlag, New York, 1991.
12. R. Hull and R. King. Semantic database modeling: Survey, applications and research issues. *ACM Computing Surveys*, 19(3):201–259, 1987.
13. Network Development Library of Congress and MARC Standards Office. MARC standards. http://lcweb.loc.gov/marc/.
14. C. Meghini, F. Sebastiani, and U. Straccia. A model of multimedia information retrieval. *JACM*, 48(5):909–970, 2001.
15. J. Mylopoulos and A. Borgida. Some features of the Taxis data model. In *Proc. of the 6th VLDB*, pages 399–410, Montreal, CA, 1980.
16. K.G. Saur. Functional requirements for bibliographic records. Final report. Technical report, Munchen, 1998. http://www.ifla.org/VII/s13/frbr/frbr.pdf.

The TREC2001 Video Track: Information Retrieval on Digital Video Information

Alan F. Smeaton[1], Paul Over[2], Cash J. Costello[3], Arjen P. de Vries[4], David Doermann[5], Alexander Hauptmann[6], Mark E. Rorvig[7], John R. Smith[8], and Lide Wu[9]

[1]Centre for Digital Video Processing, Dublin City University, Dublin, 9, Ireland.
[2]National Institute for Standards and Technology, Gaithersburg, Md., USA.
[3] Johns Hopkins University Applied Physics Laboratory, Laurel, Md., USA.
[4]CWI, Amsterdam, The Netherlands.
[5] Laboratory for Language and Media Processing, University of Maryland, College Park, MD. USA
[6]School of Computer Science, Carnegie Mellon University, USA
[7]School of Library Information Sciences, University of North Texas, Tx., USA
[8]IBM T. J. Watson Research Center, Hawthorne, NY, USA.
[9]Dept. of Computer Science, Fudan University, Shanghai, China..

The development of techniques to support content-based access to archives of digital video information has recently started to receive much attention from the research community. During 2001, the annual TREC activity, which has been benchmarking the performance of information retrieval techniques on a range of media for 10 years, included a „track" or activity which allowed investigation into approaches to support searching through a video library. This paper is not intended to provide a comprehensive picture of the different approaches taken by the TREC2001 video track participants but instead we give an overview of the TREC video search task and a thumbnail sketch of the approaches taken by different groups. The reason for writing this paper is to highlight the message from the TREC video track that there are now a variety of approaches available for searching and browsing through digital video archives, that these approaches do work, are scalable to larger archives and can yield useful retrieval performance for users. This has important implications in making digital libraries of video information attainable.

1. Introduction

The technical challenges associated with generation, storage and transmission of digital video information have received much attention over the last few years and we are now at the stage where we can regard these engineering problems as having made significant progress. This now allows us to create large libraries of digital video information and with that comes the associated challenge of developing effective, efficient and scalable approaches to searching and browsing through video digital libraries.

TREC is an annual activity which has been ongoing for the last decade and which has been benchmarking the retrieval effectiveness of a variety of information retrieval

M. Agosti and C. Thanos (Eds.): ECDL 2002, LNCS 2458, pp. 266-275, 2002.

tasks. This has included retrieval on text documents, documents in a variety of natural languages, spoken audio, web documents, documents corrupted by an OCR process, and so on. In 2001, TREC included a „track" or activity line which explored different approaches to searching through a collection of digital video information. The goal of the TREC2001 video track was to promote progress in content-based retrieval from digital video by using open, metrics-based evaluation and using publicly available video.

The TREC2001 video track had 12 participating groups, 5 from US, 2 from Asia and 5 from Europe and was divided into two distinct tasks namely shot boundary detection and searching. Shot boundary detection is the task of automatically determining the boundaries between different camera shots which is usually used as a fundamental component of video structuring and further details of the shot boundary detection task can be found in [1]. The searching task involved running queries against the video collection and what made the queries particularly interesting and challenging was that they were true multimedia queries as they all had video clips, images, or audio clips as part of the query, in addition to a text description. Participating groups used a variety of techniques to match these multimedia queries against the video dataset, some running fully automated techniques and others involving users in interactive search experiments. 11 hours of MPEG-1 data was collected and distributed as well as 74 topics or queries.

The rest of this paper is organised as follows. In the next section we give an introduction to the search task, covering the video data used, the topics and how they were formed, the evaluation mechanism and the evaluation metrics adopted. In section 3, each of the main groups who participated in the search task give an overview of the approach that they have taken in the search task. Section 4 includes a brief summary and comparison across the approaches as well as including some indicative evaluation results in order to allow the reader to gauge the absolute performance levels of the video retrieval systems. A concluding section assesses the contribution that the TREC2001 video track has made.

2. The TREC2001 Video Track

Like most of the TREC activities, the video track in TREC2001 was coordinated by the National Institute for Standards and Technology (NIST) though participating groups contributed significant amounts of work towards the definition and running of the track. The search tasks in the video track were extensions of their text analogues from previous TRECs. Participating groups were asked to index a test collection of video data and were asked to return lists of shots from the videos in the test collection which met the information need for a set of topics. The boundaries for the units of video to be retrieved were supposed to be shots and were not predefined and each system made its own independent judgment of what frame sequences constituted a relevant shot.

Participants were free to use whatever indexing and retrieval techniques they wished though the search task was divided into two distinct classes, one for interactive retrieval which involved some human in the search loop, and one for automatic retrieval where the retrieved shots were determined completely automatically. This distinction arose because the search task was designed to replicate the situation where a user uses a video information retrieval system to satisfy an information need, sometimes using interactive retrieval, sometimes completely automated. Another feature of the search task, which also reflects its real world nature, is that topics are either „known item" or „general". In the case of known item retrieval, the user knows that there is at least one relevant shot in the test collection and the task is to find those shots known to satisfy the information need, while the case of general searching reflects the situation where the user does not know whether or not there are shots in the collection which satisfy the information need.

Although the track decided early on that it should work with more than text recognised from spoken audio, systems were allowed to use transcripts created by automatic speech recognition (ASR) and any group which did this had to submit a run without the ASR or one using only ASR as a baseline. Three groups used ASR.

The test collection for the search task consisted of 85 video programmes representing over 11 hours of video, encoded in MPEG-1 and totalling over 6 Gbytes in size. The content came from the OpenVideo project [2], the NIST organisation itself, and the BBC who provided some stock footage. Further details of the collection can be found on the web pages for the video track [3]. The videos are mostly of a documentary nature but vary in their age, production style, and quality. The only manually created information that search systems were allowed to use was that which was already as part of the test collection, namely the existing transcripts associated with the NIST files and the existing descriptions associated with the BBC material, though most groups did not use this information.

The search topics were designed as multimedia descriptions of an information need, such as someone searching an archive of video might have in the course of collecting material to include in a larger video or to answer questions. While today this may be done largely by searching associated descriptive text created by a human when the video material was added to the archive, the track's scenario envisioned allowing the searcher to use a combination of other media in describing his or her information need. How one might do this naturally and effectively is an open question. Thus topics in the TREC2001 video track contained not only text but possibly examples (including video, audio, images) which represent the searcher's information need. The topics expressed a very wide variety of needs for video clips: of a particular object or class of objects, of an activity/event or class of activities/events, of a particular person, of a kind of landscape, on a particular subject, using a particular camera technique, answering a factual question, etc.

For a number of practical reasons, the topics were created by the participants which is an example of the significant contribution to running the track made by those participants. Each group was asked to formulate several topics they could imagine being used by someone searching a video archive. NIST submitted topics as well, did some selection and pruning, and negotiated revisions. All the topics were pooled and all systems were expected to run on all of these if possible.

All topics contained a text description of the user information need and examples in other media were optional. There were indicators of the appropriate processing (automatic, manual or either) and finally, if the topic was a hunt for one or more known-items, then the list of known-items was included. If examples to illustrate the information need were included then these were to come from outside the test data.

74 topics were produced in this manner and Table 1 gives a summary of the use of example media in those topics.

Table 1. Distribution of other media in topics

Number of topics	74
No. topics with image examples / Avg. number of images	26 / 2.0
No. topics with audio examples / Avg. number of audio	10 / 4.3
No. topics with video examples / Avg. number of videos	51 / 2.4

In the case of the known-item search submissions, these were evaluated by NIST but the evaluation of known item retrieval turned out to be more difficult than anticipated. One reason for this was because each group was able to define the start/stop boundaries of the shots they returned we had to use a parameterised matching procedure between known item and submitted results. Matching a submitted item to a known-item defined with the topic was a function of the length of the known-item, the length of the submitted item, the length of the intersection, and two variables which measured the amount of desired overlap among these. Evaluations were run with different settings of these overlaps. The measures calculated for the evaluation of known-item searching were precision and recall with the ground truth or relevant video clips from the collection being provided by the participants who formulated the topics. The number of known-items across the topics varied from 1 to 60 with a mean of 5.63, so the upper bound on precision in a result set of 100 items was quite low.

Submissions for the general search topics were evaluated by retired information analysts at NIST. They were instructed to familiarize themselves with the topic material and then judge each submitted clip relevant if it contained material which met the need expressed in the topic as they understood it, even if there was non-relevant material present, otherwise they were told to judge the clip as not relevant. They used web-based software developed at NIST to allow them to (re)play the video, audio, and image examples included in the topic as well as the submitted clips. A second set of relevance judgments of the submitted materials was then performed and overall, the two assessors agreed 84.6% of the time. The measure calculated for the evaluation general searching was precision but we have also calculated a partial recall score.

The detailed performance scores from the 8 groups who submitted a total of 21 runs are available online at http://www-nlpir.nist.gov/projects/trecvid/results.html but before we address retrieval performance, the next section will give a thumbnail sketch of the different approaches to video indexing and retrieval taken by the TREC2001 video track participants.

3. Participants in the TREC2001 Video Track Search Task

Of the 12 groups who took part in the TREC2001 video track, most completed the shot boundary detection task and 8 completed the search task and the approaches that each of these groups have taken is described here. Further descriptions on all of the participants work can be found in their papers in the TREC2001 proceedings [4]

3.1 Carnegie Mellon University

The CMU Informedia Digital Video library's standard processing modules were used for the TREC2001 Video evaluations. Among the processing features that were utilized in Video TREC were: shot detection using simple color histogram differences, keyframe extraction, speech recognition using the Sphinx speech recognizer with a 64000 word vocabulary, face detection, video OCR, and image search based on color histogram features in different color spaces and textures.

The Informedia interface was used in the interactive track with only minor modifications, most of which involved user preference settings. For example, users found they wanted to see as many shot results for each query as could fit on the screen, while geographic maps were irrelevant. The main modification was the addition of multiple image search engines, which allowed a user to switch between image retrieval approaches, when nothing relevant could be found using a given image retrieval approach.

For the automatic track, Informedia image retrieval was modified to process I-frames instead of merely keyframes for the image retrieval. We also added a speaker identification component, which determined whether a given segment of audio might have originated from the same speaker as the query audio. Post-mortem analysis of the results showed that image retrieval and video OCR had the largest impact on performance.

3.2 Dublin City University (Ireland)

The group from Dublin City University explored interactive search and retrieval from digital video by employing more than 30 users to perform the search tasks under controlled, timed conditions. In the Físchlár system developed at DCU [5], several keyframe browser interfaces have been developed and the task DCU performed was to evaluate the relative effectiveness of three different keyframe browsers. One of these keyframe browsers was based on a timeline of groups of related keyframes, a second browser interface simply played the keyframes on screen as a kind of slideshow, and the final browser interface was a 4-level hierarchical browser which allowed dynamic navigation through the keyframe sets. In the DCU experiments, 30 users (either final year undergraduates or research students) were employed to spend between 5 and 10 minutes on each topic, and each volunteer did interactive searching on 12 topics using one of the 3 different browsers per topic in round robin fashion. This gave the DCU group the opportunity to compare the relative performances of the three keyframe browser interfaces.

3.3 Fudan University (China)

The group from Fudan University tried 17 topics, including people searching, video text searching, camera motion etc. In order to do the search they also developed several feature extracting modules. These are qualitative camera motion analysis module, face detection and recognition module, video text detection and recognition module, and a speaker recognition and speaker clustering module. In addition they also used the speech SDK from Microsoft to get transcripts. Based on the above feature extraction modules, the Fudan retrieval system consists of two parts. One is the off-line indexing sub-system and the other is on-line searching sub-system.

For the face detection and recognition modules, face detection consists of skin-color based segmentation, and motion and shape filtering; face recognition uses a new optimal discrimination criterion to get features for recognition [6]. For the video text detection and recognition module, the group used vertical edge based methods to detect text blocks and an improved logical level technique to binarize the text blocks. The recognition was done by commercial software after binarization..

3.4 IBM Research[1]

The IBM Research team developed a system for automatic and interactive content-based retrieval of video using visual features and statistical models. The system used IBM CueVideo for computing automatic shot boundary detection results and selecting key-frames. The system indexed the key-frames of the video shots using MPEG-7 visual descriptors based on color histograms, color composition, texture and edge histograms. The MPEG-7 visual descriptors were used for answering automatic searches using content-based retrieval techniques. The system also used statistical models for classifying events (fire, smoke, launch), scenes (greenery, land, outdoors, rock, sand, sky, water), and objects (airplane, boat, rocket, vehicle, faces). The classifiers were used to generate labels and corresponding confidence scores for each shot. The features and models were then used together for answering interactive searches where the user constructed query/filter pipelines that cascaded content-based and model-based searches. This allowed integration of multiple searches using different methods for each topic, for example, to retrieve „shots that have similar color to this image, have label 'outdoors' and show a 'boat.'"

The IBM team also developed a system based on automatic speech recognition (ASR) and text indexing. The speech-based system was used as a baseline for the content-based/model-based system. The overall results showed that the content-based/model-based system performed relatively well compared to the speech-based system and to other systems. In some cases the speech-based system provided better results, for example, to retrieve „clips that deal with floods." In other cases, the content-based/model-based system provided better results, for example, to retrieve „shots showing grasslands." In two cases, the best result was obtained by combining speech-based and content-based/model-based methods, for example, to retrieve „clips of Perseus high altitude plane." The results show promise in particular for the approach based on statistical modeling for video content classification. The overall results show that significant improvements are still needed in retrieval effectiveness in general to develop usable systems. The NIST video retrieval benchmark is helping to accelerate the necessary technology development.

---

1 The IBM Research Team consisted of members from IBM T. J. Watson Research Center and IBM Almaden Research Center.

3.5 Johns Hopkins University

The JHU/APL research group developed an automatic retrieval system for the TREC2001 video track that relied on the image content of the digital video frames. Each keyframe in the video collection was indexed by its color histogram and image texture features. The texture measures were calculated using a descriptor proposed by Manjunath [7]. Ignoring audio clips or text descriptions, the query representation consisted of the image and video portions of the information need. A weighted distance between the image features of the query representation and the keyframes in the index served as a similarity measure. The shots that were retrieved for a particular query minimized this distance measure.

3.6 Lowlands Group (Netherlands)

A 'joint venture' between research institutes and universities in the Netherlands approached the challenge offered by the Video Track as the 'Lowlands Team'[2]. The group submitted pure automatic as well as 'interactive' runs, investigating the influence of human interaction on retrieval results.

The visual automatic system heuristically selected a set of filters based on specialized detectors, by analyzing the query text with WordNet; e.g., the face detector is associated to categories 'person, human, individual'. The retrieval system included a face detector, a camera motion detector (pan, tilt, zoom), a monologue detector, and a detector for text found in the keyframes using OCR. The filtered results are ranked with query example images or keyframes from example videos. A transcript-based automatic system used speech transcripts provided by CMU in a retrieval model based on language models. A trivial combination of these two automatic systems has also been tried.

The first interactive run investigated whether better articulated queries are helpful; e.g., Lunar Rover scenes are characterized by 'a black sky', and the Starwars scene by 'shiny gold'. A second interactive run studied whether a user could improve, with limited effort, the results by combining the four other approaches.

A (somewhat disappointing) lesson from the retrieval results was that the transcript-only run outperformed all other approaches, including the interactive runs.

3.7 University of Maryland

The University of Maryland, working with visiting researchers from the University of Oulu, extended methods used for image retrieval based on the spatial correlation for colors by using a novel color content method, the Temporal Color Correlogram, to capture the spatio-temporal relationship of colors in a video shot using co-occurrence statistics. The temporal correlogram is an extension of HSV color correlogram, and

---

[2] The Lowlands Team consisted of the database group of the CWI, the multimedia group of TNO, the vision group of the University of Amsterdam, and the language technology group of University of Twente.

computes an autocorrelation of the quantized HSV color values from a set of frame samples taken from a video shot.

To implement the approach the video material was segmented to create shots using VideoLogger video editing software from Virage and our own MERIT system. From each shot, the first frame was selected as a representative key frame, and the static image color correlogram was obtained. In order to calculate the temporal correlogram non-exhaustively and to keep the number of samples in equal for varying shot lengths, each shot was sampled evenly with a respective sampling delay so that the number of sample frames did not exceed 40. After segmentation, shot features were fed into our CMRS retrieval system and queries were defined using either example videos or example images depending on the respective VideoTREC topic specification. VideoTREC result submission contained retrieval results of two system configurations. The first configuration was obtained using the temporal color correlogram for the retrieval topics that contained video examples in the topic definition and the second configuration used the color correlogram for topics that contained example images in their definition.

3.8 University of North Texas

The University of North Texas team extracted frames from the collection at regular five-second intervals. These frames were then run through a keyframe extraction process, which removed the redundance of highly similar frames and ensured the presence of frames outside the prescribed normal distribution limits. The resulting keyframes were placed into UNT's Brighton Image Searcher application, which is based on mathematical measures that correspond to primitive image features. Two members of the team independently used this application to attempt to retrieve relevant keyframes for 13 of the original search topics. For each topic, the two people performing the searches selected a keyframe that appeared to answer the question. The chosen keyframe was then used as an exemplar to find keyframes similar to it. Precision scores were better than expected due to the human judgment presence.

4. Summary and Analysis of Approaches

The brief review of the approaches to video indexing and retrieval taken by track participants shows those approaches to be very varied indeed. Some sites ran interactive searching with real users (DCU) while others did their query processing entirely automatically (JHU). Some used automatic speech recognition transcripts (CMU, IBM, Lowlands) while others based their retrieval entirely on the visual aspects of video (UNT, UMd). Some groups used many automatically extracted video features as part of their retrieval (CMU, IBM, Fudan, Lowlands) while others used only a limited set of identified features (UMd, UNT). Some groups were experienced in the video indexing field and were able to leverage upon previous experience and background in working with video (IBM, CMU) while for other groups, this was their first real experience of doing video indexing and retrieval (JHU, UNT).

As might be expected for the first running of an evaluation framework still very much under construction, the results are probably most useful for small-scale comparisons - within-topic and between closely related system variants. Plausible cross-system comparison will have to wait on better consistency in topic formulation, agreement on better measures, larger numbers of comparable data points. We expect some of the participants will do further investigation and analysis of their own TREC2001 video track results and such analysis may give further insights which will be of benefit to those participants.

In terms of performance results, overall the absolute performance figures were very mixed. In the known item search tasks the mean average precision for the best 2 interactive runs (1 site) was a little over 0.6, across ~31 topics, while another group submitted two runs over the same topics and scored a consistent 0.23. Scores for comparable automatic runs ranged from 0.002 to 0.609. The use of averages may be misleading, particularly given the large number of topics for which any given system found no relevant clips. For the general search tasks the results were generally even poorer with mean partial average precision scores (based on half the collection) ranging from 0.03 to 0.23 for interactive runs on 12 topics and from 0.02 to 0.11 for automatic runs on 28 topics. The multiplicity of factors makes success as well as failure analysis a real challenge. Ongoing examination will try to explain differences in performance, but it may be that the first running of any TREC track will always be the one which irons out the difficulties and throws up the unforseen problems and that was certainly true here.

5. Conclusions and Contribution of the TREC2001 Video Track

The TREC2001 video track revealed that there are still a lot of issues to be addressed successfully when it comes to evaluating the performance of retrieval on digital video information. It was very encouraging to see interest from the community who specialise in evaluation of interactive retrieval, in what was achieved in the video track.

Overall, the track was successful with more participants than expected and the promise of even more groups this year (2002). However the real impact of the track was not in the measurement of the effectiveness of one approach to retrieval from digital video libraries compared to another approach but was the fact that we have now shown that there are several groups working in this area worldwide who have the capability and the systems to support real information retrieval on significant volumes of digital video content. As an indication of what our field is now capable of and of the potential we have for future development, the TREC2001 video track was a wonderful advertisement. There have also been many lessons learned from the track, for example the technical issues related to defining frame numbers in video which are consistent across the decoders used by different participants.

One of the interesting questions thrown up by the general search task was to do with the complexity of the topics and the relationship between the text and non-textual parts of the topic where topics had image/audio/video examples. Often it was not clear that all of the example was exemplary, but there was no way to indicate, even to a human, what aspects of the example to emphasize or ignore. We're not sure what to do about this but it may be that by making the topics more focussed, as we are planning this year, this issue may disappear.

For this year we will use a new dataset which is greater in size, and more challenging in nature – at the time of writing it appears that the TREC2002 video track will have over 20 participating groups and that we will repeat the searching task with a more focussed set of topics, some with multimedia topic descriptions.

We are also expecting to have a variety of detection tasks such as the occurrence and number of faces, identifying text in the image and then submitting it for OCR, categorising the audio as either speech, audio or silence, and so on. The search task will be as before, namely emulating the scenario where a user approaches a video retrieval system with some information need which is satisfied by the retrieval of some number of video clips from the video archive and the evaluation will, as before, be done in terms of precision and recall.

Authors' Note: The authors wish to extend our sympathies to the family and friends of our co-author, Mark E. Rorvig, who passed away shortly before this paper was submitted. We thank Diane Jenkins from UNT for helping us to clarify some of the contributions from University of North Texas.

References

1. Smeaton, A.F., Over, P. and Taban R. The TREC-2001 Video Track Report, in NIST Special Publication 500-250: The Tenth Text REtrieval Conference (TREC 2001) (available at http://trec.nist.gov/pubs/trec10/t10_proceedings.html)
2. The OpenVideo Project. Available at http://www.open-video.org/ (last visited 30 April 2002).
3. The TREC Video Track. Available at http://www-nlpir.nist.gov/projects/t01v/t01v.html (last visited 30 April 2002)
4. Proceedings of the Tenth Text REtrieval Conference (TREC-2001), Gaithersburg, Maryland, November 13-16, 2001 Available at http://trec.nist.gov/pubs.html (last visited 30 April 2002).
5. Lee, H. *et al.*: Implementation and Analysis of Several Keyframe-Based Browsing Interfaces to Digital Video. In *Proceedings of the Fourth European Conference on Digital Libraries (ECDL)*, Lisbon, Portugal, Springer-Verlag LNCS 1923, J. Borbinha and T. Baker (Eds), pp.206-218, September 2000.
6. Yuefei Guo, Lide Wu.„A novel optimal discriminant principal in high dimensional spaces", *Proc. International Conference on Development and Learning*, June 2002, MIT
7. Manjunath, B. Wu, P. Newsam, S. and Shin, H. A Texture Descriptor for Browsing and Similarity Retrieval.' *Journal of Signal Processing: Image Communication*, 16(1), pp. 33-43, September 2000.

Automated Alignment and Annotation of Audio-Visual Presentations

Gareth J.F. Jones and Richard J. Edens

Department of Computer Science, University of Exeter
Exeter, EX4 4PT, United Kingdom
{G.J.F.Jones,R.J.Edens}@exeter.ac.uk

Abstract. Recordings of audio-visual presentations are a potentially valuable component of digital libraries. These recordings can be archived to enable remote access to audio presentations including lectures and seminars. Recordings of presentations often contain multiple information streams involving visual and audio data. If the full benefit of these recordings is to be realised these multiple media streams must be properly integrated to enable rapid navigation. This paper describes the application of information retrieval techniques within a system to automatically synchronise an audio soundtrack with electronic slides from a presentation. A novel component of the system is the detection of sections of the presentation unsupported by prepared slides, such as discussion and question answering, and automatic development of keypoint slides for these elements of the presentation.

1 Introduction

The increasing availability of audio-visual recording equipment and the ease with which recordings can be made available online via the World Wide Web, means that it is becoming common practice in organisations to routinely record presentations such as lectures and seminars. One important application of this technology is the recording of university and college lectures. These are often made available online by lecturers for private study by those attending the lectures, but are also increasingly being utilised for distance learning by students physically remote to the institution.

At present recordings are generally made available for playback in the manner of a convention video recording, for example features such as fast forward and preview are often supported. However the full potential of these recordings will only be realised when the full content of the recordings is made available to enable individuals to search for interesting sections of the presentation.

As these collections of recordings grow they are beginning to form valuable digital libraries often containing material not otherwise available. Information delivered by speakers will often be unplanned, particularly when answering questions or taking part in discussions. These elements of a presentation are sometimes referred to as containing *tacit knowledge*; information which is based on

M. Agosti and C. Thanos (Eds.): ECDL 2002, LNCS 2458, pp. 276–291, 2002.

personal experiences, know how, values and beliefs [1]. Being able to automatically search these presentations will make this valuable resource much more accessible. At present, the only way to gain this type of expert insight is often to attend a lecture or speak with the presenter personally, but the ephemeral nature of these comments in their context means that the speaker may never articulate the particular unique analysis from an individual presentation again.

The technology used to make these recordings varies greatly. Well funded lecture halls may be equipped with multiple high quality audio and video capture points and record all images projected onto screens. More often a single portable video camcorder or audio recorder is used to capture the presentation. Even at institutions equipped with some state-of-the-art facilities, the majority of their lecture halls are less well equipped, and for the foreseeable future most recordings will be made in existing lectures halls equipped with portable digital recorders.

There is excellent existing work investigating the integration of multiple sources in well equipped lecture halls to provide a combined presentation, for example [2] [3]. While this work concentrates on presentation and metadata, in our work we focus on synchronisation of digital audio recordings and slide presentations using linguistic content to provide searching of the actual information delivered in the lecture. Our system demonstrates the application of a combination of techniques from information retrieval to segment and align slides with the spoken contents of the audio presentation. In addition, recognising that lectures often do not follow the planned structure exactly, the system is able to detect slides within a presentation not covered in the audio presentation, and sections of the presentation unsupported by slides, and then process these sections to identify keypoints and automatically form these into a new slide. The system can operate fully automatically or to provide support to a technician preparing presentation packages. While at present this is a freestanding application, we discuss later in the paper how it might be integrated into a larger knowledge management infrastructure to support student learning.

The remainder of the paper is organised as follows: Section 2 outlines the background to the project and describes our recording environment and system requirements, Section 3 describes the technologies used for information management, Section 4 describes the integration of the technologies to form our complete system, and Section 5 considers how the system might be extended for greater integration with personal learning and digital libraries.

2 Audio-Visual Presentations

The background to this project is an ongoing project at the *University of West England, U.K.* for the preparation and delivery of *eLectures*. The concept of eLectures is to provide a means of capturing and delivering audio recordings of lectures alongside the electronic visual aids used by the lecturer. In the basic eLectures system the slides and audio recordings are manually aligned and packaged for delivery over the Internet. eLectures are then available to students unable to attend the lecture, for private study and revision, and can be used for distance learning. Lectures are digitally recorded using a MiniDisc recorder and slides are prepared using a standard MS PowerPoint application. The processing of the recordings involves two components:

- Conversion of visual aids into a standard format for Internet delivery, this includes features such as applying standard templates and addition of features such as "next slide" and "previous slide" buttons. This process is easily automated and very fast.
- Processing the audio recordings is much slower. Sections of audio corresponding to each slide are identified manually and the audio recording segmented using *Cool Edit Pro*.

Even experienced technicians take approximately two hours to segment each recording. While the number of recordings is small this load is manageable, but as the proportion of recordings within an institution increases this procedure will rapidly become uneconomic.

Further problems can arise due to the dynamic nature of lecture presentations. The lecturer may skip a slide, perhaps due to time constraints or a change of plan while delivering the lecture. Also the lecturer may expand on a topic to provide further explanation in answer to a question or engage in discussion. The current system enables slides without audio to be marked and for new slides to be generated to support spontaneous material. Both of these processes, particularly the latter are very time consuming.

The system described in this paper supports the alignment of slides with the audio soundtrack of the lecture, identifies slides not covered in the lecture, and detects audio material without planned slides. New slides are then automatically developed for this material. The output of the system is then available for checking by an editor who is able to correct any mistakes and tidy up the automatically generated slides. The system can operate fully automatically, however because there are often not definitive segmentation points, the output of the system is improved by human verification. Thus the main objective of our system is to significantly increase the efficiency with which lectures can be prepared for Internet delivery.

3 Segmentation and Alignment Techniques

Automated audio-visual alignment systems need to perform two key tasks: the segmentation of the audio stream into sections corresponding to individual slides and the alignment of the slides with the audio segments. Our system uses a number of separate components in a tightly integrated way to perform these procedures. The system makes use of digital audio processing and the application of statistical *Information Retrieval (IR)* techniques. IR methods typically satisfy a user's information need by returning a number of potentially useful relevant documents in response to their search request. IR systems are exemplified by Web search engines, into which a user enters a simple unstructured query in response to which a list of documents is returned ranked in order of likely relevance. In the automated alignment system IR techniques are used to segment the audio transcription and match the segmented audio to the slides. This section introduces the transcription of the audio stream and the IR algorithms used, and describes the individual components of the alignment and segmentation systems. The following section then shows how they are integrated to form the complete system.

3.1 Automatic Speech Transcription

Manual transcription of spoken audio is a very time consuming process often being several times slower than the recording itself. Thus in order for the automated alignment system to be practical automatic transcription must be carried out using a speech recognition system. Speech recognition technologies have advanced rapidly in the last 10 years, and a number of commercial transcription systems have been released in recent years. The accuracy of these systems is highly dependent on the linguistic structure of the material to be recognised and quality of the audio recording. Recognition of clearly spoken linguistically well formed sentences in a quiet environment using a good quality microphone held at a constant close distance from the speakers mouth can often achieve error rates of less than 10%. However, performance decreases rapidly as the structure of the speech becomes more spontaneous and disfluent, background noise level increases and when the microphone is in a fixed position away from the speaker. As such the transcription of lecture recordings represents a very challenging recognition task.

For our system we performed transcription using the *Dragon Naturally Speaking (Professional)* software. Using the basic system we encountered recognition performance of only 20-30%. This result is quite poor, but is comparable to results reported by others for a task of similar difficultly [4]. Slightly higher performance could be expected with current research systems, but one of our objectives is to develop a system which can operate successfully using technology currently available for use in a lecture hall. Performance can be improved by training the acoustic models to individual lecturers using an enrolment session. Also we noted that many of the technical terms appearing in the lectures, and in the slides, are outside the recognition vocabulary of the slides. This suggests that it may be useful to consider the application of a open-vocabulary indexing system such as *phone lattice scanning* [5]. Research in the retrieval of spoken documents for which the transcription accuracy was around 75% indicates that retrieval performance similar to accurate manual text transcriptions can be achieved via the application of appropriate compensation techniques [6]. The high error level we encounter with out current system will impact on both slide alignment and searching of the transcription. But evidence from the related research in spoken document retrieval indicates that even with current speech recognition levels our system can produce useful performance levels.

For the development and testing of our system we manually transcribed 6 one hour lectures and compared these transcriptions with behaviour for the automated transcriptions.

3.2 Information Retrieval Techniques

The system uses standard IR techniques of stop word removal, suffix stripping and term weighting [7].

Stop Word Removal. The transcript is first filtered to identify *stop words*, typically short high frequency function words such as *it*, *and*, and *but*. These contribute little to the identification of the most relevant document in an IR system and can safely be ignored in the retrieval process.

Suffix Stripping. The objective of a suffix stripping or stemming algorithm is to reduce different forms of a word to a common stem form. This encourages matching of different forms of the same word between queries and documents. In this system we use the standard Porter algorithm [8]. This applies a set of predefined to rules to reduce different forms of a word to a common root form. Words reduced to their root form are referred to as search *terms*.

Term Weighting. Term weighting is an important component of IR systems. The objective is to give high weights to terms which are able to select the, generally few, relevant documents from among the, generally many, non-relevant documents. Our system adopts the standard Okapi BM25 *combined weight (cw)* probabilistic term weighting model which is widely used in current IR systems. This model was originally developed in [9] and further elaborated in [10]. The BM25 *cw* weight for a term is calculated as follows,

$$cw(i,j) = \frac{cfw(i) \times tf(i,j) \times (K1+1)}{K1 \times ((1-b)+(b \times ndl(j))) + tf(i,j)}$$

where $cw(i,j)$ represents the weight of term i in document j, $cfw(i) = \log N/n(i)$ is the standard collection frequency (inverse document frequency) weight, where N is the total number of documents in the collection, $n(i)$ is the total number of documents containing term i, $tf(i,j)$ is the document term frequency, and $ndl(j) = dj(j)/\text{Av. } dl$ is the normalised document length, where $dl(j)$ is the length of j. $K1$ and b are empirically selected tuning constants for a particular collection. Investigation of values for these constants in our algorithms showed that best results were found with $K = 2.0$ and $b = 0.75$. A matching score is computed between the query and each document by summing the weights of terms common to both the query and the document.

3.3 Slide Matching

A key component of our system is the correct alignment of the audio with the electronic slides. In these procedures material on individual slides is used as an IR search query to find the best matching documents from within sections of the audio transcription. The audio transcription is broken into fixed length windows which act as the documents that are then matched against the slide. Two sources of alignment information are generated by the slide matching procedures.

Phase 1: Slide Alignment. The whole contents of each slide including the title are formed into a single query. Queries are then matched against fixed length window documents. The windows are then ranked in decreasing query-document matching score. The slide is then linked to the highest scoring window. Queries here are generally very rich comprising a number of very good search terms associated with the topic of the slide. These queries are found to identify a segment associated with the correct region of the transcription at the highest rank with an accuracy of 85-90%.

Phase 2: Bullet Point Alignment. Slides often comprise a number of individual bullet points or sentences. A second phase of the slide alignment algorithm extracts individual sentences or bullet points from the slides and uses these as search queries. These much shorter queries give a more focused statement of information need typically related to a section of transcript within a slide. This shorter query statement seeks to identify a smaller target section of the transcript associated with the query and gives finer alignment granularity, but it is also a harder task and accuracy falls to between 60-65%. However, this can be integrated very effectively with the slide level alignment, as described in the next section.

3.4 Segmentation and Alignment Algorithms

A further key element of the system is the automated segmentation of the audio recording into segments where ideally each relates to a single slide. In order to do this, techniques are used based on both features of the audio itself and the words spoken. The segmentation of audio is an uncertain process, for example the number of segments required is not known in advance. Thus the output of the segmentation algorithms are combined with the slide alignment algorithms described in the last section in a fully integrated system to decide the most likely number of separate slide segments.

Audio segmentation involves two procedures: *TextTiling* and Silence Detection. Within a written text, semantic segment boundaries would typically fall at the end of a paragraph, often grouping together a number of paragraphs on the same topic. *TextTiling* algorithms are designed to brake up a written text into semantically coherent segments [11]. Without a means to exploit natural segmentation points such as paragraph and sentence ends in the audio processing, an alternative means of finding natural break points is required. Based on observation of recorded lectures is was found that long silences are a very good indicator of a slide change.

TextTiling. Essentially TextTiling is designed to search for points in the text where the vocabulary shifts from one topic to another. The TextTiling algorithm proceeds as follows:

- The transcription is broken into pseudo-sentences of size w referred to as *token sequences*.

- Token sequences are grouped together into a groups of *blocksize* to be compared against an adjacent group of token-sequences.
- The similarity between adjacent blocks b_1 and b_2 is then calculated using a cosine measure. This matching score is then assigned to the *gap* between the two blocks.

$$sim(b_1, b_2) = \frac{\sum_t w_{t,b_1} w_{t,b_2}}{\sqrt{\sum_t w_{t,b_1}^2 \sum_t w_{t,b_2}^2}}$$

  where t ranges over all the terms from the tokenisation stage, w_{t,b_1} is the weight assigned to term t in block b_1. The weights are simply the frequency of terms within the block using the function.

$$\begin{aligned} w_{t,b_i} &= 1 + \log tf(t, b_i) \quad \text{if } tf(t, b_i) \geq 1 \\ &= 0 \end{aligned}$$

  This produces a matching score in the range 0 to 1.
- Boundaries are determined by changes in the sequence of similarity scores. For a given token-sequence gap i, the algorithm looks at the scores of the token-sequence gaps to the left of i as long as their values are increasing. When the peak is reached the difference between the score at the peak and the score at i is recorded. The same procedure takes place with the token-sequence gaps to the right of i. The relative height of the peak to the right of i is added to the relative height of the peak to the left. A gap occurring at a peak has a score of zero since neither of its neighbours is higher than it. These new scores, called *depth scores*, are the sorted. Segment boundaries are assigned to the token-sequence gaps with the largest corresponding scores. In the original text-based algorithm these boundaries are then adjusted to correspond to true paragraph breaks. This is not possible in the case of automatically transcribed audio and we thus make use of the Silence Detection method described in the next section.

An alternative transcription segmentation method is described in [12]. We have not so far explored the application of this technique to our segmentation task, but it would be interesting to contrast this with TextTiling. In particular it would be interesting to find out whether the proposal of break points at a certain point if suggested by both algorithms is a more reliable classification than either method in isolation, we hope to explore this possibility in future work.

Silence Detection. The blocks used in the TextTiling procedure will usually cross the exact point of a slide change. By locating silence points well correlated with these change points, it is possible to assign an exact location in the audio source where the slide change is most likely to have occurred. It was observed that lecturers do sometimes talk across slide changes, for example when completing a point relating to a slide or connecting the slides, but even in these cases there is almost inevitably a pause for breath somewhere near the slide change point.

In determining "silence" points we are looking not for complete silence, but rather for a point where the audio energy level drops to that of the ambient background noise caused by projection machinery and the audience. Our system adopts the following simple digital audio processing procedure:

- Read in the entire sampled audio waveform noting the sampling rate.
- Compute the square of each sample value and take the positive square root to give the energy level of the sample.
- Place the samples in running 0.5 second bins. 0.5 seconds was determined empirically as being long enough to avoid classifying small intraword and intrasentence pauses as significant silence points for slide changes.
- For each bin compute the mean power level.
- Find the lowest mean power level for the recording. This is assumed to correspond to the background noise power level. To allow for small changes in background noise level assume a threshold 5% higher to correspond to the ambient noise level.
- Classify all bins below the ambient noise level as silence points.

3.5 Automated Slide Construction for New Material

In this section we describe our procedure for automatically forming new slides for parts of the transcript that do not match well with the existing lecture slides. Extracting key points from a segment of the transcription is related to the established field of summarisation. Rather than attempt to interpret the transcription and use text generation to form summary keypoints, we adopt the simpler strategy of identifying significant token sequences from within a segment and use these as bullet points for the new slide. We are not aware of existing work which attempts to perform this task from audio presentations. The most closely related work appears to be for the automatic generation of titles for spoken broadcast news [13].

Keyword Identification. The first stage in the procedure is to identify a set of keywords for the segment. The term frequency of all terms occurring in the segment is calculated within the segment and within the whole transcription. A significance factor for each word is then computed by dividing the segment tf by the transcript tf. Any word with a significance value above an empirically determined threshold is defined as a keyword for the section. A higher threshold value defines more words as keywords, while a lower gives less. After experimentation we set a threshold of 0.05.

Sentence Significance. The segment is divided into overlapping fixed length token sequences. For a token sequences of length w words, the first sequence is from word 1 to word w, the second word 2 to word $w+1$, etc. The number of keywords appearing in each token sequence is then calculated. After experimentation a token sequence length of 15 terms was generally found to give a good compromise between sequences which are too short to capture a concept description and those which are too long and cover more than one concept, whilst also providing a long enough sequence that can easily be understood and manipulated by an editor.

- new one one of the early hypertext systems was a system called guide it ran
- the systems you now get the operator would ask questions as prompted by the system
- programmed expert systems hypertext came in and replaced it out performs not only human experts

Guide

- One of the early hypertext systems was a system called Guide, developed at ICL.
- The operator asks questions as prompted by the system to perform over the phone troubleshooting.
- The hypertext system can out-perform both expert systems and human experts.

Fig. 1. Automatically developed lecture slide and manually corrected version.

Slide Generation. The 3 highest scoring non-overlapping token sequences are then taken as the bullet points for the new slide. Heuristic rules and constraints are applied to select the centre token sequence from a run of same scoring sequences, and to select 3 token sequences from across the transcription segment. The 3 sequences are placed on a new PowerPoint slide and automatically integrated into the complete presentation. Slides generated in this way are generally found to give a good gist of key points covered in this segment by the speaker. Clearly these will not be as well structured as manually developed slides. As part of a post-processing stage our system enables the operator to edit the automatically generated slides to improve clarity and correct any mistakes. Figure 1 shows an example of a slide formed automatically from a region correctly selected by our system as outside the planned slide structure, and a manually tidied up version of the slide. This post-processing editing procedure is found to be much easier and faster than listening to the entire soundtrack and then manually developing a complete new slide.

4 Complete Audio-Visual Annotation System

This section describes the integration of the techniques introduced in the previous section to form the complete alignment and annotation system. The techniques themselves are integrated into an overall framework with a number of heuristics. The system assumes that lectures work sequentially through the prepared slides for a lecture. Before the alignment procedures begin, the transcription is first broken up into token sequence "documents" of length w. After testing we set the value $w = 25$ for the system.

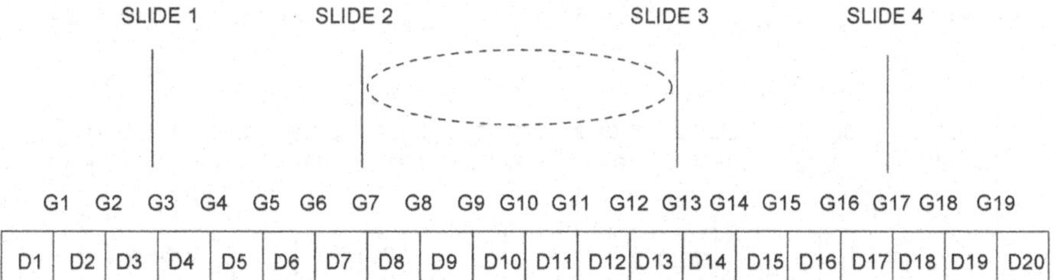

Fig. 2. Alignment of whole slides with transcription "documents".

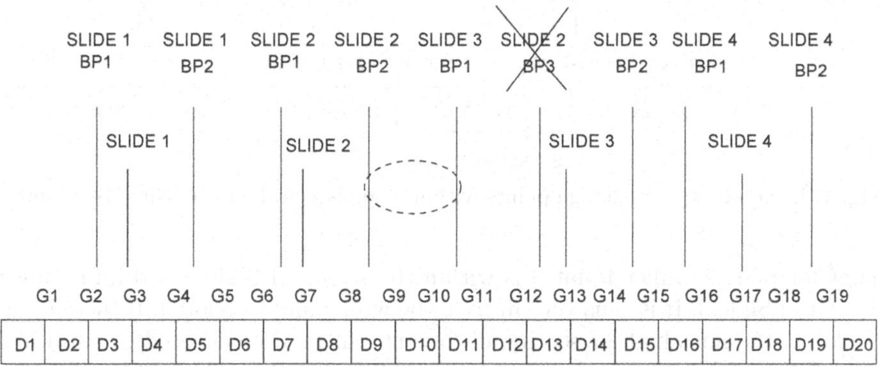

Fig. 3. Alignment of slide bullet points with transcription "documents".

4.1 Stage 1: Slide Alignment

The Slide Alignment method is used to provide a base for the other procedures. Adjacent token sequence pairs are used as documents of length $2w$ in this stage of the alignment procedure. These large documents are better able to match with the contents of complete slides. The scope of the search query means that it is able to locate documents on the topic of the slide. However, the wide coverage of the query means that it often also matches reasonably well with other documents as well. This can result in some errors, but these are usually easily resolved using heuristic rules. Figure 2 shows an example of transcript documents and the highest matching slides. The Slide Alignment procedure lays a basic framework which reliably identifies the region in which a slide change must occur. Thus in the example the change between slide 2 and slide 3 must occur somewhere in the region of gaps 8 to 12.

4.2 Stage 2: Bullet Point Alignment

Operated on its own Bullet Point Alignment is not very accurate. However, its usefulness can be greatly increased by constraining it using results from the Slide Alignment stage to only consider documents within the region associated with the whole slide. Figure 3 extends the previous example to show Bullet Point matching with individual documents. Thus Bullet Points 1 and 2 from Slide 2 are successfully located in the region of Slide 2. However, the best matching

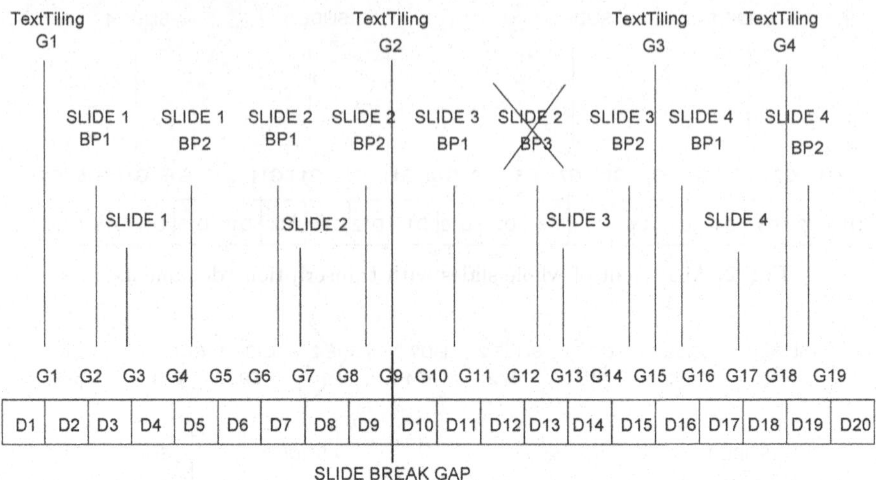

Fig. 4. Location of slide change points within alignment framework using TextTiling.

point for Slide 2 Bullet Point 3 is within the region of Slide 3 and after Bullet Point 1 of Slide 3. It is thus very likely to be wrong and is ignored. If there is one available, the next highest scoring document can then be checked to see if it is valid. Thus, if feasible, in the example Slide 2 Bullet Point 3 could be allocated to Document 10.

This finer level of granularity enables the actual slide change points to be identified more closely for further processing. From the information in Figure 3 the slide change marker between Slide 2 and Slide 3 can now be placed in the region of gaps 9 and 10.

4.3 Stage 3: Incorporating TextTiling Information

The TextTiling algorithm identifies possible break points in the semantic content of the transcription. When used independently it was found to locate slide transitions with an accuracy of only about 40%. (The same token sequence length $w = 25$ is used here with a blocksize of 2.) However, using it in the context of the slide transition information derived in Stage 1 and Stage 2, since we are expecting to find slide changes in given regions, a gap identified by the TextTiling algorithm falling between the last point of one slide and the first point of the next one is labelled as the slide change point. Figure 4 illustrates this combination of information showing how TextTiling gaps not consistent with the Stages 1 and 2 are ignored and the break between Slide 1 and Slide 2 assigned to Gap 9. Other semantic transition points proposed by TextTiling may relate to topical changes within a slide, for example addressing different bullet points.

4.4 Stage 4: Locating Approximate Slide Change Positions in the Soundtrack

The slide change gap points located in the previous sections relate to word blocks in the transcription. Stage 4 seeks to locate the actual location of the slide change in the audio recording. The output of Dragon Naturally Speaking Professional and other commercial speech recognition systems does not give the actual locations of the transcribed words. In order to find the approximate position of each word in the soundtrack we adopt the following procedure.

The average length of a word is calculated as follows,

$$\text{Average Word Length (words/second)} = \frac{\text{Total Recording Time (seconds)}}{\text{Total Number of Words}}$$

The approximate position of each word in the soundtrack was then found by multiplying its position by the average word length. Testing this procedure for a number of test words within a 26 minute lecture recording showed an average error in word location of 10.8 seconds.

Thus the approximate location for each slide change point proposed by the previous stages in the soundtrack can be located. As will be clear from Stage 5, locating an approximate position for this word is sufficient for our segmentation procedure.

4.5 Stage 5: Locating Slide Change Positions in the Soundtrack

This Stage uses the silence detection procedure described in earlier to locate silence points in the region of each proposed slide change point. Such silences are taken to be the position of the actual slide change.

In operation the Silence Detection procedure takes each of the break point times proposed in Stage 4 and searches a region 15 seconds either side for silence points. The longest silence point located in this region is then marked as the silence change point.

4.6 Heuristic Rules for Alignment Checking

Although the procedure described was found to accurately identify most slide changes, when errors occurred in Stage 1 or Stage 2 they were found to have a significant impact on the final result. Thus while part of our development work concentrated on improving the reliability of the slide-matching algorithms in the context of the complete system. It was recognised that statistical algorithms of this type will make mistakes, and checks were inserted within the system to attempt to identify likely errors and prevent them from cascading through the alignment of the complete presentation. These checks not only detect probable errors, but take action to develop solutions to them. The checking procedures also incorporate functionality to detect slides which have been skipped and areas not covered by a slide for which a new slide needs to be created.

Checking Stage 1. It is observed that regions of the soundtrack associated with a single slide often have more than one high scoring document within a small distance. Thus rather than taking the single highest scoring document, the procedure links the slide with a document only if the second highest scoring is found within 3 documents of it.

A second procedure is used to link the remainder of the slides not assigned in the first stage. Each unclassified slide is linked to the highest scoring document above a predefined threshold between the document classifications for the previous and next slides assigned so far. If a slide is not classified by either of these procedures it is not assigned to any documents and is marked as a potentially skipped slide.

Based on our assumption that lecturers work through material sequentially the ordering of assigned slides is checked. If possible any slide that is out of sequence is reclassified to a document within the correct range. If this is not possible the slide is marked as possibly missed.

Checking Stage 2. Bullet points are evaluated in the available range from Stage 1. If the first bullet point on one slide is matched to a location before the last bullet point on the next slide then the lower scoring one is removed as a misclassification.

Checking Stage 3. This section seeks to identify a slide change point in the transcript using the TextTiling results. If there is a single prediction transition point in the identified document range, then the position is fixed. However, a series of further checks are required if another situation is encountered.

– 0 TextTile results in the range: the slide change point is assigned to the end of the last document discussing the previous slide.
– 1 TextTile result in the range: the slide change marker is set to this point.
– 2 TextTile results in the range: based on observations the slide change point was set to the second of the predicted points. Intuitively this makes sense since the lecturer is more likely to start a new slide with the topic of the bullet point, and end the previous slide not discussing the final bullet point.
– 3+ TextTile results in the range: This suggests that material outside the slides is being discussed and that a new slide is required. The area between the second and last TextTile is marked as a new region and passed to the automatic slide construction procedure.

4.7 System Evaluation

The IR techniques showed impressive results in testing and in most cases successfully matched slides and bullet points. Performance was better with the manual transcriptions, but also produced promising the results with the automated transcriptions.

There were occasions however when an incorrect slide is matched by part of the transcription with a very high score. This typically happens with summary or concluding slides which feature a high density of keywords, which can incorrectly match with any section of the transcription. Once a misclassification of this type has occurred the system cannot recover from it. Further development of the system needs to be considered to attempt to prevent single errors early in the alignment process occasionally causing significant problems later on.

Another problem relates to the observation that some slides match very poorly with any part of the transcript, even though they were covered in the presentation. This was most often because the slide contains little text, for example if the slide contains a figure, or if the lecturer happens to use different vocabulary to describe the topic covered by the slide. One way to address this latter issue might be use a thesaurus to expand the keywords on an unmatched slide. Thesaurus expansion has generally not been found to be useful in conventional IR searching, however this alignment environment is highly constrained by the existing alignment evidence, and in this context use of a thesaurus may prove effective. The issue of little text on a slide is difficult to address. A lecturer may discuss at length a slide showing a graph or image, but there is no information to match to the transcription. One idea would be to ask the lecturer to provide annotation to slides, but this would be intrusive to their work and would rely on them taking time to do this.

5 Extensions to the eLectures System

Although complete in itself, the system described in this paper could be used to provide the starting point for a more complete knowledge management system for eLecture delivery. Existing work in knowledge integration suggests a number of possible directions in which the system could be extended both to support individual student use of lecture material and to enrich the lecture content itself with related information.

Connection to Individual Notes. Students typically make their own notes relating to the contents of a lecture. These notes obviously consist of notes taken during a lecture, but students may also make additional related notes during private study. An earlier study explored the connection of students own paper notes to lecture recordings by linking points where notes are made on the paper to the timing of the lecture [14]. Playback of the lecture is enabled by pressing a pen on a particular location on a page. Such a system could be integrated into the eLecture system described in this paper. Developments in web technologies and the increasing use of electronic means of note taking by students mean that ideas of this type are becoming technically easier to implement. This technology could also be applied to notes taken in private study with a lecture recording to integrate the student's information sources related to topics covered by individual slides or lecture segments.

Enriching Lecture Content. The lecture slides and the aligned content of the the transcript provide a rich source of topic descriptions that could be used to search for related information. In this scenario search queries could be generated from bullet points in the slide and related material from the transcription. These could then be used to search related material for additional content to enrich the eLecture. For example, electronic versions of textbooks, research papers, other eLectures and general World Wide Web content could be searched for related material. Sources which match well could then be attached to this point in the lecture, possibly with a simple summary of the content. Students studying the lecture could then follow these paths to sources giving further information and examples illustrating the points covered. A system of this type for automatically augmenting the spoken contents of meetings is described in [1]. Adopting a strategy of this type could greatly enrich the experience of those using digital libraries as a study resource.

6 Concluding Remarks

This paper has described a system for the automatic alignment of electronic lecture slides and the audio recording of the lecture. This system demonstrates that current audio processing and statistical information retrieval techniques can be integrated to form an effective alignment system using inexpensive computing resources. The system is not always correct and the output should ideally be checked by a human operator. However, the accuracy of the system is sufficient that the manual checking and correction is many times faster than the existing completely manual approach. The system also has the advantage that the slides and lecture transcript can now be integrated into a system for interactive searching of an lecture, and that lectures could be placed in a searchable archive allowing sections of lectures and associated slides to be located. Even with high levels of recognition errors in automatic transcriptions, the complete accuracy of the contents of the slides themselves should enable reliable searching of the lectures. This latter observation indicates that this system can make this sort of tacit knowledge within lectures available much more easily, and remove the need to view the complete contents of all lectures to find useful information not articulated or expressed elsewhere. A limitation of the current system is our assumption that lecturers follow the slide sequence of the PowerPoint lecture plan. Further work is needed to explore the possibilities of detecting out of sequence slides, although incorporating this flexibility may adversely affect correct alignment of sequentially delivered material.

The system could potentially be integrated with students personal lecture notes and also into a richer knowledge management environment incorporating searching of related resources such as text books, related lectures and resources available on the Internet. Overall technology of the type introduced in this paper has the potential to integrate knowledge resources for learning, both for students and instructors, both within lectures and in private student, and for distance learning where lectures can be used as a searchable digital library of learning resources.

Acknowledgement. We are grateful to Masoud Yazdani and the other members of the *eLectures* team at the University of the West Of England, for their encouragement and provision of the lecture materials used in this work.

References

[1] E. W. Brown, S. Srinivasen, A. Coden, D. Ponceleon, J. W. Cooper, and A. Amir. Towards Speech as a Knowldge Resource. *IBM Systems Journal*, 40(4):985–1001, 2001.

[2] S. Mukhopadyay and B. Smith. Passive Capture and Structuring of Lectures. In *Proceedings of the 7th ACM International Conference on Multimedia (Part 1)*, pages 477–487, Orlando, Florida, 1999. ACM.

[3] J. Hunter and S. Little Building and Indexing a Distributed Multimedia Presentation Archive Using SMIL. In *Proceedings of the 5th European Conference on Research and Advanced Technology for Digital Libraries (ECDL 2001)*, pages 415-428, Darmstadt, 2001.

[4] A. G. Hauptmann and M. J. Witbrock. Informedia: News-on-Demand Multimedia Information Aquistion and Retrieval. In M. T. Maybury, editor, *Intelligent Multimedia Information Retrieval*, pages 215–239. AAAI/MIT Press, 1997.

[5] M. G. Brown, J. T. Foote, G. J. F. Jones, K. Sparck Jones, and S. J. Young. Open-vocabulary speech indexing for voice and video mail retrieval. In *Proceedings of ACM Multimedia 96*, pages 307–316, Boston, 1996. ACM.

[6] J. S. Garafolo, C. G. P. Auzanne, and E. M. Voorhees. The TREC Spoken Document Retrieval Track: A Success Story. In *Proceedings of the RIAO 2000 Conference: Content-Based Multimedia Information Access*, pages 1–20, Paris, 2000.

[7] C. J. van Rijsbergen. *Information Retrieval.* Butterworths, 2nd edition, 1979.

[8] M. F. Porter. An algorithm for suffix stripping. *Program*, 14:130–137, 1980.

[9] S. E. Robertson and S. Walker. Some simple effective approximations to the 2-Poisson model for probabilistic weighted retrieval. In *Proceedings of the 17th Annual International ACM SIGIR Conference on Research and Development in Information Retrieval*, pages 232–241, Dublin, 1994. ACM.

[10] S. E. Robertson, S. Walker, M. M. Beaulieu, M. Gatford, and A. Payne. Okapi at TREC-4. In D. K. Harman, editor, *Overview of the Fourth Text REtrieval Conference (TREC-4)*, pages 73–96. NIST, 1996.

[11] M. Hearst. Multi-Paragraph Segmentation of Expository Text. In *Proceedings of ACL'94*, Las Cruces, New Mexico, U.S.A., 1994.

[12] D. Ponceleon and S. Srinivasen. Structure and Content-Based Segmentation of Speech Transcripts. In *Proceedings of the 24th Annual International ACM SIGIR Conference on Research and Development in Information Retrieval*, pages 404–405, New Orleans, 2001. ACM.

[13] R. Jin and A. G. Hauptmann. Automatic title generation for spoken broadcast news. In *Proceedings of Human Language Technology Conference (HLT 2001)*, San Diego, 2001.

[14] L. J. Stifelman. Augmenting Real-World Objects: A Paper-Based Audio Netbook. In *Proceedings of CHI'96*, Vancouver, Canada, 1996.

OpenDLib: A Digital Library Service System

Donatella Castelli and Pasquale Pagano

Istituto di Elaborazione dell'Informazione
Consiglio Nazionale delle Ricerche
Pisa - Italy
{castelli,pagano}@iei.pi.cnr.it

Abstract. OpenDLib is a software toolkit that can be used to create a digital library easily, according to the requirements of a given user community, by instantiating the software appropriately and then either loading or harvesting the content to be managed. OpenDLib consists of a federation of services that implement the digital library functionality making few assumptions about the nature of the documents to be stored and disseminated. If necessary, the system can be extended with other services to meet particular needs. The main focus of the paper is the openness and extendibility of the system. This feature has been obtained by applying a systematic approach to the design of the toolkit. A model of the system architecture has been defined in order to support this approach. The paper presents OpenDLib through this model.

1 Introduction

The term "digital library" (DL) is used nowadays to indicate both the system that implements the services of a globally accessible library and the digital content of the library itself, i.e. the set of documents that are maintained and disseminated [1,2,3]. This overlapping of meanings reflects the current status of the majority of digital libraries, which are implemented as ad-hoc services created to disseminate specific collections of documents.

However recently, this view has started to change. One of the first steps towards this change was made by the Open Archives Initiatives (OAI) [4]. OAI proposed a different model for publication and dissemination, which distinguishes between data providers - the providers of the content, and service providers - those that implement high level services for accessing and manipulating the content. The OAI model relaxes the one-to-one correspondence between services and content that characterizes existing digital libraries. With this model, the same collection of documents can be disseminated through different services, and the same service can be instantiated in order to work on different collections of documents. A recent DELOS brainstorming meeting entitled "Digital Libraries: Future Directions for a European Research Programme" [5] reinforced this distinction. The digital library was conceptualized as a system which comprises three major components: the *Content*, i.e. the set of documents and metadata records that are maintained and disseminated, the *Core System*,

M. Agosti and C. Thanos (Eds.): ECDL 2002, LNCS 2458, pp. 292-308, 2002.

responsible for the management of the content and for providing the necessary functionality, and the *User Interface*, which deals with all aspects of the interaction between the user and the system.

This framework opens new perspectives for the creation of digital libraries. In particular, it establishes the premises for the building of systems that implement the functionality of the Core System while making few assumptions about the content to be managed. We call a system of this type a *digital library service system (DLSS)*. Using a DLSS, a DL can be created by configuring and instantiating this system and then either loading or harvesting the relevant digital document collection(s).

According to this vision, a DLSS coordinates service and resource sharing in dynamic, multi-institutional virtual organizations. For this reason a DLSS has to be open, i.e. its functionality must be extendible, and able to handle different collections of documents. A DLSS must be open since the functionality it offers may not always be sufficient to satisfy the requirements of a particular digital library user community. Additional services may be required to cover specific user needs or to treat specific content formats. For example, a digital library that serves a research community may require a co-operative work service, whereas a digital library that serves a worldwide community of TV programme makers may need a video summarization service. The openness makes it possible to extend the generic functionality provided by the DLSS to meet the needs of a particular application area. A DLSS must also be capable of working with a wide range of document types, structures, media, etc., and/or be able to rely on existing archives in order to, again, be able to satisfy the needs of different user communities and institutions that may want to both disseminate and access documents of heterogeneous types stored in different formats.

This paper introduces a DLSS, named OpenDLib, which is the result of the work carried out in the last three years at the DLib Center of IEI-CNR in Pisa. OpenDLib provides a set of basic digital library functions: acquisition, storage and preservation, search, browse and retrieval, selection and dissemination of documents, authorization and authentication of the users. From the architectural point of view, OpenDLib is a federation of interoperating services, which can be distributed and/or replicated on different servers. These services communicate through an open protocol. The allocation of the services to the servers can change over the digital library lifetime, as can the communication paths among the services.

The paper describes OpenDLib by focusing mainly on the design choices that support the openness of the system. These choices are the result of a preliminary study that aimed at formalizing the design of OpenDLib. In particular, we have constructed a model that specifies the system components, their architectural relations and a number of constraints that hold among them. By reasoning on this model, we have been able to systematically design an open system that can be customized with respect to several dimensions of functionality. We present OpenDLib through this model and show how it has been exploited to design an open digital library service system.

The rest of the paper is organized as follows: Section 2 provides an overview of OpenDLib; Section 3 describes the OpenDLib architecture through its model; Section 4 presents the communication protocol and shows how its definition has been derived from the model; and finally, some conclusions are drawn in Section 5.

2 An Overview of OpenDLib

The design of OpenDLib has been deeply influenced by our experience in building the Ercim Technical Reference Digital Library (ETRDL) [6]. This digital library, initially intended as the European branch of NCSTRL [7, 8], now maintains grey literature published by seven ERCIM institutes. ETRDL was implemented using an enhanced version of Dienst [9], the software developed to support NCSTRL. Dienst was one of the first systems to build a digital library as an open federation of distributed services. However, it cannot be considered as a DLSS because it is not easily generalizable, as it was tailored to meet the needs of the NCSTRL application, e.g. the documents that can be archived and disseminated are unstructured texts described through a subset of the RFC 1807 metadata format [10]. Moreover, Dienst does not adopt any explicit systematic approach to the design of the services and the protocol. As a consequence there are no rules on the way in which new service types can be added to the architecture not on how the communication protocol can be extended.

In designing OpenDLib we maintained the choice made by Dienst of building a digital library as an interoperable and communicating federation of services as we considered this to be appropriate solution for achieving an extendible system. Having made this choice, we worked on creating a dynamic and highly configurable digital library service system. Considerable effort was dedicated to understanding how to systematically design such a system. In particular, we tried to make explicit the rules that govern the federation, i.e. the rules which must be satisfied by all the services that belong to the federation, whether native OpenDLib, or extensions of it. This process led us to begin defining the OpenDLib DLSS architecture. Theoretically we started by defining a formal model of the architecture and of the services that provide the DL functionality.

The model enabled us to identify the service requests to be supported by the communication protocol and to uniformly design the components of the federation. It also permitted us to clearly establish the parametric dimensions and to identify which of them have to be chosen at the time of the creation of the DL and which instead depend on the status of the other services of the federation. As a side effect of the definition of the model, we produced a characterization of the legal configurations of the OpenDLib system. The system was implemented to support any of these legal configurations dynamically.

The present version of OpenDLib provides a number of interoperating services that implement the basic functionality of a digital library. This set of services is not fixed but can be extended to provide additional functionality.

The OpenDLib services can be centralized or distributed and/or replicated on different servers. This means that an OpenDLib federation may comprise multiple instances of the same service type. Each service may require the functionality of other services in order to carry out its processing. In this case, a service instance communicates with the other service instances via the OpenDLib Protocol (OLP) [11]. OLP protocol requests are expressed as URLs embedded in HTTP requests. All structured requests or responses are XML-based.

An OpenDLib federation is managed by a particular service, called *Manager Service* (see Figure 1), which always maintains updated information about its status. This service is completely parametric with respect to the type and number of managed services. The only prerequisite for these services is that they must be able to respond to an established set of OLP protocol requests. The information maintained by the Manager is partially provided by the digital library administrator when he/she instantiates the DLSS; the rest is collected by the Manager Service by periodically sending appropriate protocol requests to the service instances.

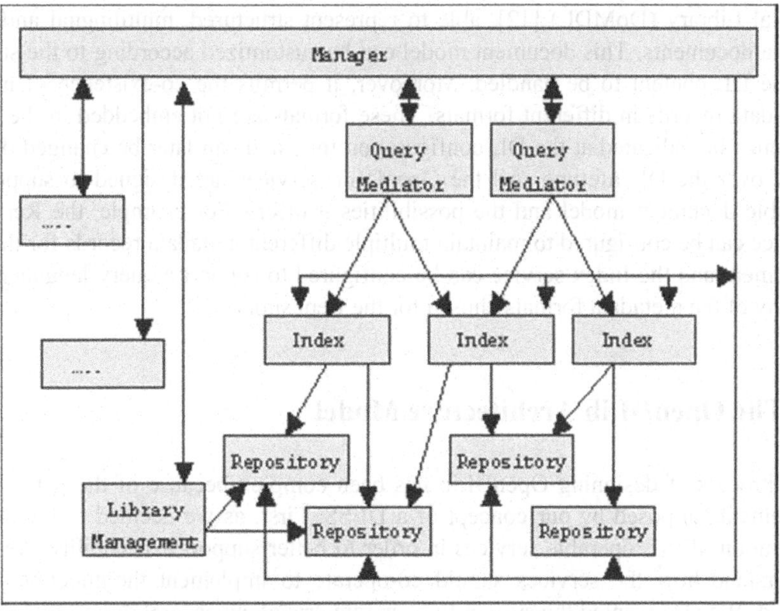

Fig. 1. An example of OpenDLib services interaction.

Each service instance responds to the Manager by providing information about its state, structure, and functionality. A service instance, in turn, may ask the Manager for information about the location and characteristics of any other instance of the federation. This exchange of information between the Manager and the other services makes it possible to create co-operating services that have no built-in knowledge of the location of their instances. It also permits a dynamic allocation of the service instances according to the needs and availability of the servers in the architecture. Note that this co-operation is more complex than a simple client-server application. A service can act both as a provider and as a consumer, and sharing relationships can exist a priori among any subset of the services. Services, in fact, may be combined to support different functionality, and the same services may be used in different ways, depending on the restrictions placed on the sharing and the goal of the sharing.

OpenDLib services are customizable along several dimensions. The initial configuration of an OpenDLib digital library, i.e. the number of service instances, their allocation and the topology of the communication paths, is decided when the digital library is created. This configuration may be changed later either automatically, for example to recover from a server crash, or as an effect of an explicit request formulated by the digital library administrator. For example, the administrator can decide to extend the architecture by adding new servers, and/or mounting new service instances, in order to reduce the workload on the existing services; a service instance can shift its requests from one service instance to another; a service instance can change its role from master to slave; etc.

The services support a powerful document model, called Document Model for Digital Library (DoMDL) [12], able to represent structured, multilingual and multimedia documents. This document model can be customized according to the structure of the DL content to be handled. Moreover, it permits the co-existence of multiple metadata records in different formats. These formats are not embedded in the system but must be indicated at the DL configuration time and can later be changed dynamically over the DL lifetime. All the OpenDLib services are designed to support this flexible document model and the possibilities it offers. For example, the Repository service can be configured to maintain multiple different metadata records for the same document and the Index service can be configured to support a query language based on any of the metadata formats chosen for the Repository.

3 The OpenDLib Architecture Model

The process of designing OpenDLib has been complex because of the particular requirements imposed by our concept of a DLSS. First, as we decided to build it as a federation of interoperable services in order to better support extensibility, we had to understand how the services should co-operate to implement the functionality required. We also wanted the system to be parametric along several dimensions in order to support customization. These dimensions had to be identified and their interrelations had to be clarified and maintained consistent. Finally, we required a system able to support changes on the selections made with respect to the values of the parameters, the types of services provided, and last but not least, the organization of the service instances in the federation. This system should be dynamically modifiable in order to meet quality criteria such as performance, fault tolerance, etc. A specification of the legal configurations and of the consistency rules to be checked was also needed in order to control these dynamic changes.

As first step towards managing this complexity, we formalized the problem of representing the OpenDLib architecture by defining a model, named the OpenDLib Model. This model allowed us to systematize the design of both the services and the protocol. In particular, it was extensively used in designing the Service Manager and that part of the protocol dedicated to the management of the federation. This section presents the OpenDLib architecture through this model. Due to the limited space, we will introduce the main components of the model, through a semi-formal presentation style. The complete definition of this model can be found in [13].

The DL architectures that can be created using the OpenDLib DLSS are specified by a set-theoretic model. This model represents the universe of the architectural elements identified during the design and the semantic that governs their co-existence and co-operation. The model has three components <S, F, P>

- S models the significant classes of objects of the OpenDLib Architectural Universe. Each class is represented by a set.
- F represents the attributes associated with each class. Each attribute is modeled by a function defined on the set that models the associated class.
- P models the properties that hold among the different elements in this universe.

In this model, we can distinguish a *kernel*, which models the basic elements of the OpenDLib DLSS architecture and its instances, e.g. services and servers, and a *service types specification*, which models the service types that implement the OpenDLib functionality, e.g. Repository, Index, etc. The kernel establishes the architectural framework dedicated to the handling of the services. The service types specification models the specific class of services implemented by OpenDLib. This specification can be extended to represent enhanced versions of OpenDLib, i.e. versions containing additional service types.

For the sake of clarity, we present these parts of the model in two separate subsections. In each part we will introduce the elements of the three sets S, F, and P.

3.1 The Architecture Kernel

Services and Servers are the basic elements of an OpenDLib architecture. A service is a building block that contributes to the implementation of the DLSS functionality; a server is a network device that is able to provide services to the network users by managing shared resources.

Two given sets, Services and Servers, model these classes of architectural elements. A number of functions are defined over these sets to represent the attributes associated with these basic elements. Table 1 lists these functions.

The format of the description that characterizes each service is defined according to the attributes associated with the Services. This description is the specification of the service that is disseminated to the other services of the federation on demand. It provides different kinds of information about the service. For example, it specifies information for identifying the service, e.g. serviceTypeName and server_url; information that describes the service functionality, e.g. verbsInfo and protocolVersion; and information on how the service can be used, e.g. useRestrictions.

The servers are identified by their address expressed as a pair (url, http_port), called base_url for brevity. Each server can host several services of different types. A server is characterized by a computational power, called capacity, that represents the average number of accepted contemporary accesses and therefore is not service dependent. Even though many other server descriptive attributes could have been used [14], the present version of OpenDLib uses this value in order to automatically optimize the distribution of services on servers.

Table 1. Services and Servers

S	F	P
Services	serviceTypeName server_url textualDescription submissionProcedure harvestingProcedure managerServiceURL useRestrictions protocolVersion adminEMail verbsInfo usedServiceTypes	$\forall$x,y,z,k,w | (x,y), (z,y) $\in$ serviceTypeName $\wedge$ (x,k), (z,w) $\in$ server_url $\Rightarrow$ k $\neq$ w $\forall$(x,y) $\in$ server_url $\exists$s $\in$ Servers (s,y) $\in$ base_url
Servers	base_url capacity	

Specific properties, modeled as elements of the set P, are associated with these functions to define their domain, range, multiplicity, etc. Due to limited space, in this paper we will present only a few examples of these properties. For instance, the first property reported above states that the URL associated with a service must be the URL of one of the registered servers; and the second property says that the same server cannot host two service instances with the same service type.

The instances of Services and Servers are decided when the DLSS is instantiated. The services chosen define the functionality that is implemented by the DL, the servers specify the physical distribution, and the server_url attribute indicates the allocation of these services to the servers. The initial choices can change over the DL lifetime. A server, for example, can be added to reduce the workload of the others or because a new publisher has adhered to the federation; a service can be moved from a server to another in order to improve performance, and so on.

OpenDLib services are centralized or distributed and/or replicated. This means that there can be multiple service instances in the architecture offering the same service functionality, e.g. there can be multiple instances of a Repository service, and each mounted on a different server. The set Services actually model the service instances. For each instance, the function serviceTypeName specifies the type of the service, i.e. its functionality class.

The OpenDLib model represents the centralized, distributed and replicated services as subsets of the set Services. Table 2 lists these subsets, each of which is an element of S, and the corresponding functions and properties.

The *Centralized* services are those that must be mounted (instantiated) on exactly one server in any OpenDLib DL. A service is usually centralized when the security and the privacy of its content is an issue.

Table 2. Centralized, Distributed and Replicated service instances

S	F	P
		Services = Centralized ∪ Distributed ∪ Replicated
Centralized		Centralized ⊆ Services Centralized ∩ (Distributed ∪ Replicated) = ϕ ∀x,y,k,w | x, y ∈ Centralized ∧ x ≠y ∧ (x,k), (y,w) ∈ serviceTypeName ⇒ k ≠ w
Distributed	authorityNames	Distributed ⊆ Services
Replicated		Replicated ⊆ Services Replicated=NoInput ∪CentralizedInput∪DistributedInput
NoInput		NoInput ⊆ Replicated NoIput ∩ (CentralizedInput ∪ DistributedInput) = ϕ
Centralized Input	c_masterYesNo c_masterURL	CentralizedInput ⊆ Replicated CentralizedInput ∩ (NoIput ∪DistributedInput) = ϕ ∀x,y,w,z | x, y ∈ CentralizedInput ∧ x ≠y ∧ (x,'yes'),(y,'yes') ∈ c_masterYesNo ∧ (x,w), (y,z) ∈ serviceTypeName ⇒ z ≠ w
Distributed Input	d_masterYesNo d_masterURL instancesSet	DistributedInput ⊆ Replicated DistributedInput ∩ (NoInput ∪ CentralizedInput) = ϕ ∀x,y,w,z | x, y ∈ DistributedInput ∧ x ≠y ∧ (x,'yes'), (y,'yes') ∈ d_masterYesNo ∧ (x,w), (y,z) ∈ serviceTypeName ⇒ z ≠ w

The *Distributed* services are those that implement the service functionality through multiple instances, each of which manages data stored on a different server. The data are distributed according to a set of criteria that may differ from service to service. For example, in the basic version of OpenDLib that we are illustrating, the services that are distributed are those that maintain a huge amount of data. The distribution criteria are based on the document publishing institutions (authorities). The publishing institutions usually prefer to maintain their own documents on their own server to have a physical control over them. Moreover, each institution usually has its own rules for document submission/withdrawal, or content management, and therefore prefers to maintain these procedures also in a shared environment. Each instance of a distributed service thus serves a subset of institutions. This subset is maintained in the model by the function authorityNames.

Note that distributed instances of the same service type are independent, i.e. they do not know each other. An instance receives requests and serves them without knowing anything about the selection criteria that have been adopted by the client.

The *Replicated* services are those whose functionality is implemented by a set of service instances, where each instance is able to cover completely the service functionality over the entire set of data. In the present version of OpenDLib we have chosen to replicate those services that are either not constrained by any proprietary (see distributed services), security or privacy (see centralized) constraint. This replication makes it possible to improve service efficiency and to increase robustness. This is, for example, the case of the replication of indexes that has been introduced to enhance content access, or the replication of meta information that has been introduced to improve digital library service access.

The OpenDLib model distinguishes three kinds of replicated services. Each kind is modeled by a subset of the set Replicated:

- *NoInput* services are pure copies of each other, i.e. the different instances are never distinguishable since they handle the same data and behave in the same way.
- *CentralizedInput* services have one replication, which acts as a master, and a set of replicates which act as slaves. The master is a special instance of the service whose only purpose is to maintain and distribute on demand an updated version of the information handled by the service. The slave instances update their content by periodically invoking the master. The master and slave roles are not statically assigned but can be changed in order to achieve a better connectivity or to overcome a temporary crash. The function c_masterYesNo models these roles, while the function c_masterURL identifies the service, among those of the same type, which is acting as master.
- *DistributedInput* services also have one replication, which acts as a master, and a set of replicates which act as slaves. Both the master and slave replicates can accept new information and serve information requests. The master maintains the global state of the service information: each time a slave updates its local information, the slave communicates the change to the master, which merges the new information with its own information. Periodically, each slave updates its state by invoking the master. As with the CentralizedInput services the master and slaves roles can change dynamically.

Disjunction and subclass relations relate the classes of services identified above. For example, a centralized service cannot be either a distributed or replicated service, a replicated service must belong to just one of the classes NoInput, CentralizedInput and DistributedInput. A number of other properties express rules on the possible values of the functions. Table 2 reports one example of these kinds of rules. The rule shown states that for each CentralizedInput or DistributedInput service type there is exactly one service instance that acts as a master.
In this section, we have described the OpenDLib architectural kernel. We have introduced the services as architectural elements identified by certain information and located on particular servers. We have not made any distinction according to the functionality they implement. In the next section we refine the notion of services by introducing classes of services, called service types, that group together service instances which implement the same functionality.

3.2 The Service Types

The current version of OpenDLib provides a set of service types that cover the basic digital library functionality such as acquisition, description, and storage, search, browse, selection and dissemination of documents, authorization and authentication of the users [15]. These services are embedded in the architecture framework specified in the previous section. They represent the way in which we have logically decided to partition the OpenDLib functionality. Other services can be added to this set to create more powerful digital library systems provided that these satisfy the rules that govern the architecture kernel. It is also possible to create another digital library system by replacing a service, or a group of services. Again, this is possible only if the new service/services satisfy the OpenDLib architecture kernel rules. Each OpenDLib service type is modeled by a subset of the leaf sets identified in the previous section. Subset relations represent the architectural choices of centralizing, distributing and/or replicating the given services.

Table 3 shows the OpenDLib services types and some of their functions and properties.

Table 3. The OpenDLib service types

S	F	R
Repository	contentDescription authorities sets metadataFormats documentStructure	Repository $\subseteq$ Distributed
Multimedia Storage	compositeDocumentFormats nonCompositeDocumentFormats multimediaDocumentFormats	Multimedia Storage $\subseteq$ Distributed
Library Manage-ment	authority set documentStructure metadataFormat	Library Management $\subseteq$ Distributed
Index	metadataFormat indexedFields resultFormats language	Index $\subseteq$ Distributed Index $\subseteq$ Replicated
Query Mediator	searchMethods resultFormats	Query Mediator $\subseteq$ Replicated
Manager	serviceDescriptionFormat	Manager $\subseteq$ Replicated
Browse	metadataFormat browsableFields resultFormats	Browse $\subseteq$ Replicated
Registry	userProfileFormat groupProfileFormat	Registry $\subseteq$ Centralized
Collection	collectionMetadataFormat	Collection $\subseteq$ Replicated
User Interface	frameset	User Interface $\subseteq$ Replicated

In the rest of this section we will describe the services that are implemented by the present version of the OpenDLib software referring again to the OpenDLib model. For simplicity, in the rest of the presentation we will use the term "service" instead of "service type" when the semantics of the term is clear from the context.

- *Repository*

This service stores documents that conform to the OpenDLib document model, named DoMDL. We have chosen to distribute it on multiple servers because authorities, or group of authorities, may want to store their documents in their own Repository service. The Repository service is parametric with respect to document formats and metadata. A set of these formats is supported by default but new formats can be easily added and managed.

- *Multimedia Storage*

This service supports the storage, the streaming (real-time) and the download delivery of the stored video manifestations of a document (according to the DoMDL document model). Furthermore, it supports their dissemination either as whole documents or as aggregations of scenes, shots and frames. We have chosen to distribute it on multiple servers because authorities, or group of authorities, may want to store their documents in their own Multimedia Storage service. The Multimedia Storage service is parametric with respect to the formats of document manifestations.

- *Library Management*

This service supports the submission, withdrawal, and replacement of documents. We have chosen to distribute it on multiple servers because authorities, or group of authorities, may want to manage their documents according to their own rules. The Library Management service is parametric with respect to the metadata formats and each of its instances can manage multiple metadata formats, helping the users to compile and submit them to the Repository.

- *Index*

This service accepts queries and returns lists of document identifiers matching those queries. It can be distributed and replicated on multiple servers. It is distributed because an Index service can index documents published by different authorities that are stored in different Repositories. It is replicated because documents published by different authorities can be indexed by different Index service. The Index service is parametric with respect to the metadata formats, to the set of indexed fields, and to the set of result sets formats.

- *Query Mediator*

This service dispatches queries to appropriate Index service instances. It can be replicated on multiple servers. The Query Mediator service adapts its behavior by taking into account the available Index Service instances, and therefore it completely exploits the potentially of the Index service.

- *Browse*

This service supports the construction of browsing indexes and the actual browsing of those indexes on library contents. It can be replicated on multiple servers. The Browse service is parametric with respect to the metadata formats, to the set of browsable fields, and to the set of result sets formats.

- *Registry*

This service supports the storage and access of information about authors, individual users, and user groups. It is centralized, i.e. one server always hosts it. The Registry service is parametric with respect to the user and group profiles that can be set up at the service configuration time. It also maintains information about the access rights and the privilege of the users.

- *Manager Service*

This service organizes the set of services, configures replicated services - joining information prepared by the DL administrator with information harvested from the different instances -, and verifies and maintains the infrastructure in a consistent state. It is replicated on multiple servers.

- *Collection Service*

This service provides a virtual organization of the documents stored in the repositories. It supplies the information necessary to manage these virtual document aggregations. This information is used by the other services in order to handle the collection objects allowing, for example, the Query Mediator to perform a query on a specified collection, or the Browse to perform a browse on a collection, and so on. It can be replicated on multiple servers.

- *User Interface*

This service mediates human interaction with these services and their protocols. It is replicated.

Each service has descriptive attributes that specify its content: Table 3 lists the specific attributes associated with each service type. Note that, as an implicit consequence of the representation given, all the functions defined on the set Services are also defined on its subsets. This means, for example, that the Repository instances are described by the functions on the Repository set (see Table 4), and by those associated with both the Distributed and Services sets (see Tables 2 and 1, respectively).

All the above services have been designed parametric with respect to several dimensions. For example, the Query Mediator and Index services can support different types of search operations, e.g. simple, fielded, ranked, multilingual, etc., and different query languages. Furthermore, all the services that manage documents support the DoMDL flexible document model, which can represent a wide range of document structures and a variable and dynamic set of metadata formats.

The provision of these parametric dimensions, integrated with the ability to select the number of replicated and distributed services and the possibility to add new service types, makes it possible to create a wide variety of DLs by customizing OpenDLib. The specific customization must be chosen at DL creation, but can also vary over the DL lifetime to better meet the requirements of the user community.

In presenting the OpenDLib architectural model above we have made a distinction between the generic architectural framework, called *kernel*, and the *service type specifications* that model the detailed functionality classes of a particular version of the system. It should be noted that this distinction has also been maintained in the software: there are modules that implement the handling of the kernel and others that implement the specific services chosen to provide the basic digital library functionality. This separation, together with the systematic design of these modules, is the key feature that realizes the openness of OpenDLib.

The next section discusses how the definition of the communication protocol has been driven by this model.

4 The Open Digital Library Protocol

In order to facilitate the openness of the system, we have introduced a Manager service, which maintains an updated status of the federation and disseminates it on demand to all the other services, and a common service-independent set of service requests to describe the state and the functionality of a service.

The Manager[1] harvests information about services by periodically sending appropriate protocol requests to the instances of the federation. It then elaborates the information gathered and takes decisions about the organization of the federation, e.g. the communication paths. These decisions can change over time according to the value of different parameters, such as the workload of a server or the status of the connection, etc. In turn, at service start-up, the service instances harvest information from the Manager on how to self-configurate. They also ask the Manager periodically for information about the organization of the federation, and about the status of the other service instances. By exploiting this information, the instances of federation "know" each other and can start the co-operation required to serve the DL user requests.

All these communications occur through the Open Digital Library Protocol [OLP]. This protocol defines the format of the data exchanged between two services, including the syntax of messages, character sets, and sequencing of messages. It does not specify how the services prepare the responses and in which programming languages the services are written. The purpose of the protocol is to provide interoperability between existing services, allowing new services to be easily added in the same time.

OLP protocol requests are embedded in HTTP and responses are in an XML-encoded byte stream. The complete specification of the OLP protocol for the OpenDLib service system can be found in [11]. We can distinguish three classes of protocol requests in the information flow described above:

- *OLP_Config*

These are the protocol requests implemented by the Manager to disseminate information about the status of the federation and about the configuration of all replicated services needed to maintain the infrastructure consistent with respect to the OpenDLib Model reported in the previous section. They include all the requests needed to configure the services, to identify their addresses, and to exchange meta information between services.

- *OLP_Explain*

These protocol requests are implemented by each service. They provide information about its state and its content to the other members of the federation. These protocol requests inherit from the Z39.50 Explain [16] functionality the idea that a consumer of resources can configure itself taking into account the characteristics of the producer but overcome the rigidity and complexity of Z39.50 Explain with a more flexible and provider adaptable service. They provide a structured adaptable mechanism for the service provider to publish information about the capabilities of the server software, and about the characteristics of the information stored and managed on the server. The rich set of information elements defined by the OLP_Explain facility includes contact

[1] We are actually speaking of its instances since it is a replicated service.

information for the host institution, as well as specifications of the available access points to harvest service state information and to access service functionalities.

• *OLP_Service_Specific*

These are the service requests that are service dependent and are related to the functionality of each service.

The service requests belonging to the OLP_Config protocol class are provided by the Manager. All of them have been defined systematically by working on the model of the OpenDLib architectural kernel. Therefore, for each element belonging to the set `S` reported in the previous section, a service request disseminating the elements of the set has been introduced. The OLP protocol thus supports service requests such as ListServices, ListServers, ListIndices, ListRepositories, and so on. The semantics of each service request is made explicit by the model: the ListServices service request reports the list of instantiated service instances of the OpenDLib service system at a given time; the ListServers service request reports the list of the mounted servers; the ListIndices service request reports the list of Index service instances, and so on.

Each of the above service requests supports parameters that, for each element of the specified set, allow the retrieval of the value of its attributes. For example ListServers supports a parameter, called *services*, that makes it possible to know the list of services hosted by each server; ListRepositories supports a parameter, called *authorities*, that makes it possible to know the list of authorities hosted by each repository server; ListCollections supports a parameter, called *verbose*, that makes it possible to know the state, master/slave, of each instance of the Collection service.

All these kinds of service requests are not dependent by the service type, Repository, Index, etc., but are strictly related to the service class, Distributed, Replicated, CentralizedInput, etc. The *authorities* parameter, for example, is supported by all Distributed services, as far as all DistributedInput or CentralizedInput services support the *verbose* parameter.

Other service requests belonging to this first class of the protocol are those needed to configure each service. It is clear that if Replicated services are implemented by a set of service instances, where each instance is able to cover completely the same service functionality over the same entire set of data, each instance must be configured in the same way. For this reason, the configuration of this class of services is hosted by the Manager service that supports the ServiceConfigDescription service request for each replicated service.

The service requests belonging to the OLP_Explain protocol class are implemented by each service. This class includes service requests about the protocol itself, such as ListVerbs (reports the list of supported service requests) and DescribeVerb (reports detailed information about a single service request), and about the service instance, such as Identify (reports a complete description of the service indicating how to access the content, how to interpret its state, and so on). The information reported in the Identify service request are no more than the attribute values, belonging to `F`, reported in the tables of the previous section, or the indication of the service requests that allow these values to be accessed.

The OLP_Service_Specific protocol class including service dependent requests has been driven by the specification of the model for each specific service. This set of service requests defined for each service makes it possible to access the service functionality. Its definition has been simplified by the standardization of the service presentation, realized with the OLP_Explain protocol class, and of the infrastructure description, realized with the OLP_Config protocol class.

The OpenDLib model has not only driven and simplified the definition of the overall set of OLP service requests, but has permitted the partition of the protocol into service classes, each of which dispatches in a standard way information about the infrastructure, the service configuration, and the service functionalities, respectively.

Finally, the openness of the digital library service system is rendered explicit: new services that want to join OpenDLib know exactly how to interact with the infrastructure, how to communicate with existing services and, more important, how to present their own state, features, and functionalities so that existing services can use them.

The OpenDLib Manager is a good example of how the openness is now embedded in the system: new services can easily be added to the infrastructure specifying the service type, distributed and/or replicated or centralized, and adopting a very small set of mandatory service requests, which belong to the OLP_Explain protocol class.

5 Conclusion

At present, the digital library research community is starting to recognize the need for digital library service systems. There are some attempts under way to build generic architectural service systems [17,18,19], but so far none of them has proposed a systematic approach to their construction. We strongly believe that in the future the pressing need for new DL services coming from a wide variety of disciplines, not necessarily accustomed building complex software systems, will stimulate the further development of advanced digital library service systems. This will necessitate the definition of a digital library theory that establishes the principles and the rules that govern the design and development of these complex systems. One of the aims of this paper has been to give a first contribution in this direction.

In particular, the paper has introduced OpenDLib, a DLSS whose architecture has been formalized by a set theoretic model. By reasoning on this model we have been able to manage the complexity of designing an open system which can be customized along several dimensions.

The first version of OpenDLib [21] is now running and we plan to make it available as Open Source soon. This first version has been employed in the Scholnet project [20] in order to construct a DLSS able to support the communication and collaboration within scholarly communities. The Scholnet system extends the basic OpenDLib version with additional services that support annotation on documents, cross-language search and personalized information dissemination. The experience made in Scholnet has validated the openness of OpenDLib and has demonstrated the usefulness of the systematic approach in facilitating the building by extension of new DLSS.

Our next step is to extend the functionality of OpenDLib by adding more powerful services. In particular, we are working at the implementation of an extended Query

Mediator which will allow us to support queries on terms taken from different metadata formats or specifically defined by the community of DL users.

We are also adding further elements to what we have called the "theory of DLSS" in order to formalize other aspects related to the DL environment. For example, we are formalizing the query language [22]. This formalization will permit us to clearly establish the conditions under which the query language can be customized and will give us indications on how to implement it in a way that will support its customization.

References

1. NCSTRL: Networked Computer Science Technical Reference Library. http://www.ncstrl.org
2. NDLTD: Networked Digital Library of Theses and Dissertations. http://www.theses.org
3. NZDL: The New Zealand Digital Library. http://www.nzdl.org
4. Carl Lagoze, Herbert Van de Sompel: The Open Archives Initiative: Building a low-barrier interoperability framework. In Proc. Joint Conference on Digital Library (JCDL). June 2001. Roanoke, VA, USA.
5. Digital Libraries: Future Research Directions for a European Research Programme. DELOS Network of Excellence Brainstorming Workshop. June 2001. Alta Badia (Dolomites), Italy
6. Maria Bruna Baldacci, et al.:Developing a European Technical Reference Digital Library. In "Research and Advanced Technology for Digital Libraries : third European Conference; proceedings / ECDL '99, Paris.". (Lecture notes in computer science; Vol. 1696), 1999
7. Naomi Dushay, James C. French, Carl Lagoze: A Characterization Study of NCSTRL Distributed Searching. Cornell University Computer Science, Technical Report TR99-1725, January 1999.
8. B. M. Leiner: The NCSTRL Approach to Open Architecture for the Confederated Digital Library. In D-Lib Magazine, December 1998.
9. J. R. Davis, Carl Lagoze: Dienst: an Architecture for Distributed Document Libraries. In Communications of the ACM, 38 (4) April 1995.
10. R. Lasher, D. Cohen: A Format for Bibliographic Records. In Internet Engineering Task Force, RFC 1807, June 1995.
11. Donatella Castelli, Pasquale Pagano: OLP: The Open Digital Library Protocol. Istituto di Elaborazione dell'Informazione, Technical Report. 2002.
12. Donatella Castelli, Pasquale Pagano: A flexible Repository Service: the OpenDLib solution. To be published in: Proc. Elpub 2002 Conference, Karlovy Vary, Czech Republic, Nov. 2002.
13. Donatella Castelli, Pasquale Pagano. The Open Digital Library Model. Istituto di Elaborazione dell'Informazione, Technical Report. 2002.
14. Ian Foster. et al.: The Physiology of the Grid: An Open Grid Services Architecture for Distributed Systems Integration, January 2002. http://www.globus.org/research/papers.html
15. Carl Lagoze, Sandra Payette. An Infrastructure for Open-Architecture Digital Libraries. Cornell University Computer Science, Technical Report TR98-1690. 1998.
16. Z39.50: International Standard Maintenance Agency. http://lcweb.loc.gov/z3950/agency

17. Edward A. Fox, Hussein Suleman. A Framework for Building Open Digital Libraries. In D-Lib Magazine Volume 7 Number 12, December 2001
18. Andy Powell, Liz Lyon. The JISC Information Environment and Web services. In Ariadne, Issue 31. March-April 2002. http://www.ariadne.ac.uk/issue31/
19. A. Bartelt, D. Faensen, et al. Building Infrastructures for Digital Libraries. In Proc. 3rd DELOS Workshop on Interoperability and Mediation in Heterogeneous Digital Libraries. 8-9 September 2001. Darmstadt, Germany
20. SCHOLNET: A Digital Library Testbed to Support Networked Scholarly Communities. http://www.ercim.org/scholnet
21. OpenDLib. http://www.opendlib.com
22. Donatella Castelli, Carlo Meghini, Pasquale Pagano: Foundations of a Multidimensional Query Language for Digital Libraries. In Proc. Maristella Agosti, Costantinio Thanos (eds), Proc. ECDL'02 Conference, Lecture Notes in Computer Science, Sprinter-Verlag, 2002.

Prototyping Digital Library Technologies in *zetoc*

Ann Apps and Ross MacIntyre

MIMAS, Manchester Computing, University of Manchester,
Oxford Road, Manchester, M13 9PL, UK
ann.apps@man.ac.uk, ross.macintyre@man.ac.uk

Abstract. *zetoc* is a current awareness and document delivery service providing World Wide Web and Z39.50 access to the British Library's Electronic Table of Contents database of journal articles and conference papers, along with an email alerting service. An experimental prototype version of *zetoc* is under development, based on open standards, including Dublin Core and XML, and using the open source, leading-edge Cheshire II information retrieval technology. Enhancements investigated in this prototype include request and delivery of discovered articles, location of electronic articles using OpenURL technology, and additional current awareness functionality including the exposure of journal issue metadata according to the Open Archives Initiative protocol. These experimental developments will enhance the *zetoc* service to improve the information environment for researchers and learners.

Keywords. Electronic table of contents, current awareness, document delivery, alerting, OpenURL, Open Archives Initiative, Z39.50.

1 Introduction

The *zetoc* [1] current awareness service provides access to the British Library's [2] Electronic Table of Contents of journal articles and conference papers. It is available to researchers, teachers and learners in UK Higher and Further Education under the BL/HEFCE 'strategic alliance' [3], and to practitioners within the UK National Health Service. Access may be via the World Wide Web or the NISO Z39.50 [4],[5] standard for information retrieval which defines a protocol for two computers to communicate and share information. An experimental prototype of an enhanced version of *zetoc*, built on open standards and using open source, leading-edge software, is under development. The enhancements include ordering of copies of discovered articles, location of electronic articles and additional current awareness functionality including the exposure of journal issue metadata according to the Open Archives Initiative [6] protocol. Some of the enhancements trialled in this prototype are now implemented in the 'live' *zetoc* service. As well as being a development of a popular service, based on a significant quantity of data, the *zetoc* enhancement prototype provides a platform to explore the introduction of new technological advances to improve the information environment for researchers and learners.

M. Agosti and C. Thanos (Eds.): ECDL 2002, LNCS 2458, pp. 309–323, 2002.

2 The *zetoc* Service

The ***zetoc*** database contains details of articles from approximately 20,000 current journals and 16,000 conference proceedings published per year and is updated daily. With 20 million article and conference records from 1993 to date, the database covers every imaginable subject in science, technology, medicine, engineering, business, law, finance and the humanities. Copies of all the articles recorded in the database are available from the British Library's Document Supply Centre [7]. The service was developed, and is hosted, by MIMAS [8] at the University of Manchester, UK. The ***zetoc*** Web-Z gateway is based on that developed for the COPAC [9] research library online catalogue service which is familiar to ***zetoc***'s target audience. Z39.50 compliance is provided by reworking of the COPAC application code, which utilises CrossNet's ZedKit software, developed as part of the ONE project [10], and an Open Text BRS/Search database [11]. The database is updated daily with 5000-10000 records by automatic FTP download and data conversion from the SGML format supplied by the British Library.

Searches for articles in ***zetoc***, by fields such as title, author, subject and journal, may be made through the World Wide Web interface, or via Z39.50 and return details of the articles found. Currently the search results do not include abstracts for the majority of articles but there are plans to include abstracts for some articles in the future. For example, one of the results following a search in ***zetoc*** for articles by an author 'apps a', has a full record which includes:

```
Article Title:    Studying E-Journal User Behavior Using Log Files
Author(s):        Yu, L.; Apps, A.
Journal Title:    LIBRARY AND INFORMATION SCIENCE RESEARCH
ISSN:             0740-8188
Year:             2000
Volume:           22
Part:             3
Page(s):          311-338
Dewey Class:      020
LC Class:         Z671
BLDSC shelfmark: 5188.730000
ZETOC id:         RN083430771
```

Following a Z39.50 search, records may be retrieved as Simple Unstructured Text Record Syntax (SUTRS), both brief and full records, full records being similar to the above example, GRS-1 (Generic Record Syntax) and a simple tagged reference format. In addition ***zetoc*** is compliant with the Bath Profile [12], an international Z39.50 specification for library applications and resource discovery, and provides records as Dublin Core in XML according to the CIMI Document Type Definition [13].

zetoc includes a popular journal issue alerting service. Users may request email table of contents alerts to be sent to them when issues of their chosen journals are loaded into ***zetoc***. These email journal issue alerts, which are in plain text at present, list the articles and their authors within the journal issue in addition to the journal issue information. Along with each article listed is a URL which provides direct entry into the ***zetoc*** Web service, thus enabling the user to take advantage of the document delivery functionality of ***zetoc***. Currently nearly 8000 alerts are sent out every night, and there are more than 12,500 registered users of the alerting service. Of ***zetoc*** Alert, Douglas Carnall in the British Medical Journal's 'Website of the week' said "The 800lb gorilla of such services in the United Kingdom is zetoc" [14].

An enhancement to the ***zetoc*** Alert service has been the introduction of alerts based on pre-defined search criteria. Users may set up an alert search request based on keywords in the article title or an author's name. These saved searches are performed on new data when it is loaded into ***zetoc*** each night, users being emailed with the records of articles which matched. The search-based alert is performed separately from the journal issue table of contents alert and the searches are run against all the data loaded into ***zetoc***, including conference paper records.

3 The *zetoc* Enhancement Prototype

A prototype enhanced version of ***zetoc*** is being developed by MIMAS. It was decided to investigate a solution based on open standards and using open software. Within this version of ***zetoc*** the data is stored as Dublin Core [15] records, using XML syntax, generated from the SGML data supplied by the British Library. The mapping of the ***zetoc*** data to Dublin Core, and some of the problems associated with encoding bibliographic data using Dublin Core are described in [16].

This prototype version of ***zetoc*** is being used to try out enhancements before they are introduced into the service. Enhancements already added to the service, which are described in more detail below, include document delivery and subject-based alerts. In other cases, experimental enhancements employing leading-edge technology may be tested in this ***zetoc*** prototype but will not become part of the 'live' ***zetoc*** service if they are too immature. It has been found simpler to experiment with and implement these enhancements within the ***zetoc*** enhancement prototype, which has a flexibility provided by its use of open standard data formats and open software, rather than in the ***zetoc*** service which is built on proprietary data formats. It is possible that at some point in the future this ***zetoc*** enhancement prototype will replace the current ***zetoc*** service, but there is currently no timescale for this changeover.

4 The Cheshire II Information Retrieval System

The software platform used for the ***zetoc*** enhancement prototype is Cheshire II [17] which is a next generation online catalogue and full text information retrieval system, developed using advanced information retrieval techniques. It is open source software, free for non-commercial uses, and was developed at the University of California-Berkeley School of Information Management and Systems, underwritten by a grant from the US Department of Education. Its continued development by the University of Berkeley and the University of Liverpool receives funding from the Joint Information Systems Committee (JISC) of the UK Higher and Further Education Funding Councils and the US National Science Foundation (NSF). Experience and requirements from the ***zetoc*** Cheshire prototype have been fed back into the continuing Cheshire development. Although using evolving software has caused some technical problems, the Cheshire development team has been very responsive to providing new functionality, and this relationship has proved beneficial to both projects. Examples of facilities implemented in Cheshire for ***zetoc*** development include sorting of result sets within the Cheshire Web interface and implementation of 'virtual' databases described below in section 4.3.

4.1 *zetoc* Z39.50 via Cheshire

Cheshire provides indexing and searching of XML (or SGML) data according to an XML Document Type Definition (DTD), and a Z39.50 interface. The underlying database is currently either a single file or a set of files within a directory structure, along with a set of indexes onto the data. The ***zetoc*** XML data is mapped to the Z39.50 Bib-1 Attribute Set [18] for indexing and searching. The Z39.50 search results formats replicate the ***zetoc*** service, as described above. The mapping from the ***zetoc*** data to the GRS-1 Tagset-G [19] elements is defined in the Cheshire configuration file for the database, and this information is used by Cheshire to return GRS-1 to a requesting client. The other Z39.50 result formats are implemented by bespoke filter programs which transform the raw XML records returned by Cheshire.

4.2 The Cheshire *zetoc* Web Interface

Cheshire also provides 'webcheshire' which is a basic, customisable World Wide Web interface. The web interface for the ***zetoc*** enhancement prototype is built on webcheshire as a bespoke program written in OmniMark (version 5.5) [20]. This ***zetoc*** web program provides a search interface which replicates that of the ***zetoc*** service, including saving session information between web page accesses, and sorting result records according to date (numeric) or title (alphabetic) using underlying Cheshire functionality. It transforms retrieved records from XML to XHTML (version 1.0) for web display. OmniMark was chosen as the programming language for this interface because it is XML (or SGML) aware according to a DTD, a knowledge which is employed for the XML translations involved. OmniMark was also chosen because of existing expertise, and the free availability of OmniMark Version 5.5 at the start of the project (but it is no longer available). Other suitable languages for the web interface implementation would have been Perl, or TCL which is the basic interface language to Cheshire.

The ***zetoc*** web interface provides search results in discrete 'chunks', currently 25 at a time, with 'next' and 'previous' navigation buttons. This is implemented by using the Cheshire capability to request a fixed number of records in the result set, beginning at a particular number within that set. The Cheshire/***zetoc*** application remembers the ***zetoc*** identifiers of the results in the retrieved 'chunk', and extracts the record corresponding to a particular ***zetoc*** identifier when an end-user selects a 'full record display'.

4.3 Indexing and Searching a Large Number of Records

Two problems were encountered when using Cheshire as a platform to implement ***zetoc***, as a consequence of the very large and continually increasing number of records involved. These were the ordering of the returned results after a search and the size of the index files.

Sorting Result Sets. ***zetoc*** being a current awareness service, researchers accessing the database wish to see the most recent records first in their search results. Cheshire returns the most recently indexed results first. This is obviously not a problem for new 'update' data when the service is built and running, provided some thought is given to the data organisation within a directory structure. But it does mean that, if all data were in one Cheshire database, it would be necessary to load the backdata in order, with the oldest loaded first. This problem was partially resolved by the introduction of a sort capability into Cheshire which is able to return sorted results sets. By default, results returned to the user are sorted by reverse date (year of publication) order. The ***zetoc*** web interface provides the end-user with the option to re-sort the results by ascending date and title, and also by journal title following a journal article search. However, it becomes impractical to sort results within a very large result set, for instance of more than 500 results. Sorting larger result sets, which a dataset the size of ***zetoc*** could produce, would mean poor performance. Thus the problem of having to load the back data in order still remained.

Virtual Databases. Until recently all data for an application had to be indexed within a single Cheshire database. Because of concerns about this approach given that Cheshire had never been proven on this scale, a full volume test back data load was undertaken. After more than 10 million records had been indexed, performance during indexing deteriorated seriously. The problem was probably exacerbated by the fact that ***zetoc*** is run on the shared MIMAS service machine which is used simultaneously by other applications which process large amounts of data. By the time this experimental bulk data load was stopped, the largest of the Cheshire index files was 6 gigabytes in size. Although the operating system (Solaris 8) was able to cope with very large files, manipulation of files this size has implications for swap space and disk input/output, and hence performance.

Both of the above problems have now been addressed by the introduction of new Cheshire functionality which allows the definition of a *virtual database*.

A Cheshire virtual database contains no data itself, but is configured to search across a list of physical databases, on the same machine. A search request to a virtual database, via either Z39.50 or webcheshire, is fanned out across the underlying physical databases, and the results are assembled appropriately before display. This implementation of virtual databases supports result sets and result sorting as for a single physical database.

Using a Cheshire virtual database made it possible to load the ***zetoc*** data across several physical databases, one per publication year. This architecture has overcome indexing performance and index file size problems. Because the order of unsorted returned results reflects the order of the physical databases within the configuration of the virtual database, it is no longer a requirement for the back data to be loaded in publication date order, beginning with the oldest.

5 Article Delivery

5.1 Ordering from the British Library

Having discovered an article of interest in ***zetoc***, a researcher will then wish to acquire the article. The ***zetoc*** service includes a web link to the British Library Document Supply Centre (BLDSC) which enables a user to purchase a copy of the article directly by credit card payment. ***zetoc*** sends the ***zetoc*** identifier on this link providing the BLDSC with the information it requires to locate the article within the British Library and send a copy to the customer. Within the ***zetoc*** enhancement prototype a demonstration link has also been included to the BLDSC Articles Direct service, for journal articles. Unlike the direct link to BLDSC, article details are filled into a web form by ***zetoc***, the rest of the form being completed by the customer. In both these cases, the payment required by the British Library includes a copyright fee. Methods of delivery include mail, fax, courier, and electronic where available and agreed with the publisher concerned. This last method is currently subject to a level of paranoia amongst publishers who are refusing permission or insisting on encryption, severely constraining the usability. Exceptions are Karger, Kluwer and Blackwell Science, all of whom have given the British Library permission to supply the customer with the article in their preferred format including electronic.

5.2 Ordering via Inter-library Loan

Within the communities which are granted access to ***zetoc***, the majority of users will be entitled to order copies of articles through their own institution's Inter-Library Loan department without payment of a copyright fee, i.e. by 'library privilege', if the copy is solely for their own research or private study. In fact, 'Inter-Library Loan' is rather a misnomer, because in the case of an article a 'copy' will be supplied rather than a loan. However, the term Inter-Library Loan (ILL) is used because it is commonly understood, and it distinguishes this order method from the direct document ordering described above.

To assist researchers in making ILL requests for discovered articles, a link has been added to the ***zetoc*** service, following some prototyping of the facility within the ***zetoc*** enhancement prototype. The result of following this link depends on the institution to which the researcher belongs. Before this facility was designed, discussions were held with several ILL librarians to discover their current procedures and their opinions on what functionality ***zetoc*** should provide. It became apparent that there were many variations in current practices. It was also clear that some institution libraries who had developed their own forms and instructions for ILL document supply requests would want to continue to use these. On the other hand they could see the value in a researcher being able to provide the ILL department with an authoritative citation for the requested article, which also includes the British Library 'shelf location' information. Thus it was decided to allow institutions to choose one of two options *ILL Form* or *Local*, with a third default option for users where ***zetoc*** has no recorded information about their institution.

Authentication for use of ***zetoc*** is performed by IP address checking, and failing that by Athens [21], the UK Higher and Further Education authentication system. The Athens three-letter prefix, which is specific to each institution, is used as the institution identifier for ***zetoc*** ILL. ILL information from institutions and details of their library catalogue is supplied to ***zetoc*** support staff at MIMAS who enter the information via a bespoke administration web form. Within the ***zetoc*** application, this information, including the institution identifier, is saved in an XML format 'Institution Information' file. When a user selects the ILL request web link, their institution identifier is determined from their login authentication and the institution information is processed as XML to provide customisation of the web pages displayed. Wording on the web pages encourages good practice, advising users to check the catalogue to determine whether their library has the article available locally, either electronically or in print, before making an unnecessary ILL request.

ILL Form Option. If an institution has requested the 'ILL Form' option, when a user selects the web link "Request a copy from your Institution's Library (for research/private study)" at the foot of a ***zetoc*** 'full record' display, they are presented with a web form which includes the citation information for the discovered article. This form is in a separate web browser window to enable the user to 'keep their place' in ***zetoc***. The user is asked to complete the form with personal details such as name, department and library card number. Selecting 'Submit' on this form results in a further web page containing all the captured details along with a 'Copyright Declaration'. The user is instructed to print this form, sign it to indicate that they agree with the copyright declaration, and take it to their ILL department with the required payment. From this point onwards, the ILL request is processed according to the library's normal procedures.

Local Option. Where an institution has requested the 'Local' option, selection of the ILL web link results in a page containing citation information about the discovered article along with details of the library's ILL department. Users are instructed to use the citation information to fill out the institution's own ILL forms and follow their instructions to make the request. The 'default' option is similar, except that ***zetoc*** is unable to provide users with details of their ILL department.

zetoc* Order Number.** It is possible to request only one article at once from ***zetoc, which is the article whose 'full record' displayed the selected link. This fits with ILL practice where a separate signature and payment are required for each item ordered. For all accesses to the ***zetoc*** ILL option, a unique ***zetoc*** order number is generated and appears on forms printed by the user. It was introduced following a suggestion by one institution and could have possible uses in the future. For instance if ILL requests were emailed to an institution's ILL department as well as printed by a user, the order number would allow correlation between the two modes of request.

Interoperable ILL. It is important to stress that this is the first stage only in developing a ***zetoc*** ILL facility. But it has set the foundations for future developments being based on: good practice; a definitive full citation for an article; existing practices; and no extra work for any party. With a view to future enhancements of this ILL facility within ***zetoc***, usage will be monitored and comments from both researchers and librarians will be noted. It is likely that enhancements will be introduced incrementally as they appear to be acceptable to the community. The future vision would be to enable researchers to send their ILL document requests for articles discovered within ***zetoc*** directly to the British Library using a ***zetoc*** web form, and for the requested items to be returned using an electronic document delivery method. Recent advances such as development of a profile of the ISO ILL request format standard (ISO 10160/10161) by the Interlibrary Loan Protocol Implementers Group (IPIG) [22], which the British Library is already able to handle, and digital signatures make this vision technically nearer to realisation. But it will also be necessary to work within the existing structure of institution ILL procedures to authenticate requests and process payments from institution department budgets, which necessitates the introduction of change in a measured way.

6 Article Linking

An obvious development for a current awareness table of contents service such as ***zetoc*** is to provide links to the full text of an article where it is available electronically. The problem of providing such a link is two-fold if the user is to be given a link which will not be a dead end. Firstly the citation information for an article must be translated into a URL which will link to an article. Secondly this link must, if possible, be to a version of an article which is available free to the user maybe via a valid institution subscription. The latter problem is known as that of the 'appropriate copy' [23]. A user would not be happy if linked to a publisher's web site where a copy of an article was available for a substantial fee if they were entitled to read the same article through a service where they have a subscription.

6.1 OpenURL

One solution to the first of these problems is to encode a link to the full text of an article as an OpenURL [24]. OpenURL provides a syntax for transmitting citation metadata using the Web HTTP protocol and is in the process of becoming a NISO standard. The NISO committee who are developing the OpenURL standard have 'pinned down' the draft OpenURL as version 0.1 [25], to enable its use by early implementers, and where possible are allowing for backwards compatibility in the first version of the standard (1.0).

Within the *zetoc* enhancement prototype, OpenURLs are generated from journal article records and used for various experimental links. An OpenURL encoding using version 0.1 syntax for the journal article example shown above in section 2 would be as follows. This example shows only the 'query' part of the OpenURL which contains the metadata for the referent (i.e. the entity about which the OpenURL was created) and omits the resolver (BaseURL). Syntax differences between versions of OpenURL should be noted here. In a version 0.1 OpenURL the type of the referent is indicated by the label '`genre`', as in this example. In a version 1.0 OpenURL, which may contain further entities in addition to the referent, the referent type will be defined by a 'metadata description schema' registered with NISO, possibly as '`ref_valfmt=NISOArticle`' but this is not definite at the time of writing. Within this example spaces have been escape-encoded as '%20' for HTTP transmission and line breaks are for clarity only.

```
?genre=article&title=LIBRARY%20AND%20INFORMATION%20SCIENCE
&atitle=Studying%20E-Journal%20User%20Behavior%20
     Using%20Log%20Files
&aulast=Yu&auinit=L
&date=2000&volume=22&issue=3
&pages=311-338&issn=0740-8188
```

6.2 Context Sensitive Linking

A solution to the 'appropriate copy' problem is to provide the user with a link via an OpenURL resolver which has knowledge of article subscriptions relevant to that user. Currently the best known such context sensitive reference linking service is SFX [26] from Ex Libris [27]. MIMAS are evaluating SFX as part of a separate project, 'Implementing the DNER Technical Architecture at MIMAS' (ITAM) [28], which includes the development of a UK academic 'national default' resolver. An OpenURL link to this resolver from the full record display for a journal article has been included within the *zetoc* enhancement prototype.

Following this link shows the user a range of 'extended services', which will include a link to the full text of the article where it is available free. Other extended services may be: a free abstract for the article; a general web search using words from the article title; a non-bibliographic function such as a library service like 'on-line, real-time reference' (ORR) [29]; and certain widely licensed services such as ISI 'Web of Science' [30] and JSTOR [31].

A link to an OpenURL resolver would be even more useful if it pointed to a resolver specific to the user's institution. The 'Institution Information' XML file, described above for ILL, will be extended to include details of an institution's OpenURL resolver, and this resolver will be used for a context sensitive link in preference to the 'national default' resolver.

6.3 Other OpenURL Links

OpenURL links are used to pass information internally within the ***zetoc*** enhancement prototype, for the 'Articles Direct' order and ILL order links described in section 5. Another experimental OpenURL link from a full article record in the ***zetoc*** enhancement prototype is to ZBLSA [32], an article discovery tool which indicates to an end-user where the full text of the article may be found, but with no guarantee of free access. An 'OpenURL like' link, but using proprietary labels within the URL query syntax, has been included to LitLink [33], an article linking tool from MDL Information Systems.

7 The JISC Information Environment Architecture

zetoc is part of the JISC 'Information Environment' [34], which provides resources for learning, teaching and research to UK Higher and Further Education, and thus must be consistent with its architecture. The Information Environment will enable article discovery through the various portals in its 'presentation layer', including the discipline specific Resource Discovery Network (RDN) hubs [35]. Content providers in the 'provision layer' are expected to disclose their metadata for searching, harvesting and by alerting. Currently the ***zetoc*** service provides the requisite Web and Z39.50 (Bath Profile compliant) search interfaces and an alert capability albeit in plain text. Other interfaces required of ***zetoc*** are OAI (Open Archives Initiative) for metadata harvesting and OpenURL for article discovery and location.

7.1 *zetoc* as an OpenURL Target

The OpenURL developments within ***zetoc*** described above are concerned with implementing ***zetoc*** as an OpenURL 'source', to link out from the display of the full metadata record of an article to its full text. It is also planned to implement ***zetoc*** as an OpenURL 'target' providing linking 'in' to the record for a specific article. It is already possible to discover an article from its metadata with a Z39.50 search to determine its ***zetoc*** identifier, followed by a direct web link into ***zetoc*** using that identifier. Enabling ***zetoc*** as an OpenURL target would provide a direct web link into a particular article's record using its citation metadata. ***zetoc*** would then become a 'reference centre' allowing an application to provide its end-users with the ability to discover an article by a definitive citation search and then locate that article along with other relevant services.

7.2 *zetoc* as an OAI Repository

The Open Archives Initiative (OAI) has specified a Metadata Harvesting Protocol [36] which enables a data repository to expose metadata about its content in an interoperable way. The architecture of the JISC Information Environment includes the implementation of OAI harvesters which will gather metadata from the various collections within the Information Environment to provide searchable metadata for portals and hence for end-users [38]. Portals would select metadata from particular subject areas of relevance to their user community. Thus there is a requirement for collections and services within the Information Environment to make their metadata available according to the OAI protocol, including a minimum of OAI 'common metadata format', i.e. simple Dublin Core, records.

Providing an OAI interface for ***zetoc*** presents several problems and questions. The ***zetoc*** data itself is in fact metadata for the articles, and there are a very large number of records. Allowing an OAI harvester to gather all the ***zetoc*** records would not be sensible considering machine resources required for both the ***zetoc*** machine and the harvester. Harvesting ***zetoc*** data to provide a searchable interface would be nonsensical when the ***zetoc*** service itself is available for searching. In addition ***zetoc*** data is commercially sensitive, access restricted and owned by the British Library. There may however be some merit in making available journal issue records for harvesting. In particular, this could be useful for current awareness applications which would benefit from information about the most recent issues of journals. Thus it is intended to implement an experimental OAI interface into the ***zetoc*** enhancement prototype, or a data subset of it, which provides journal issue level and conference proceedings records, rather than records for articles or papers. But there is no guarantee that this will ever become a generally available service within the JISC Information Environment. Such a service would require negotiation between owners of the data and services.

A possible simple Dublin Core record provided to an OAI service for the journal issue containing the article shown above in section 2 may be as follows. An issue-level record would never contain a 'creator' but it may contain a 'contributor' if the journal issue has a named editor. The first 'identifier' in the example is the shelf location within the British Library.

```
<title>LIBRARY AND INFORMATION SCIENCE 22(3)</title>
<subject>(DDC)020</subject>
<subject>(LCSH)Z671</subject>
<date>2000</date>
<identifier>5188.730000</identifier>
<identifier>(ISSN)0740-8188</identifier>
```

```
<rights>All Rights Reserved
   http://zetoc.mimas.ac.uk/zetoc/terms.html</rights>
```

Currently ***zetoc*** processes article level records, holding no specific records for journal issues. In order to provide only one record for each journal issue, it will be necessary to mark the first article of an issue as such during the data load process, and include this information in the Cheshire indexes. With this data tag in place it will be possible to select issue level records when an OAI request is processed. A specific display format within the Cheshire configuration of the ***zetoc*** database will process the XML search result records to transform them into journal issue information.

Date Ranges. The OAI protocol allows harvesters to specify they want records 'from' a certain date and/or 'until' a certain date. Because the ***zetoc*** back data has been loaded recently for years gone by, using the 'date loaded' would not lead to sensible results. So records will be supplied according to the year of publication of the journal issue for most requests. However, it is likely that some harvesters accessing a current awareness service will want information about the latest issues of journals, which would not be readily provided using 'year' as the granularity. Thus if a 'from' date includes a month, and it is not more than two months ago ***zetoc*** will provide journal issues which have been added since that date. Selecting records added to the ***zetoc*** Cheshire database after a certain date, in response to an OAI request, is implemented easily when a Cheshire index has been created for the 'date loaded' field.

Acceptable Use. Implementing an OAI interface onto a very large database such as ***zetoc***, which is mounted on a machine running many services, raises some concerns. With no restrictions, OAI harvesting could result in effective 'denial of service' attacks because of the machine resources required, and so there is a need for an 'acceptable use' policy. Thus there will be restrictions on how many records may be harvested at one time. When supplying only part of a result set, the OAI protocol allows for the return of a '`resumptionToken`' which the harvester uses to make repeat requests. The format of this `resumptionToken` is not defined in the OAI protocol but by the source application. The `resumptionToken` from ***zetoc*** will include the number of the next record in the result set, along with any 'from/until' date information from the original request. There will be further restrictions, advertised in the information returned in response to an OAI 'Identify' request, on how soon a harvester can repeat the request, maybe allowing a particular harvester access only once per day. This information will also be encoded in the `resumptionToken`, to enable ***zetoc*** to refuse too frequent repeat requests using an HTTP 'Retry-After' response, or an OAI version 2 error code.

Access to the ***zetoc*** database through the Web and Z39.50 is restricted to particular communities by agreement with the British Library, and is authenticated either by IP address or Athens. Thus there will be tight restrictions, requiring British Library agreement, on which services will be allowed to harvest ***zetoc*** data, even at the journal issue level. OAI access will be validated using IP addresses.

7.3 Current Awareness Alerting

At present the data feed for the ***zetoc*** Alert service is the BRS-format ***zetoc*** update file. In line with the other ***zetoc*** enhancement developments, this data feed will be changed to an XML file containing Dublin Core ***zetoc*** records. The search-based alerts will operate on XML records retrieved from a Cheshire database. Changing the alert data feed into an open standard format opens up the possibility of offering ***zetoc*** alerts in several standard formats such as XML, Dublin Core, RDF Site Summary (RSS) [37], and a tagged bibliographic format in addition to the current plain text. Providing alerts in RSS, required in the 'Information Environment', would enable their use for news feeds, whereas a tagged bibliographic format may be imported directly into personal bibliographic databases.

8 Conclusion

zetoc aims to provide researchers with a means to find and access published research material to aid in the furtherance of their own research, thus assisting in the advancement of knowledge. Within an internet cross-referencing paradigm of 'discover – locate – request – deliver' [39], the initial ***zetoc*** service provided discovery of research articles in a timely fashion. Enhancements to the ***zetoc*** service have provided 'request and deliver' through document supply directly from the British Library, and indirectly through traditional inter-library loan routes. Some of the experimental enhancements described in this paper indicate ways in which ***zetoc*** may provide 'location' of 'appropriate copies' of articles, and internet methods of 'request and deliver', or access, via web links.

An orthogonal purpose of ***zetoc*** is to provide a current awareness service through its Alert function. This service has been improved with the inclusion of search-based alerts. Further current awareness enhancements could be the provision of a choice of alert format including RSS for news feeds. The implementation of ***zetoc*** as an OAI repository providing journal issue records will also augment its current awareness support.

zetoc, being a popular service with a significant quantity of data, has provided a platform to prototype new technologies and possible additions to the service. One aim of the '***zetoc*** Enhancement Project' was to develop a solution based on open standards and using leading-edge, open source technology. This has been successfully achieved within a prototype environment using a Cheshire II software platform to index ***zetoc*** Dublin Core records encoded in XML. A spin-off has been improvements to Cheshire following ***zetoc*** feedback. Other experimental technologies such as OAI and OpenURL will enable ***zetoc*** to be integrated into the JISC 'Information Environment', thus providing a valuable service to the stakeholders within that environment.

Acknowledgements. The authors wish to acknowledge the contribution to the development of ***zetoc*** by their colleagues at the British Library, including Stephen Andrews and Andrew Braid, at MIMAS, Ashley Sanders, Jane Stevenson, Andrew Weeks and Vicky Wiseman, and the Cheshire development team, Ray Larson at the University of California–Berkeley and Paul Watry and Robert Sanderson at the University of Liverpool. The initial development of the ***zetoc*** service was funded by the British Library who own and supply the Electronic Table of Contents data. The '***zetoc*** Enhancement Project' is funded by the British Library and by the Joint Information Systems Committee (JISC) [40] for the UK Higher and Further Education Funding Councils, as part of the 'Join-Up' programme [41] within the Distributed National Electronic Resource (DNER) development programme [42].

References

1. ***zetoc***, Electronic Table of Contents from the British Library. `http://zetoc.mimas.ac.uk`
2. The British Library. `http://www.bl.uk`
3. Strategic alliance emphasises British Library's central role in support of higher education. Press Release, 19 March 2002. `http://www.bl.uk/cgi-bin/press.cgi?story=1231`
4. Z39.50, the North American National Information Standards Organisation (NISO) standard for information retrieval. `http://www.niso.org/standards/resources/Z3950.pdf`
5. Miller, P.: Z39.50 for All. Ariadne **21** (1999). `http://www.ariadne.ac.uk/issue21/z3950`
6. Open Archives Initiative (OAI). `http://www.openarchives.org/`
7. British Library Document Supply Centre (BLDSC). `http://www.bl.uk/services/document/dsc.html`
8. MIMAS, a UK Higher and Further Education data centre. `http://www.mimas.ac.uk`
9. The COPAC research library online catalogue service. `http://copac.ac.uk`
10. CrossNet ZedKit software. `http://www.crxnet.com`
11. Open Text BRS/Search. `http://www.opentext.com/dataware/`
12. The Z39.50 Bath Profile. `http://www.nlc-bnc.ca/bath/bp-current.htm`
13. The Consortium for the Computer Interchange of Museum Information (CIMI) Dublin Core Document Type Definition. `http://www.nlc-bnc.ca/bath/bp-app-d.htm`
14. Carnall, D.: Website of the week: Email alerting services. British Medical Journal **324** (2002) 56
15. The Dublin Core Metadata Initiative. `http://www.dublincore.org`
16. Apps, A., MacIntyre, R.: ***zetoc***: a Dublin Core Based Current Awareness Service. Journal of Digital Information **2**(2) (2002). `http://jodi.ecs.soton.ac.uk/Articles/v02/i02/Apps/`
17. The Cheshire II Information Retrieval System. `http://cheshire.lib.berkeley.edu`
18. The Z39.50 Bib-1 Attribute Set. `http://lcweb.loc.gov/z3950/agency/defns/bib1.html`

19. The Z39.50 Generic Record Syntax (GRS-1) Tagsets.
`http://lcweb.loc.gov/z3950/agency/defns/tag-gm.html`
20. OmniMark Technologies. `http://www.omnimark.com`
21. Athens Access Management System. `http://www.athens.ac.uk`
22. Interlibrary Loan Protocol Implementers Group (IPIG) Profile for the ISO ILL Protocol. `http://www.nlc-bnc.ca/iso/ill/ipigprfl.htm`
23. Caplan, P., Arms, W.Y.: Reference Linking for Journal Articles. D-Lib Magazine **5**(7/8) (1999). `doi://10.1045/july99-caplan`
24. OpenURL, NISO Committee AX. `http://library.caltech.edu/openurl/`
25. OpenURL Syntax Description (v0.1).
`http://www.sfxit.com/OpenURL/openurl.html`
26. Van de Sompel, H., Beit-Arie, O.: Open Linking in the Scholarly Information Environment Using the OpenURL Framework. D-Lib Magazine **7**(3) (2001).
`doi://10.1045/march2001-vandesompel`
27. Ex Libris, SFX Context Sensitive Reference Linking. `http://www.sfxit.com`
28. 'Implementing the DNER Technical Architecture at MIMAS' (ITAM) project.
`http://epub.mimas.ac.uk/itam.html`
29. Moyo, L.M.: Reference anytime anywhere: towards virtual reference services at Penn State. The Electronic Library **20**(1) (2002) 22-28.
30. ISI Web of Science Service for UK Education. `http://wos.mimas.ac.uk`
31. JSTOR, the Scholarly Journal Archive (UK). `http://www.jstor.ac.uk`
32. ZBLSA – Z39.50 Broker to Locate Serials and Articles.
`http://edina.ac.uk/projects/joinup/zblsa/`
33. LitLink, MDL Information Systems. `http://www.litlink.com`
34. Powell, A., Lyon, L.: The JISC Information Environment and Web Services. Ariadne **31** (2002).
`http://www.ariadne.ac.uk/issue31/information-environments/`
35. Resource Discovery Network (RDN). `http://www.rdn.ac.uk`
36. Warner, S.: Exposing and Harvesting Metadata Using the OAI Metadata Harvesting Protocol: A Tutorial. High Energy Physics Libraries Webzine **4** (2001).
`http://library.cern.ch/HEPLW/4/papers/3/`
37. Powell, A.: RSS FAQ, JISC Information Environment Architecture.
`http://www.ukoln.ac.uk/distributed-systems/dner/arch/faq/rss/`
38. Cliff, P.: Building ResourceFinder. Ariadne **30** (2001).
`http://www.ariadne.ac.uk/issue30/rdn-oai/`
39. MODELS – Moving to Distributed Environments for Library Services.
`http://www.ukoln.ac.uk/dlis/models/`
40. The Joint Information Systems Committee (JISC). `http://www.jisc.ac.uk`
41. The Join-Up programme. `http://edina.ed.ac.uk/projects/joinup/`
42. The UK Distributed National Electronic Resource (DNER).
`http://www.jisc.ac.uk/dner/`

Employing Smart Browsers to Support Flexible Information Presentation in Petri Net-Based Digital Libraries

Unmil P. Karadkar, Jin-Cheon Na[*], and Richard Furuta

Center for the Study of Digital Libraries and Department of Computer Science
Texas A&M University
College Station, TX 77843-3112, USA
{unmil, jincheon, furuta}@csdl.tamu.edu

Abstract. For effective real-life use, digital libraries must incorporate resource and system policies and adapt to user preferences and device characteristics. The caT (context-aware Trellis) hypertext model incorporates these policies and adaptation conditions within the Petri net specification of the digital library to support context-aware delivery of digital documents in a dynamically changing environment. This paper describes extensions to the caT architecture for supporting adaptation via smarter browsers and an external resource store to provide greater flexibility in information presentation. Browsers request resources that they can best display with their knowledge of intrinsic capabilities and constraints imposed on them by the devices that they run on. The data store returns the most appropriate version of a resource in response to browser requests, thus allowing maintainers of libraries to add, modify and remove resources without any changes to the structure, presentation or document pointers in the digital library.

1 Introduction

Libraries are dynamically changing social spaces that provide access to collections of resources, physical as well as digital. In addition to the resources, libraries provide reference and other services to patrons, some all the time and others during specific hours. Patrons may incur costs for using some of these services, while others may be available at no cost. Actions of patrons affect others who access the libraries. For example, checking out the last available copy of a resource by one patron for finishing a class assignment will render the resource inaccessible to others until someone returns their copy of this resource. To ensure smooth functioning libraries set policies that must be followed by all patrons. In the case of resources being unavailable, users must wait until a copy is available for their use. Libraries must also abide by the licensing regulations set by creators of resources that they contain. For example,

---

[*] Jin-Cheon Na's current address is: Division of Information Studies, School of Communication & Information, Nanyang Technological University, 31 Nanyang Link, Singapore 637718 (tjcna@ntu.edu.sg).

M. Agosti and C. Thanos (Eds.): ECDL 2002, LNCS 2458, pp. 324-337, 2002.

libraries may not photocopy the books they buy or make copies of digital resources like VHS tapes, CDs, or DVDs.

When porting this model to the digital world, it is essential to support the dynamism of the environment created by the presence of other users in the space as well as the policies of the service provider. At the same time, the service must be convenient to access, easy to use and must account for the needs and preferences of various users and characteristics of the devices used to access the resources. Digital library support for these features can be better managed at the architecture level than at the application level. Integrating the policy and adaptation support in the architecture simplifies the development of the library application.

This paper describes extensions to the caT architecture to support flexible information presentation by incorporating smart browsers, an externally accessible resource store to decouple information resources from the digital library that includes them, and mechanisms to retrieve the most optimal resources available at the time of user access. Na and Furuta developed caT (context-aware Trellis) [14] by augmenting the Trellis Petri net-based system [21] to support context-aware adaptation and delivery of digital documents in a dynamically changing environment. We are building on the strengths of the caT model by incorporating browsers that are aware of their capabilities (that is, the media types that they support) and the constraints imposed on them by the devices that they operate on (display resolution, size, network bandwidth). Further, they may possibly be controlled by a remote manager to present information to the user on the most suitable devices in the given situation.

The remainder of the paper is organized as follows: In section 2, we review relevant aspects of our earlier work. Section 3 presents the architecture of the system along with extensions that may go into it shortly. Section 4 describes an example of how the system will serve users who are trying to access information about the bus system on a University campus in different situations. Section 5 reviews related work and systems. Section 6 provides a discussion of the various issues involved and outlines avenues for future work in providing information to users that best suits their context of use at the right time in the best possible format. Section 7 summarizes and concludes the paper.

2 Trellis and caT

caT has a long history, draws from concepts in automata theory and has applications in a variety of areas. In this section we have only tried to present the features that are essential for understanding the current system and that help punctuate the strengths of this system for implementation and use of Digital libraries and other complex structures and systems. We provide pointers to relevant literature that explains the concepts in greater detail.

2.1 Trellis

The Trellis project [21, 22] has investigated the structure and semantics of human-computer and human-human interaction in the context of hypermedia systems, computer-supported collaborative work (CSCW), program browsers, visual programming notations, and process models. Trellis uses a Petri net [15] based representation of hypermedia documents and applications. Information elements map to *places* (denoted by circles) in a Petri net and links to *transitions* (denoted by bars). *Tokens* in places represent the current location of users in the hyperdocument in terms of the information elements that they see. When a place is *marked* (contains a token), the corresponding content is displayed, and when a transition is *enabled* (all places leading to the transition contain a token for each arc that connects the two), the corresponding link can be selected (*firing* the transition; i.e., removing a token per arc from each place that leads to the transition and adding one to each place that is led to from the transition). Due to lack of identity for tokens, the basic Petri net is not convenient for representation and analysis of complex systems. Trellis uses colored timed Petri nets (CPN) [10] where colors represent various users, thus allowing different access specifications for various (groups of) users. The timing values on transitions can be set to enable and fire transitions automatically. Thus, Trellis treats users and processes identically as processes may browse the hypertext by waiting for automatic firing of the transitions. We can conceive of the CPN as the task description and the associated contents as the information required by the task. A detailed overall description of how Trellis works is given in [7].

The dual nature of Petri nets allows specification of document structure as well as the browsing semantics. While the graph structure describes the nodes and links in a hypertext, the associated automaton semantics, when applied, specify its browsing semantics or the sequence of information elements displayed and the links made available while browsing. Trellis browsing semantics are said to be programmable [6] since localized change to the specification can be used to change the browsing behavior. As the behavior of a document depends on its initial state, a virtual change in the document specification can modify the browsing semantics for the document.

Trellis browsing semantics provide a mechanism by which a hypertext can respond to events in its environment. As examples, Trellis hypertexts can be designed to dynamically permit or limit access to information, to select different information for presentation on initial and subsequent accesses for information elements, and to respond differently if multiple readers are viewing a section of a hypertext simultaneously. This feature can be used to implement specification of dynamically changing access policies for documents. The system implementation makes no assumptions about these but simply interprets the document specification.

Trellis documents incorporate parallelism, in that multiple information elements can be displayed simultaneously. The parallelism allows synchronous as well as asynchronous traversal of multiple content elements. The document specification can direct simultaneous display of multiple information threads, each of which can be accessed independently or synchronized display of related components of a multimedia presentation, all of which must change together.

The Petri net structure is based on formal specification and can be analyzed for behavioral properties as well as performance assessment [25]. Thus, the Petri net structure can be formally analyzed to test the reachability of specific nodes starting with various initial states and for finding nodes that match specific properties to analyze and debug complex systems, for example, finding all nodes that do not have any outgoing links.

Over the years, the Trellis document specification has been applied to a wide variety of domains. These include applications in quick prototyping of process protocols in the areas of software engineering for specifying control algorithm for an elevator [4] and Computer Supported Collaborative Work for simulating virtual meetings that follow various protocols [5].

2.2 caT (context-aware Trellis)

Like Trellis, caT [14] is a document-centric system and directly inherits all its advantages mentioned earlier. caT was developed to support context-aware information delivery by augmenting Trellis with a high-level Petri net specification, context-awareness, user models and a fuzzy knowledge engine. The high-level Petri net tokens in caT include additional state information that expresses a user's context and preferences such as time, location, available bandwidth, acceptable costs and so on, thus enabling adaptation based on changes in the user's environmental information. caT also enhances the support for authoring, browsing and analysis of complex hypertexts by incorporating an authoring and analysis tool that supports hierarchical Petri Nets [14]. The fuzzy engine allows authors of documents to specify behavior based on abstract conditions like "if the user is on-campus", "if it is daytime". The Petri net engine forwards the inputs received from environmental sensors to the fuzzy engine, which infers new information with the specific inputs and a specified rulebase.

caT also includes a HTTP interface [3] for tapping into the potential of the WWW. The interface allows creators of caT nets to specify templates; essentially HTML files with placeholders indicating where information is to be embedded when the corresponding places are marked and transitions enabled. From caT's point of view, the template file is simply another content type. It takes control when its corresponding place is marked. The template file specifies whether and how to render the active content and transitions. The node that contains a template file can be viewed as specifying the directions by which a virtual composite node is constructed from the active content elements. As the composite node only displays elements that are currently active the content of the composite node changes as the user browses the hypertext.

A formal definition of caT and more information about the system prototype can be found in [13, 14].

3 Architecture

caT supports RPC-based client-server interaction in a 4-layer architecture comprising of the server, services, clients and devices. The server layer stores global data like Petri net structures, resources, user profiles, etc. Various processes in the server

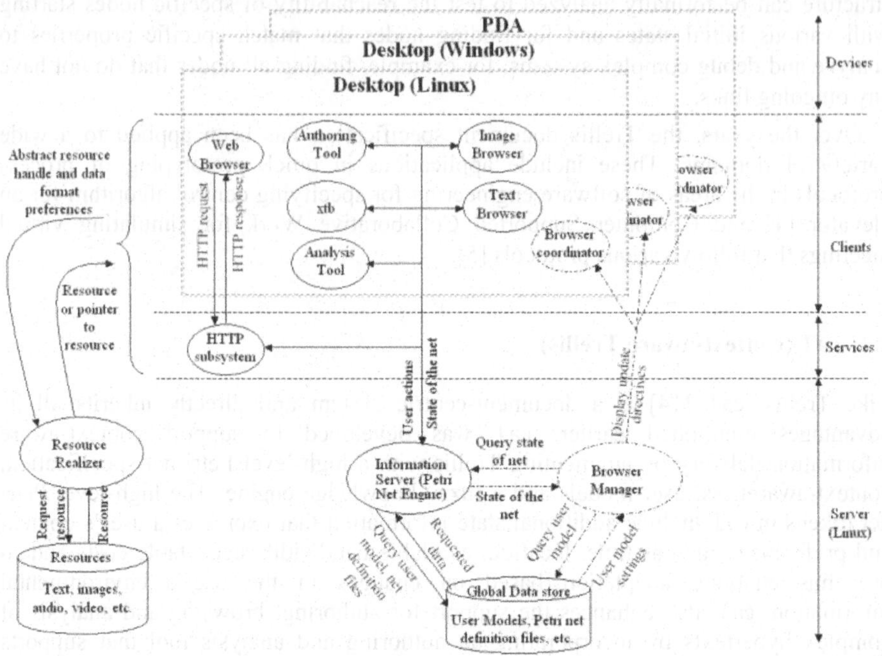

Fig. 1. Extended caT Architecture

provide access mechanisms for the clients to support user browsing of the hypertext by executing the Petri nets, help clients realize resources from abstract handles and in the near future may aid in adaptation of the hypertext by directing browsers to display resources based on various parameters. The services layer provides an HTTP interface for accessing the Petri net engine via Web browsers. Web-specific and other browsers located on a variety of devices display the hypertext structure and resources to the users. This section describes the architecture shown in Figure 1 from the perspective of its importance in structuring and accessing resources in a caT-based digital library. Technical aspects pertaining to the implementation of various components are explained in greater detail by Na and Furuta in [13, 14].

3.1 Information Server

The Information Server (also called the Petri net engine) provides function interfaces for creation, editing, annotation and execution of Petri nets to remote processes and to any client applications that may be running. It runs in the background and has no visible user interface. The Petri net engine reads in the Petri net structure that may define the structure and browsing semantics pertaining to the digital library along with user models from the Global Data Store. These are used to define, constrain, and reflect user actions, in effect the Petri net engine executes user browsing of hypertext structures. While creating and analyzing hypertexts, the authoring tool updates the net structure stored in the server. As users browse the hypertexts the clients facilitate two-way communication between users and the Information Server. The net's document specification refers to resources available in the library by their conceptual and semantic content (in the form of abstract resource handles) that are passed on to clients that must then procure the appropriate resources.

3.2 Browser Clients

The browsers are the only part of the system that the users interact with directly. Users receive resources and information contained in caT hypertext nets via the browsers. The browsers convey actions performed by the users (for example, following active links) that may result in a change to the current state of the net. As actions of other users in the environment affect a user and change the state of the document, the browsers periodically check with the server for any updates to the state of the net that result in changes to the display. The server provides the current state of the browser and returns abstract handles for resources that are to be displayed. The browser must then contact the Resource Realizer and retrieve the resource in a format that it best supports or is most optimal for presentation to the user in the current context.

3.3 Resource Realizer

The Resource Realizer provides dual advantage by incorporating a layer of abstraction between specification of various resources in a digital library and their physical manifestation in various formats. Conceptually, it encapsulates all resources that contain similar or interchangeable information irrespective of the presentation format. Thus, a photograph of the launch of a space shuttle, its video and its text description may all be stored as a single conceptual unit and information in either or multiple formats may be presented to the user upon request by a browser. Practically, it decouples the hypertext structure that includes the resource from the location and representation of the resource. Thus, if the video file of the shuttle, in the earlier example, were to be corrupted later, it could be removed from the corpus or replaced with another video without the need to modify any other part of the system including the net structure that refers to it.

Operationally, the Resource Realizer receives an abstract resource handle from various browsers along with the browsers' preferred media type(s). The browser requests the resources based on the knowledge of its intrinsic capabilities (for example, a text browser may request text file while an image browser may request a jpeg file). The Resource Realizer returns the resource to be displayed along with the access method to be used by the browser. The Realizer could either return the contents of the resource (which can be directly processed by the browser), or with a location pointer within the browser's file system (disk path) or via a globally accessible location pointer (a URL).

3.4 Browser Manager

The Browser Manager and Coordinators (sections 3.4 and 3.5) are not yet operational and hence considered as a future extension. Figure 1 shows these components differently than the system that is currently in place, with dotted lines. However, these sections are included here for the sake of completeness and coherence.

The Browser Manager is expected to function as the centralized display controller. It will communicate with the Browser coordinators on various devices to manage the routing of information based on use and user information from user profiles, current tasks and status of the user, system policies, and knowledge about other users in the system and their actions, among other factors. For example, it may send critical information to a user's cell phone instead of send it to the PDA or a notebook computer if the user is driving. The Browser Coordinator is responsible for invoking browsers on the local device upon the Browser Manager's instructions.

In order for the Browser Manager to be effective, the Information Server treats it like it treats all other clients. The Manager must ensure that it receives updates to the state of the net and decide if it needs to act upon these, based upon the user's current state (available from the net), user profile (available from the Global Data Store) and other policies that may be specified in the net.

3.5 Browser Coordinators

The Browser Coordinators are device-specific clients that contain information about capabilities of the device and various browsers available on the device. They invoke these browsers when the Browser Manager directs them to present the contents of a marked place or a set of places. The browser that is opened must then communicate with the Information Server and the Resource Realizer to present information to the user.

The following section describes a scenario to illustrate an example of user interaction with caT. The scenario is presented from the user's perspective with tie-ins to the architecture at relevant points.

4 Example of Browsing a caT-Based Digital Library

Large Universities often provide information resources for students, employees and visitors via their Web servers. These University-wide information systems include resources on academic information, organizational and administrative information, catalogs of books in the libraries, networking and computing information, shuttle and commuter information and overview of reasearch among other things. In spite of the availability of these resources students, employees and visitors on large university campuses often have trouble getting from one place to another. Typically, the users must ensure that all needed information is available to them before they set out and stick to their planned route as much as possible. However, little support is provided for shuttle users to access the information while they using the system. The users must

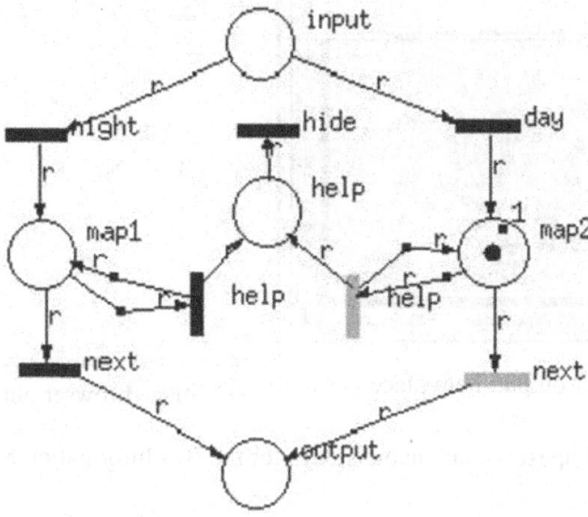

Fig. 2. Bus Information Service: subnet specification

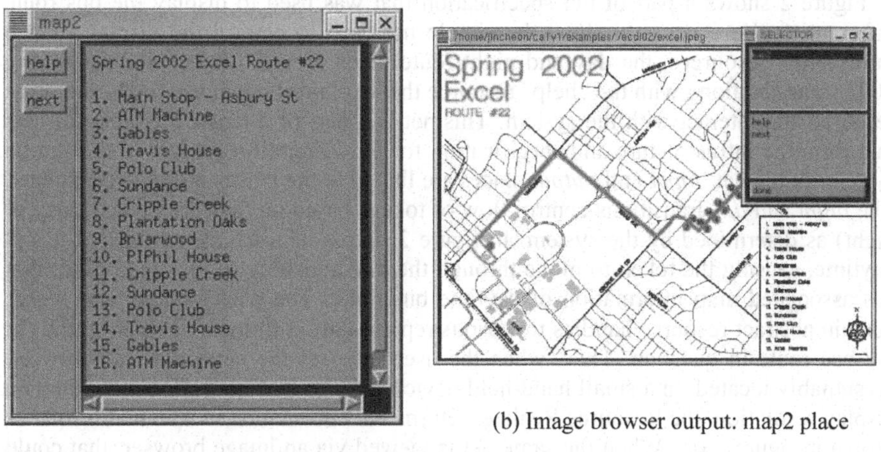

(a) Text browser output: map2 place

(b) Image browser output: map2 place

Fig. 3. Text and image displays for the Bus Information Service

rely on information from others around them, who may also not know answers to the users' specific questions. The recent surge in browsing the Web via PDAs or cell phones is yet to make its mark on campus information systems. Here, we show how a user may access information on the go using any of the various available network-enabled devices and caT infrastructure that is currently available.

The user starts a session when she accesses the information pages for the caT-based shuttle and commuter information pages. At the start of the session, caT identifies the user and the state of the user, for example whether the user is a student

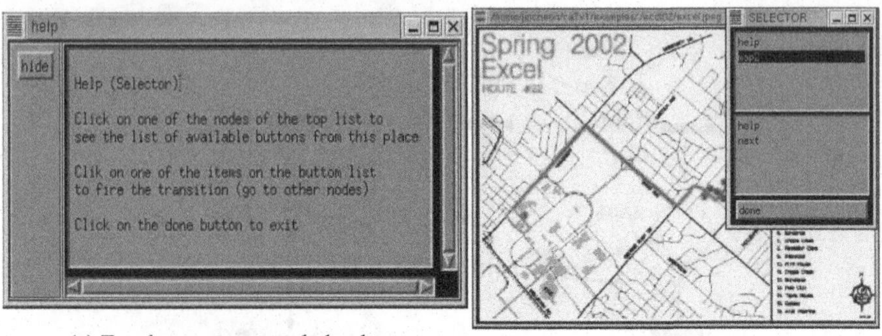

(a) Text browser output: help place (b) Image browser output: map2 place

Fig. 4. Help (text) and map displays for the Bus Information Service

or employee, the current time is day or night and if the student is on or off campus. Not all information that caT gathers may be used during an interaction.

Figure 2 shows a part of net specification that was used to display the bus route information. Here we only show the simple net used to control the display of two information resources, the day and night route maps for #22, Excel, for the Spring 2002 semester along with the "help" resource that explains how to use the information resource and interact with the system. This net is a part of a larger hierarchy of nets that form the infrastructure and specification for browsing all resources in the shuttle system. In the net, *input* and *output* places are linked to the places in its parent subnet. The *night* and *day* transitions control flow of tokens based on the current state (day or night) as determined by the system. In figure 2, the system has determined that it is daytime, causing the token to move through the *day* transition to the *map2* place that has associated map information of daytime bus route. The places, *map1* and *map2*, contain abstract resource handles to various representation formats of information for the bus route in question. Thus, when the user accesses the net via a text browser, presumably located on a small hand-held device with limited network bandwidth and display resolution, the Resource Realizer returns the information in a textual format as shown in figure 3 (a). When the same net is viewed via an image browser, that could be located on a networked notebook computer possibly with higher bandwidth, the resource handle resolves to an image file of the bus route as shown in figure 3(b). Thus, caT-based hypertexts provide good separation between the net structure and its related contents with the help of Resource Realizer.

The selector shown on top of the route image in figure 3(b) is the main browser that allows firing transitions (the caT equivalent of following links) to browse the hypertext.

When the user selects (or fires) the *help* transition for acquiring help information the system moves the token into the *help* place, causing the browser to display its contents. In this example, the help information is only available as a text file and the image browser is unable to display this information. Figures 4(a) and 4(b) show the display of the text and image browsers, respectively, when the user views the help information. In the future the Browser Coordinator could help resolve such situations by negotiating with the various browsers and the Resource Realizer to either obtain the best resource or invoke the most capable browser for presenting the information that is available.

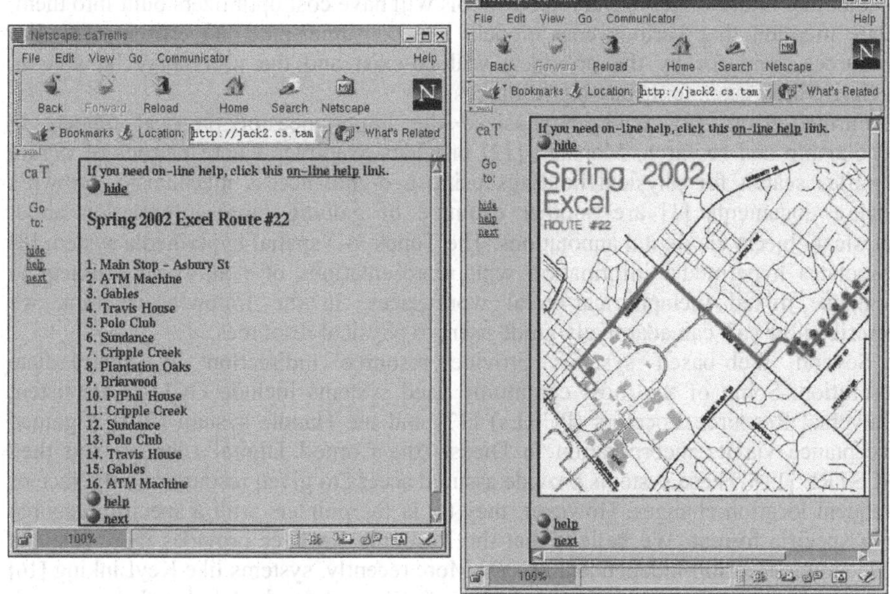

(a) Display on mobile devices

(b) Display on desktop computers

Fig. 5. Web browser displays for the Bus Information Service

Browsers that are capable of processing information in multiple formats may use their full capability to provide optimal information to the user. If the user prefers to view the information via a Web browser, the HTTP interface assists with presentation of the information in figure 3 in a suitable format. Figure 5 shows composite views of the information when viewed via a Web browser. The system may display the textual information as shown in figure 5(a) when a browser running off of a PDA requests information considering the lesser bandwidth, while it may display the image of the bus route as shown in figure 5(b) when the user views the information from a desktop system connected to a fast network.

5 Related Work

Various project groups have researched aspects of digital library infrastructure, policies, and access mechanisms among other aspects. Schilit, et al. [18], envision widespread use of mobile appliances for accessing digital repositories in the near future. We can already see the surge in wireless connectivity via the notebook computers, cell phones and PDAs. We believe that in the near future there is an urgent need to support information work via a plethora of appliances and have aimed the development of caT towards supporting users in various work settings armed with a variety of devices.

Sistla, et al. [19], propose various cost structures for accessing digital libraries and predict that future digital library access tools will have cost optimizers built into them. They mention that various cost models like consumer-paid, advertiser paid, free resources (paid for by the provider) will co-exist and the users may be able to optimize their costs for accessing resources.

Furuta, et al. [2], have emphasized the importance of physical objects in scholarship and research. Marshall [12] provides examples where patrons of digital libraries search for physical holdings using a digital access mechanism. Brown's stick-e documents [1] are another example of gaining more information about physical objects via digital annotations. The Topos 3-D spatial hypermedia system [8] associates hypermedia information with representations of real world artifacts to compose mixed metaphorical-literal workspaces. In the following section, we describe how caT can adaptively guide users to physical resources.

Several Web-based systems provide resource indirection by intermediate resolution. Some of the most commonly used systems include OCLC's Persistent Universal Resource Locators (PURLs) [17] and the Handle system [9] that gained acceptance via its incorporation in Dienst (the Cornell Digital Library) and then NCSTRL [11]. These systems provide assured access to given resources in the face of frequent location changes. However, they tie in the pointers with a specific resource in a specific format. We believe that the Resource Realizer provides more features than simple location-independent access. More recently, systems like KeyLinking [16] provide facilities for dynamic resolution of soft and implied links. This research focuses on "providing access to the most appropriate available resource at the time of usage". Though the phrase sounds similar to what the Resource Realizer does, it differs from KeyLinking in that the Resource Realizer makes no judgment about what is appropriate but leaves the decision to the browser.

Among the contemporary multimedia presentation systems, SMIL [20] provides mechanisms that permit flexible specification of multimedia presentations that can be defined to respond to a user's characteristics. However, this support is restricted to an instantiation of the presentation. Once instantiated, the changes in browsing state cannot be reflected to other browsers that the user may open later, or to other devices. Similarly, XML [23] and XSLT [24] implementations allow flexible translations of given static structures, but these transformations are static and irreversible. Generation of a new transformation requires repetition of the process with a different XSLT template.

6 Discussion and Future Work

The Resource Realizer decouples the conceptual resource from its instantiation. It enables creators of digital libraries to package all resources that are semantically equivalent. The abstract resource may then be appropriately resolved to retrieve its most suitable presentation for each user taking into account the user's preferences, task environment and other factors like the presence and location of other users in system. This encapsulation can be further extended to support versioning in digital libraries. All versions of a resource may also be linked together, to be resolved to present the right version(s) at access time. For the example in section 4, traffic pattern analyzers could compare the bus routes for various semesters to plot trends and assess the future needs of the campus.

The Realizer also may act as a resource catalog that points to various resources owned by different entities, some or all of which may charge the users for providing access. The Resource Realizer could then act as the cost optimizer [19] for caT and negotiate the costs for resources to provide the best possible deal for the users depending on their preferences.

The resources that the system includes also may include physical resources, for example, books on shelves in a physical library. The resource realizer may also provide the location of the physical resources. The Resource Realizer is simply the gatekeeper for accessing resources. It does decide if or how the resource will be used by the entity that requests it. Thus, the information regarding location of physical resources, if provided by the Realizer, may or may not be presented to the users depending on their context.

While browsing, caT maintains the current state of the net in the server. This state is reflected in all browsers that connect to the server and request updates. Users only see their state (the places that they are viewing) even though others may be accessing the system simultaneously. However, this permits interactions between users. For example, caT net specifications may allow only a certain number of users to access a resource simultaneously, thus providing support for access control policies. Once all available copies of a resource are in use, the system may temporarily prohibit access, and indeed, cause the resource to vanish (if the designer of the system so desires) until a license of the resource is available for use.

As the browsing state is maintained on the server, users accessing it via multiple browsers on various devices see the same information on all devices. Also, when the user browses the digital library, the changes effected via an action in one browser are reflected (almost) instantaneously in all other browsers on all devices. Thus, our user who is trying to find out more about the bus system, may start viewing the shuttle pages on her desktop, locate the nearest bus stop for the bus she wants and realize that she needs to hurry to get onto the next bus and leave without closing her browsing session on the desktop computer. On her way to the bus stop, she can open another browser, presumably from her PDA to check on the fare, the bus route and decide if she can get other things done during this trip. While coming back home, she can start reading an article that interests her and after coming home, continue reading it on her desktop, where she may also be able to watch relevant videos or see images that her PDA could not adequately display.

The Browser Management system described in sections 3.4 and 3.5 (Manager and the Coordinators) is still in the design stage. Upon integration, the Browser Manager is expected to communicate with the Browser Coordinators on the devices in order to present various active information elements on different devices, in response to user profiles, device capabilities and the current state of the user. The user may configure the behavior of the Manager and the Coordinators through configuration files. For example, the user may decide to allow the manager to open all possible browsers that are capable of displaying an information element, or to allow it to open only the browser that can best present it. Thus, in the example in section 4, the first case would allow the Manager to open both, the text as well as the image browsers, and if it exists, the Web browser. This implies that the user viewing the bus route via the image browser would still be able to get the textual help information. The latter case would however require that the Manager opens only the Web browser as it can handle all media types, if the device supports the high bandwidth and display resolution.

If two or more browsers are capable of displaying a media type, the Browser Coordinator may act as the local conflict resolver by closing one of the applications. Media types do not have to match the conventional types. Creators of resources may create multiple media types for a conventional type, for example, to support Web-based browsing from different devices, creators of the digital library may support different versions of an html document (i.e., "full html" and "short html"). Web browsers on mobile devices may request and display "short html" files while desktop computers may present "full html" files.

The interaction between the browser and the Realizer can be further enhanced to enable them to reach a mutually acceptable resolution for a given resource handle. Currently, the Realizer either provides a resource, or does not. For the earlier example, the *help* resource could not be realized for the image browser. The proposed enhancement would cause the Realizer to respond with the best available resource, which can then be displayed by another browser that may be capable of presenting this resource. This negotiated resource resolution may probably be better handled by the Browser Coordinators than the browsers themselves.

7 Conclusion

In this paper we have described extensions to caT (context-aware Trellis) for supporting flexible information presentation in digital information repositories via browsers on a variety of devices. caT provides a consistent display of the current browsing state on multiple browsers and reflects the changes caused by user actions in one browser to all open browsing instances. Browsers are aware of their capabilities and the constraints of the devices that they run on. The browsers receive abstract handles for resources they must present to the users from the server. An abstract handle may point to possibly many equivalent instantiations all of which are semantically identical and hence interchangeable. The Resource Realizer resolves abstract handles to return resources in a media formats described by the browser. This architecture can be further extended by the incorporation of a central Browser Manager and device-specific Coordinators to deliver information to browsers on various devices and presumably at specified time in order to help users view the relevant information in its most suitable form based on their preferences and the immediate task at hand.

Acknowledgements. This material is based upon work supported by the National Science Foundation under Grant No. DUE-0085798.

References

1. Brown, P.J.: The stick-e Document: A Framework for Creating Context-Aware Applications. Proceedings of EP '96 (Palo Alto, CA, 1996) 259-272
2. Furuta, R., Marshall, C., Shipman, F.M., Leggett, J.: Physical objects in the digital library. Proceedings of the first ACM conference on Digital Libraries (Bethesda, Maryland, United States, 1996) 109-115

3. Furuta, R., Na, J-C.: Applying Programmable Browsing Semantics Within the Context of the World-Wide Web. Proceedings of the thirteenth conference on Hypertext and hypermedia, Hypertext '02 (College Park, Maryland, USA, June 11-15, 2002) 23-24
4. Furuta, R., Stotts, P.D.: A hypermedia basis for the specification, documentation, verification, and prototyping of concurrent protocols. Technical Report TAMU-HRL 94-003, Texas A&M University, Hypertext Research Lab, (June 1994)
5. Furuta, R., Stotts, P.D.: Interpreted Collaboration Protocols and their Use in Groupware Prototyping. Proceedings of ACM 1994 Conference on Computer Supported Cooperative Work, ACM (Oct. 1994) 121-132
6. Furuta, R., Stotts, P.D.: Programmable Browsing Semantics in Trellis. Proceedings of Hypertext '89, ACM, New York (1989) 27-42
7. Furuta, R., Stotts, P.D.: Trellis: a Formally-defined Hypertextual Basis for Integrating Task and Information. Lawrence Erlbaum Associates (2001) 341-367
8. Grønbæk, K., Vestergaard, P. P., Ørbæk, P.: Towards Geo-Spatial Hypermedia: Concepts and Prototype Implementation. Proceedings of the thirteenth conference on Hypertext and hypermedia, Hypertext '02 (College Park, Maryland, USA, June 11-15, 2002) 117-126
9. Handle: The Handle System. http://www.handle.net/ (2002) accessed April 2002
10. Jensen, K.: Coloured Petri Nets: Basic Concepts, Analysis Methods and Practical Use Volume 1. EATCS Monographs on Theoretical Computer Science, Springer-Verlag (1992)
11. Lagoze, C., Fielding, D. Payette, S.: Making global digital Libraries work: collection services, connectivity regions, and collection views. Proceedings of the third ACM conference on Digital Libraries (Pittsburgh, Pennsylvania, United States, 1998) 134-143
12. Marshall, C., Golovchinsky, G., Price, M.: Digital Libraries and mobility. Communications of the ACM 44, 5 (May 2001) 55-56
13. Na, J-C.: Context-aware Hypermedia in a Dynamically Changing Environment, Supported by a High-level Petri Net. Ph.D. Dissertation, Texas A&M University (December 2001)
14. Na, J-C., Furuta, R.: Dynamic documents: Authoring, browsing, and analysis using a high-level Petri net-based hypermedia system. Proceedings of the ACM Symposium on Document Engineering (DocEng '01), ACM (2001) 38-47
15. Peterson, J.L.: Petri Net Theory and the Modeling of Systems. Prentice-Hall, Englewood Cliffs, N.J. (1981)
16. Pritchett, B.: KeyLinking: dynamic hypertext in a digital library. Proceedings of the fifth ACM conference on Digital Libraries (San Antonio, Texas, United States, 2000) 242-243
17. PURL: OCLC's Persistent Universal Resource Locators. http://www.purl.org/ (2002) accessed April 2002
18. Schilit, B.N., Price, M.N., Golovchinsky, G.: Digital library information appliances. Proceedings of the third ACM conference on Digital Libraries, ACM (Pittsburgh, Pennsylvania, United States, 1998) 217-226
19. Sistla, A. P., Wolfson, O., Yesha, Y., Sloan, R.: Towards a theory of cost management for digital Libraries and electronic commerce. ACM Transactions on Database Systems (TODS) 23, 4 (December 1998) 411-452
20. SMIL: Synchronized Multimedia Integration Language (SMIL 2.0) specification. http://www.w3.org/TR/smil20/, W3C Proposed recommendation (2001)
21. Stotts, P.D., Furuta, R.: Petri-net-based hypertext: Document structure with browsing semantics. ACM Transactions on Information Systems, 7, 1 (January 1989) 3-29
22. Stotts, P.D., Furuta, R.: Dynamic Adaptation of Hypertext Structure. Proceedings of Hypertext '91, (1991) 219-231
23. XML: Extensible Markup Language (XML) 1.0 (Second Edition). http://www.w3.org/TR/2000/REC-xml-20001006, W3C Recommendation (2000)
24. XSLT: XSL Transformations (XSLT) Version 1.0. http://www.w3.org/TR/xslt, W3C Recommendation (1999)
25. Zurawski, R., Zhou, M.: Petri Nets and Industrial Applications: A Tutorial. IEEE: Transactions on Industrial Electronics, vol. 41, no. 6, (December 1994)

On the Use of Explanations as Mediating Device for Relevance Feedback

Ian Ruthven

Department of Computer and Information Sciences
University of Strathclyde
Glasgow
G1 1XH
Scotland
Ian.Ruthven@cis.strath.ac.uk

Abstract. In this paper we examine the role of explanations as a means of facilitating the use of relevance feedback in information retrieval systems. We do this with particular reference to previous experimental work. This demonstrates that explanations can increase the user's willingness to interact more fully with the system. We outline the general conclusions from this experimental work and discuss the implications for interactive IR systems that incorporate relevance feedback.

1 Introduction

The World Wide Web and Digital Libraries provide large repositories of electronically stored information whose content can be accessed by any computer user. Although the field of Information Retrieval (IR) has provided many effective search tools for such collections of diverse data and media, the *interaction* between an IR system and a searcher is still problematic [11]. Search systems that are difficult to use, or which lead to low levels of interaction, can cause poor retrieval results and low user satisfaction.

One of the major interactive tasks in searching is selecting search terms. This is usually held to be one of the most difficult tasks for searchers, [6]. This is because searchers will usually not be aware of what information is available and, consequently, they will not know which query terms will retrieve relevant documents. The result is that the searchers will have to iteratively refine the content of their queries. This method of searching – repeated querying – is expensive in terms of time and the effort a user must expend in searching.

In traditional IR systems this problem has been addressed by the technique of Relevance Feedback (RF) [5]: using the content of pages that the searcher has assessed as being relevant to improve the content of the searcher's query. The strength of RF is that the system can suggest query terms to the searcher or directly add them to the searcher's query. RF has been shown to be a powerful, practical technique for improving the retrieval of relevant information [10].

M. Agosti and C. Thanos (Eds.): ECDL 2002, LNCS 2458, pp. 338-345, 2002.

However the interaction between the RF functionality and the user is generally poorly defined. In particular, IR systems generally offer the user little guidance in how to use RF effectively; for example when to use RF in a search, what RF will do to their search and how new query terms are used to retrieve documents. The result is that users are often reluctant to use RF as a general search technique [4].

In earlier work, [8], we explored the use of *explanations* as a technique for helping users understand RF as it applies to their search and for encouraging users to employ RF more often in their searches. In this paper we use the main findings from these experiments as the basis for a discussion on the use of explanations as a mediating device in IR. In particular we provide a more detailed account, than in [8], of the form explanations took in our experiments and how these were perceived by users.

In the following section we shall motivate the general use of explanations in IR, in section 3 we shall discuss how we used explanations and in section 4 we shall discuss the experiments and main findings from our experiments. In section 5 we provide a discussion on the use of explanations for RF.

2 Explanations

Explanations serve to mediate between a system's function and the user's interpretation of those functions [1]. That is, explanations are used to reduce the conceptual gulf between how the system operates and how the user thinks the system operates. This form of mediating device is especially suitable for interactive information retrieval systems as the functions by which IR systems retrieve documents are not always obvious to users, [11].

Systems with explanatory power have traditionally incorporated two main components: dialogue models, [1], and domain knowledge representation, [2]. The dialogue model controls what is to be explained and at what stage in the dialogue explanations are to be given, whereas the domain knowledge determines the content of the explanation.

In our experiments we wanted to investigate the use of explanations that do not rely on these components. We not use domain knowledge representations because most IR collections do not have a strong domain that can be exploited for tailoring explanations. We not use dialogue models because of the strong evidence that techniques that force users to employ specific search strategies are often not taken up by users, [3]. What is required instead are techniques, such as the ones we propose, which support the searchers' existing search strategies.

In our system several RF techniques were available for use by the system. For each iteration of RF, the choice of which RF technique to deploy was selected by a simple expert system which analysed features of the user's relevance assessments such as the number of documents marked relevant, the similarity of the relevant documents and where in the document ranking the relevant documents appeared. The use of relevance assessments to select a RF technique was evaluated separately in [7]. What is important for this paper is that each RF technique corresponds to a separate explanation and it is this use of explanations for describing RF that is under investigation here.

The explanations formed within our system were composed of three components: the reason, action and indicative components. The *reason* component tells the user *why* a particular RF decision has been made. This is either based on the user's search behaviour (e.g. the user has found few relevant documents) or the system's processing (e.g. the system does not have enough information to make a RF decision). The *action* component tells the user what particular effect the RF is intended to have on their query, e.g. to increase recall or to improve the quality of the retrieved documents. Finally the *indicative* component is an indication to the user of how they can undo the effect of the RF decision, or help the system make better decisions, e.g. remove search terms that are not useful or add more search terms. The individual types of explanations are therefore *personalised* to the user's individual search and to the search stage. In the next section we present the explanations used in our system.

3 Explanations for Feedback

In our work we concentrated on developing explanations for RF. There were two main areas upon which we concentrated: the automatic addition of search terms to the query (*query expansion*) and choosing how the search terms are used to retrieve new documents (*term weighting*). In the following two sections we describe the explanation types developed for our system.

3.1 Query Expansion

Our system could generate five types of explanation relating to query expansion. Below we summarise the types of explanation, and the reason, action and indicative components of each. We should note here that this set of explanations are not intended to be comprehensive, rather they are examples of the types of explanations a RF system could present to the user.

i. *Little relevance explanation.* In this case the user has only marked a few documents relevant. The explanation tells the user that, as they have only found a few documents (*reason*), it will add a large set of terms to the query to try to attract more documents (*action*). The indicative component in this case is simply to suggest that the user removes any search terms that do not appear useful to the search.

ii. *Reweighting explanation.* If the original search terms are very good at retrieving relevant documents then the system may decide not to add any search terms. In this case the explanation tells the user that as their search terms are good, it is concentrating on deciding which terms are the best at retrieving relevant documents (*reason*), to try to improve the quality of the retrieved documents (*action*) and the indicative component is to suggest the user removes any terms that are being treated inappropriately. This type of explanation uses same information as the term weighting explanations, section 3.2.

iii. *Similarity explanation.* In this case the relevant documents are judged as being consistent (similar to each other) and the system tells the users that as the documents as similar (*reason*), it will add terms that appear in *most* of the relevant documents (*action*), i.e. those terms that help make the relevant documents similar to each other. The indicative suggestion is to remove any terms that are not central to the search.

iv. *Discriminatory explanation.* If the relevant documents are not very similar then the system will concentrate on adding terms that are good discriminators of relevance. In this case the system tells the user that as the relevant documents cover a range of topics (*reason*), it is concentrating on terms that appear important to the search (*action*). The indicative component is, again, simply to suggest the user removes any terms that it does not regard as useful to their search.

v. *Can't tell explanation.* In this case the system cannot choose which kind of query modification is appropriate for the search. The reason is that there is insufficient evidence to distinguish between the types of explanation outlined above or the evidence is contradictory. In this case the system will tell the user that it is not sure what the user wants (*reason*), it has not changed the query (*action*) and asks the user provide more evidence either by selecting more documents as relevant or adding more search terms (*indicative* component).

In each explanation the reason, action and indicative component are linked; the reason component is chosen from the user's relevance assessments, the action component is selected as being the best RF technique for this particular set of assessments and the indicative component is a method of altering the specific action decision made by the system. Each action component has an associated indicative suggestion.

3.2 Explanations for Reweighting

These explanations are based on how search terms are used for retrieving new documents. The explanations provided all had a similar form. This tells the user that, based on how the terms are used within the relevant and non-relevant documents (*reason*), the system has decided how each term is to be used to retrieve new documents (*action*). The action component is tailored for each term according to how the term is to be used, there are three ways in which a term can be used for retrieval: if the term is related to the main topic of the document, if the term occurs frequently within documents and if the document mentions the term at all.

The system may choose any of these methods or some combination of methods. The action component is therefore of the form 'I am looking for any documents in which **macbeth** seems important to the main topic of the document'. This relates the term (*macbeth*), to its function in retrieval (*important to main topic*) to the and to the new set of documents that will be retrieved. This is intended to help the user understand the results of the new retrieval. The indicative component suggests the user removes any term that is being treated inappropriately by the system. An obvious extension is to allow the user to change how terms are used to retrieve new documents.

In the next section we shall introduce the main points of the experiments we carried out on these principles and the main findings from the experiments.

4 Experiments

Six subjects participated in our experiments. The subjects were 4 male and 2 female subjects. These subjects had relatively high experience of on-line searching (average 4 years), which was mostly gained through library search facilities and web search engines. The subjects reported good experience on these two forms of IR system but little experience of any other search system. The subjects were also relatively frequent searchers searching daily or at least weekly. No subject reported experience of an IR system that offered RF functionality.

The systems used allowed the users to search using natural language query expressions, titles of retrieved documents were displayed in pages of 10 titles, and query terms were highlighted in the text of retrieved documents. Other than RF, and issuing a new search, there were no other query modification options. The interface, therefore, was a similar as possible to the most common IR system used by our subjects: internet search engines. All searching was performed on the same set of newspaper collections.

In our experiments the six subjects were each asked to complete six search tasks. The same six search tasks were given to each subject but the order in which the tasks were given, and the allocation of task to system was randomised across subjects. The search tasks were devised by the experiment designer but the subjects were given complete freedom on how they defined relevant information; they were no given criteria for relevance. This decision was made to create a more realistic searching task where there are no set criteria for classifying a document as relevant. Three search tasks were completed on a control system. This system offered the subjects the opportunity to start a new search or perform an RF iteration. If the subjects asked for RF, the system selected new query terms and weighted the search terms according to their utility in retrieving the relevant documents.

The remaining search tasks were completed on an experimental system. The experimental system used the same RF algorithms and the subjects requested RF in a similar manner; the only difference between the two systems was that the experimental system presented the user with explanations after RF. Only the query expansion explanation was automatically shown to the user, the term reweighting explanation had to be explicitly requested by the user. The reason for this was to *layer* the role of explanations; the query expansion explanation was presented automatically at the same time as the new query was presented, whereas the term reweighting explanation was an additional source of evidence on RF.

The results were analysed according to three sets of criteria: overall search behaviour, search effectiveness and users' perceptions of the two systems. The results regarding the search effectiveness showed that neither system was better at retrieving relevant documents. This is to be expected as both systems were using the same retrieval and relevance feedback algorithms. The results regarding the search behaviour – how the subjects interacted with the systems showed that the subjects using the experimental system not only used RF more often but were more likely to use it in preference to starting a new search; that is they trusted RF more when using the explanation-based system.

More pertinent to this paper are the results regarding the users' perceptions of the two systems. The subjects were asked to assess on a scale from 1 to 5[1] how useful were various features of the system. The results showed that the users regarded the query expansion explanation as more useful than RF, and RF more useful that the term reweighting explanation. This was a general finding that held over the majority of search topics. In the next section we shall examine in what ways the explanations were useful.

5 On the Use of Explanations

All subjects were interviewed after each search and after the experiment as a whole. In these interviews we sought to elicit both positive and negative views on the use of explanations for RF.

One of the most common views was that the query expansion explanations were useful because of the reason component. That is, the explanations provided some kind of justification for the particular decisions that RF made, e.g. adding terms to the query. One important point is that explanations were regarded as being useful even if RF itself was not successful. So, even if RF added unusual terms or added terms that were regarded as poor by the user, the explanation could still provide useful information on *why* the terms were added. Although this did not improve retrieval effectiveness it engendered a greater degree of trust in RF as a process because it the users could recognise what RF was trying to do. The main criticisms regarding the explanations were that the users wanted more personalised explanations; ones directed particularly to their search. Partly this finding results from the small set of explanations we used in this experiment. A more diverse set of explanation types could counter this criticism.

The term reweighting explanations were rated lower than the query expansion explanations. Partly this may be because the term reweighting explanations had to be requested. This fits with empirical evidence from studying human-human intermediary sessions that *umprompted* explanation is often the most appropriate form of explanation [1]. It also seems to be because the term reweighting explanations are relative to the success of RF itself. That is, if RF adds good search terms to the query then the term reweighting explanation can be useful source of evidence for assessing the retrieved set of documents. However, if RF adds poor search terms then additional information on how these terms are used in retrieval is generally not useful because the users have already ruled out the new search terms.

[1] 1 represents the category 'Not useful', 5 represents the category 'Very useful'

In our explanations we used three components: reason, action and indicative. The relative success of these three components depended on the nature of the individual search. For example, the reason component was useful in situations where the users were less confident in how RF operated relative to their search. That is, the reason component was more useful in situations where there was a poor connection between the users' relevance assessments and the RF decision. The action component was most useful in situations where the connection between the RF technique and the new retrieval was not clear, e.g. when unusual search terms were added to the query. This is a use of explanations that could be more fully exploited as apparently unusual RF decisions can put users off using RF [9]. The indicative component was useful to an extent in encouraging users to modify rather than replace an existing query. However, as the indicative component was not very developed in our experiments, this observation requires more thorough investigation before we would claim it as a general finding.

Overall the use of explanations were successful in that they engendered a greater degree of trust in the RF process. They did this in two ways: by making explicit the connection between the user's searching and the function of RF, and by making explicit the connection between RF and the new retrieval. To fully exploit this approach we need to carry out a more detailed study of how user search behaviour can be integrated into explanation-based interfaces. Nevertheless what our study has shown is that methods of explanation can increase the uptake and awareness of RF functionality. A separate, and more extensive study, is being planned to investigate a wider set of explanations. This study will also investigate *when* in a search it is most appropriate, or useful, to provide automatic explanations of system decisions.

References

1. Belkin, N. J. On the nature and function of explanation in intelligent information retrieval. Proceedings of the 11th Annual International ACM SIGIR Conference on Research and Development in Information Retrieval. Grenoble. (1988) 135 –145
2. Cawsey, A. Explanation and interaction: the computer generation of explanatory dialogues. MIT Press. (1992)
3. Dennis, S., McArthur, R. and Bruza, P. Searching the WWW made easy? The Cognitive Load imposed by Query Refinement Mechanisms. Proceedings of the Third Australian Document Computing Symposium. (1998)
4. Fowkes, H. and Beaulieu, M. Interactive searching behaviour: Okapi experiment for TREC-8. IRSG 2000 Colloquium on IR Research. electronic Workshops in Computing. Cambridge. (2000)
5. Harman, D. Relevance feedback and other query modification techniques. Information Retrieval: Data Structures & Algorithms. Englewood Cliffs: Prentice Hall. (W.B. Frakes and R. Baeza-Yates ed). Chapter 11. (1992) 241-263
6. Ingwersen, P. and Willett, P. An introduction to algorithmic and cognitive approaches for information retrieval. Libri. 45, 3/4. (1995) 160-177
7. Ruthven, I. Abduction, explanation and relevance feedback. PhD Thesis. University of Glasgow. (2001)
8. Ruthven, I., Lalmas, M. and van Rijsbergen, C. J. Incorporating User Search Behaviour into Relevance Feedback. 2002 (Submitted for Publication).

9. Ruthven, I., Tombros, A. and Jose, J. A study on the use of summaries and summary-based query expansion for a question-answering task. 23rd BCS European Annual Colloquium on Information Retrieval Research (ECIR 2001). Darmstadt. (2001)
10. Salton, G. and Buckley, C. Improving retrieval performance by relevance feedback. Journal of the American Society for Information Science. 41. 4. (1990) 288-297
11. Shneiderman, B., Byrd, D. and Croft, W. B. Sorting out Searching: A User-Interface Framework for Text Searches. Communications of the ACM. 41. 4. (1998) 95-98

Qualitative Evaluation of Thesaurus-Based Retrieval

D. Blocks, C. Binding, D. Cunliffe, and D. Tudhope

Hypermedia Research Unit, School of Computing, University of Glamorgan,
Pontypridd CF37 1DL, UK
{dblocks; cbinding; djcunlif; dstudhope}@glam.ac.uk
Telephone: +44 1443 482271
Fax: +44 1443 482715

Abstract. This paper reports on a formative evaluation of a prototype thesaurus-based retrieval system, which involved qualitative investigation of user search behaviour. The work is part of the ongoing 'FACET' project in collaboration with the National Museum of Science and Industry and its collections database. The main thesaurus employed in the project is the Getty Art and Architecture Thesaurus. The aim of the evaluation is to analyse at a micro level the user's interaction with interface elements in order to illuminate problems and inform interface design decisions. Data gathered included transcripts of think-aloud sessions, screen capture movie files, user action logs and observator notes. Key incidents from the sessions are analysed and the qualitative methodology is discussed. The evaluation analysis informs design issues concerning the allocation of search functionality to sub-windows, the appropriate role of thesaurus browsing in the search process, the formation of faceted queries and query reformulation. The analysis suggests that, although the prototype interface supports basic level operations, it does not provide non-expert searchers with sufficient guidance on query structure and when to use the thesaurus. Conclusions are drawn that future work should further support and suggest models of the search process to the user.

1. Introduction

As Digital Libraries and subject gateways grow, it becomes increasingly important to structure access for end-users to avoid the problems associated with Web search engines and their lack of terminology control. One useful tool in this quest is the thesaurus [1]. Thesauri are used in Library, Museum and Archive contexts as both indexing and search tools. While thesauri can also be used to expand free text search queries, in this paper we are concerned with a controlled vocabulary application. Users select search terms from a thesaurus which has been used to index the collection. This approach avoids false hits and provides users with a model of the domain which can facilitate term selection [2, 3], although they may need assistance to identify terms which are relevant and effective in retrieval [4]. Various studies have investigated issues concerning the role of the thesaurus in information seeking but there have been few empirical evaluations of thesaurus use in search systems by end-users. This paper reports on a formative evaluation of a prototype thesaurus-

M. Agosti and C. Thanos (Eds.): ECDL 2002, LNCS 2458, pp. 346–361, 2002.

based retrieval system with semantic term expansion and the paper also discusses the qualitative methodology employed to study user search behaviour.

Fidel has investigated thesaurus use by professional searchers to construct knowledge bases for IR systems which could inform term selection of less experienced searchers [5-7]. Iivonen and Sonnenwald [8] conducted investigations into term selection in end-user-intermediary searching. They postulated that the processes should not simply be seen as a substitution of user terms for thesaurus terms, but that different ways of viewing and representing topics contribute to the selection of terms. Pollitt's HIBROWSE [9] assists users with faceted thesauri and other knowledge patterns in medicine. The user selects terms from hierarchical menus which correspond to various facets, e.g. „Physical disease" and „Therapy". Postings of documents that are indexed with all these terms are shown. For each facet, a new window with a list of narrower terms is opened, so that the number of results can progressively be reduced. The semantic links in a thesaurus can also be used in query expansion. Previous work at Glamorgan has investigated the potential of associative and spatial relationships [10]. The Okapi project has looked at the balance between system and user as to term selection. After automatic and interactive versions, they designed the Enquire interface which combines the two approaches [11]. Selecting from suggested terms was found to be difficult for users as they lacked an understanding of the impact terms might have on their query (see also[12]).

In this paper, we present key results from the formative evaluation and discuss their impact on design decisions. Quantitative evaluation methods can prove useful in analysing system performance and user attitudes identified via questionnaires [13]. However, the general aim of this study was to use qualitative methods to pinpoint problems at different search stages in order to better integrate the thesaurus into the search process. This is important as many potential users have little or no training in online searching and the use of complex tools. Making these tools available will however become more important as Digital Library collections grow and demand for more precise searching increases. The study was part of a larger project (FACET), being a formative, evaluation of a working prototype of the system. The qualitative evaluation methodology was informed by a previous study of the work practices of commercial software developers which followed an ethnographic approach [14]. Ethnographic techniques can also be employed in studies of information seeking behaviour [e.g. 15]. Although the time scale of our formative evaluation did not permit a longitudinal study, we wished to adapt elements of an ethnographic approach, working with potential users in their own settings, at realistic tasks (within the constraints of an experimental prototype) and, crucially, capturing rich detail of the fleeting events of user sessions. Data gathered included transcripts of think-aloud sessions, screen capture movie files, user action logs and participant observer notes. Combining several data gathering methods allows triangulation between them. The aim was to analyse at a micro level the user's interaction with interface elements and reasoning in order to illuminate tacit sources of problems and inform iterative interface design decisions. This requires representations of session events that combine the different modalities of data capture.

2. The Facet Project

FACET is an experimental system [16] which is being developed at the University of Glamorgan in collaboration with the National Museum of Science and Industry (NMSI) which includes the National Railway Museum [17]. The research project investigates the possibilities of term expansion in faceted thesauri based on measures of semantic closeness. The main thesaurus employed in the project is the Art and Architecture Thesaurus (AAT) developed by the J. Paul Getty Trust [18]. With a view to making their collections more accessible to the public, NMSI is indexing parts of its collections database using the AAT. An export of these records is used as the underlying dataset for the system (some 400,000 records). The evaluation focused on the Railway Furniture and Railway Timepieces collections, although other collections are available.

The AAT is a faceted thesaurus; concepts are organised into a small number of high level, exclusive, fundamental categories or 'facets': *Associated Concepts, Physical Attributes, Styles & Periods, Agents, Activities, Materials, Objects* (with optional facets for *Time* and *Place*). As opposed to attempting to include all possible multi-concept headings explicitly in the thesaurus (e.g. *painted oak furniture),* they are synthesised as needed by combining terms from different facets [19]. This can be performed either by the cataloguer when indexing or the searcher when constructing queries. One of the goals of the FACET project is to investigate matching between multi-concept headings that takes advantage of semantic term expansion. The semantic relationships between thesaurus terms provide a system with information on how similar two terms are by calculating the traversal cost from the number and type of traversals necessary to move from one term to the other [e.g. 10, 20, 21, 22]. Various possibilities need to be considered, e.g. the absence of a query term from the indexing terms of a record, the presence of further indexing terms, exact matches of terms and partial matches of a query terms with semantically close indexing terms. For a more detailed discussion of these issues and how FACET deals with them, refer to [19]. Thus, it is not necessary for the users to construct a query that exactly matches a record's set of index terms or to exhaustively browse trying different combinations of terms to achieve the exact match. FACET calculates a match value between a query term and an index term depending on traversal cost. This in turn feeds into a matching function that produces ranked results, including partial matches, from a multi-term query. The system is implemented in C++ with a Visual Basic interface using a SQL Server database. An in-memory representation of the network of thesaurus relationships permits an efficient term expansion algorithm. The focus of this paper, however, is on the formative evaluation of the prototype interface and the role of the thesaurus in that interface.

Figures 1 and 2 illustrate the initial prototype of the interface, which was modified as a result of the first evaluation session conducted in this study as discussed below. This initial interface contains a number of elements, assigned to separate windows or subpanes including a Thesaurus Browser for users to browse through the hierarchies of the thesaurus using a mouse and a string search facility (Term Finder) that attempts to map an initial string to vocabulary terms (Figure 1). All terms can be dragged into the Query window. A ranked list of summaries appears in a results pane and details can be viewed. The record opens in a new window in the foreground and shows the full description and the indexing terms (Figure 2). Double-clicking on any term will open the Thesaurus Browser, centred on that term.

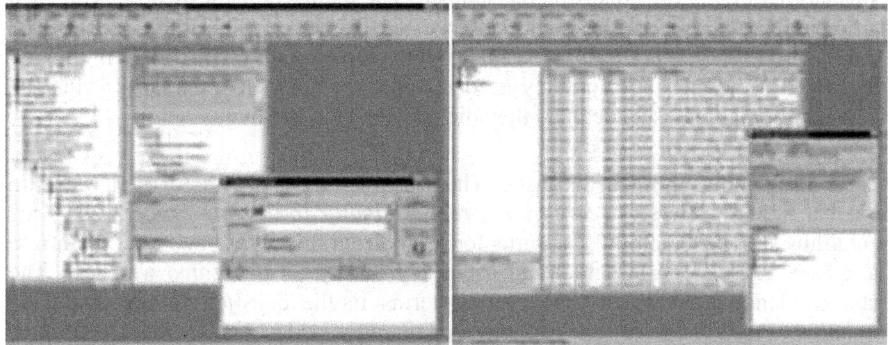

Fig. 1. Thesaurus Browser and Term Finder **Fig. 2.** Query window and results record

3. Methodology

Researchers in the fields of HCI, library and information science use a number of qualitative and quantitative data collection and analysis methods (see [23-26] for overviews). In this study, we were interested in users' reasoning in addition to the interaction sequences, in order to have a better insight into motivation and to reveal potential problems. This requires a dialog between evaluator and participants during and/or after the search sessions. This dialog and other interactions need to be recorded in detail for thorough analysis. One drawback of working with people's thoughts is that users need to be encouraged to „think aloud" so their thoughts can be recorded. Some people find this difficult and if they are silent it is not always easy for the evaluator to ask them about their actions without giving the impression of criticism (e.g.[27]).

Although a recording of conversation itself can normally be followed without problems, it is not always possible to identify the incident or precise interface element the speakers refer to. It is therefore desirable to have a comprehensive history of interactions. The FACET system records critical user and system actions in a log, which is further processed to be readable. Screen capture tools proved useful to remind the evaluator of the events of the session. We used Camtasia [28] which creates movie files as a visual record of the session. In future evaluations, playback of incidents may also be used as a basis for discussion with participants. The main evaluator took notes after sessions to record any information not otherwise captured, e.g. uncertainty on the part of the user or evaluator or observations of particularly notable events for later analysis. For some sessions, notes from additional observers are also available.

Over the summer of 2001, six museum professionals from various institutions, one IT and one library professional from University of Glamorgan participated in the study. The evaluators travelled to participants, taking a laptop with the experimental system. Thus each session took place in an environment familiar to the participants. Before the sessions, they were given a demonstration of the interface including an explanation of the term expansion mechanism. The main evaluator then sat with each participant at a table so she could observe the events on the laptop screen. The participants were given a training scenario with step-by-step instructions. It covered all aspects of the interface that they needed to know to complete the tasks. After the demonstration, three users decided they did not need the training.

A second handout outlined the tasks. The session started with a focused warm-up task that required users to *search for a record similar to the one printed out.* They could thus simply search the thesaurus for terms from this record and drag them into the query. The second task required users to *find objects decorated with text.* The main challenge here was to move from terms in the question to more suitable thesaurus terms. The third task was more open and was designed to require the user to identify thesaurus terms which were not included in the task description. Participants were given a picture of a chair, and asked to *find a matching record.* One problem with this task was that the records did not include images, and the chair in the picture was not from the collection. However, matching records existed in the collection, and participants were successful in their search. The last task asked users to *generally explore the interface.* Not all users completed this task due to time restrictions.

The set-up was similar but not exactly the same for each session. Minor modifications were made to logging and the prompt strategy to encourage think-aloud. Occasionally, users felt uncomfortable with the audio recording, so none was taken during these sessions. Travelling to different locations meant the environment varied, e.g. it was not always possible to conduct the evaluation session in a separate room. Sometimes additional evaluators observed the session. The participants also had different levels of knowledge of the project. However, the differences were noted and considered in the data analysis.

The sessions totalled eight hours. Data for analysis include transcripts of audio tapes, screen capture files, the log created by the application and a number of sets of observer notes. The log files were post-processed both automatically and manually for clarity of presentation. The tapes were transcribed word for word in the large part, although sections not relating to the evaluation or interface were summarised. The evaluator watched the screen capture files and generated descriptions of events. Transcripts of tapes and screen capture files were collated together with log data and comments from the notes. This resulted in a rich set of data for each session. The notation used to describe the incidents selected for discussion clearly identifies the contribution of each data source:

Descriptive summary of screen capture files	Log file (post-processed)
`Transcript of audio recording`	Post-hoc evaluator notes

Initially, the tape transcripts were the primary source of interest, as they explicitly and implicitly revealed problematic situations. These were identified and analysed in more detail, e.g. by examining the log and the screen recording. Other incidents analysed included those the evaluator noted during the sessions and when looking at screen capture files. For each important or problematic incident, the evaluator considered the different data sources from the session. Juxtaposing incidents allowed further identification of possible reasons behind problems. Lower level interface issues were identified, however this paper focuses on issues particularly relevant to the search process.

4. Selected Key Incidents from the Evaluation

4.1 Window Switching

At the interface level, one initial issue was switching between windows. The initial prototype comprised a number of individual windows for searching the thesaurus, browsing it, constructing the query and viewing the results (Figures 1 & 2). This profusion of separate windows caused problems in the first evaluation session. In the example shown, the participant is trying to find objects decorated with text (Task 2). Figure 3 shows the corresponding extract from the post-processed log. The indentation of the second column indicates the interface form in use. It can be seen that the user interacts very little with forms before changing to another form. Note that the user has to return to the background window or main form to execute the query (e.g. 11:04:40). The user activates windows (e.g. 11:04:38) simply to move them. Screen dumps of the original screen capture file provide a visual representation of the events (Figures 4-9).

The user has opened the Term Finder window and enters „Text". He executes the search and uses the menu to open a new query (fig. 4). He then drags the result, „Text" from the Term Finder into the query and goes back to the Term Finder to search for „Text decoration" and then just „Decoration". He drags the term „Decoration" into the query. He moves the query window up on the screen (fig. 5) and executes the query by clicking the „Start button" on the main form. The results appear (fig. 6) and the user double-clicks one to bring up the record (fig. 7). On the record form, he then double-clicks the term „Lettering (layout features)" which brings up the Thesaurus Browser (fig. 8). Note that the user then has to move the record form in order to uncover the right hand side of the Thesaurus Browser which is obscured (fig. 9 and around 11:10:05). (Descriptive summary of screen capture)

As a consequence of this first evaluation, the interface was modified to attempt to reduce window context switching. Underlying these problems appears to be a lack of intrinsic order in the user's progress through the search. The user has to interact with a number of components all contained in separate windows which could be opened in any sequence and moved anywhere on the screen. The lack of sequence was further reinforced by the general toolbar which contained the menus and buttons referring to different windows. The user cannot anticipate easily which windows will follow, continually having to move/adjust existing windows as new ones appear.

In the revised interface used for the subsequent sessions in this evaluation, Term Finder and Thesaurus Browser are integrated into one window using tabs. The Browser can be seen in Figure 10. The query is no longer in a separate window but forms the background of the interface (with query terms on the left and results on the right). These modifications were an attempt to reflect the logic of users' search behaviour better and to reinforce stages of search behaviour as identified e.g. by Kuhlthau [29]. The use of overlapping windows remained an issue though, e.g. if the Thesaurus Browser window was not minimised before executing the search, it covers the results.

11:02:44	Main form: Click (Open Term Finder)	
11:02:44	Term Finder: Activate window	
11:03:01	Term Finder: Click „Find now“	Text
11:03:13	Main form: Click (Open new Query form)	
11:03:13	Query form: Activate window	
11:03:17	Term Finder: Activate window	
11:03:39	Query form: DragDrop Expression [fig. 4]	Text
11:03:59	Term Finder: Click „Find now“	Text decoration
11:04:17	Term Finder: Click „Find now“	Decoration
11:04:34	Query form: DragDrop Expression	Decorations
11:04:38	Query form: Activate window [fig. 5]	
11:04:40	Main form: Click (Execute Query)	
11:04:40	Query form: QueryStart [fig. 6]	Text, Decorations
11:05:13	Query form: Double click Result record	217474
11:05:15	Catalogue record: Activate window [fig. 7]	
11:05:35	Catalogue record: Double click	lettering (layout features)
11:05:37	Thesaurus Browser: GetData	Thesaurus term: lettering (layout features)
11:05:38	Main form: Activate window	
11:05:38	Thes. Brows.: Activate window [fig. 8]	
11:10:05	Catalogue record: Activate window [fig. 9]	

Fig. 3. Extract from the post-processed log

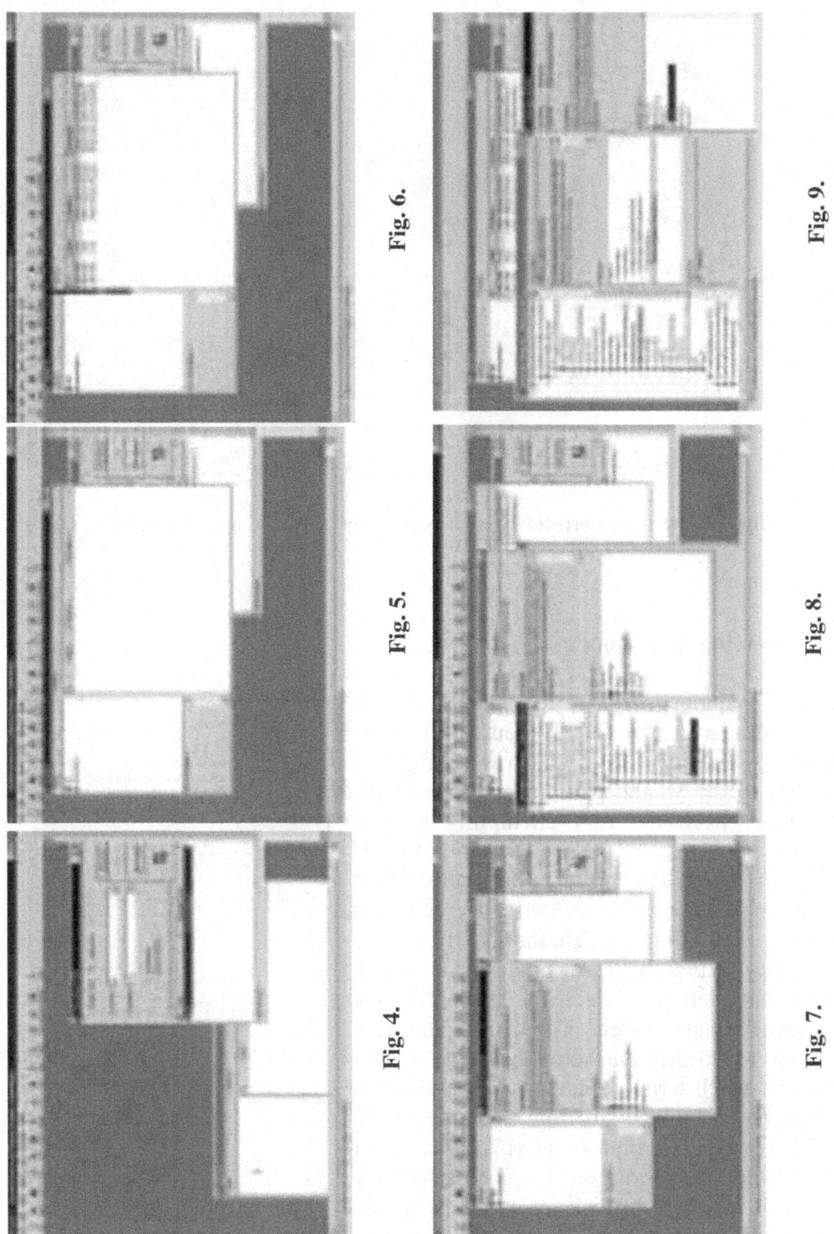

Fig. 4 – 9 Windowing issues

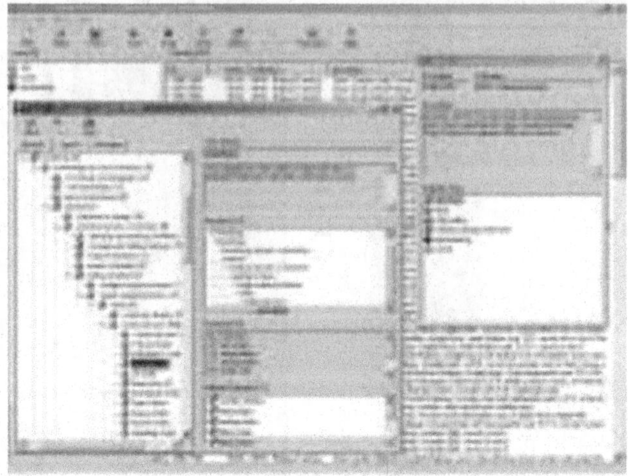

Fig. 10. Revised interface: Thesaurus Browser (left) and record in front of query

4.2 Browsing Behaviour

This example from a later session demonstrates use of the Thesaurus Browser. While searching for a chair matching the picture (Task 3), the participant browsed the thesaurus from the root attempting to find „Wood". It is unclear precisely what motivated the user to opt for this approach rather than initially searching for „Wood". He had just added a term from the Thesaurus Browser to the query so that the Term Finder pane, which might have led to a search for „Wood" in the thesaurus, was hidden. The participant was unable to locate the term because it was unclear which terms to navigate through. This might be due to the structure and size of the AAT (over 28,000 preferred terms). The closer to the root the terms, the more abstract they are. This makes it difficult for users, especially those who are not familiar with the AAT, to distinguish between them. Guide terms can also be difficult for the non-expert to interpret. Figure 11 shows the path (six levels deep) that leads to „Wood" in the Thesaurus Browser.

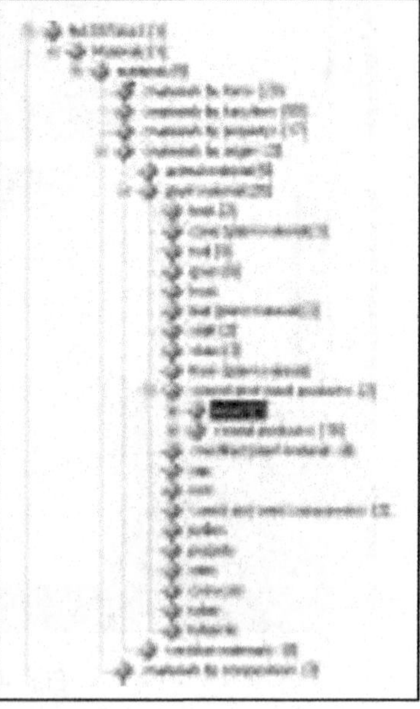

Fig. 11. „Wood" in the hierarchy

Figure 12 shows a log excerpt of this incident. The first three clicks are actually on the same term. The user initially clicked twice so that the hierarchy contracted and had to be expanded again. Note the user did not get close to the hierarchy of the term „Wood“ and even decided to browse a second facet, („Physical attributes“). After another sequence of unsuccessful browsing, the user thought of searching the thesaurus with Term Finder and instantly found „Wood“.

07:04.6	Thes. Browser: Double click Term	Thesaurus term: {Materials}
07:09.8	Thes. Browser: Double click Term	Thesaurus term: {Materials}
07:17.3	Thes. Browser: Double click Term	Thesaurus term: {Materials}
07:19.0	Thes. Browser: Double click Term	Thesaurus term: {Materials}
07:27.0	Thes. Browser: Double click Term	Thesaurus term: {materials}
07:34.7	Thes. Browser: Double click Term	Thesaurus term: {<materials by composition>}
07:50.6	Thes. Browser: Double click Term	Thesaurus term: {organic material}
08:03.3	Thes. Browser: Double click Term	Thesaurus term: {<materials by form>}
08:19.9	Thes. Browser: Double click Term	Thesaurus term: {<materials by function>}
08:47.7	Thes. Browser: Double click Term	Thesaurus term: {Physical attributes}
08:56.5	Thes. Browser: Double click Term	Thesaurus term: {Design Elements}
08:58.9	Thes. Browser: Double click Term	Thesaurus term: {<design elements>}

Fig. 12. Browsing from the root to find the term „Wood“

The following example stands in contrast to this unprofitable thesaurus browsing. For the final open task (exploration of the interface), the participant first searched for a term and then inspected its local context in the Thesaurus Browser.

The user brings up two results for „Trains„ in the Term Finder – „Trains (vehicle groupings)“ and „Trains (costume components)“. The user double-clicks „Trains (vehicle groupings)“ and clicks the „Browse“ tab to look at the term's local context. The user scrolls down a bit, then double-clicks „Trains (vehicle groupings)“ and then one of its more specific terms, „Passenger trains“. It has one more specific term, „High speed trains“. The user then drags „Passenger trains“ into the query, deletes the terms from the previous query and executes it.

The main difference between this browsing and the incident previously described is that the user's entry point into the thesaurus is much lower. Within three clicks, the user reaches the bottom of the hierarchy. The term is six levels away from the Facet (root) level – as is „Wood“. Finding this seemingly obvious term by browsing down from the root would probably have been just as difficult. For example, the hierarchy to select after „Objects“ would have been „Object groupings and systems“. While a user may sometimes browse to explore the structure of a thesaurus, this incident suggests an insight into the role of thesaurus browsing when part of a specific query. It seems fair to assume that thesaurus browsing to find a particular term is useful as long as the entry point is low enough so that users navigate within the term's local context and do not face highly abstract categories near the root. Not only is the cognitive load for the user reduced, but the process is faster (particularly so for large thesauri such as the AAT). While the browsing in the first example took almost 2 minutes and did not result in a term selection, the user in the latter example found a term within 20 seconds. These examples show that browsing the local context of a term can be useful to fine-tune the query and reassure the user that they are on the right track. The contrast between the incidents also suggests that the interface provides the right functionality, but perhaps still does not sufficiently model the query process, given that the problematic browsing occurred.

4.3 Breaking a Task down into Concepts

For faceted retrieval, users have to identify individual query components corresponding to thesaurus terms. One participant wanted to find a wooden table in the database (Task 1). He first searched the Term Finder for „Tables“ and then browsed the local context of this term in the thesaurus in an attempt to locate a compound term for the query.

```
Participant: So you want a table to go with the chair… right… so you know that… okay, take this. So … you can just go through and if you see … Tables by … Just trying to think. It obviously tells you … „Tables by design". But I was looking for „Tables by materials". Because you know you are trying to match it with an oak chair.
```

We see that he does not fully break the task down into concepts. He should look for „Wood“ (or even „Oak“) and „Tables“ separately as these are two different concepts represented by different terms in different facets („Materials“ and „Objects“ respectively). This misunderstanding also occurred in some other sessions. Following this study, the next version of the interface will provide more support in faceted query formulation by matching terms entered into the Term Finder individually and in combination and by a more structured Query Builder.

4.4 Reformulation of Query

Task 2 required the users to find items decorated with text. The challenge was to move away from the terms in the task description to more suitable thesaurus terms. One participant had a particularly persistent difficulty in that he reformulated the query repeatedly, but the same results were returned each time. A collated extract from different data sources is shown in Figure 13. It is not completely clear why this session was unsuccessful in reformulating the query, although it partly depends on the terms employed. Two closely related terms (e.g. „Text“ and „Words“) cover each other through the expansion algorithm, so there is no need to include them both in the query. To use a term from an initial result is generally speaking a good approach, and would have retrieved more results if this term („Lettering“) had not been used to index only the three records already retrieved. It is unclear why the participant rejected the term „Embossing“. Additional records with more potentially suitable terms would have been retrieved, which could have broken the impasse.

The user searches the thesaurus for „text":

52:08.1 Thesaurus form: Click „Find now" Text

The user then adds „text" to the query. After this, he looks at the related terms, and drags the (only) related term („words") also into the query. The user executes the query.

53:06.4 Query form: QueryStart Start Query: Text, Words

53:12.0 Query form: Results: 3

Three records come up as a result:

ID	*Match*	*Collection*	*Description*
1999-7588	*23.2%*	*NRM Railway Furniture*	*Station Seat: ex Market Weighton Passenger Station Cast Iron frame...*
1986-7908	*23.2%*	*NRM Railway Furniture*	*Station seat, GER, Slatted bench on cast-iron supports decorated with...*
1986-7948	*23.2%*	*NRM Railway Furniture*	*Station Seat, Great Central Railway, Wooden bench on log-design cas...*

The user looks at the first record. The indexing terms are: cast iron, embossing, inlays, lettering (layout features), seating, wood.

53:57.0 Catalogue record: Activate window

`Participant: Right, okay, so you've got the words „embossing". Ah, okay. That's just a different tense, isn't it? … Participant: So I can now try that and see if it will get me anything more.`

He then drags „lettering" from the record into the query.

54:40.9 Query form: Toolbar Start Query: Text, Words, Lettering

54:46.5 Query form: Results: 3

The same results as above now have a 50.0% match. The user deletes „text" and re-runs query. He then also removes „words" The results remain the same with 66.7% and 100% matches respectively.

`P: Yes. Still the same three benches. I wonder whether there is other words that I can use. It's because of the words that I'm picking, I'm only bringing up the three. Benches do have the station name on and the crest, it's the railway furniture. So, I'll try … Which word … [typing] You've not had that before, have you?`

The user opens the thesaurus browser and searches for „decorations":

56:29.7 Query form: Toolbar Thesaurus

56:29.7 Query form: Click „View Thesaurus"

56:48.4 Thesaurus form: Click „Find now" Decoration

56:55.1 Query form: DragDrop Expression

He drags „decorations" into the query – now „decorations" and „lettering".

`P: Right, so I could try that…`

The query returns the same three results as above, this time with a 66% match. (Note: „Decorations" is not matched by any indexing terms even with term expansion, which decreases the match value.)

`P: And I've still got the same three benches. I think I'm just going to have to admit - three benches.`

Fig. 13. Collated data of unsuccessful query reformulation

The term „Decorations" did not improve the query due to a misunderstanding. The user believed that „Decorations" refers to additions for aesthetic purposes. As he did not check the scope note or the local context but directly dragged the term into the query (Figure 13; 56:55.1), he remained unaware that this term actually refers to medals or badges. This incident demonstrates the risk that when a term's meaning is supposedly known, the user may not take the time to double-check the local context. Training might not be a solution because this participant applied this knowledge in other situations. Providing more context in Term Finder, e.g. the broader term, might have helped the user realise the ambiguity. However, this information would have to be visible without any further action by the user, which raises issues of space and information overload in the Term Finder display.

Overall, the user employed reasonable, advisable strategies to modify the query. It was not the strategies themselves that led to unsuccessful results. The results would indeed have fulfilled the task requirements. That the user *wanted* to find more results and was unable to do so constitutes the problem. This situation is especially problematic as the local context of the terms did not lead to other appropriate terms, such as „Inscriptions", which was very effective in retrieval. Other users made the leap to this term, or searched for objects, such as plaques or posters which they imagined could be decorated with text.

Mechanisms to support moves similar to that from „Text" to „Inscriptions" would be complex, but users could generally speaking be encouraged by appropriate prompts to search for objects that may have useful terms. The nature of the data collections implies this approach, and users commented accordingly when asked about the authenticity of the tasks. However, it cannot be denied that users could still commence a search with inappropriate terms from which they cannot easily move on to more suitable ones without additional help.

5. Conclusions

Collecting data from various sources was valuable, despite the fact that transcribing the tape and analysing the screen capture files was very time consuming. The collated representation (e.g. Figure 13) together with screen dumps combine the different sources. To some extent, such representations also serve to provide a record of the basis for reported findings. (We hope to include relevant screen capture video files with the electronic version of the proceedings). Triangulation of different data sources provides a fuller picture of user's reasoning and interactions. Users' interactions on a micro level could be put in the context of their reasoning and the specific features of the interface. As discussed in Section 4, the rich picture provided by the qualitative evaluation data of user sessions served to inform analysis of important issues, including the allocation of search functionality to sub-windows, the appropriate role of thesaurus browsing in the search process, the formation of faceted queries and query reformulation. Additional lower level interface issues were noted but lack of space prevents discussion here. The findings discussed are currently contributing to a further iteration of the user interface.

Certain aspects of the methodology still need to be resolved however. Not all participants are comfortable with audio recording, so an alternative method of collecting data needs to be developed for these cases. A type of shorthand notation might be suitable to capture as much detailed information as possible while conducting the evaluation and observing the user. The evaluator's prompts to encourage thinking-aloud need to be developed further. Alternatively, a session set-up with two collaborating users might encourage them to confer verbally on their steps and the individual might feel less under observation. The evaluator has to reassure users and give them appropriate pointers when they are unsure of how to proceed.

Looking at the problems that occurred during the sessions, it becomes apparent that despite some minor issues, interaction techniques used by FACET are successful in allowing a person with little knowledge of the interface to use the functionality. However, constructing a good query that returns satisfactory results is more challenging. It is during the search process itself that most users encounter problems of a conceptual nature. These range from breaking down the query into concepts that match thesaurus terms, to improving results through repeated reformulation. The analysis suggests that the prototype interface does not provide non-expert searchers with sufficient guidance as to query structure and when to use the thesaurus in the search process. The potential of the thesaurus and term expansion mechanism is also not explicit enough. We are currently working on a model of thesaurus informed searching which includes potential methods to resolve common problems. Users often have a choice of approaches, e.g. searching or browsing the thesaurus. At times, both options might be equally valid, but at other times use of the thesaurus should be channeled so that users employ techniques at search stages where they benefit most from them. This would for example mean discouraging browsing the thesaurus from the root level to find a term on a relatively low level or including a number of closely related terms in a query. Approaches which could assist users include more initial training and providing initial template queries and results. This would provide information on indexing practice. Users could modify the given queries according to their requirements so that they do not start with a blank sheet. A search wizard would be another method of channeling search activities in (likely) productive ways. An initial user profile might help determine which search technique would be the most appropriate to follow. In the long run, more information on the stages and options of the search process could be integrated into the interface.

However, problems in achieving results can arise even when people demonstrate textbook searching behaviour. In these cases, users might require more background information on how and why results are retrieved. In one example described above, the user performed reasonable interactions, but the results would not expand. The user was not aware of other approaches such as modifying the term expansion ratio because this feature was not intended for the participants' use in this interface version. Particularly in versions for non-specialists, the system might provide more active support and possibly automatic query refinement. Further options for thesaurus integration and support thus remain to be explored. Query histories would allow comparisons of query versions and give an opportunity to easily return to the best result set. Users could have the opportunity to modify query options, e.g. the term expansion ratio. This would be helpful in fine-tuning queries, although the cognitive load would also increase.

The next version of the interface under development will facilitate query formulation. An integrated Query Builder tool, which combines searching/browsing with query formulation and maintains the top level facets, will better reflect the search process and the thesaurus as a source of terms for the query. This presentation should assist users in breaking down their query into faceted components and in forming a better mental model of the thesaurus. More feedback will be available on the effects of semantic term expansion on the query and on query results (why records were retrieved). This should allow users to establish a better understanding of how to construct and reformulate a query according to their priorities. Thus, it is intended that the next version of the system will further support and suggest models of the search process to the user.

Acknowledgements. We would like to acknowledge the support of the UK Engineering and Physical Sciences Research Council (grant GR/M66233/01) and the support of HEFCW for the Internet Technologies Research Lab. We would like to thank Geoff Elliot and Traugott Koch for helpful comments; the J. Paul Getty Trust for provision of their vocabularies; the NMSI for provision of their collection data; and the participants in the study for their time, effort and input.

References

1. Aitchison, J., A. Gilchrist, and D. Bawden. *Thesaurus construction: a practical manual.* (4th ed.), London: AsLib. 2000.
2. Bates, M. Where Should the Person stop and the information search interface start. *Information Processing & Management*, 26(5), 1990, 575-591.
3. Fidel, R. and E.N. Efthimiadis. Terminological knowledge structure for intermediary expert-systems. *Information Processing & Management*, 31(1), 1995, 15-27.
4. Spink, A. and T. Saracevic. Interaction in information retrieval: selection and effectiveness of search terms. *Journal of the American Society Information Science*, 48(8),1997, 741-761.

5.,6.,7. Fidel, R. Searchers' selection of search keys: I The selection routine; II Controlled vocabulary or free-text searching; III Searching styles. *Journal of the American Society for Information Science*, 42(7), 1991, 490-500, 501-514, 515-527.

8. Iivonen, M. and D.H. Sonnenwald. From translation to navigation of different discourses: a model of search term selection during the pre-online stage of the search process. *Journal of the American Society for Information Science*, 49(4), 1998, 312-326.
9. Pollitt, A.S., M.P. Smith, and P.A.J. Braekevelt. View-based searching systems - a new paradigm for IR based upon faceted classification and indexing using mutually constraining knowledge-based views. in C. Johnson and M. Dunlop (Eds.) *Joint workshop of the Information Retrieval and Human Computer Interaction Specialist Groups of the British Computer Society*. Glasgow University. 1996. 73-77.
10. Alani H., C. Jones and D. Tudhope. Associative and spatial relationships in thesaurus-based retrieval. in J. Borbinha, T. Baker (eds.). *Proceedings (ECDL 2000) 4th European Conference on Research and Advanced Technology for Digital Libraries,* (J. Borbinha, T. Baker eds.), Lecture Notes in Computer Science, Berlin: Springer, 2000, 45-58.

11. Beaulieu, M. Experiments on interfaces to support query expansion. *Journal of Documentation*, 53(1), 1997, 8-19.
12. Oakes, M.P. and M.J. Taylor. Automated assistance in the formulation of search statements for bibliographic databases. *Information Processing & Management*, 34(6), 1998, 645-668.
13. Berenci, E., C. Carpineto, V. Giannini and S. Mizzaro. Effectiveness of keyword-based display and selection of retrieval results for interactive searches, *Proceedings (ECDL 1999) 3rd European Conference on Research and Advanced Technology for Digital Libraries,* (S. Abiteboul and A. Vercoustre eds.). Lecture Notes in Computer Science, Berlin: Springer, 1999, 106 - 125.
14. Tudhope D., P. Beynon-Davies, H. Mackay and R. Slack. Time and representational devices in Rapid Application Development.*Interacting with Computers*,13(4),2001,447-466
15. Kuhlthau C.C. and M.J. McNally. Information seeking for learning: a study of librarians' perceptions of learning in school libraries. *Proceedings 3rd International Conference on Information Seeking in Context (ISIC III), New Review of Information Behaviour Research*, Vol. 2, 2001, 167-177.
16. FACET Project, University of Glamorgan: Pontypridd, 2000. http://web.glam.ac.uk/schools/soc/research/hypermedia/facet_proj/index.php
17. National Museum for Science and Industry http://www.nmsi.ac.uk/
18. Art and Architecture Thesaurus, J. Paul Getty Trust, 2000. http://www.getty.edu/research/tools/vocabulary/aat
19. Tudhope D., C. Binding, D. Blocks and D. Cunliffe. Compound descriptors in context: a matching function for classifications and thesauri, *Proceedings Joint Conference on Digital Libraries (JCDL'02),* Portland, ACM Press, forthcoming, 2002.
20. Rada, R., H. Mili, E. Bicknell, and M. Blettner, Development and application of a metric on semantic nets. *IEEE Transactions on Systems, Man and Cybernetics*, 19(1), 1989, 17-30.
21. Tudhope, D. and C. Taylor. Navigation via similarity: Automatic linking based on semantic closeness. *Information Processing & Management*, 33(2), 1997, 233-242.
22. Chen H. and Dhar V. 1991. Cognitive process as a basis for intelligent retrieval systems design. *Information Processing & Management*, 27(5), 405-432.
23. Harter, S.P. and C.A. Hert. Evaluation of information retrieval systems: Approaches, issues, and methods. *Annual Review of Information Science and Technology*, 32,1997, 3-94.
24. Savage-Knepshield, P.A. and N.J. Belkin. Interaction in information retrieval: Trends over time. *Journal of the American Society for Information Science*, 50(12), 1999, 1067-1082.
25. Seymour, S. Online public-access catalog user studies - a review of research methodologies, March 1986 - November 1989. *Library & Information Science Research*, 13(2), 1991, 89-102.
26. Tague-Sutcliffe, J. The pragmatics of information-retrieval experimentation, revisited. *Information Processing & Management*, 28(4),1992, 467-490.
27. Branch, J.L. The trouble with think alouds: Generating data using concurrent verbal protocols. in A. Kublik (ed.) *Proc. of CAIS 2000: Dimensions of a global information science*. Canadian Association for Information Science. 2000.
28. Camtasia, TechSmith Corporation, 2000, http://www.camtasia.com/products/camtasia/camtasia.asp
29. Kuhlthau, C.C. Inside the search process - Information seeking from the users perspective. *Journal of the American Society for Information Science*, 42(5),1991, 361-371.

Meta-data Extraction and Query Translation. Treatment of Semantic Heterogeneity

Robert Strötgen

Social Science Information Centre, Bonn
stroetgen@bonn.iz-soz.de

Abstract. The project *CARMEN*[1] (*"Content Analysis, Retrieval and Metadata: Effective Networking"*) aimed among other goals at improving the expansion of searches in bibliographic databases into Internet searches. We pursued a set of different approaches to the treatment of semantic heterogeneity (meta–data extraction, query translation using statistic relations and cross–concordances). This paper describes the concepts and implementation of this approaches and the evaluation of the impact for the retrieval result.

1 Treatment of Semantic Heterogeneity

Nowadays, users of information services are faced with highly decentralised, heterogeneous document sources with different kinds of subject indexing. Semantic heterogeneity occurs e.g. when resources using different documentation languages for content description are searched by using a single query system. It is much harder to deal with this semantic heterogeneity than the technological one. Standardization efforts such as the *Dublin Core Metadata Initiative* (DCMI)[2] are a useful precondition for comprehensive search processes, but they assume a hierarchical model of cooperation, accepted by all players.

Because of the diverse interests of the different partners, such a strict model can hardly be realised. Projects should consider even stronger differences in document creation, indexing and distribution with increasing "anarchic tendencies". [1,2] To solve this problem, or at least to moderate it, we introduce a system consisting of an automatic meta–data generator and a couple of transformation modules between different document description languages. These special agents are able to map between different thesauri and classifications.

Semantic heterogeneity in our context is different from the discussion on "semantic heterogeneity" in the database community, which deals with more technological problems concerning data model/terminological mapping and integrated (mediated) schemas. [3,4]

The first step in handling semantic heterogeneity should be the attempt to enrich the semantic information about documents, i.e. to fill up the gaps in

[1] Funded by the German Federal Ministry of Education and Research in the context of the programme *"Global Info"*, FKZ 08SFC08 3.

[2] http://dublincore.org/

M. Agosti and C. Thanos (Eds.): ECDL 2002, LNCS 2458, pp. 362–373, 2002.

the documents meta–data automatically. Section 2 describes a set of cascading deductive and heuristic extraction rules, which were developed in the project *CARMEN* for the domain of Social Sciences.

The mapping between different terminologies can be done by using intellectual, statistical or neural network transfer modules. Intellectual transfers use cross– concordances between different classification schemes or thesauri. Section 3.1 describes the creation, storage and handling of such transfers.

Statistical transfer modules can be used to supplement or replace cross–concordances. They allow a statistical crosswalk between two different thesauri or even between a thesaurus and the terms of automatically indexed documents. The algorithm is based on the analysis of co–occurrence of terms within two sets of comparable documents. A similar approach of using relations between descriptors have been used in the project *AIR/PHYS*. [5] The *"EuroSpider"*[3] systems use related methods for multilingual databases. [6,7,8] Such methods have also been investigated in the *"Interspace"*[4] prototype. [9,10] The main principles of this approach are discussed in section 3.2.

Query expansion has been discussed for relevance feedback information. [11] We used intellectually and statistically created semantic relations between terms for query translation between different documentation languages (cf. section 3.3) and evaluated the impact of this translation on the query result (cf. section 3.4).

2 Meta-data Extraction

2.1 Approach

The goal of extracting meta–data during the gathering process is to enrich poorly indexed documents with meta–data, e.g. author, title, keywords or abstract — while the other methods described in the following section run during the retrieval process. This meta–data should be available for retrieval along with certain intellectually added meta–data, but with a lower weight.

The actual algorithms for meta–data extraction depend on file formats, domain properties, site properties and style properties (layout). No stable and domain independent approach is known so far. Until conventions for creating HTML documents change and become standardized towards a semantic web only temporary and limited solutions can be found.

Internet documents from the Social Sciences are mostly structured HTML files, but they use html features mainly for layout reasons, not as mark–up for content. Meta tags are infrequently used, and their syntax is often not correct. Different institutions use different ways of creating their Internet documents and a large number of documents contain no information about author or institution at all. This makes extraction of meta–data very difficult. Nevertheless we developed a set of heuristics for identifying some meta–data in this heterogeneous set of documents.

[3] `http://www.eurospider.ch/`

[4] `http://www.canis.uiuc.edu/projects/interspace/`

Because operating on (frequently incorrect) HTML files is not very comfortable, we transformed the documents into (corrected) XHTML and implemented our heuristics on these XML trees using XPath queries. [12]

The following exemplary algorithm for title extraction ($< x >$ shows an internal method number, *[x]* the weight of the extracted meta data) processes the parts of the document that have been identified and extracted with XPath before:

```
If (<title>-tag exists && <title> does not contain ''untitled'' &&
  any set of (possibly paired) <hx>-tags exist) {
  If (<title>==<hx>-tags) {
    <1> title[1]=<title>
  } elsif (<title> includes <hx>-tags) {
    <2> title[0.8]=<title>
  } elsif (<hx>-tags include <title>) {
    <3> title[0.8]=<hx>-tags
  } else {
    <4> title[0.8]=<title> + <hx>-tags
  }
} elsif (<title> exists && pset (a set of specially marked paragraphs)
    exists) {
    <5> title[0.5]=<title> + pset
} elsif (<title> exists) {
    <6> title[0.5]=<title>
} elsif (<hx>-tags exist) {
    <7> title[0.3]=<hx>-tags
} elsif (S exists) {
    <8> title[0.1]= pset
  }
}
```

Fig. 1. Heuristic for title extraction

2.2 Evaluation

The test corpus for the Social Sciences contains 3,661 HTML documents collected from Web servers from different research and education institutions. The documents are of different types (e.g. university calendars, project descriptions, conference proceedings, bibliographies). We analysed these documents and used them as basis for the creation and improvement of the extraction heuristics.

From these documents 96 % contain a correctly coded title; 17.7 % of the rest contain an incorrectly marked title, the other documents contain no title at all. Only 25.5 % contain keywords, all of them are marked properly. Not more than 21 % contain a correctly coded abstract, 39.4 % of the rest contain a differently marked abstract. This survey is the base for the evaluation of the meta–data extraction. Of course meta–data can only be extracted, if it is present in the document at all — we did try to implement automatic classification or automatic abstracting.

For the evaluation of the extracted meta–data we created a random sample containing every tenth document (360). We intellectually rated the relevance and correctness of the extracted data in four grades (accurate and complete; accurate in detail, but not complete or inaccurate parts; not accurate; not rateable).

We found that 80 % of the extracted titles are of medium or high quality; almost 100 % of the extracted keywords are of high quality; and about 90 % of the extracted abstracts are of medium or high quality. [13]

3 Query Translations Using Semantic Relations

Intellectual and statistical semantic relations between terms or notations expand or modify the query during retrieval. The translation of the user's query, which was formulated for one of the document collections, leads to specific queries for each target document collection considering the different systems for content analysis.

3.1 Intellectual Transfer Relations (Cross-Concordances)

Intellectual transfers use cross–concordances between different controlled documentation languages like thesauri and classifications. These languages have a limited number of indexing terms or classes used to describe document subjects.

To build cross–concordances documentary and professional experts created semantic relations between thesaurus terms or classes with similar meanings. Different kinds of inter–thesaurus or inter–classification relations are defined: "exact equivalence", "inexact equivalence", "narrower equivalence" and "broader equivalence". These relations can be annotated with weight information ("high", "medium", "low") reflecting the relevance of the relations for retrieval quality. In the project *CARMEN* cross–concordances are provided between universal or special classifications and thesauri in the domains involved (mathematics, physics, social sciences). These cross–concordances allow safe transfers between different documentation languages and the document sets using them.

Problems may arise if there are insufficient resources (time, money, domain experts) to create and maintain such cross–concordances; furthermore not all documents — particularly Internet documents — are indexed with a controlled vocabulary. Therefore additional approaches like statistical transfers based on the analysis of co-occurrence of terms (cf. section 3.2) are necessary. The software tool *SIS–TMS*[5] proved useable for creation of cross–concordances between different thesauri. *CarmenX*[6] has proved to be equally useful for creating relations between different classifications.

3.2 Statistical Transfer Relations

Quantitative statistical methods offer a general, automatic way to create transfer relations on the basis of actual bibliographic data. Co–occurrence analysis is one

[5] `http://www.ics.forth.gr/proj/isst/Systems/sis-tms.html`

[6] `http://www.bibliothek.uni-regensburg.de/projects/carmen12/`

of those methods. It takes advantage of the fact that the content analysis from two different libraries on a single document held in both collections will represent the same semantic content in different content analysis systems. The terms from content analysis system A which occur together with terms from content analysis system B can be computed. The assumption is that the terms from A have (nearly) the same semantics as the related ones from B, and thus the relation can be used as a transfer relation. The prerequisite for such computations is a parallel corpus, where each document is indexed by two different content analysis systems.

The classical parallel corpus is based on two different sets of documents, e.g. two different library catalogues. Each is indexed with a specific thesaurus/classification. To be able to create co–occurrence relations between the terms of these thesauri, the indexations of the documents have to be brought into relation. This is done by finding identical (or at least equivalent) documents in both catalogues. Considering print media, the problem of identity can be solved quite easy. An identical ISBN in combination with at least one identical Author should be a sufficient criterion for the identity of two documents. But the situation is worse, if the underlying data sets are not bibliographic ones, e.g. if text data should be combined with fact data or if Internet texts are considered.

In dealing with the World Wide Web we are concerned with many Web pages that are not indexed by a specific (given) thesaurus or classification system. The only terms we can rely on are the full–text terms supplied by a full–text indexing machine. Taking into account that a user might start his search with controlled vocabulary obtained from a thesaurus, relevant Internet documents should be retrieved as well as well–indexed documents stored in a database. In order to facilitate this, we have to realize a transfer from classification terms, thesaurus terms respectively, to full–text terms, and vice versa. As long as we cannot fall back to any standards of classifying Internet documents, we have to use a weaker strategy of combining keywords and full–text terms. Note that intellectual indexing would result in enormous costs. This weaker strategy is simulating parallel corpora for supplying semantic relations between keywords and Internet full–text terms.

First of all, in order to provide a simulated parallel corpus, we have to simulate intellectual keyword indexing on the basis of a given thesaurus. Simulating intellectual indexing implies that a method is used that produces vague keyword–document–relationships, i.e. unlike intellectual indexing, where each assignment is (usually) un–weighted (weighted 1 respectively) simulated keyword–document–ties are weighted on a [0,1]–scale. This yields a situation as indicated in Fig. 2: Unlike the situation in public databases (like the German Social Science literature database *SOLIS*[7]), where we have exact assignments of keywords and documents, we produce vague keyword indexing as well as vague full–term indexing.

Parallel corpora simulation via vague keyword and full–text term assignments is described for the *CARMEN* test corpus. This corpus is a collection

[7] `http://www.gesis.org/en/information/SOLIS/`

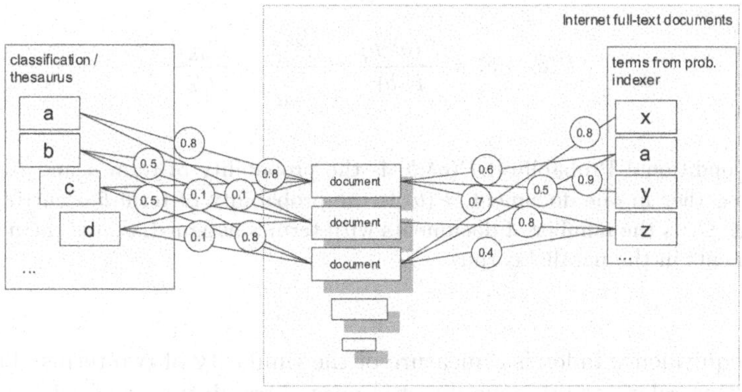

Fig. 2. Parallel Corpus Simulation with vague keywords and full–text terms

of about 6,000 Social Science Internet documents that have no keyword assignments. For the assignment of controlled vocabulary (keywords) to non–classified Internet documents a given thesaurus is used, i.e., in the case of the *CARMEN* corpus, the "Thesaurus Sozialwissenschaften"[8]. As a basic method assigning thesaurus keywords to Internet documents we consider each single keyword of the thesaurus as a query that is "fired" against a full–text indexing and retrieval machine maintaining the *CARMEN* corpus. The full–text retrieval engine *Fulcrum SearchServer 3.7* is used to provide ranking for values the documents in the corpus according to their similarity to the query vector. Each document in the result set that has a ranking value greater then a certain minimum threshold is then indexed by the keyword requested. The ranking values supplied by *Fulcrum* are considered the weights for the keyword assignments. This basic method has been improved to consider the relevance of a keyword for the document retrieved. [14]

Full–text terms are obtained by tokenising the full–text of an Internet document, eliminating stop words, and stemming the remaining terms using a Porter stemmer.[9] For weighting the terms the inverse document frequency is used. [15] The full–text is then indexed with full–text terms having a weight greater than a certain minimum threshold.

During the last two decades various mathematical models have been suggested for the analysis of the co–occurrence of terms. Their application was on automatic indexing mainly, [5,16] but they have been used for term expansion and clustering also. [17] The conditional probability and the equivalence index achieved some of the best results.

Basically the conditional probability is the probability of the occurrence of a term b from thesaurus B, if the same document has been indexed by term a from thesaurus A. Thus stating that there is a probable transfer relation between term a and term b. Fig. 3 shows the according computations.

[8] `http://www.gesis.org/en/information/support/`

[9] `http://www.tartarus.org/~martin/PorterStemmer/`

$$P(a \rightarrow b) = \frac{P(a\&b)}{P(b)} = \frac{\frac{C_{a\&b}}{C_{all}}}{\frac{C_b}{C_{all}}} = \frac{C_{a\&b}}{C_b}$$

Fig. 3. Conditional Probability; $P(a\&b)$ is the probability of term a and term b occurring together in one document, $P(b)$ is the probability of term b occurring in one document, C_x is the number of documents with term x assigned, C_{all} is the number of all documents in the parallel corpus

The equivalence index is a measure of the similarity of two terms. Therefore the resulting relations are none directed ones. The advantage of this equality is that very closely related terms can be filtered out easily (they will have a very high equivalence index). The disadvantage is that loosely related terms are very hard to find, because of their very low equivalence index (cf. Fig. 4).

$$P(a \leftrightarrow b) = E_{ab} = \frac{{C_{ab}}^2}{C_a * C_b}$$

Fig. 4. Equivalence Index

Those mathematical models are quite simple, but their advantage is, that they are easy to scale, which allows a wide range of applications. The next section describes a tool for modifying the summation algorithm and to find the appropriate threshold values.

In the context of the project *ELVIRA*, a tool for generating statistical correlation relations based on parallel corpora was implemented. *JESTER* (the *Java Environment for Statistical Transformations*) is a general workbench that allows the interactive selection of parameters for optimising the transfer relation between a pair of classification systems. *JESTER* also employs a number of heuristics for the elimination of systematic errors, introduced by the simulation of an actual parallel corpus as described before. [18]

In particular, the graphical representation of the term–document frequencies permits the eliminations of documents and/or terms from the following steps, based on their occurrence. In the case of a simulation of a parallel corpus, some documents got too many terms assigned. This happens, when the probabilistic search engine erroneously returns the same document on almost every query because some domain specific phrase appears verbatim.

The analysis results in a term–term–matrix that represents the term relations. This matrix is used for query translation.

3.3 Query Translation

Once the transfer relations have been realized, the question remains how to incorporate them into information retrieval systems. As a query term manipulating methodology they have to be placed somewhere between the user interface and the databases. Transfer relations, or — to be precise — transfer modules, become necessary, if data sets have to be combined, which are indexed by different content analysis systems. Usually those data sets reside in different databases. In a classical coordination layer the user query is simply distributed — unchanged — to the different databases and the results are combined to an overall result set. Most of the meta search engines in the Web work this way.

But this procedure is not applicable to data with heterogeneous indexing systems. To send one and the same query to all databases would lead to a lot of zero results in the connected databases. This is due to the fact that e.g. a queried classification is available in only one database, but not in the others. At this point the transfer relations come into play. Through their ability to transform controlled vocabulary, they are able to adapt the users query to the different requirements of the database. Therefore the query the user has issued will be transformed into different queries fitting the different content description systems (cf. Fig. 5).

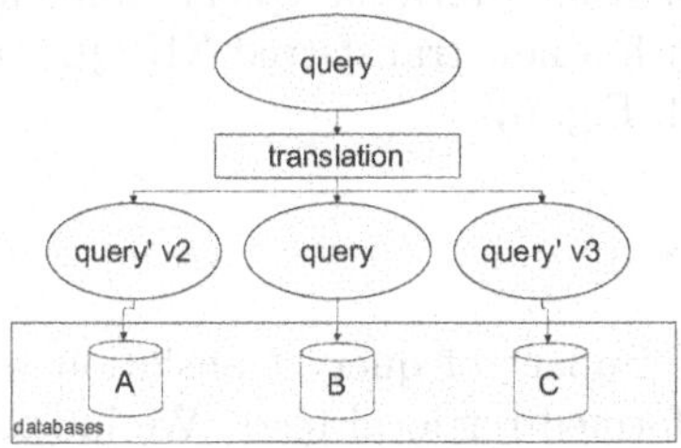

Fig. 5. Query Translation Process

During the actual transformation the relevant part of the users query (e.g. the classification terms from system A) is separated from the other parts. The terms of this separated part act as the input for the different transformation modules. After the transformation, the resulting output forms the new, transformed query part. This new part consists of terms from system B, and is combined with the rest of the users query (e.g. author/title query) to form the new, transformed query. Afterwards the query is sent to the corresponding database.

This procedure follows the so–called "two step model" [19] developed by the Social Science Information Centre (IZ) in the context of different projects. [10] We did not follow the ontology based approach that results into a global schema

[10] *ELVIRA*, *CARMEN*, *ViBSoz* and *ETB*, [14] cf. `http://www.gesis.org/en/research/information_technology/heterogeneity.htm`

by merging ontologies. [14] We prefer bilateral semantic relations between terms from two different databases.

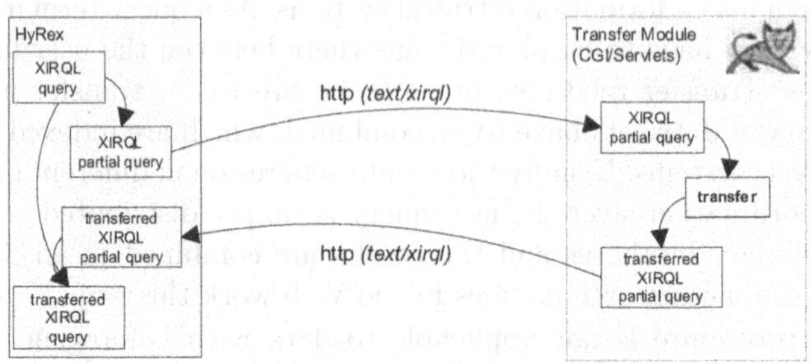

Fig. 6. Query Transfer Architecture

For *CARMEN* this approach was implemented in the project's architecture. The retrieval system *HyRex*[11] is part of a package developed at the *University of Dortmund.* [20] This search engine uses transfer services running remotely on servers at the Social Science Information Centre. Relevant parts of the complete query (e.g. author is no transferable query type) are sent to the transfer service as *XIRQL* (XML *Information Retrieval* Query Language) statements by http request and answered with a new transferred XIRQL statement that represents the transferred query (cf. Fig. 6).

3.4 Evaluation

In order to evaluate the impact of query translation with statistically created transfer relation we performed retrieval tests. We indexed about 10,000 HTML documents using *Fulcrum SearchServer.* Our scenario consisted of a search starting from the bibliographic database *SOLIS* using the "Thesaurus Sozialwissenschaften" as documentation language for query formulation. This query was supposed to be expanded to Internet documents. For this purpose the query is translated from the controlled thesaurus term to free terms. In this special case no translation of one controlled language to another leads to a replacement of terms; the uncontrolled free terms as translation target allow the addition of semantically related terms.

We executed the search in two ways: We sent both the original *SOLIS* query and the translated (expanded) query to the retrieval engine and compared the results. We have not been able to perform representative tests but exemplary spot tests. For each of three domains from the Social Sciences (women studies, migration, sociology of industry) we carried out two searches. Two of them are described exemplarily: One query used the *SOLIS* keyword *"Dominanz"* (*"dominance"*) and returned 16 relevant documents from the test corpus. Using the

[11] `http://ls6-www.informatik.uni-dortmund.de/~goevert/HyREX.html`

query translation 9 additional terms were found.[12] With this expanded query 14 new documents were found; 7 of them were relevant (50 %, a gain of 44 %). The precision of this search is 77 %. In this case without too much noise a significant number of new documents could be reached with the query translation.

Another, less successful example: A query using the keyword *"Leiharbeit"* (*"temporary employment"*) returned 10 relevant documents. The query translation added 3 new terms[13] and produced a result of 10 new documents, but only 2 of them were relevant (20 %, a gain of 20 %). The precision of this search is 60 %. In this example the translated query results in very little gain of new relevant documents but 80 % noise.

Summerising all examples we can state that we always found new relevant documents using the translated query compared with the original query. The precision of the additionally found documents ranges between 13 % and 55 %. Without being already able to find systematic conditions we find rather successful and weaker query results.

4 Outlook

The modules for meta–data extraction proved to be satisfactory. Meta–data was extracted tolerably from Web documents. They have been integrated in the gathering system (*"CARA"*)[14] and can be used for other projects. It seems promising to transfer the heuristics for HTML documents to other domains than the Social Sciences. Probably the weighting component will need some adjustment. The modules and heuristics are in general functioning; some improvement is conceivable by tuning the heuristics. Because of the transient Web standards and the fast changes in Web style very high effort for maintenance seems necessary to keep the heuristics up to date. It seems questionable if this effort can be raised. The query transfer modules using statistically created semantic relations proved able to improve the query result in retrieval test. New relevant documents were found using the transfer from a thesaurus to free terms for an Internet search, but some queries produce more noise then useful documents.

Some aspects remain unanswered and require more research and tests. How can the document corpus, used for computing the semantic relations, be improved; e.g. what kind of documents create bad artefacts or which properties does a corpus need to be representative? Probably the statistical methods need some refinement.

In the project's context intellectually created cross–concordances have been created and evaluated separately. The tested transfer modules can handle both kinds of semantic relations, and both should be compared directly. Also methods of combining both ways should be implemented and evaluated.

[12] "Messen", "Mongolei", "Nichtregierungsorganisation", "Flugzeug", "Datenaustausch", "Kommunikationsraum", "Kommunikationstechnologie", "Medienpädagogik", "Wüste"

[13] "Arbeitsphysiologie", "Organisationsmodell", "Risikoabschätzung"

[14] `http://cara.sourceforge.net/`

Of course the user interaction remains an important topic. By now the transfer process is a black box for the user. An user interface is needed that allows the user to understand and to influence this process and its parameters without handling incomprehensible numbers like statistical thresholds. The outcome of an interactive retrieval using transfer modules must be evaluated with real user tests. An output of the project are services and software modules for query translation, which are offered to interested users. We already integrated them into existing services like *"ViBSoz"* (Virtuelle Fachbibliothek Sozialwissenschaften); [21] other new services like *"ETB"* (European Schools Treasury Browser) and *"Informationsverbund Bildung — Sozialwissenschaften — Psychologie"* will follow.

References

1. Krause, J., Marx, J.: Vocabulary switching and automatic metadata extraction or how to get useful information from a digital library. In: Information Seeking, Searching and Querying in Digital Libraries: Pre - Proceedings of the First DELOS Network of Excellence Workshop. Zürich, Switzerland, December, 11-12, 2000, Zürich (2000) 133–134
2. Krause, J.: Informationserschließung und -bereitstellung zwischen Deregulation, Kommerzialisierung und weltweiter Vernetzung ("Schalenmodell"). IZ-Arbeitsbericht; Nr. 6. IZ Sozialwissenschaften, Bonn (1996)
3. Hull, R.: Managing semantic heterogeneity in databases. a theoretical perspective. In: ACM Symposium on Principles of Databases. Proceedings. ACM (1997) 51–61
4. Bright, M.W., Hurson, A.R., Pakzad, S.H.: Automated resolution of semantic heterogeneity in multidatabases. ACM Transactions on Database Systems (TODS) **19** (1994) 212–253
5. Biebricher, P., Fuhr, N., Lustig, G., Schwantner, M., Knorz, G.: The automatic indexing system air/phys. from research to application. In Chiaramella, Y., ed.: SIGIR'88, Proceedings of the 11th Annual International ACM SIGIR Conference on Research and Development in Information Retrieval, Grenoble, France, June 13-15, 1988. ACM (1988) 333–342
6. Schäuble, P.: An information structure dealing with term dependence and polysemy. In Chiaramella, Y., ed.: SIGIR'88, Proceedings of the 11th Annual International ACM SIGIR Conference on Research and Development in Information Retrieval, Grenoble, France, June 13-15, 1988. ACM (1988) 519–533
7. Braschler, M., Schäuble, P.: Multilingual information retrieval based on document alignment techniques. In Nikolaou, C., Stephanidis, C., eds.: Research and Advanced Technology for Digital Libraries, Second European Conference, ECDL '98, Heraklion, Crete, Greece, September 21-23, 1998, Proceedings. Volume 1513 of Lecture Notes in Computer Science. Springer (1998) 183–197
8. Braschler, M., Schäuble, P.: Using corpus-based approaches in a system for multilingual information retrieval. Information Retrieval **3** (2000) 273–284
9. Chung, Y.M., He, Q., Powell, K., Schatz, B.: Semantic indexing for a complete subject discipline. In: Proceedings of the fourth ACM conference on Digital libraries, ACM Press (1999) 39–48
10. Chang, C.T.K., Schatz, B.R.: Performance and implications of semantic indexing in a distributed environment. In: Proceedings of the eighth international conference on Information and knowledge management, ACM Press (1999) 391–398

11. Harman, D.: Towards interactive query expansion. In Chiaramella, Y., ed.: SIGIR'88, Proceedings of the 11th Annual International ACM SIGIR Conference on Research and Development in Information Retrieval, Grenoble, France, June 13-15, 1988. ACM (1988) 321–331
12. Strötgen, R., Kokkelink, S.: Metadatenextraktion aus internetquellen: Heterogenitätsbehandlung im projekt carmen. In Schmidt, R., ed.: Information Research & Content Management: Orientierung, Ordnung und Organisation im Wissensmarkt; 23. Online-Tagung der DGI und 53. Jahrestagung der Deutschen Gesellschaft für Informationswissenschaft und Informationspraxis e.V., DGI, Frankfurt am Main, 8. bis 10. Mai 2001; Proceedings. Tagungen der Deutschen Gesellschaft für Informationswissenschaft und Informationspraxis; 4. DGI, Frankfurt am Main (2001) 56–66
13. Binder, G., Marx, J., Mutschke, P., Strötgen, R., Plümer, J., Kokkelink, S.: Heterogenitätsbehandlung bei textueller Information verschiedener Datentypen und Inhaltserschließungsverfahren. IZ-Arbeitsbericht; Nr. 24. IZ Sozialwissenschaften, Bonn (2002)
14. Hellweg, H., Krause, J., Mandl, T., Marx, J., Müller, M.N., Mutschke, P., Strötgen, R.: Treatment of Semantic Heterogeneity in Information Retrieval. IZ-Arbeitsbericht; Nr. 23. IZ Sozialwissenschaften, Bonn (2001)
15. Salton, G., McGill, M.: Introduction to Modern Information Retrieval. McGraw-Hill, New York (1983)
16. Ferber, R.: Automated indexing with thesaurus descriptors: A co-occurence based approach to multilingual retrieval. In Peters, C., Thanos, C., eds.: Research and Advanced Technology for Digital Libraries. First European Conference, ECDL '97, Pisa, Italy, 1-3 September, Proceedings. Volume 1324 of Lecture Notes in Computer Science. Springer (1997) 233–252
17. Grievel, L., Mutschke, P., Polanco, X.: Thematic mapping on bibliographic databases by cluster analysis: A description of the sdoc environment with solis. Knowledge Organisation **22** (1995) 8
18. Hellweg, H.: Einsatz von statistisch erstellten transferbeziehungen zur anfragetransformation in elvira. In Krause, J., Stempfhuber, M., eds.: Integriertes Retrieval in heterogenen Daten. Text-Fakten-Integration am Beispiel des Verbandinformationssystems ELVIRA. Volume 4 of Forschungsberichte des IZ Sozialwissenschaften. IZ Sozialwissenschaften, Bonn (2002)
19. Krause, J.: Virtual libraries, library content analysis, metadata and the remaining heterogeneity. In: ICADL 2000: Challenging to Knowledge Exploring for New Millennium: the Proceedings of the 3rd International Conference of Asian Digital Library and the 3rd Conference on Digital Libraries, Seoul, Korea, December 6 - 8, 2000, Seoul (2001) 209–214
20. Fuhr, N., Großjohann, K., Kokkelink, S.: Cap7: Searching and browsing in distributed document collections. In Borbinha, J.L., Baker, T., eds.: Research and Advanced Technology for Digital Libraries, 4th European Conference, ECDL 2000, Lisbon, Portugal, September 18-20, 2000, Proceedings. Volume 1923 of Lecture Notes in Computer Science. Springer (2000) 364–367
21. Marx, J., Müller, M.N.: The social science virtual library project. dealing with semantic heterogeneity at the query processing level. In: Third DELOS Network of Excellence Workshop "Interoperability and Mediation in Heterogeneous Digital Libraries". Darmstadt, Germany, September 8-9, 2001, Darmstadt (2001) 19–23

MetaDL: A Digital Library of Metadata for Sensitive or Complex Research Data

Fillia Makedon[1], James Ford[1], Li Shen[1], Tilmann Steinberg[1], Andrew Saykin[2], Heather Wishart[2], and Sarantos Kapidakis[3]

[1] The Dartmouth Experimental Visualization Laboratory,
Department of Computer Science, Dartmouth College,
Hanover, NH 03755, USA
{makedon,jford,li,tilmann}@cs.dartmouth.edu

[2] Brain Imaging Laboratory, Dartmouth Medical School,
Lebanon, NH 03756, USA
{saykin,wishart}@dartmouth.edu

[3] Department of Archive and Library Sciences,
Ionian University, Greece
sarantos@ionio.gr

Abstract. Traditional digital library systems have certain limitations when dealing with complex or sensitive (e.g. proprietary) data. Collections of digital libraries have to be accessed individually and through non-uniform interfaces. By introducing a level of abstraction, a Meta-Digital Library or MetaDL, users gain a central access portal that allows for prioritized queries, evaluation and rating of the results, and secure negotiations to obtain primary data. This paper demonstrates the MetaDL architecture with an application in brain imaging research, BrassDL, the Brain Support Access System Digital Library. BrassDL is currently under development. This paper describes a theoretical framework behind it, addressing aspects from metadata extraction and system-supported negotiations to legal, ethical and sustainability issues.

1 Introduction

Traditional digital library systems have certain limitations when dealing with complex or sensitive (e.g. proprietary) data. This is true especially in cases where this data may be very useful to a large group of users but the owners have certain valid restrictions in allowing ubiquitous sharing of the data. Examples of such data can be found in medical, scientific, commercial, entertainment, security and other applications. Distributed access to this information necessitates alternative mechanisms of sharing. This paper describes a new type of digital library (DL) model framework called **MetaDL** that allows information sharing even when distribution limitations are present.

A MetaDL contains only data about data, referred to as *metadata*, and not the data themselves. Through a standard of metadata representation, sensitive objects can be securely and efficiently accessed, traded, and evaluated in a summary form. This not only protects the original data from malicious abuse but

M. Agosti and C. Thanos (Eds.): ECDL 2002, LNCS 2458, pp. 374–389, 2002.

also makes highly heterogeneous objects interoperable and amenable to being pooled for various purposes. MetaDLs are user-centered because they provide the user with a one-stop interactive interface that is personalizable (user defines priority and mode of data access), focused on satisfying user needs (built-in evaluation [10] operates on this basis) and lightweight (not dealing with cumbersome primary data).

This paper describes a MetaDL implementation in the area of neuroscience where there is a perceived need [6,21] for sharing valuable human brain data to facilitate meta-analysis, integrative investigations and data mining, and thus make progress towards the larger goal of understanding the brain. Proponents of data access have called for public dissemination of scientific data sets for a decade [33,15]. This kind of access has been attempted in certain fields, for example genomics [31], while it is still largely under discussion in other fields like neuroscience [35]. Among the concerns researchers face is that unfettered access to raw data may work against the interests of the data suppliers, as when their own data is used to anticipate their research [26]. The MetaDL approach proposed here can be applied to protect the interests of the data suppliers but still allow information sharing at several different levels.

The example MetaDL implementation is called **BrassDL**, the **Brain Access Support System Digital Library**. In it, different types of data are represented by metadata: multiple types of scans and datasets, subject data, experiments, methods and results. BrassDL is intended to provide the members of the brain imaging community with a resource that addresses many needs. It allows them to gain an overview of each other's work, search a metadata library of this work, and formulate requests for data sets that augment their available data. It is also designed to provide a negotiation and feedback system between data owners and data users that benefits the users (by making more data available) and the owners (by evaluating the data and thus making it more valuable). The philosophy of the design aims at providing user flexibility (e.g., user can revise or withdraw metadata once posted), simplicity (e.g., simple and uniform method of data entry and simplicity in data sharing), security and ethics in data sharing, and automation.

The rest of paper is organized as follows. Section 2 describes related work. Section 3 presents the MetaDL architecture. Section 4 describes the BrassDL system. Section 5 provides an incentive model. Section 6 concludes the paper.

2 Related Work

The concept of using metadata in place of desired data for indexing and searching is not a new one. The earliest use of the idea may have been in public records offices employing *collection level description* over a century ago [34], motivated by the desire to have remote (albeit limited) access to voluminous records data by way of summaries of holdings. Museums and libraries continue to use collection level description to allow indexing and searching of materials that have not yet been extensively examined or annotated, such as the archives of a famous person

[29], which might be described in a catalog by the number and dates of letters, diaries, and photographs that the collection contains.

In more recent digital collections, where the pooling of large amounts of digital information might seem to obviate the need of using metadata descriptions as a "stand-in" for data, metadata remains valuable for its abstraction of data. Scientific data repositories like GenBank [16], the European Computerized Human Brain Database (ECHBD) [9], and the fMRI Data Center [18] typify this new kind of system. GenBank is the NIH genetic sequence database, an annotated collection of all publicly available DNA sequences. Records in GenBank contain sequences and data such as sequence description, source organism, sequence length, and references. ECHBD is a 3D computerized database for relating function to microstructure of the cerebral cortex of humans. ECHBD collects homogeneously processed data, and then distributes these back to the submitters. The fMRI Data Center is a database established specifically for the storage and sharing of fMRI data from cognitive studies published in specific journals. It also allows for the mining of highly heterogeneous and voluminous fMRI data. Our proposed MetaDL architecture is also a digital collection; however, it differs from the above projects is that it collects only metadata and links to actual data resources. In the case of BrassDL, the advantages are twofold. On one hand, due to the compactness of metadata, the system is more scalable, can cover different brain science areas such as studies using fMRI, MRI and PET, and stores metadata from studies of different types such as journal publications, scientific meeting presentations, and formal but unpublished studies, and thus can provide a more complete research information repository for neuroscience study. On the other hand, since the structured metadata capture the important features of the raw data, our system does not lose functionality in terms of finding information. Actually, it collects exactly all the information that is expected to help users find what they look for.

Similar ideas are present in the Stanford Digital Library metadata architecture [2], the Alexandria Digital Library architecture [12], and the Common Data Model [13,14], and in the BrainMap [11], BioImage Database Project [5], MARIAN [17], ARION [19], SenseLab [7], and GEREQ [1] systems. In all of these, metadata descriptions are used to link to data from external sources that are never themselves integrated into the system. The Stanford architecture was designed with traditional text-based library documents in mind, and sets up a multi-source metadata index that allows users to search many repositories with a single query. The Alexandria architecture was demonstrated with earth science data, and features metadata-based indexing and searches on a centralized server with ties back to data repositories. The Common Data Model is a framework for integrating neuroscience data from the perspective of mediating data exchange between independent and heterogeneous data resources. BrainMap is a software environment for meta-analysis of the human functional brain-mapping literature. Its purpose is to help researchers understand the functional anatomy of the human brain and the studies that have been done on it through access to current imaging-derived research. The BioImage Database Project stores biological data obtained using various microscopic techniques. Data are stored along with metadata describing sample preparation, related work, and keywords. Issues of data access and ownership are discussed in [5], but no specific system of access and usage control is offered. MARIAN is a system for integrating data from various repositories of theses and dissertations into a single view. ARION facilitates better searching and retrieval of digital scientific collections containing data sets, simulation models and tools in various scientific areas. SenseLab is a repository of chemosensory receptor protein and gene sequence data that integrates sequences from 100 laboratories studying 30 species. GEREQ (GEography REsource discovery and Querying management project) is a system for indexing and searching large geographic databases using metadata representations. All the systems mentioned here can be considered "special cases" of MetaDLs, although they lack some proposed MetaDL features. All are centralized indexes of distributed data sources, as with a MetaDL, but a MetaDL adds sophisticated access control and control of metadata indexing by data source owners.

Metadata descriptions are used as a means to organize, index, and query medical or similarly sensitive data in the NeuroGenerator project [32], the fMRI Data Center [18], mentioned above, current pharmaceutical data warehouses [3], and a system proposed by researchers at Rutgers in 2000 [24]. The NeuroGenerator database system is based on the concept of storing raw data at a central site and making processed versions of it available. Researchers submit raw PET and fMRI data, along with detailed metadata describing its collection, and the central site uses current methods for data processing to integrate it into homogeneous collections. Users can then access collections that correspond to the data and processing type they are interested in. The fMRI data center receives data in concert with publications in certain journals that require a contribution of data to the center as a condition of publication. Data formatting and metadata tagging is done by the originating sites. Pharmaceutical data warehouses use metadata records to integrate various existing stores of data and allow for data indexing and advertisement for sale. The proposed Rutgers system aims to facilitate peer-to-peer sharing of datasets by using a centralized site to allow researchers to register what data is available, and under what conditions. The central site would use cryptographically signed exchanges between data providers and users to create a binding agreement before data is released. Although described in news format in 2000 in *Science*, publications have not yet been made on the proposed system.

Considerable work has been done on the development and promotion of metadata standards for creation and dissemination of metadata. The Dublin Core Metadata Initiative [8] is an organization dedicated to promoting the widespread adoption of interoperable metadata standards and to developing specialized metadata vocabularies for describing resources. The so-called "Dublin core" of metadata elements is used as a basis for many metadata schemas. The METAe project [27] aims to ease the automated creation of (technical, descriptive, and structural) metadata during capture or digitization. The aim of the Metadata Tools and Services project [28] — also known as MetaWeb — is to develop indexing services, user tools, and metadata element sets in order to promote the metadata on the Internet. The BrainML [4] project is creating a language and organizational ontology for metadata for neuroscience. The MetaDL model adapts techniques from these previous studies and systems to the task of providing a comprehensive digital information service for domains with complex or sensitive information.

3 MetaDLs

A MetaDL exists within a two-tier architecture (Figure 1) that supports two endeavors: searching for data via metadata, and sharing these data in a secure fashion. Tier 1 consists of autonomous DLs containing data, while Tier 2 systems contain data about the Tier 1 DLs and permit browsing and searching for primary data that are contained in Tier 1 DLs. Tier 1 DL systems by definition must contain actual data, while Tier 2 MetaDL systems by definition must contain only metadata. For this reason, the two tiers contain non-overlapping sets of systems.

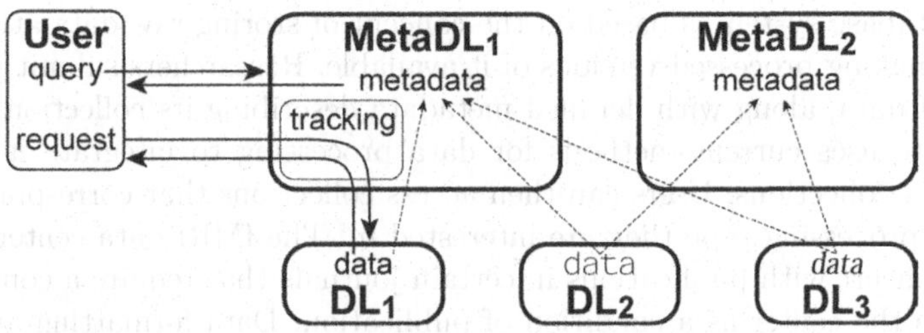

Fig. 1. How MetaDLs improve use of digital libraries (DLs). Rather than accessing every DL separately using each DL's individual interface (and possibly finding no matches or accessing a DL that is not appropriate), a user can query multiple DLs via a MetaDL that has collected metadata from each DL (dashed arrows), giving the user a homogeneous interface. Requests for actual data are facilitated and tracked by the MetaDL. Multiple MetaDLs can exist with individual priorities and interfaces, reflecting different purposes of each MetaDL.

The naming of the tiers reflects the distance from the primary data, Tier 1 being the closest. Any provider can set up and operate her own Tier 1 system, and a wrapper can be used to make existing systems conform to the model. Each system is independent and autonomous, allowing for flexibility in organization and configuration. As an example, a group of Tier 1 providers (e.g. some hospitals in the same country) may create their own Tier 2 system (with information for their Tier 1 DLs — and possibly some other important Tier 1 DLs that they also want to access). In practice, a single universal usage system may not be as efficient because of bandwidth or policy reasons (e.g. national laws). Therefore, the MetaDL model allows for any number of MetaDL systems providing coverage for possibly overlapping or redundant sets of digital libraries.

Tier 2 systems use metadata submitted by Tier 1 systems to provide an overview of data resources. General users access Tier 2 systems. Local users of a Tier 1 system have the option to query their Tier 1 system directly (for local operations only) or to access a Tier 2 system (for accessing data from many providers). If the user needs to access any of Tier 1 DLs, then she can use a Tier 2 system to authenticate herself, negotiate conditions and access the data. In what follows, a more detailed description of the tier functions is provided.

3.1 Tier 1 – Primary Data Management

A Tier 1 system does the following: (a) keeps track of the ownership, status and access rights of its objects; (b) authenticates its users, to verify and determine their access rights; (c) records user requests; (d) validates and serves the requests of its interactive users and of Tier 2; (e) can store alert conditions, for notifying the users on specific conditions — like insertions of new data sets; (f) supports different modes of data interchange between the data requester and the data owner; and (g) provides object information (usually public metadata), and optionally user and object usage information to Tier 2. Every data provider is encouraged to provide metadata by a mechanism of incentives and a built-in negotiation system that supports data exchanges in Tier 2. General users of a MetaDL always connect first to Tier 2, which provides a friendly one-stop (graphical) interface and transparently forwards requests to the appropriate Tier 1 DLs. All object handling is done in Tier 1, and the object accessibility is actually a property of each object (object-oriented design) and can be different in different objects in the same collection.

Tier 1 systems set conditions on sharing the data, and Tier 2 provides a front-end interface to these conditions, as well as support for a notification system connected to relevant legislation and other appropriate resources. The amount of the information, including both metadata and data, which are given to a user will depend on the specific Tier 1 DLs that contain the information, and their configuration and even on the data and metadata themselves. For example, a Tier 1 DL may contain some public-access sets for promotional purposes or an educational Tier 1 DL may contain and provide only public-access sets of "clean datasets" or benchmarks donated for educational purposes.

Tier 1 functionalities are implemented through a software tool distributed from the MetaDL website. This software can help data owners index their autonomous DLs while formatting metadata for Tier 2 systems in a uniform way.

3.2 Tier 2 – Meta-data Information Service

The contents in a Tier 2 system are (a) static descriptions of Tier 1 DLs — what Tier 1 servers exist, which collections they contain, information (in structured metadata and free text descriptions) about them, etc.; (b) dynamically generated descriptions for Tier 1 DLs and their objects, as they are produced by the public metadata that Tier 1 systems provide; (c) dynamically generated object usage and user information (such as object tracking, data use statistics, user alert data, etc.), both provided by Tier 1 systems and obtained from Tier 2 usage monitoring; and (d) other public data such as generic demographic information on relevant research activities. All these are actually metadata that relate user requests to Tier 1 DLs and objects in them. In Tier 2, a user searches, browses and manipulates information through a common interface, not accessing the original data directly. Once a user has identified a dataset he would like, he enters a request through Tier 2. A Tier 2 negotiation component (see Section 3.3) supports user-to-user data interchange: authenticate users, mediate between Tier 1 and Tier 2 components, manage transactions, and track condition.

3.3 Negotiation Model

The negotiation system [20] is composed of a set of transactions, see Section 4.3 for an example. The Negotiations between users and Tier 1 DLs need to fulfill the following requirements:

- *Proof of completion*: provide both parties with proof that each stage of the negotiation has completed.
- *Privacy of communication and security of transmission*: keep users' searches of and requests from DLs confidential, since this information may allow outsiders to draw conclusions as to the nature of this research. It is also obvious that data transmitted must not be usable by outsiders.
- *Verification of identity*: allow a data provider to verify a recipient, and allow a recipient to verify a data source. Especially over the Internet, both parties need to be certain about the other's identity. On the machine level, this is an old problem; for specific MetaDLs (such as BrassDL), there is the additional layer of being certain about the other side's credentials (e.g. recipient is a PhD).
- *Conditions of use*: allow the owner to make distinctions between users or their use of the data (e.g. a doctor may be allowed access to help solve a particular patient's problem, but access for researchers in general may be denied). Without this flexibility, the data owner would be forced to the lowest common denominator: deny access to everybody.
- *Comment on data quality*: protect the user from being given inadequate or substandard data by allowing the user to provide feedback on the data.

For example, two clinicians want to test their experiment on a larger number of subjects, and query a MetaDL geared towards their research for similar subject data. Of the descriptions they receive back, they pick one dataset and request it. The MetaDL forwards this request to the dataset's owner, who demands that the clinicians sign a privacy and nondisclosure agreement, as well as list the owner in any publication resulting from their use of this dataset. The clinicians agree, and the dataset is sent to them. They work on their combined data, and find that the new data augments the old very nicely, so they send a favorable review of the dataset back to the MetaDL. The owner of the data is notified that this review has been added onto the dataset's history. Later, the clinicians write a paper about their work but omit to list the owner of the dataset they requested. The owner spots the publication and complains, using the tracking information from the MetaDL and the digitally signed agreements as proof that his data was unproperly used.

There is a stage at which a public Tier 2 system would like some financial support in order to continue to offer services. One option is to charge a membership fee, which is variable according to entity (institution, lab, researcher, student) on an annual basis. A payment scheme would be beneficial for large data suppliers but detrimental to students who have very little to contribute to the system (aside from their potential as future members of the community). For users, there is some compensation in the form of reputation: data owners gain reputation by producing good datasets, while users gain by providing helpful feedback. Good datasets benefit the users directly; quality feedback improves the accuracy of queries.

4 BrassDL

Recent non-invasive scanning techniques in neuroscience have resulted in an explosive growth of research, the aim of which is to discover how the brain functions. Mapping structure/function relationships is a grand challenge problem in neuroscience [30]. Using brain multi-sensor technologies, such as Magnetic Resonance Imaging (MRI), Positron Emission Tomography (PET), Magnetic Resonance Spectroscopy (MRS), functional MRI (fMRI), Single-Photon Computed Tomography (SPECT), etc., novel discoveries can emerge with appropriate access and analytic strategies [36]. BrassDL aims to provide researchers with a moderated forum for exchanging data, ideas, and commentary in neuroscience.

Primary neuroscience data is very expensive and difficult to share. Most remain inaccessible to researchers outside of a particular project [21,22,25]. Currently, a traditional digital library containing original brain data is not realistic or practical due to the issue of data ownership. While researchers may be willing to exchange data in some circumstances, many are not willing to embrace a system that will allow unfettered access to and use of their hard-won data. In spite of many efforts to share this data [11,13,14,18,24,35], the state of the art is that each laboratory follows its own methodology, collects its own data and shares this data only through publications or in a limited manner [24]. New technologies have also resulted in an explosion of new research findings. A huge number of diverse, and possibly non-interoperable datasets and methods are being accumulated in various laboratories, often not known to other labs. From the standpoint of efficiency, it would be good to share these datasets, especially due to the very expensive equipment required and the high cost of each scan (on the order of several hundred to thousand US dollars [23]). In addition, to increase statistical power of analyses, it may be useful to integrate existing data with newer data where possible. For most labs right now, one must find old datasets on local disc archives. Although assumptions and technologies have changed, much of the collected information is in raw format and can be reinterpreted.

There are two reasons behind this lack of a comprehensive collection point. One is technical: due to data complexity, the diversity of formats, diverse experimental assumptions and scanner conditions, it is often requires considerable effort to combine data or results [32]. For example, if two studies aimed to measure the same phenomenon, but collected data from different scanners, it may be difficult or undesirable to combine the data depending on the research context. The second obstacle is non-technical and involves ownership, security, and privacy concerns that make direct data access non-feasible except in small-scale situations among a small number of users. To overcome these obstacles, the MetaDL concept is a good choice. Its two-tier organization permits better scalability, allows autonomous operations on each data provider, eases adoption of the system, and is able to integrate different providers while not sacrificing data ownership and access rights.

4.1 BrassDL Model

We propose a MetaDL implementation in the area of neuroscience that we call **BrassDL**, for the **BRain Access Support System Digital Library**. BrassDL not only catalogs data of different types and from different sources, but also provides a negotiation and feedback system to facilitate multi-level data sharing and data evaluation. Unlike existing data sharing models [11,18], BrassDL does not restrict itself to published data but starts bottom up, from the datasets that exist or are being developed in a laboratory. BrassDL can attempt to evaluate metadata according to different criteria, such as consistency and reasonableness. It also monitors user interaction with the system and mediates different types of negotiations among users.

As a MetaDL, BrassDL exists within a two-tier architecture, as shown in Figure 2. Tier 1 consists of autonomous DLs controlled by data providers (or BrassDL Partners). These DLs contain primary data, metadata and information about their access conditions. BrassDL is a Tier 2 system and contains data about the Tier 1 DLs. Tier 2 provides functionalities including browsing and searching for data that are contained in Tier 1 DLs as well as tracking the primary data exchange between users and BrassDL Partners.

A user usually interacts with BrassDL in the following way: initially, to query content of all data providers by searching the metadata that BrassDL has collected from each provider; subsequently, to request data sets from a particular provider; and finally, to submit feedback about the data sets that were received from the provider as additions to the provider's track record.

The collection of metadata for BrassDL is shown in Figure 3. BrassDL cataloger is used to organize the different data in a local DL and at the same time extract metadata, both for the benefit of the local site and, optionally, for submission to BrassDL to benefit the community. A data provider can use the cataloger to enter experiments, methods, tasks and datasets locally and in a uniform way with other data providers. The cataloger then enables metadata

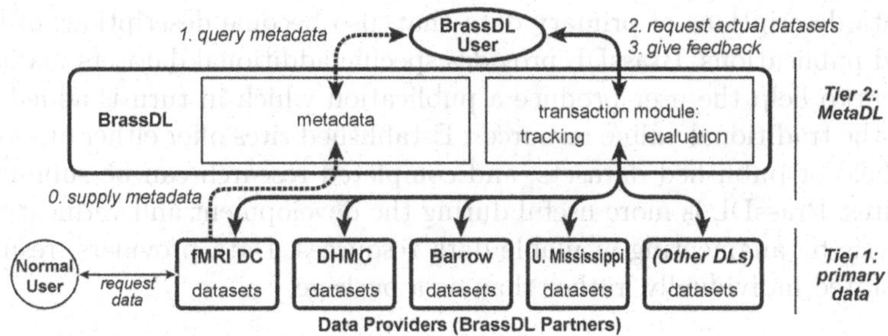

Fig. 2. User-BrassDL interactions. Tier 1 interactions are between the user and a data provider only: the user requests data; the data provider verifies the request and returns data if the request is granted. In Tier 2, the user interacts with BrassDL: initially, to query content of all data providers by searching the metadata that BrassDL has collected from each of its providers (dashed arrow); subsequently, to request datasets from a particular data provider; and finally, to submit feedback about the datasets which are passed on to the provider as additions to the provider's track record.

extraction from the local entries and with the consent of the owner. Each data provider can formulate policies to restrict usage to acceptable terms; specific agreements are made when a user requests a data set.

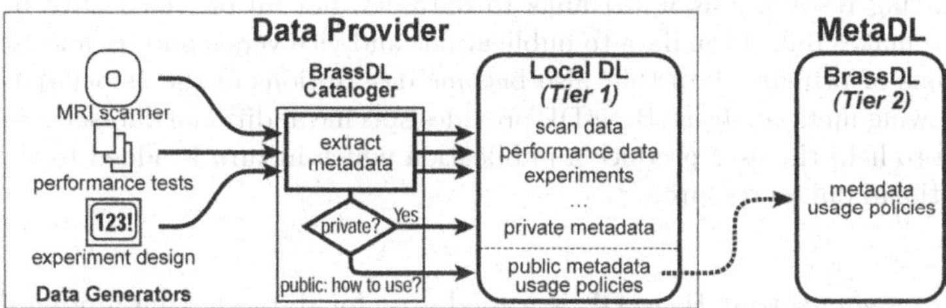

Fig. 3. Contributing to BrassDL. A BrassDL data provider uses an organizer tool provided by BrassDL to manage its data (e.g. scans, performance data, experiment descriptions) in a local DL. As data are added, metadata descriptions are created (e.g. scan kind and size, high-level descriptions of experiments) and stored together with the actual data. To contribute to BrassDL, metadata descriptions are submitted to the BrassDL system, together with any preliminary or general restrictions of use (e.g. "academic use only, except by arrangement").

From the user's point of view, there are two options for accessing information about a given topic in brain imaging (see Figure 4). On one hand, he can visit individual online resources, such as BrainMap or fMRI Data Center. On the other hand, he can visit BrassDL for a synergistic superset to existing brain imaging resources; since BrassDL (a) links to datasets, not all of which have been published, (b) makes links from data to publications and vice versa, and (c) adds metadata descriptions of primary data that also become descriptions of the associated publications. BrassDL provides specific additional datasets via its data providers to help the user produce a publication which in turn is added to the pool of the traditional online resources. Established sites offer either an overview of the field or published datasets, and completed research can be submitted to these sites. BrassDL is more useful during the development and verification of a hypothesis by augmenting available data resources. Data providers' results are incorporated individually, rather than as a package.

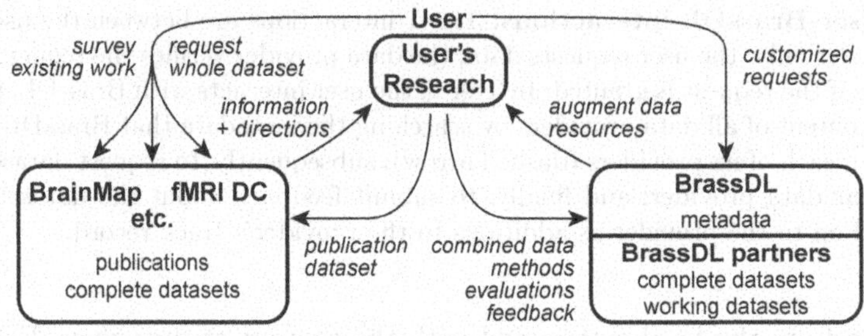

Fig. 4. Information flow in brain imaging research. A user researching a given topic can look at BrainMap, the fMRI Data Center, and other resources to get an overview of existing, published work. BrassDL is a synergistic superset to existing brain imaging resources as it (a) links to datasets, not all of which have been published; (b) makes links from data to publications and vice versa; and (c) adds metadata descriptions of primary data that also become descriptions of the associated publications, allowing meta-analysis. BrassDL provides specific additional datasets via its data providers to help the user produce a publication which in turn is added to the pool of the traditional online resources.

Figure 4 shows that BrassDL is a mediator for data sharing among different types of repositories. Similarly, BrassDL also acts as a mediator between different types of users, each of whom may contribute different services to the whole community (Figure 5). As the foundation of the system, data providers contribute metadata to the system (but keep the actual data). System subscribers can use these metadata in their research and return feedback in form of results, or make requests for specific data types. Evaluators classify data according to quality with regards to different criteria. Clinicians use actual cases for comparison and add expert knowledge to the system. Student users learn from textbook cases and can post their questions. Finally, the comments about the datasets flow back into each data provider's track record.

4.2 BrassDL Query and Data Evaluation

One strength of the abstraction layer that a MetaDL (and thus BrassDL) provides is the ability of the user to specify queries with different weights on prop-

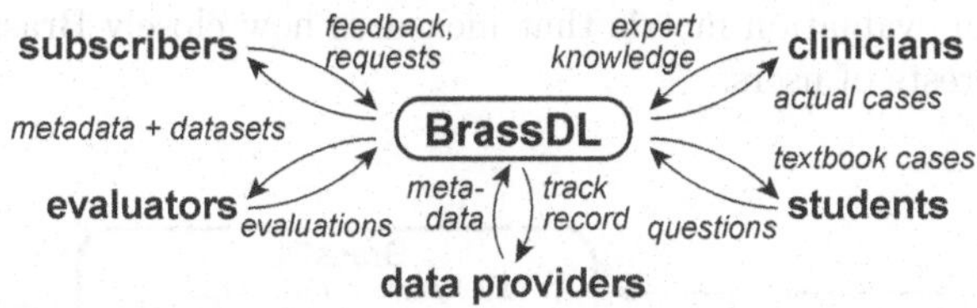

Fig. 5. Usage of BrassDL by different users and providers. Each type of user benefits differently from BrassDL and contributes parts that are useful for other users. For example, a case available from a data owner is evaluated as useful for a certain condition. A clinician then uses this case to treat a patient with the condition and adds her experiences, elevating the case to a textbook case used by medical students.

erties of the metadata being searched (see Figure 6 for a simplistic example). The user can choose which attributes to prioritize in a query in order to match his experiments. The system helps the user find the closest desired dataset based on the criteria he defines.

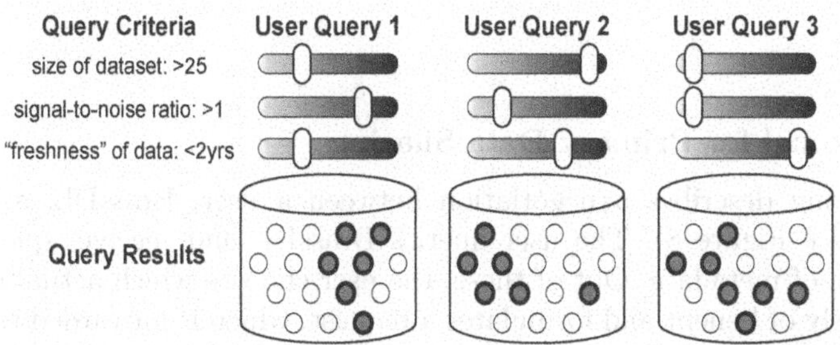

Fig. 6. User-weighted queries. By giving search criteria different weights, the user can customize a query to match the priorities of a research topic. For example, query 1 prefers datasets with a very high signal-to-noise ratio; query 2 selects large new datasets, with size more important than age; while the last query looks for datasets based on their age only.

Metadata queries (Tier 2) are evaluated separately from negotiations of actual datasets (Tier 1), yet can influence each other, as Figure 7 caption explains. Queries also influence the results of future queries: the metadata of frequently requested datasets will rank higher than unused datasets given equal values for the search parameters. A negotiation may take into account previous queries for datasets so as to not produce a compromising set in the hands of the user (e.g. sufficient data to identify a patient in conjunction with that on file at an insurance company, leading to higher insurance rates) — based on what data the user already has requested and obtained (through BrassDL), the negotiation offer from a data provider may include additional requirements. In [10], we describe a built-in evaluation metric that measures how closely BrassDL contents match the interests of users.

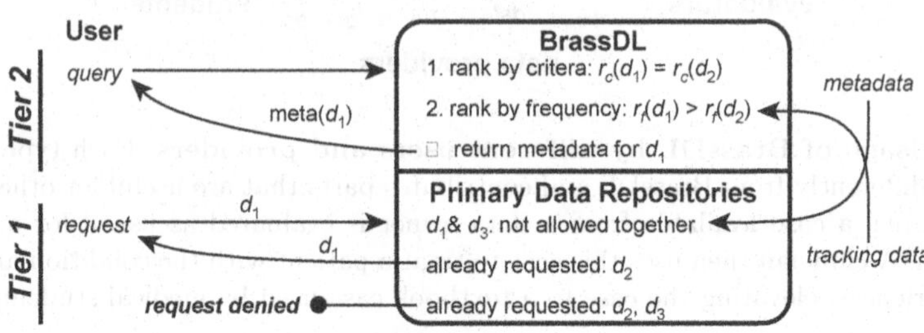

Fig. 7. Evaluation on each tier influences user queries and requests. Results to user queries are primarily ranked by search criteria, but in case of ties, the ranking can include the frequency of use, determined by the tracking data from all previous accesses. Similarly, restrictions of use (e.g. "datasets 1 and 3 constitute a compromising set") can be incorporated at the query level, hiding or flagging those datasets that would violate the restriction.

4.3 Protocol for Primary Data Sharing

The following describes a negotiation between a user, BrassDL, and a data provider (see Figure 8). The user queries BrassDL and receives query results in the form of metadata. Out of these, the user chooses which actual dataset(s) is most likely of benefit and formulates a request, which is forwarded to the data provider. The provider replies with a set of usage requirements (e.g. nondisclosure, clearances, co-authorship). The user signs this binding agreement and returns it to the partner, who then releases the actual dataset to the user. This dialogue of transaction is facilitated and tracked at each stage by BrassDL. Once the research has been concluded and is published by the user, the results are shared with BrassDL in form of evaluations and general feedback, giving the data provider a source of feedback and a record of collaboration.

5 Incentive Model

BrassDL supplements its use of the MetaDL model with a strong incentive model that overcomes the non-technical issues and can be adapted to other MetaDL applications. Since a MetaDL is based on metadata and the user's interaction with this data, a MetaDL would not survive without a good incentive for users to participate. The BrassDL incentive model is designed to answer the following question: "Why would a large neuroimaging laboratory go into the trouble of entering its metadata and why would a researcher want to access it (and enter her own)?" Below we briefly list several incentives for participation:

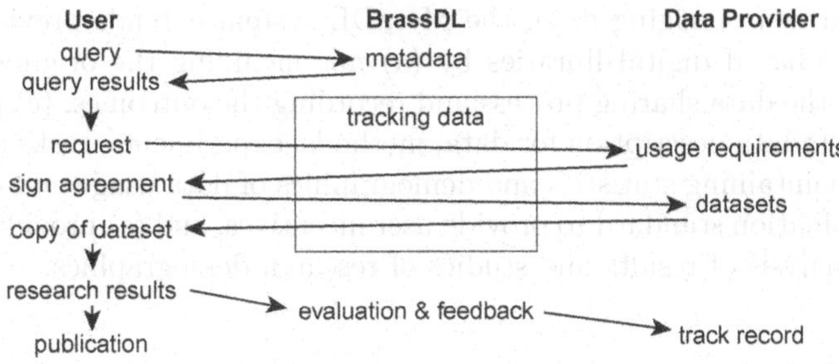

Fig. 8. Sketch of the protocol for data sharing and feedback. BrassDL acts as a mediator between user and data provider (BrassDL partner), initially to narrow the search for a good dataset, then to document the actual negotiation, and finally to store comments about the dataset.

- Visibility - The research activity of a data provider becomes visible to the community. This helps attract potential funding, patients or collaborators.
- Feedback - User feedback on the use of data may provide another means of data evaluation, as well as valuable advice on the improvement of data generation and data quality.
- Software support - BrassDL distributes a software tool to implement Tier 1 functionality. This software can help data providers build their own autonomous DLs, organizing data as they like, and create metadata in a standard fashion.
- Value assessment - Built-in evaluation mechanisms [10] assess the popularity of a dataset based on user demand and user feedback, resulting in automatic dataset ranking.
- Security - BrassDL helps provide for secure direct data exchanges by a mechanism of brokering, mediation, rights management and data tracking. This allows data sharing flexibility and the protection of data ownership and access rights.
- Notification and consultation - A user who places a query can receive future notifications of "similar" work, as defined by her profile, when new datasets are inserted; alternatively, she may receive consultation on how to proceed with future queries. BrassDL facilitates collaboration between organizations who create primary data and organizations who perform advanced data analysis.
- Data sharing management - BrassDL stores and manages each negotiation of data exchange. This helps owners manage their data-sharing activities, since it records cases or evidence of possible misuse and protects owners' rights.

6 Conclusion

We have presented a new framework for digital libraries managing sensitive datasets that have limitations on distribution, and a specific implementation.

For medical neuroimaging data, the MetaDL system extends previous notions of metadata-based digital libraries by (a) not including the original data; (b) supporting the data sharing process and recording the outcomes, (c) providing a uniform metadata description for data, methods, experiments, tasks and subject data, (d) maintaining statistics and demographics of data usage and providing a built-in evaluation standard to provide user incentives, and (e) providing support for meta-analysis of results and studies of research demographics.

References

[1] F. Andres, N. Mouaddib, K. Ono, and A. Zhang. Metadata model, resource discovery, and querying on large scale multidimensional datasets: The GEREQ project. In *Kyoto International Conference on Digital Libraries*, pages 83–90, 2000.

[2] M. Baldonado, C.-C. K. Chang, L. Gravano, and A. Paepcke. The Stanford Digital Library metadata architecture. *International Journal on Digital Libraries*, 1(2):108–121, 1997.

[3] J. S. Barrett and S. P. J. Koprowski. The epiphany of data warehousing technologies in the pharmaceutical industry. *International Journal of Clinical Pharmacology and Therapeutics*, 40(3):S3–13, March 2002.

[4] BrainML functional ontology for neuroscience. brainml.org.

[5] J. M. Carazo and E. H. K. Stelzer. The BioImage database project: Organizing multidimensional biological images in an object-relational database. *Journal of Structural Biology*, 125:97–102, 1999.

[6] M. Chicurel. Databasing the brain. *Nature*, 406:822–825, August 2000.

[7] C. Crasto, L. Marenco, P. Miller, and G. Shepherd. Olfactory Receptor Database: a metadata-driven automated population from sources of gene and protein sequences. *Nucleic Acids Research*, 30(1):354–360, 2002.

[8] The Dublin Core Metadata Initiative. dublincore.org.

[9] European Computerised Human Brain Database (ECHBD). fornix.neuro.ki.se/ECHBD/Database.

[10] J. Ford, F. Makedon, L. Shen, T. Steinberg, A. Saykin, and H. Wishart. Evaluation metrics for user-centered ranking of content in MetaDLs. In *Fourth DELOS Workshop on Evaluation of digital libraries: Testbeds, measurements, and metrics*, Budapest, Hungary, June 2002.

[11] P. T. Fox and J. L. Lancaster. Mapping context and content: the BrainMap model. *Nature Reviews Neuroscience*, 3(4):319–321, 2002.

[12] J. Frew, M. Freeston, N. Freitas, L. Hill, G. Janee, K. Lovette, R. Nideffer, T. Smith, and Q. Zheng. The Alexandria Digital Library architecture. *International Journal on Digital Libraries*, 2(4):259–268, 2000.

[13] D. Gardner, M. Abato, K. H. Knuth, R. DeBellis, and S. M. Erde. Dynamic publication model for neurophysiology databases. *Philosophical Transactions of the Royal Society of London: Biological Sciences*, 356(1412):1229–1247, 2001.

[14] D. Gardner, K. H. Knuth, M. Abato, S. M. Erde, T. White, R. DeBellis, and E. P. Gardner. Common data model for neuroscience data and data model exchange. *Journal of the American Medical Informatics Association*, 8(1):103–104, 2001.

[15] M. Gelobter. Public data-archiving: a fair return on publicly funded research. Psycoloquy: 3(56) Data Archive (3), 1992.

[16] GenBank genetic sequence database. www.ncbi.nlm.nih.gov/Genbank.

[17] M. A. Gonçalves, R. K. France, and E. A. Fox. MARIAN: Flexible interoperability for federated digital libraries. In *Proceedings of ECDL 2001, the 5th European Conference on Research and Advanced Technology for Digital Libraries*, pages 173–186, Darmstadt, Germany, September 2001. Springer.

[18] J. S. Grethe, J. D. Van Horn, J. B. Woodward, S. Inati, P. J. Kostelec, J. A. Aslam, D. Rockmore, D. Rus, and M. S. Gazzaniga. The fMRI Data Center: An introduction. *NeuroImage*, 13(6):S135, 2001.

[19] C. Houstis and S. Lalis. ARION: An advanced lightweight software system architecture for accessing scientific collections. *Cultivate Interactive*, 4, May 2001.

[20] S. Kapidakis, F. Makedon, L. Shen, T. Steinberg, and J. Ford. A negotiation model for mediated sharing of private digital data, 2002. In preparation.

[21] S. H. Koslow. Should the neuroscience community make a paradigm shift to sharing primary data? (editorial). *Nature Neuroscience*, 3:863–865, September 2000.

[22] S. H. Koslow. Sharing primary data: A threat or asset to discovery? (editorial). *Nature Reviews Neuroscience*, 3:311–313, April 2002.

[23] D. Krotz. PET and MRI race to detect early Alzheimer s. *AuntMinnie.com*, January 2001.
www.auntminnie.com/index.asp?Sec=nws&sub=rad&pag=dis&ItemId=50098.

[24] E. Marshall. Downloading the human brain with security. *Science*, 289(5488): 2250, September 2000.

[25] E. Marshall. A ruckus over releasing images of the human brain. *Science*, 289(5484):1458–1459, September 2000.

[26] E. Marshall. DNA sequencer protests being scooped with his own data. *Science*, 295(5558):1206–1207, February 2002.

[27] The MetaE metadata engine project. meta-e.uibk.ac.at.

[28] The Metadata Tools and Services Project (MetaWeb).
www.dstc.edu.au/Research/Projects/metaweb.

[29] P. Miller. Collected wisdom. *D-Lib Magazine*, 6(9), September 2000.

[30] The Organization for Human Brain Mapping (OHBM).
www.humanbrainmapping.org.

[31] L. Roberts, R. J. Davenport, E. Pennisi, and E. Marshall. A history of the Human Genome Project. *Science*, 291(5507):1195, 2001.

[32] P. Roland, G. Svensson, T. Lindeberg, T. Risch, P. Baumann, A. Dehmel, J. Frederiksson, H. Halldorson, L. Forsberg, J. Young, and K. Zilles. A database generator for human brain imaging. *Trends in Neuroscience*, 24(10):562–564, 2001.

[33] J. R. Skoyles. FTP internet data archiving: A cousin for psycoloquy. Psycoloquy: 3(29) Data Archive (1), 1992.

[34] M. Sweet and D. Thomas. Archives described at collection level. *D-Lib Magazine*, 6(9), September 2000.

[35] J. D. Van Horn, G. J. S., P. Kostelec, J. B. Woodward, J. A. Aslam, D. Rus, D. Rockmore, and M. S. Gazzaniga. The Functional Magnetic Resonance Imaging Data Center (fMRIDC): The challenges and rewards of large-scale databasing of neuroimaging studies. *Philosophical Transactions of the Royal Society of London: Biological Sciences*, 356(1412):1323–1339, 2001.

[36] D. A. Wagner. Early detection of Alzheimer s disease: An fMRI marker for people at risk? *Nature Neuroscience*, 3(10):973–974, 2000.

Importing Documents and Metadata into Digital Libraries: Requirements Analysis and an Extensible Architecture

Ian H. Witten[1], David Bainbridge[1], Gordon Paynter[2], and Stefan Boddie[1]

[1] Computer Science Department, University of Waikato, New Zealand
{ihw, davidb, sjboddie}@cs.waikato.ac.nz
[2] Universtiy of California Science Library, Riverside, California, United States of America
gordon.paynter@ucr.edu

Abstract. Flexible digital library systems need to be able to accept, or "import," documents and metadata in a variety of forms, and associate metadata with the appropriate documents. This paper analyzes the requirements of the import process for general digital libraries. The requirements include (a) format conversion for source documents, (b) the ability to incorporate existing conversion utilities, (c) provision for metadata to be specified in the document files themselves and/or in separate metadata files, (d) format conversion for metadata files, (e) provision for metadata to be computed from the document content, and (f) flexible ways of associating metadata with documents or sets of documents. We argue that these requirements are so open-ended that they are best met by an extensible architecture that facilitates the addition of new document formats and metadata facilities to existing digital library systems. An implementation of this architecture is briefly described.

1 Introduction

Flexible digital library systems need to be able to accept documents and metadata in a variety of different forms. Documents may be available in web-oriented formats such as HTML and XML, word-processor formats such as Microsoft Word and RTF, page description languages such as PostScript and PDF, or media-rich formats such as JPEG images and MPEG video. Metadata may also be available in a variety of different forms: embedded in the documents, in separate metadata files, in spreadsheets, even encoded into file naming conventions; or it may be computable from the documents themselves. Digital library designers must either insist that users adopt a particular prescribed scheme for document and metadata specification, or face the challenge of coming up with flexible, extensible, ways of accommodating new and different formats.

Of course, there are standards for representing metadata, just as there are standards for representing documents. Metadata might be embedded in documents in the form of *meta* tags in HTML, *\info* attributes in RTF, or *\title* and *\author* commands in LaTeX. Or it may be expressed externally as MARC records or in some standard encoding of Dublin Core metadata. While it might be desirable to enforce the use of a particular

M. Agosti and C. Thanos (Eds.): ECDL 2002, LNCS 2458, pp. 390–405, 2002.

standard, as most digital library systems do, in practice there are many different standards to choose from! Furthermore, legacy data will always present conversion problems. This paper explores a different approach that involves an extensible architecture.

2 Requirements

There are two basic elements that must be considered when importing material into a digital library. The first comprises documents, where the term is interpreted in a suitably general way. Documents form the raw material of any library. The second is metadata: summary information, in structured form, about the documents. This is the basis for the organization of material. Librarians are expert in creating metadata and using it to facilitate access to large information collections.

When a large collection of documents and metadata is made available for import into a digital library, questions arise as to the structure within which the documents are presented, and how the relationship between the documents and the metadata is expressed—which metadata pertains to which documents.

2.1 Documents

We use the term "document" to denote any information-bearing message in electronically recorded form. In a digital library, a document is a particular electronic encoding of what in library science is called a "work." A pressing practical problem is the wide variety of ways in which such encodings may be expressed. We focus in this paper on textual documents and media-rich formats supported by metadata; similar considerations arise when dealing with direct manipulation of multimedia content.

There are four principal styles of format in which electronic documents are expressed. The first style is web-oriented, and includes HTML, XHTML and various XML forms (such as the Text Encoding Initiative and Open eBook format). One difficulty is that such documents are not always self-contained: they frequently include explicit links to other resources such as images or other documents. These raise questions about the identity of the document—where are its boundaries?

Some such formats are designed around a strong notion of a "work." For instance, an Open eBook document contains a manifest of all external resources that constitute a single book—such decisions are straightforward to make. However, in other cases—and HTML is the archetypal example—some resources referred to by a document, such as images, are generally considered as part of it, while others, such as linked documents, are considered to have separate identity.

When a set of documents is imported into a digital library, it is necessary to carefully consider the question of what to do with links. For example, when a link is to another document that is also being imported, it is often appropriate to replace it by a link to the library copy of the target document instead of a link to the original external resource. Such decisions will depend on the digital library's aim and context.

The second style of expression comprises word-processor formats such as Microsoft Word or RTF ("rich text format"). RTF is designed to allow word-processor documents to be transferred between applications, and uses ASCII text to describe page-based documents that contain a mixture of formatted text and graphics. In contrast, the native Word format is intended for use by a single word processor. Strictly speaking, it is inappropriate to use this format to convey documents to digital libraries; nevertheless, users often want to do that.

There are two key difficulties with word-processor formats: they continually evolve to meet new demands, and they are often proprietary, with no public documentation. These problems are less severe with RTF: it is documented, and has an explicit and well-defined mechanism for adding new commands in a backwards-compatible manner that allows reasonable results to be obtained when new documents are processed by old software. However, with native Word the situation is different. Word is really a family of formats rather than a single one, and has nasty legacy problems. Although Microsoft have published "as is" their internal technical manual for the Word 97 version, the format continues to evolve. A serious complication is that documents can be written to disk in "fast save" mode, which no longer preserves the order of the text. Instead, new edits are appended, and whatever program reads the file must reconstruct its current state. Even Microsoft products sometimes can't read Word documents properly.

The third style of expression for documents comprises page description languages like PostScript and PDF. These combine text and graphics by treating the glyphs that express text as little pictures in their own right, and allowing them to be described, denoted, and placed on an electronic "page" alongside conventional illustrations. Page description languages portray finished documents, ones that are not intended to be edited, and are therefore more akin to traditional library documents than word-processor formats. Most of the time digital libraries can treat documents in these languages by processing them using standard "black boxes": generate this report in a particular page description language, display it here, transfer it there, and print. However, richer and more coherent collections can be built from such documents if text can be extracted for indexing, and elements of document structure can be extracted for browsing purposes. These are challenging problems.

The fourth style of expression is media-rich documents such as sound, pictures and video. When accompanied by textual descriptions, their treatment becomes one of associating metadata with documents. This provides a baseline approach that unifies the different media types and permits all the metadata methods discussed below for the general case to be applied. Direct manipulation of content is also possible, but lies beyond the scope of this paper.

We have described these four groups as "styles" because in practice their boundaries overlap. For example, although PDF is a page description language it supports hyperlinks akin to web-based documents and annotations comparable with word-processor documents. Proprietary eBook formats exhibit web characteristics, but distinctive issues arise because of their closed specifications. This means that an architecture for importing documents should not be compartmentalized based on these categories, but instead should be flexible enough to respond to a range of document features regardless of their origin.

Aside from document format, another key question for digital libraries is the librarian's traditional distinction between "work" and "document". This arises when we have to deal with different versions of a particular work. Digital representations are far easier than printed ones to both copy and change. It is necessary to decide when two documents are to be considered the same and when they are different. Digital collections often contain exact duplicates; should duplicate copies be retained? When a new version of a document appears, should it supersede the old one, or should both be kept? The answers will depend on the purpose of the collection. Archival or historical records must not be allowed to change, but errors in collections of practical or educational information must be correctable.

A further complication that affects the identity of documents is that interactions with digital libraries are often sustained over time—for example, by keeping records of each individual user's work to facilitate future interaction. When identifiers are allocated to documents, decisions must be made about whether duplicates are significant and when new versions of documents supersede old ones. For example, one way of assigning identifiers is to compute a signature from the word sequence that makes up the document. This is attractive because exact copies receive the same identifier and are therefore mapped into the same object. However, it is sometimes necessary to make an updated version of a document supersede the original by giving it exactly the same identifier even though its content is slightly different, and in this case identifiers cannot simply be computed from the content.

2.2 Metadata

Metadata may be conveyed in three basically different ways. It may be *embedded* in the particular documents to which it pertains, contained in *auxiliary* metadata files, or *extracted* automatically from the textual content of the documents themselves. The final category extends the traditional definition of the term metadata, but it does so in a way that we find helpful.

Embedded metadata. Formats such as HTML and RTF allow documents to state metadata explicitly: in the former case using *<meta>* tags and in the latter with an *\info* statement. These provide a mechanism for specifying that certain "attributes" have certain "values". However, it is rather limited. HTML imposes no checks or constraints on the attributes that are used, while RTF restricts them to a small fixed set. Metadata values are strings with no other structure.

XML, in contrast, is specifically designed for expressing both document structure and metadata in a very flexible way. Document type definitions (DTDs) can be created that enforce appropriate constraints over the metadata that is present in an entire family of documents, including rules that govern the syntactic nesting of nodes. Metadata can be expressed as an "enumerated" type with a particular set of valid values, particular attributes can be declared to be "unique" within the document to act as identifiers, and so on. Even more comprehensive facilities for defining data structures are provided in the related standard XML Schema. As well as describing what structure is allowed in an XML file, this provides a rich array of basic types including year, date, and URI, as well as textual patterns and ways of subtyping and defining new types.

Other document formats have their own particular way of embedding metadata. Microsoft Office documents have "Summary" metadata that comprises title, date, subject, author, manager, company, category, keywords, comments. E-mail documents have sender, recipient, date, subject, and so on. PDF documents have title, date, subject, author, keywords, and binding (left or right edge). Music files may have title, date, composer, copyright, and description.

Auxiliary metadata. Metadata pertaining to a document collection is commonly expressed in the form of a separate metadata file. There are two widely-used standard methods for representing document metadata: the "machine-readable cataloging" (MARC) format and the Dublin Core. They represent opposite ends of the complexity spectrum. MARC is a comprehensive, well-developed, carefully-controlled scheme intended to be generated by professional catalogers for use in libraries. Dublin Core is an intentionally minimalist standard applicable to a wide range of digital library materials by people who are not necessarily trained in library cataloging. These two schemes highlight diametrically opposed underlying philosophies. There are two other bibliographic metadata formats that are in common use amongst document authors in scientific and technical fields, namely BibTeX and Refer.
As well as being able to express complete, self-contained documents along with their metadata, the XML language is capable of representing metadata alone in the form of auxiliary files. The information in any of the above metadata formats could easily be expressed as an XML file.

Extracted metadata. Whereas explicit metadata is determined by a person after careful examination and analysis of the document, "extracted" metadata is obtained automatically from the document's contents. This is usually hard to do reliably, and although extracted metadata is cheap, it is often of questionable accuracy. Relatively few documents today contain explicitly-encoded metadata, although the balance will shift as authors recognize the added value of metadata, standards for its encoding become widespread, and improved interfaces reduce the mechanical effort required to supply it.
"Text mining" may be defined as the process of analyzing text to extract information that is useful for particular purposes, and is a hot research topic nowadays. The ready availability of huge amounts of textual information on the web has placed a high premium on automatic extraction techniques. In this area there is hardly any underlying theory, and existing methods use heuristics that are complex, detailed, and difficult to replicate and evaluate.

2.3 Associating Metadata with Documents

Several challenging practical issues arise when large collections of documents and metadata are made available for import into a digital library. Any large collection of files is almost always stored in some kind of hierarchical directory space. And the structure of the file hierarchy is hardly likely to be completely random: it invariably represents some aspects of the structure of the document collection itself.

Large collections are usually created by amalgamating smaller subcollections, and the upper levels of the hierarchy are likely to reflect this structure. This may have important implications for metadata assignment. Ideally, one assumes that all metadata associated with a document is explicitly coded into it, or into a separate metadata file along with an explicit link to the document itself (e.g., its source URL). However, this is often not the case in practice. Particular pieces of metadata may be associated with the position of documents in the directory hierarchy. For example, all works published by one organization may be grouped together into a subdirectory, and within this works may be grouped by author into subordinate directories. In a collection formed by amalgamating diverse subcollections, different parts of the hierarchy are likely to have their own special organization. And certain pieces of metadata—publisher and author, in this example—may be defined implicitly rather than being explicitly stated along with each document.

It may be that directory and file names have been chosen to reflect particular metadata values. Perhaps more likely is that auxiliary files will be provided that state what metadata values are to be assigned to which parts of the hierarchy. In our experience with building digital library collections, metadata is more likely to be presented in the form of spreadsheet files than as MARC records. And these spreadsheets have an *ad hoc* structure that often relates to the directory hierarchy containing the documents.

The lower levels of the hierarchy may have their own structure too, in this case determined by the documents themselves. For example, image files associated with a particular HTML document are usually placed together in a subdirectory. Different types of files call for different treatment. Some contain documents, others images, others metadata in various forms, and still others should be ignored completely.

2.4 Metadata at Other Levels

We have tacitly assumed that metadata is associated with individual documents, and this is certainly the normal case. However, it is frequently present at other levels.

At the subdocument level, metadata may be associated with parts of documents. Chapter and section headings are a kind of metadata, and different sections of a document frequently have different authors. In general, any kind of metadata may be associated with any logical level of a document. Unless explicitly stated otherwise, subparts of a document inherit the document-level metadata.

At the supra-document level, metadata may be associated with a document collection as a whole. It might comprise a general statement of the topics covered by the collection, principles that govern the inclusion or exclusion of documents, principles according to which the collection is organized, collection editor and creation date, as well as particular information relevant to the collection, such as time period covered by a historical collection.

3 Architecture

The requirements that we have identified above are so varied that they can only be accommodated by a flexible architecture, one that is extensible in that new facilities can easily be added as new document and metadata formats arise. The architecture that we propose has three main components: an internal document format to which all documents are converted when they are brought into the system; a set of parsers that process document and metadata formats (and the directory structure in which they are presented) and whose functionality can be combined by cascading them, and a scheme for "designing" individual digital library collections by providing a specification of the kind of documents and metadata they are to contain, and what searching and browsing facilities they provide.

3.1 Internal Document Format

Collections of disparate documents in assorted formats are best accommodated by converting them into a standard internal representation for processing. There are many reasons, amongst them:

- as a fallback for presentation
- to support full-text searching
- as a vessel for metadata
- to resolve the issue of document identity
- to facilitate rapid processing.

A standardized internal document format need not imply a uniform *presentation* format, because a link to the original document can be retained and that original presented when the user calls for the document. In a Web-based digital library, HTML documents can be presented directly; XML documents can be presented using an appropriate stylesheet; PDF documents can be presented through the Acrobat reader; PostScript ones by invoking a suitable viewer; Word and RTF documents by invoking Word itself. However, if the necessary viewing utility is not available (e.g., Word on a Linux platform), a convenient fallback is to display the document's standard internal representation instead, with a concomitant reduction in display quality.

One purpose of the internal document format is to support full-text searching. It should be expressed in the form of as electronic text; preferably using Unicode (say UTF-8 or UTF-16) to accommodate different languages and scripts. The requirements of full-text search may mean that the internal format must preserve certain document components. For example, if searching is required at a paragraph, section, or chapter level, those structural units must be represented in the internal document format. Search terms can easily be highlighted in found documents if they are presented using the internal representation; otherwise some word-by-word positional mapping back to the original may be needed. Note that search engine operations such as stemming and case-folding may preclude highlighting by re-scanning the retrieved documents for the search terms.

The internal document format is a convenient vessel for storing the document's metadata. Whether metadata is embedded in the original document file, specified in an auxiliary file, or computed from the document text itself—or a mixture of all three—it can be pulled out into a standard form and saved as part of the internal document representation. This allows subsequent operations on document metadata to proceed in the same way irrespective of its source. XML is a suitable way of expressing metadata along with the document's textual content and some structuring information.

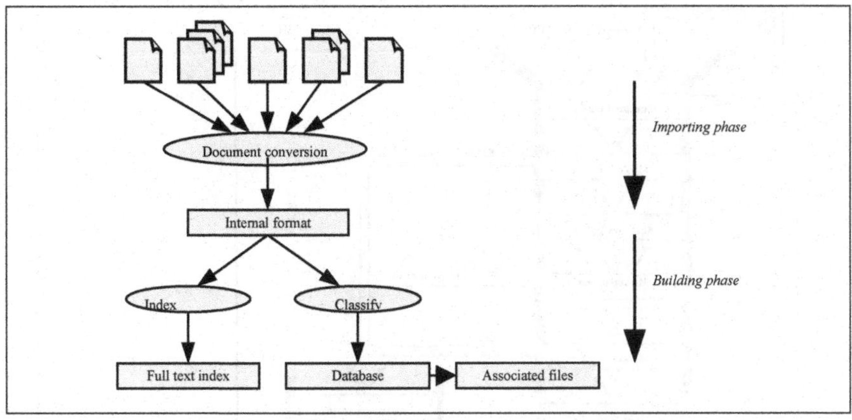

Fig. 1. Creating a digital library collection within the proposed architecture

Another purpose of the document format is to resolve issues of document identity. The simplest way to identify each document within the system is to assign it a unique label. It is important that labels persist over time, so that they can be used to record the history of individual users' interactions. Duplicate copies of documents can be eliminated by assigning them the same label. One way to do this, suggested above, is to compute a signature from the document's internal representation. Assuming that this representation is plain, unformatted text, this conveniently ignores differences that are merely formatting. However, for some collections, other ways of assigning document identifiers will be more appropriate—for example, when suitable labels pre-exist, when differently-formatted versions of identical documents are to be distinguished, or when there are special requirements for structured labels. Once obtained, a document's identifier can be stored within it as metadata; then, the signature method simply becomes the default way of calculating this metadata value.

Finally, the internal format should facilitate rapid processing of documents. Most digital library collections are large, and processing speed is often critical. Each document is converted to the internal format just once: subsequently all operations work on this representation.

Figure 1 gives an overview of how a digital library collection is created. The importing phase converts documents to the internal format, which forms the basis for subsequent operations. This improves efficiency when working with large collections (the normal case) by caching documents and metadata in a uniform format. We return to the remainder of the procedure shortly.

3.2 Plug-Ins

The proposed architecture adopts a flexible scheme of parser modules, called plug-ins, to process document and metadata formats. Each collection may involve documents and metadata in several different formats, and a plug-in must be included for each type. Plug-ins fit together into a cascaded pipeline structure that provides a highly configurable workflow system.

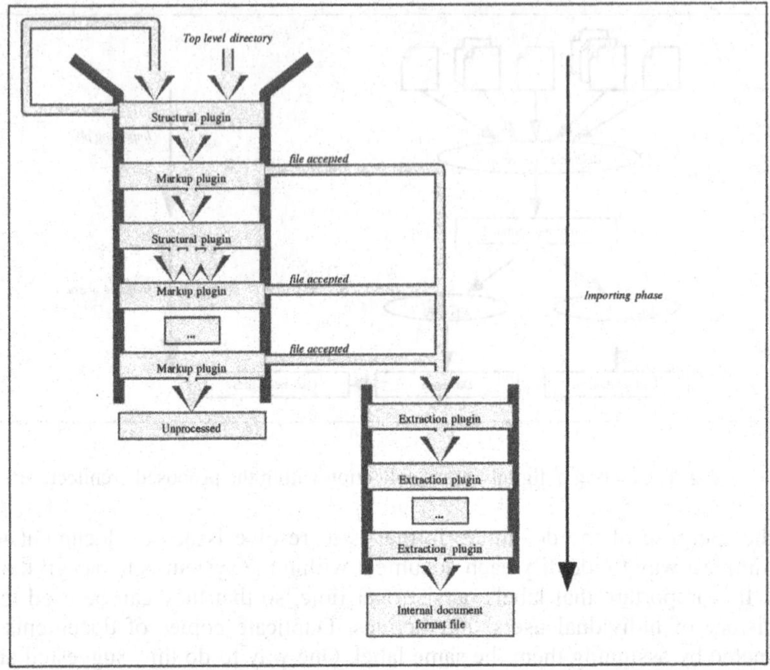

Fig. 2. The generic plugin pipeline architecture (idealized: see text)

Plug-in pipeline. Figure 2 shows the pipeline in generic terms. There are three types of plug-in: structural, markup, and extraction. The processing order in the pipeline is part of the collection design.

The import process is initiated by feeding the name of the top-level directory that contains the source documents into the pipeline. This name is passed down until one of the plug-ins signals that it is able to process it.

If an item reaches the end of the pipeline without being processed by any plug-in, the system generates a warning message and moves on to the next item. The process stops when no more items remain in the queue.

```
<!DOCTYPE GreenstoneArchive [
  <!ELEMENT Section (Description,Content,Section*)>
  <!ELEMENT Description (Metadata*)>
  <!ELEMENT Content (#PCDATA)>
  <!ELEMENT Metadata (#PCDATA)>
  <ATTLIST Metadata name CDATA #REQUIRED>
]>
```

Fig. 3. Greenstone internal document format

Structural plug-ins. Structural plug-ins operate on the generic file structure rather than on particular document formats. For example, under normal operating conditions, any filename that names a directory is processed by a structural plug-in that lists all files in the named directory and feeds their names, one by one, into the pipeline. In general this list includes further subdirectories, and they will be processed in the same way. This is the default way in which a collection's directory structure is traversed. However, when certain files or directories need special treatment, or when directory names are significant for metadata assignment purposes it must be possible to adapt this behavior. For example, it is often necessary to handle archived input formats in a digital library. Using this architecture, these can be expanded and their contents fed into the pipeline one by one. In other cases each source file may contain several documents (common E-mail formats do this) and need to be split into separate documents for the processing pipeline.

Markup plug-ins. Markup plug-ins process particular document or metadata types. To take one example of a document type, Microsoft Word documents require a markup plug-in that can parse this syntax. In this case, as in many others, the plug-in will call external format conversion utilities to do the work. The result may be in a form such as HTML or text, which must be further transformed to the internal format using a subsequent plug-in.

To supply the necessary flexibility, plug-ins will need to take various options that modify their behavior. One example is the input encoding used for the source files: in addition to ASCII, Unicode, and various other ISO standards, special-purpose techniques used for encoding particular languages such as Chinese, Cyrillic, Greek, Hebrew, and standards accommodated by particular operating systems (e.g. Windows) are required if the architecture is to operate internationally. Another option is to specify which files a plug-in can process, in terms of a set of file extensions. The plug-in for HTML, for example, should accept filenames with the extension *.htm* or *.html*. It is also useful for a plug-in to block particular files and prevent them from being further down the pipeline—the same HTML plug-in will need to block files with such extensions as *.gif*, *.png* and *.jpg* because they do not contain any text or metadata but are embedded in documents when they are viewed.

Plug-ins for document formats that include metadata extract this information and transfer it to the document's internal-format file. One of the requirements identified above is to be able to assign metadata to documents from files that have been created manually (or automatically). For example, information pertaining to a document collection might be available in a standard form such as MARC records. A metadata markup plugin processes this by placing the metadata into each individual document's internal file during the import process. Once there, it can be used to define searchable indexes and browsing structures.

Extraction plug-ins. The identified text and metadata are passed into a secondary pipeline of "extraction" plug-ins, whose contents are again part of the collection's design. These extract metadata from the plain text of the document and add it to the internal format. In this subsection we stretch the term "metadata" beyond its conventional usage to include any useful structured information about the contents of a document collection that can be extracted automatically.

One important piece of metadata that can be readily and reliably derived from a document's content is the language that it is written in. This can be added as *language* metadata. The same techniques can be used to identify the encoding scheme used for the document, which was mentioned above as an example of something that ought to be explicitly specifiable. This example illustrates that the sequential pipeline structure illustrated in Figure 2, while useful for conceptualizing what goes on, may be something of an idealization in implementation terms. We expand on this in the implementation section below.

It is often necessary to extract title metadata from documents wherever possible. When titles are unavailable, the document's opening words are often used as a substitute. E-mail addresses are a good example of information that can be extracted automatically; they can be added to the document as *emailAddress* metadata. More challenging is to identify all dates (e.g., in years) relating to the content of historical documents and add them as *Coverage* metadata.

Technical, commercial and political documents make extensive use of acronyms. A list of acronyms and their definitions can assist document presentation by allowing users to click on an acronym to see its expansion, and help check whether acronyms are being used consistently in a document collection. Heuristic procedures can be used to extract acronyms and their definitions, and add them as *Acronym* metadata

Table 1. Document processing plugins

TEXTPlug	Plain text.
HTMLPlug	HTML, replacing hyperlinks appropriately.
WordPlug	Microsoft Word documents.
PDFPlug	PDF documents.
PSPlug	PostScript documents.
EMAILPlug	E-mail messages, recognizing author, subject, date, etc.
BibTexPlug	Bibliography files in *BibTex* format.
ReferPlug	Bibliography files in *refer* format.
SRCPlug	Source code files.
ImagePlug	Image files for creating a library of images.
BookPlug	Specially marked-up HTML.
GBPlug	Project Gutenberg E-text.
TCCPlug	E-mail documents from Computists' Weekly.
PrePlug	HTML output from the PRESCRIPT program.

[1]. It is sometimes useful to annotate all occurrences of acronyms with links to their definitions.

In the scientific and technical literature, keywords and keyphrases are often attached to documents to provide a brief synopsis of what they are about. Keyphrases are a useful form of metadata because they condense documents into a few pithy phrases that can be interpreted individually and independently of each other. Again, heuristic procedures are available that obtain keyphrase metadata automatically from documents with a considerable degree of success [2, 3].

Table 2. Metadata extraction plugins

first	Extract the first characters of text and add it as metadata.
email	Extract E-mail addresses.
date	Extract dates relating to the content of historical documents and add them as *Coverage* metadata.
language	Identify each document's language.
acronyms	Extract acronym definitions.
acronyms	Add acronym information into document text.
keyphrases	Extract keyphrases from the full text and add them as *Subject* metadata.

3.3 Relationship to Other Work

The flexible architecture that we have described fits well with other initiatives, both practical and conceptual, in the digital library field. For example, it can be connected to digital libraries that export document data, gracefully handling a range of popular formats that are used for this task—such as the MARC record format and the Open Archives Initiative for metadata harvesting [4]. The plug-in mechanism turns such data into a form that is more malleable for the destination digital library. The modular nature of the architecture means that it can be used in different ways. For example, when working with a digital library system that expects its documents to be in a particular homogeneous format, the plug-in mechanism we have described can be used in a preprocessing step that converts all documents to the chosen internal representation. Note, however, that the design does not solve the problem of equivalent document representation between formats, which is a more fundamental issue.

Finally, the functionality described here has a strong relationship with the independently-designed Ingest component of the Open Archival Information System (OAIS) [3], an initiative whose focus is on long-term preservation of data. We find the fact that different considerations have led to similar architectures rather encouraging.

4 An Implementation

The Greenstone digital library software is an implementation of large parts of the architecture that has been described above [5]. In Greenstone, the design of a collection is encapsulated in a "collection configuration file" that directs both the import and build phases. This file contains the list of plug-ins for processing the source information, along with appropriate options for each, which is used during the import procedure. The remainder of the configuration file includes information pertinent to the build phase—what searchable indexes the collection contains, what browsing facilities there should be, how the various pages should be formatted, and so on. We have described this mechanism in a previous paper [4] and will not dwell on it here.

(a)
```
<!DOCTYPE DirectoryMetadata [
  <!ELEMENT DirectoryMetadata (FileSet*)>
  <!ELEMENT FileSet (FileName+,Description)>
  <!ELEMENT FileName (#PCDATA)>
  <!ELEMENT Description (Metadata*)>
  <!ELEMENT Metadata (#PCDATA)>
  <ATTLIST Metadata name CDATA #REQUIRED>
  <ATTLIST Metadata mode (accumulate|override) "override">
]>
```

(b)
```
<?xml version="1.0" ?>
<!DOCTYPE DirectoryMetadata SYSTEM
"http://greenstone.org/dtd/DirectoryMetadata/1.0/DirectoryMe
tadata.dtd">
<DirectoryMetadata>
  <FileSet>
    <FileName>nugget.*</FileName>
    <Description>
      <Metadata name="Title">Nugget Point, The Catlins
        </Metadata>
      <Metadata name="Place" mode="accumulate">Nugget Point
        </Metadata>
    </Description>
  </FileSet>
  <FileSet>
    <FileName>nugget-point-1.jpg</FileName>
    <Description>
      <Metadata name="Title">Nugget Point Lighthouse
        </Metadata>
      <Metadata name="Subject">Lighthouse</Metadata>
    </Description>
  </FileSet>
</DirectoryMetadata>
```

Fig. 4. XML metadata format: (a) DTD; (b) Example

4.1 Inheritance

Digital libraries process vast collections of documents, and one overriding requirement is that they operate reasonably efficiently. The processes that we are discussing are performed off-line, of course; and so do not affect the response to interactive library users. Nevertheless, even off-line collection building must take place expeditiously.

The pipeline architecture in Figure 2 has the potential to be rather sluggish. A document must pass through many stages. It may be expanded from a compressed archive, converted to a different format (e.g., Word to HTML), reconverted (e.g. HTML to the internal format), have an identifier calculated (e.g. by hashing the full text), and the resulting representation passed to a whole succession of extraction plug-ins that extract language and various other types of metadata. While the actual processing components are unavoidable, significant overhead will be incurred by repeatedly passing the document around. For example, if a Unix pipeline mechanism were used, the proposed architecture has the potential to be rather inefficient.

For this reason, the pipeline metaphor of Figure 2 is not taken completely literally. The Greenstone implementation of the architecture utilizes an inheritance structure to provide the necessary flexibility while minimizing code duplication, without repeatedly passing document representations around. All plug-ins derive from the same basic code, which performs universally-required operations like creating a new internal document object to work with, assigning an object identifier, and handling a document's subsection structure.

It is also more efficient to implement the automatic extraction procedures as part of the basic plug-in rather than as separate steps in the pipeline. This makes it easy for a markup plug-in to pass a document on to an automatic extraction plug-in for further processing. It also allows structural plug-ins to be enhanced with markup capabilities and *vice versa*. This is a useful ability when, for example, metadata and documents are represented separately in the file system. It allows more flexible dependencies to occur than the pipeline model, as when an extraction plug-in identifies both language and encoding and the latter is used in the early stages of converting the document to Unicode. Finally, it increases efficiency of operation because there is no need to physically pass large volumes of textual data from one extraction plug-in to the next.

4.2 Internal Document Format

The internal format divides documents into sections and stores metadata at the document or section level. One design requirement is to be able to represent any previously marked-up document that uses HTML tags, even if the markup is sloppy. Another is to be able to parse documents very rapidly. The internal format is an XML-compliant syntax that contains explicit commands for sectioning and metadata assignment, and can also embed HTML-style markup that is not interpreted at the top XML level.

In XML, markup tags are enclosed in angle brackets, just like HTML tags. The internal format encodes HTML tags by escaping any embedded <, >, or " characters within the original text using the standard codes *<*, *>* and *"*.

An XML *<Section>* tag signals the start of each document section, and the corresponding closing tag marks the end of that section. Each section begins with a metadata block that defines pertinent metadata. There can be any number of metadata specifications; each gives the metadata name and its value. In addition to regular metadata, the file that contains the original document can be specified as *gsdlsourcefilename*, and files that are associated with the document, such as image files, can be specified as *gsdlassocfile*.

Figure 3 gives the XML Document Type Definition (DTD) for the internal document format. The basic document structure is preserved by allowing it to be split into *Sections*, which can be nested. Each *Section* has a *Description* that comprises zero or more *Metadata* items, and a *Content* part (which may be null)—this is where the actual document's content goes. A name attribute and some textual data are associated with each *Metadata* element (the name can be anything). Making both parts optional enables collections to be built purely on content or purely on metadata. For instance, this allows multimedia-based content described by metadata, and also encompasses traditional electronic library catalogue systems.

In XML, *PCDATA* stands for "parsed character data," that is, text which may involve further markup. To include characters such as '<' the XML entity form must be used— *<* in this case.

4.3 Plug-Ins

Table 1 lists the document processing plug-ins Greenstone provides, while Table 2 shows the metadata extraction plug-ins. As previously mentioned, all plug-ins that extract metadata from full text are implemented as features of the basic plug-in object, and consequently all derived plug-ins inherit them. Extraction plug-ins, therefore, are specified as options to markup and structural plug-ins. This has the advantage that they can, if desired, be used selectively to extract information from certain types of document.

The structural plug-in that traverses directory hierarchies incorporates a way of assigning metadata to documents from XML files that contain auxiliary metadata. It checks each input directory for an XML file called *metadata.xml* and applies its contents to all the directory's files and subdirectories.

Figure 4a shows the XML Document Type Definition for the metadata file format, while Figure 4b shows an example *metadata.xml* file. The example contains two metadata structures. In each one, the *filename* element describes files to which the metadata applies, in the form of a regular expression. Thus *<FileName>nugget.* </FileName>* indicates that the first metadata record applies to every file whose name starts with "nugget". For these files (sourced from a collection of photos), *Title* metadata is set to "Nugget Point, The Catlins."

Metadata elements are processed in the order in which they appear. The second structure sets *Title* metadata for the file named *nugget-point-1.jpg* to "Nugget Point Lighthouse, The Catlins," overriding the previous specification. It also adds a *Subject* metadata field.

Sometimes metadata is multi-valued and new values should accumulate, rather than overriding previous ones. The *mode=accumulate* attribute does this. It is applied to *Place* metadata in the first specification above, which will therefore be multi-valued. To revert to a single metadata element, write *<Metadata name="Place" mode= "override">New Zealand</Metadata>*. In fact, you could omit this mode specification because every element overrides unless otherwise specified. To accumulate metadata for some field, *mode=accumulate* must be specified in every occurrence.

5 Conclusions

This paper has analyzed the requirements for importing documents and metadata into digital libraries and described a new extensible architecture that satisfies these requirements. It also includes a brief sketch of the Greenstone digital library system as an example implementation of this architecture. The proposed structure converts heterogeneous document and metadata formats, organized in arbitrary ways in the file system, into a uniform XML-compliant file structure. This simplifies the construction of the indexes, browsing structures, and associated files that form the basis of the runtime digital library system. Object oriented design further enhances capabilities whilst maximizing code reuse. The result is a comprehensive, flexible and extensible architecture.

Further details, and many examples, can be obtained from *nzdl.org*. The Greenstone software is available under the terms of the GNU General Public License from *greenstone.org*.

References

1. Dumais, S.T., Platt, J., Heckerman, D. and Sahami, M.: Inductive learning algorithms and representations for text categorization. Proc ACM Conf on Information and Knowledge Management. (1998) 148–155
2. Frank, E., Paynter, G.W., Witten, I.H., Gutwin, C. and Nevill-Manning, C.: Domain-specific keyphrase extraction. Proc Int Joint Conference on Artificial Intelligence, Stockholm, Sweden. San Francisco, CA: Morgan Kaufmann Publishers. (1999) 668–673
3. Lavoie, Brian. Meeting the Challenges of Digital Preservation: The OAIS Reference Model. OCLC Newsletter, No. 243. (2000) 26-30
4. Van de Sompel, H. and Lagoze, C.: The Santa Fe convention of the Open Archives Initiative. D-Lib Magazine, Vol 6, No 2. (2000)
5. Witten, I.H., Bainbridge, D. and Boddie, S.J.: Power to the people: end-user building of digital library collections. Proc Joint Conference on Digital Libraries, Roanoke, Virginia. (2001) 94–103
6. Witten, I.H., Bainbridge, D., Paynter, S. and Boddie, S.J.: The Greenstone plugin architecture. Proc Joint Conference on Digital Libraries, Portland, Oregon. (2002)
7. Yeates, S., Bainbridge, D. and Witten, I.H.: Using compression to identify acronyms in text. Proc Data Compression Conference, edited by J.A. Storer and M. Cohn. IEEE Press Los Alamitos, CA. (2000) 582

The Mellon Fedora Project

Digital Library Architecture Meets XML and Web Services

Sandra Payette[1] and Thornton Staples[2]

[1]Department of Computer Science, Cornell University
payette@cs.cornell.edu
[2] University of Virginia Library
staples@virginia.edu

Abstract. The University of Virginia received a grant of $1,000,000 from the Andrew W. Mellon Foundation to enable the Library, in collaboration with Cornell University, to build a digital object repository system based on the Flexible Extensible Digital Object and Repository Architecture (Fedora). The new system demonstrates how distributed digital library architecture can be deployed using web-based technologies, including XML and Web services. The new system is designed to be a foundation upon which interoperable web-based digital libraries can be built. Virginia and collaborating partners in the US and UK will evaluate the system using a diverse set of digital collections. The software will be made available to the public as an open-source release.

1 Introduction

In September of 2001 The University of Virginia received a grant of $1,000,000 from the Andrew W. Mellon Foundation to enable the Library, in collaboration with Cornell University, to build a sophisticated digital object repository system based on the Flexible Extensible Digital Object and Repository Architecture (Fedora) [1][2][3]. Fedora was originally developed as a research project at Cornell University, and was successfully implemented at Virginia in 2000 as a prototype system to provide management and access to a diverse set of digital collections [4].

The Mellon grant was based on the success of the Virginia prototype, and the vision of a new open-source version of Fedora that exploits the latest web technologies. Virginia and Cornell have joined forces to build this robust implementation of the Fedora architecture with a full array of management utilities necessary to support it. A deployment group, representing seven institutions in the US and the UK, will evaluate the system by applying it to testbeds of their own collections. The experiences of the deployment group will be used to fine-tune the software in later phases of the project.

The motivation for the new system specification is to create an implementation of Fedora that is highly compatible with the web environment - one that uses web stan-

M. Agosti and C. Thanos (Eds.): ECDL 2002, LNCS 2458, pp. 406-421, 2002.

dards, and is built with freely available technologies. The original Fedora research implementation was built in a distributed object paradigm using the Common Object Request Broker Architecture (CORBA). The Virginia reinterpretation proved that the model could be adapted to run as a web application, specifically using Java Servlet technology with relational database underpinnings. However, the prototype sacrificed some of the advanced interoperability features of Fedora. The new Mellon Fedora has been carefully designed to recreate a full-featured Fedora system that can become a foundation upon which interoperable web-based digital libraries can be built.

With the advent of XML and web services, a new paradigm for web-based applications is emerging. The new Mellon Fedora open-source system offers the opportunity to deploy interoperable digital libraries using mainstream web technology. The Fedora access and management systems are described using the Web Services Description Language (WSDL), as are all auxiliary services included in the architecture. The system communicates over HTTP and supports the Simple Object Access Protocol (SOAP). The project has adopted the Metadata Encoding and Transmission Standard (METS) [9] as the means to encode and store digital objects as XML entities.

This paper is a report on the status of the Mellon Fedora project. The design phase is complete and the detailed system specification is available from the project web site [10]. The alpha release of the software will be available for download by deployment partners in October 2002. We are planning a public release date of January 2003.

2 Virginia Requirements for Managing Large Digital Collections

The University of Virginia Library has been building digital collections since 1992. The Library has amassed large collections that include a variety of SGML encoded etexts, digital still images, video and audio files, and social science and geographic data sets that are being served to the public from a set of independent web sites that have very little cross-integration. By 1999 it became clear that the Library's future involved very large-scale collections in all media and content types.

Like many other libraries, Virginia initially sought a vertical vendor solution that provided a complete, self-contained package for delivering and managing all digital content needs. A number of commercial solutions were considered, including IBM's Digital Library Software system (later renamed Content Manager) and SIRSI's Hyperion digital media archive system. The investigation started with the requirement for a digital content repository with a wide variety of features, including scalability to handle hundreds of millions of digital resources, flexibility to handle the ever expanding list of digital media formats, and extensibility to facilitate the building of customizable tools and services that can interoperate with the repository. It is clear that such repository functionality must be at the core of a digital library system, providing a means of uniquely identifying each piece of digital content, as well as identifying groups of related content or collections. The remaining services and functionality of a digital library system would then be built on top of this core.

The Virginia search revealed a number of shortcomings in commercial digital library products:

- Most products are narrowly focused on specific media formats that offer good solutions for managing and delivering video or images but lack adequate tools and support for structured (e.g., XML or SGML) electronic texts or the ability to intermingle media types.
- Many products perform well at document management but offer no features for dealing with video or images.
- None of the products we examined adequately addressed the need to track and manage the array of ancillary programs and scripts that play an essential role in the delivery of that digital content.
- Many products fail to effectively deal with the complex interrelationships among digital content entities. As an example, consider an electronic text in the form of a five hundred-page book. The book consists of a single file containing all five hundred pages of text, marked up using XML. In addition to the XML file, there are also five hundred images that represent the scanned pages from the original hardcopy edition of the book. There are also twenty-five audio files that provide a recording of the book's content read aloud. To the librarian, all of these digital media are digital manifestations of the intellectual object known as the "book" and all are closely related to one another.
- Few of the products attended to the critical issue of interoperability, failing to provide an open interface to allow sharing services and content with systems from other vendors at other libraries.

In the summer of 1999, early in the design process, the Library's research and development group discovered a paper about Fedora written by Sandra Payette and Carl Lagoze of Cornell's Digital Library Research Group. Fedora was designed on the principle that interoperability and extensibility is best achieved by architecting a clean and modular separation of data, interfaces, and mechanisms (i.e., executable programs). With Cornell's help, the Virginia team installed the research software version of Fedora and began experimenting with some of Virginia's digital collections. Convinced that Fedora was exactly the framework they were seeking, the Virginia team reinterpreted the implementation and developed a prototype that used a relational database backend and a Java servlet that provided the repository access functionality. The prototype provided strong evidence that the Fedora architecture could indeed be the foundation for a practical, scalable digital library system.

3 Fedora: The Basic Architectural Model

The Fedora architecture has been discussed at length elsewhere [1][2][3]. Similar architectures have also been described including Kahn/Wilensky [5], CNRI [6], Mönch [7], and Nelson [8]. We will review the basic Fedora architectural abstractions and introduce a slightly modified vocabulary to facilitate the discussion of the UVA prototype and the new Mellon implementation.

The two fundamental entities in Fedora are the *digital object* and the *repository*. As depicted in Figure 1, a digital object has a unique persistent identifier (*PID*), one or more `disseminators`, one or more `datastreams`, and system metadata. One significant characteristic of the Fedora digital object is that it aggregates both content (i.e., data and metadata) and behaviors (i.e., services); both can be distributed and referenced via a URI. As shown in Figure 1, `datastreams` represent content and `disseminators` represent services. A Fedora repository provides both access and management services for digital objects.

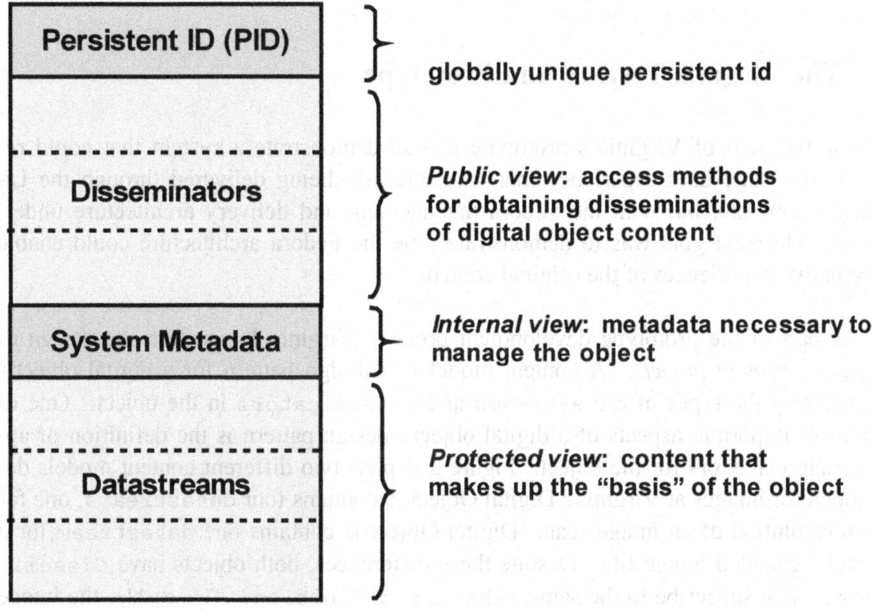

Fig. 1. Fedora Digital Object Model

From an access perspective, the architecture fulfills two basic functions: (1) it exposes both generic and extensible behaviors for digital objects (i.e., as sets of method definitions), and (2) it performs *disseminations* of content in response to a client's invoking these methods. A dissemination is defined as a stream of data that manifests a view of the digital object's content.

Disseminators are used to provide public access to digital objects in an interoperable and extensible manner. Object-specific access control policies can also be applied to disseminators [3]. Essentially, each disseminator will define a set of methods through which the object's datastreams can be accessed. For example, there are simple disseminators that define methods for obtaining different renditions of images. There are more complex disseminators that define methods for interacting with complex digital creations such as multi-media course packages (e.g., GetSyllabus, GetLectureVideo). Finally, there are disseminators that define methods for transforming content (e.g., such as translating a text between different languages). A disseminator is said to "subscribe" to a behavior definition, which is an abstract service definition consisting of a set of methods for presenting or transforming the content of a digital object. A disseminator uses a behavior mechanism, which is an external service implementation of the methods to which the disseminator subscribes. A disseminator also defines the binding relationships between a behavior mechanism and datastreams in the object. The mechanics of how disseminators enable digital objects to interface with external services will be discussed later in Section 5.

4 The Virginia Testbed and Prototype

The initial goal of Virginia's prototype was to demonstrate a system that could recreate the same user experience that was currently being delivered through the Library's web site, but with the Fedora management and delivery architecture underneath. The next goal was to demonstrate how the Fedora architecture could enable alternative experiences of the original content.

As part of the prototype development process, Virginia focused on the design of different *content models*. A content model is a design pattern for a digital object - particularly the types of datastreams and disseminators in the object. One of the most important aspects of a digital object's design pattern is the definition of appropriate behaviors for the object. Figure 2 depicts two different content models developed for images at Virginia. Digital Object A contains four datastreams, one for each resolution of an image scan. Digital Object B contains one datastream for a wavelet-encoded image file. Despite these differences, both objects have disseminators that subscribe to the same behavior definition. This enables the image objects to be accessed from one abstract point of view (i.e., via methods like GetThumbnail and GetHighResolution). The objects are also said to have *functional equivalency,* which means that clients can interact with them in an interoperable manner.

Within a year, the Virginia testbed had grown to include 500,000 objects including digital images, numeric data, and XML objects. The team developed a variety of disseminators that provide functionality for electronic finding aids, TEI-encoded e-texts (letters and books), and structured XML-encoded art and archeology image collections. Another interesting disseminator provides access to a social science dataset. This object model includes datastreams to represent an XML codebook and an SQL dataset for a group of CBS news polls, with disseminators that allow investigation of the codebook and extraction/download of the data.

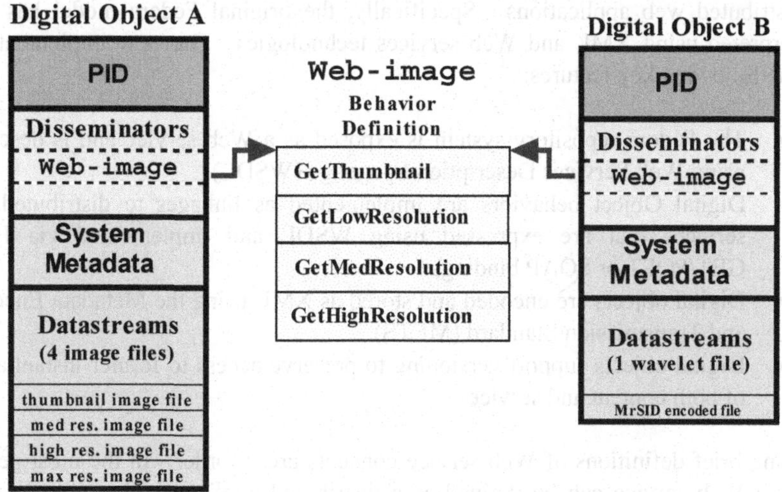

Fig. 2. Functional equivalency between digital objects

In addition to Library digital collections, the testbed included two "born-digital" projects created by humanities scholars in the Institute for Advanced Technology in the Humanities (IATH) at Virginia: the Salisbury Cathedral project and the Rossetti Archive. These two projects alone consist of approximately 6,000 digital images of art and architecture, and over 5,000 XML transcriptions of texts. The Supporting Digital Scholarship (SDS) project, jointly undertaken by the Library and IATH, focuses on collecting such projects in a Fedora repository.

The Virginia Fedora prototype was stress-tested using Apache's JMeter software [11]. Tests were conducted to simulate the load from a group of users simultaneously issuing a mixture of dissemination requests. These tests provided a simple proof of concept that the Fedora architecture can perform very efficiently in a production setting. On a Sun Ultra80 two-processor workstation, simulations of 20 simultaneous users, each making requests with an average delay of 300 milliseconds, yielded an average response time of approximately one half second per request. Note that most of the XML object transactions included a server-side rendering of XML into HTML, a relatively processor-intensive action. The repository was then moved to a four-processor, dedicated server, and the testbed was scaled up by repeatedly duplicating the existing 500,000 objects. Within a range of 1,000,000 to 10,000,000 objects, the same simulation yielded an average response time of approximately 1.5 seconds per transaction. We will use this data as the benchmark for performance in the new Mellon Fedora implementation.

5 The New Mellon Fedora: XML, Web Services, Versioning

Building on Virginia's extensive collections experience, the Virginia prototype and testbed, and the original Fedora research implementation, the Mellon Fedora team has developed an updated Fedora system specification that exemplifies a new generation of distributed web applications. Specifically, the original Fedora model has been reinterpreted using XML and Web services technologies. Our new implementation has the following key features:

- The Fedora repository system is exposed as a Web service and is described using Web Services Description Language (WSDL).
- Digital Object behaviors are implemented as linkages to distributed web services that are expressed using WSDL and implemented via HTTP GET/POST or SOAP bindings.
- Digital objects are encoded and stored as XML using the Metadata Encoding and Transmission Standard (METS).
- Digital objects support versioning to preserve access to former instantiations of both content and services.

Some brief definitions of Web service concepts are in order. In the most general sense, a Web service can be defined as a distributed application that runs over the internet. Web services are typically configured to use HTTP as a transport protocol for sending messages between different parts of the distributed application. The use of XML is a key feature of such applications, serving as a standard for encoding structured messages that are sent to and from the distributed applications. WSDL is an XML format for describing network services as a set of abstract operations that are realized as a set of *endpoints* that are able to receive and respond to structured messages [12]. Each endpoint communicates over a specific network protocol and uses a specific message format. There is currently some debate as to the preferred way to implement Web services. Some argue that messages can be exchanged in a simple manner over HTTP using GET and POST operations that return XML[13]. Others argue for the use of SOAP [14], which was originally conceived of as a way to do Remote Procedure Calls (RPC) with XML messaging. SOAP assumes no particular transport protocol, although it is common to send SOAP messages over HTTP.

The Mellon Fedora system will expose its services in both manners. An overview of the design of the new Fedora system is depicted in Figure 3. We will discuss the architecture diagram from the top down.

5.1 Fedora Web Service Exposure Layer

The new Fedora system is exposed as two related web services, the Fedora Management service (API-M) and the Fedora Access service (API-A). The service interfaces

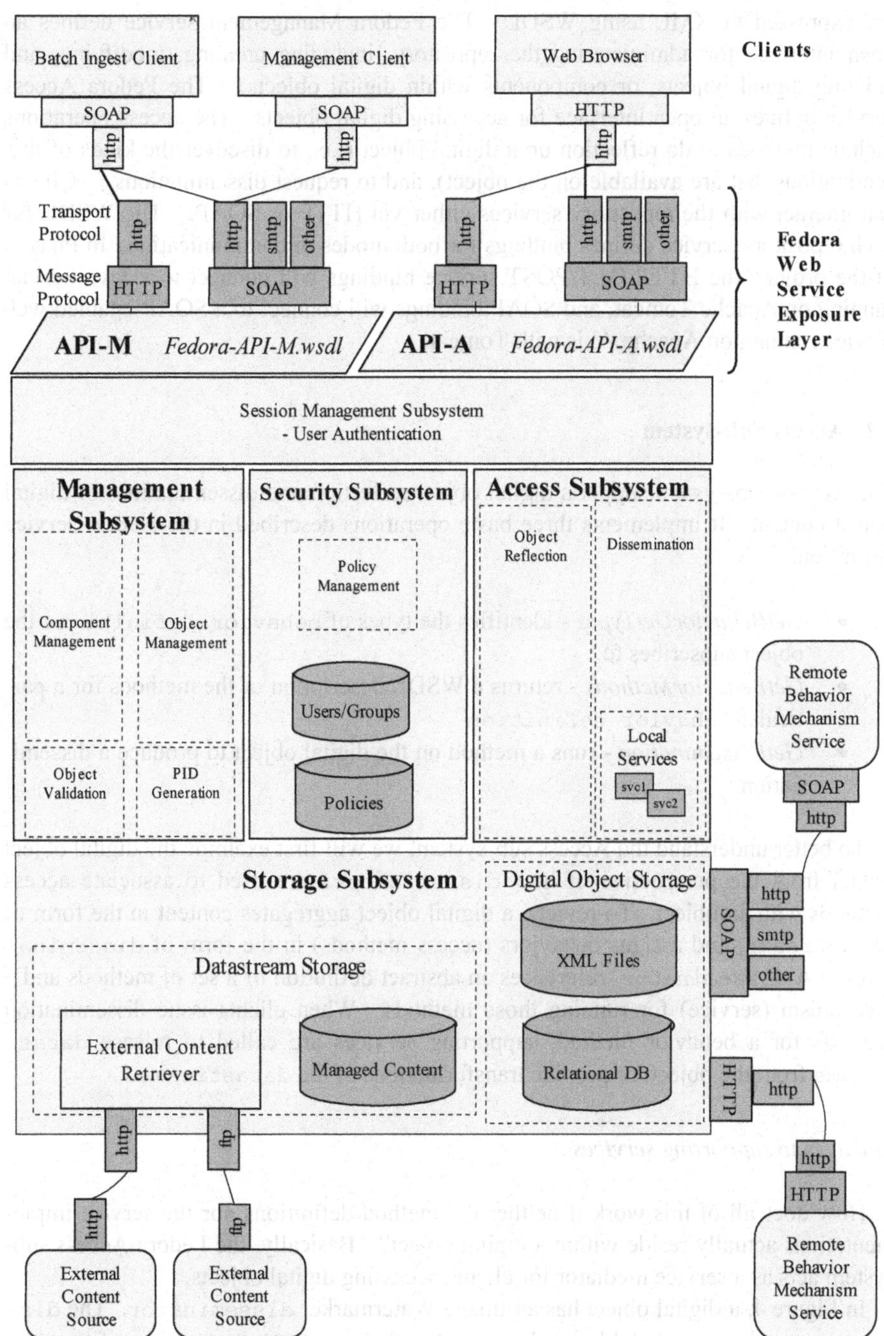

Fig. 3. Mellon Fedora System Diagram

are expressed in XML using WSDL. The Fedora Management service defines an open interface for administering the repository, including creating, modifying, and deleting digital objects, or components within digital objects. The Fedora Access service defines an open interface for accessing digital objects. The access operations include methods to do reflection on a digital object (i.e., to discover the kinds of disseminations that are available on the object), and to request disseminations. Clients can interact with the repository services either via HTTP or SOAP. The WSDL for each repository service defines bindings for both modes of communication. In Phase I of the project, the HTTP GET/POST service bindings will connect to a Java Servlet running on Apache Tomcat, and SOAP bindings will connect to a SOAP-enabled web service running on Apache Axis with Tomcat.

5.2 Access Sub-system

The Access sub-system supports digital object reflection and disseminations of digital object content. It implements three basic operations described in the Access service definition:

- *GetBehaviorDefTypes* - identifies the types of `behavior definitions` the object subscribes to.
- *GetBehaviorMethods* - returns a WSDL description of the methods for a particular `behavior definition`
- *GetDissemination* - runs a method on the digital object to produce a dissemination

To better understand the Access sub-system, we will first examine the digital object model from the perspective of how `disseminators` are used to associate access methods with an object. To review, a digital object aggregates content in the form of `datastreams`, and assigns behaviors (access methods) in the form of `disseminators`. A `disseminator` references an abstract definition of a set of methods and a mechanism (service) for running those methods. When clients issue dissemination requests for a behavior method, supporting services are called to release `datastreams` from the object, or provide transformations of the `datastreams`.

Linkages to supporting services

How does all of this work if neither the method definitions nor the service implementations actually reside within a digital object? Basically, the Fedora Access subsystem acts as a service mediator for clients accessing digital objects.

In Figure 4, a digital object has an Image Watermarker `disseminator`. The `disseminator` has two notable attributes: a `behavior definition` identifier and a `behavior mechanism` identifier. These identifiers are actually *persistent identifiers to other Fedora digital objects*. These are special digital objects that are *surrogates* for external services, for example, a service for obtaining watermarked images at different resolutions. A behavior definition object contains a special datastream whose content is a WSDL definition of abstract methods for images (e.g., GetThumbnail, GetWatermarked). A behavior mechanism object contains a special datastream that is a WSDL definition describing the run-time bindings to an external service for these methods (operations). Service bindings can be via HTTP GET/POST or SOAP.

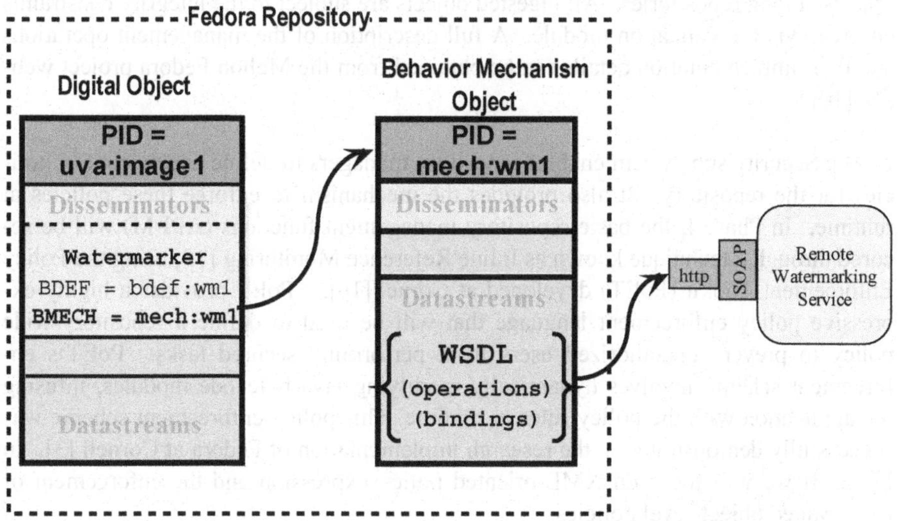

Fig. 4. Digital Object Association to External Service

Thus, a key function of the Fedora Access sub-system is to fulfill a client's request for dissemination by evaluating the behavior associations specified in a digital object, and figuring out how to dispatch a service request to an external service with which the digital object associates. The Access sub-system facilitates all external service bindings on behalf of the client, simply returning a dissemination result. Note that a client can be a web browser, a web application with embedded dissemination requests, or a custom client built to interact with Fedora.

5.3 Management and Security Sub-systems

The Management sub-system implements an array of operations for creating and maintaining digital objects. This sub-system mediates the creation and manipulation of XML-encoded digital objects, in response to service requests from clients via API-M. The component management module is responsible for maintaining version control within digital objects, as described in Section 7. The validation module ensures that each operation performed on a digital object is valid from the METS schema perspective. It also validates objects against a set of Fedora-specific integrity rules, especially referential integrity between digital objects and the behavior service entities to which they refer. A PID generation module is responsible for dispensing unique persistent identifiers for digital objects.

It should be noted that the object management module provides an ingestion function that will accept METS-encoded digital objects created outside the context of the repository system. This facilitates batch loading of digital objects and movement of objects among repositories. All ingested objects are subject to the integrity constraints enforced via the validation module. A full description of the management operations and their implementation details can be obtained from the Mellon Fedora project website [10].

The Security sub-system enables repository managers to define access control policies for the repository. It also provides the mechanism to enforce these policies at runtime. In Phase I, the basic repository management functions (API-M) will be secured through a technique known as Inline Reference Monitoring [15] using the Policy Enforcement Tookit (PoET) developed at Cornell[16]. PoET provides a highly expressive policy enforcement language that will be used to define a repository-wide policy to prevent unauthorized users from performing secured tasks. PoET's enforcement scheme involves dynamically modifying java bytecode modules, infusing the application with the policy rules at runtime. This policy enforcement scheme was successfully demonstrated in the research implementation of Fedora at Cornell [3]. In Phase, II we will focus on XML-oriented policy expression and the enforcement of fine-grained object-level policies.

5.4 Storage Sub-system

The Storage sub-system manages all aspects of reading, writing, and deleting data from the repository. Within it we find the actual data store for the XML-encoded digital objects, and the `datastreams` to which the digital objects refer.

Digital objects are stored as XML files. All digital objects conform to the METS XML schema, as described in Section 6. Digital object XML files aggregate one or more `datastreams`. `Datastreams` are of two types: those under the custodianship of the repository system (i.e., managed content) and those that are references to external content (i.e., represented as a URI to a remote content source). The Storage sub system is responsible for managing content files stored within its domain, and for interfacing with remote content sources to obtain external content at runtime. The Phase 1 implementation supports retrieval of external content via back-end HTTP and FTP; however, in later phases, other protocol gateways will be introduced. For example, we envision `datastreams` that are stored SQL queries, stored SOAP requests, and even stored dissemination requests to other Fedora digital objects.

The Phase I Storage sub-system supports a relational database as an alternate form of storage for digital objects. This is a redundant storage scheme that enables us to guarantee the performance benchmark set by the Virginia prototype. The team created a relational database schema that expresses a Fedora digital object from an access point of view. The Storage sub-system is responsible for replicating the XML-encoded digital objects into the database schema format.

The relational database is a *temporary* feature that will service disseminations while we optimize performance for querying the XML-based digital objects.

6 Encoding Digital Objects Using METS

A major goal of the new Mellon Fedora project was to define an XML schema for the Fedora digital object model. Early in the project, the team discovered the Metadata Transmission and Encoding Standard (METS), a Digital Library Federation [17] initiative focused on developing an XML format for encoding metadata necessary to manage digital library objects within a repository and to facilitate exchange of such objects among repositories. METS is expressed using the XML Schema language [18] and is freely available from the METS website [9]. The METS standard is maintained by the Network Development and MARC Standards Office of the Library of CongressFrom the Fedora perspective, the METS schema provided much of the functionality required to encode digital objects. However, the concept of associating behaviors or services with objects was not initially supported by METS. The Fedora project joined the METS specification effort, and was instrumental in effecting additions to the METS schema to support the Fedora notion of a `disseminator`. The Mellon Fedora project now uses METS as the official encoding format for digital objects stored in a Fedora repository.

All major components of a Fedora digital object can be mapped to elements defined in the METS schema. The relationships among digital object components are also easily expressed in METS. Table 1 shows the translation of the major Fedora digital object components to their equivalent METS entities. The XML samples in the METS column are abbreviated for readability.

7 Digital Object Versioning Strategy

The Mellon Fedora system supports versioning within digital objects to preserve former instantiations of content and services. Specifically, the system creates versions of `datastreams` and `disseminators` within a digital object. From a management perspective this provides a mechanism to track changes in objects over time. From an Access perspective, this enables users to view digital objects from a historical perspective.

Table 1. Mapping Fedora Digital Object to METS

Fedora	METS Encoding
Persistent Identifier	<METS:mets OBJID="***PID***" />
System Metadata	<METS:metsHdr/> <METS:amdSec/>
Datastreams	
Implementer Metadata	<METS:amdSec/> <METS:dmdSec/>
Managed Content + *External Referenced Content*	<METS:fileGrp ID="***dsID***" <METS:file ID="***dsVersionID***> <METS:Flocat LOCTYPE="URL" xlink:href="***dsLocation***"/> </METS:file> </METS:fileGrp>
Dissemina-tors	
Behavior Definition + *Service*	<METS:behaviorSec ID="***dissID***" STRUCTID="***dsMapID***"> <METS:interfaceDef xlink:href="***bdefID***"/> <METS:mechanism xlink:href="***bmechID***" /> </METS:behaviorSec>
Datastream Relationships	<METS:structMap ID="***dsMapID***"> <METS:div TYPE="***dsBindName***" ORDER="***dsSeq***"> <METS:fptr FILEID="***datastreamID***" /> </METS:div> </METS:structMap>

As previously mentioned, the Management sub-system will be responsible for the versioning task. Rather than maintaining multiple instances of digital object XML files, the system will maintain versions of `datastreams` and `disseminators` *within* a digital object. The system will also insert audit trail records describing the changes. This strategy enables individual object components to evolve at their own pace, and provides a container for the entire object history. `Datastreams` are versioned whenever a modification request is issued via the management API. The METS <fileGrp> is used to group versions of the same `datastream`. Each `datastream` version will be represented by a METS <file> element. The CREATED attribute of the <file> provides the date and time that a version was created.

Versioning to reflect changes in behavior services is a more difficult task, since it can involve versioning of `disseminators`, as well as components within `behavior definition` and `mechanism` objects. We have designed a versioning strategy to record changes such as the addition of new methods to a `behavior definition`, and the release of an upgrade to a behavior service implementation (i.e., a better mousetrap). The details of this scheme, as well as sample objects with component versioning, are found in the Mellon Fedora Technical Specification document available at the project website [10]. Again, the net effect of the digital object versioning strategy is to enable clients to obtain disseminations that reflect how a digital object looked at different points in time. To facilitate this, the Fedora Access service will support a date-time-stamped variant of the GetDissemination request.

8 Software Release Plan and Deployment Partnerships

The Phase 1 goals of the Mellon Fedora project are to publish the full system specification and to deploy the first open-source release the new Fedora software. The specification document has been published and can be accessed on the project web site. In October 2002, the team will release the alpha version of the software package for use by the deployment partners. A public release of software will be available on the project website in January 2003.

Phase 2, will entail working closely with our partners in testing and evaluating the system. Their experience will inform the development of subsequent releases of the software. The partners include: the Digital Library group at Indiana University; the Humanities Computing group at New York University; the Digital Collections and Archives Department at Tufts University; the Humanities Computing group at Kings College, London; the Oxford Digital Library group and the Refugee Studies Center, both at Oxford University; and the Motion Picture Broadcasting and Recorded Sound Division at the Library of Congress; and a library/academic computing team from Northwestern University. Although not officially part of the deployment partnership, two other Mellon-funded projects underway at the University of Virginia will provide additional test implementations of the new Fedora system. The Digital Imprint project at the University of Virginia Press plans to experiment with Fedora as a means of publishing of born-digital scholarly projects. The Library's American Studies Information Community project, one of the seven Open Archives Initiative (OAI) projects recently funded by Mellon, will integrate American Studies information harvested from OAI servers into the Library's Fedora repository.

As previously mentioned, Phase 2 will entail performance optimization, especially for XML querying. This will be an important prerequisite for phasing out the supplemental relational database storage scheme for digital objects. Security and access control will be significantly enhanced. Interoperability experiments among deployment partners will be conducted to realize the full goals of the distributed Fedora system. The final phase will concentrate on providing more sophisticated delivery of end-user experiences. This will include extending the functionality of `disseminators` by adding new services that are important for collecting scholarly projects and publications. The project team also plans to map the major functions of the Fedora system to the OAIS reference model [19] and to develop a strategy for managing the open source software over time.

9 Concluding Statement

The Fedora collaboration between University of Virginia and Cornell University has been a model for moving digital library research into a production environment that is motivated by the needs of scholars, librarians, and other information communities. The Mellon project serves as an example of how to bridge computer scientists doing digital library research and institutions that are building large digital collections. The cycle of research, reference implementation, technical transfer, prototyping, redesign, and production implementation has ensured that the Mellon Fedora project is grounded in the requirements of real collections and users.

Acknowledgements. The authors would like to give special thanks to Ross Wayland for his keen analysis and leadership. Also, we wish to acknowledge the Fedora development team members for their excellent contributions to the design and implementation of the new system. The team includes (alphabetically): Paul Charlton, Ronda Grizzle, Carl Lagoze, Bill Niebel, Tim Sigmon, Ross Wayland, Chris Wilper. We would also like to thank Jerry McDonough of NYU for his support regarding METS. Finally, we are grateful to the Andrew W. Mellon Foundation for its generous grant that has made this project possible.

References

1. Payette, Sandra and Carl Lagoze: Flexible and Extensible Digital Object and Repository Architecture. Second European Conference on Research and Advanced Technology for Digital Libraries. Lecture Notes in Computer Science, Vol. 1513. Springer-Verlag, Berlin Heidelberg New York (1998) 41-59
2. Payette, Sandra, Christophe Blanchi, Carl Lagoze, and Edward Overly: Interoperability for Digital Objects and Repositories: The Cornell/CNRI Experiments. D-Lib Magazine. (May 1999) http://www.dlib.org/dlib/may99/payette/05payette.html
3. Payette, Sandra and Carl Lagoze: Policy-Carrying, Policy-Enforcing Digital Objects. Fourth European Conference on Research and Advanced Technology for Digital Libraries. Lecture Notes in Computer Science, Vol. 1923. Springer-Verlag, Berlin Heidelberg New York (2000) 144-157
4. Staples, Thornton, and Ross Wayland: Virginia Dons Fedora: A prototype for a digital object repository. D-LIb Magazine (July 2000) http://www.dlib.org/dlib/july00/staples/07staples.html

5. Kahn, Robert and Robert Wilensky: A Framework for Distributed Digital Object Services. Corporation for National Research Initiatives. (1995) http://www.cnri.reston.va.us/k-w.html
6. Arms, William Y., Christophe Blanchi, and Edward A. Overly: An Architecture for Information in Digital Libraries. D-Lib Magazine. (February 1997) http://www.dlib.org/dlib/february97/cnri/02arms1.html
7. Mönch, Christian: INDIGO - An Approach to Intrastructures for Digital Libraries. Fourth European Conference on Research and Advanced Technology for Digital Libraries. Lecture Notes in Computer Science, Vol. 1923. Springer-Verlag, Berlin Heidelberg New York (2000)
8. Nelson, Michael L. and Kurt Maly: Buckets: Smart Objects for Digital Libraries. Communications of the ACM. 44(5) (May 2001) 60-62
9. Metadata Encoding and Transmission Standard (METS), http://www.loc.gov/standards/mets/
10. The Mellon Fedora Project, http://www.fedora.info, http://comm.nsdlib.org/projects/fedora/
11. Apache JMeter, http://jakarta.apache.org/jmeter/
12. Web Services Description Language (WSDL) 1.1, http://www.w3.org/TR/wsdl
13. Prescod, Paul:Google's Gaffe. O'Reilly XML.com. April 24, 2002 http://www.xml.com/pub/a/2002/04/24/google.html
14. Simple Object Access Protocol (SOAP), http://www.w3.org/TR/SOAP/
15. Schneider, Fred B.: Enforceable Security Policies. Computer Science Technical Report #TR98-1664. Department of Computer Science, Cornell University (1999) http://cs-tr.cs.cornell.edu:80/Dienst/UI/1.0/Display/ncstrl.cornell/TR98-1664
16. Erlingsson, Ulfar and Fred B. Schneider: IRM Enforcement of Java Stack Inspection. Computer Science Technical Report #TR2000-1786. Department of Computer Science, Cornell University (2000)
17. Digital Library Federation, http://www.diglib.org/
18. XML Schema Language, http://www.w3.org/XML/Schema
19. Open Archival Information System (OAIS), http://www.ccsds.org/RP9905/RP9905.html

Hybrid Partition Inverted Files: Experimental Validation

Wensi Xi[1], Ohm Sornil[2], Ming Luo[1], and Edward A. Fox[1]

[1]Computer Science Department, Virginia Polytechnic Institute and State University VA, 24060, U.S.A.
{xwensi, lming, fox}@vt.edu

[2]Information Systems Education Center, The National Institute of Development Administration, Bangkok 10240, Thailand
osornil@nida.nida.ac.th

Abstract. The rapid increase in content available in digital forms gives rise to large digital libraries, targeted to support millions of users and terabytes of data. Efficiently retrieving information then is a challenging task due to the size of the collection and its index. In this paper, our high performance "hybrid" partition inverted index is validated through experiments with a 100 Gbyte collection from TREC-9 and -10. The hybrid scheme combines the term and the document approaches to partitioning inverted indices across nodes of a parallel system. Experiments on a parallel system show that this organization outperforms the document and the term partitioning schemes. Our hybrid approach should support highly efficient searching for information in a large-scale digital library, implemented atop a network of computers.

1. Introduction

In a digital library, a collection is searched to identify documents that are relevant to a user's information need. Indexes help speed up the search. Building these indexes incurs time and space overhead. However, the overhead is usually amortized over a large number of searches; thus indexing is adopted in almost every system. Two major indexing techniques are inverted indices and signature files. Zobel et al. [16] conduct a comparison of inverted indices [4] and signature files [3]. They show that inverted indices are more flexible and outperform signature files for most applications.

An inverted index is a term-oriented indexing mechanism. It contains an entry for every term in the collection lexicon – a list of pointers to occurrences of that term in the collection. The entry also is known as an inverted list, and the pointers are referred to as postings. In order to handle very large collections and achieve good performance for information retrieval (IR) tasks, the index should be distributed across the nodes of a parallel (e.g., cluster) computing system.

A partitioning scheme is used to properly distribute postings of the inverted file across system nodes. Effective data partitioning across multiple nodes is crucial to the performance of an IR system since it affects the load distribution. But the data usage pattern is unpredictable [5].

M. Agosti and C. Thanos (Eds.): ECDL 2002, LNCS 2458, pp. 422-431, 2002.

1.1 Related Work

There are 2 main methods for partitioning the data: *document partitioning* and *term partitioning* [2, 5]. In document partitioning, an inverted file is decomposed into sub-files according to the physical locations of the documents. Sub-files for a batch of documents are stored together on a node. In term partitioning, an inverted file is partitioned into a disjoint set of inverted lists. All postings of a term are stored on a single node, regardless of the physical locations of the documents in which they appear.

Document partitioning allows searching to be performed locally at each node. In term partitioning, each node returns its local results to brokers that combine and compute globally consistent document scores.

Both of these schemes have been studied in various environments [5, 7, 11, 13, 14]; we discuss them further in [9, 10].

1.2 System Architecture

We have carried out studies with the VT-PetaPlex-1 system, provided by Knowledge Systems, Inc. The VT-PetaPlex-1 system consists of 100 nodes and an IR server (IBM R/S6000 system) connected through a 100BaseT network. Each node is a single PC and contains one 25 Gbyte disk and one 200MHz CPU.

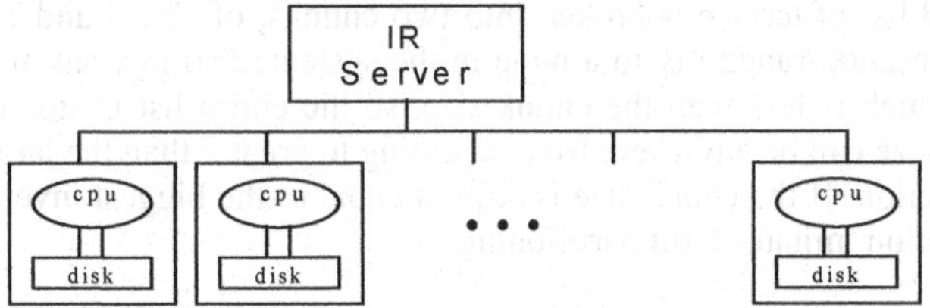

Fig. 1. Architecture of VT-PetaPlex-1 System

The inverted file is distributed across the nodes according to a partitioning scheme. When a query enters the system, the IR server extracts terms from the query and sends requests to appropriate nodes, to obtain the inverted list for every term. Each node fetches each appropriate partial list from its local disk and returns that to the server. After the IR server receives lists for every term in the query, the processing is completed from the index system standpoint. To focus our research, we deal only with returning the entire inverted lists to the IR server. Further processing, e.g., searching and ranking, can be carried out inside the IR server.

2. Partitioning Scheme

We explore three partitioning schemes, each illustrated for the data in Figure 2(a). In the term partitioning approach, the inverted list of a term, regardless of the physical location of documents it indexes, is entirely stored in one node. Figure 2(b) shows an example of this scheme. In the document partitioning approach, an inverted file is decomposed into sub-files according to physical locations of the documents. An example of this scheme is shown in Figure 2(c); the document partitioning scheme balances the load by using as many nodes as possible to process a query term. The term partitioning scheme is not trying to balance the load for a term even in highly skewed environments.

(a) Given: 4 disks (d1-d4) Collection (documents d1-4 and terms a-e) d1 <a,b,a,c,d> d3 <b,c,a,b> d2 <a,d,e,a> d4 <b>	**(b) Term Partitioning** Node1: a = (d1:1), (d1:3), (d2:1), (d2:4), (d3:3) Node2: b = (d1:2), (d1:5), (d3:1), (d3:4), (d4:1) Node3: c = (d1:4), (d3:2) Node4: d = (d2:2) e = (d2:3)
(c) Document Partitioning Node1: a=(d1:1), (d1:3),b=(d1:2),c=(d1:4),d=(d1:5) Node2: a = (d2:1), (d2:4),d = (d2:2),e = (d2:3) Node3: a = (d3:3),c = (d3:2),b = (d3:1), (d3:4) Node4: b = (d4:1)	**(d) Hybrid Partitioning** (chunk size = 4) Node1: a = [(d1:1), (d1:3), (d2:1), (d2:4)] Node2: b = [(d1:2), (d1:5), (d3:1), (d3:4)] Node3: a = (d3:3) c = (d1;4),(d3,2) Node4: b = (d4:1) d = (d2:2) e = (d2:3)

Fig. 2. Inverted Index Partitioning Schemes

In the hybrid scheme (introduced in Sornil's dissertation [9] and briefly discussed in [10]), we divide an inverted list into a number of chunks. Chunks are allocated to different nodes. They are equal in size, except for the last chunk, which can be less full. The hybrid partitioning scheme takes a moderate approach to balancing load among the nodes in the system. It is a middle-ground between the term and document approaches, hence its name "hybrid".

As shown in Figure 2(d), term *a* has 5 postings. If the chunk size is 4 postings, then the inverted list of term *a* is broken into two chunks, of size 4 and 1. Each chunk is distributed pseudo-randomly to a node in the system. Term *c*ψhas an inverted list of length 2, which is less than the chunk size, so the entire list is stored in one chunk. The chunk size can be anywhere from 1 posting to greater than the largest inverted list in the collection. If the chunk size is at least equal to the biggest inverted list size, the hybrid partition imitates term partitioning.

3. Research Methodology

In prior work, summarized in Section 3.1, we carried out initial analytical and simulation studies, starting with 2 Gbytes of text from the Text Retrieval Conference (TREC) [14] [15] collection. In Section 3.2 we describe our efforts to validate our earlier results with larger collections.

3.1 Previous Simulations

In Sornil's dissertation [9], briefly summarized in [10], we introduced the hybrid partition inverted file and demonstrated its value through simulations, implemented with YACSIM [6]. In those simulations, Sornil proposed the Hybrid Partitioning Scheme's Chunk Size Model. This model includes term-frequency distribution *Z*(*i*), query distribution q(*i*), chunk size *c*, number of query terms *T*, and number of nodes in the system *N*. The average number of chunks required from a node to retrieve an average term, *C*, is:

$$C = \frac{\left\lceil \frac{\sum_{i=1}^{V} q(i) \cdot Z(i)}{c} \right\rceil}{N}$$

where *i* is the rank of a term and V is the vocabulary size.

Using the model above, Sornil generated 200 Gbyte of pseudo-collection. The number of nodes in the simulation was 100. The chunk size was 16384 postings per chunk. Figure 3 illustrates the node utilization of the system.

Document partitioning distributes loads best, but hybrid partitioning leads to more balanced loading than term partitioning. Document partitioning leads to node utilization close to 100%, saturating the nodes, so in reality hybrid partitioning is the preferred utilization situation.

Another key parameter is multiprogramming level, which indicates the number of queries in the system at a particular time. If a system can support a higher multiprogramming level, then higher throughput can result, and it is less likely that nodes will remain idle. From Figure 4 we see that hybrid partitioning leads to the highest throughput. Term partitioning does less well, but much better than document partitioning.

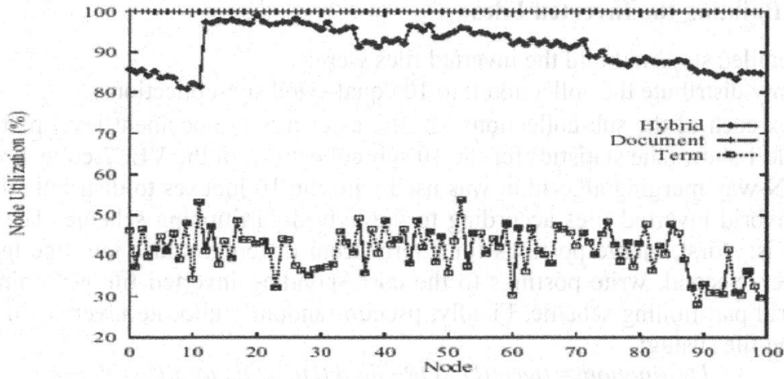

Fig. 3. Node Utilization of Previous Simulation

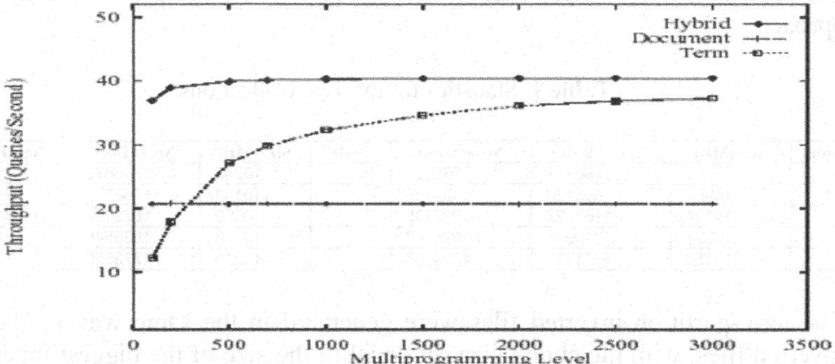

Fig. 4. Effect of Multiprogramming Levels

3.2 Collection Selection

In our current study, we make use of a real web collection: the Very Large Collection (VLC2) used by the Text Retrieval Conference (TREC) [13, 14]. The VLC2 collection is a partial snapshot of the Web of 1997. It is about 100 Gbyte in size and contains 18,571,671 web pages. It was used in TREC-9 as the standard collection for ad-hoc query retrieval tasks.

In our work, the VLC2 collection is divided into 10 roughly equal-sized sub-collections, since we are using 10 nodes to develop the hybrid partition inverted files. Each sub-collection represents the local collection of one node. Statistics regarding these 10 sub-collections are shown in Table 1.

We also chose a query collection from TREC, namely the 245 homepage-finding queries from TREC-10. These queries were originally used to search for web-site entry pages.

3.3 Building the Inverted Files

The detailed steps to build the inverted files were:

1. Evenly distribute the collection into 10 equal-sized sub-collections.
2. Index each of the sub-collections locally, as occurs in document level partitioning. Table 1 shows the statistics for the 10 sub-collections of the VLC2 collection.
3. An N-way merging algorithm was used with the 10 indexes to distribute them into 10 hybrid inverted files according to the hybrid partitioning scheme. The detailed step is: First, merge postings for a term from different nodes into one temporary buffer. Second, write postings to the corresponding inverted file according to the hybrid partitioning scheme. Finally, pseudo-randomly allocate inverted file chunks to the files using:

   Destination = (termID XOR chunkID) MOD totalDiskNodes

   where termID and chunkID are integers. The chunk sizes selected were 1024, 16384, and 102400 postings per chunk. Figure 5 illustrates the procedure used to generate the hybrid inverted files. In the future we may use a better randomization approach.

Table 1. Statistics for the Test Collections

Node	Size (MB)	No. of Docs	No. of terms	Node	Size (MB)	No. of Docs	No. of terms
0	10140	1788015	3165639	5	10242	1706812	3580158
1	10224	1803126	4320497	6	10153	1760376	3998057
2	10194	1767227	3847435	7	10099	1672666	4490571
3	10238	1710956	4126778	8	10178	1838545	3874397
4	10150	1671738	4000053	9	10220	1773990	3710154

4. The term-partition inverted files were generated in the same way as the hybrid inverted files, with the chunk size set equal to the size of the biggest inverted list. The inverted files were generated using a Linux box with twin 850Mhz CPUs, 1G Byte RAM, and 300G of hard disk. The indexing procedure took about 20 hours.

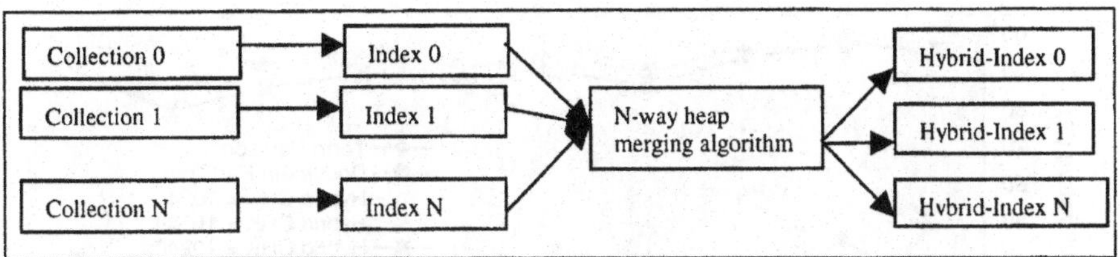

Fig. 5. Procedure for Generating the Hybrid Inverted Files

4. Results and Analysis

With the collections discussed above, we sought to validate our earlier simulation results. As is shown in the next subsections, we focused on two crucial measures of the performance of a parallel IR system: the degree to which loads are distributed across the nodes, and the throughput achieved when increasing numbers of simultaneous queries are processed.

4.1 Load Balancing Analysis

Load balancing is a crucial characteristic for parallel inverted indices. We use node utilization to measure the degree of load balancing in this research. Node utilization is defined as the total amount of time the node is serving requests from the IR server, divided by the total amount of time of the entire experiment. The node utilization graphics shown below illustrate how well the postings for the query terms are distributed across the nodes in the system. Figures 6 and 7 illustrate the node utilization for each of the 10 nodes in the system; small fluctuation in node utilization among nodes indicates good load balancing. From the figures below, we see that document partitioning achieves better load balancing than does term partitioning. Hybrid partitioning achieves better load balancing than does document partitioning. The only exception is that hybrid partitioning with chunk size = 102400 postings is worse than the document partitioning. This is because the chunk size is too big to allow the hybrid partitioning scheme to be effective. From the figures below, we also see that for the hybrid partitioning scheme with different chunk sizes, the smaller the chunk size the better the load balancing. Statistical information for the load balancing analysis can be found in Table 2.

Table 2. Statistics for Load Balancing Analysis

Partition Scheme	Mean Time Spend (s)	STDDEV for Time Spend	Mean Node Utilization (%)	STDDEV for Node Utilization
CHK=1024	2387.45	1.516360775	99.726	0.063340049
CHK=16384	2387.46	19.66503228	98.168	0.808595077
Document Partition	2414.48	81.5619464	95.02	3.209836537
CHK=10240	2385.41	130.2441937	90.083	4.918587376
Term Partition	2385.99	972.6108187	29.319	11.95147234

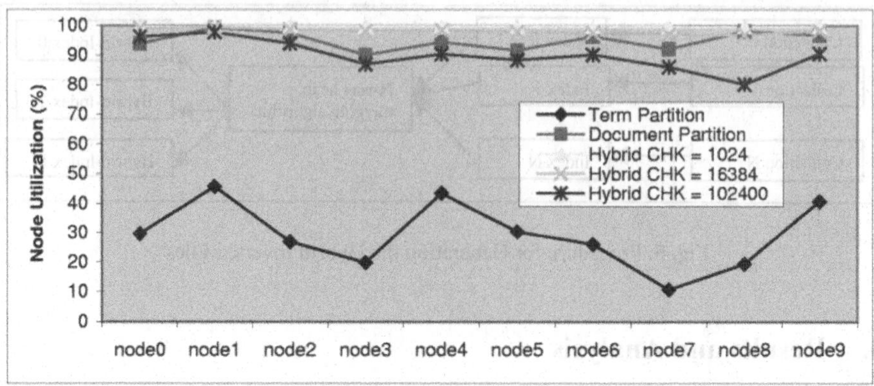

Fig. 6. Node Utilization

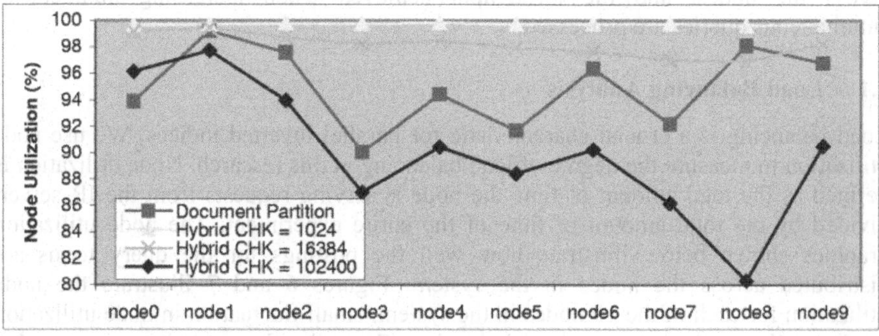

Fig. 7. Node Utilization (without term partitioning)

4.2 Multiprogramming Analysis

With multiprogramming, multiple queries can be processed concurrently. The multiprogramming level indicates the number of queries in the system at a particular time. Multiprogramming increases the throughput of the system by utilizing nodes better. In this research, we only use 200 queries to perform the multiprogramming analysis. The multiprogramming levels we experimented with are 10, 20, 50, 100, and 200. Figures 8 and 9 illustrate the effect of multiprogramming levels.

The figures below confirm our previous simulation results that the hybrid partitioning performs better than the other two schemes and the throughput of term partitioning tends to approach that achieved by the hybrid partitioning scheme at high multiprogramming level. We also note that for the hybrid partitioning schemes, the smaller the chunk size, the better the performance.

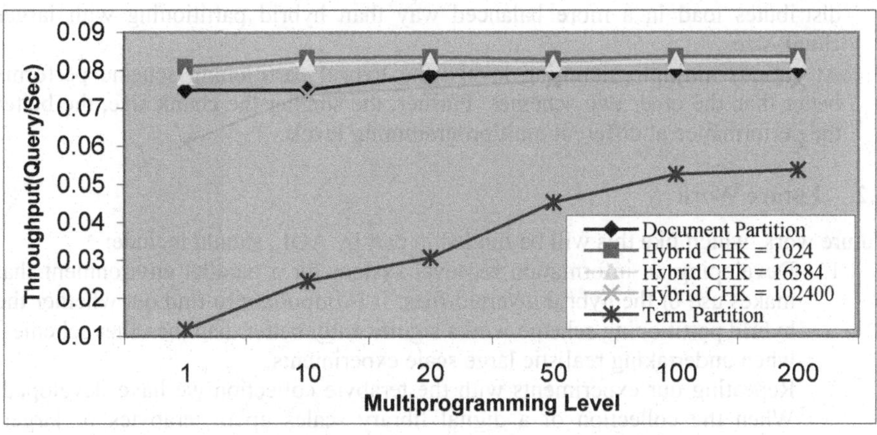

Fig. 8. Effect of Multiprogramming Levels

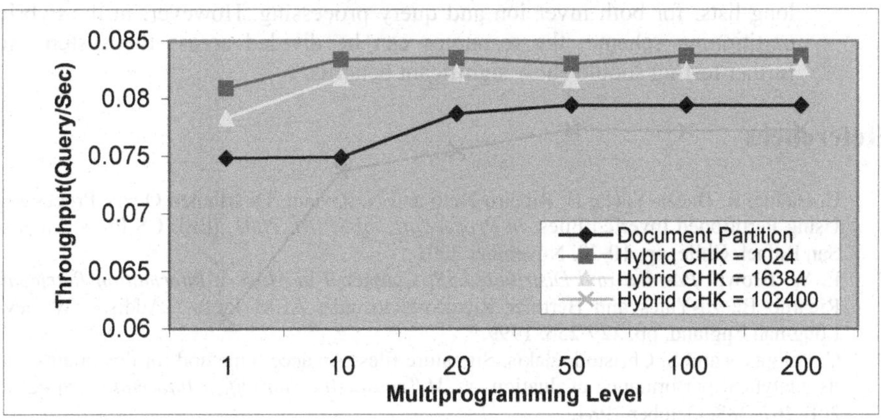

Fig. 9. Effect of Multiprogramming Levels (without term partitioning)

5. Conclusion and Future Work

5.1 Conclusion

In this paper, we explain and validate the hybrid inverted index partitioning scheme which combines the document and term approaches to partitioning inverted indexes. The new hybrid decomposition scheme is suitable for very large digital library collections. The VLC2 100 Gbyte collection was used to generate hybrid partition inverted files based on 10 nodes. We compared the experimental results using these collections with results from our previous simulations. Our earlier results were validated for the cases tested. Particular findings include:

1. Hybrid partitioning distributes load in a more balanced way than document partitioning or term partitioning. Hybrid partitioning, with smaller chunk sizes,

distributes load in a more balanced way than hybrid partitioning with larger chunk size.

2. At various multiprogramming levels, the hybrid partitioning scheme performs better than the other two schemes. Further, the smaller the chunk size, the better the performance at different multiprogramming levels.

5.2 Future Work

Future work, which like this will be funded in part by AOL, should include:

1. Developing an information retrieval system for a parallel environment that makes use of the hybrid inverted files. It is important to find out whether the hybrid partitioning scheme works significantly better than the other schemes, when undertaking realistic large scale experiments.
2. Repeating our experiments with the terabyte collection we have developed. When the collection of a digital library scales up to terabytes or larger, storing a very long list completely in one node may not be efficient. A large amount of storage and computation is required at the nodes containing very long lists, for both inversion and query processing. However, in the hybrid partitioning scheme, the resources can be divided across the system, so further testing should show significant benefits.

References

1. C. Badue, R. Baeza-Yates, B. Ribeiro-Neto and N. Ziviani. Distributed Query Processing Using Partitioned Inverted Files. *In Proceedings of SPIRE 2001*, IEEE CS Press, Laguna San Rafael, Chile, pp. 10-20, November 2001.
2. E. W. Brown. *Parallel and Distributed IR,* Chapter 9 in *Modern Information Retrieval,* Ricardo Baeza-Yates and Berthier Ribeiro-Neto, eds, ACM Press / Addison Wesley-Longman England, pp. 229-256, 1999.
3. C. Faloutsos and S. Christodoulakis. Signature files: An access method for documents and its analytical performance evaluation. *ACM Transactions on Office Information Systems,* 2(4):267–288, October 1984.
4. D. Harman, E. Fox, R. Baeza-Yates, and W. Lee. *Inverted Files*, Chapter 2.1 In *Information Retrieval: Data Structures & Algorithms*, editors W. Frakes & R. Baeza-Yates, Prentice-Hall, pp. 28-43, 1992.
5. B.-S. Jeong and E. Omiecinski. Inverted file partitioning schemes in multiple disk systems. *IEEE Transactions on Parallel and Distributed Systems,* 6(2): 142–153, 1995.
6. J. R. Jump. YACSIM: *Reference Manual*. Rice University, version 2.1 edition, March 1993.
7. B. A. Ribeiro-Neto and R. A. Barbosa. Query performance for tightly coupled distributed digital libraries. In *Proceedings of the 3rd ACM Conference on Digita Libraries,* pp. 182–190, 1998.
8. B. A. Ribeiro-Neto, E. S. Moura, M. S. Neubert, and N. Ziviani. Efficient distributed algorithms to build inverted files. In *Proceedings of ACM SIGIR'99,* pp. 105–112, 1999.
9. Ohm Sornil. Parallel Inverted Index for Large-Scale, Dynamic Digital Libraries. Ph. D. Dissertation, Virginia Tech Dept. of Computer Science, 2001.
10. Ohm Sornil and Edward A. Fox. Hybrid Partitioned Inverted Indices for Large-Scale Digital Libraries. In *Proceedings of the 4th International Conference on Asian Digital Libraries, ICADL 2001*, Bangalore, India, Dec. 10-12, 2001
11. A. S. Tomasic. *Distributed Queries and Incremental Updates in Information Retrieval Systems.* Ph.D. thesis, Princeton University, June 1994.

12. A. S. Tomasic and H. Garcia-Molina. Caching and database scaling in distributed shared-nothing information retrieval systems. In *Proceedings of SIGMOD'93*, Washington, D.C., May 1993.
13. A. S. Tomasic and H. Garcia-Molina. Performance of inverted indices in shared-nothing distributed text document information retrieval systems. In *Proceedings of PDIS'93,* 1993.
14. E. M. Voorhees and D. K. Harman. NIST special publication: *The 9th Text REtrieval Conference (TREC-9),* November 2000.
15. E. M. Voorhees and D. K. Harman. NIST special publication: *The 10th Text REtrieval Conference (TREC-10),* November 2001.
16. J. Zobel, A. Moat, and K. Ramamohanarao. Inverted files versus signature files for text indexing. *ACM Transactions on Database Systems*, 23(4):453–490, December 1998.

Digital Library Evaluation by Analysis of User Retrieval Patterns

Johan Bollen, Somasekhar Vemulapalli, and Weining Xu

Computer Science Department,
Old Dominion University,
Norfolk VA
{jbollen,svemulap,wxu}@cs.odu.edu

Abstract. We propose a methodology to evaluate the impact of a Digital Library's (DL) collection and the characteristics of its user community by an analysis of user retrieval patterns. Patterns of journal and document co-retrievals are reconstructed from DL server logs and used to generate proximity data for journals and documents, resulting in a weighted relation defined over the DL document collection represented by a network of document and journals. A measure of discrepancy between user-defined measures of document impact and the Journal Citation Record (JCR) Impact Factor (IF) published by the Institute for Scientific Information (ISI) is used to analyze characteristics of the DL user community. A preliminary analysis of the Los Alamos National Laboratory (LANL) Research Library (RL) server logs registered in 2001 demonstrates the potential of this approach.

1 Introduction

The recent growth in the number and size of Digital Library applications has introduced the issue of evaluating DL services and collections [10]. Given the proliferation of new services such as the integration of collections [19], information linking, advanced DL recommendation systems [3,18], it has become increasingly important to determine whether these services indeed match user preferences and characteristics, and consequently what these preferences are. A similar issue related to the evaluation of DL collection is whether a given DL collection matches the characteristics and preferences of its user community. In this case as well, it has become important to analyze the unique preferences of a given user community.

Some attempts have been made to evaluate DL services and collections by the use of citation analysis and citation frequency. Traditionally, the impact of a given journal is assessed by counting the number of citations to articles appearing in the journal over a given period. This number is normalized by dividing this count by the number of citable articles that appeared in the journal during the same period [8]. The Institute for Scientific Information (ISI) publishes the

M. Agosti and C. Thanos (Eds.): ECDL 2002, LNCS 2458, pp. 432–447, 2002.

Impact Factor (IF) for a given journal for a given year x which is determined as the ratio between two quantities A and B as follows.

$$IF = \frac{A}{B} \tag{1}$$

where
A = number of citations to journal during last 2 years preceding x
B = number of articles that appeared in journal during last 2 years preceding x

ISI publishes a yearly database containing the determined Impact Factors for a large number of journals. These impact factors have, by lack of other data sets, become the de facto standard by which to judge the impact of a given journal and have found use in the evaluation of the quality of individual researchers and entire research departments by proxy of the impact of the journals they have published in. They have become an integral part of the evaluation of scholarly publications and research, and may thus be applied to the evaluation of DL services and collections.

However, we can identify at least the following problems with this approach:

1. The extent to which citation frequencies and the IF actually indicate impact or usefulness has not been equivocally established [11,13,14,17]
2. Citation records apply only to scholarly publications and do not reflect the impact of technical reports, digital publications, multimedia documents, etc.
3. Citations are universally defined and can not be adapted to the preferences of a specific DL user community.

Our approach to the analysis of the characteristics of specific user communities is founded on the use of user document retrieval requests in DL's WWW interfaces. We generate document and journal networks from user retrieval sequences as they can be reconstructed from DL WWW server logs. These networks are held to express a collective "mental map" of the preferred relations among documents and journals as they exist among a specific community of DL users, namely those for which the DL server logs have been registered.

Our central assumption is that when users retrieve a sequence of digitalized documents in temporal proximity, an event referred to as co-retrieval, they thereby implicitly indicate a certain degree of similarity between the retrieved document. The strength of relation between the retrieved articles, and journals in which they appeared, corresponds to the frequency of their co-retrieval. A set of weighted document and journal relations is thereby determined from user co-retrieval frequencies. The generated document and journal relations can then be combined to form document and journal networks. An analysis of these networks will yield measures of journal impact for a specific user community which can be used to evaluate the characteristics of this community as well aid in evaluating the extent to which the DL has responded and catered to these interests.

2 The Derivation of Journal and Document Relations from DL Server Logs

The proposed methodology to derive large document networks from user co-retrieval patterns was first developed for adaptive hypertext linking and has been modified for applications to DL document linking and DL evaluation [3]. It has in this context recently been tested on the server logs of the Los Alamos National Laboratory [1]. In both simulations and the mentioned applications, the methodology has been shown to reliably and validly generate document networks that represent the collective preferences of a specific user community, namely those whose recorded retrieval patterns have been used to generate the network. These results will be briefly discussed in section 4.

2.1 Reconstruction of Co-retrieval Events from DL Web Server Logs

Most DL services record user document retrieval requests, in fact it is one of the most underutilized resources in DL research. Specifically, DL services accessible by a WWW interface generally register user retrieval requests for documents in their WWW server logs. These logs generally do not contain co-retrieval data, but this information can be derived from data such as the originating IP number, a document identification (in many DLs this includes the publishing journal's ISSN number) and a date and time on which the retrieval request was issued.

We define a document co-retrieval event as a pair of any two retrieval requests by the same user within a given period of time labeled Δ_t. From that definition, co-retrieval events can be reconstructed from DL server logs by simply scanning time sorted document retrieval requests issued from the same IP number, and determining that any two subsequent requests whose date and time stamps differ less than the quantity Δ_t constitute a co-retrieval event.

An example of this procedure is shown in tables 1 and 2. Table 1 lists a sequence of user retrieval requests for document as they were registered in June to October 2001 for the Los Alamos National Laboratory Science Server DL service. In this case, Δ_t, the defined threshold to decide whether any two subsequent requests constitute a co-retrieval event, has been set to 3600 seconds. These sequences of retrieval requests were transformed to the set of co-retrieval events shown in table 2.

This approach to the construction of co-retrieval events is highly similar to the TimeOut-IP method discussed by [15] who discuss the benefits and short-comings of deriving retrieval paths from WWW server logs in this manner. It is known to be particularly difficult to derive adequate usage data from WWW server logs [16]. However, the objective is not to perfectly accurately reconstruct

Table 1. An example of the transformed Science Server log used to reconstruct journal and document co-retrieval events.

userID	data/time	Document ID	Service
100	24/Aug/2001:17:12:52	02721716;14;4;69_ddacfrtip	SciServer
100	24/Aug/2001:17:14:41	01689274;25;4;499_prtuauma	SciServer
100	24/Aug/2001:17:15:43	00978493;19;2;281_apiaaaortars	SciServer
101	18/Jun/2001:12:03:04	00207225;38;3;347_otfrim	SciServer
101	18/Jun/2001:12:04:40	02780062;19;3;211_aotdfmfct	SciServer
101	18/Jun/2001:13:13:40	08956111;25;2;113_asrgt3tr	SciServer

Table 2. Co-retrieval events derived from set of user retrieval requests in table 1.

100	(0272-1716, 0168-9274) (0168-9274, 0097-8493)
101	(0020-7225, 0278-0062) (0278-0062, 0895-6111)

user retrieval paths, but reconstruct sufficient pairs of co-retrieved documents or journals for a valid estimate of the strength of their mutual relation.

2.2 Generation Document Relations from Co-retrieval Patterns

The set of reconstructed co-retrieval events can then be used to generate document or journal networks by a methodology that relates strongly to one previously developed by [2] to implement adaptive hypertext linking based on user hyperlink traversal frequencies [4,6].

Our document and journals networks are represented by a directed, weighed graph which implies that the defined relations are similar to those found in citation graphs: they represent a directional relation existing between an entire document and another, and the existence of a link between document b and document a does not follow from the existence of a link between document a and document b. As an exception to citation relations, links are associated with a weight value which expresses the strength or the validity of the link, and they are derived from user co-retrieval patterns rather than citation frequencies.

We thus represent a journal network[1] as the directed weighted graph as $G = (V, E, W)$ where the set of n journals is denoted $V = \{v_0, v_1, \ldots, v_n\}$ and E represents the edges between pairs of journals; $E \subseteq V^2$. A weight function is defined over all pairs of journals $(v_i, v_j) \in E$ so that $W : E \rightarrow \mathcal{R}_0^+$. The weight values in graph G are represented as the $n \times n$ matrix M whose entries m_{ij} correspond to $W(v_i, v_j)$. Next we denote the set of co-retrieval events derived from a given web logs as $E = \{e_1, e_2, \cdots, e_k\}$. Each co-retrieval event e_i is

[1] This representation is also suitable for document networks generated from document co-retrieval data, however for brevity we will only make reference to journals.

represented by the triplet $e_i = (v_i, v_j, t(v_i, v_j))$ where $t(v_i, v_j)$ represents the time in seconds elapsed between the retrieval requests for document v_i and v_j, and $t(v_i, v_j) < \Delta_t$. Each co-retrieval for the documents v_i and v_j corresponds to a small increase of journal relation strength, r, which is added to m_{ij} and defined as $r = f(e_i)$. $f(e_i)$ is referred to as the reinforcement function and can be varied according to the nature of dataset on which the algorithm is operating.

For all applications discussed in this article, we will define $f(e_i) = 1$ which means m_{ij} will correspond exactly to the frequency with which a given co-retrieval will occur over the retrieval requests of a set of users as registered in a DL's WWW server log.

We can then formalize the algorithm to produce the weight values for matrix M as follows.

$\forall_{ij} m_{ij} = 0$
for (i=1; i<n+1; i++){
  $e_i = (v_i, v_j, t(v_i, v_j))$: $m_{ij} += f(e_i)$
}

Every co-retrieval $c_i = (v_i, v_j, t(v_i, v_j))$ corresponds to a small reinforcement value r added to the matrix entry m_{ij} which represent the strength of the relation between the journals v_i and v_j. In this sense, the set of all overlapping "trails" of user retrieval sequences, or co-retrievals, gradually generates a journal network that can be held to represent the overlapping preferences of individuals in the user community for which the set of co-retrievals has been generated.

3 Analysis of Journal Networks

The generated matrices are assumed to represent the implicit preferences of a user community as they were expressed in their document or journal retrieval patterns. From the generated networks we can construct measures of journal impact as well as measures of how the structure of journal relations points to shift and changes in user preferences and the composition and structure of the user community itself. The results of such analysis is of much use to the evaluation of DL services, the evaluation of research and publications, analysis of scientometric evolution in the general scientific community [5] and as a tool for DL management to inform policy decisions.

3.1 Journal Consultation Frequency

The definition of $f(e_i)$ in this proposal is a simple one, namely $f(e_i) = 1$. Therefore each value m_{ij} corresponds exactly to the frequency by which v_i and v_j were involved in a co-retrieval event. The frequency by which an article in the journal v_i has been requested, $F(v_i)$, is thus defined in equation 2. We will refer to F as the Journal Consultation Frequency (JCF).

$$F(v_i) = \sum_{j=1}^{n} m_{ij} + \sum_{j=1}^{n} m_{ji} \tag{2}$$

Clearly this frequency will indicate the extent with which a given journal has been consulted over a specific DL WWW server log sample, and therefore it represents a measure of journal impact among readers defined independently from citation frequencies. Since the JCF has been defined independent from citation relations, it is not limited to scholarly publications, it reflects the preferences of users rather than authors and it can be adapted to specific user communities.

3.2 Impact Factor Discrepancy Ratio

Journal usage frequency confounds two distinct factors:

1. Journal relevance or impact to a specific user community.
2. General impact or relevance of a journal to the larger scientific community.

For example, the journal Science may have a high frequency of usage at the Los Alamos National Laboratory, but this is true for any scientific community given the generally high impact of this journal. The detection of a high frequency of usage for this journal therefore does not indicate a specific feature of the LANL user community, but confounds general journal impact and impact specific to the LANL user community.

Given that general journal impact is expressed by the ISI IF (it is based on the citation frequencies of researchers who are not confined to a specific community), the JCF values determined for a specific community can differ from the established IF values for the same set of journals. We assume these differences or discrepancies to be most significant for journals that best correspond to the specific characteristics of this community. In other words, the set of journals most frequently used by the LANL user community in spite of their IF rating may be the set of journals most indicative of the nature of the LANL RL user community. To determine the journals whose JCF deviates most from the IF we define the Impact Factor Discrepancy Ratio (IFDR), $r_f(v_i)$, for a journal v_i as the ratio between the JCF and the ISI IF as shown in equation 3.

$$r_f(i) = \frac{JCF(i)}{IF(i)} \tag{3}$$

The journals with highest IFDR values are those for which the highest discrepancy between the IF and the JCF exists, and are therefore assumed to be the journals most characteristic of a given user community.

4 A Test Case for the Los Alamos National Laboratory Research Library

The Los Alamos National Laboratory (LANL) Research Library (RL) was used as a test-bed for the proposed methodology. A large portion of the RL catalog is available in digital format and readers can download most journal articles to their desktops from the RL's web site. We have focused specifically on users of the LANL RL SciSearch service because its server kept the most complete records of user article retrieval requests. The set of registered logs has however for 2001 been expanded to all LANL RL services.

The Los Alamos National Laboratory SciSearch database is based on the Science Citation Index, a product of the Institute of Scientific Information that provides indexing, citation and meta-data for articles published in the large number of scientific domains such as e.g. astronomy, biology, physics, computer science, engineering, etc. The LANL Research Library has subscriptions to a large number of publisher databases containing digital copies of the documents bibliographically indexed in the SciSearch database. SciSearch users can thereby not only search and retrieve an article's bibliographic information, but can also download the actual article from any of these subscribed databases so that they can be read or printed from the users' own desktops. The database contains over 17,000,000 records at present and is updated on a weekly basis.

4.1 User Interaction

Fig.1 shows the Los Alamos National Library's web page offering access to the SciSearch database. A number of text fields allow the user to search on several kinds of bibliographic information such as "author name", "title", "publication year", "ISSN", etc.

When a search request is issued, the SciSearch database returns a list containing the abbreviated meta-data for all matching articles and links to the electronic versions of those articles. The abbreviated meta-data is hyperlinked to a consequent information page that offers more extended meta-data for the selected article, accompanied by another hyperlink pointing to the digital version of that article. The user can download a given article by selecting the hyperlink pointing to the digital version of the article. A new browser window will open and the PDF file containing the article will be downloaded and displayed (fig. 1).

4.2 Co-retrieval Event Reconstruction from Science Server Retrieval Logs

All user requests to download the digital version of an article are recorded and stored in the LANL RL server logs in the sequence in which they occurred. The server logs register a request's originating IP number, date and time of the

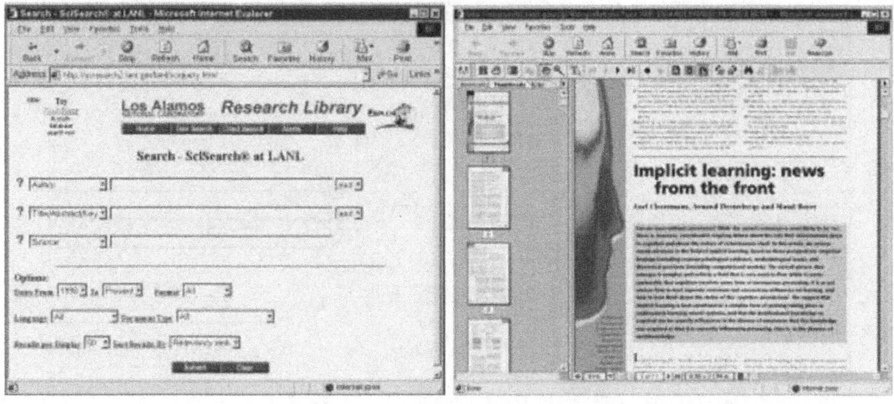

Fig. 1. The Los Alamos National Laboratory SciSearch database WWW article search service page (left) and PDF file displayed (right) after user article retrieval request.

request, an identification of the down-loaded article (including ISSN number) and an identification of the service for which the server logs has been registered[2]. One set of server logs recorded in 2001 for retrieval requests from the LANL Science Server services was selected for further analysis. These web logs had registered 40,847 retrieval requests for 20,720 unique documents published in a total of 1829 unique journals, issued by 1,858 unique users.
The selected logs were transformed by replacing all user names or IPs by a unique, numerical identifier for privacy considerations and sorting the log file according to user and date/time of the request. The latter would cluster all retrieval requests according to user ID, and data and time of the request. A small Java application would scan all sorted requests and generate a set of co-retrieval events. In this case Δ_t was, lacking information on the typical time delay between subsequent requests, chosen to be 3600s.

This procedure is computationally very undemanding and was completed in less than 20s on a computer equipped with a Pentium IV 1.6Ghz and 128mb RAM. A Java application was implemented for the automated analysis of large DL server logs. The application can at present read any DL server logs which contains at least a data and time stamp, user ID and document ID for every user request. Document and journal matrices can be generated according to a number of different learning methods, and saved in a variety of formats. The application allows the user to examine the generated document and journal matrices by the use of a dynamic graph visualization. We expect to develop this application as a generally available tool for the analysis of DL server logs. A screenshot of the application is show in figure 2.

[2] The objective of this item is future disambiguation of server logs registered for different services

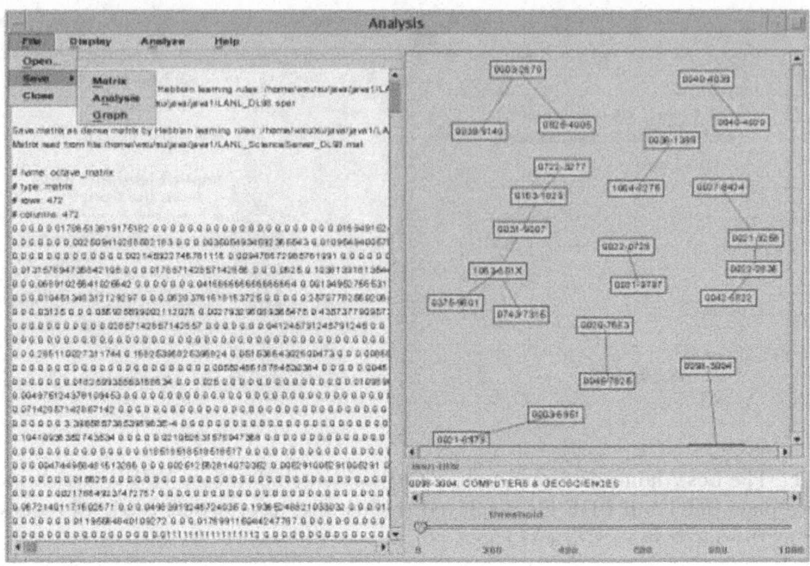

Fig. 2. Java application developed to generate document and journal matrices from DL server logs.

4.3 Journal Matrix Generation

The generated set of document co-retrieval events was subsequently used to generate a journal relation network. Although the above described methodology could be applied to the generation of a document relation network, we chose to generate a journal network for a first prototype since the number of documents (20,720) greatly exceeded the number of journals (1829). We found the latter number would produce more manageable data sets for a first prototype. Nevertheless, the described methodology could in principle efficiently be applied to the generation of document networks or any set of items for which co-retrieval events can be reconstructed from DL server logs.

A network of journal relations was generated for all 1829 journals according to the algorithm described in 1, and represented by a 1829 $\times$ 1829 matrix M. A sample of the resulting matrix is shown in table 3 for the 15 most frequent journals occurring in the SciServer logs. A visual representation of the generated journal network is shown in figure 3.

The generated matrix was a highly sparse matrix (density 0.176%), indicating user retrieval behavior focused on a limited number of journals, or that only a limited set of journals share meaningful relations. The distribution of values in matrix M_t indicated the same: the mean of link weights was found to be 1.196 with a standard deviation of 0.821 for all $m_{ij} : m_{ij} > 0$. The minimum and

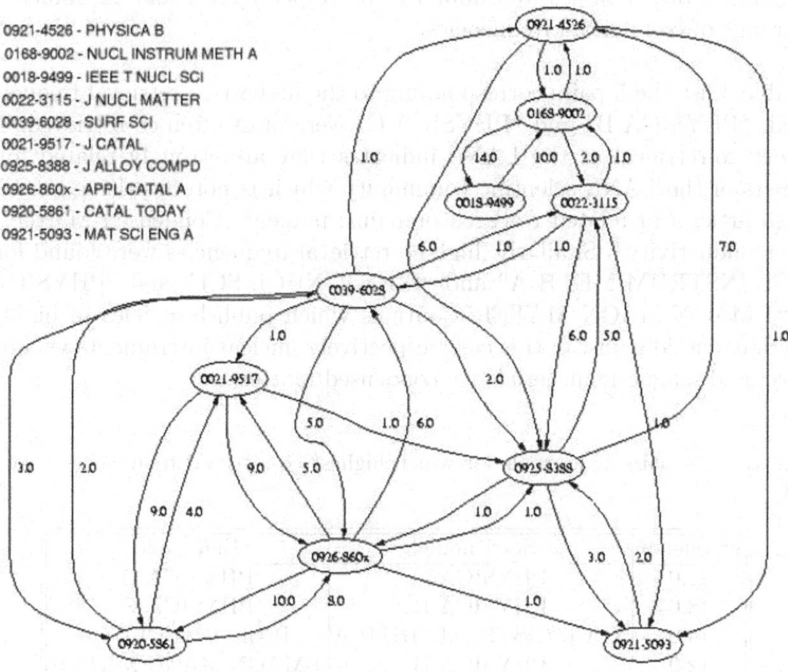

Fig. 3. Graph displaying generated connections between ten most frequently consulted journals

Table 3. Sample of generated journal relations matrix for 15 journals associated with highest JCF scores.

Journal Title	Index	01	02	03	04	05	06	07	08	09	10	11	12	13	14	15
PHYSICA B	01	0	1	0	1	6	0	0	0	0	0	0	18	0	1	1
NUCL INSTRUM METH A	02	1	0	0	0	0	14	0	0	0	2	0	0	0	0	2
APPL CATAL A-GEN	03	0	0	0	1	1	0	10	5	6	0	4	0	0	0	0
MAT SCI ENG A-STRUCT	04	0	0	0	0	2	0	0	0	0	0	0	0	6	0	0
J ALLOY COMPD	05	7	0	1	3	0	0	0	0	0	5	2	1	0	0	1
IEEE T NUCL SCI	06	0	10	0	0	0	0	0	0	0	0	0	0	0	1	1
CATAL TODAY	07	0	0	8	0	0	0	0	4	2	0	0	0	0	0	0
J CATAL	08	0	0	9	0	1	0	9	0	0	0	3	0	0	0	0
SURF SCI	09	1	0	5	0	2	0	3	1	0	1	1	0	0	0	0
J NUCL MATER	10	0	1	0	1	6	0	0	0	1	0	0	0	1	0	1
APPL SURF SCI	11	1	1	1	0	1	0	0	0	6	0	0	0	0	0	0
PHYSICA C	12	22	0	0	0	0	0	0	0	0	0	0	0	0	0	0
ACTA MATER	13	0	0	0	10	0	0	0	0	0	1	1	0	0	0	0
J COMPUT PHYS	14	0	0	0	0	0	0	0	0	0	0	0	0	0	0	0
J RADIOANAL NUCL CH	15	0	3	0	0	1	0	0	0	0	1	1	0	0	0	0

maximum recorded values were found to be respectively 1 and 22, indicating a wide range of co-retrieval frequencies.

Table 4 list the 5 pairs corresponding to the highest co-retrieval frequencies. Indeed, "PHYSICA B" and "PHYSICA C" were most often co-retrieved. Their frequent co-retrieval at the LANL indicates they are strongly related for the members of the LANL scientific community which is not surprising since they publish articles in related research domains, namely "Condensed Matter" and "Superconductivity". Similarly, high co-retrieval frequencies were found for the "NUCL INSTRUM METH A" and "IEEE T NUCL SCI", and "PHYSICA B" and "J MAGN MAGN MATER" journals which publish articles in highly related research domains, in this case respectively nuclear instruments vs. nuclear science, and magnetic materials vs. condensed matter.

Table 4. Five pairs of journals for which highest co-retrieval frequencies have been found.

Frequency	Start node	End Node
22.0	PHYSICA C	PHYSICA B
18.0	PHYSICA B	PHYSICA C
14.0	NUCL INSTRUM METH A	IEEE T NUCL SCI
12.0	PHYSICA B	J MAGN MAGN MATER
11.0	J MAGN MAGN MATER	PHYSICA B

4.4 Analysis

JCF values were calculated for all 1829 journals and IF values were retrieved from the Institute for Scientific Information Journal Citation Records database. The 15 journals corresponding to the highest JCF values in the generated network are shown in table 5, followed by the respective IF values.

Evidently, this list of journals does not correspond to what could otherwise be expected to be the most frequently consulted journals for other institutions or the scientific community in general. At least 4 of the listed journals correspond to nuclear science, which clearly relates to the general LANL mission. A large majority of the listed journals furthermore corresponds to physics and material science, which is another indication that our use of journal consultation frequency has validly characterized a characteristics of the LANL research community, namely its focus on physics and more specifically on nuclear physics.

We retrieved year 2000 ISI IFs[3] for the same set of the 15 highest JCF scoring journals which are listed in table 5. Although most journals do carry relatively

[3] The 2001 IF have not yet been published

Table 5. List of 15 most frequent journals in LANL RL Science Server network and 1998 Impact Factors.

Frequency	IF	Journal Title
176.00	0.893	PHYSICA B
134.00	0.964	NUCL INSTRUM METH A
132.00	1.576	APPL CATAL A-GEN
112.00	0.897	MAT SCI ENG A-STRUCT
107.00	0.845	J ALLOY COMPD
106.00	1.060	IEEE T NUCL SCI
104.00	1.933	CATAL TODAY
96.00	3.030	J CATAL
93.00	2.198	SURF SCI
92.00	1.241	J NUCL MATER
82.00	1.222	APPL SURF SCI
79.00	1.489	PHYSICA C
77.00	2.166	ACTA MATER
77.00	1.550	J COMPUT PHYS
75.00	0.488	J RADIOANAL NUCL CH

high IFs, IFs do not seem to correspond well to the ranking of these journals according to their LANL JCF score. We computed the correlation between JCF and ISI IF, where available. IFs could be retrieved for 1033 out of 1829 journals. The Spearman rank order correlation between JCF and IF scores was determined to be 0.13 ($p < 0.05$), indicating a statistically significant but weak relation between JCF and ISI IF scores for journals. A scatterplot of retrieved IF values and JCF values is shown in figure 4 and illustrates the weak relation between JCF and IF values for this user community.

r_f (Impact Factor Discrepancy Ratio) values were determined for the set of 1033 journals for which IF values were available. Table 6 lists the 15 journals corresponding to the highest r_f values. The rank ordering of journals according to their r_f values differs strongly from the generated rank ordering according to JCF values. The list shown in table 4 is characterized by the presence of journals in the domains of physics, nuclear physics as well as aeronautics and space science. In particular, the high r_f ranking of the journals "ASTROPHYS SPACE SCI", "ADV SPACE RES", "ACTA ASTRONAUT" and "AEROSP SCI TECHNOL" indicate the specific impact or importance of these journals for the LANL research community in spite of their low IF ranking.

Similarly, a number of nuclear science journals which did not achieve high rank according to their JCF values nevertheless corresponded to high r_f values, e.g. "NUCL ENG DES" and "PROG NUCL ENERG". A notable exception to the prevalence of nuclear science and physics journals in both JCF and r_f ranks is the high r_f score of the "COMPUT EDUC" journal which in spite of a very low IF factor still claims a relatively high JCF. This journal has thereby shown

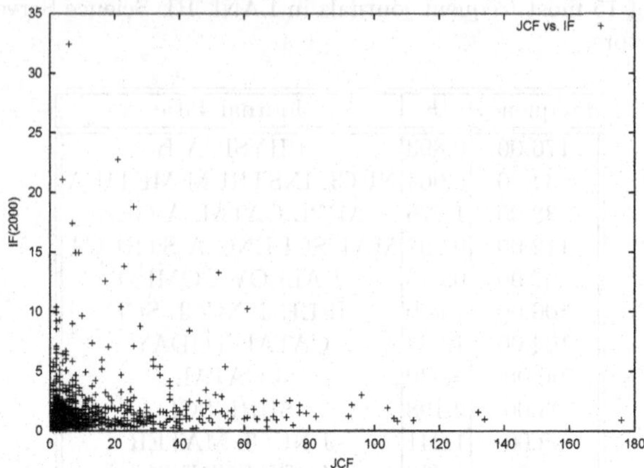

Fig. 4. Scatterplot of retrieved IF values over JCF values for set of 1033 journals.

Table 6. List of 15 journals for which highest ratio of JCF and ISI IF has been found.

r_f	JCF	IF	Journal Title
232.804	44	0.189	ASTROPHYS SPACE SCI
199.005	40	0.201	NUCL ENG DES
197.088	176	0.893	PHYSICA B
189.873	45	0.237	J MATER PROCESS TECH
189.802	67	0.353	ADV SPACE RES
172.043	32	0.186	ACTA ASTRONAUT
153.689	75	0.488	J RADIOANAL NUCL CH
143.939	38	0.264	PROG NUCL ENERG
139.004	134	0.964	NUCL INSTRUM METH A
128.676	35	0.272	MATH COMPUT SIMULAT
126.627	107	0.845	J ALLOY COMPD
124.861	112	0.897	MAT SCI ENG A-STRUCT
100.000	106	1.060	IEEE T NUCL SCI
95.808	16	0.167	AEROSP SCI TECHNOL
86.667	26	0.300	COMPUT EDUC

to be more characteristic of the LANL research community or at least a certain subsection of this community than could have been expected from its JCF or IF ranking.

These preliminary results indicate we have indeed isolated a set of journals that strongly relate to the specific characteristics and composition of the LANL research community by means of the JCF and r_f values, and have been able to ranked these journals according to measures of their impact among that community. Although a similar assessment could have been made based on the experience and intuition of DL management, this methodology provides a quantitative means of comparing the impact and importance of a given set of journals, or documents, for a specific community of users, and thereby allows a quantitative evaluation of the characteristics of this community as well.

5 Conclusion

We proposed a methodology to produce a set of journal and document impact measures which reflect the characteristics of a given user community. The methodology relies on the reconstruction of co-retrieval events from DL server logs to generate document or journal networks. From these networks we derived measures of journal impact among users, such as JCF and r_f. However, the presented analysis does not exhaust the many possibilities the generated networks offer in terms of the evaluation of DL services and user communities.

Recent efforts have focused on exploiting the specific graph-theoretical characteristics of the generated document networks by hierarchical cluster analysis and Latent Semantic Analysis.

First, a cluster analysis will enable us to not only rank journals and document according to their user-determined impact, but also to generate journal clusters which can be related to specific clusters of DL users. Although the present log data is anonymized for privacy reasons, the data will nevertheless reveal certain features of the structure of the underlying user community. This information can inform DL policies in terms of adapting existing services to accommodate for the needs of specific subgroups of users which would otherwise have gone undetected. Indeed, it is quite plausible that the organizational structure of a research institution only partially overlaps with the many implicit user groups defined by common interests and preferences which this method would reveal.

Second, a Latent Semantic Analysis (LSA) [7,12] can be used to reveal the underlying semantic structure of document and journal relations and aid in the adaptive subject categorization of a DLs collection. Furthermore, as data sets grow in size, so will the generated journal and document matrices. Although the generated matrices are expected to be extremely sparse, LSA may also benefit analysis by enabling the generation of lower-rank approximations which demand less storage and can be more efficiently analyzed.

The proposed methodology has proven to yield results relevant to the evaluation of DL collections and the assessment of user characteristics. We envision to expand the present range of applications. The present analysis was conducted on a rather small set of DL server logs and focused on a specific search service. However, the Los Alamos National Laboratory DL, as many DLs do, generate server logs many times the discussed size. Given our present experiences we are confident the present methodology and tools can accommodate data sets several orders of magnitude larger than the ones that have been processed at present. The analysis of larger data sets is a requirement to establish the validity and reliability of this approach. In a similar fashion, DL server logs registered at different times can be analyzed, so that the generated document and journal networks can be used to detect changes in the user communities and consequent changes in journal impact. Such analysis may allow DL management to anticipate future developments and respond by appropriate changes in services and acquisition policies.

We believe further experimentation with different learning functions and parameters is warranted. [9] discusses similar mechanisms for the generation of word and document relations which derive measures of user interests from time spent reading a document, and modulates link weight adaptation according to user interest. Although the proposed learning method was developed for applications to the WWW, it can be adapted to a DL context.

The generated document and journal networks can be applied to the construction of novel recommendation services such as Spreading Activation [4] which propagates activation values across network connections to retrieve relevant documents. This type of retrieval is independent from text-content and meta-data since it relies on document and journal relations established from user retrieval patterns. A prototype of such service has been developed and can be tested at http://biosis.lanl.gov:8077/jserv-bin/SpreadAct_SciS_loop.

Acknowledgment. The authors wish to thank the Los Alamos National Laboratory for the disposition of its DL server logs and most specifically Rick Luce, Herbert van de Sompel and Luis Rocha for their many contributions to the ideas developed in this article.

References

[1] Johan Bollen. Group user models for personalized hyperlink recommendation. In *LNCS 1892 - International Conference on Adaptive Hypermedia and Adaptive Web-based Systems (AH2000)*, pages 39–50, Trento, August 2000. Springer Verlag.

[2] Johan Bollen and Francis Heylighen. A system to restructure hypertext networks into valid user models. *The New Review of Hypermedia and Multimedia*, 4:189–213, 1998.

[3] Johan Bollen and Luis M. Rocha. An adaptive systems approach to the implementation and evaluation of digital library recommendation systems. In *LNCS - Fourth European Conference on Research and Advanced Technology for Digital Libraries (ECDL2000)*, Lisbon, September 2000. Springer Verlag.

[4] Johan Bollen, Herbert Vandesompel, and Luis M. Rocha. Mining associative relations from website logs and their application to context-dependent retrieval using spreading activation. In *Proceedings of the Workshop on Organizing Webspaces (ACM-DL99)*, Berkeley, California, 1999. in preparation.

[5] Christine L. Borgman and Ronald E. Rice. The convergence of information science and communication: A bibliometric analysis. *Journal of the American Society for Information Science*, 43(6):397–411, 1992.

[6] Philip K. Chan. Constructing web user profiles: a non-invasive learning approach. In Brij Masand and Myra Spiliopoulou, editors, *Web Usage Analysis and User Profiling - LNAI 1836*, San Diego, CA, August 1999. Springer.

[7] Peter W. Foltz. Using latent semantic indexing for information filtering. In R. B. Allen, editor, *Proceedings of the Conference on Office Information Systems*, pages 40–47, Cambridge, MA, 1990.

[8] Eugene Garfield. *Citation Indexing: Its Theory and Application in Science, Technology, and Humanities.* John Wiley and Sons, New York, 1979.

[9] Francis Heylighen. Mining associative meanings from the web: from word disambiguation to the global brain. In R. Timmerman and M. Lutjeharms, editors, *Proceedings of the International Colloqium: Trends in Special Language and Language Technology*, pages 15 – 44, Antwerpen, Belgium, 2001. Standaard Editions.

[10] Nancy R. Kaplan and Michael L. Nelson. Determining the publication impact of a digital library. *Journal of the American Society of Information Science*, 51:324–339, 2000.

[11] R. N. Kostoff. The use and misuse of citation analysis in research evaluations. *Scientometrics*, 43(1):27–43, 1998.

[12] Todd A. Letsche and Michael W. Berry. Large-scale information retrieval with latent semantic indexing. *Information Sciences*, 100:105–137, 1997.

[13] Michael H. MacRoberts and Barbara R. MacRoberts. Problems of citation analysis: A critical review. *Journal of the American Society for Information Science*, 40(5):342–349, 1989.

[14] Tobiasa Opthof. Sense and nonsense about the impact factor. *Cardiovascular Research*, 33:1–7, 1997.

[15] P. Pirolli and J. E. Pitkow. Distributions of surfers' paths through the world wide web:empirical characterization. *World Wide Web*, 2(1,2):29–45, 1999.

[16] James Pitkow. In search of reliable usage data on the www. In *Proceedings of the Sixth International WWW Conference*, Santa Clara, California, April 7-11 1997.

[17] Jan Reedijk. Sense and nonsense of science citation analyses: comments on the monopoly position of isi and citation inaccuracies. risks of possible misuse and biased citation and impact data. *New J. Chem.*, pages 767–770, 1998.

[18] Luis Mateus Rocha. Talkmine and the adaptive recommendation project. In *Proceedings of ACM Digital Libraries 99*, Berkeley, California, August 1999.

[19] Herbert Vandesompel. Reference linking in a hybrid library environment (i). *D-Lib Magazine*, 5(4), 1999.

Interactive Search Results

Ioannis Papadakis[1], Ioannis Andreou[1], and Vassileios Chrissikopoulos[2]

[1] University of Piraeus, Computer Science Department, Karaoli & Dimitriou 80, 18534 Piraeus, Greece
{jpap, gandreou}@unipi.gr

[2] University of Ionio, Department of Archives and Library Sciences, Plateia Eleytherias, 49100 Corfu - Greece
vchris@ionio.gr

Abstract. In this paper, we address the issue of interactive search results manipulation, as provided by typical Web-based information retrieval modules like search engines and directories. Many digital library systems could benefit a lot from the proposed approach, since it is heavily based on metadata, which constitute the building block of such systems. We also propose a way of ranking search results according to their overall importance, which is defined as a weighted combination of the relevancy and popularity of a resource that is being referenced in a search results list. In order to evaluate this model, we have developed an interactive search results manipulation application, which is executed at the client's workspace through a Web browser without any further interaction with the server that provided the initial search results list. The prototype implementation is based on the XML standard and has been evaluated through an adequate evaluation process from which useful conclusions have been obtained.

1 Introduction

Traditionally, information retrieval modules at the Web as well as at the field of Web-based digital libraries, are evaluated according to their ability to fetch search results that are relevant to users' queries. Two factors are employed for such a task, namely *precision* and *recall* [17]. Precision measures how well the retrieved documents match the referred query and recall reveals the percentage of relevant documents that are retrieved by the module [15]. However, as it will be argued throughout this work, such an evaluation could prove to be inaccurate, since there are cases where users may be dissatisfied with the output of such modules even if they contain references to resources of high relevancy to the corresponding query.

In a search results list of many items, documents are usually ranked according to their relevancy to the query that triggered the creation of the list. Many times though, users don't know exactly what they are looking for when submitting a query to a search engine. Instead, they just enter a vague description of the knowledge they pursue and try to locate the corresponding resource(es) by harvesting long lists of search

M. Agosti and C. Thanos (Eds.): ECDL 2002, LNCS 2458, pp. 448-462, 2002.

results. Thus, in the case of long lists with more or less relevant results, there is rarely any option on screen to manipulate the list items (except maybe by scrolling down the list or moving across pages) in a way that would allow users to "play around" with them in order to choose the most appropriate resource with minimum effort. Providing just a static visualization of search results ranked by relevancy, prevents users from retrieving useful information located anywhere else apart from the top of such lists.

In this paper, we introduce the notion of interactive search results as applied to existing Web-based information retrieval modules like search engines. The proposed approach depends on metadata and therefore could prove to be particularly useful at the field of digital libraries, where metadata are most commonly met. The deriving functionality is provided as a separate software component located in an intermediate layer between existing information retrieval modules and their users. According to this concept, search results lists are dynamic documents, which may be manipulated in various ways in order to provide a better understanding of their content.

We also argue that the importance of a resource should not only be estimated from its relevancy to the corresponding query. Instead, we propose a method for measuring the importance of a resource by also taking into consideration the number of times it has been accessed (i.e. selected from a search results list) during it's lifecycle.

A distinctive feature of applications based on the notion of interactive search results, apart from the fact that they should operate supplementary to the search engine, is that they should preferably rely on the client computer's resources without putting additional strain to the server. Such a requirement is possible to be fulfilled through the employment of the XML standard, as it will be discussed later in this paper.

The above thoughts have been applied to a prototype implementation of an interactive search results manipulation system based on XML/XSLT technology, which extends the functionality of the search engine of a working digital library system. Furthermore, useful remarks about the proposed functionality have been obtained from the evaluation process of the prototype system.

The rest of this paper is organized as follows: in the next section, related work in the field of interactive information retrieval applications is presented. Section 3 describes the proposed Interactive Search Results architecture, focusing on metadata elements and execution space. Section 4 illustrates a prototype implementation of the above architecture while section 5 outlines the results that have been extracted from an evaluation process of the corresponding implementation. Finally, section 6 concludes this paper.

2 Related Work

The importance of the way search results should be displayed and the need to accommodate them with dynamic manipulation functionality has been the issue of many researchers before the advent of Web-based information retrieval modules. Based on the cluster hypothesis of van Rijsbergen [26], Bead [3] and Lyberworld [5] are two systems that provide extended functionality to search results. Scatter/Gather [4] goes one step further by observating that "the same sets of documents behave differently in different contexts". The idea behind this system is to cluster retrieval results in *k* clusters, scatter the documents inside and then partition the document set into another *k* clusters. Some other systems would (statically) present search results based on two-[19] or three-[1] dimensional visualization schemes.

Such solutions however, although they are relatively popular at the field of traditional digital libraries, cannot be easily applied to the entire Web and specifically to Web-based digital libraries that employ the Web browser to host their User Interface, for a number of reasons. Thus, most of these systems require either sophisticated graphical software, or are difficult to scale, or require excessive system resources, or most frequently, combine the above features [2].

The particular needs of Web-based information retrieval and, most importantly, the need to decouple search engine logic from manipulation of search results are regrettably difficult to be found in the information retrieval literature [24].

Zamir and Etzioni [27] proposed a method for re-ranking and tagging the most relevant documents returned by search engines, based on a clustering algorithm. The VIEWER system [2] provides an intermediate layer between the query formulation stage and the display of search results. According to this system, users are able to dynamically interact with search results by manipulating various "views", where a view is defined as the subset of retrieved documents that contain a specified subset of query terms. However, in order to get a different view of the search results, users have to reformulate their query and reinvoke the search engine.

Apart from the above references to the information retrieval literature, a number of commercial and non-commercial information retrieval modules on the Web have apparently realized the problems of current search results presentation [21]. However, most of the search engine development performed by companies, comes with little or no publication of technical details. This causes search engine technology to remain largely a black art [13].

The Google search engine [13] relies on PageRank [14] to rank search results lists. According to PageRank, a resource is highly ranked if the sum of the ranks of its backlinks (i.e. links that point to a given resource) is high. This system utilizes the link graph of the Web [6] to estimate the importance of a Web page (in terms of relevancy and popularity in the graph). Although the employment of PageRank for ranking resources has proved to be useful in the sense that it objectively ranks sites according to their importance, still no interaction with users on the search results list is allowed.

In the field of Web-based digital libraries, ResearchIndex [20] and the Open Journal Project [10] have their own definitions of importance for ranking search results. ResearchIndex is a digital library of scientific literature that measures the importance of documents based on the Autonomous Citation Indexing (ACI) system. This implicit Recommender System maintains an index that automatically catalogues documents' citations by linking them with the cited works. Thus, documents within the search results list are ranked according to the citations they have. Furthermore, ResearchIndex takes under consideration the elapsed time since a document was first published [18]. A similar approach (though not as applicable as ResearchIndex since it relies on specific document format) is followed by the Open Journal project. According to this project, a link service that associates every journal with the rest through its citation links is defined. Links are provided through a publicly available link database. However, just like in the previous cases, interaction with users is not supported.

The NCSTRL [22] Web-based digital library has recently employed a methodology for a priori interactive manipulation of search results. Specifically, upon construction of a query, users have the opportunity to group and rank the expected results according to their relevancy, discovery date and archiving. Users are not able to dynamically change the grouping and/or ranking of search results without re-submitting their query.

3 Interactive Search Results

3.1 The Architecture

In this work, we introduce the notion of Interactive Search Results. It refers to a methodology according to which information retrieval functionality continues to be available even after the construction of search results lists. Such functionality requires active participation from users and execution space at the client's Web browser through adequate applications. Search results lists are considered as dynamic, homo-

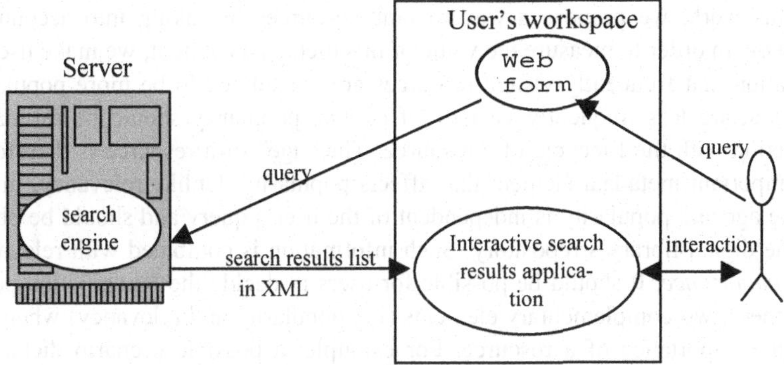

Fig. 1. Interactive Search Results architecture

geneous lists of references to resources with metadata (i.e. descriptive data about other data [16]) that are common to the items of such lists. Such information is provided by the search engine, which, in turn, collects the metadata from the digital library's repository. In the case of search engines on the Internet, the provided metadata set is reasonably smaller. Users are able to transform the original lists by exploiting the information provided by the corresponding metadata, thus making quick and accurate decisions about the usefulness of the referred resources. Long lists may be rapidly transformed to shorter ones and provide users with more comprehensive information about the included items. Moreover, faster and more accurate transactions result in saving of network bandwidth and server-side system resources. The proposed interactive manipulation may be provided in terms of grouping, filtering and/or rearranging of the items that constitute the original search results list.

In order to develop applications capable of employing the proposed functionality, an adequate architecture should be followed. Thus, as illustrated in fig. 1, the output of a search engine is directed to a complementary application that is executed at the client-side.

Users are able to interact with the application and accordingly change the ranking and/or population of the search results list items. The number of transformations that may be applied to such lists depends on the amount of metadata that are provided by the search engine. A rich set of metadata results in a similarly rich set of interaction possibilities.

3.2 Metadata Elements

The most common criterion for ranking search results is by far the relevancy of the resources to the initial query. For many years, search engines at the Web relied entirely on relevancy to rank search results. However, in an attempt to improve quality of search results, search engines have evolved to consider a number of alternative ways of ranking search results [21].

In this work, we propose a way to rank resources by taking into account their *popularity*. In order to measure the value of this metadata element, we make use of the observation that frequently visited resources are considered to be more popular than others that are less frequently visited. Of course, popularity should be estimated in conjunction with the lifecycle of a resource. The “age” of a resource is therefore another important metadata element that affects popularity. Unlike relevancy, information like age and popularity is independent of the user’s query and should be obtained from the digital library’s repository. Such information is combined with relevancy to define *importance*. It should be possible for users to decide the participation percentage of these two complementary elements (i.e. popularity and relevancy) when calculating the importance of a resource. For example, a possible scenario dictates that search results are ranked according to their importance, which is defined as a sum of 90% of relevancy plus 10% of popularity.

Apart from the above metadata elements that are common to virtually all Web resources, there are a number of metadata that are specific to certain collections. For example, when referring to a Web-based digital library of technical reports (e.g. NCSTRL [22]), we come against metadata like author, date of submission, title, etc. Moreover, Web-based digital libraries of specific formats (e.g. image, video and sound) have their own specific metadata. It is therefore the interactive search results application’s responsibility to exploit the information provided by the information retrieval module (in terms of metadata elements) in order to provide extended functionality to its users.

3.3 The Execution Space

According to this work, the proposed functionality requires availability of adequate execution space at the client-side. Information retrieval functionality (e.g. search engines and directories) is by far the most popular feature of the majority of today's Web-based digital libraries. Relying on the server for such tasks demands even greater processing power and consume large amounts of additional network bandwidth for the exchange of data between server and clients. In order to avoid this additional cost, it is necessary to provide the requested functionality at the client-side.

A few years ago, it was very difficult, if not impossible, to find a technology capable of fulfilling the requirements for a unified way of processing search results across the diversity of the Web in terms of computer platforms and software. Fortunately, the emergence of XML as a Web standard for exchanging and presenting information and its wide adoption from the major Web browsers, renders XML as a suitable technology for the implementation of the proposed model. Additionally, the ability of XML-based applications to separate content from presentation and to transform documents from one form to another are two very important features that are applicable to interactive Web models like the one that is presented in this work.

4 Prototype Implementation

4.1 The Application

In order to test the proposed Interactive Search Results model, we have implemented a search results manipulation application, which we have applied to the University of Piraeus Lecture Notes (UPLN) digital library [25]. This prototype application acts as a Recommender System [12] in the sense that it provides assistance to its users in locating useful resources. UPLN is a Web-based digital library that provides common search facilities to its users. The underlying repository contains teaching material from nine departments within the University. The actual content of the digital library is the lecture notes of each course, which may be stored in various formats (pdf, doc, jpg, html, etc). UPLN's search engine indexes bibliographic information like "author", "date of acceptance" and "title", which exists in a separate bibliographic file for each set of lecture notes:

```
BIB-VERSION:: CS-TR-v2.1
ID:: unipi.csd//csd-001
TITLE:: "Database Systems"
ENTRY:: February 12, 1999
AUTHOR:: George Chondrokoukis
ABSTRACT:: ="Homework for Relational Schemas..."
END:: unipi.csd//csd-001
COUNTER:: 624
```

Such data is directly associated to the metadata elements that are needed for the interactive manipulation of search results. The prototype application utilizes metadata elements like Title, Author, Entry, Abstract and Counter, where "Counter" monitors the number of times the corresponding resource has been accessed from the users of the digital library.

In order to apply the proposed functionality, the output of the UPLN's search engine has been modified to export the search results list not as a static html stream but as a XML structure containing the aforementioned metadata elements (i.e. author, date, counter, etc), as illustrated below:

```
<?xml version="1.0" encoding="ISO-8859-7"?>
<?xml-stylesheet type="text/xsl" href= "hits.xsl"
xmlns:xsl= "http:// www.w3.org/ TR/WD-xsl"?>
<list>
<resource date="November 13, 1999" counter="450"…
url="http://thalis.gr/Rep/U.I/prod-001/index.html"
relevancy="7.654" popularity="15.3"
abstract="Database Systems..." id="prod-001"
importance="1">
<author>George Hondrokoukis</author>
</resource>
<resource date="November 13, 1999" counter="353"…
url="http://thalis.cs.unipi.gr/a.html"
relevancy="7.654" popularity="12"
abstract="Homework for Rel. Schemas..." id="csd-003"
importance ="0.7">
<author>George Vassilakopoulos    </author>
</resource>
</list>
```

Each item of the search results list corresponds to a "resource" element containing the URL and other information about the resource according to its bibliographic file. "Relevancy" refers to the relevancy score provided by the underlying search engine.

The "popularity" attribute represents the access rate in terms of hits per month for the specified resource. The "importance" attribute is obtained from the equations 1-3, where imp_i is the importance factor for resource i, rel_i is the relevancy of resource i (0•i•n, where n is the total number of search results) as obtained transparently from the search engine, pop_i is the popularity of a resource expressed in hits per month (counter/30), k is the weighting factor of relevancy in importance and (1-k) is the weighting

$$\overline{imp_i} = rel_i \cdot k + pop_i \cdot (1 - k), \tag{1}$$

$$imp_{\max} = \max(\overline{imp_i}), \tag{2}$$

$$imp_i = \overline{imp_i} / imp_{\max} \tag{3}$$

factor of popularity in importance. k's value ranges from 0 to 1 ($0 \le k \le 1$). k decides which of the two elements (i.e. relevancy and popularity) will mostly affect the overall importance. Values near "0" are in favor of popularity, whereas values near "1" are in favor of relevancy. The user should be able to adjust k's value according to her/his particular needs. However, for simplicity reasons, we have decided to assign k with the fixed value of 0.8. Finally, imp_i is normalized to the range of [0,1].

The deriving XML tree is fed to our prototype application, which transforms it to HTML according to the directives included in an adequate XSL file. The list items are initially sorted by relevancy.

As illustrated in fig.2, the left frame on the screen contains the provided functionality.

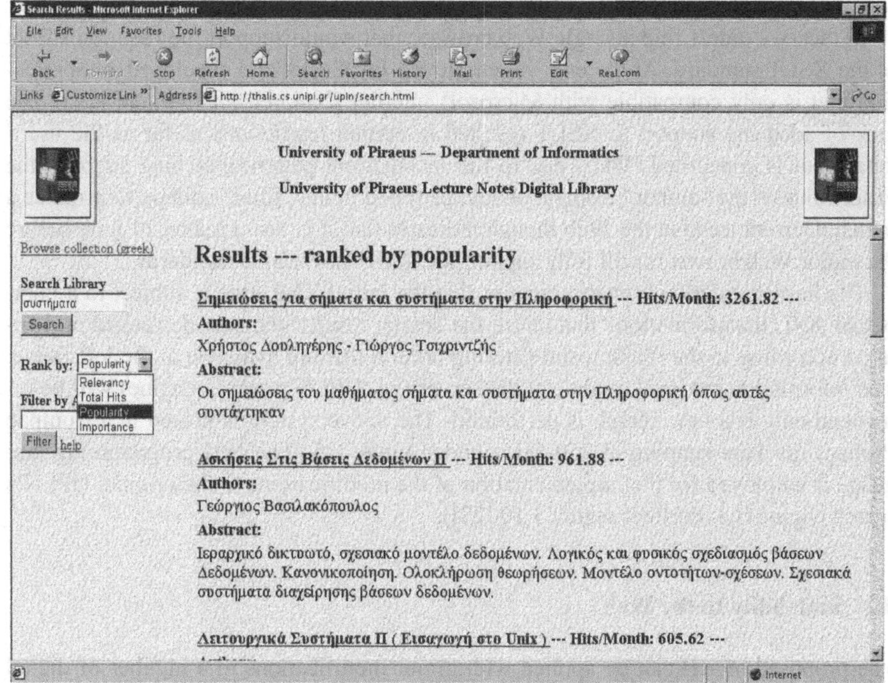

Fig. 2. Search Results, ranked by popularity

Users are able to re-rank search results according to a) their popularity, b) the total number of times they have been accessed (i.e. "total hits") and c) their importance, as it has been previously defined. Moreover, users may choose to view the results items that refer to a specified author, by clicking the "Filter" button. Specifically, fig. 2 illustrates a re-ranked search results list according to the popularity of the documents it contains. In the case of a user wishing to view the lecture notes of just one author in the above list, she/he may filter search results by filling the "Author" field and by clicking the "Filter" button.

4.2 Implementation Issues

The proposed application consumes client-side system resources through the employment of JavaScript and XSLT. The initial goal was to rely just on XSLT for the implementation of the project, since most of the currently available Web browsers claim to be XML-compatible.

However, we soon realized that it was impossible to develop an application compatible with all the XML-capable Web browsers, due to the fact that each Web browser supported a different subset of a different version of the XSLT recommendation.

In fact, we didn't find a single Web browser that would support the required subset of the XSLT standard. At the end, we employed JavaScript and developed an application that is only compatible with Microsoft Internet Explorer ver. 5.0 and later. The lack of adequate support to XSLT resulted in certain restrictions as far as the users' data input is concerned. Thus, due to the inconsistent pattern-matching support, the exact value of the "author" element should be typed in the "filter" editbox to produce a match. Current trend at the Web though indicates that it is just a matter of time before the major Web browsers will fully support the XML and related standards.

The implementation scenario dictates that the initial XML tree is subject to a number of XSL transformations that cause the search results items to be ranked and filtered according to the ranking and filtering criteria that are available at the left frame. The information retrieval module at the server (i.e. UPLN's search engine) will be re-invoked only if a new search is performed. The above system is hosted in a Compaq Proliant machine running at 350 MHz under Linux OS. The Perl programming language is employed for the implementation of the modifications to the original UPLN's search engine (i.e. Perlfect search 3.10 [23]).

4.2 Scalability to the Web

The proposed model can be applied with minor modifications to a number of digital libraries, since resources within such systems traditionally employ rich sets of metadata. Despite the fact that Web resources rarely employ metadata, Web search engines could also benefit from the employment of such functionality. For example, apart from importance and relevancy ranking, items in a search results list could be filtered according to their Web location or language. The only requirement is that search results should be provided in XML format. Moreover, the hierarchical structure of XML data and the rapid growth of hardware development (current PC workstations are remarkably powerful while maintaining their price at reasonable levels), ensure that manipulation of very long and diverse search results lists will be equally effective.

5 Evaluation

5.1 The Evaluation Method

According to Nielsen [11], methods for evaluation can be separated into usability testing methods, where users are involved and usability inspection methods, where users are not involved. Usability is related to how well a user could use the provided functionality.

In order to evaluate the proposed system, we have developed a questionnaire, which we have distributed to a group of users who had previously used the prototype system. Then, a discussion took place with each subject separately about their overall impression of the system. The advantage of this evaluation method is that it can easily involve numerous users and, in addition, is an inexpensive survey method. On the other hand, it is difficult to get 100% accurate results when using questionnaires since users' answers are usually based on what they think they do, not on what they actually do [11]. However, the specific questionnaire is heavily based on a questionnaire that is specially adopted for digital libraries [24] and is claimed to be highly reliable by the authors. Questions that are targeted to both style and content have been avoided, since they usually confuse users [8]. Finally, it should be kept in mind that our main goal is to evaluate the usability of interactive search results through the use of our system and not the system itself.

5.2 The Experiment

The goal of the evaluation process was to realize the usefulness of the principles of interactive Web-based information retrieval modules that have been addressed throughout this paper. In particular, we have conducted an experiment in which the subjects were asked to submit a number of random as well as predefined queries to the search engine of a digital library of teaching material through our prototype application. The predefined queries were designed in a way to return relatively long search results lists. Then, the subjects had the opportunity to interact with the results through the provided functionality of our system. The next step of the experiment was to distribute a questionnaire among the subjects, which they were asked to fill-in. At the end of this process, we had a five to ten minutes conversation with each subject in order to obtain their overall opinion about the system.

5.3 The Testbed

The extensive employment of metadata in digital libraries and specifically in the UPLN, renders this system as a suitable testbed for our evaluation process. The UPLN's search engine has been operational since 1998 and proved to be a very popular and efficient information retrieval module for the UPLN's digital library users. Another reason for the employment of the specific system for the evaluation process was the familiarity of the subjects with its content and search facilities. Such familiarity resulted in the development of an easy to understand and use questionnaire, which facilitated the overall process.

5.4 The Subjects

Nine subjects participated in the evaluation process. Four of them were Ph.D. candidates at the Informatics department and the remaining five were undergraduate (senior) students at various departments within the University of Piraeus in Greece. All of the subjects had previous experience with the specific digital library. The evaluation process took place in a laboratory containing ten PC workstations running at 350 MHz under Windows NT, equipped with Internet Explorer 5.5, which supports XML ver. 1.0.

5.5 The Questionnaire

The questionnaire was comprised of six categories that contained up to four questions each. The categories were namely:

1. Overall reactions to the system
2. Screen display
3. Learning
4. System capabilities and user control
5. Navigation
6. Completing tasks

and were inspired by Yin Leng Theng's et al. [24] classification scheme which, in turn, was heavily based on Lingaard's classification of usability defects in interactive systems [9]. Specifically, questions belonging to the first category evaluate users' overall perception of the system's performance in terms of satisfaction, completion of tasks and appeal. The "Screen display" category contains questions about the organization and screen display of the overall information. "Learning" refers to the ease of use of the system, "System capabilities and control" examines it's response time and reliability and "Navigation" investigates whether the user is lost in the underlying environment. Finally, the "Completing tasks" category examines the extent of usefulness for the provided facilities in helping users to complete their tasks.

All of the questions were closed questions, since they are generally easier to analyze than open ones [9]. As proposed by [24], users' responses were given through a 7-point scale except from question 4.3 (which requested an ordering of five options-see appendix). A value of "1" represented the most negative response whereas a number of "7" represented the most positive one for the particular question. Finally, a mid-value of 4 was considered to be a neutral response.

5.6 Results and Analysis

On the whole, questionnaire results were not surprising. A first glance at fig. 3 reveals that the subjects were generally satisfied with the application.

Fig. 3 shows the average value of the nine different answers that correspond to the six categories of the distributed questionnaire.

The subjects were particularly satisfied with the ease of use of the prototype (category 3). Despite the fact that during the previous years they were used to working on a simple User Interface for the same digital library, they quickly adapted (the training of the subjects on the new User Interface lasted in all nine cases no more than ten minutes) to the more complex system and realized the advantages of the provided functionality.

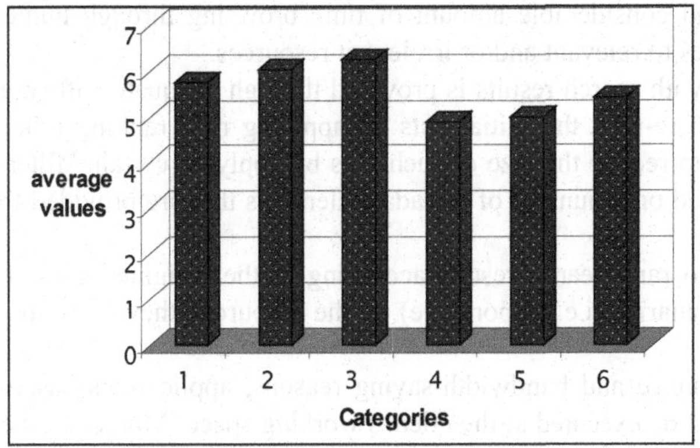

Fig. 3. Average values for received answers

The subjects were asked, through the questionnaire, to rate the importance of the ranking and filtering criteria, as compared to the traditional static, exhaustive browsing of search results for locating useful resources. The results suggest that users made repeated use of all the ranking and filtering possibilities provided by the system. This may also be witnessed from the replies to question 4.3 (see appendix), where the participating subjects decided that "ranking by relevancy" was not a very satisfactory ranking criterion, as compared to the other criteria that were provided from the prototype application. Specifically, "ranking by popularity" was the most appealing ranking option according to the subjects, followed closely by "ranking by importance". The "ranking by relevancy" and "filter by" options came third and fourth respectively and last, came the "ranking by total hits" option.

Moreover, the proposed model shifted user habits from inspection to interaction with the search results, reducing the time and effort spent to examine them and increasing the user satisfaction. It is also important to notice that the extended functionality didn't cost additional execution time. In fact, the overall impression is that without the provided functionality at the left frame, users would complete their ultimate goal for retrieving useful results in longer time. The relatively low average for questions belonging to the fourth category (i.e. system capabilities and user control) is due to the restriction according to which, only the exact author's name may be entered for filtering (XSLT pattern matching functions are not well supported in this version of the employed Web browser). Users probably felt uncomfortable with the fact that just the surname of an author wouldn't work. As it has already been mentioned though, such inconsistencies will most likely disappear in upcoming versions of current Web browsers.

6 Conclusions

This paper introduced the notion of Interactive Search Results on the Web, which provides an alternative way of locating references to useful resources in search results lists. The proposed model is particularly applicable to long lists, where users are forced to spend considerable amount of time browsing through numerous pages of short summaries to relevant and/or irrelevant resources.

Interaction with search results is provided through adequate software modules that enable users to re-rank the initial lists by applying new ranking criteria. Moreover, users are able to reduce the size of such lists by applying certain "filters". Such functionality is based on a number of metadata elements that are provided from the search engine.

A method to rank search results according to the weighted combination of relevancy and popularity (i.e. importance) of the resources they refer to, has also been proposed.

For performance and bandwidth-saving reasons, applications based on the above thoughts should be executed at the client's working space. Moreover, the effectiveness of such applications heavily depends on the Web browser's ability to support XML and related standards.

A prototype implementation has been developed in order to evaluate the concepts that have been presented in this paper. According to the results obtained from the evaluation process, the proposed functionality seems to help users accomplish their information retrieval-related tasks in Web search results lists in a shorter time with minimum effort. However, current support from the major Web browsers to the XML and related standards is probably inadequate for the development of applications that would exploit the full potential of the proposed principles of interactive search results. There are though strong indications in the field of Web technologies that future versions of Web browsers are most likely to overcome such inconsistencies.

References

1. Allan, J., Leuski, A., Swan, R., and Byrd, D.: Evaluating Combinations of Ranked Lists and Visualizations of Inter-document Similarity. Information Processing and Management (IPM), 37, 2000, 435-458
2. Berenci, E., Carpineto, C., Giannini, V., and Mizzaro, S.: Effectiveness of keyword-based display and selection of retrieval results for interactive searches. in Proceedings of ECDL '99 (Paris, September 1999), 106-125
3. Chalmers, M., and Chitson, P.: Bead: Explorations in information visualization. in Proceedings of SIGIR '92 (Copenhagen, June 1992), 330-337

4. Hearst, M.A., Pedersen, J.O.: Reexamining the Cluster Hypothesis: Scatter/Gather on Retrieval Results. in Proceedings of SIGIR '96 (Zurich, August 1996), 76-84
5. Hemmje, M., Kunkel, C., and Willet, A.: Lyberworld - A visualization user interface supporting full text retrieval. in Proceedings of SIGIR '94 (Dublin, July 1994), 249-259
6. Kleinberg J.M.: Authoritative Sources in a Hyperlinked Environment. in Proceedings of ACM-SIAM Symposium on Discrete Algorithms (San Francisco, January 1998), 668-677
7. Lawrence, S., Giles, C.L., and Bollacker, K.: Digital Libraries and Autonomous Citation Indexing. IEEE Computer, 32, 6, 67-71, 1999
8. Lif, M.: Adding usability: A case study. Uppsala University Technical Report No. 87, (Uppsala-Sweden, 1998)
9. Lindgaard, G.: Usability testing and system evaluation: A guide for designing useful computer systems. Chapman & Hall, 1994
10. Liu, Y-H., Dantzig, P., Sachs, M., Corey, J., Hinnebusch, M., Sullivan, T., Damashek, M., and Cohen, J.: Visualizing Document Classification: A search Aid for the D.L. in Proceedings of ECDL '98 (Herakleion-Crete, September 1998), 555-567
11. Nielsen, J.: Usability Engineering. Academic Press Inc., 1993
12. Oard, D.W., Kim, J.: Implicit feedback for Reccommender Systems. in Proceedings of the AAAI Workshop on Recommender Systems (Madison, July 1998), 81-83
13. Page, L., Brin, S.: The Anatomy of a Large-Scale Hypertextual Search Engine. in Proceedings of the Seventh WWW '98 (Brisbane, April 1998), 14-18
14. Page, L., Brin, S., Motwani, R., and Terry Winograd, T.: The Pagerank citation ranking: Bringing order to the web. Technical report, Stanford (Santa Barbara, CA 93106, January 1998). http:// www-db.stanford.edu/ ~backrub/ pageranksub.ps
15. Pinkerton, B.: Finding What People Want: Experiences with the WebCrawler. in Proceedings of the WWW '94 (Geneva, May 1994), Elsevier Science BV, 17-20. http://info.webcrawler.com/bp/WWW94.html
16. Rusch-Feja, D.: Metadata: Standards for retrieving WWW documents. Library and Information Services in Astronomy III, 153, 157-165, 1998
17. Salton, G.: Automatic text processing: The transformation, analysis and retrieval of information by computer. Addison Wesley, 1989
18. Salton, G., Wong, A., and Yang C.S.A.: Vector Space Model for Automatic Indexing. Communications of the ACM 18, 613-620, 1975
19. Shneiderman, B., Feldman, D., Rose, A., and Ferre Grau, X.: Visualizing Digital Library Search Results with Categorical and Hierarchical Axes. in Proceedings of ACM ICDL '99 (San Antonio, June 2000), 57-66
20. Singh, M., and Valtorta, M.: Efficient Learning of Selective Bayesian Network Classifiers. in Proceedings of ICML '96 (Bari, July 1996), 453-461
21. The BEST Search Engines.: http:// lib.berkeley.edu/ TeachingLib/ Guides/ Internet/ SearchEngines.html
22. The Networked Computer Science Technical Reference Library: http://www.ncstrl.org
23. The PerlfectSearch search engine.: http://www.perlfectsearch.com
24. Theng, Y.L., Duncker, E., Mohd-Nasir, N., Buchanan, G., and Thimbleby, H.: Design Guidelines and User-Centered Digital Libraries. in Proceedings of ECDL '99 (Paris, September 1999), 167-183
25. University of Piraeus Lecture Notes (UPLN) digital library.: http://thalis.cs.unipi.gr/upln/search.html
26. Van Rijsbergen, C.J.: Information Retrieval. Butterworths, London, 1979 Zamir, O., and Etzioni, O.: Web document clustering: a feasibility demonstration. in Proceedings of SIGIR '98 (Melbourne, August 1998), 46-54

Appendix: Questionnaire

1.1 How helpful did you find the options "filter" and "rank by" in locating useful resources?

1.2 Do you believe that the provided functionality at the left frame of the UI is a good alternative to exhaustive browsing of search results?

1.3 How often did you change the default option of ranking search results?

2.1 Is the functionality provided by the system easy to access?

2.2 Do you feel comfortable with the overall screen layout?

3.1 How long did it take you to get used to the provided User Interface of the system?

3.2 How often did you use the provided help?

4.1 How long did it take for your actions at the left frame of the Use Interface to be applied at the main frame?

4.2 Did you feel confident with the filter and the rank by criteria of the system?

4.3 Please order the ranking and filtering possibilities provided at the left frame in an order that describes the usefulness of each choice regarding the top items of the corresponding search result lists (i.e. which choice ranks search results more efficiently?).

A. Relevancy
B. Importance
C. Total hits
D. Popularity
E. Filter by

5.1 How easy was to move from one view of the search results to another (e.g. from the filtered view to the rank by importance view)?

6.1 Did you feel that in some cases, exhaustive browsing could be a faster method for locating useful search results?

6.2 Provided that the queries returned relatively long search results lists, did you locate any useful resources in other pages except the first one?

6.3 In cases where the search engine didn't return any useful results, do you think that the functionality provided at the left frame was helpful in deciding quicker that you had to rephrase the original query in order to get useful results?

6.4 Do you feel that ranking by relevancy should be the only ranking criterion in a search results list?

An Investigation of Mixed-Media Information Retrieval

Gareth J.F. Jones and Adenike M. Lam-Adesina

Department of Computer Science, University of Exeter
Exeter, EX4 4PT, United Kingdom
{G.J.F.Jones,A.M.Lam-Adesina}@exeter.ac.uk

Abstract. Digital document archives are increasingly derived from various different media sources. At present such archives are stored and searched independently. The Information Retrieval from Mixed-Media Collections (IRMMC) project is investigating retrieval from combined document collections composed of items originating from differing media forms. Experimental investigation of a "mixed-media" retrieval task based on the existing TREC Spoken Document Retrieval task combining Text, Spoken and Scanned Image is described. Results show that non-text media perform well within the mixed-media collection. Also while pseudo relevance feedback is extremely effective for spoken documents, its behaviour for document image retrieval is more complex.

1 Introduction

Growth in the availability of electronic documents derived from sources other than typed text has led to significant interest in areas such as Spoken Document Retrieval (SDR) and scanned Document Image Retrieval (DIR). Searching for material within these collections of documents is clearly an important topic for multimedia digital libraries. The Text REtrieval Conference (TREC) programme has included relevant tasks such as retrieval of scanned documents in the TREC-5 Confusion Track [1] and SDR in TREC-6 onwards [2]. These studies and others exploring retrieval of documents originating in non-text media have led to a greater understanding of the associated indexing and retrieval issues, and the proposal and investigation of a wide variety of techniques to address these. In practice, users of retrieval systems are often primarily interested in addressing their information need. The user may find the relevant information they are looking for in documents originating in any available media source, while not all available single media archives will necessarily contain the relevant information.

One approach to addressing this problem is to combine index information from documents originating in different media sources into a single collection. We refer to such collections containing *different* documents from various single media sources as *mixed-media* collections. We distinguish the concept of a mixed-media collection, where an individual document exists in only one media form, from *multi-media* collections where an individual document may be represented by multiple media streams, e.g. audio and video.

M. Agosti and C. Thanos (Eds.): ECDL 2002, LNCS 2458, pp. 463–478, 2002.

This paper describes work from the *Information Retrieval for Mixed-Media Collections (IRMMC)* project at the University of Exeter which is studying retrieval from document collections containing different typed electronic text, spoken data and scanned paper documents. An underlying assumption in this work is that a user is seeking information and that this information is equally valid if it is found in any of the available media sources. If a user requires their relevant information to be contained in a video source, then mixed-media retrieval is not appropriate; but it may be that the information they require is not contained in a video source or that studying documents from other media sources will inform their information need to assist them in locating relevant video documents. In these cases the availability of potentially relevant documents from other sources from a mixed-media collection may be useful.

The remainder of the paper is organised as follows. Section 2 reviews existing work in spoken and scanned document retrieval, Section 3 describes the design of our mixed-media test collection, Section 4 summarises the IR techniques used in our current experimental investigation with the results in Section 5, and finally Section 6 gives conclusions and outlines further work.

2 Related Research in Non-text Retrieval

The principal difference between standard typed text retrieval (TR) and retrieval from other media is the need to index the document contents. Spoken documents are indexed using a Speech Recognition (SR) process and scanned paper documents using Optical Character Recognition (OCR). While both SR and OCR have advanced considerably in recent years, they are both still prone to make recognition errors. Unsurprisingly these indexing errors have been shown to impact disadvantageously on retrieval performance. While both technologies make indexing errors the form of these errors is often found to be different. It is the presence of indexing errors within mixed-media collections, the impact of differing error forms associated with different media, and how to address them that is the main research focus of the IRMMC project.

2.1 Spoken Document Retrieval (SDR)

Various methods of speech recognition have been explored for SDR, including subword feature indexing [3], phone lattice spotting [4] and, most commonly for the TREC evaluations [2], document transcriptions generated using large vocabulary recognition (LVR) systems.

Errors in indexing for spoken documents may arise from various sources. The speech may be inherently hard to transcribe due to effects such as poor articulation, spontaneous speech issues such as phrase and word restarts, and acoustic channel noise, However, a potentially important issue in speech recognition systems for SDR is the indexing vocabulary. Standard word-based speech recognition systems have a restricted recognition vocabulary meaning that any words present in a spoken document, but not in the recognition vocabulary, cannot, by definition, be recognised correctly. The out-of-vocabulary issue has not been found to be a significant problem in the TREC SDR tasks where LVR transcription has shown the best retrieval results. Since the IRMMC investigation is based on a modified form of the TREC-8 task, LVR indexing is adopted for spoken document indexing. Several methods have been successfully explored to compensate for the general problem of reduced retrieval performance due to recognition errors, including standard pseudo (or blind) relevance feedback for query expansion and document expansion [2].

The only previous work describing an exploration of mixed-media collection retrieval was reported by Sanderson and Crestani in [5] for text and spoken documents. In this experiment the reference text transcription and an LVR transcription for the TREC-6 SDR known-item task were combined into a single collection. Their results suggest that retrieval of text transcriptions is favoured over the LVR transcriptions when using a standard $tf * idf$ weighting scheme. It was further shown that this mismatch is primarily due to the tf function adopted in their work leading to lower term weights for spoken documents. A slightly more surprising result is that using *idf* only weighting, retrieval from both sources is almost identical, it might be expected that indexing misses in the spoken transcriptions would lead to lower matching scores. The reason for this result was not explored in their analysis.

2.2 Document Image Retrieval (DIR)

Unlike speech recognition systems, OCR techniques tend to misrecognise individual characters from within words. This can lead to matching problems between terms within documents and queries, and also to inappropriate term weights being assigned to the recognised indexing units where single character errors produce rare terms with high weights.

Research in retrieval of scanned images of paper documents has been ongoing for a similar period to that in SDR. However, this work has not been so widespread and although a large number of approaches to using OCR output in retrieval have been proposed, they have not been explored in detail. The only comparative experiments were carried out in the TREC-5 Confusion track [1], the results of which are summarised in this section, along with those of studies carried over a number of years at the University of Nevada, Las Vegas [6] and ETH Zurich [7].

TREC-5 Confusion Track. The TREC-5 Confusion track consisted of a "known-item" search, a task in which the system attempts to find a single, partially-remembered, target document from with a document collection. The corpus contained approximately 55,000 documents. Participants in the track were provided with three text versions of the data: the original electronic typed text which was regarded as a baseline, a second version with an estimated error rate of 5% obtained by scanning the hardcopy, and a third version obtained by downsampling the original page images and having an error rate of around 20%.

Groups participating in this task adopted a variety of indexing strategies and best-match term weighted retrieval. The indexing strategies used can generally be divided into the following: n-gram character string matching string, fuzzy matching of word and character strings, and automated "correction" of words using a dictionary. In addition, several participants explored the use of automated feedback strategies to perform a second retrieval pass. Results using these different indexing methods were generally inconclusive; the track co-ordinators were unsure as to whether retrieval effectiveness was affected more by the indexing method or the retrieval strategy adopted [1]. However, overall as would expected, increasing error rates in indexing reduced retrieval performance.

University of Nevada, Las Vegas. A large number of experimental studies have been carried out at the University of Nevada, Las Vegas over a period of years. Results of many of these experiments are summarised in [6]. Relevant conclusions from these studies include: term frequency functions have to be chosen carefully for this task, and that relevance feedback is less reliable than for text retrieval.

ETH Zurich. Mittendorf working at ETH Zurich carried out a careful analysis of the impact of recognition errors on retrieval behaviour [7]. Working with the TREC-5 Confusion Track collection, she concluded that in general the impact of recognition errors on retrieval will be less for long verbose documents. While this is an important result, it suggests that the adverse affect on retrieval of recognition errors on the relatively short documents in the TREC-8 SDR collection used in our experiments may be significant. She also suggests that adopting word-based indexing is best for lightly corrupted data, such as that used in the investigation described in this paper.

3 Test Collections

The cost of developing new test collections for information retrieval research is considerable. In the case of ad hoc retrieval tasks it requires development of a document set, but also a set of search requests and corresponding manual relevance assessments. Although methods such as pooling are typically used to reduce the number of documents which must be checked for relevance, the cost is very high for more than very small collections. The cost of developing multimedia retrieval collections is higher still since, in addition to the steps required for text collections, the document set must be manually verified to check the contents.

Since it was beyond the resources of the IRMMC project to develop a new multimedia retrieval collection, it was decided to adapt the existing TREC-8 SDR collection to enable a study in mixed-media retrieval to be conducted. The TREC-8 SDR collection is based on the English broadcast news portion of the TDT-2 News Corpus. In order to develop a mixed-media collection the existing SDR collection of text and spoken document sets was augmented by forming a corresponding scanned document collection.

The remainder of this section outlines the structure of the TREC-8 SDR collection set, SDR retrieval task, the implementation of our printed document collection and the design of our mixed-media test collection.

3.1 TDT-2

The TREC-8 SDR portion of the TDT-2 News Corpus covers a period of 5 months from February to June 1998. The news data is taken from 4 sources as follows: CNN "Headline News" (about 80 stories in 4 programmes per day), ABC "World News Tonight" (about 15 stories in 1 programme per day), PRI "The World" (about 20 stories in one programme per day) and VOA English news programmes (about 40 stories from 2 programmes per day). The sampling frequencies are approximate and all sources were prone to some failures in the data collection process.

Each broadcast is manually segmented into a number of news stories which form the basic document unit of the corpus. Each news story is uniquely identified by a "DOCNO" indicating the source, date and time of the broadcast, and the location of the story within the broadcast. An individual news story was defined as containing two or more declarative statements about a single event. Miscellaneous data including commercial breaks, music interludes, and trailers were ignored. The collection contains a total of 21,754 stories with an average length of 180 words totalling about 385 hours of audio data.

There is no high-quality human reference transcription available for TDT-2 - only "closed-caption" quality transcriptions for the television sources and rough transcripts quickly made for the radio sources by commercial transcription services. These transcriptions are used to assess baseline retrieval performance. A detailed manual transcription of a randomly selected 10 hour subset was carried to enable speech recognition and baseline transcription accuracy to be evaluated. The television closed-caption sources were found to have a Word Error Rate of approximately 14.5% and radio sources to have a Word Error Rate of around 7.5%. These error rates are significant with the television closed caption error rates approaching those for state-of-the-art broadcast news recognisers [2].

3.2 TREC-8 SDR Test Collection

The TREC-8 SDR retrieval test collection was completed by forming a set of 50 search topics and corresponding relevance assessments. The goal in creating the topics was to devise topics with a few (but not too many) relevant documents in the collection to appropriately challenge test retrieval systems. Retrieval runs submitted by the TREC-8 SDR participants were used to form document pools for manual relevance assessment [2]. The average topic length was 13.7 words and the mean number of relevant documents for each topic was 36.4. Note: only 49 of the topics were ultimately adjudged to have relevant documents within the TREC-8 SDR corpus [8].

3.3 Spoken Documents

The Spoken Document transcriptions used in our experiments are taken from the TDT-2 version 3 CD-ROMs. The transcription set used is designated `as1` on this release and was generated by NIST using the BBN BYBLOS Rough'N'Ready transcription system using a dynamically updated rolling language model. This transcription was designated "B2" in the official NIST TREC-8 SDR documentation and "B1" in the corresponding TREC-9 SDR documentation. Full details of this recognition system are contained in [9]. The recognition performance of this transcription is shown in Figure 1

Table 1. Word Error Rate (WER) on 10 hour subset of the TREC-8 SDR evaluation set for "B2" baseline transcription.

Correct	Substitutions	Deletions	Insertions	Word Error Rate
76.5%	17.2%	6.2%	3.2%	26.7%

3.4 Scanned Document Collection

The scanned document collection was based on the 21,759 "NEWS" stories in TDT-2 Version 3 (December 1999). The objective in the design of the printed version of the collection was to create story hardcopy similar in style to newspaper clippings. In order to simulate the differences in formatting of stories from different newspaper sources it was decided to print each story in one of four fonts: *Times*, *Pandora*, *Computer Modern* and *San serif*. The stories were divided roughly equally between these font types. Material from ABC, PRI and VOA was assigned to each font on a sequential basis evenly over the time span of the collection. The stories were printed in one of 6 different widths as follows and in 1 of 3 different font sizes. The text column width and font size was assigned sequentially from the beginning of each broadcast. These were printed in single column format running onto a second page if necessary. The stories were printed using a Epson EPL-N4000 laser printer. Further details of the collection design are contained in [10].

Since the stories had been newly printed onto white paper using a high quality laser printer, the best available current OCR technologies would have been able to provide almost perfect transcriptions. However, the operational target of scanned document retrieval is more usually legacy documents printed using mechanical methods, and for which the print quality is usually inferior to current printings. In order to explore retrieval behaviour with a more errorful transcription an OCR transcription was performed with suboptimal system settings. After some ad hoc exploration of OCR accuracy versus the system parameters, the transcription was created as follows. All documents were scanned using an HPScanJet ADF at 200 dpi in Black & White at a threshold of 100. OCR was carried out using Page Keeper Standard Version 3.0 (OCR Engine Version 271) (SR3). Errors include typical OCR mistakes such as the recognition of `journal` as `joumal`. This obviously assumes that the type of errors created will be similar to those observed for legacy documents with high quality OCR, however this has not been experimentally verified. The OCR process introduced some errors into document titles, these were all manually verified and errors corrected in order to ensure accuracy of document titles. Document titles are regarded as metadata which must be accurately recorded in order to manage the archive reliably.

The underlying inaccuracy of the baseline transcription means that a comparison of retrieval behaviour between SDR and DIR is affected both by the differing accuracy levels and error behaviour of SR and OCR, but also by the observation that SR is attempting to transcribe the actual spoken data and the OCR seeks to recognise the images of the inaccurate baseline transcriptions. The DIR retrieval results thus provide a direct measurement of the effect of OCR errors on retrieval behaviour, while the relationship between the SDR results and the baseline is less clear. Intuitively it would appear that DIR will never be better than the reference transcription, while if the recognition accuracy of SR is better than that of the reference, the SDR retrieval performance might actually be better than that of the reference. Measuring the actual recognition performance of the OCR system relative to the reference transcription is a topic of current work.

3.5 Design of the Mixed-Media Collection

The experimental mixed-media collection is based on a partition of the existing mono-media documents collections of electronic text, spoken data and scanned document images. There are many different ways in which the data could be partitioned, but an individual document must be present in only one media. For the current mixed-media collection design it is assumed that the collection contains similar proportions from each media source. In practice this latter assumption will often not be true for real collections, and will depend on the operating domain of the system. However, this decomposition is designed to enable retrieval behaviour of the different media forms within the mixed-media collection to be explored without bias towards or against the proportions of individual media.

The mixed-media collection partition is based on a further subdivision of each of the existing scanned document images subsets into a further 3 subsection. Thus broadcasts for each source for each font are partitioned sequentially into subcollections i, ii, iii. The name of each broadcast and story for each media was augmented to indicate its subcollection. The partitions i, ii, iii are then gathered together to form three overall subsets of the complete document collection. To form the mixed-media collection i, ii, iii are assigned to individual media as follows:

	Media		
Mixed-Media Collection	i	ii	iii
MMC1	T	I	S
MMC2	T	S	I
MMC3	S	I	T

Key: T = text, S = spoken, I = image.

Once the structure of the mixed-media collection was decided, copies of the broadcasts were made with their names augmented to indicate the media source. Similarly the label of each story within each broadcast was augmented to indicate its media. Thus individual stories and their original media could easily be identified within the collection and within retrieved document lists. Thus each of the collections defined above had a unique list of names stories indicating their media. A separate relevance file was formed for each collection and for each media type within each mixed-media collection to enable the retrieval behaviour of each media subcollection to be explored.

4 Information Retrieval Methods

The basis of the experimental system is the City University research distribution version of the Okapi system [11]. The retrieval model used in Okapi has been shown to be very effective in a number comparative evaluation exercises in recent years and has been adopted in many IR research systems.

The retrieval strategy adopted in this investigation follows standard practice for best-match ranked retrieval. The documents and search topics were first processed to remove common stop words from a list of around 260 words, suffix stripped using the Okapi implementation of Porter stemming [12] to encourage matching of different word forms, and terms were further indexed using a small set of synonyms.

4.1 Term Weighting

Following preprocessing document terms are weighted using the Okapi *combined weight* (cw), often known as BM25, [11]. The BM25 cw for a term is calculated as follows,

$$cw(i,j) = \frac{cfw(i) \times tf(i,j) \times (K1+1)}{K1 \times ((1-b) + (b \times ndl(j))) + tf(i,j)}$$

where $cw(i,j)$ represents the weight of term i in document j, $cfw(i) = \log(N/n(i))$ the standard collection frequency (inverse document frequency) weight, $n(i)$ is the total number of documents containing term i, and N is the total number of documents in the collection, $tf(i,j)$ is the document term frequency, and $ndl(j) = dl(j)$ Av. dl is the normalised document length where $dl(j)$ is the length of j. $K1$ and b are empirically selected tuning constants for a particular collection. The matching score for each document is computed by summing the weights of terms appearing in the query and the document, which bare then returned in order of decreasing matching score. BM25 has performed well in SDR evaluations [2], and has been shown to be effective for DIR [13].

4.2 Pseudo-Relevance Feedback

The performance of IR systems can often be improved by a process of Relevance Feedback (RF) query expansion, which adds terms to the original query to better describe the information need. Full RF relies on true user relevance judgements, the alternative Pseudo RF (PRF) method assumes a number of top ranked documents from the initial to be relevant. PRF is on average found to give improvement in retrieval performance, although this is usually smaller than that observed for true user based RF. The main implementational issue for PRF is the selection of appropriate expansion terms. In the standard Okapi approach potential expansion terms are ranked using the Robertson selection value (rsv) [14], defined as,

$$rsv(i) = r(i) \times rw(i)$$

where $r(i)$ is again the number of relevant documents containing term i, and $rw(i)$ is the standard Robertson/Sparck Jones relevance weight [11] defined as,

$$rw(i) = \log \frac{(r(i)+0.5)(N-n(i)-R+r(i)+0.5)}{(n(i)-r(i)+0.5)(R-r(i)+0.5)}$$

where $n(i)$ and N have the same definitions as before and R is the total number of relevant documents for this query. The top ranking terms are then added to the query.

Problems can arise in PRF when terms taken from assumed relevant documents that are actually non-relevant, are added to the query causing a drift in the focus of the query. Standard RF and PRF methods treat the whole document as relevant, the implication of this being that using terms from non-relevant sections of these documents for expansion may also cause query drift. To reduce the number of expansion terms taken from non-relevant material, we have developed a term selection method for PRF based on document summarisation [15]. Results using this method have been very encouraging and we adopt it in this investigation. By focusing on the key elements of the document our method seeks to exclude possible expansion terms not closely associated with the main focus of the document. The summary is formed by taking a fixed number of sentences from each document selected using a combination of statistical and heuristic techniques [15].

5 Experimental Investigations

This section describes our current investigation of retrieval from the three separate media collections: text, spoken and scanned image, and retrieval from the mixed-media collections. In both case initial experiments give results for baseline retrieval and then results for the application of PRF for query expansion. Results for the mixed-media collections give overall collection performance and for the individual media subsets within the collections.

Results are shown for retrieval precision at 10 document cutoff, standard TREC average precision and the total number of relevant documents retrieved. The number of relevant documents retrieved in each case can be compared to the total number of relevant documents across all topic statements in the TREC-8 SDR test set of 1818.

Table 2. Baseline mono-media collection retrieval results.

Media	Text			Speech			Image		
	P10	AvP	RelRet	P10	AvP	RelRet	P10	AvP	RelRet
No Fbk	0.551	0.468	1608	0.396	0.329	1222	0.557	0.454	1581
chg. media	—	—	—	-28.1%	-29.7%	-386	+1.0%	-3.0%	-27

Table 3. Mono-media collection retrieval results with summary based feedback.

Media	Text			Speech			OCR		
	P10	AvP	RelRet	P10	AvP	RelRet	P10	AvP	RelRet
Fbk 5	0.580	0.506	1639	0.451	0.396	1544	0.574	0.448	1578
chg. media	—	—	—	-22.2%	-21.7%	-95	-1.0%	-1.6%	-61
chg. bl.	+5.3%	+8.1%	+31	+13.9%	+20.4%	+322	+3.1%	+9.7%	-3
Fbk 20	0.598	0.514	1631	0.516	0.432	1503	0.534	0.440	1385
chg. media	—	—	—	-13.7%	-16.0%	-128	-10.7%	-14.4%	-246
chg. bl.	+8.5%	+9.8%	+23	+30.3%	+31.3%	+281	-4.1%	-3.1%	-196

5.1 Mono-Media Retrieval

Baseline Results. Table 2 shows baseline retrieval results for each media type. These results confirm the expected result that best performance in terms of both 10 document cutoff and average precision, and the number of relevant documents retrieved is achieved for TR with the original electronic documents. For SDR and DIR average precision is reduced by around 30% and 3% respectively. The difference in retrieval performance between SDR and DIR is related to the accuracy of indexing and thus no direct comparison is possible between the figures for the different media.

Pseudo-Relevance Feedback. Table 3 shows retrieval results for each media type with summary-based feedback. In all cases the summary uses 6 sentences, 5 documents for feedback terms and 20 documents for term selection. The table shows results for feedback with 5 and 20 expansion terms. The weight of the original query terms was in each data multiplied by 1.5. It can be seen that while TR and SDR perform best with 20 expansion terms, best performance for DIR is observed when only 5 expansion terms are used. It is important to understand this difference in retrieval behaviour in order to develop more effective feedback techniques for each media type, and in particular so that the most appropriate strategies can be adopted in the case of mixed-media collections.

One question that arises in analysing these results is whether DIR performs better with less expansion terms because poor expansion terms are selected as the number increases, or because of matching issues between the query terms and the errorful OCR output based on the scanned document images. In order to explore this effect a further set of experiments were performed. The best baseline retrieval results are observed with the electronic text data, thus the expansion terms selected here are likely to be the best of those for the three collections. In order to see whether a better set of expansion terms has a significant impact

Table 4. Text Collection retrieval results with summary-based feedback using 20 expansion terms from different baseline sources.

	Text exp. terms			SDR exp. terms			DIR exp. terms		
	P10	AvP	RelRet	P10	AvP	RelRet	P10	AvP	RelRet
Fbk 20	0.598	0.514	1631	0.602	0.506	1608	0.608	0.518	1630
chg. media	—	—	—	+0.7%	-1.6%	-23	+1.7%	+0.8%	-1

Table 5. SDR retrieval results with summary-based feedback using 20 expansion terms from text baseline retrieval.

	SDR exp. terms			Text exp. terms		
	P10	AvP	RelRet	P10	AvP	RelRet
Fbk 20	0.516	0.432	1503	0.580	0.479	1515
chg. media	—	—	—	+12.4%	+10.9%	+22

Table 6. DIR retrieval results with summary-based feedback using 5 and 20 expansion terms from text baseline retrieval.

	DIR exp. terms			Text exp. terms		
	P10	AvP	RelRet	P10	AvP	RelRet
Fbk 5	0.574	0.498	1578	0.567	0.490	1610
chg. media	—	—	—	-1.2%	-1.6%	+32
Fbk 20	0.534	0.440	1385	0.516	0.420	1364
chg. media	—	—	—	-3.4%	-4.5%	-21

on retrieval performance the electronic text expansion terms were added to the queries for SDR and DIR, with the reverse experiments being performed using the electronic text data with expansion terms taken from initial runs using the spoken data and the scanned image data.

Table 4 shows the effect on text retrieval with PRF of using expansion terms from baseline SDR and DIR runs. It can be seen that these alternative expansion sets give a very small variation in performance. The small difference is interesting because it gives a strong indication that the expansion method is very robust to the indexing errors in individual documents present in both spoken document transcriptions and OCR output.

Table 5 shows SDR retrieval with summary-based PRF comparing expansion terms derived from SDR and text retrieval baseline runs. In this case text retrieval derived expansion terms improve retrieval in the feedback run both in terms of average precision and the number of relevant documents retrieval. It should be noted that the +10% improvement arising from use of the TR derived expansion terms is *in addition* to the +30% relative to the baseline when using the SDR derived expansion terms. This result indicates that the level of improvement in SDR due to query expansion can be significant, but is heavily dependent on the selected expansion terms. The reason for this effect relates to the high word error rate in the transcription, use of an effective expansion set is able to exploit redundancy in the document transcription to match with

Table 7. Baseline mono-media collection retrieval results for mixed-media collection partitions.

	MMC1			MMC2			MMC3		
	P10	AvP	RelRet	P10	AvP	RelRet	P10	AvP	RelRet
Text	0.202	0.227	578	0.202	0.227	578	0.225	0.253	636
Speech	0.170	0.203	551	0.169	0.201	340	0.159	0.161	428
Image	0.188	0.222	397	0.221	0.239	630	0.185	0.221	395

Table 8. Mono-media collection retrieval results with 20 term summary-based PRF for mixed-media collection partitions.

	MMC1			MMC2			MMC3		
	P10	AvP	RelRet	P10	AvP	RelRet	P10	AvP	RelRet
Text	0.224	0.263	590	0.224	0.263	590	0.243	0.264	642
chge	+10.9%	+15.9%	+12	+10.9%	+15.9%	+12	+8.0%	+4.3%	+6
Speech	0.212	0.226	599	0.185	0.224	370	0.180	0.200	533
chge	+24.7%	+11.3%	+48	+9.5%	+11.4%	+30	+13.2%	+24.2%	+105
Image	0.156	0.201	355	0.230	0.233	546	0.154	0.200	353
chge	-17.0%	-9.5%	-42	+4.1%	-2.5%	-84	-16.8%	-9.5%	-42

correctly recognised terms. The more terms are matched by the expanded query the more effective is the retrieval.

Table 6 shows DIR performance using DIR and text baseline retrieval derived expansion terms produce a small reduction in DIR retrieval. Interestingly for 5 expansion terms the number of relevant documents retrieved increases, while for 20 expansion terms it is reduced.

Thus the differences in retrieval behaviour for the different sources must be related to differences in indexing, and how this relates to the query-document matching, and perhaps in some way to the effect on term weights that result from the indexing errors. These effects need to be examined in more detail by further experimentation.

5.2 Mixed-Media Retrieval

The initial results show retrieval performance for the mixed-media subsets with the mono-media collections used in the previous section. These results are then compared against results in the next section for the true mixed-media collections.

Tables 7 and 8 summarise the mono-media subset results for baseline and PRF respectively for the media partitions in collections MMC1, MMC2 and MMC3. Thus the results in these tables do not show results for a single collection, but merely bring together the results relevant documents for single media collections in the the media that actually appear in the mixed-media collections. Tables 9 and 10 show results for the actual mixed-media collections. The results show performance for the complete collections and for the individual media subsets within the collections.

Table 9. Baseline mixed-media collection retrieval results.

	MMC1			MMC2			MMC3		
	P10	AvP	RelRet	P10	AvP	RelRet	P10	AvP	RelRet
Text	0.226	0.236	569	0.211	0.236	568	0.245	0.258	631
chge mono	+11.9%	+4.0%	-9	+4.5%	+4.0%	-10	+8.9%	+2.0%	-5
Speech	0.204	0.208	619	0.136	0.192	366	0.150	0.165	526
chge mono	+20.0%	+2.5%	+68	-19.5%	-4.5%	+26	-1.7%	+2.5%	+98
Image	0.190	0.226	397	0.234	0.242	624	0.193	0.217	396
chge mono	+1.0%	+1.8%	+0	+5.9%	+1.3%	-6	+4.3%	-1.8%	+1
All	0.565	0.450	1583	0.531	0.445	1558	0.537	0.434	1553

Table 10. Mixed-media collection retrieval results with 20 term summary-based PRF.

	MMC1			MMC2			MMC3		
	P10	AvP	RelRet	P10	AvP	RelRet	P10	AvP	RelRet
Text	0.222	0.244	557	0.224	0.244	564	0.247	0.245	598
chge bl	-1.8%	+3.4%	-3	+6.2%	+3.4%	-4	+0.8%	-5.0%	-33
chge mono	-0.9%	-7.2%	-33	0.0%	-7.2%	-26	+1.6%	-7.2%	-44
Speech	0.266	0.291	641	0.182	0.245	384	0.189	0.234	576
chge bl	+30.4%	+39.9%	+22	+33.8%	+27.6%	+18	+26.0%	+41.8%	+50
chge mono	+25.5%	+28.8%	+42	-1.6%	+9.4%	+14	+5.0%	+17.0%	+43
Image	0.181	0.203	384	0.238	0.239	620	0.181	0.225	381
chge bl	-4.7%	-10.2%	-13	+1.7%	-1.2%	-4	-6.2%	-3.7%	-1
chge mono	+16.0%	+1.0%	+29	+3.5%	+2.6%	+74	+17.5%	+12.5%	+28
All	0.612	0.506	1580	0.582	0.490	1568	0.565	0.473	1555
chge bl	+8.3%	+12.4%	-3	+9.6%	+10.1%	+10	+9.0%	+9.0%	+2

Baseline Results. Table 9 shows baseline mixed-media results. The row "chge mono" shows the change in performance for relevant documents in this media relative to the mono-media results in Table 7. These results show a number of interesting features. The first overall comment is that similar behaviour is observed for all three mixed-media collections MMC1, MMC2 and MMC3; thus the results observed in this table can be attributed to features of the document media rather than documents themselves and the relevance data.

For TR there is a consistent small increase in both precision at 10 document cutoff and average precision, also in all cases there is a very small reduction in the number of relevant documents retrieved. For SDR there are small positive and negative changes in average precision, and large positive and negative variations in precision at 10 document cutoff. In all cases there is a large increase in the overall number of relevant documents retrieved. There is little change in DIR performance. Comparing the overall results in the final row with the mono-media results for TR, SDR and DIR in Table 2 it can be seen that overall mixed-media results are lower than those for TR and DIR, but better than those for SDR. The overall results can be anticipated from the subset results in Table 9. The differences between the mono-media and mixed-media retrieval results can be attributed to one or more of a number of factors:

- Variation in the $cfw(i)$ values. Compared to the mono-media collections the N value will be the same; $n(i)$ will be less accurate than for TR due to indexing errors in the other media, but more accurate than for SDR and DIR.
- There will be a small variation in the "Average *dl* for all documents" compared to all collections.
- Differences in query-document matching for the different media may interact to cause overall variations in behaviour for the mixed-media collection.

Determination of the way in which these factors interact will require further experimental investigation. However, some analysis of these results can be carried out at this point. For TR, the indexing errors in the other media will reduce the reliability of the $cfw(i)$ values which would be expected to reduce retrieval effectiveness. However, the small increase in results here probably arises from indexing errors in other media leading to increased rank of some text documents despite the less reliable term weights.

Pseudo-Relevance Feedback. Table 10 shows results for mixed-media retrieval with the application of summary-based PRF with 20 expansion terms. The row "chge mono" shows the the change in performance for relevant documents in this media relative to the mono-media results in Table 8, and the row "chge bl" shows the change in mixed-media performance itself relative to the baseline results shown in Table 9.

For TR PRF gives a small improvement over baseline in 2 cases and a decrease in the other. Relative to TR performance for the mono-media collections the mixed-media results are consistently lower by -7.2% for average precision, but little changed with respect to precision at cutoff of 10 documents and number of relevant documents retrieved. This contrasts with baseline performance where mixed-media text results were slightly improved. There is no change in either case in term weights between the baseline and PDF results. Further the results in Table 4 show that differences in selected expansion terms have little effect on retrieval behaviour for TR. The reasons for the difference in the mixed-media case may result from one or both of two sources. Term weights for some of the selected expansion terms may be slightly less reliable in the mixed-media collection. Thus some added terms while actually good selections in terms of expressing information need, may adversely affect retrieval behaviour since they have poorly estimated $cfw(i)$ values. The other effect relates to the behaviour of documents in other media and how they interact with Text documents. Since the indexing of the Text documents is the most accurate and therefore the expected average number of query-document term matches the highest, it would be expected that the matching scores of these documents would dominant the mixed list. In view of this observation the term weighting explanation is probably the more likely.

Retrieval precision for SDR with PRF improves both with respect to the mixed-media baseline on average by more than +30% and also with respect to the mono-media result, but less uniformly by between +10% and +25%, although in the latter case improvement in precision at cutoff 10 is much lower and in one case actually falls slightly. The improvement relative to the baseline is to be expected from the behaviour for the mono-media in Table 3, in addition Table 5 indicates that further improvement can be achieved using a better expansion terms. The baseline performance for mixed-media retrieval is closer to TR than SDR, so the added expansion terms are likely to be closer to those for TR, and thus very effective for SDR.

Looking at DIR it can be seen that retrieval performance with application of PDF is reduced. However, comparing with the result for 20 term expansion for the mono-media result, it can be seen that the reduction in the mixed-media collection is much reduced. The reason that the degradation in performance is much less for mixed-media may again relate to the improved term weights and also indexing characteristics of the Text and Spoken documents which behave well with PRF. Another interesting feature is the increase in the number of Scanned Image documents retrieved with PRF in the mixed-media collection. Note, it would have been possible to use 5 term expansion for the Scanned Image documents in the mixed-media collection, however, the matching score of documents will be related to the length of the queries and use of 5 term expansion term would bias retrieval against Scanned Image documents.

6 Conclusions and Further Work

This paper has described the first comparative experimental investigation of the retrieval from parallel Text, Spoken and Scanned Image document collections both within separate mono-media collections and also combined together as unique subsets within mixed-media collections. Query expansion via summary-based PRF is shown to provide large improvements in performance for SDR, good improvements for TR, but surprisingly can lead to significant reduction in performance for DIR.

Mixed-media retrieval performs well without compensation for media specific indexing problems. Baseline mixed-media retrieval results for all media improve relative to mono-media performance. In addition, PRF is again highly effective for the spoken documents, useful for text documents, but DIR is again reduced.

Investigation and analysis only represents the first part of the process. The final objective must be to improve retrieval performance for the mixed-media collection. The performance is already quite close to TR in some cases which can probably be regarded as a upper limit on performance (without application of additional techniques to improve general retrieval performance). However, there are clearly issues, such as the failure of PRF for DIR, that once properly understood may be addressed by suitable indexing correction or compensation techniques.

Acknowledgement. The IRMMC project was supported by UK EPSRC grant GR/N04034.

References

[1] P. B. Kantor and E. M. Voorhees. The TREC-5 Confusion Track: Comparing Retrieval Methods for Scanned Text. *Information Retrieval*, 2:165–176, 2000.

[2] J. S. Garafolo, C. G. P. Auzanne, and E. M. Voorhees. The TREC Spoken Document Retrieval Track: A Success Story. In *Proceedings of the RIAO 2000 Conference: Content-Based Multimedia Information Access*, pages 1–20, Paris, 2000.

[3] M. Wechsler, E. Munteanu, and P. Schauble. New Techniques for Open-Vocabulary Spoken Document Retrieval. In *Proceedings of the 21st Annual International ACM SIGIR Conference on Research and Development in Information Retrieval*, pages 20–27, Melbourne, 1998. ACM.

[4] G. J. F. Jones, J. T. Foote, K. Sparck Jones, and S. J. Young. Retrieving spoken documents by combining multiple index sources. In *Proceedings of the 19th Annual International ACM SIGIR Conference on Research and Development in Information Retrieval*, pages 30–38, Zurich, 1996. ACM.

[5] M. Sanderson and F. Crestani. Mixing and merging for spoken document retrieval. In *Proceedings of the 2nd European Conference on Digital Libraries*, pages 397–407, Heraklion, Greece, 1998. Springer Verlag.

[6] K. Taghva, J. Borsack, and A. Condit. Evaluation of Model-Based Retrieval Effectiveness with OCR Text. *ACM Transactions on Information Systems*, 14(1):64–93, 1996.

[7] E. Mittendorf and P. Schauble. Information Retrieval can Cope with Many Errors. *Information Retrieval*, 3:189–216, 2000.

[8] S. E. Johnson, P. Jourlin, K. Spark Jones, and P.C. Woodland. Spoken Document Retrieval for TREC-8 at Cambridge University. In D. K. Harman and E. M. Voorhees, editors, *Proceedings of the Eighth Text REtrieval Conference (TREC-7)*, pages 157–168, Gaithersburg, MD, 2000. NIST.

[9] C. Auzanne, J. S. Garafolo, J. G. Fiscus, and W. M. Fisher. Automatic Language Model Adaptation for Spoken Document Retrieval. In *Proceedings of the RIAO 2000 Conference: Content-Based Multimedia Information Access*, pages 1–20, Paris, 2000.

[10] G.J.F.Jones and M.Han. Information Retrieval from Mixed-Media Collections: Report on Design and Indexing of a Scanned Document Collection. Technical Report 400, Department of Computer Science, University of Exeter, January 2001.

[11] S. E. Robertson, S. Walker, S. Jones, M. M. Hancock-Beaulieu, and M. Gatford. Okapi at TREC-3. In D. K. Harman, editor, *Overview of the Third Text REtrieval Conference (TREC-3)*, pages 109–126. NIST, 1995.

[12] M. F. Porter. An algorithm for suffix stripping. *Program*, 14:130–137, 1980.

[13] G. J. F. Jones and M. Han. Retrieving scanned documents from a mixed-media document collection. In *Proceedings of the BCS-IRSG European Colloquium on IR Research*, pages 136–149, Darmstadt, April 2001.

[14] S. E. Robertson. On term selection for query expansion. *Journal of Documentation*, 46:359–364, 1990.

[15] A. M. Lam-Adesina and G. J. F. Jones. Applying Summarization Techniques for Term Selection in Relevance Feedback. In *Proceedings of the 24th Annual International ACM SIGIR Conference on Research and Development in Information Retrieval*, pages 1–9, New Orleans, 2001. ACM.

Alignment of Performances with Scores Aimed at Content-Based Music Access and Retrieval

Nicola Orio

Department of Information Engineering
University of Padova
nicola.orio@unipd.it

Abstract. Music digital libraries pose interesting and challenging research problems, in particular for the development of methodologies and tools for the retrieval of music documents. One difficult aspect of content-based retrieval of musical works is that only scores can be represented by a symbolic notation, while performances, which are of interest for the majority of users, allow for access based on bibliographic values only. The research work reported in this paper proposes to index and retrieve music performances through an automatic alignment of acoustic recordings with the music scores. Alignment my allow for: automatic recognition of performances, aimed at cataloging large collections of recordings; automatic tagging of performances, aimed at an easy access to long recordings. The methodology is based on the use of hidden Markov models, a powerful tool that has been successfully used in many research areas, like speech recognition and molecular biology. The approach has been tested on a collection of acoustic and synthetic performances, showing good results in the recognition and in the tagging of performances. The proposed approach can be used to increase the functionalities of a music digital library, allowing for content-based access to scores and recordings.

1 Introduction

There is an increasing interest towards music stored in digital format, which is witnessed by the widespread diffusion on the Web of standards for audio like MP3. There are a number of reasons to explain such a diffusion of digital music. First of all, music is an art form that can be shared by people with different culture because it crosses the barriers of national languages and cultural backgrounds. For example, tonal Western music has passionate followers also in Japan and many persons in Europe are keen on classical Indian music: all of them can enjoy music without the need of a translation, which is normally required for accessing foreign textual works. Another reason is that technology for music recording, digitalization, and playback, allows for an access that is almost comparable to the listening of a live performance, at least at the level of audio quality, and the signal to noise ratio is better for digital formats than for many analog formats. This is not the case of other art forms, like painting or sculpture, for which the digital format is only an approximate representation

M. Agosti and C. Thanos (Eds.): ECDL 2002, LNCS 2458, pp. 479–492, 2002.

of the artwork. The access to digitized paintings can be useful for studying the works of a given artist, but cannot substitute the direct interaction with the "real world" works. Moreover, music is an art form that can be both cultivated and popular, and sometimes it is impossible to draw a line between the two, as for jazz or for most of ethnic music.

These reasons, among others, may explain the increasing number of projects involving the creation of music digital libraries. A music digital library allows for, and benefits from, the access by users from all over the world, it helps the preservation of cultural heritage, and it is not tailored only to scholars' or researchers' needs. Yet, music has some peculiarities that have to be taken into account when developing a music digital library.

A musical work can be represented in two main forms: the music score, which is a symbolic notation of the music events, and the recording of a performance, which is an audio signal as captured by one or more microphones. Both forms may be of interest for the users of a music digital library, because music is both a composing and a performing art. For the aims of a music digital library, the music score is an easier form to deal with, because it is a structured representation made of a finite number of symbols. On the other hand, most of the users are probably interested in accessing to music performances. Since the recording of a performance is an unstructured sequence of sound events, users cannot benefit from tools for music browsing, and the evaluation of documents relevance in a retrieval session can be a time-consuming task. A more detailed discussion on the peculiarities of music and their impact on the access to a music digital library is reported in Section 2.

This paper addresses the problems arising from the dual nature, symbolic and acoustic, of music and from the time constraints of its access. An approach is presented for overcoming the problem of indexing music performances digitally stored as plain, untagged audio signals. The approach is based on the automatic recognition of performances when their scores are available, through the use of hidden Markov models, a powerful tool that has been extensively used in many different research areas. Automatic alignment and tagging allow for automatic cataloging of hours of music recordings. When an audio signal is recognized to be the performance of a score, it can be automatically indexed through its symbolic notation using techniques that have been developed for music information retrieval. After performances are associated to scores, it is also possible to develop tools for an easier access to music documents. The score is used to superimpose a fine grained structure to the audio signal, allowing for a fast access to different parts of the music document. The methodology for the automatic alignment is presented in Section 3, while Section 4 reports a preliminary study on a prototype system.

2 Music Digital Libraries

There are a number of relevant issues related to accessing to music digital libraries. Apart from the problem of digital acquisition of music works and the creation of a database of music documents, which are a challenging problem by themselves as reported in [1] and [5], a crucial aspect is the development of methodologies and tools for the content-based indexing and retrieval of music documents. Methodologies should be developed according to the peculiarities of the music language [7].

2.1 Formats of Music Documents

The communication in music is achieved at two levels: the composer translates his emotions into a musical structure, that is represented by a music score, and the musician translates the written score into a performance, that is represented by a flow of acoustic events. Thus the same music work can be represented in two main *forms*: the symbolic notation of the score and the acoustic recording of the performance. A number of different digital *formats* correspond to each form. It can be noted that, as musicians can interpret scores, the resulting performances differ and therefore more than one performance correspond to a single score. Even if the two forms can be considered as instantiations of the same object, they substantially differ in the information that can be manually or automatically extracted from their respective formats.

- The *score* is a structured organization of symbols, which correspond to acoustic events; the score is a direct representation of all the dimensions of music – i.e., melody, harmony, and rhythm – and it usually contains all the information that is relevant for classifying and cataloging: type of movement, time and key signatures, composer's notes, and so on. The symbolic nature of the score allows for an easy representation of its content, and many proposed formats represents score in the form of a textual markup language, for instance ABC and GUIDO.
- The *performance* is made of a sequence of gestures performed by musicians on their musical instruments; the result is a continuous flow of acoustic waves, which correspond to the vibration induced on musical instruments. Even if all the dimensions of music are embedded in a performance, it requires high-level information processing to recognize them. In particular, only experienced musicians can recognize all the dimensions of music from listening to a performance and, at the state of the art, there is no automatic system that can recognize them from an acoustic recording, apart from trivial cases. The nature of a performance does not allow for an easy representation of its content. The formats adopted to digitally represent performances, such as AIFF (Audio Interchange File Format, proposed by Apple Computers) or MP3 (MPEG 1, Layer 3), are a plain digital coding of the acoustic sound waves, with a possible data compression.

Content-based indexing and retrieval of symbolic representations of music documents have been addressed by several research works. Some interesting work on content-based music retrieval, mostly based on the use of MIDI format, are reported in [2], [6], [8], [9], and [16].

A Note on MIDI. A format that can be considered as a compromise between the score and the performance forms is MIDI (Musical Instrument Digital Interface), which was proposed in 1982 for data exchange among digital instruments [14]. MIDI carries both information about musical events, from which it is possible to reconstruct an approximate representation of the score, and information for driving a synthesizer, from which it is possible to listen to a simplified automatic performance. It seems then that MIDI draws a link between the two different forms for music representation. This characteristics, together with the fortune of MIDI as an exchange format in the early times of the Internet, can explain why many music digital libraries and most projects regarding music indexing and retrieval refer to it. Some of the research work on music information retrieval take advantage of the availability of MIDI files of about all the different musical genres and styles. MIDI files are parsed in order to extract a representation of the music score, and then indexed after different preprocessing.

Nevertheless, MIDI is becoming obsolete and users on the Internet increasingly prefer to exchange digital music stored in other formats such as MP3 or RealAudio, because they allow for a good audio-quality with a considerably small dimension of the documents size. Moreover, if the goal of a music digital library is to preserve the cultural heritage, more complete formats for storing both scores and performances are required. Being a compromise between two different needs – i.e., to represent symbols and to be playable – MIDI turns out to fit neither the needs of users who want to access to a complete digital representation of the score, nor to users who want to listen to high-quality audio performances.

2.2 Users of a Music Digital Library

The two forms, and the corresponding formats in which they are stored, may be of interest for different classes of *users*. For the sake of simplicity, users may be divided in two typologies, even if users' expertise and information needs span in a continuum.

At one extreme, musicians, composers, and music scholars may wish to access to digital representations of scores, because they are interested in finding particular compositions to perform, in studying particular musical structures used by well-known composers, or in drawing parallels among different styles. These users, which can be considered *expert users*, are able to extract the needed information from the score thanks to their musical background. Expert users are likely to clearly express their information needs when accessing to a music digital library, because of their knowledge of music structure, dimensions, and styles. The musical background may also allow for a good knowledge of the bibliographic information normally used when cataloging musical works, such as name of the composer, title of the composition, period, style, and so on. Nevertheless, as expressed in [9], a content-based retrieval of musical works can be useful also for this class of uses.

At the other extreme there are *casual users*, which may not be able to read music scores, and who can only access to, and are basically interested in, recordings of performances. Casual users may whish to listen to a particular performance of a given music work, to performances of works of a given composers or of a given musical genre, and so on. In contrast with expert users, casual users are likely to express their information needs vaguely, mainly because they may not know the music language, and also because they may not have a good knowledge of bibliographic values. Casual users may remember a melody, for instance heard at the radio, and they may wish to retrieve and to listen to it by accessing and querying, such as "query by humming", a music digital library. It is likely that a content-based indexing and retrieval of performances would be particularly useful for these users.

Accessing and retrieval of music documents present a small paradox. On the one hand, expert users, who are likely to know bibliographic values of music document, are interested in scores and they can benefit for automatic indexing of music content. On the other hand, the majority of potential users are likely to have little knowledge about music literature, but they can not take advantage for automatic tools for content-based indexing and retrieval.

2.3 Dissemination of Music Documents

The effectiveness of a retrieval session depends also on the ability of users to judge whether retrieved documents are relevant to their information needs. The evaluation step, in a classical presentation-evaluation cycle, for an information retrieval session of textual documents usually benefits from tools for browsing the document (e.g., the "find" function), in particular when the size of documents is large. Moreover, a general overview of the textual content may help users to judge the relevance of most of the retrieved documents.

Users of a music digital library cannot take advantage of these "shortcuts" for the evaluation of documents relevance, when they are retrieving music performances. This is due to the central role played by *time* in the listening to music. A music performance is characterized by the organization of music events along the time axis, which concatenates the single sounds that form the whole performance. Changing playback speed of more than a small amount may result in a unrecognizable performance. In other words, it requires about 20 minutes to listen to a performance that lasts 20 minutes. It may be argued that many music works are characterized by their incipit, that is by their first notes, and hence a user could be required to listen only to the first seconds of a performance before judging its relevance to his information needs. Anyway, the relevant passage of a music document – e.g., a theme, the refrain – may be at any position in the time axis of the performance.

A tool that is often offered by playback devices is the "skip" function, that allows for a fast access to a sequence of random excerpts of the audio files, to help listeners looking for given passages. Everyone who tried to find a particular passage in a long music performance, knows that the aid that the skip function gives when accessing to music documents is not even comparable with the find function for textual documents. This is partially due to the fact that auditory information does not allow a "snapshot" view of the documents as visual information does. The evaluation of relevance of retrieved music documents may then be highly time-consuming, if tools for a faster access to document content are not provided.

3 Automatic Indexing of Music Performances

It is proposed to partially overcome the problems arising for the indexing and the access to music performances. The basic idea is to use the structured information on a given music work, that is available from the score, for indexing the corresponding performances. This is achieved through a technique for *automatic performance recognition* based on the modeling of performances from symbolic events in the score. Recognition is achieved through the use of hidden Markov models (HMMs), which are shortly reviewed in Section 3.1. Performances modeling can be used to automatically align them to their corresponding score, aimed at automatically tag performances through the information on musical structure that is readily available from scores. The methodology for automatic recognition and alignment is described in Section 3.2, where the application of HMMs to this particular problems is introduced. In Section 3.3 the applications of the methodology to content-based indexing and retrieval of music performances are discussed, together with the integration with an existing methodology for music information retrieval.

3.1 Overview on Hidden Markov Models

HMMs are probabilistic finite-state automata, where transitions between states are ruled by probability functions. At each transition, the new state emits a value with a given probability. Emissions can be both symbols from a finite alphabet and continuous multidimensional values. Transition probabilities are assumed to depend only on a finite number of previous transitions (usually one) and they may be modeled as a Markov chain. The presence of transitions with probability equal to zero defines a topology of the model, limiting the number of possible paths across states. States $Q = \{q_1, q_2, \ldots, q_N\}$ are not observable, thus these models are defined hidden. What can be observed are only their emissions $O_T = \{o_1, o_2, \ldots, o_T\}$ from time 1 to time T, which are called observations.

A HMM with N states is completely described by a set of parameters, called λ, that includes:

- the set of transition probabilities from state q_i to state q_j, with $1 \leq i, j \leq N$
- the set of emission probabilities of state q_j, with $1 \leq j \leq N$

For completeness, it should be added also the probability of being in state i at time 1, but usually an additional state is added and it is considered to be always the first state.

Once the set of parameters λ is defined, a HMM can be used for recognition tasks. Given a sequence of observations O_T, the probability $P(O_T|\lambda)$ that the model λ emitted that particular sequence of observations can be computed. HMMs proved to be a powerful tool for classifying and recognizing data sequences and, because of this, they are extensively used in different areas, such as speech recognition, hand-writing recognition, and biological sequence analysis.

The probability $P(O_T|\lambda)$ is computed considering all the possible sequences of states, which are by definition hidden. The problem of finding, given a sequence of observations O_T, which is the optimal (in some sense) corresponding sequence of states $q_1, \ldots, q_T$ is called *decoding*. Decoding is the attempt to uncover the hidden part of the model, and it can be used to align couples of sequences. There are a number of possible criteria for the optimality of decoding, the most widely used being Viterbi decoding.

The set of parameters λ of a HMM, namely transition and emission probabilities, can be *trained* to maximize the probability of emitting a given set of observation sequences. Training is based on a set of known observations, which are used as examples, and it is usually carried out through the Baum-Welch technique. A complete discussion on theory and applications of HMMs can be found in [4] and [12].

3.2 Recognition and Alignment of Performances

HMMs can be used to model a hidden process that can be observed only through its emissions. A sequence of observations is considered as an instance of one underlying process: computing which is the most probable hidden process, among a set of potential hidden processes that may have generated the observations, is a recognition task; computing the most probable sequence of states of the recognized process is a decoding task. The basic idea of the method proposed in this paper is that scores are the hidden processes and performances are the observed sequences. It can be noted that this approach is coherent with the way music is composed and performed: the score can be thought as a model from which performances are created.

The first papers on automatic alignment of music performances with scores appeared in 1984, reporting work on automatic computer accompaniment of solo performances. Early works on alignment were based on MIDI performances, and the alignment was achieved using string matching techniques [3]. The first paper on automatic alignment based on HMMs was presented by Raphael [13]. The technique proposed in this paper is based on Raphael's work, with substantial changes in the modeling of the performances and extended to polyphonic scores.

Creation of the HMM. The first step of the method proposed in this paper is the automatic creation of a HMM that represents a music score. A score contains a sequence of notes each one with a given pitch and a given duration; polyphonic scores are modeled considering possible parallel events. When performed and recorded, a note can be considered as a sequence of acoustic parameters, corresponding to the attack of the sound, the sustain phase, the release, and an eventual silence depending on articulation. Preliminary research showed that note release does not need to be modeled. Hence, each event of the score can be represented by a segment of a HMM, that is by a sequence of states connected with a left-to-right geometry, with:

– one state modeling the attack
– a set of states modeling the sustain
– one state that modeling the eventual silence

According to this approach, there are three sets of specialized states, connected in a chain. Figure 1 depicts how specialized states are connected, where states are bounded by two null states for clarity of presentation.

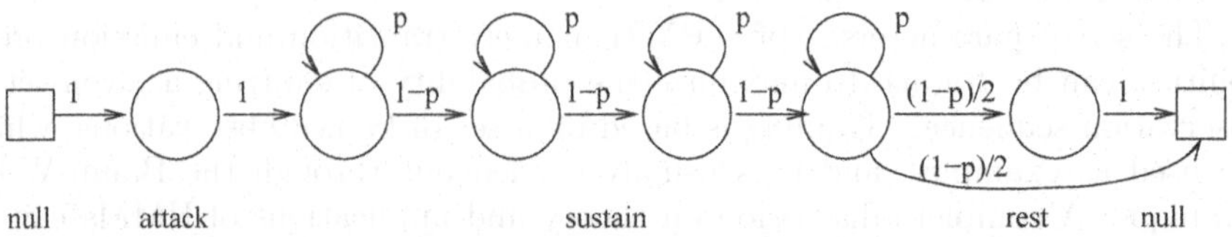

Fig. 1. Graphical representation of states of the HMM corresponding to a single note in the score, transition probabilities are reported over each allowed transition

As can be seen in Figure 1, event duration is modeled using a cluster of sustain states with non-null self-transition probability. Given n the number of states in a cluster and p their self-transition probability, the probability of having a given duration has the form of the negative binomial law:

$$P(d) = \binom{d-1}{n-1} p^{d-n}(1-p)^n \tag{1}$$

The values n and p can be chosen for setting the position of the maximum and the shape of the curve, and they are computed from the expected duration of score events.

The transition probabilities from the attack state to the first sustain state is set to 1, while the transition probabilities from the last sustain state to the silence state and to the null state are arbitrarily set to $(1-p)/2$. After modeling each single event in the score, the complete score can be modeled by just connecting in a single chain all the different events. Events may correspond to single notes in case of monophonic scores, and to parallel notes in the case of polyphonic scores. Given these choices, the transition probabilities of the HMM are completely defined by score inspection.

Emission probabilities need to be defined for a complete specification of the HMM. In the proposed approach, emissions are continuous multidimensional features, related to the probability of emitting a given audio spectrum. Harmonic audio signals, as the ones produced by most of musical instruments, have a spectrum where the fundamental frequency and its integer multiples carry most of the signal energy. Since the fundamental frequency can be computed from the note pitch in the score, for each sustain state of a note the expected spectrum is known. The probability that the energy carried by the first partials is a given percentage of the overall signal energy is then used as one of the emission probabilities. This operation can be performed by slicing the audio signal in frames of fixed lenght and computing the energy output of a bank of rectangular bandpass filters, centered on the harmonic sequence of the expected note, divided by the global energy of the signal. Figure 2 shows the superimposition of the expected frequency bands with a correct (a) and an incorrect (b) spectrum of a performance frame.

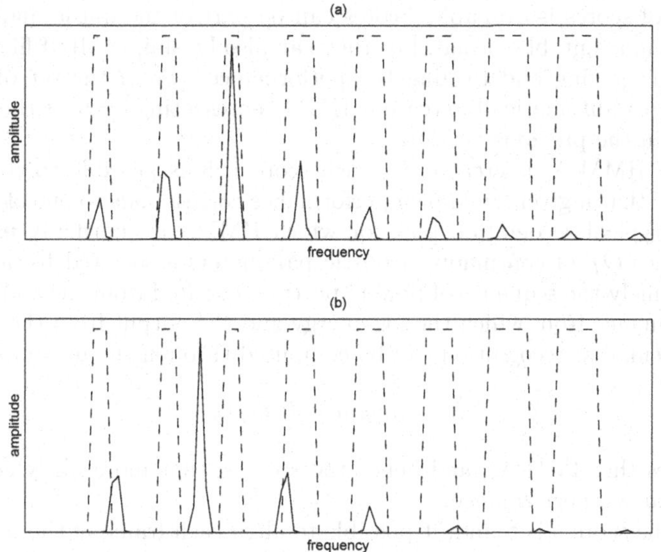

Fig. 2. The expected frequency bands superimposed with a good (a), and a bad (b) matching performance spectrum.

Emissions also include the first derivative of this parameter, in order to model changes in the spectrum. Moreover, the log-energy of the signal, together with its derivative, are considered as emissions in order to better deal with the characteristics of signal attack. Each of the three classes of specialized states emits the same four features, with different probabability density functions.

Once the kind of emissions are defined, their probabilities need to be computed. This is normally achieved through training, which requires a set of performances of the given score to be used as examples. In the current approach, it is proposed to train separately the emission probabilities, using a database available on the Web [15]. The database contains samples of all the orchestral instruments, played with different techniques and with different dynamics. The continuous multidimensional features of the signal, modeled by HMM emissions, are assumed to be statistically independent. After a number of tests, the exponential probability density function has been chosen to model each of the features.

The approach allows for modeling of polyphonic signals, with the only difference that the filterbank is set according to the superposition of the different notes in the polyphony. Moreover, it is possible to model the spectral features of more complex musical gestures, as trills and frequency vibrato just changing the bandwidth of the filters.

Recognition and Alignment. For the recognition task, it is assumed that a collection of scores is available. Scores can be part of the music digital library, if they are in a suitable format, but they can also be simple MIDI files and used just for recognizing and tagging the performances. From the set of scores, it is possible to automatically create a HMM representing each of the scores, as explained in the previous Section.

Once a HMM λ_i is created for each score i, it is possible to compute the probability that a given, unknown performance corresponds to one of the scores. This is a typical recognition task for which HMMs are normally used. Given the sequence O_T of continuous acoustic parameters associated to performance frames, namely the sequence of power spectra computed from the audio signal of the performance from which the log-energy and the output from the filterbanks can be calculated, recognition can be computed through the maximization

$$\lambda_s = argmax_\lambda P(O_T|\lambda_i) \tag{2}$$

which gives the HMM λ_s, and hence the score s, that more likely corresponds to the unknown performance.

Once the score s is found, it possible to align each frame of the performance with the corresponding event in the score. This is a typical decoding task, and the Viterbi decoding technique can be used. Given the sequence O_T and the model λ_s, decoding can be computed through

$$q^* = argmax_q P(q, O_T|\lambda_s) \tag{3}$$

which gives the most probable state sequence q^* corresponding to the sequence of performance frames. The frames aligned with the attack state of events in the score can be tagged by that events or, alternatively, events in the score can be associated with the position on the time axis of the corresponding performance frame.

3.3 Integration with Previous Research

This methodology can integrate previous research on music information retrieval, which is in great part aimed at accessing music scores, normally in MIDI format. The automatic association of a database of performances with scores in a digital collection can be used to allow users for accessing to unstructured audio recordings (the performances) while having the facilities of content-based access to structured symbolic notations (the scores).

Moreover, the automatic alignment of performances with scores can integrate previous work carried out by Massimo Melucci and the author [9]. The research work, for which a prototype was developed [10], regards a novel technique for music information retrieval based on segmentation of melodies in their musical phrases, which can be considered as the lexical units of the music language. The segmentation affects both documents in the collection and users' musical queries. A study on the perceptual basis of this approach can be found in [11].

The alignment of score notes with performance frames can be used to automatically tag the audio file containing the digital recording of the performance. Once a user's query is segmented in its musical phrases and the most potentially relevant documents are retrieved, the user can be able to browse the retrieved performance for listening to the excerpts that contain the phrases of the query. The time needed to evaluate the documents relevance can then be significantly reduced, because the user may listen only to those excerpts that are potentially relevant to his information needs. Furthermore, it can be implemented a tool for an easy access to performances similar to the find function for textual documents. The search of a given musical phrase can be carried out on the score and, if the phrase is found, its time positions on the performance can be reported for a fast access and playback.

4 Results

The methodology has been tested on an experimental setup. Two analyses have been carried out: a qualitative analysis on a relatively small number of real performances and a quantitative analysis on automatically generated performances of music excerpts.

4.1 Qualitative Analysis

A prototype implementing the methodology has been developed. The prototype aligns on-line the performance to the score, during recording playback, under the supervision of an expert musician. The prototype highlights any new match on the computer screen while playing a short sound. The supervisor was asked to listen to the performance while looking at the computer screen and to report any mismatch. In this way it was possible to test the methodology in a reduced amount of time, without requiring particular skills to the supervisor.

Twenty works for monophonic and polyphonic instruments, and for the voice, were used. Works contain fast passages, trills and vibrato, chords, and imprecise tuning for the voice. When available, different performances of the same music score were used. The recordings were in digital format, at audio CD quality. The average duration of performances was about 5 minutes.

When the recording did not correspond to the score, the system tried to find an alignment in any case, skipping great part of the score or jumping almost at random from one position to another. Apart from this behavior, that can be used as an heuristic for early rejections of scores when recognizing an unknown performance, the probability of the global alignment was always lower than when the recording corresponded to the score. In all these latter cases the supervisor judged that the alignment was globally correct, even if there were local mismatches. According to him, mismatches affected about 5% of the notes in the score.

4.2 Quantitative Analysis

A quantitative analysis has been carried out using short music scores played by a synthesizer. Synthetic performances were automatically catalogued and tagged while they were created, giving a direct reference. Unfortunately, synthetic sounds are only partially representative of real acoustic sounds and the methodology needs more extensive testing once a collection of performances manually catalogued and tagged will be available.

About 600 automatic performances were played by a synthesizer and sampled at 11 kHz, using 16 bits for sample. In order to test robustness to different sound sources and articulations, 14 different sounds played at 4 different degrees of staccato were used. The music scores were 4 different short excerpts, of monophonic and polyphonic music. Performances were very short, with an average length of 10 seconds.

The system wrongly recognized 8.4% of the excerpts. Further analysis showed that most of the misplaced recordings were performed using a bell-like sound, which inharmonic spectrum is not taken into account by the emission model. The error rate drop to 1.3% after these recordings were removed. It has to be noted that the good performances may be the result of the particular experimental setup, and further investigation using a larger number of scores is advisable.

Another important aspect for audio browsing applications is the number of notes that were wrongly aligned to performance frames: if local alignment is wrong, even if the performance is correctly recognized, it will not be possible to correctly browse the document. An error was reported each time the real position, along the time axis, of a note attack differ of more than 200 ms from the position computed through alignment. Of all the files, only 9.4% had at least one error. The percentage of alignment errors over all the notes in the 600 performances were 2.5%.

5 Conclusions

The method presented in this paper allows for automatic matching of an unknown music performance with the corresponding score stored in a database. The approach allows also for automatic alignment of the audio frames of the digital recording of the performance with the notes in the score. Alignment can be used in combination with techniques for melody segmentation to browse music documents during the evaluation phase in a retrieval session, for a fast judgment of documents relevance. A preliminary test, on a reduced set of scores and performances, gave encouraging results, which should be verified through further investigation.

The methodology can be applied for automatic cataloging of big collection of performances, for instance recordings of radio broadcasts, providing that the corresponding score are available in digital format.

A music digital library, which is likely to contain both music scores and performances, can take advantage from the proposed method. In fact, automatic classification of hours of music recordings can help, if not replace, manual cataloging. Moreover, content-based indexing and retrieval of recordings, through the corresponding score, can permit also to non expert user to access the digital library even if they do not know exact bibliographic values.

Acknowledgments. The research work presented in this paper has been carried out in collaboration with the Real-time System Group at Ircam (Institut de Recherche et Creation Acoustique/Musique) in Paris. The author wish to thank all the members of the group, and in particular its chief François Déchelle, for their support. A special thank to Diemo Schwarz of the Analysis-Synthesis Group at Ircam, who supplied the examples used in the quantitative analysis and who participated to the testing of the proposed methodology.

References

1. Agosti, M., Bombi, F., Melucci, M., and Mian, G.: Towards a digital library for the Venetian music of the eighteenth century. In Anderson, J., Deegan, M., Ross, S., & Harold, S. (Eds.), DRH 98: Selected papers from Digital Resources for the Humanities, Office for Humanities Communication (2000) 1–16
2. Bainbridge, D., Nevill-Manning, C.G., Witten, I.H., Smith, L.A., and McNab,R.J.: Towards a digital library of popular music. In *Proceedings of ACM Digital Libraries (DL) Conference*, Berkeley, CA (1999) 161–169
3. Dannenberg, R.B.: Recent Work In Real-Time Music Understanding By Computer. In Sundberg, Nord, and Carlson (Eds.), *Music, Language, Speech, and Brain*, Macmillan Publishers, London, UK (1991) 194–202
4. Durbin, R., Eddy, S., Krogh, A., Mitchison, G.: *Biological sequence analysis.* Cambridge University Press, Cambridge, UK (2000) 46–133
5. Ferrari, E. and Haus, G.: The musical archive information system at Teatro alla Scala. In Proceedings of the IEEE International Conference on Multimedia Computing and Systems (ICMCS"99), volume II, Florence, IT (1999) 817–821
6. Ghias, A., Logan, J., Chamberlin, D., and Smith, B.C.: Query by humming: Musical information retrieval in an audio database. In *Proceedings of ACM Digital Libraries (DL) Conference*, New York, NY (1995) 231–236
7. McLane, A.: Music as information. In Williams, M. (Ed.), *Annual Review of Information Science and Technology (ARIST)*, American Society for Information Science, volume 31, chapter 6 (1996) 225–262
8. McNab, R.J., Smith, L.A., Witten, I.H., Henderson, C.L., and Cunningham, S.J.: Towards the digital music library: Tune retrieval from acoustic input. In *DL'96: Proceedings of the 1st ACM International Conference on Digital Libraries*, Multimedia Digital Libraries, (1996) 11–18
9. Melucci, M. and Orio, N.: Musical information retrieval using melodic surface. In *Proceedings of ACM Digital Libraries (DL) Conference*, Berkeley, CA (1999) 152–160
10. Melucci, M. and Orio, N.: SMILE: a system for content-based musical s information retrieval environments. In *Proceedings of Intelligent Multimedia Information Retrieval Systems and Management (RIAO) Conference*, Paris, FR (2000) 1246–1260
11. Melucci, M. and Orio, N.: Evaluation of Automatic and Manual Melody Segmentation for Music Information Retrieval. In *Proceedings of Joint Conference on Digital Libraries*, Portland, OR (2002) in press

12. Rabiner, L. and Juang, B.H.: *Fundamentals of speech recognition* Prentice Hall, Englewood Cliffs, NJ (1993) 321–389
13. Raphael, C.: Automatic Segmentation of Acoustic Musical Signals Using Hidden Markov Models. IEEE Transactions on Pattern Analysis and Machine Intelligence, **21**(4) (1999) 360–370
14. Rothstein, J.: *MIDI: A comprehensive introduction.* A-R Editions, Madison, WI (1991)
15. Studio On Line, `http://sol.ircam.fr`, visited on 3 May 2002
16. Uitdenbogerd, A. and Zobel, J.: Manipulation of music for melody matching. In *Proceedings of ACM Multimedia Conference*, Bristol, UK (1998) 235–240

Alternative Surrogates for Video Objects in a Digital Library: Users' Perspectives on Their Relative Usability

Barbara M. Wildemuth, Gary Marchionini, Todd Wilkens, Meng Yang, Gary Geisler, Beth Fowler, Anthony Hughes, and Xiangming Mu

Interaction Design Lab, School of Information and Library Science
University of North Carolina at Chapel Hill, Chapel Hill, NC 27599-3360
wildem@ils.unc.edu

Abstract. In a digital environment, it is feasible to integrate multimedia materials into a library collection with ease. However, it seems likely that non-textual surrogates for multimedia objects, e.g., videos, could effectively augment textual representations of those objects. In this study, five video surrogates were evaluated in relation to their usefulness and usability in accomplishing specific tasks. The surrogates (storyboards with text or audio keywords, slide shows with text or audio keywords, fast forward) were created for each of seven video segments. Ten participants, all of whom watch videos at least monthly and search for videos at least occasionally, viewed the surrogates for seven video segments and provided comments about the strengths and weaknesses of each. In addition, they performed a series of tasks (gist determination, object recognition, action recognition, and visual gist determination) with three surrogates selected from those available. No surrogate was universally judged "best," but the fast forward surrogate garnered the most support, particularly from experienced video users. The participants expressed their understanding of video gist as composed of three components: topicality, the story of the video, and the visual gist of the video. They identified several real-world tasks for which they regularly use video collections. The viewing compaction rates used in these surrogates supported adequate performance, but users expressed a desire for more control over surrogate speed and sequencing. Further development of these surrogates is warranted by these results, as well as the development of mechanisms for surrogate display.

1 Introduction

In a digital environment, it is feasible to integrate multimedia materials into a library collection with ease because they can be delivered as bit streams, just as textual materials can be delivered. This feasibility is demonstrated daily by the addition of collections of multimedia materials, such as video, to the World Wide Web and digital libraries. While delivery of digital video is possible over the Web, it is costly in download time. Thus, library users would benefit from the ability to assess the relevance of the available videos prior to downloading. While textual surrogates for the videos (such as the video title or a desription of its content) can assist in this process, it seems likely that non-textual surrogates for the available videos could effectively augment textual surrogates. Unfortunately, because video is a relatively

M. Agosti and C. Thanos (Eds.): ECDL 2002, LNCS 2458, pp. 493-507, 2002.

new medium, we have not yet developed surrogates analogous to the abstracts, reviews, tables of contents, prefaces, etc., that help people understand the gist of texts before reading the full objects. Although there is an enormous amount of technical research directed at creating such surrogates, there is little work on understanding how people can and will actually use such summaries. The emphasis to date has been on using the surrogates as metadata objects for the purposes of retrieval. We aim to understand broader issues such as how these surrogates are used to extract meaning and to make ongoing decisions that guide browsing within a library of digital videos. More specifically, in the current study we are concerned with understanding which surrogates are useful for which types of tasks and how people are able to incorporate these surrogates into their information processing strategies.

2 Background

Surrogates "stand for" objects. Abstracts, titles, and keywords are all familiar surrogates for complete documents or objects. Surrogates support both retrieval and gist extraction and have long been central to library and information science research (e.g.,[1,13]). In browsing, surrogates provide an important alternative to primary objects as they take far less time to examine and provide enough semantic cues to extract gist and allow users to assess the need for further examination of other surrogates and the primary object. In digital libraries and archives, surrogates are crucial for browsing large distributed collections that result from filtering programs or analytical queries of the data space.

Key frames are a natural analogue to keywords in text and much of the effort has focused on identifying and extracting key frames. O'Connor [20] suggested that key frames—still images representative of scenes extracted from the video itself—could be used to construct video abstracts or "contour maps." Rorvig [22] demonstrated the feasibility of creating visual surrogates based on extracted key frames and the creation of specific summaries has become an important aspect of the information retrieval research community's interest in multimedia (e.g., [17,25]).

Results of studies of people interacting with surrogates [8,11,29] have suggested that keywords and key frames each contribute unique elements to understanding and each reinforces the other. Text contributes iconographic, thematic information and images contribute preiconographic details and affective impact. These results parallel the Robertson et al. [21] work with thumbnail images for Web pages that showed that combining text and thumbnails led to fewer errors and failed trials than text or thumbnails alone. It seems logical that providing more and more varied information will lead to better results. However, an important question is how much the additional processing "costs" the browser and how this affects the overall browsing experience.

The temporal nature and multiple channels of video content exacerbate the need for search and browsing mechanisms that offer more representation facets than text. Some researchers have begun by developing structured interfaces for video surrogates (e.g., [7,10,32-34] and there has been excellent progress on the engineering of video surrogates and designing display structures (e.g., [9,18,27]), but there has been very little work on studying how people interact with and use such surrogates. The

Informedia Project is an important exception, having both constructed innovative interfaces for video retrieval and conducted studies of how people use alternative surrogate implementations [2,3,26]. In addition, Goodrum [12] has examined users' perspectives on the congruence between videos and several surrogates. Marchionini and his colleagues have conducted user studies to identify key parameters for video browsing [7,8,14,24,28] and have developed a set of methodologies that may be used in other video browsing efforts. However, these studies mainly focused on surrogates for specific video objects and item recall types of tasks. The current study focuses on the general tasks of reviewing and extracting salience (operationalized in gist determination, object recognition, action recognition, and visual gist performance tasks) from surrogates of the items retrieved from video collections.

3 Research Questions

Our long-term goals are to understand surrogates within the context of digital library use. The current study focuses on particular characteristics of the surrogates and their effects on user preferences and performance. Specifically, this study addresses two research questions:

- What are the strengths and weaknesses of each surrogate, from the user's perspective?
- Are any of the surrogates better than the others in supporting user performance?

4 Methods

Five surrogates were created for each of seven video segments. The surrogates included two storyboards (one with text keywords and one with audio keywords), two slide shows (one with text keywords and one with audio keywords) and fast forward. Ten participants, all of whom watch videos at least monthly and search for videos at least occasionally, viewed the surrogates and provided comments about their strengths and weaknesses. In addition, they performed a series of tasks (gist determination, object recognition, action recognition, and visual gist determination) with three surrogates selected from those available. The methods used in the study are described in more detail below.

4.1 The Videos

The video segments were selected from the repository of the Open Video Project (http://www.open-video.org/), a shared digital video repository and test collection created at the Interaction Design Lab at the University of North Carolina at Chapel Hill. The collection currently is more than a half terabyte and contains video and metadata for more than 1600 video segments.

For the current study, seven video segments were selected from the collection. They included both color and black & white videos and represented several genre (documentaries, educational, promotional). They were:

- Apollo, Segment 4006 (2:07),
- Chevrolet Promotional Videos: Master Hands, Segment 1 (4:54),
- Challenge at Glen Canyon, BOR03, Segment 2 (3:00),
- Educational Films: A Date with Your Family (9:59),
- Moon, Segment 2 (3:43),
- Hurricanes, Segment 1 (3:54), and
- New Indians, Segment 101 (2:11).

4.2 The Surrogates

With support from the Mpeg Encoded Retrieval and Indexing Toolkit (MERIT, http://documents.cfar.umd.edu/LAMP/Media/Projects/MERIT/) and customized Java and Perl programs, we manually created five surrogates to be evaluated in this study. Two of our surrogates were storyboards, each consisting of no more than 36 frames, laid out in a 6x6 grid. Users were allowed to view the storyboard for a limited amount of time, allowing 500 milliseconds per key frame. For example, if a storyboard included 20 key frames, the user was allowed to view it for 10 seconds. One of the storyboards was augmented with text keywords (consolidated from those independently assigned by two members of the research team), visible under the storyboard, at the bottom of the grid. The other was augmented with audio keywords (the same set); an audio recording of them was played during the viewing. The audio recording was generated by a speech synthesizer, so that standardization of pace and pronunciation could be ensured. Audio was repeated as necessary for the duration of the visual display. Two of the surrogates were slide shows incorporating the same set of key frames as were included in the storyboards. They were displayed at the rate of 250 milliseconds per frame. The entire set was displayed twice, with no pause between the two repetitions. The slide shows were augmented with textual and audio keywords, parallel to the augmentation of the storyboards. The fifth surrogate was a fast forward version of the video segment, mimicking the fast forward function of a VCR player. For this study, the target video segment was played at four times its original speed, so that it would "run" for about the same amount of time that the storyboard and slide show for the same video segment were displayed. Each participant viewed it once. No keywords augmented this surrogate.

4.3 Participants

Study participants were recruited through the distribution of flyers in several UNC-CH classes related to video production and the posting of the same flyers near the video collection in the UNC-CH libraries. Participants were included in the study only if they had some experience in searching video libraries or collections. The set of ten participants included five men and five women ranging in age from their early 20's to early 40's. All of them used computers daily. The frequency with which they watch videos varied from daily to monthly and the frequency with which they search for videos varied from daily to occasionally.

4.4 Procedures

Each study session was conducted in three phases. First, the concept of a surrogate was explained to the participants as something that "might be used in place of viewing the whole video for certain purposes such as selecting a particular video for full viewing or sorting the videos into a certain order." During the first phase, the study participant worked with the Apollo and Master Hands segments (order of presentation was counter-balanced). Each participant first viewed the full segment, and then viewed three surrogates of that video. The surrogates were assigned to participants so that all participants could comment on all surrogates, with the medium of the keywords (text versus audio) counterbalanced to minimize order effects. While the participant worked with each surrogate, s/he was asked to identify its strengths and weaknesses, tasks for which it might be most appropriate, and its usefulness under time constraints.

In the second phase, the participants interacted with the Glen Canyon and Date with Your Family segments. The procedures were the same as the first phase, except that the full video segment was ***not*** viewed. Thus, participant comments and understanding were based solely on the surrogates.

In the third phase, each participant was asked to complete several assigned tasks while interacting with each of three surrogates. Each participant selected the surrogate with which to perform the tasks, for each of three video segments: Moon, Hurricanes, and New Indians. The participant was free to use the same surrogate each time, or to select a different surrogate for each segment. In the 30 trials (three for each of the 10 participants), the storyboard with audio keywords was used four times, the storyboard with text keywords and the slide show with audio keywords were each used six times, and the fast forward surrogate was used 14 times.[1] Participants were asked to think aloud while completing the assigned tasks.

Some of the assigned tasks have been used in previous studies, while others were created for this study. All of the tasks are closely related to reviewing and extracting salience from the surrogates—a task that is typical in digital library settings. First, the participant completed two gist determination tasks. In the first, the participant was asked to write a brief summary (a few sentences) of the video content; in the second, the participant was asked to select the summary that best represented the video content from five brief text summaries presented. The gist statements generated in the first task were scored using the method reported in Tse et al. [28]. The statements were independently scored by two members of the research team and any differences were resolved by a third member of the team. Next, the participant completed two object recognition tasks. In the first, the participant was presented with a list of 12 object names and asked to mark those objects seen in the surrogate. Six of the 12 had been seen (i.e., were correct). Three of the correct and three of the incorrect were concrete objects, e.g., "astronaut" for the Moon video, while the remaining objects were more abstract, e.g., "space program" for the Moon video. In the second object

[1] The participants' selection of surrogates for use in phase 3 should not be interpreted as an indicator of their preferences for those surrogates. Several of the participants explicitly stated that they selected a surrogate to use in phase 3 because they did *not* like it and wanted to confirm their negative judgment of it.

recognition task, 12 key frames were presented to the study participant. Six of them were randomly selected from the key frames used in the creation of the storyboard and slide show surrogates (i.e., were correct), three were selected from other segments of the same video, and three were selected from other videos in the Open Video repository. The participant was asked to mark those frames seen in the surrogate. An action recognition task was newly developed for this study. Six mini-segments (each 2-3 seconds long) were displayed to the study participant. Two of the mini-segments were from the video segment represented in the video surrogate (i.e., were correct), two were from another segment of the same video, and two were from a different video. In response to each mini-segment, the participant was asked whether s/he believed it to be from the same video segment as represented in the surrogate. The final task was developed for this study, and is intended to assess the participant's ability to determine visual gist: a combination of topic, story line, and style. Twelve frames were displayed to each study participant, ***none*** of them from the surrogate. Three were other frames from the video segment (considered correct); three were selected from other segments of the same video (also considered correct); three were selected from other videos of a similar style (e.g., black and white versus color), and three were selected from videos of other styles. The study participant was asked to select those frames that s/he believed "belong" in the video segment for which the surrogate was seen. For the object recognition, action recognition and visual gist determination tasks, the total score was the sum of the correct items marked and the incorrect items not marked.

All phases of the study were videotaped, using the usability workstation in the UNC-CH Interaction Design Lab. The videotape included a face shot, a keyboard/mouse shot, and screen capture. Participant comments from the videotapes were transcribed and analysed by inductively identifying themes in the comments and categorizing the comments by these themes. The phase 3 data were analysed quantitatively; descriptive statistics will be reported here. In addition, the effects of surrogate and video segment on participant performance were investigated with analysis of variance.

5 Results and Discussion

After the participants' preferences for particular surrogates are summarized, this section will focus on participants' understanding of what gist might encompass, and their ability to determine the gist of the video from viewing the surrogate. This will be followed by a discussion of the tasks for which surrogates might be used and the relationship between those tasks and the phase 3 performance tasks, the efficiency gained through use of the surrogates, and the effects of differences in the video segments on participant performance.

5.1 User Preferences

At the end of each phase of data collection, each of the participants was asked which surrogate s/he preferred. While not all participants expressed a preference, most did. Participant preferences tended to change over time, and some preferred particular surrogates for particular purposes. Some participants (David, Ling)[2] preferred the fast forward surrogate, and several additional participants (Matt, Ryan, Cheryl, Pam) suggested that they would prefer a fast forward surrogate if audio keywords were added. The others who stated a preference were divided among storyboard with audio keywords (Jan) and the slide show with audio keywords (Bettie, Steven). These results indicate that the fast forward surrogate should be further developed with the addition of audio keywords.

5.2 Gist from a User's Perspective

Determining the gist of the video was the most important function of the surrogates, from the users' perspective. Three different understandings of gist were present in their discussions of using the surrogates to determine gist. The first was the view that the surrogate could help the user to understand what the video was about, i.e., the topic of the video. This understanding is parallel to the concept of topical relevance [5,23]. Participants referred to this concept by describing the surrogate as providing an "overview," describing the "content" of the video, or "what it's about." This function of the surrogates was the one for which keywords played the most prominent role. In the words of Jan, as she was using the fast forward surrogate (with no keywords): "If you don't have the [key]words, you'll think it's about something else, not as it was supposed to be." The participants found the keywords that were proper nouns to be particular useful, as Cheryl commented: "The common noun keywords are debatable, but the proper noun keywords would be really good to have."

Secondly, the participants found the surrogates most useful when they told the "story" of the video or had a narrative structure. As Cheryl commented: "It's in chronological order, so that makes sense and you can kind of follow the story line through." Ryan criticized one of the storyboard surrogates for lacking this information: "I didn't get much of a sense of the flow of the story." This desire for a narrative structure is most likely associated with the temporal nature of video. In addition, the users' interactions with the surrogates are consistent with van Dijk and Kintsch's [30,31] model of discourse comprehension. In it, they postulate that readers use macrostrategies to form an initial hypothesis about the gist of a text based on initial cues from the text, and then interpret additional cues from the text in light of their initial hypothesis concerning its gist. This cognitive process was most apparent while participants viewed the video segment, A Date with Your Family, produced in 1950. The keywords included the term "date," yet the video depicted a family meal and was oriented toward etiquette. A number of the participants were disturbed by the conflict between the expected scenario of a date (i.e., their initial hypothesis of the video's gist) and the family scene they were viewing. As expressed by Pam, "When the voice said 'date,' there was a picture of 'dad,' kind of crazy to me. It wasn't an image of 'date' to me." A more positive example supporting van Dijk and Kintsch's theory was Ryan's viewing of the Apollo segment: "I got, pretty early on, that it was training for the mission to the moon. Once I had that, I could figure out what each of the pieces were in the training."

---

[2] Names used in the paper are pseudonyms assigned to protect the participants' confidentiality.

The third understanding of gist presented by the study participants is what we are calling visual gist. Based on the participant comments, it is a combination of topicality, narrative structure, and visual style. While this concept needs additional clarification, participant comments clearly indicated that they formed a more holistic view of gist, beyond topic and narrative. Most of the positive comments related to visual gist were associated with the fast forward surrogate, such as Matt's comments: "The motion really added a lot... I have a stronger sense of what the movie's like... It definitely gave it a whole different feel... It gave me more of a sense of what to expect from watching [the entire video]."

During the third phase of the study, participants performed two gist determination tasks: one in which they generated a statement of the gist of the video and one in which they selected a gist statement from five presented to them. Scores on the participant-generated statements could range from 0 to 3. The participants' mean score was 1.68 (s.d. = 0.75); their actual scores covered the entire range possible. There were no differences between surrogates in this score (F=0.39 with 3, 26 df,[3] p=0.7643). Further comparisons with analysis of variance indicated that there were no differences by the basic form of the surrogate (storyboard v. slide show v. fast forward; F=0.58 with 2, 27 df, p=0.5653) or by the medium with which the keywords were presented (F=0.35 with 2, 27 df, p=0.7050). On the second gist determination task, participants were correct on 80% of their statement selections. Again there were no differences by surrogate (p=0.85, Fisher's exact test), by the basic form of the surrogate (p=0.83, Fisher's exact test), or by keyword medium (p=0.72, Fisher's exact test).

5.3 Tasks for Which Video Surrogates Might Be Used

One of the weaknesses in our basic knowledge of people interacting with digital video libraries is in our understanding of the tasks for which video collections might be used. As the study participants used the various surrogates, they were asked about possible uses for which the surrogate might be useful. The results of these interviews revealed a number of tasks associated with video use.

The task originally envisioned in the research design (as expressed in the definition of surrogates provided to the participants) was the classic information retrieval task of selecting videos from the collection. Jan described the possibilities of looking for particular content or particular visual techniques. When working with the fast forward surrogate, Cheryl said, "You get a pretty good sense of whether or not you wanted to actually see the whole thing and take the time to pursue it further." Matt made a more fine-grained distinction, noting that he was more likely to use the surrogates for school projects and reference tasks than for entertainment-oriented searching. Bettie commented that surrogates would be useful for determining whether a particular video would be appropriate for children.

In addition to selection decisions related to the entire video, a number of participants pointed out the possibility of using the surrogates for selecting particular

---

[3] For this and other analyses of the effects of the surrogates, there are only 3 degrees of freedom associated with the model, since participants used only four of the available surrogates during the third phase of the study.

frames or clips for later use. Participants noted differences between the surrogates for these types of tasks. For example, Ryan contrasted the utility of the storyboard with text for identifying a particular image, but would prefer the slideshow if he was looking for particular visual elements. David, a very experienced video user, preferred the fast forward surrogate for "picking out highlights", but most of the participants believed that the storyboards would be most useful for identifying particular frames or sections of the video. Participants also pointed out that "sometimes you need to compare images" (David), for which the storyboard would work most effectively. David also noted that, "ultimately they're going to have to organize what they're viewing," and that users will need ways to manipulate portions of a segment.

The motion in a video and the video's style were also attributes about which the participants wanted information in the surrogates. They differentiated between "long shots" and "zooms," and described a desire to search for particular "film techniques" and "camera angles." In all these cases, seeing the movement in a video was critical. As David pointed out, "With motion pictures, you want to see how it moves at some point in the process."

In summary, participants expected the surrogates to provide the capability to select videos from the collection, to select and organize particular frames or clips, and to evaluate the style or identify particular stylistic techniques. For selecting videos, different surrogates were judged to have particular advantages or disadvantages. There was general agreement that storyboards were most useful for selecting and organizing particular frames or clips and that the fast forward surrogate was most useful when focusing on the video's style.

5.4 Performance Tasks in Relation to User-Defined Tasks

During the third phase, in addition to gist determination, the participants performed object recognition, action recognition, and visual gist tasks. Object recognition, in which the participant is provided with a set of stimuli and asked which were seen in the surrogate, is related to the user-defined task of selection of particular frames. If a person performs well in the object recognition task, it can be argued that the surrogate supports the task of frame selection well. There is a parallel relationship between action recognition and the selection of particular clips. The visual gist performance task, which asks users to predict whether a particular frame is from the same video segment as shown in the surrogate, incorporates both content and stylistic considerations. This performance task is most closely related to users' desire to evaluate the movement or style in a video.

Participants performed two object recognition tasks. For the first, the 12 stimuli were names of objects that may have been represented in the surrogate viewed. The mean score was 9.0 (s.d. = 1.6), and scores ranged from 6 to 12. Analysis of variance indicated that the effect of the surrogate approached significance (F=2.70 with 3, 26 df, p=0.0664). A post hoc Duncan's multiple range test indicated that the effect was associated with the difference between the storyboard with text keywords (mean = 10.2) and the storyboard with audio keywords (mean = 7.5). For the second object recognition task, the stimuli were 12 video frames. The mean score was 9.0 (s.d. =

1.8) and scores ranged from 3 to 12. The effect of the surrogate was not significant (F=0.36 with 3, 26 df, p=0.7823). The mean score on the action recognition task was 4.6 (s.d. = 1.0), and scores ranged from 2 to 6. The effect of the surrogate was statistically significant for this task (F=3.36 with 3, 26 df, p=0.0340). A post hoc Duncan's multiple range test indicated that the fast forward surrogate outperformed the rest of the surrogates. The means, by surrogate, are shown in Table 1. For the visual gist task, the participants were presented with 12 frames and asked to select the frames that "belonged" in the target video segment. The mean score was 9.7 (s.d. = 1.4), and scores ranged from 7 to 12. The effect of the surrogate was not significant (F=0.08 with 3, 26 df, p=0.9709). For two of the performance tasks, a particular surrogate seemed to provide better support than others: the fast forward surrogates in support of the action recognition task and the storyboard with text keywords in support of the object recognition task (with textual stimuli). In terms of user performance, it is reasonable to view at least these two surrogates as promising for future investigation.

Table 1. Action recognition performance, by surrogate*

Surrogate	n	Mean score
Fast forward	14	1.6
Storyboard with audio keywords	4	1.0
Storyboard with text keywords	6	0.8
Slide show with audio keywords	6	0.8

* No participant selected the slide show with text keywords for use during phase 3 of the study.

Of more import for future research is the validation of the performance measures used in this study. Of the two gist determination tasks presented earlier, each has its strengths and weaknesses. The scoring method used for the user-generated gist statements still needs refinement. While there was a significant amount of interrater agreement on the scoring (Cohen's kappa = 0.354 [4]), it was far from ideal. We expect that the problems experienced in scoring may be minimized if a clearer distinction is made between scores of 2 and 3 and if scorers are clearly instructed to base their judgments on their viewing of the entire video segment. The multiple-choice gist determination task can be objectively scored, but care must be taken in developing distractor statements that are at an appropriate level of difficulty. A similar challenge exists for the remaining performance tasks–selecting distractors that are appropriate. In this study, specific criteria were established for selecting a set of distractors that were of varying levels of difficulty. As more is known about people's interactions with video material, it is likely that these criteria can be further refined. In spite of these challenges, it is fair to conclude that the measures developed and used in this study provide a basic set of valid approaches to the measurement of performance in interacting with video materials. Their psychometric properties seem reasonable (means just above the midpoint of the possible range of scores; appropriate variability in the scores). In addition, they are clearly related to the real-world tasks that users expect to perform with video collections.

5.5 Efficiency as a Function of Viewing Compaction

One of the goals of creating surrogates is to allow the user to review retrieved items and make decisions about their relevance more quickly than if they were required to review the complete item [15]. For video materials, this concept can be instantiated in the human-centric idea of viewing compaction, i.e., the ratio of time to view the full video segment to the time to view the surrogate. In the current study, the viewing compaction rate was approximately 15:1 (ranging from 8:1 for the fast forward surrogates for Moon and New Indians to 29:1 for the storyboards and slide shows of A Date with Your Family). These compaction rates were expected to be acceptable for users to be able to determine the gist of the video segment, based on Ding et al.'s [8] work with slide shows.

From the phase 3 data, we can conclude that this viewing time was reasonable. Mean scores on all performance measures were above the midpoint of the range of possible scores. However, participant comments often related to a desire for spending more time with the surrogate. Ryan was one of the people who commented on the brevity of his view of the storyboard: "For the amount of time, it was a lot of pictures – I couldn't take it all in." Almost all of the participants felt the slide show was too fast, e.g., Kevin's comment: "It still goes too fast, I think. It's too much information in too little time." Opinions of the speed of the fast forward were more mixed, and tended to be related to the participant's level of prior experience in using video. David, an experienced video user, spoke positively about the speed: "Another strength is that it's fast – you can see what it is and move on." Ling, a less experienced video user, believed that selection decisions would suffer because of the speed of the fast forward surrogate: "It's so fast, I think a lot of people [might be] interested in this [video], but it's shown so fast, you cannot [be] sure." The discrepancy between performance and satisfaction has often been reported in usability studies [19], and this study is no exception. Future studies should investigate surrogate use in a more naturalistic setting, with adequate user control over the speed of each surrogate and the number of times each surrogate can be viewed and where other contextual cues are present such as titles or an articulated query.

5.6 Effects of Video Content and Style

For this study, video segments were purposively selected from the Open Video repository to represent a variety of genre and styles. Based on participant comments and some of the performance data from phase 3, both user perceptions and performance can be affected by characteristics of the video segment itself. Of the three videos used in phase 3, New Indians was least well represented by its surrogates. There was a significant difference in the mean gist determination scores ($F=7.07$ with 2, 27 df, $p=0.0034$) and in the visual gist scores ($F=8.01$ with 2, 27 df, $p=0.0019$). In both cases, New Indians had lower performance than the other two videos (see Table 2).

Table 2. Differences in phase 3 performance, by video

Video	Mean gist determination score	Mean visual gist score
Moon	2.2	10.1
Hurricanes	1.7	10.5
New Indians	1.1	8.6

Two themes came out in participants' comments about video characteristics and their effects on use of the surrogates. The first theme was concerned with the variability in the key frames derived from the video segment. If the video was relatively homogeneous visually, none of the surrogates were very effective. For example, David, contrasted Master Hands, "It was easier to deal with [Master Hands] because there was more variety in the images, I think," with Apollo, "The interesting thing about this video is that the footage for this video is all very similar in value, so those frames are kind of hard to distinguish." It is likely that the homogeneity of content in the key frames from New Indians accounted for at least some of the difference in performance during phase 3. The second theme expanded on the first, as a stronger preference for keywords when the visual portions of the surrogate were not as useful. The low performance of the New Indians surrogates in phase 3 may also be attributable to the quality of the keywords associated with those surrogates. Matt pinpoints the importance of keywords for some videos in his comments about Apollo and Glen Canyon: "You're pretty much looking at so much of the exact same thing – I mean, it's not the exact same thing but really similar things – water going down or a plane flying around – that it would really help to have some additional idea of what's happening… Like more than just a visual stimulus – like audio [keywords] on top." It may be possible to take these differences in video style into account as surrogates are created, e.g., through some frame similarity adjustment analogous to IDF.

6 Conclusion

While the current study is an early and exploratory effort to understand how people interact with video collections and surrogates of video objects, its findings will be useful in shaping further research. Though no surrogate triumphed as the "best," the fast forward surrogate garnered substantial support from the study participants, particularly from experienced users of videos and video collections. The participants expressed their understanding of video gist as composed of the content or topic of the video, the story or narrative structure of the video, and the visual gist of the video (a combination of topicality, story, and visual style). The participants were successful in using the surrogates to determine gist, recognize objects and actions they had seen in the surrogates, and identify frames that "belonged" in a particular video (i.e., determine visual gist). Participants were able to identify several tasks for which surrogates would be useful, such as selecting videos from a collection, selecting and organizing frames and clips from a particular video, and identifying particular visual techniques used in a video. The compaction rates used in the surrogates allowed users to efficiently interact with them, but users expressed a preference for slowing them down or controlling their viewing in other ways. Participants also noted some differences in which types of surrogates might be most useful for particular types of videos.

From these findings, several conclusions can be drawn. First, all the surrogates tested in this study are candidates for further development. The weakest was the slide show with text keywords (not preferred by anyone, rarely spoken of positively, not selected by anyone for use in phase 3), so its development is of lowest priority. Of highest priority is the further development of a fast forward surrogate (or surrogates) with audio keywords. In addition, research is needed to determine which information compaction rates result in the best viewing compaction rates for users (taking into account the tradeoff between viewing time and level of understanding).

The role of keywords is another area warranting further research. The participants in this study used the keywords for several purposes: to understand the content of the video (as expected), as advance organizers for viewing the visual portion of the surrogate, and as a source of ideas for terms to use in future searches. These last two uses were most clearly stated by Bettie, "It was telling me 'Neil Armstrong' and 'astronauts,' pointing me to what to look for, what to grasp" and by Kevin, "It tells you some of the topics, then you could go look those up online or in an encyclopedia or something." These surrogates are a hybrid of verbal and non-verbal information and the value of each type of information in representing video materials is worthy of additional study.

Once a suite of useful surrogates has been developed, the next step is to develop mechanisms with which users can control the display of the surrogates. First, users would like to have control over the display of each surrogate, e.g., the starting, stopping, and speed of the fast forward and slide show surrogates and the display time for the storyboard. As David said, "It all comes down.. to flexibility and control. You need to do different things at different moments." In addition, users would like to be able to move from surrogate to surrogate. They viewed different surrogates as being more or less useful for different types of tasks, and so would like to move from one to another easily. While some participants had a particular sequence in mind (e.g., David expressed the desire to search on text indexing, then move to storyboard, then move to fast forward), others expected the sequence of surrogate use to vary from situation to situation. It is in response for this need for flexibility that we are pursuing the development of the AgileViews user interface framework [16]. This framework defines several different views of a collection (including overviews, previews, reviews, peripheral views, and shared views), as well as control mechanisms that facilitate low-effort actions and strategies for coordinating the views. This and similar work, when implemented, will provide digital video library users with the tools they need for effectively retrieving, reviewing and extracting salience from video materials.

Acknowledgements. The research team would like to thank David Doermann, University of Maryland, for his assistance with the use of the Merit software and Curtis Webster for the additional support he has provided for this project. This research was supported by grant NSF IIS-0099638 from the National Science Foundation.

References

1. Borko, H., Bernier, C.: Abstracting Concepts and Methods. Academic Press, New York (1975).
2. Christel, M., Smith, M., Taylor, C. R., Winkler, D.: Evolving Video Skims into Useful Multimedia Abstractions. In: Proceedings of CHI '98: Human Factors in Computing Systems (Los Angeles, April 1998). ACM Press, New York (1998), 171-178.
3. Christel, M., Winkler, D., Taylor, C. R.: Improving Access to a Digital Video Library. Paper presented at the Human-Computer Interaction: INTERACT97, the 6th IFIP Conference on Human-Computer Interaction, Sydney, Australia, July 14-18, 1997.
4. Cohen, J.: A Coefficient of Agreement for Nominal Scales. Educational and Psychological Measurement **20** (1960), 37-46.
5. Cooper, W. S.: A Definition of Relevance for Information Retrieval. Information Storage & Retrieval **7** (1971), 19-37.
6. Ding, W.: Designing Multimodal Surrogates for Video Browsing and Retrieval. Unpublished doctoral dissertation, University of Maryland (1999).
7. Ding, W., Marchionini, G., Soergel, D.: Multimodal Surrogates for Video Browsing. In: Proceedings of Digital Libraries '99: the Fourth Annual ACM Conference on Digital Libraries (Berkeley, CA, August 1999). ACM Press, New York (1999), 85-93.
8. Ding, W., Marchionini, G., Tse, T.: Previewing Video Data: Browsing Key Frames at High Rates Using a Video Slide Show Interface. In: Proceedings of the International Symposium on Research, Development and Practice in Digital Libraries (Tsukuba, Japan, 1997), 151-158.
9. Elliot, E.: Watch, Grab, Arrange, See: Thinking with Motion Images via Streams and Collages. MSVS thesis document., MIT Media Lab, Cambridge MA (1993).
10. England, P., Allen, R. B., Sullivan, M., Bianchi, M., Heybey, A., Dailianas, A.: Ibrowse: The Bellcore Video Library Toolkit. In: Proceedings of the SPIE Photonics West '96: Electronic Imaging Science and Technology '96: Storage and Retrieval for Image and Video Database IV (San Jose CA, January 1996).
11. Goodrum, A.: Evaluation of Text-Based and Image-Based Representations for Moving Image Documents. Unpublished doctoral dissertation, University of North Texas (1997).
12. Goodrum, A. A.: Multidimensional Scaling of Video Surrogates. Journal of the American Society for Information Science **52** (2001), 174-182.
13. Heilprin, L.: Paramorphism versus Homomorphism in Information Science. In: Heilprin, L. (ed.): Toward Foundations of Information Science. Knowledge Industry Pub., White Plains NY (1985), 115-136.
14. Komlodi, A., Marchionini, G.: Key Frame Preview Techniques for Video Browsing. In: Proceedings of the ACM Digital Libraries Conference '98 (Pittsburgh, PA, June 24-26, 1998). ACM Press, New York (1998).
15. Li, F., Gupta, A., Sanocki, E., He, L., Rui, Y.: Browsing Digital Video. In: CHI 2000 Conference Proceedings: Human Factors in Computing Systems (The Hague, Netherlands, April 3-6, 2000). ACM Press, New York (2000), 169-176.
16. Marchionini, G., Geisler, G., Brunk, B.: AgileViews: A Human-Centered Framework for Interfaces to Information Spaces. In: ASIS 2000: Proceedings of the 63rd ASIS Annual Meeting, Volume 37 (Chicago, November 12-16, 2000). Information Today, Medford, NJ (2000), 271-280.
17. Maybury, M.: Intelligent Multimedia Information Retrieval. MIT Press, Cambridge MA (1997).
18. Mills, M., Cohen, J., Wong, Y.: A Magnifier Tool for Video Data. In: Proceedings of CHI '92: Human Factors in Computing Systems (Monterey, CA, May 3-7, 1992). ACM Press, New York (1992), 93-98.

19. Nielsen, J., Levy, J.: Measuring Usability: Preference vs. Performance. Communications of the ACM **37** (April 1994), 66-75.
20. O'Connor, B.: Access to Moving Image Documents: Background Concepts and Proposals for Surrogates for Film and Video Works. Journal of Documentation **41** (1985), 209-220.
21. Robertson, G., Czerwinski, M., Larson, K., Robbins, D., Thiel, D., van Dantzich, M.: Data Mountain: Using Spatial Memory for Document Management. In: Proceedings of the 11th Annual ACM Symposium on User Interface Software and Technology (San Francisco, November 1998), 153-162.
22. Rorvig, M. E.: A Method for Automatically Abstracting Visual Documents. Journal of the American Society for Information Science **44** (1993), 40-56.
23. Saracevic, T.: The Concept of "Relevance" in Information Science: A Historical Review. In: Saracevic, T. (ed.): Introduction to Information Science. Bowker, New York (1970), 111-151.
24. Slaughter, L., Shneiderman, B., Marchionini, G.: Comprehension and Object Recognition Capabilities for Presentations of Simultaneous Video Key Frame Surrogates. In: Research and Advanced Technology for Digital Libraries: Proceedings of the First European Conference (EDSL '97, Pisa, Italy, 1997), 41-54.
25. Smeaton, A.: Content-based Access to Digital Video: The Físchlár System and the TREC Video Track. Paper presented at MMCBIR 2001 - Multimedia Content-based Indexing and Retrieval (INRIA, Rocquencourt, France, September 2001). http://www.cdvp.dcu.ie/Papers/MMCBIR2001.pdf. Last accessed January 26, 2002.
26. Smith, M., Kanade, T.: Video Skimming and Characterization through the Combination of Image and Language Understanding. In: Proceedings of the 1998 IEEE Workshop on Content-based Access of Image and Video Databases (Bombay, India, January 1998). IEEE, Los Alamitos CA (1998), 61-70.
27. Tonomura, Y., Akutsu, A., Otsuji, K., Sadakata, T.: VideoMAP and VideoSpaceIcon: Tools for Anatomizing Video Content. In: Proceedings of INTERCHI '93: Human Factors in Computing Systems (Amsterdam, April 1993), 131-136.
28. Tse, T., Marchionini, G., Ding, W., Slaughter, L., Komlodi, A.: Dynamic Key Frame Presentation Techniques for Augmenting Video Browsing. In: Proceedings of AVI '98: Advanced Visual Interfaces (L'Aquila, Italy, May 1998), 185-194.
29. Turner, J.: Determining the Subject Content of Still and Moving Image Documents for Storage and Retrieval: An Experimental Investigation. Unpublished doctoral dissertation, University of Toronto (1984).
30. van Dijk, T. A., Kintsch, W.: Strategies of Discourse Comprehension. Academic Press, New York (1983).
31. van Dijk, T. A., Kintsch, W.: Toward a Model of Text Comprehension and Production. Psychological Review **85** (1978), 363-394.
32. Wactlar, H., Christel, M., Gong, Y., Hauptmann, A.: Lessons Learned from Building a Terabyte Digital Video Library. Computer **32** (2, 1999), 66-73.
33. Yeo, B.-L., Yeung, M.: Retrieving and Visualizing Video. Communication of the ACM **40** (December 1997), 43-52.
34. Zhang, H. J., Low, C. Y., Smoliar, S. W.: Video Parsing and Browsing Using Compressed Data. Multimedia Tools and Applications **1** (1995), 89-111.

Word Alignment in Digital Talking Books Using WFSTs

António Serralheiro, Diamantino Caseiro, Hugo Meinedo, and Isabel Trancoso

L^2F Spoken Language Systems Lab.
INESC-ID/IST
Rua Alves Redol 9, 1000-029 Lisbon, Portugal

Abstract. This paper describes the motivation and the method that we used for aligning digital spoken books, and the results obtained both at a word level and at a phone level. This alignment will allow specific access interfaces for persons with special needs, and also tools for easily detecting and indexing units (words, sentences, topics) in the spoken books. The tool was implemented in a Weighted Finite State Transducer framework, which provides an efficient way to combine different types of knowledge sources, such as alternative pronunciation rules. With this tool, a 2-hour long spoken book was aligned in a single step in much less than real time.

1 Introduction

The framework of this paper is a national project known as IPSOM, whose main goal is to improve the access to digitally stored spoken books by the visually impaired community. Spoken books have been mainly provided by the National Library (BN, *Biblioteca Nacional*) in analogue format (cassette) and have lately been under a gradual conversion process to digital format (CDROM). To improve the usability of these spoken books, the IPSOM project aims to provide both specific access interfaces for persons with special needs, and also tools for easily detecting and indexing *units* (words, sentences, topics) either written or spoken. Therefore, a good word-by-word synchronization between the text and its audio recording is mandatory for unit access and thus spoken book alignment is a major task of the IPSOM project. This time alignment can be further complicated by the co-articulation and the vowel reduction problems that occur in natural speech. Therefore, different pronunciations of each word should be taken into account by using either an enlarged lexicon or phonological rules. We have chosen the latter approach, which was implemented in a *WFST* (Weighted Finite State Transducer) framework. *WFSTs* have been successfully used in many written and spoken language applications, providing an efficient and elegant way of combining different types of knowledge sources, which makes them good candidates for alignment purposes.

From the point of view of research in the area of speech processing, one of the most interesting aspects of the IPSOM project is the fact that indexed spoken

M. Agosti and C. Thanos (Eds.): ECDL 2002, LNCS 2458, pp. 508–515, 2002.

books provide an invaluable resource for data-driven prosodic modeling and unit selection in the context of text-to-speech synthesis. This is a good motivation to perform the alignment not only on the basis of words but also of sub-word units. Simultaneously, the project also aims to broaden the usage of multimedia spoken books (for instance in didactic applications, etc.), by providing multimedia interfaces for access and retrieval.

Throughout this paper, we preferred avoiding the standard designation of Digital Talking Books (*DTB*), as the spoken books available from BN do not yet have the associated text or navigation structure and, as such, can only be regarded as a simplified form of a type *1-DTB* [1] [2]. *DTBs* may provide the "talking" capability by means of a text-to-speech synthesizer, allowing a direct access to each text word within the book. Our automatic aligner easily provides this same word synchronized access for books read by a human voice, with all the naturalness and emotions that current synthesizers are still unable to convey, which causes them to invariably induce some fatigue to the listeners.

2 Pilot Corpus

Existing spoken books at BN have been recorded by volunteers (non-professional readers) and stored in analogue tapes, that by their sequential access mode, results in an extremely slow (and error-prone) information retrieval process. This handicap could be easily overcome through their conversion to CDROM, if other problems had not been found, namely: low audio quality (multiple copies and damaged masters), and audible differences of quality through the same book (manual spectral equalization, and uncalibrated multiple recording sessions). These problems, together with the non-systematic reading of tables, figures, chapter numbers, footnotes, preface, etc., made the current material not suitable for automatic text-to-speech alignment. Consequently, it was decided to record a new spoken book - "O Senhor Ventura" by Miguel Torga, to serve as a *pilot corpus* for the new recording and alignment procedure. This fiction book was read by a professional speaker in a sound-proof booth. It was recorded directly to DAT and later down-sampled to 16kHz. The digital audio file was then manually edited to remove some reading errors and extraneous noises (although breathing sounds were kept to enhance naturalness), resulting in 2h 15m of audio. The pilot corpus text, amounting to 137,944 words, was pre-processed to deal with abbreviations, numbers and special symbols, resulting in a lexicon with around 5k different forms. Although very intelligible, as expected from a professional speaker, the speaking rate was relatively high, averaging more than 174 words per minute. At this stage, we decided to make a plain text-to-speech alignment without dealing with the textual structure (punctuation marks, paragraphs, sections, chapters, etc.).

3 Alignment System

Although the purpose of our alignment is directed to spoken books, figure 1 shows a diagram of a generic alignment system without the navigation structure associated to *DTBs*. The feature extraction block maps the input samples of the audio signal into a lower-rate time sequence of acoustic parameters, as described in the next subsection. The forced-alignment block is further detailed in another subsection.

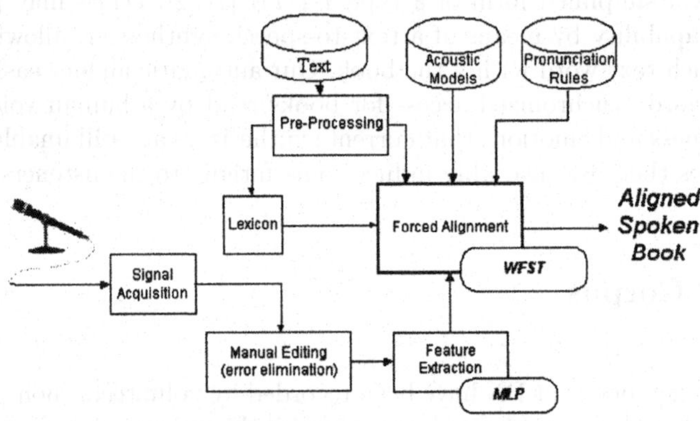

Fig. 1. Alignment System Diagram.

3.1 Acoustic Modeling

The hybrid acoustic models used in the alignment of spoken books were originally developed for a dictation task [3], in an effort to combine the temporal modeling capabilities of *HMMs* (Hidden Markov Models) with the pattern classification capabilities of *MLPs* (Multi-Layer Perceptrons). The models have a topology where context-independent phone posterior probabilities are estimated by three *MLPs* given the acoustic parameters at each frame. The streams of probabilities are then combined using an appropriate algorithm [4]. The processing stages are represented in Figure 2. The *MLPs* use the same basic structure and were trained with different feature extraction methods: *PLP* (Perceptual Linear Prediction) [5], *Log-RASTA* (log-RelAtive SpecTrAl) [5] and *MSG* (Modulation SpectroGram) [6]. *PLP* modeling is based on some specific human hearing characteristics, namely: non-linear frequency resolution, asymmetry of auditory filters, unequal hearing sensitivity at different frequencies and intensity-loudness non-linear relation. *RASTA* modeling attempts to model the sensitivity of human speech perception to preceding context and also to model the apparent insensitivity to absolute spectral shape. The *MSG* is a technique that models the slow modulations in speech signals across time and frequency, emphasizing amplitude modulations in critical bands at rates of 0 to 8Hz. For the first two processes, the features are log-energy and *PLP/Log-RASTA* 12th order coefficients and their first temporal derivatives summing up to 26 parameters. The *MSG* method uses 28 coefficients. Each *MLP* classifier incorporates local acoustic context via a multi-frame input window of 7 frames. The resulting network has a single hidden layer with 500 units and 39 output units (38 phones for European Portuguese plus silence).

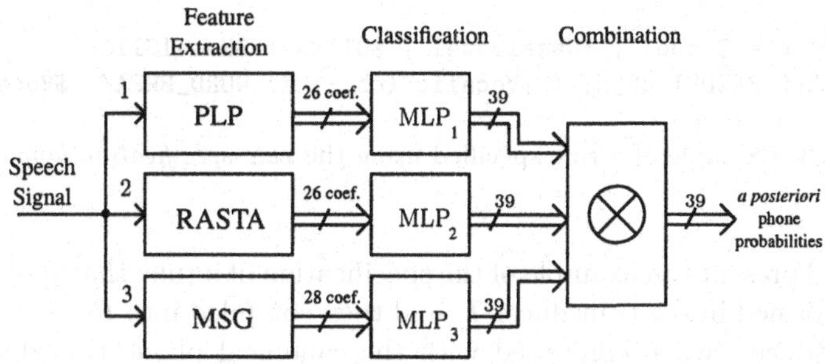

Fig. 2. Acoustic modeling combining several MLPs.

3.2 Alignment

An aligner is just a decoder that keeps track of the time boundaries between words or phones. Our decoder is based on *WFSTs* [7] in the sense that its search space is defined by a distribution-to-word transducer that is built outside the decoder. That search space is usually constructed as $H \circ L \circ G$, where H is the *HMM* or phone topology, L is the lexicon and G is the language model. For alignment, G is just the sequence of words that constitute the orthographic transcription of the utterance. The main advantage is that no restrictions are placed on the construction of the search space, which means that it can easily integrate other sources of knowledge, and the network can be optimized and replaced by an optimal equivalent one. This last advantage is a disadvantage from the perspective of alignment, as there are no warranties that the output and input labels are synchronized. To solve this problem, the decoder was extended to deal with special labels, on the input side, that are internally treated as epsilon labels, but are used to mark time transitions or boundaries. Whenever such end-of-segment labels are crossed, the time is stored in the current hypothesis. The user may choose to place those labels at the end of each phone *WFST* or at the end of each word *WFST*.

Phonological Rules. Instead of building a lexicon with multiple pronunciations per word, our goal is to develop phonological rules that can be used with a lexicon of canonical forms, in order to account for alternative pronunciations. These rules are specified using a finite-state grammar whose syntax is similar to the Backus-Naur-form augmented with regular expressions. Each rule is represented by a regular expression, and to the usual set of operators we added the operator $\rightarrow$, simple transduction, such that $(a \rightarrow b)$ means that the terminal symbol a is transformed into the terminal symbol b. The language allows the definition of non-terminal symbols (e.g. *$vowel*). All rules are optional, and are compiled into *WFSTs*.

```
$Vocalic = $Vowel | $NasalVowel | $Glide | $NasalGlide;
DEF_RULE SANDHI_ch_z, ( $Vocalic (ch -> z) WORD_BREAK  $Vocalic)
```

Fig. 3. Example of a rule specified using the *rule specification language.*

Figure 3 presents an example of the specification of a rule; that specification is first transformed into a transducer T, and then compiled into $R_T = \Sigma^*(T\Sigma^*)^*$[1]. That transducer, when composed with the canonical phone transducer S will produce $S_T = \pi_2(S \circ R_T)$ that allows new pronunciation alternatives.

We do not apply the rules one by one on a cascade of compositions, but rather build their union $R = R_{T_1} \cup R_{T_2} \cup \cdots \cup R_{T_n}$. R is applied 3 times ($S_R = \pi_2(S \circ R \circ R \circ R)$), to allow the application of one rule to the results of another. By performing the union of the rules we avoid the exaggerated growth of the resulting transducer, which can be exponential with the length of the composition cascade.

The main phonological aspects that the rules are intended to cover are vowel reduction and word co-articula-tion phenomena. Vowel reduction is specially important for European Portuguese, being one of the features that distinguishes it from Brazilian Portuguese and that makes it more difficult to learn for a foreign speaker. In our experiments, we used 37 such rules.

4 Experimental Results

The tests described in this section involve both word level and phone level experiments. The pilot corpus allows us to do alignment tests at a word level, but not at a phone level, as required for text-to-speech research. In order to evaluate the quality of the phone level transcriptions obtained using the pronunciation rules, we used a fragment of the EUROM.1 corpus [8], for which we have manual phone level alignment. In addition, we also performed recognition experiments with spoken books.

[1] Σ is the identity transducer, that converts each input symbol into itself.

4.1 Alignment Experiments with Spoken Books

A major advantage of our approach is that it allowed us to align the full audio version of the book in a single step. This is specially important if we take into account that the memory limitations of our previous alignment tool imposed a maximum of 3-minute audio segments. We thus avoid the very tedious task of manually breaking-up the audio into smaller segments with their associated text.

The word segmentation of the book ran in 0.024 real-time (RT), requiring 200MB of RAM. The phone level alignment of the book ran at 0.027 xRT when using the canonical pronunciations of the lexicon, and 0.030 xRT when using also the pronunciation rules.

An informal evaluation of the alignment procedure at word level was done using the publicly available Transcriber tool[2], which allowed us to subjectively access the good quality, by simultaneously listening and seeing on a word-by-word basis. Figure 4 illustrates the use of this tool.

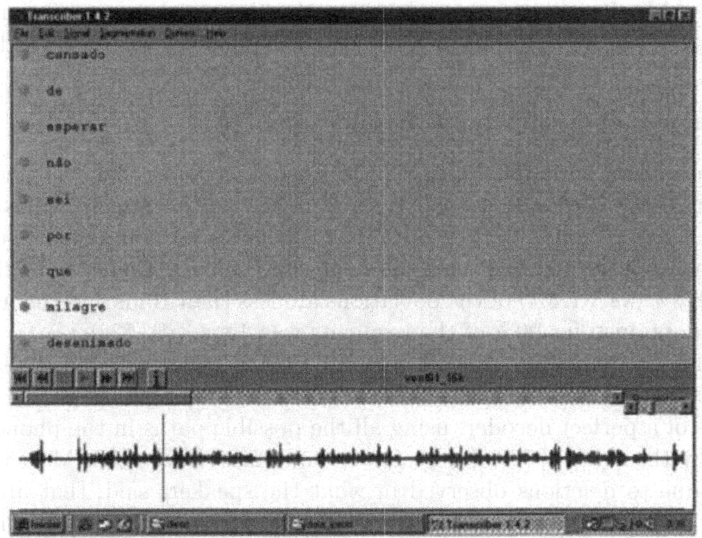

Fig. 4. Illustration of the word-level alignment of spoken books.

4.2 Recognition Experiments with Spoken Books

The edition of recordings to remove reading errors and extraneous noises produced by the speaker is also a very labor intensive task. As a first step to automate this procedure, we tried to match text recognized using a dedicated

[2] http://www.etca.fr/CTA/gip/Projets/Transcriber/

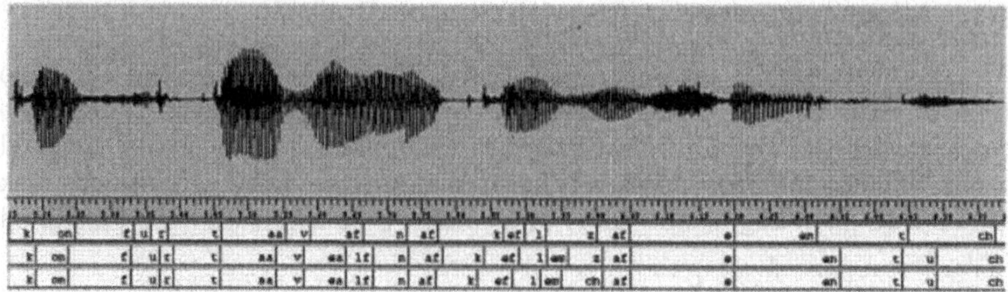

Fig. 5. Illustration of the phone level alignment of the EUROM.1 corpus.

recognizer with the original text in order to detect incorrect audio portions. The dedicated recognizer uses a lexicon and an n-gram language model estimated from all the book's text and achieved a word error rate (*WER*) of 17.2%.

Significant improvements were obtained by using spea-ker adaptation. That was done by retraining the acoustic models on 80% of the available audio, using the time stamps provided by the automatic aligner. The adapted models obtained with the alignment made using the canonical pronunciation lexicon achieved a *WER* of 7.8%, and the one using the phonological rules yielded 7.1%.

4.3 Phone Level Alignment Evaluation

Our experiments with the EUROM.1 corpus showed us that the phone level alignment using the phonological rules is closer to the manual transcriptions than the canonical one (95.62% vs. 93.65% phone correction, respectively). The same conclusion was drawn when we analyzed the time deviation of the alignments: 38.6% (vs. 37.4%) of the deviations are less than 10ms and the maximum deviation obtained for 90% of the segments was 44ms (vs. 52ms).

We also compared the *WFSTs* generated by the rules with the manual transcriptions, in order to obtain the oracle performance of the rules (i.e. the performance of a perfect decoder, using all the possible paths in the phone lattices allowed by the rules): 97.73% correctness and 82.11% accuracy. Most of the errors are due to deletions observed in what the speakers said, that are neither allowed by the canonical lexicon nor by the rules. Figure 5 illustrates the phone level labels obtained with and without rules (middle and bottom layers), which can be compared with the manually assigned labels (top layer).

5 Conclusions and Future Work

The paper described our work on spoken books in the framework of the IPSOM project, emphasizing the problems of the actual repository and the alignment tools that were developed. We verified that, with proper recording procedures, the alignment task can be fully automated in a very fast single-step procedure, even for a 2-hour long recording. This is specially important if we take into account that the memory limitations of our previous alignment tool imposed a maximum of 3-minute audio segments. With this new tool, we avoid the very tedious process of partitioning audio and text into corresponding segments. In addition, the use of a dedicated recognizer can also contribute to speeding up the manual process of removing reading errors.

The word boundaries computed using the *WFST*-based alignment will allow for the development of more sophisticated browsing tools for spoken books, which is one of our next tasks in the IPSOM project. Such browsing and indexing tools can be specially important for non-fiction, technical books, for which there is a great request from the visually impaired community.

The use of phonological rules seems to provide reasonably good alternative pronunciations, specially accounting for vowel reduction and inter-word co-articulation phenomena. However, a more exhaustive comparison with manual labeling still needs to be conducted in order to improve these rules. The better phone level alignment of spoken books achieved with these rules will also be crucial for our research in text-to-speech synthesis, namely for prosodic modeling and unit selection, using data-driven approaches.

Acknowledgments. This work was partially funded by FCT projects POSI/ 3452/ PLP/2000 and POSI/33846/PLP/2000. INESC-ID Lisboa had support from the POSI Program of the "Quadro Comunitário de Apoio III". The authors would like to thank Isabel Bahia and João Lopes Raimundo for their kind cooperation in reading the book and our colleagues from CLUL, Céu Viana and Isabel Mascarenhas, for their help with the phonological rules and manual labeling.

References

1. ANSI/NISO Z39.86 - 2002 Specifications for the Digital Talking Book, *http://www.niso.org/standards/index.html*
2. DAISY 2.02 Specification, Formal Recommendation, Feb. 28, 2001. *http://www.daisy.org/products/menupps.htm*
3. Neto, J., Martins, C. and Almeida, L., *A Large Vocabulary Continuous Speech Recognition Hybrid System for the Portuguese Language*, in Proc. ICSLP 98, Sydney, Australia, 1998.
4. H. Meinedo and J. Neto, "Combination of acoustic models in continuous speech recognition hybrid systems", In Proc. ICSLP 2000, Beijing, China, 2000.
5. H. Hermansky, N. Morgan, A. Baya and P. Kohn, "RASTA-PLP Speech Analysis Technique", In Proc. ICASSP 92, San Francisco, USA, 1992.
6. B. E. Kingsbury, N. Morgan, and S. Greenberg, "Robust speech recognition using the modulation spectrogram", Speech Communication, 25:117–132, 1998.
7. M. Mohri, M. Riley, D. Hindle, A. Ljolje, F. Pereira, "Full Expansion of Context-Dependent Networks in Large Vocabulary Speech Recognition", In Proc. ICASSP 98, Seattle, Washington, 1998.
8. C. Ribeiro, I. Trancoso and M. Viana, *EUROM.1 Portuguese Database*, Report of ESPRIT Project 6819 SAM-A, 1993.

Migration on Request, a Practical Technique for Preservation

Phil Mellor, Paul Wheatley, and Derek Sergeant

CAMiLEON Project*, Edward Boyle Library, The University of Leeds, Leeds LS2 9JT, UK
{P.R.Wheatley, D.M.Sergeant}@leeds.ac.uk

Abstract. Maintaining a digital object in a usable state over time is a crucial aspect of digital preservation. Existing methods of preserving have many drawbacks. This paper describes advanced techniques of data migration which can be used to support preservation more accurately and cost effectively.
To ensure that preserved works can be rendered on current computer systems over time, "traditional migration" has been used to convert data into current formats. As the new format becomes obsolete another conversion is performed, etcetera. Traditional migration has many inherent problems as errors during transformation propagate throughout future transformations.
CAMiLEON's software longevity principles can be applied to a migration strategy, offering improvements over traditional migration. This new approach is named "Migration on Request." Migration on Request shifts the burden of preservation onto a single tool, which is maintained over time. Always returning to the original format enables potential errors to be significantly reduced.

1 Introduction

In a digital library a new problem has surfaced, collections of digital objects become obsolete and unusable while technology rapidly evolves. Meanwhile, the field of digital preservation is only just beginning. Surely it is safest to wait for the advice to mature? However, in doing so many current digital objects that needed preserving will have already been lost (irretrievably).

Maintaining a digital object in a usable state over time is a crucial aspect of digital preservation. In order to preserve successfully, action must be taken to ensure that digital objects can be easily rendered on current computer platforms over time. Migration has been widely used to move obsolete data into current data formats. When a data format becomes obsolete, a migration tool is used to transform the digital object into a data format which can be rendered and used on a current computer platform. When this format becomes obsolete, another

* Research for this paper was supported in part by the National Science Foundation, Award #9905935, Digital Library Initiative - International, Emulation Options for Digital Preservation and by the Joint Information Systems Committee in the UK.

M. Agosti and C. Thanos (Eds.): ECDL 2002, LNCS 2458, pp. 516–526, 2002.

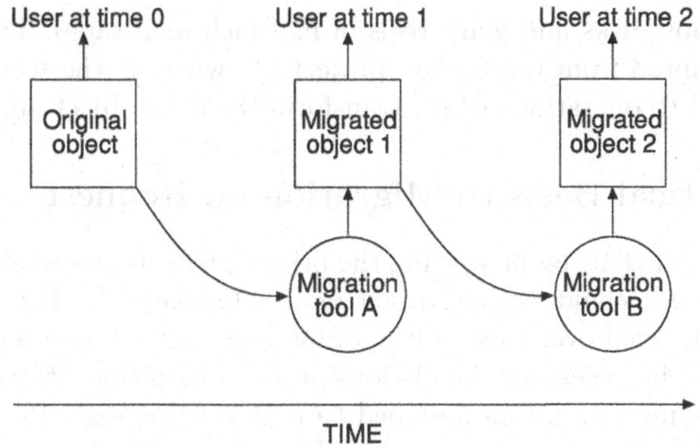

Fig. 1. A digital object preserved using traditional migration

transformation is performed, and so on. There are many drawbacks with this strategy of "traditional migration" (see figure 1). Any errors or omissions from a transformation will propagate throughout and hence be present in all future transformations (see figure 2). Existing methods of preserving digital data often fall short of accurately preserving and authentically rendering an original digital document. Continually producing new migration tools whenever a transformation is required and then applying them to possibly very large data holdings is costly. This paper describes some advanced techniques of data migration which can be used to support preservation work more accurately and cost effectively.

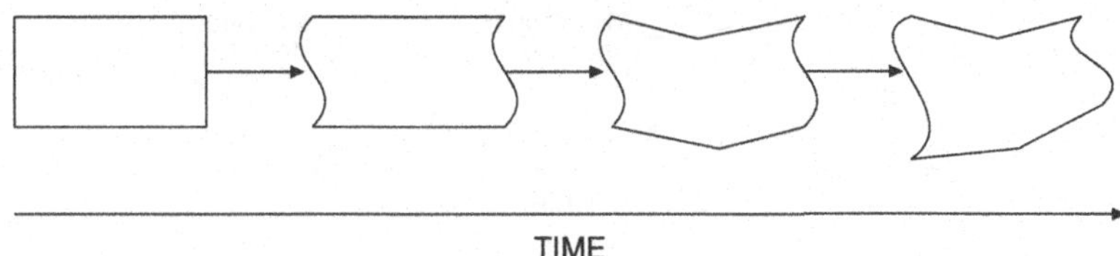

Fig. 2. Errors propagating through each conversion step of traditional migration

Traditional migration has been widely used to convert obsolete data into current data formats. In the short term this offers a way of keeping digital materials current, but it is not an effective long term strategy. This research performed by the CAMiLEON project[1] has investigated a way of applying migration in a more sensible and effective way. This new approach is named "Migration on Request." The CAMiLEON project has implemented a real Migration on Request tool to ensure that this theoretical work is truly practical. This paper explains this technique and presents findings from the experimental implementation. The Digitale Bewaring project is an excellent resource about migration [2].

Underpinning this approach is the notion of indefinite retention of an abstract byte-stream. This means preserving the original data object (not preserving eight-inch floppy disks and giant reels of half-inch mag tape). These principles have been adopted from the Cedars project [3], whereby the term "migration" is only applied to operations which transform the data object [4].

2 Theoretical Basis to Migration on Request

Cedars suggested that, by preserving the original bytestream of a digital object, preservation work could be performed more effectively [5]. If a bytestream is preserved unchanged over time, a way of interpreting or rendering that original format will also be necessary. An obvious problem with this strategy is the short lifetime of any migration tool designed to perform this task. Previous research on the CAMiLEON project has developed techniques for software longevity [6]. While these techniques were originally developed to maintain software emulators over generations of platform, they equally apply to implementing migration tools. Combining these methods of software longevity with the principle of always maintaining the original bytestream, we see a new form of migration taking shape.

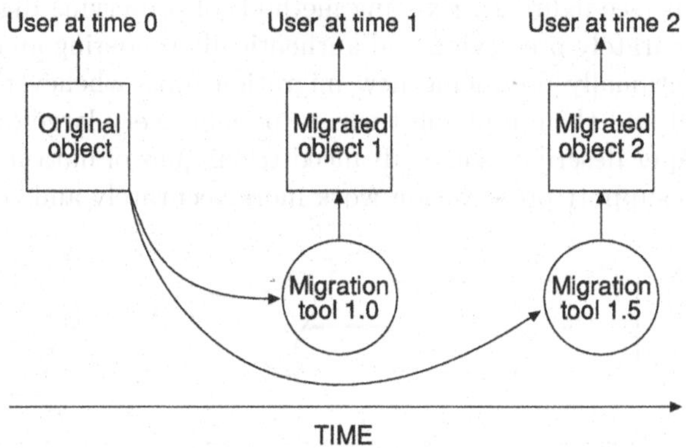

Fig. 3. Applying a Migration on Request tool over time

This foundation work points the way to a practical method of implementing a more useful migration strategy. Migration on Request shifts the burden of preservation from handling vast quantities of digital objects to a single tool for each class of data format in the archive. This tool renders all of the digital objects and is maintained over time (see figure 3) using the previously mentioned software longevity techniques. A digital object is simply archived in its original format. New output modules can be added to the tool to produce newer data formats as previously supported formats become obsolete. Always returning to the original digital format enables Migration on Request to significantly reduce the possibility of errors being introduced during the conversion process (see figure 4). There is always only one transformation step from the original to the current format. In any case the original is what is retained in the archive.

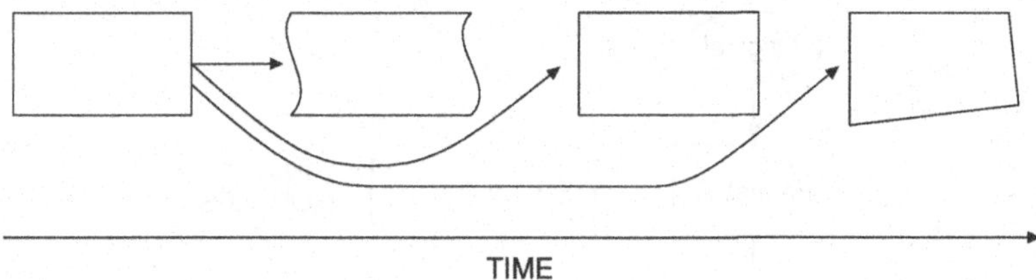

Fig. 4. Migration on Request may introduce minor errors, but these do not propagate

Migration on Request offers several key benefits over a traditional migration approach:

- The code which reads in and interprets a particular file format need only be implemented once.
- Using only one migration step increases migration accuracy.
- Issues of authenticity are greatly simplified as a digital object is preserved in its original form.
- The modular design of a migration tool makes the implementation of a "reversible migration" test much simpler and cheaper.
- The migration tool is only deployed "on request" and so offers massive savings where a large number of digital objects are preserved.

3 Migration on Request Tool Design

Figure 5 shows how a Migration on Request tool breaks down the elements required to migrate a digital object. This design is extensible, so as supported output formats become obsolete new output modules can be added without having to re-write existing input modules. This provides a major cost saving in comparison to a traditional migration approach.

The Consultative Committee for Space Data Systems OAIS Reference Model [7] reminds us that the only way of ensuring a migration step has been completed without error is by the proof of a reversible migration. If we can convert a migrated object back to its original form, and it matches the original object then no data has been lost. With a traditional migration approach the effort required to implement a reversible migration test effectively doubles the overall implementation required. On top of that, all this work must be repeated at each subsequent migration step! With Migration on Request, the modular framework allows us to make substantial savings in implementation time. The addition of an input and output module provides support for a new data format with the opportunity for a reversible migration test. When we add support for subsequent formats we make use of existing input modules. This represents a cost saving over the complete re-implementation at each step of a traditional migration process.

The ability to have a number of input as well as output modules means that one Migration on Request tool can support a number of different input formats.

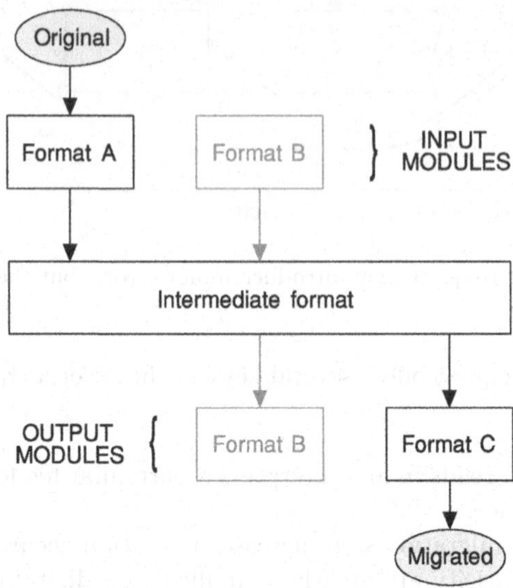

Fig. 5. The Migration on Request process

For example, an archive may contain textual data in a number of word processing formats, which are sufficiently similar for one Migration on Request tool to support them. Again, we see massive cost savings over traditional migration. A Migration on Request tool is maintained over time by adding new output modules as supported output formats become obsolete. These output formats can be used with all the supported input formats, stripping away all the wasteful implementation redundancy found in traditional migration.

The modularised design of a migration tool makes it easier to maintain and provides us with a functional record of the file format in which our preserved data is maintained.

4 Testing the Theory

The aim was to provide a practical test of a Migration on Request approach. A successfully working Migration on Request tool would provide strong evidence that this approach is useful, and also highlight any difficulties which became apparent during the implementation. It was important to make this test hard enough to tease out these implementation issues. Since vector graphic formats are sufficiently complex (unlike text or bitmap graphics), they were chosen as the focus of this test. This ensures that the Migration on Request strategy is tested thoroughly before progressing to other classes of digital objects.

Three formats covering a cross section of existing vector formats were chosen for implementation: WMF [8], Draw [9] and SVG [10]. Windows Meta Files (WMF) were developed by Microsoft. Images are represented by a series of instructions that match the calls made by applications to the Windows Graphics

Device Interface. The Draw file was invented by Acorn Computers in the early 1990's and is commonly used for exchanging data between applications on the RISC OS platform. In the UK a lot of educational material still exists in this format. Scalable Vector Graphics (SVG) are a new XML based format developed by the W3O, and is mainly used for web site imagery. Figure 6 shows how an oversimplified vector diagram of a face is represented in these formats. Several vector graphics files, of varying complexities, were used in order to test the Migration on Request tool.

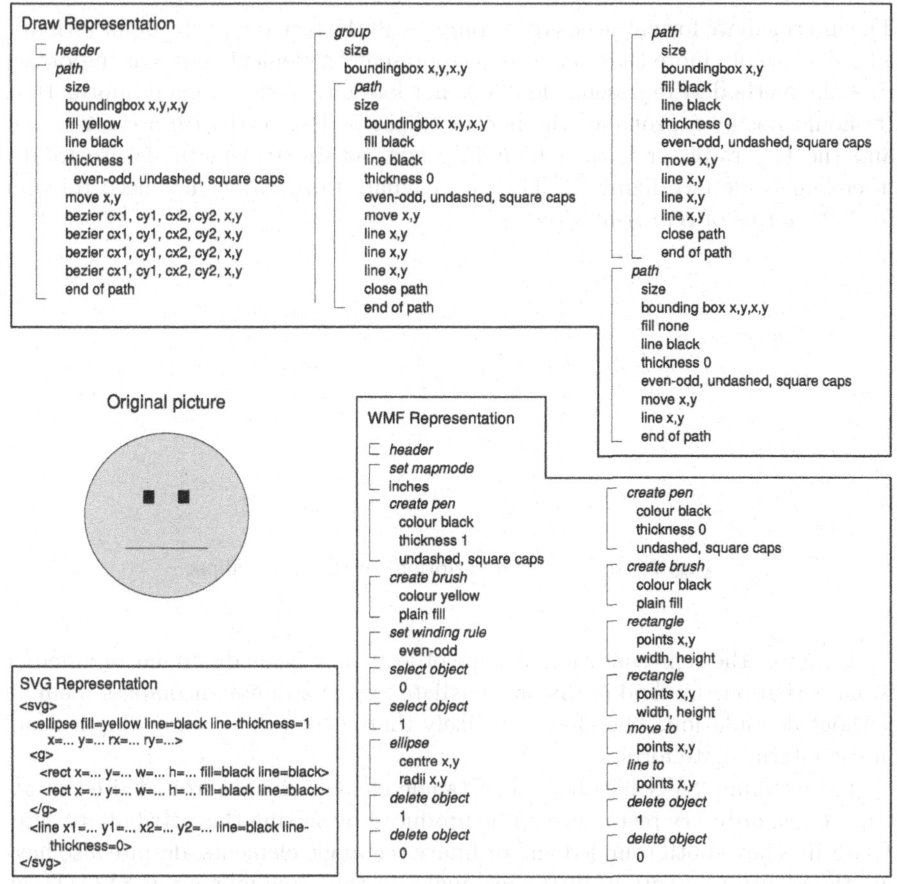

Fig. 6. WMF, Draw, and SVG representations for a simple face

The migration tool was constructed in a modular way. Separate functions were used to input each format and return an intermediate structure, a hierarchy of elements such as lines, ellipses and polygons. This structure could be passed to an output module, but it is likely to contain elements unsupported by the output format. To solve this the output module passes the structure on to a series of functions that downgrade or convert any unsupported elements into ones that the format can handle. In order to minimise the amount of conversion routines that are needed, a chain of conversions can be applied; for example a curved path could be converted to a straight line path, and then to a series of individual lines; there is not need to create a special routine or clause to convert curved paths directly into individual lines.

5 Data Formats and Their Interpretation

The intermediate format needs to encompass all the features of the input formats. There is usually more than one way to represent an element, but it is important that the method of representation does not lose any of the original information. It should not be a problem whether an ellipse is described with a centre point and the two radii, or with a bounding box, as the two methods are totally interchangeable (see figure 7). The intermediate format does not need to cater for both forms of representation.

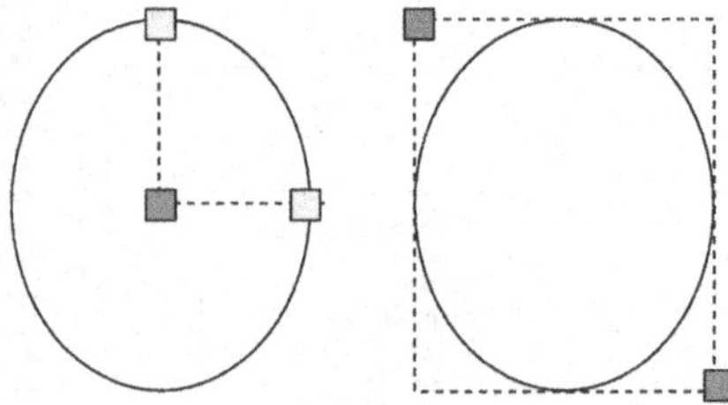

Fig. 7. Alternative descriptions of the same ellipse

However, the representation of some objects may be so dissimilar in different formats that one method in the intermediate format will not encompass them all without degradation. Therefore it is likely that there will be some 'duplication' in the intermediate format.

For example, SVG files have a rectangle element with a 'rounded edge' attribute. An ordinary rectangle can be produced by setting this attribute to zero. WMF files have both rounded and ordinary rectangle elements, despite also having the ability to create ordinary rectangles in the same manner as SVG. Draw files do not support rounded rectangles; instead a path of lines and curves would be needed.

The WMF structure is oriented in favour of the implementation of rendering rather than the content of the graphic itself. This means there are lots of elements specific to WMFs which are unlikely to be needed by file formats in the future and would get ignored or 'flattened out' by the output modules anyway. WMF files allow the presence of lots of redundant instructions. For example, a series of instructions to set the mapping mode to inches, millimetres, then back to inches again with no objects being drawn in the meantime, would be pointless but possible. This is just a simple example but the possibilities are tremendously wasteful. The WMF is basically a simple programming language, and very poor, inefficient programs can be written with it.

Retaining any of this seemingly redundant information would only serve to clutter the intermediate format, thereby making it more complex, less intuitive, and increasing the risk of bugs or incompatibilities that are hard to track down. It seems reasonable, therefore, that such elements are not made part of the intermediate format and are dealt with and converted into more suitable representations by the WMF input module. The limitation of this approach would be that reversible migration of WMFs would become impossible.

5.1 Internal Number Representation

The Draw format measures values in OS units (1/180th of an inch), stored as fixed point 32-bit numbers with an 8 bit fractional part. WMFs offer a choice of units for a value, which is stored in 16 bits. Furthermore, an offset and scaling can be applied. SVG numbers are written as a string of ASCII characters, usually in base 10.

Care needs to be taken when storing such numbers in memory. Errors in precision can occur when numbers are stored in a floating point representation, particularly when storing exceptionally large or small numbers. However, the range of fixed point numbers is more constrained and can cause greater imprecision errors, usually through truncation of the fractional part.

There are many different units of measurement that could be used — inches, millimetres, pixels, and so on. These values need to be kept in their original units for as long as possible, since unnecessary conversion could lose accuracy.

In our Migration on Request tool a structure is defined to store a unit of measurement and a value (as either an integer or floating point number). Various functions can extract the value in different units. The design could go so far as to simulate various number representations itself, such as 16 and 32 bit integers, even ASCII strings. This would require a lot of maths routines to be implemented by hand, such as addition and multiplication, perhaps even square root functions.

6 Reversible Migration

The reversible migration test compares a migrated version of the digital object to the original digital object. This is done by migrating the migrated version back into the original format, see figure 8. A Migration on Request tool can be used to perform all of the migrations required for the reversible migration test. CAMiLEON has performed a reversible migration test successfully with the Draw format, and a reversible migration was achieved (bar some minor information such as user interface preferences). It would even be possible to reversibly migrate WMF files, if its features were integrated with the intermediate format. Such features would significantly increase the complexity of the intermediate format, making the tool harder to maintain. A choice between complexity and reversibility must be made. It seems unlikely that the rendering structure found in WMF will also appear in future vector graphic formats, so it seems logical not to support this style here. ASCII formats such as SVG raise an interesting quandary. The amount of white space (new lines, spaces etc) is irrelevant to the information stored in the file, but is often used to indent nested items or to separate different sections to enable human readability. For true reversible migration (using a "diff" tool), this white space would also have to be preserved in the internal format. Alternatively a parsing tool could be used to remove this non-essential information before applying the "diff" test. Migration on request certainly makes the 'holy grail' of reversible migration easier to reach than through conventional migration techniques.

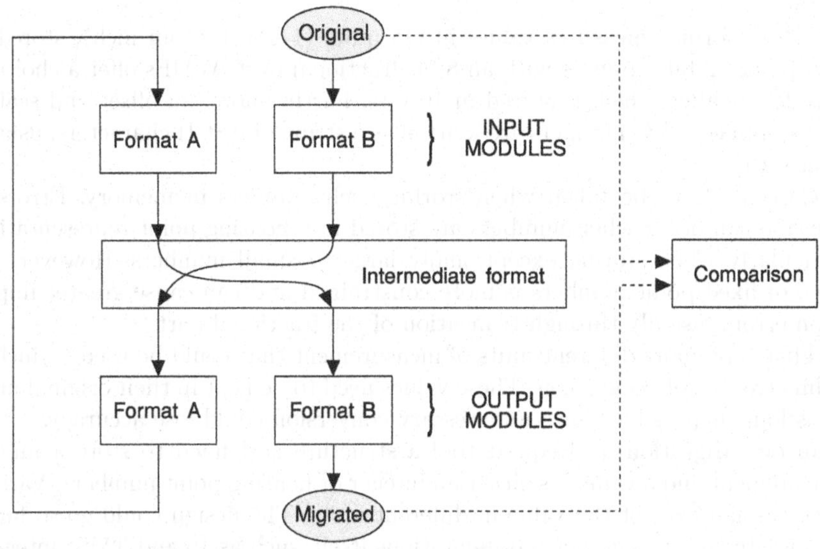

Fig. 8. The reversibility test

7 Reliance on Original Evidence

When developing the tool, it was essential to view the output from the migration tool in a graphics application (rather than a file editor), and compare this with a rendering of the original file. A simple visual check was used to confirm whether elements had migrated properly. Although not particularly accurate, this method allowed obvious errors to be identified quickly.

Imagine a collection of abstract paintings by Mondrian existed only in a poorly documented, (now) unused vector format. If the colours were mixed up or some shapes distorted during migration, without a true comparison to the original, these errors may go unnoticed. Technically it would be possible to examine each file manually to determine what it would look like, but for large or complex files this would be an arduous task.

Once the migration tool can be shown to be working correctly, the need for such evidence is less necessary, but still relevant. Later modifications to the tool would require all the modules to be tested again for any discrepancies in the migration. Such modification might be, for example, adding new features to the intermediate format to support a new input module. Evidence of an original rendering of test files would again be useful here, perhaps via emulation.

Using the original applications need not be the only way to acquire this evidence; screenshots, written documents, etc, are other useful sources. These resources may also have to be preserved as time passes. Implementation of a Migration on Request tool should be done when the format is still in a usable form and such evidence can be gathered. This echoes Holdsworth and Wheatley's observations on the timeliness of emulation for preservation [6].

8 The Evolution of File Formats

In order to prepare any Migration on Request tools for the future, study into trends of data formats is needed. Vector graphics used to be the preserve of design and publishing, but it is a reasonable assumption that in a few years their most widespread deployment will be on the World Wide Web. Designers of migration tools should concentrate on preserving features that are most likely to be used in future developments of their format genres.

The development of open standards is interesting. If the trend is to define and follow standards, then choosing an internal format similar to one of these standards would be a sensible way forward. SVG seems a good basis for the intermediate format in a vector migration tool. Unfortunately it seems unlikely that relying on standards will be sufficient to ensure preservation. The need to maintain a commercial advantage over competitors has meant in the past that standards are extended or not adhered to, HTML being a case in point. We have to accept that standards can change over time and will at some point become obsolete. Fortunately a Migration on Request strategy can benefit from the stability and longevity of open standards but is not tied to them. It must also be remembered that a format is not necessarily a good design just because it is a standardised format [11].

9 Evaluation

The practical implementation of a Migration on Request tool was a valuable test of our theoretical strategy. The modular migration tool successfully imports, converts and exports a number of vector graphic formats. The experiences encountered in developing a tool of this kind were useful in raising problem areas and providing the chance to develop solutions to tackle these difficulties. In particular, implementing a reversible migration test was not as easy in practice as was originally thought but this was not a specific problem with Migration on

Request. Ordering of data elements, non-critical information and multiple methods of representing the same data are problems likely to be encountered with most data formats, using any migration strategy.

The implementation work showed that the initial development of a Migration on Request tool is not overly laborious or costly. Over a short to medium term period Migration on Request should offer major cost savings in comparison to a traditional migration strategy, even where standard/open formats are utilised.

10 Conclusions

The CAMiLEON project has developed a Migration on Request tool which shows that a preservation strategy of this kind can work in a practical environment. Migration on Request provides a more accurate and cost effective strategy for preserving digital objects than traditional migration. Because Migration on Request relies on the preservation of the original bytestream of a digital object it can effectively work alongside an emulation strategy. If open source emulation and Migration on Request tools become available, a digital repository can effectively offer different ways of rendering its digital materials at a very low cost. The time is right to move forward from the "thinking" to the "doing" and provide the preservation community with well designed, but cost effective tools for the preservation of digital materials.

References

1. The CAMiLEON Project http://www.si.umich.edu/CAMILEON/
2. Testbed Digitale Bewaring: Migration : Context and Current Status (2001) http://www.digitaleduurzaamheid.nl/bibliotheek/Migration.pdf
3. Cedars Guide To : Digital Preservation Strategies (2002) http://www.leeds.ac.uk/cedars/guideto/dpstrategies/
4. Wheatley, P: Migration - a CAMiLEON discussion paper Ariadne **29** (2001) http://www.ariadne.ac.uk/issue29/camileon/
5. Holdsworth, D and Sergeant, D M: A blueprint for Representation Information in the OAIS Model (1999) http://www.personal.leeds.ac.uk/~ecldh/cedars/ieee00.html
6. Holdsworth, D and Wheatley, P: Emulation, Preservation and Abstraction. RLG Dignews **5,4** http://www.rlg.org/preserv/diginews/diginews5-4.html#feature2
7. Consultative Committee for Space Data Systems: Reference model for an Open Archival Information System (OAIS) (2001) http://www.ccsds.org/documents/pdf/CCSDS-650.0-R-2.pdf
8. GFF Format Summary: Microsoft Windows Metafile O'Reilly's Encyclopedia of Graphics File Formats http://www.oreilly.com/centers/gff/formats/micmeta/download.htm
9. (RISC OS) Programmers Reference Manual: Acorn Computers Technical Publications **5** (1994)
10. World Wide Web Consortium: Scalable Vector Graphics (SVG) 1.0 Specification September (2001) http://www.w3.org/TR/SVG/
11. Hedstrom, M and Lee, C: Digital Objects: Definitions, Applications, Implications. Proc 3rd DLM Forum, Barcelona, May (2002) (forthcoming)

Information Alert in Distributed Digital Libraries: The Models, Languages, and Architecture of DIAS*

M. Koubarakis, T. Koutris, C. Tryfonopoulos, and P. Raftopoulou

Dept. of Electronic and Computer Engineering
Technical University of Crete
73100 Chania, Crete, Greece
{manolis,koutris,trifon,rautop,}@intelligence.tuc.gr
www.intelligence.tuc.gr/~manolis

Abstract. This paper presents DIAS, a distributed alert service for digital libraries, currently under development in project DIET. We first discuss the models and languages for expressing user profiles and notifications. Then we present the data structures, algorithms and protocols that underly the peer-to-peer agent architecture of DIAS.

1 Introduction

Users of modern digital libraries can keep themselves up-to-date by searching and browsing their favourite collections, or more conveniently by resorting to an *alert service*. Recently, the participants of project HERMES [15] have argued very convincingly that an alert service which integrates information from a wide variety of information providers can be indispensable to users. It relieves them from the tedious and cumbersome task of searching and browsing, or even from subscribing to individual alert services such as Springer Link Alert[1] or Elsevier Contents Direct[2].

In this paper, we discuss the models, languages and architecture of DIAS, a *D*istributed *I*nformation *A*lert *S*ystem currently under development in the context of the European project DIET [24,27,18]. DIAS adopts the basic ideas of project HERMES [15] and extends them in various interesting ways.

Our main technical contributions can be summarized as follows. First, we introduce the peer-to-peer (P2P) agent architecture of DIAS which has been inspired by the event dissemination system SIENA [6]. We also discuss the requirements imposed by this architecture on the data models and languages to

* This work was carried out as part of the DIET (Decentralised Information Ecosystems Technologies) project (IST-1999-10088), within the Universal Information Ecosystems initiative of the Information Society Technology Programme of the European Union.

[1] http://link.springer.de/alert

[2] http://www.elsevier.nl

M. Agosti and C. Thanos (Eds.): ECDL 2002, LNCS 2458, pp. 527–542, 2002.

be used for specifying user profiles/queries and notifications.[3] Then we develop formally the data models $\mathcal{WP}$, $\mathcal{AWP}$ and $\mathcal{AWPS}$, and their corresponding languages for specifying queries and notifications. Data model $\mathcal{WP}$ is only briefly presented and more details can be found in [19,20]. $\mathcal{WP}$ is based on free text and its query language is based on the *boolean model with proximity operators.* The concepts of $\mathcal{WP}$ extend the traditional concept of proximity in IR [2,8,9] in a significant way, and utilize it in a query language targeted at information alert for distributed digital libraries. Data model $\mathcal{AWP}$ is based on *attributes* or *fields* with finite-length strings as values. Its query language is an extension of the query language of data model $\mathcal{WP}$. Our work on $\mathcal{AWP}$ complements recent proposals for querying textual information in distributed event-based systems [6,4] by using linguistically motivated concepts such as *word* and not arbitrary strings. This makes $\mathcal{AWP}$ very appropriate in information alert systems for digital libraries[4]. Finally, the model $\mathcal{AWPS}$ extends $\mathcal{AWP}$ by introducing a "similarity" operator in the style of modern IR, based on the vector space model [2]. The novelty of our work in this area is the move to query languages much more expressive than the one used in the information dissemination system SIFT [29] where documents and queries are represented by free text. The similarity concept of $\mathcal{AWPS}$ is essentially the similarity concept pioneered by IR systems [2], database systems with IR influences (e.g., WHIRL [11]) and more recently by the XML query language ELIXIR [10]. We note that both WHIRL and ELIXIR target information retrieval and integration applications, and pay no attention to information dissemination and the concepts/functionality needed in such applications. The first presentation of model $\mathcal{AWPS}$ is the one given in this paper and [21].

In the second part of our paper, we present the detailed protocols and algorithms of our architecture and discuss its implementation in the context of project DIET [24,27,18]. Contrary to project HERMES [15], we develop a distributed information alert service from scratch based on the ideas of SIENA [6] and do not rely on any pre-existing message-oriented middleware.

The rest of the paper is organised as follows. Section 2 introduces the DIAS architecture, and discusses the requirements for data models and languages to be used in this context. Section 3 presents data model $\mathcal{WP}$ and its semantics. Then Sections 4 and 5 build on this foundation and develops the same machinery for data models $\mathcal{AWP}$ and $\mathcal{AWPS}$. Section 6 discusses some interesting details of the DIAS architecture and implementation. Finally, Section 7 gives our conclusions and discusses future work.

[3] In this paper, the terms *query* and *profile* will be used interchangeably. We are in an information alert setting where a profile is simply a *long-standing query*.

[4] Also, for other commercial systems where similar models are supported already for retrieval.

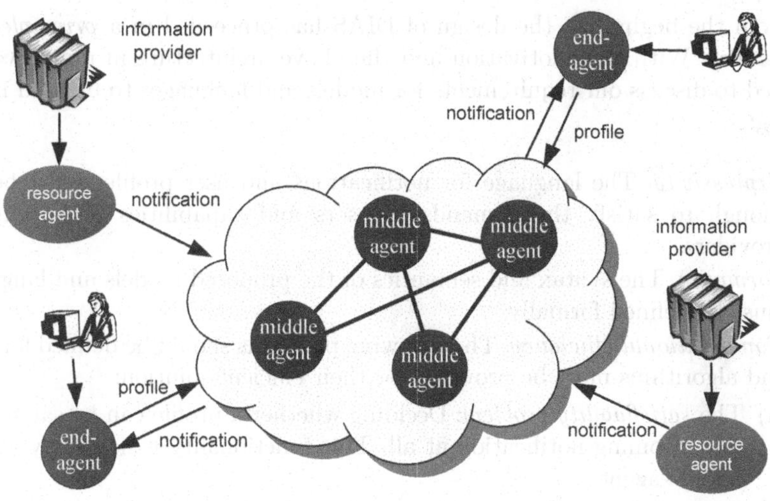

Fig. 1. The architecture of DIAS

2 DIAS: Architecture and Requirements

A high level view of DIAS is shown in Figure 1. *Resource agents* integrate a number of information providers to produce streams of notifications that are send to some *middle-agent(s)*. Resource agents are similar in functionality to observers as defined in project HERMES [15]. Users utilize their *personal agents* to post profiles to some middle-agent(s). The P2P network of middle-agents is the "glue" that makes sure that published notifications arrive at interested subscribers. To achieve this, middle-agents forward posted profiles to other middle-agents using an appropriate P2P protocol. In this way, matching of a profile with a notification can take place at a middle-agent that is as close as possible to the origin of the incoming notification. Profile forwarding can be done in a sophisticated way to minimize network traffic e.g., no profiles that are less general than one that has already been processed are actually forwarded.

Most of the concepts of the architecture sketched above have been explicit (or sometimes implicit) in the agent literature for some time (especially, the literature on KQML and subsequent multi-agent systems based on it [16]. Unfortunately the emphasis in most of these systems is on a single central middle-agent, making the issues that would arise in a distributed setting difficult to appreciate. In our opinion, the best presentation of these concepts available in the literature can be found in [6] where the distributed event dissemination system SIENA is presented.[5] Some core ideas of SIENA have been adopted by DIAS as we will explain in Section 6.

[5] SIENA does not use terminology from the area of agent systems but the connection is obvious.

From the beginning, the design of DIAS has proceeded in a *principled* and *formal* way. With this motivation and the above architecture in mind, we now proceed to discuss our requirements for models and languages to be used in this setting:

1. *Expressivity.* The language for notifications and user profiles must be rich enough to satisfy the demands of users and capabilities of information providers.
2. *Formality.* The syntax and semantics of the proposed models and languages must be defined formally.
3. *Computational efficiency.* The following problems should be defined formally and algorithms must be provided for their efficient solution:
   a) The *satisfiability problem*: Deciding whether a profile can be satisfied by any incoming notification at all. This functionality is necessary at each middle-agent.
   b) The *satisfaction* (or *matching*) *problem*: Deciding whether a notification satisfies (or matches) a profile.
   c) The *filtering problem*: Given a database of profiles db and a notification n, find all profiles $q \in db$ that match n. This functionality is very crucial at each middle-agent and it is based on the availability of algorithms for the satisfaction problem. We expect deployed information alert systems to handle hundreds of thousands or millions of profiles.
   d) The *entailment* or *subsumption problem*: Deciding whether a profile is more or less "general" than another. This functionality is crucial if we want to minimize profile forwarding as sketched above.

Previous research has shown that the above formal perspective is shared by other researchers in the area of information dissemination.[6] Various papers proposing sophisticated filtering algorithms in the area of event dissemination have defined the syntax and semantics of their languages carefully [1,25,14]. The developers of the distributed event dissemination system SIENA in particular have carefully defined the syntax and semantics of their language for events and profiles, and have formalised the notions of satisfaction and entailment (called "covers" in [6]). The same has been done for a much more expressive language in [4] where only satisfaction and filtering have been considered. To the best of our knowledge, no work has been done so far on addressing the satisfiability problem.

In the rest of this paper, we concentrate on information alert in distributed digital libraries and define the models $\mathcal{WP}$, $\mathcal{AWP}$ and $\mathcal{AWPS}$ that are suitable for this job. Then we discuss the architecture of DIAS and show how the theoretical concepts discussed above become crucial for its efficient implementation.

[6] However, to the best of our knowledge, no one has applied this formal perspective in a distributed digital library context.

3 Text Values and Word Patterns

The model $\mathcal{WP}$ assumes that textual information is in the form of *free text* and can be queried by *word patterns* (hence the acronym for the model).

We assume the existence of a finite *alphabet* $\mathbf{\Sigma}$. A *word* is a finite non-empty sequence of letters from $\mathbf{\Sigma}$. We also assume the existence of a (finite or infinite) set of words called the *vocabulary* and denoted by $\mathcal{V}$.

Definition 1. *A* text value *s of length n over vocabulary $\mathcal{V}$ is a total function $s : \{1, 2, \ldots, n\} \to \mathcal{V}$.*

In other words, a text value s is a finite sequence of words from the assumed vocabulary and $s(i)$ gives the i-th element of s. Text values can be used to represent finite-length strings consisting of words separated by blanks. The length of a text value s (i.e., its number of words) will be denoted by $|s|$.

We now give the definition of word-pattern. The definition is given recursively in three stages.

Definition 2. *Let $\mathcal{V}$ be a vocabulary. A* proximity-free word pattern *over vocabulary $\mathcal{V}$ is an expression generated by the grammar*

$$WP \to \mathbf{w} \mid \neg WP \mid WP \wedge WP \mid WP \vee WP \mid (WP)$$

where terminal $\mathbf{w}$ *represents a word of $\mathcal{V}$. A proximity-free word pattern will be called* positive *if it does not contain the negation operator.*

Example 1. In all the examples of this paper, our vocabulary will be the vocabulary of the English language and will be denoted by $\mathcal{E}$. The following are proximity-free word patterns that might appear in queries of a user of an information alert system interested in articles on constraints:

$$\textit{constraint} \wedge \textit{programming} \wedge \neg\textit{e-commerce},$$
$$\textit{constraint} \wedge (\textit{optimisation} \vee \textit{programming})$$

We now introduce a new class of word patterns that allows us to capture the concepts of *order* and *distance* between words in a text document. We will assume the existence of a set of *(distance) intervals* $\mathcal{I}$ defined as follows:

$$\mathcal{I} = \{[l, u] : \ l, u \in \mathbb{N}, l \geq 0 \text{ and } l \leq u\} \cup \{[l, \infty) : \ l \in \mathbb{N} \text{ and } l \geq 0\}$$

The symbols $\in$ and $\subseteq$ will be used to denote membership and inclusion in an interval as usual.

The following definition uses intervals to impose lower and upper bounds on distances between word patterns.

Definition 3. *Let $\mathcal{V}$ be a vocabulary. A* proximity word pattern *over vocabulary $\mathcal{V}$ is an expression $wp_1 \prec_{i_1} wp_2 \prec_{i_2} \cdots \prec_{i_{n-1}} wp_n$ where $wp_1, wp_2, \ldots, wp_n$ are positive proximity-free word patterns over $\mathcal{V}$ and $i_1, i_2, \ldots, i_{n-1}$ are intervals from the set $\mathcal{I}$. The symbols $\prec_i$ where $i \in \mathcal{I}$ are called* proximity operators. *The number of proximity-free word patterns in a proximity word pattern (i.e., n above) is called its* size.

Example 2. The following are proximity word patterns:

$$constraint \prec_{[0,0]} programming, \quad artificial \prec_{[0,0]} neural \prec_{[0,0]} networks,$$
$$algorithms \prec_{[0,3]} (satisfaction \vee filtering), \quad induced \prec_{[0,\infty)} constraints$$
$$repairing \prec_{[0,10]} querying \prec_{[0,10]} (inconsistent \wedge databases)$$

The proximity word pattern $wp_1 \prec_{[l,u]} wp_2$ stands for "word pattern wp_1 is *before* wp_2 and is separated by wp_2 by *at least* l and *at most* u *words*". In the above example $algorithms \prec_{[0,3]} satisfaction$ denotes that the word "satisfaction" appears after word "algorithms" and at a distance of at least 0 and at most 3 words. The word pattern $constraint \prec_{[0,0]} programming$ denotes that the word "constraint" appears exactly before word "programming" so this is a way to encode the string "constraint programming". We can also have arbitrarily long sequences of proximity operators with similar meaning (see the examples above). Note that proximity-free subformulas in proximity word-patterns can be more complex than just simple words (but negation is *not* allowed; this restriction will be explained below). This makes proximity-word patterns a very expressive notation.

Definition 4. *Let $\mathcal{V}$ be a vocabulary. A* word pattern *over vocabulary $\mathcal{V}$ is an expression generated by the grammar*

$$WP \rightarrow PFWP \mid PWP \mid WP \wedge WP \mid WP \vee WP \mid (WP)$$

where non-terminals $PFWP$ and PWP represent proximity-free and proximity word patterns respectively. A word pattern will be called positive *if its proximity-free subformulas are positive.*

Example 3. The following are word patterns of the most general kind we allow:

$$applications \wedge (constraint \prec_{[0,0]} programming) \wedge \neg e\text{-}commerce,$$
$$algorithms \wedge (complexity \prec_{[0,10]} (satisfaction \wedge filtering)),$$
$$learning \wedge ((neural \prec_{[0,0]} networks) \vee (neuromorphic \prec_{[0,0]} systems))$$

It is not difficult to see now how to define what it means for a text value s to *satisfy* a word pattern wp (denoted by $s \models wp$). The exact definition is given in [19,20,21].

Example 4. Let s be the following text value:

"*Interaction of constraint programming and*
local search for optimisation problems"

The text value s satisfies the following word patterns:

$$local \prec_{[0,0]} search \prec_{[0,5]} optimisation$$
$$(global \vee local) \prec_{[0,5]} search \prec_{[1,1]} optimisation,$$
$$(constraint \wedge programming) \prec_{[0,10]} optimisation \prec_{[0,0]} problems$$

The text value s also satisfies word pattern:

$$optimisation \wedge (constraint \prec_{[0,0]} programming)$$

Finally we define entailment (conversely: subsumption) of two word patterns.

Definition 5. *Let wp_1 and wp_2 be word patterns. We will say that wp_1* entails *wp_2 (denoted by $wp_1 \models wp_2$) iff for every text value s such that $s \models wp_1$, we have $s \models wp_2$. If $wp_1 \models wp_2$, we also say that wp_2* subsumes *wp_1.*

Example 5. The word pattern $constraint \wedge programming$ entails $programming$. The word pattern $learning \wedge (artificial \prec_{[0,0]} neural \prec_{[0,0]} networks)$ entails the word pattern $learning \wedge (neural \prec_{[0,0]} networks) \wedge artificial$. The word pattern $algorithms$ subsumes the word pattern $algorithms \wedge satisfaction \wedge filtering$. Similarly, $satisfaction \vee filtering$ subsumes $filtering$.

4 An Attribute-Based Data Model and Query Language

Now that we have studied the data model $\mathcal{WP}$,we are ready to define our second data model and query language. Data model $\mathcal{AWP}$ is based on *attributes* or *fields* with finite-length strings as values (in the acronym $\mathcal{AWP}$, the letter $\mathcal{A}$ stands for "attribute"). Strings will be understood as sequences of words as formalized by the model $\mathcal{WP}$ presented earlier. Attributes can be used to encode textual information in a notification (e.g., author, title, abstract of a paper and so on). $\mathcal{AWP}$ is somewhat restrictive since it offers a flat view of a notification, but it will suffice in many cases that arise in digital library environments. A similarly flat view of a notification has successfully been adopted in project HERMES [15].

We start our formal development by defining the concepts of notification schema and notification. Throughout the rest of this paper we assume the existence of a countably infinite set of attributes $\mathbf{U}$ called the *attribute universe*.

Definition 6. *A* notification schema *$\mathcal{N}$ is a pair $(\mathcal{A}, \mathcal{V})$ where $\mathcal{A}$ is a subset of the attribute universe $\mathbf{U}$ and $\mathcal{V}$ is a vocabulary.*

Example 6. An example of a notification schema for information alert in a digital library is

$$\mathcal{N} = (\{AUTHOR,\ TITLE,\ ABSTRACT\}, \mathcal{E}).$$

Definition 7. *Let $\mathcal{N} = (\mathcal{A}, \mathcal{V})$ be a notification schema. A* notification *n over schema $\mathcal{N}$ is a set of attribute-value pairs (A, s) where $A \in \mathcal{A}$, s is a text value over $\mathcal{V}$, and there is at most one pair (A, s) for each attribute $A \in \mathcal{A}$.*

Example 7. The following is a notification over the schema of Example 6:

{ (*AUTHOR*, "*John Brown*"),
(*TITLE*, "*Interaction of constraint programming and*
local search for optimisation problems"),
(*ABSTRACT*, "*In this paper we show that*
adapting constraint propagation...") }

Notice that *only* textual information is allowed in notifications as defined in this paper. In the DIAS implementation to be discussed in Section 6, we eventually plan to support other kinds of information (e.g., numerical, dates, etc.). However, at the moment, we concentrate only on textual information.

The syntax of our query language is given by the following recursive definition.

Definition 8. *Let $\mathcal{N} = (\mathcal{A}, \mathcal{V})$ be a notification schema. A* query *over $\mathcal{N}$ is a formula in any of the following forms:*

1. *$A \sqsupset wp$ where $A \in \mathcal{A}$ and wp is a* positive *word pattern over $\mathcal{V}$. The formula $A \sqsupset wp$ can be read as "A contains word pattern wp".*
2. *$A = s$ where $A \in \mathcal{A}$ and s is a text value over $\mathcal{V}$.*
3. *$\neg\phi$ where ϕ is a query containing no proximity word patterns.*
4. *$\phi_1 \vee \phi_2$ where ϕ_1 and ϕ_2 are queries.*
5. *$\phi_1 \wedge \phi_2$ where ϕ_1 and ϕ_2 are queries.*

The queries in the first two of the above cases are called *atomic.*

Example 8. The following are queries over the schema of Example 6:

$$AUTHOR \sqsupset (John \prec_{[0,2]} Smith),$$
$$\neg AUTHOR = \text{“}John\ Smith\text{”} \wedge$$
$$(TITLE \sqsupset (optimisation \wedge (constraint \prec_{[0,2]} programming)))$$

Let us now define the semantics of the above query language in our information alert setting. We start by defining when a notification satisfies a query.

Definition 9. *Let $\mathcal{N}$ be a notification schema, n a notification over $\mathcal{N}$ and ϕ a query over $\mathcal{N}$. The concept of notification n* satisfying *query ϕ (denoted by $n \models \phi$) is defined as follows:*

1. *If ϕ is of the form $A \sqsupset wp$ then $n \models \phi$ iff there exists a pair $(A, s) \in n$ and $s \models wp$.*
2. *If ϕ is of the form $A = s$ then $n \models \phi$ iff there exists a pair $(A, s) \in n$.*
3. *If ϕ is of the form $\neg\phi_1$ then $n \models \phi$ iff $n \not\models \phi_1$.*
4. *If ϕ is of the form $\phi_1 \wedge \phi_2$ then $n \models \phi$ iff $n \models \phi_1$ and $n \models \phi_2$.*
5. *If ϕ is of the form $\phi_1 \vee \phi_2$ then $n \models \phi$ iff $n \models \phi_1$ or $n \models \phi_2$.*

Example 9. The first query of Example 8 is not satisfied by the notification of Example 7 while the second one is satisfied.

Finally we define entailment (conversely: subsumption) of two queries.

Definition 10. *Let ϕ_1 and ϕ_2 be queries over schema $\mathcal{N}$. Then ϕ_1* entails *ϕ_2 (denoted by $\phi_1 \models \phi_2$) iff every notification n over $\mathcal{N}$ that satisfies ϕ_1 also satisfies ϕ_2. If ϕ_1 entails ϕ_2 then we also say that ϕ_2* subsumes *ϕ_1.*

Example 10. The query
$(AUTHOR \sqsupset John \prec_{[0,1]} Brown) \wedge (TITLE \sqsupset constraint \wedge programming)$
entails (equivalently: is subsumed by) $TITLE \sqsupset programming$.

5 Extending $\mathcal{AWP}$ with Similarity

Let us now define our third data model $\mathcal{AWPS}$ and its query language. $\mathcal{AWPS}$ extends $\mathcal{AWP}$ with the concept of *similarity* between two text values (the letter $\mathcal{S}$ stands for similarity). The idea here is to have a "soft" alternative to the "hard" operator $\sqsupset$. This operator is very useful for queries such as "I am interested in papers written by John Brown" which can be written in $\mathcal{AWP}$ as

$$AUTHOR \sqsupset (John \prec_{[0,0]} Brown)$$

but it might not be very useful for queries "I am interested in papers about the use of local search techniques for the problem of test pattern optimisation".

The desired functionality can be achieved by resorting to an important tool of modern IR: the *weight* of a word as defined in the Vector Space Model (VSM) [2,23,28]. In VSM, documents (text values in our terminology) are conceptually represented as vectors. If our vocabulary consists of n distinct words then a text value s is represented as an n-dimensional vector of the form $(\omega_1, \ldots, \omega_n)$ where ω_i is the weight of the i-th word (the weight assigned to a non-existent word is 0). With a good weighting scheme, the VSM representation of a document can be a surprisingly good model of its semantic content in the sense that "similar" documents have very close semantic content. This has been recently demonstrated by many successful IR systems [2] or database systems adopting ideas from IR (see for example, WHIRL [11]).[7]

In VSM, the weight of a word is computed using the heuristic of assigning higher *weights* to words that are frequent in a document and *infrequent* in the collection of documents available. This heuristic is made concrete using the concepts of word frequency and the inverse document frequency defined below.

Definition 11. *Let w_i be a word in document d_j of a collection C. The* term frequency *of w_i in d_j (denoted by tf_{ij}) is equal to the number of occurrences of word w_i in d_j. The* document frequency *of word w_i in the collection C (denoted by df_i) is equal to the number of documents in C that contain w_i. The* inverse document frequency *of w_i is then given by $idf_i = \frac{1}{df_i}$. Finally, the number $tf_{ij} \cdot idf_i$ will be called the* weight *of word w_i in document d_j and will be denoted by ω_{ij}.*

At this point we should stress that the concept of inverse document frequency assumes that there is a *collection* of documents which is used in the calculation. In our alert scenarios we assume that for each attribute A there is a collection of text values C_A that is used for calculating the *idf* values to be used in similarity computations involving attribute A (the details are given below). C_A can be a collection of recently processed text values as suggested in [29,15].

[7] Sometimes in IR systems (or systems adopting ideas from IR) word *stems*, produced by some stemming algorithm [26], are forming the vocabulary instead of words. Additionally, *stopwords* (e.g., "the") are eliminated from the vocabulary. These important details have no consequence for the theoretical results of this paper, but it should be understood that our current implementation of the ideas of this section utilizes these standard techniques.

We are now ready to define the main new concept in $\mathcal{AWPS}$, the similarity of two text values. The similarity of two text values s_q and s_d is defined as the cosine of the angle formed by their corresponding vectors:[8]

$$sim(s_q, s_d) = \frac{s_q \cdot s_d}{\|s_q\| \cdot \|s_d\|} = \frac{\sum_{i=1}^{N} w_{q_i} \cdot w_{d_i}}{\sqrt{\sum_{i=1}^{N} w_{q_i}^2 \cdot \sum_{i=1}^{N} w_{d_i}^2}} \tag{1}$$

By this definition, similarity values are real numbers in the interval $[0, 1]$.

Let us now proceed to give the syntax of the query language for $\mathcal{AWPS}$. Since $\mathcal{AWPS}$ extends $\mathcal{AWP}$, a query in the new model is given by Definition 8 with one more case for atomic queries:

– $A \sim_k s$ where $A \in \mathcal{A}$, s is a text value over $\mathcal{V}$ and k is a real number in the interval $[0, 1]$.

Example 11. The following are some queries in $\mathcal{AWPS}$ using the schema of Example 7:

$TITLE \sim_{0.6}$ *"Local search techniques for constraint optimisation problems"*,
$(AUTHOR \sqsupseteq (John \prec_{[0,2]} Smith)) \wedge$
$(TITLE \sim_{0.9}$ *"Temporal constraint programming"*$)$,
$TITLE \sim_{0.9}$ *"Large Scale Telecommunication Network Optimisation"*

We now give the semantics of our query language, by defining when a document satisfies a query. Naturally, the definition of satisfaction in $\mathcal{AWPS}$ is as in Definition 9 with one additional case for the similarity operator:

– If ϕ is of the form $\mathcal{A} \sim_k s_q$ then $d \models \phi$ iff there exists a pair $(A, s_d) \in d$ and $sim(s_q, s_d) \geq k$.

The reader should notice that the number k in a similarity predicate $A \sim_k s$ gives a *relevance threshold* that candidate text values s should exceed in order to satisfy the predicate. This notion of relevance threshold was first proposed in an information alert setting by [17] and later on adopted by [29]. The reader is asked to contrast this situation with the typical information retrieval setting where a ranked list of documents is returned as an answer to a user query. This is not a relevant scenario in an information alert system because very few documents (or even a single one) enter the system at a time, and need to be forwarded to interested users (see the architecture sketched in Figure 1).

A low similarity threshold in a predicate $A \sim_k s$ might result in many irrelevant documents satisfying a query, whereas a high similarity threshold would result in very few achieving satisfaction (or even no documents at all). In DIAS,

[8] The IR literature gives us several very closely related ways to define the notions of weight and similarity [2,23,28]. All of these weighting schemes come by the name of $tf \cdot idf$ weighting schemes. Generally a weighting scheme is called $tf \cdot idf$ whenever it uses word frequency in a monotonically increasing way, and document frequency in a monotonically decreasing way.

users could start with a certain relevance threshold and then update it using relevance feedback techniques to achieve a better satisfaction of their information needs. Recent techniques from adaptive IR can be utilised here [7]. This update functionality has not been implemented in the current version of DIAS.

Example 12. The first query of Example 11 is likely to be satisfied by the document of Example 7 (of course, we cannot say for sure until we know the *idf* factors so that the exact weights can be calculated). The second query is not satisfied, since the author specified in the query does not match the document's author. Moreover the third query is unlikely to be satisfied since the only common word between the query and Example 7 is the word "optimisation".

6 The Current DIAS Implementation: Details

In the previous sections of this paper, we have defined appropriate models and languages for expressing profiles and notifications in DIAS. For efficiency reasons, the current implementation of DIAS supports only profiles of the form $\psi \wedge \sigma$ where

- ψ is a conjunction of atomic queries of $\mathcal{AWP}$ of the form $A = s$ or $A \sqsupset wp$ where every proximity formula in the word pattern wp contains only words as subformulas.
- σ is a conjunction of atomic similarity queries as defined in the model $\mathcal{AWPS}$.

The notion of notification supported currently in DIAS is as defined in Section 4.

The reasons for the above choices in the current DIAS implementation are as follows. In [13], we give precise bounds for the computational complexity of all problems defined in Section 2 for model $\mathcal{AWP}$. Satisfaction can always be decided in polynomial time. For the complete query language of $\mathcal{AWP}$, the satisfiability problem is NP-complete and the entailment problem is coNP-complete. Polynomial cases of these two problems have been identified and the most useful one is the conjunctive case adopted in DIAS. This theoretical analysis will appear in a forthcoming paper.

In the rest of this section we discuss the data structures, algorithms and protocols that regulate how DIAS agents work together so that all produced information is delivered to interested consumers. This is achieved with the combination of the following techniques: sophisticated forwarding of the $\mathcal{AWP}$ part of each subscription by utilizing appropriate networking algorithms [12] and a poset data structure, and very fast indexing techniques for detecting the set of profiles that match an incoming notification. Preliminary evaluation of these techniques by us (and previously by SIENA researchers [6,5]) lead us to believe that DIAS will be a robust and scalable system.

Forwarding the $\mathcal{AWP}$ Part of a Subscription. DIAS follows the lead of SIENA [6,5] and forwards subscriptions using the *reverse path forwarding algorithm* of [12]. In DIAS this algorithm works as follows. Let us assume that at one end of the information chain, a personal agent A posts a profile $p \equiv \psi \wedge \sigma$ to some middle-agent M (ψ and σ are as defined at the beginning of this section). Then, the $\mathcal{AWP}$ part ψ of p is propagated through the middle-agent network so that a *spanning tree* that connects M to all other middle-agents is formed. More precisely, a middle-agent M forwards an $\mathcal{AWP}$ profile ψ only if ψ is coming from a neighbor middle-agent N that is on the *shortest path* connecting the source of ψ with middle-agent M. If this condition is satisfied then M can forward ψ to all its neighbors except the one that originally forwarded ψ to M.

The above algorithm requires that every middle-agent M knows the identity of the neighbor middle-agent that is the next node on the shortest path from M to every other middle-agent in the network. To keep track of this information, every middle-agent maintains an appropriate routing table that associates a *source* middle-agent to a *neighbor* middle-agent and a *distance* which reflects the latency between nodes in the network. This routing table can be constructed using traditional techniques such as the asynchronous distributed version of Bellman-Ford's all-pairs shortest-path algorithm [3].

The Profile Poset. At each middle-agent, the propagation of a newly arrived $\mathcal{AWP}$ profile ψ is implemented by treating ψ as a subscription to neighboring middle-agents. This propagation step is optimized (network traffic is minimized) by allowing it only towards those agents that have not received already a more general profile ϕ (i.e., $\psi \models \phi$). To achieve this, each agent maintains a *partially ordered set* (called the *profile poset*) that keeps track of the subsumption relations among the $\mathcal{AWP}$ profiles posted to it.[9] This is possible because the relation of subsumption in $\mathcal{AWP}$ (see Section 4) is reflexive, anti-symmetric and transitive i.e., a *(weak) partial order* [22].

As $\mathcal{AWP}$ profiles arrive at a middle-agent from neighboring middle-agents, they are inserted into the local profile poset. If for two profiles ψ and ϕ of a given poset P, $\psi \models \phi$, then ϕ will be an *ancestor* of ψ (and conversely ψ will be a *descendant* of ϕ) in P. Although the relations ancestor/descendant are transitive relations, the poset maintains only *immediate* ancestor/descendant relations. Figure 2 shows an example of a profile poset.

To facilitate the routing of subscriptions and notifications, every profile ψ in a poset is associated with two sets: a set of *subscribers* that contains the identities of other middle-agents that have subscribed with profile ψ, and a set of *forwardees* that contains the addresses of neighbor middle-agents where profile ψ has been forwarded.

The insertion of an $\mathcal{AWP}$ profile ψ in the poset of a middle-agent M is performed according to the following rules:

[9] See [22] for posets and related definitions.

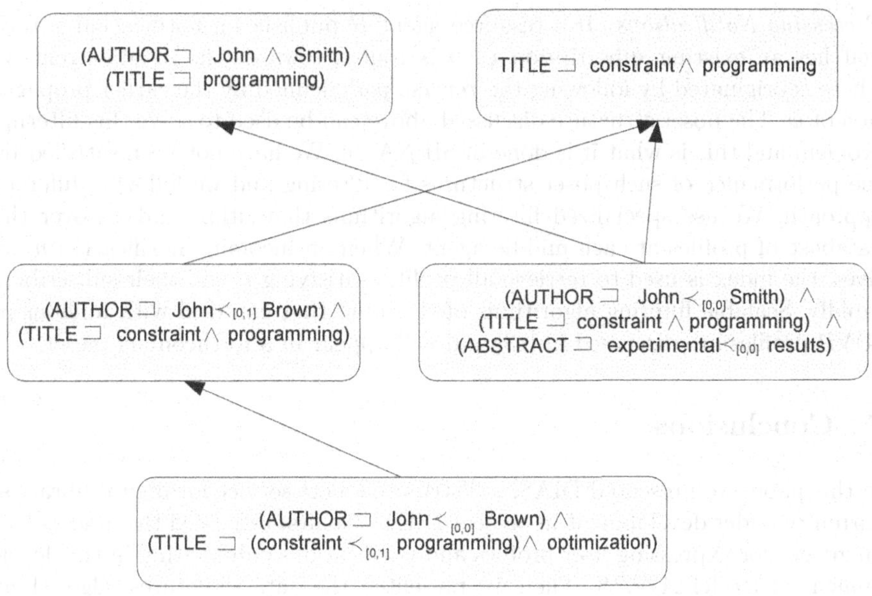

Fig. 2. A profile poset

1. If a profile subscription ϕ that subsumes ψ is already present in the poset, and has the source S of the profile among its subscribers, the insertion ends without updating the poset structure.
2. If ψ exists in the poset, and S is not among its subscribers, M simply inserts the current subscriber S in the set of subscribers of ψ.
3. If ψ does not exist in the poset, the two (possibly empty) sets f and f', representing the immediate ancestors and the immediate descendants of ψ, are computed, and ψ is inserted as a new node between f and f'.

In the latter two cases, M also removes S from all the subscriptions in the poset that are subsumed by ψ. If this process leaves a subscription with an empty set of subscribers then this subscription is removed from the poset.

After the poset is updated, M forwards ψ to all its neighbors except to those that M has already forwarded a profile that subsumes ψ (and of course except the neighbor that originally sent this profile to M). The complexity of this algorithm for inserting a profile in a poset is polynomial (the exact bound is given in [13]). Note that M could also forward the similarity part σ of a profile if an appropriate entailment relation had been defined for model $\mathcal{AWPS}$. This is currently an open problem for us and similarity queries σ participate only in filtering notifications as explained below.

Processing Notifications. If a resource agent R publishes a notification n that matches an existing subscription ψ, n is routed towards the middle-agent M where ψ originated by following the *reverse path* defined by the earlier propagation of ψ. The poset structure discussed above can be used to solve this filtering problem and this is what it is done in SIENA [6]. We have not been satisfied by the performance of such poset structures for filtering and we follow a different approach. We use specialized filtering algorithms that utilize indices over the database of profiles at each middle-agent. When an incoming notification n arrives, the index is used to retrieve all profiles satisfying n and their subscribers rapidly. Scalable filtering algorithms of this kind that can deal with millions of $\mathcal{AWP}$ profiles are discussed in [13] and will appear in a forthcoming paper.

7 Conclusions

In this paper we presented DIAS, a distributed alert service for digital libraries, currently under development in project DIET. We first discussed the models and languages for expressing user profiles and notifications culminating in the development of model $\mathcal{AWPS}$. Then we presented the data structures, algorithms and protocols that underlie the P2P agent architecture of DIAS. $\mathcal{AWPS}$ is an expressive formal model especially targeted for information alert in distributed digital libraries. However, it is fair to say that in our quest for formality and expressive power, we have overlooked the issue of adaptation of user profiles and how this would affect the design and algorithms of DIAS. In this area there is a lot of interesting IR research (e.g., see the work in the TREC filtering track[10]) but it is an open problem how such ideas can be used in distributed information alert systems such as DIAS.

Our current research concentrates on evaluating analytically and experimentally the current DIAS architecture and comparing it with other alternatives inspired by current research in P2P systems. In this way, we expect that the informal claims we made in Section 6 about scalability and robustness of DIAS will be substantiated.

Acknowledgements. This work was carried out as part of the DIET (Decentralised Information Ecosystems Technologies) project (IST-1999-10088), within the Universal Information Ecosystems initiative of the Information Society Technology Programme of the European Union. We would like to thank the other participants in the DIET project, from Departmento de Teoria de Senal y Comunicaciones, Universidad Carlos III de Madrid, the Intelligent Systems Laboratory, BTexact Technologies and the Intelligent and Simulation Systems Department, DFKI, for their comments and contributions. We would also like to thank the reviewers for their very constructive criticisms.

[10] `http://trec.nist.gov`

References

1. M. Altinel and M.J. Franklin. Efficient filtering of XML documents for selective dissemination of information. In *Proceedings of the 26th VLDB Conference*, 2000.
2. R. Baeza-Yates and B. Ribeiro-Neto. *Modern Information Retrieval.* Addison Wesley, 1999.
3. D. Bertsekas and R. Gallager. *Data Networks.* Prentice Hall, 1987.
4. A. Campailla, S. Chaki, E. Clarke, S. Jha, and H. Veith. Efficent filtering in publish-subscribe systems using binary decision diagrams. In *Proceedings of the 23rd International Conference on Software Engineering*, Toronto, Ontario, Canada, 2001.
5. A. Carzaniga. *Architectures for an Event Notification Service Scalable to Wide-area Networks.* PhD thesis, Politecnico di Milano Italy, 1998.
6. A. Carzaniga, D. S. Rosenblum, and A. L. Wolf. Achieving scalability and expressiveness in an internet-scale event notification service. In *Proceedings of the 19th ACM Symposium on Principles of Distributed Computing (PODC'2000)*, pages 219–227, 2000.
7. U. Cetintemel, M.J. Franklin, and C.L. Giles. Self-adaptive user profiles for large-scale data delivery. In *ICDE*, pages 622–633, 2000.
8. C.-C. K. Chang, H. Garcia-Molina, and A. Paepcke. Boolean Query Mapping across Heterogeneous Information Sources. *IEEE Transactions on Knowledge and Data Engineering*, 8(4):515–521, 1996.
9. C.-C. K. Chang, H. Garcia-Molina, and A. Paepcke. Predicate Rewriting for Translating Boolean Queries in a Heterogeneous Information System. *ACM Transactions on Information Systems*, 17(1):1–39, 1999.
10. T. T. Chinenyanga and N. Kushmerick. Expressive retrieval from XML documents. In *Proceedings of SIGIR'01*, September 2001.
11. William W. Cohen. WHIRL: A word-based information representation language. *Artificial Intelligence*, 118(1-2):163–196, 2000.
12. Y. Dalal and R. Metcalfe. Reverse Path Forwarding of Broadcast Packets. *Communications of the ACM*, 21(12):1040–1048, 1978.
13. M. Koubarakis et. al. Project DIET Deliverable 7 (Information Brokering), December 2001.
14. F. Fabret, H. A. Jacobsen, F. Llirbat, J. Pereira, K. A. Ross, and D. Shasha. Filtering algorithms and implementation for very fast publish/subscribe systems. In *Proceedings of ACM SIGMOD-2001*, 2001.
15. D. Faensen, L. Faulstich, H. Schweppe, A. Hinze, and A. Steidinger. Hermes – A Notification Service for Digital Libraries. In *Proceedings of the Joint ACM/IEEE Conference on Digital Libraries (JCDL'01), Roanoke, Virginia, USA*, 2001.
16. T. Finin, R. Fritzson, D. McKay, and R. McEntire. KQML as an Agent Communication Language. In N. Adam, B. Bhargava, and Y. Yesha, editors, *Proceedings of the 3rd International Conference on Information and Knowledge Management (CIKM'94)*, pages 456–463, Gaithersburg, MD, USA, 1994. ACM Press.
17. P.W. Foltz and S.T. Dumais. Personalised information delivery: An analysis of information filtering methods. *Communications of the ACM*, 35(12):29–38, 1992.
18. A. Galardo-Antolin, A. Navia-Vasquez, H.Y. Molina-Bulla, A.B. Rodriquez-Gonzalez, F.J. Valvarde-Albacete, A.R. Figueiras-Vidal, T. Koutris, A. Xiruhaki, and M. Koubarakis. I-Gaia: an Information Processing Layer for the DIET Platform . In *Proceedings of the 1st International Joint Conference on Autonomous Agents & Multiagent Systems (AAMAS 2002)*, September 15–19 2002.

19. M. Koubarakis. Boolean Queries with Proximity Operators for Information Dissemination. Proceedings of the workshop on Foundations of Models and Languages for Information Integration (FMII-2001), Viterbo, Italy , 16-18 September, 2001. In LNCS (forthcoming).
20. M. Koubarakis. Textual Information Dissemination in Distributed Event-Based Systems. Proceedings of the International Workshop on Distributed Event-Based systems (DEBS'02), July 2-3, 2002, Vienna, Austria.
21. P. Raftopoulou M. Koubarakis, C. Tryfonopoulos and T. Koutris. Data models and languages for agent-based textual information dissemination. In *Proceedings of the 6th International Workshop on Cooperative Information Agents(CIA2002), Madrid*, Lecture Notes in Computer Science. Springer, 2002. forthcoming.
22. Z. Manna and R. Waldinger. *The Logical Basis of Computer Programming*, volume 1. Addison Wesley, 1985.
23. C.D. Manning and H. Schütze. *Foundations of Statistical Natural Language Processing.* The MIT Press, Cambridge, Massachusetts, 1999.
24. P. Marrow, M. Koubarakis, R.H. van Lengen, F. Valverde-Albacete, E. Bonsma, J. Cid-Suerio, A.R. Figueiras-Vidal, A. Gallardo-Antolin, C. Hoile, T. Koutris, H. Molina-Bulla, A. Navia-Vazquez, P. Raftopoulou, N. Skarmeas, C. Tryfonopoulos, F. Wang, and C. Xiruhaki. Agents in Decentralised Information Ecosystems: The DIET Approach. In M. Schroeder and K. Stathis, editors, *Proceedings of the AISB'01 Symposium on Information Agents for Electronic Commerce, AISB'01 Convention*, pages 109–117, University of York, United Kingdom, March 2001.
25. J. Pereira, F. Fabret, F. Llirbat, and D. Shasha. Efficient matching for web-based publish/subscribe systems. In *Proceedings of COOPIS-2000*, 2000.
26. M.F. Porter. An Algorithm for Suffix Striping. *Program*, 14(3):130–137, 1980.
27. F. Wang. Self-organising Communities Formed by Middle Agents. In *Proceedings of the 1st International Joint Conference on Autonomous Agents & Multiagent Systems (AAMAS 2002)*, September 15–19 2002.
28. I.H. Witten, A. Moffat, and T.C. Bell. *Managing Gigabytes: Compressing and Indexing Documents and Images.* Morgan Kauffman Publishing, San Francisco, 2nd edition, 1999.
29. T.W. Yan and H. Garcia-Molina. The SIFT information dissemination system. *ACM Transactions on Database Systems*, 24(4):529–565, 1999.

DSpace: An Institutional Repository from the MIT Libraries and Hewlett Packard Laboratories

MacKenzie Smith, Associate Director for Technology

Massachusetts Institute of Technology Libraries, Cambridge, MA 02139, USA
kenzie@mit.edu

Abstract. The DSpace™ project of the MIT Libraries and the Hewlett Packard Laboratories[1] has built an institutional repository system for digital research material. This paper will describe the rationale for institutional repositories, the DSpace system, and its implementation at MIT. Also described are the plans for making DSpace open source in an effort to provide a useful test bed and a platform for future research in the areas of open scholarly communication and the long-term preservation of fragile digital research material.

1 Introduction

Scholarly communication among academic researchers has followed well-worn paths for much of the last century. Research is conducted, and its results are summarized in published monographs or in the formal, peer-reviewed journal literature of the academic field. Publication is evidence of scholarly significance and success, and journal editors and reviewers serve at the gatekeepers of the scholarly record, and therefore of the status of individual scholars. The advent of advanced computer technology, the prevalence of networking, and publishing media such as the World Wide Web have begun to erode some of these traditions of scholarly communication. First, there is the improved speed of delivery of research results on the Internet. Preprint archives in some branches of physics and mathematics have become the normal way in which scholars communicate – however most authors expect their results to appear in print journals eventually, as the published record. Second, there is a growing amount of important research that never sees formal publication – for example the white papers and technical reports of sponsored research in computer science and biotechnology. Third, the increasing availability of primary research material on the Web makes dependence on published summaries less satisfying – scholars want to verify and reproduce results, see the data underlying the research, experience the simulations and visualizations for themselves. The printed article is gradually becoming a sort of final imprimatur of the research: serving the gatekeeper function (i.e. an editor accepted the research into an exclusive journal thus verifying its importance) but not that of scholarly communication.

[1] DSpace project home page http://www.dspace.org/

M. Agosti and C. Thanos (Eds.): ECDL 2002, LNCS 2458, pp. 543-549, 2002.

The Massachusetts Institute of Technology (MIT) in Cambridge, Massachusetts is fertile ground for this phenomenon, producing some ten thousand unpublished preprints, technical reports, and white papers annually in almost every field of science, technology, business and economics. The Institute additionally produces large amounts of primary digital research material in the form of datasets (statistical, geospatial, etc.), image sets (from radars, sonars, satellites, etc.), software for simulations, visualizations, and other mechanisms of performing or disseminating research. Many MIT faculty make this material available on a departmental web site, and it represents a significant intellectual asset of the institution. In recognition of the growing importance of this material and of the role of the library in capturing and preserving it for future researchers, the DSpace project to build an institutional digital repository was created.

Scholarly communication among academic researchers has followed well-worn paths for much of the last century. Research is conducted, and its results are summarized in published monographs or in the formal, peer-reviewed journal literature of the academic field. Publication is evidence of scholarly significance and success, and journal editors and reviewers serve at the gatekeepers of the scholarly record, and therefore of the status of individual scholars. The advent of advanced computer technology, the prevalence of networking, and publishing media such as the World Wide Web have begun to erode some of these traditions of scholarly communication. First, there is the improved speed of delivery of research results on the Internet. Preprint archives in some branches of physics and mathematics have become the normal way in which scholars communicate – however most authors expect their results to appear in print journals eventually, as the published record. Second, there is a growing amount of important research that never sees formal publication – for example the white papers and technical reports of sponsored research in computer science and biotechnology. Third, the increasing availability of primary research material on the Web makes dependence on published summaries less satisfying – scholars want to verify and reproduce results, see the data underlying the research, experience the simulations and visualizations for themselves. The printed article is gradually becoming a sort of final imprimatur of the research: serving the gatekeeper function (i.e. an editor accepted the research into an exclusive journal thus verifying its importance) but not that of scholarly communication.

The Massachusetts Institute of Technology (MIT) in Cambridge, Massachusetts is fertile ground for this phenomenon, producing some ten thousand unpublished preprints, technical reports, and white papers annually in almost every field of science, technology, business and economics. The Institute additionally produces large amounts of primary digital research material in the form of datasets (statistical, geospatial, etc.), image sets (from radars, sonars, satellites, etc.), software for simulations, visualizations, and other mechanisms of performing or disseminating research. Many MIT faculty make this material available on a departmental web site, and it represents a significant intellectual asset of the institution. In recognition of the growing importance of this material and of the role of the library in capturing and preserving it for future researchers, the DSpace project to build an institutional digital repository was created.

The DSpace system is the result of a joint development project by the MIT Libraries and the Hewlett Packard Laboratories to build an institutional repository system for the research output of MIT faculty in digital formats. The system supports the capture, management, dissemination and preservation of this digital material. DSpace is about to be deployed at MIT, and we hope to extend its use to other institutions to facilitate the sharing of MIT's intellectual content and metadata and to allow the system to benefit from a larger community of users and developers. The system will ultimately be freely available under an open source license. DSpace consists of tools for the loading, administration, and dissemination of digital content following the Open Archival Information System (OAIS) reference model[2]. These tools include integrated subsystems for web-based and batch submission of digital material and related metadata, locally-configured submission workflow management, cross-system metadata schema, index and search, archival package management, access policy control, robust provenance and history logging, persistent identifiers, and administration.

The DSpace project is currently completing an early-adopter phase that has provided us with a large amount of material to both exercise and demonstrate the utility of the system. Early adopters at MIT have included the Sloan School of Management, the Department of Ocean Engineering, the Center for Technology, Policy and Industrial Development, and the Lab for Information and Decision Systems. In addition, two historical collections have been loaded: the out-of-print books of the MIT Press (in PDF format) and a large collection of technical reports from the NSF-funded NCSTRL project[3]. Each of these adopters has formed a community that defined its own membership, collections, workflow, metadata practices, and interface design. The system is scheduled for general release to the MIT community in September of 2002 and the MIT Libraries have developed a detailed transition plan for bringing the system into its daily operations. Shortly after the general MIT release, the system will be made available to some other institutions wishing to federate with the MIT Libraries and willing to help develop new functionality that a federated system might support (e.g. "virtual" distributed collections, new journal publications, cross-institutional searching, etc.). Since DSpace will ultimately be available under an open source distribution license, this could support the rapid development of both institutional digital archives and new modes of online scholarly communication

2 Information Model

The DSpace system implements an information model that will be familiar to many in the digital library field. The system is organized into "communities" which reflect the institution's organizational structure (i.e. at MIT these would be schools, departments, labs, centers, programs, etc.). DSpace communities can differ from each other in useful ways: each community defines one or more content "collections" that they would like to create (i.e. technical reports, preprints, datasets, white papers, images,

[2] Open Archival Information System http://ssdoo.gsfc.nasa.gov/nost/isoas/

[3] National Computer Science Technical Reports Library http://www.ncstrl.org/

etc.). These collections group material in whatever way the community chooses, based on their existing practices. Each community further defines a submission workflow that reflects its policies and procedures. The user roles currently defined in the workflow module include: submitters, approvers, reviewers, and editors. Communities register their members to play one or more of these roles, and define submission procedures that enforce their local policies. For example, one community might allow faculty to submit material directly to DSpace while another might define a few administrative staff to review faculty submissions, then have the department chair approve each reviewed submission. Material is ingested into DSpace only after it has passed all the workflow steps defined by the community. Finally, each community can tailor its user interface with a logo, explanatory text, and so on, while keeping within the general DSpace user interface paradigm.

Collections within communities consist of "items", each of which is a logical work (using the definition of "work" proposed by the Functional Requirements for Bibliographic Records[4] standard, as opposed to its "item" entity). Items are, in turn, composed of one or more bitstreams, or physical files of digital material. An item's bitstreams are defined by a "bundle" which will be implemented using the Metadata Encoding and Transfer Standard (METS)[5]. A couple of examples might help clarify the need for this. The simplest case of a DSpace item is a single bitstream, for example a digital image encoded as a TIFF file, or a digital document encoded as a PDF file. Another example, however, is of a PDF and a Microsoft Word version of the same work, and so both bitstreams (i.e. the PDF file and the Word file) make up the item. Another example is a print document that has been scanned into a set of digital TIFF image files, all of which together and in the correct sequence constitute the logical item. A final example is a digital document that consists of a set of several HTML pages and some inline JPG images. All of these are types of DSpace items, and there are undoubtedly other cases where physical files should be grouped for presentation to users. Digital preservation will presumably be done at the bitstream, or physical file, level in cases where format migration is done, and if the preservation strategy used is emulation then it may be done at the item level. The information model supports either approach.

For descriptive metadata, DSpace uses a qualified Dublin Core[6] vocabulary derived from the Library Application Profile for common description across all content types, and the METS framework for information packaging. Appropriate descriptive metadata about items is provided by submitters, rather than library staff, as part of the system's submission process. Submission also entails agreeing to a license that grants the library a non-exclusive right to store, preserve, and distribute the item (copyright is retained by the author or institution). Minimal technical metadata about items is captured during submission, and it's automatically generated from the physical file (i.e. the file format, size, checksum, etc.). MIT will be undertaking research in the future to determine what set of technical metadata is needed to support long-term preservation of various digital formats such as PDF, XML, etc. In addition to

[4] Functional Requirements for Bibliographic Records http://www.ifla.org/VII/s13/frbr/frbr.htm
[5] Metadata Encoding and Transmission Standard http://www.loc.gov/standards/mets/
[6] Dublin Core Metadata Initiative http://www.dublincore.org/

descriptive and technical metadata, DSpace uses the Harmony/ABC model-based mechanism for recording the history of changes within the system, which is implemented using RDF[7].

The assignment of persistent identifiers to digital items in DSpace is one of the great benefits that communities perceive. The phenomenon of "link rot" is becoming a well-known problem on the Web, especially with the sort of unpublished or semi-published material that will be DSpace's main content [1]. To avoid this, DSpace items are assigned a CNRI Handle[8] as part of the submission process, and the handle becomes part of the item's descriptive metadata. Since DSpace items can belong to more than one collection, the local handle resolver resolves requests to the item's metadata page without a collection context. From there, the user can link to the digital object itself. The handle is always displayed with the item's metadata, along with a recommendation to use the handle for citations to the item. A point of ongoing discussion has been the dual role of the handles in DSpace to serve as persistent URL and as a sort of globally unique accession number for the item. In future we may decide to assign a unique identifier to the work/item in addition to the handle to allow functions such as determining identity between multiple copies of an item that are distributed at several institutions running DSpace.

3 Architecture

Internally, DSpace can be thought of as a Digital Asset Management System that implements the OAIS reference model and includes subsystems that support common digital library functions (e.g. indexing and search of metadata, secure digital object access and delivery, collection management and preservation planning, etc.). The goal of the system is to provide MIT faculty with a robust, scalable, preservation-quality institutional repository for its born-digital research output, so that has been the initial focus of development rather than the support of digitally reformatted library collections. The system is primarily written in Java, and uses only free software libraries and tools, including the PostgreSQL RDBMS, the Lucene search engine, Xerces/Xalan XML tools, and Jena, an RDF tool from HP, among others.

The system has been implemented with clearly delineated modules, divided into user interface, business logic, and storage layers. Each module, or subsystem, has a well documented API so that they can be implemented differently at other institutions that have different practices for functions such as authenticating and authorizing users, or managing transaction logging and history tracking. We expect DSpace to grow over time, both in scope and functionality, and designed the system to be both flexible and extensible by MIT and other institutions.

In anticipation of its future deployment at other institutions through a federation, DSpace supports several of the current standards for interoperability: the Open

[7] Resource Description Framework http://www.w3.org/RDF/
[8] Corporation for National Research Initiatives Handle system http://www.handle.net/

Archives Initiative[9] protocol for metadata harvesting, and the OpenURL[10] standard among them. DSpace item metadata is available for harvesting by union catalog creators and other information service providers using OAI. MIT Libraries run the SFX[11] system from Ex Libris, and have successfully tested DSpace as both an SFX "source" and "target" to allow cross-linking between the library's online public catalog and it's DSpace institutional repository. One of the many local policies that MIT is considering is whether to catalog DSpace resources in its central library catalog or to rely on cross-system searching and linking to help users find library material in its various locations. Support will soon be added to the system for exporting items encoded in METS to support virtual collection building and other types of cross-institutional interoperation.

4 Business Plan

A business plan for the initial deployment and long-term sustainability of the DSpace system at MIT has been developed with the help of a grant from the Andrew W. Mellon Foundation. This will allow MIT to decide how to fund DSpace as a service of the Libraries using detailed cost information from MIT's own implementation, and will potentially help other institutions determine what the costs of running an institutional repository in their own organization might be. Cost and business models are one of the aspects of digital library research and development that has gotten the least attention, yet in the long run will be critically important to making these systems sustainable and justifying the large investments required in their development. We hope to share the information gathered in the MIT business plan, and to build on it for further research projects that investigate the actual costs of managing digital collections and performing digital preservation over the long-term. We will also document the results of our service model (including both free and for-fee services) to help the community understand where value-added services may be created to help pay for the operation of institutional repository systems.

5 Conclusion

In conclusion, MIT Libraries and the HP Laboratories have developed a new system that will serve as an institutional repository for the MIT faculty's intellectual output in digital formats. This repository will be the basis for managing the institution's digital research collections over time and for preserving this fragile material. DSpace will be tested at MIT over the coming year and will be made available to other institutions wishing to archive digital materials and possibly federate their collections. DSpace will be an important new platform in the coming years for several areas of digital library research including digital archiving and preservation, and new modes of scholarly communication.

---

9 Open Archives Initiative http://www.openarchives.org/

10 OpenURL http://library.caltech.edu/openurl/

11 SFX http://www.sfxit.com/

References

1. Kiernan, Vincent. Nebraska Researchers Measure the Extent of 'Link Rot' in Distance Education. Chronicle of Higher Education [Internet]. 2002 Apr 10 [cited 2002 May 4]: Available from http://chronicle.com/free/2002/04/2002041001u.htm

User Behavior Tendencies on Data Collections in a Digital Library

Michalis Sfakakis[1] and Sarantos Kapidakis[2]

[1]National Documentation Centre / National Hellenic Research Foundation,
48 Vas. Constantinou, GR-11635 Athens, Greece
msfaka@ekt.gr
[2]Archive and Library Sciences Department / Ionian University,
Plateia Eleftherias, Paleo Anaktoro, Corfu 49100, Greece
sarantos@ionio.gr

Abstract. We compare the usage of a Digital Library with many different categories of collections, by examining its log files for a period of twenty months, and we conclude that the access points that the users mostly refer to, depend heavily on the type of content of the collection, the detail of the existing metadata and the target user group. We also found that most users tend to use simple query structures (e.g. only one search term) and very few and primitive operations to accomplish their request. Furthermore, as they get more experienced, they reduce the number of operations in their sessions.

1 Introduction

The evolution of Digital Libraries attends great interest by researchers in a variety of disciplines during the last years. Especially the study to understand and evaluate their usage has become a centric point in a number of Digital Library projects ([9], [10]) and specifies a number of critical factors during the design, creation and development process of a Digital Library ([12]).

Depending on the study and its use, a number of appropriate qualitative or quantitative methods exist ([3], [4]) to accomplish it. An unobtrusive way to study and evaluate user behavior is the Transaction Log Analysis. Although log analysis is used as an effective method to assess how users actually interact with a working Digital Library, this method hardly provides any information about the users' reasons behind their specific behavior - which is also very difficult to extract – and it is lack of giving information on their intentions. The accuracy of this quantitative method heavily depends on the detail of the information logged (automatically by the system), the period of time used to log the information, the usage and the number of the performed transactions during the log period. Such data are not usually publicly available (especially in detail) because of privacy constraints. For these reasons and due to that large Digital Libraries have recently started developing, only a few studies exist based on this technique ([5], [7], [8], [11]).

In this work, based on the logged information, we study and evaluate the behavioral tendencies of different user groups on a variety of collections in the Digital Library of the Hellenic National Documentation Centre (*NDC*). The Digital Library of

M. Agosti and C. Thanos (Eds.): ECDL 2002, LNCS 2458, pp. 550-559, 2002.

NDC (http://theses.ndc.gr) is one of the most significant in Greece and consists of more than ten collections of diverse types. Most of these collections are unique world wide with internationally interesting content. In particular, the "Hellenic Ph.D. Dissertations Thesis" collection is part of the international Networked Digital Library of Theses and Dissertation Initiative ([2]). The Digital Library of NDC is targeted to a number of diverse types of user groups (e.g. students, researchers, professionals, librarians, etc.), mainly in Greece, from a variety of scientific domains.

In the following section we describe the goal and the methodology of this study. We also describe the collections, their characteristics, the targeted user groups they refer to and the functionality of the available operations by the system. Then we present some our most important observations from the operation distribution, the Access Points usage and how users accomplish their requests, together with our interpretation and conclusions. Finally we present a number of interesting issues arrived from this work for further evaluation and research.

2 Purpose and Methodology of the Study

The goal of this study is to compare and evaluate the differences on the usage among data collections, based on the collection content type, metadata and characteristics and also to approach the way diverse kinds of users accomplish their requests.

For a period of twenty months, we logged the operations performed by the users on the content of ten different collections of a Digital Library, using a specific web based retrieval system. Considering the content type (e.g. PhD theses, articles in a specific scientific area, Books and Periodicals Union catalogues etc.), the structure and the metadata quality of the collection (specificity, completeness of fields, syntactic correctness and consistency as implemented by authority files [6]), plus the target group they refer to, we selected the eight most used ones and classified them into four categories:

1. Hellenic Ph.D. Dissertations Thesis (*C1*) with bilingual metadata and Hellenic Scientific Libraries Serials Union Catalogue (*C2*), with a medium consistency level, targeted to diverse kinds of scientific user groups (e.g. students, researchers etc.) from all scientific domains.
2. Medical Bibliography – Hippocrates (*C3*) and Social Science Bibliography – GLAFKA (*C4*), with simple metadata structure and a low consistency level, targeted to a specific scientific user group (e.g. doctors, sociologists and researchers).
3. Hellenic Archaeological Records – grARGOS(*C5*) and International Archaeological Records – intARGOS(*C6*), including library material with diverse types of data and a good consistency level, targeted to a specific scientific user group (e.g. researchers on Archaeology).
4. Hellenic School Libraries (*C7*) and Hellenic Public Libraries Union Catalogue (*C8*), union catalogs for library materials from many domains and a very good consistency level, targeted to librarians.

All the above collections are structured using the UNIMARC format with almost the same level of quality attributes specificity, completeness of fields, syntactic correctness, but a different level of the quality consistency attribute as described in every category. From their 300,000 metadata records there are links giving online access to

14,000 digitized documents composed of 2,000,000 scanned pages and few other object formats.

The web-based retrieval system that we monitored is implementing a Z39.50 client and connects to a Z39.50 server. The users start their sessions by selecting and connecting to a collection. After connecting to a collection, a user may express his search request or browse specific *Access Points* (e.g. extracts information about metadata indexing - the terminology used for naming them is the one of the Z39.50 attribute set bib-1 as defined in [1]) and then to retrieve (*present*) the documents. In some cases, there is the ability to further access the object (document) that includes the full text, mostly in scanned images. There are seventeen available Access Points and the "search" operation supports Boolean combinations of them. When the user browse the terms from a specific Access Point, the system permits either to select a term in order to use it in a "search" operation or to retrieve ("present") the corresponding documents for display or further processing (searching and retrieving). From the more advanced searching techniques, the system also supports Boolean search combination of previously issued result sets, Search History and Selection of specific records from individual result sets.

During the study covering period, no major modifications occurred on the two basic components of the Digital Library, the collections and the retrieval system. Fig. 1 shows the number of sessions and operations for all collections on a monthly basis, where the operations have been divided by five, to be visible on the same scale. •he number of operations, sessions and users increased while maintaining an annual periodic variation, and the number of sessions and operations seem to have the same transitions.

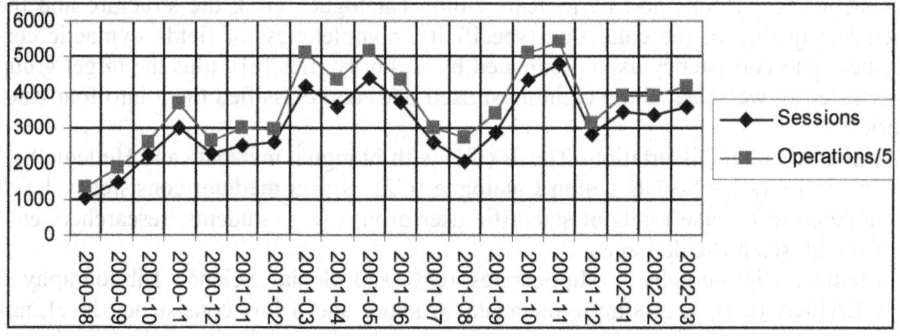

Fig. 1. Number of Sessions and Operations/5 per month

From August 2000 till March 2002, the study covering period, we recorded 490,042 operations from all the collections of the Digital Library to process and evaluate. From this set of operations we select only those that concern the eight selected collections and finally, in order to be more accurate in our study, we exclude all operations that do not affect the way the users accomplish their requests (e.g. connect to a collection in the Digital Library or request information about the collection). The final 359,157 analyzed operations belong to 60,869 sessions.

3 Operations Distribution

The distribution of the performed operations for the eight selected collections, according to their functionality and excluding the operations that do not affect the way the users accomplish their requests, as shown in fig. 2, showed that the users accomplish their requests using mainly the two basic operations: "search" (50%) and "present" (43%), to retrieve the documents. The users avoid extracting information about metadata indexing, using the "browse" operation (4%). Finally, they very rarely use the "search history" operation (1%) to combine or further refine their search results.

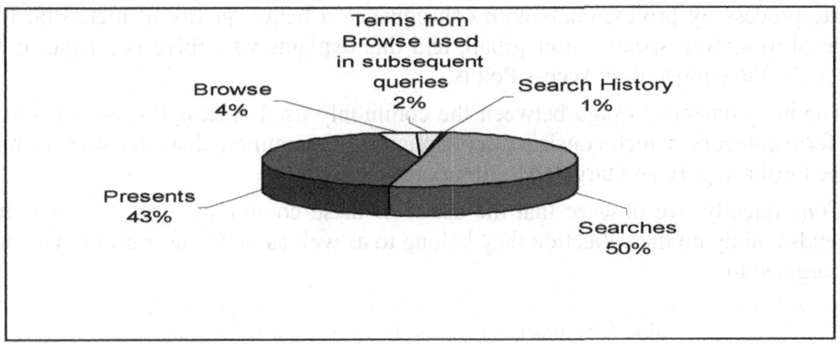

Fig. 2. Operation Distribution

The evaluation of the "search" operation usage and formulation showed that the majority (81.51%) of the logged search operations were formulated using only one search term. A small number of "search" operations were formulated using more than one search terms combined by Boolean operators (18.49%) of which a tiny portion (0.1%) were also formulated reusing previously issued result sets.

The conclusion from the distribution of the operations in the session is that the users accomplish their requests using simply the basic operations, avoiding making use of advanced (complicated but more efficient at the same time) querying techniques.

4 Evaluation of the Usage of Access Points

For the four most commonly used Access Points, Table 1 shows the order of preference and the percentage of times each Access Point has been used, for each collection and all collections together.

The evaluation of the usage of Access Points, shows that the most commonly used Access Points, for all the collections in the Digital Library, are the "Any", "Author", "Title", "Subject Heading" (Table 1), from the seventeen ones used in the metadata (the used terminology for naming Access Points is the one used by the Z39.50 attribute set bib-1), mostly in this order.

The vast majority of all users, independent of user group, used the "Any" Access Point for almost all collections. The only exception occurs at collection C6, were the most used Access Point is the "Author" which could be explained from the specialized subject area of the collection's content (Archaeological Records with detailed metadata description, where scientific work is known and searched usually by author) in combination with the specific type of its closed targeted user group's requests.

Another interesting observation with regard to the first two categories of the collections is the big usage difference between the two most used Access Points. These collections consist of content with simple metadata structure and are targeted to a number of diverse types of occasional users.

The third category, consists of collections with typical library material (e.g. more complex metadata structure, diverse kinds of material) that usually impose a more accurate process by professionals with consequence a better quality of metadata. It is targeted to a more specific user group, and this explains why there is a balance between the three most used Access Points.

The most balanced usage between the commonly used Access Points, happens at the forth category, which consists of collections with common characteristics as those in the third category and targeted to librarians.

Consequently, we observe that the usage of these commonly used Access Points depends mainly on the collection they belong to as well as on the user group type they are targeted to.

Table 1. Summary of Access Points use per Collection

AP	Total	C1	C2	C3	C4	C5	C6	C7	C8
Any	110,120 50.5%	51%	57%	78%	67%	39%	30%	30%	35%
Author	42,020 19.3%	20%	9%	5%	8%	28%	36%	23%	26%
Title	34,911 16%	13%	22%	10%	17%	26%	26%	21%	18%
Subject Heading	20,871 9.5%	10%	7%	4%	5%	4%	5%	22%	15%
		Any Auth or Title Sub- ject	Any *Title* *Autho* *r* Sub- ject	Any *Title* *Author* Sub- ject	Any *Title* *Auth* *or* Sub- ject	Any Author Title Subject	*Author* *Any* Title Sub- ject	Any Auth or *Sub-* *ject* *Title*	Any Auth or Title Sub- ject

When formulating a "search" operation, the user can specify the structure of the search term (e.g. word, words, phrase) and possibly use right or left truncation for each Access Point. The study of the most commonly used Access Point's structure used by the users to accomplish their search operations shows that, for almost all collections, the vast majority use the "Word" structure combined with the "Right Truncation" for the "Any" and "Title" Access Points and the "Phrase" structure combined also with the "Right Truncation" for the "Author" and "Subject Heading" Access Points. From the wide use of the right truncation we suspect that the majority of users are not very specific when expressing their requests accepting in most cases the system defaults.

Table 2 displays the usage of Access Point combinations for each collection and all collections together. We first observe that the Access Point "Any" is not that dominant in Access Point combinations as it was in single Access Point specifications. We also observe that the difference between the two most used Access Point combinations follows the previously observed Access Point usage pattern. Finally, for the majority of the collections, the most commonly used combination of Access Points is the "Title-Any", except for the collections C5, C6, C8. We have already seen (Table 1) that these collections have a more uniform usage on their single Access Points, without overusing the "Any" Access Point, and consequently the most commonly used combination of Access Points for them is the "Title-Author".

We also observe that the Access Point "Title" is used much more often on Access Point combinations, although it is the third one in the list of the most used Access Points, which indicate that "Title" is used in more sophisticated "search" operations and by more sophisticated users.

Table 2. Summary of Access Points Combination use per Collection

	Total	C1	C2	C3	C4	C5	C6	C7	C8
Title – Any	4,153 30.6%	**30%**	**28%**	**52%**	**59%**	16%	21%	**33%**	16%
Title – Author	2,782 20.5%	12%	13%	8.7%	5%	**58%**	**48%**	26%	**27%**
Author – Any	1,370 10.1%	13%	10%	8.4%	4%	6%	10.6%	4.8%	10%
Subject Heading - Any	939 6.9%	8.2%	8%	7%	6%	2.9%	3.3%	7.1%	7%
Title - Subject Heading	561 4.1%	4.3%	5%	2.6%	2%	2.1%	3.1%	6%	6%
Title – Author – Any	491 3.6%	4.4%	4%	3.1%	3%	1.9%	2.6%	1.3%	4%
Subject Heading - Author	482 3.5%	4%	2%	1.7%	1%	2%	2.5%	5.4%	6%

Considering the results that, the vast majority (81.51%) of the search queries consist of one search term and most users for almost all collections use a general Access Point, "Any", truncated to accomplish their requests with big usage difference from the next, more specific, Access Point, "Author" or "Title", we can infer that new users will need more operations to accomplish their requests which impacts the increase of the number of operations per session when new users enter the system.

5 User Behavior (How a User Accomplishes the Job)

Fig. 3 shows on a monthly basis the average operations per session and the number of sessions (scaled down to be shown together – its actual scale is not important and is not shown) aggregated for all eight collections studied. Similar lines correspond to each one of the studied collections.

The average number of operations per session (fig. 3) in general drops during the study period, while the number of sessions increases. Also, in August that most of the regular users are on their summer vacations, we have a smaller number of sessions, which indicates that we may have a lot of new users. Do the August data imply that new users need more operations per session to expresses their requests?

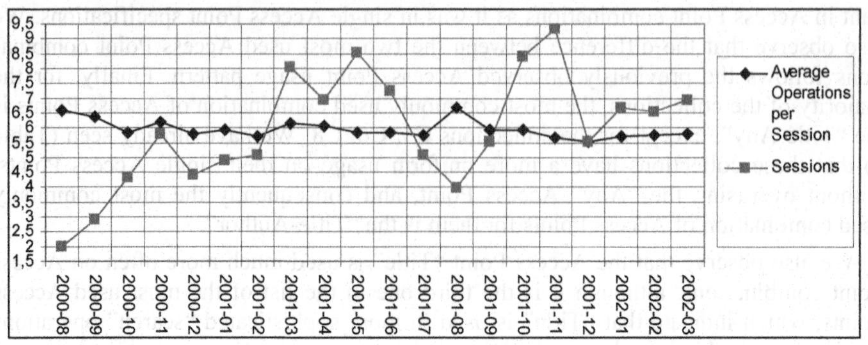

Fig. 3. Average Operations per session, Sessions

Fig. 4 shows the monthly proportion of sessions with operations less than or equal to three per session for three collections and aggregated for all eight collections studied, on a monthly basis. Similar lines correspond to the rest of the studied collections.

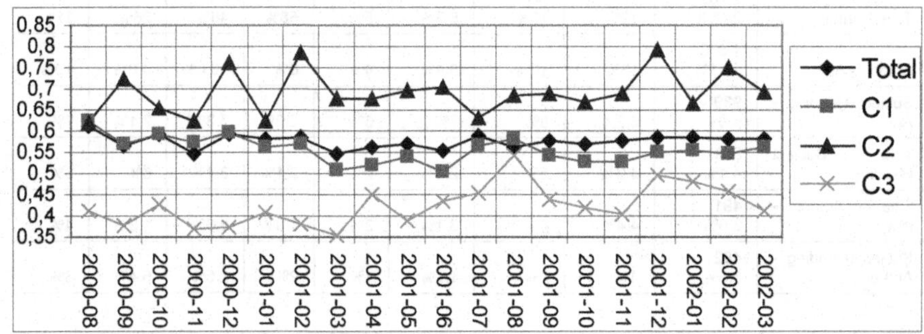

Fig. 4. Proportion of Sessions with less than or equal to 3 operations per session

We observe that in each month (Fig. 4), three operations are enough to fulfill at least half of the sessions in almost all collections – and the number of operations to fulfill at least half of the sessions on a specific collection depends on the collection. Furthermore, the number of sessions in each collection with less than or equal to three operations per session have a generally constant fluctuation, which indicates that a balance on the number of sessions with the same number of operations per session is maintained, from the new users that are added and the old users that become more experienced. We also see a slight increase to the proportion of sessions with less than or equal to 3 operations per session for the collections with mainly a closed set of users.

Please note that although the fact that only so few operations per session are enough to fulfill at least half of the sessions seem incompatible with the fact that the average number of operations per session is greater than 5 (Fig. 3), they can be explained by the existence of some sessions with a lot of operations, probably generated by some non-interactive query mechanism.

Another interesting question is how we measure the experience of the users. The experience of a specific user will certainly increase by time, but how can we distinguish it from that of a newer user, on a system that does not record the identification of the user? Are there patterns on his behavior that are related to his experience?

We assume that one aspect of the experience of the user is measured by the number of operations that are included in a session, the full sequence of operations that the user performed. We have already concluded that most users perform few operations in order to find their material, but as the users become more experienced, do they use more operations (been able to make more complex sessions) or less operations (been more specific and efficient) in their sessions? The addition of new users into the system makes the distinction more difficult.

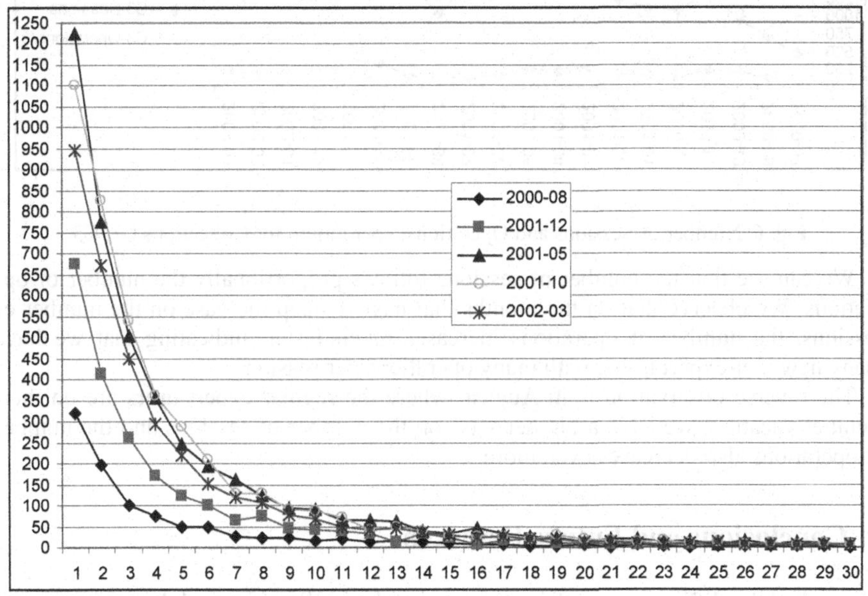

Fig. 5. Number of operations per session - Number of Sessions

Fig. 5 shows the number of sessions for each number of operations (from 1 to 30) per session for five representative months, aggregated for all collections. From fig. 5 we can see that on the later stages in our Digital Library lifetime, the increased number of users corresponds to only an increase to the number of sessions that have only one operation. We already observed, on the evaluation of Access Point usage, that new users perform queries with many operations per session. We also believe that it is unlikely that all new users perform only queries with one operation per session, and we can see from fig. 1 that the total number of sessions in the last three of the depicted months are practically the same, so we conclude that older users decrease the number of operations into their sessions, in a way that (by coincidence) corresponds to or outperforms the increase of new users performing the same number of operations per session. Thus expert users use fewer operations per session than non-expert users and the users decrease the number of operations in their sessions during the time they use the Digital Library.

In fig. 6 we depict the number of sessions and operations for two collections on a monthly basis, where the number of operations has been divided by five, to be shown on the same scale. Other collections give similar results. Fig. 1 depicts the same quantities, aggregated for all collections.

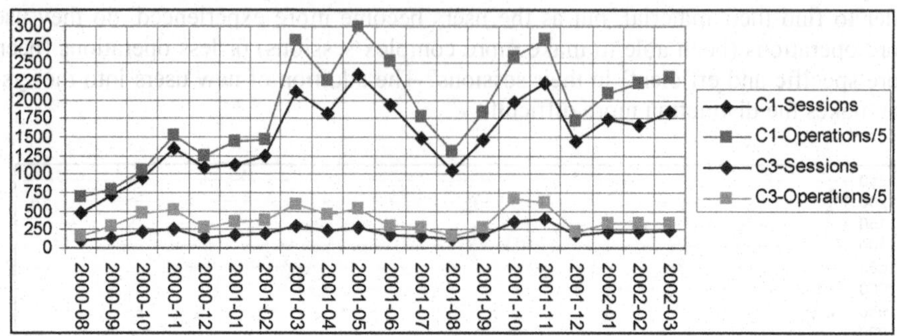

Fig. 6. Number of Sessions and Operations/5 per month for Collections C1, C3

We can see that the number of sessions follows proportionally the number of operations. We observe that on the months that have a steep increase on the number of sessions, the number of operations increases much faster, indicating that we have many new non-expert users, with many operations per session.

The reverse observation is in August, where the regular expert users are on their summer vacation, we have a big decrease on the number of sessions and the number of operations also decreases even more.

6 Conclusions and Future Research

We studied the differences on the usage among data collections and the way users accomplish their requests. We examined the relationship between the number of operations and sessions, and the distribution of the different types of operations, and we found that most users tend to use simple query structures and very few and primitive operations to accomplish their requests. We explored the usage count of the different access points and their combinations and we realized that they depend heavily on the type of the content of the collection, the detail of the existing metadata and the target user group, where the more sophisticated users use more complex structures and more specialized and informative access points. Finally, we investigated the evolution of the user behavior by the time, and we concluded that the users reduce the number of operations in their sessions, as they get more experienced.

From this work a number of interesting points arrives for future evaluation and research. A more detailed analysis for the search term formulation (e.g. word, phrase, truncation) used by a specific group of users to accomplish their search requests per collection would be interesting. Another point of interest is how different user types (e.g. professionals, ordinary users) behave under the same circumstances. What sequences (patterns) of operations (i.e. number of "Presents" follows the "Search" operation, etc.) in sessions do different types of users adopt? Finally, another interesting point of evaluation is the evolution of the query formulation complexity.

References

1. ANSI/NISO: Z39.50 Information Retrieval: application service definition and protocol specification: approved May 10, 1995.
2. E. Fox, Robert Hall, Neill A. Kipp, John L. Eaton, Gail McMillan, and Paul Mather. NDLTD: Encouraging International Collaboration in the Academy. In Special Issue on Digital Libraries, DESIDOC Bulletin of Information Technology, 17(6): 45-56, Nov. 1997.
3. Bains S., "End-User Searching Behavior: Considering Methodologies", The Katharine Sharp Review, No. 4, Winter 1997.
4. Covey, D. T., "Usage and Usability Assessment: Library Practices and Concerns", Washington, D.C., Digital Library Federation Council on Library and Information Resources, January 2002, ISBN 1-887334-89-0.
5. Jones, S., Cunningham, S. J., McNab, R. J. and Boddie, S., "A Transaction log Analysis of a digital library", International Journal on Digital Libraries, v. 3:no. 2 (2000), pp. 152-169.
6. Larsen, Ronald L., "The DLib Test Suite and Metrics Working Group: Harvesting the experience from the Digital Library Initiative". D-Lib Working Group on Digital Library Metrics Website, April 2002.
7. Mahoui, M., Cunningham, S. J., "Search Behavior in a Research-Oriented Digital Library", ECDL 2001, LNCS 2163, pp. 13-24.
8. Mahoui, M., Cunningham, S. J., "A Comparative Log Analysis of Two Computing Collections", Research and Advanced Technology for Digital Libraries: Proceedings of the 4th European Conference, ECDL Lisbon, Portugal, Sept. 2000, pp. 418-423.
9. Peterson Bishop, A., "Working toward an understanding of digital library use: a report on the user research efforts of the NSF/ARPA/NASA DLI projects", D-Lib Magazine, October 1995.
10. Payette, S.D. and Rieger, O.Y. "Z39.50 The User's Perspective", D-Lib Magazine, April 1997.
11. Sfakakis, M. and Kapidakis, S, "Evaluating User Behavior on Data Collections in a Digital Library", Forth DELOS Workshop on Evaluation of Digital Libraries: Testbeds, Measurements and Metrics, Budapest, Hungary, June 2002.
12. Van House, N.A. et. al., "User centered iterative design for digital libraries: the Cypress experience", D-Lib Magazine, February 1996.

Student Comprehension of Classification Applications in a Science Education Digital Library

Jane Greenberg,[1] Kristen A. Bullard,[2] M. L. James,[1] Evelyn Daniel,[1] and Peter White[2]

[1]School of Library and Information Science, University of North Carolina at Chapel Hill
Chapel Hill, NC 27599-3360, +1 919 962 8366
{janeg, jamem, and daniel} @ils.unc.edu
http://www.ibiblio.org/pic

[2]Department of Biology, University of North Carolina at Chapel Hill
Chapel Hill, NC 27599-3280, +1 919 962 2077
{bullardk, pswhite} @email.unc.edu

Abstract. Piaget's theory of cognitive development serves as a basis for a comparative analysis of middle school students' understanding of classification in the *physical* and *digital library*. Attention is also given to student comprehension of *scientific classification*. Results of this pilot study show that although participants had good comprehension of classification principles in the physical environment, with which they are more familiar, their understanding diminishes in the digital environment and when addressing scientific classification. Results are compared to an earlier study and implications for the design of educational science digital libraries are discussed.

Keywords: Digital Library, Classification, Science Education, Piaget, Cognitive Development.

1 Introduction

One of the most exciting developments supported by World Wide Web (web) technology is the ability to connect students to primary resources housed in botanical, zoological, geological, and other scientific research centers. Central to this development is the emergence of science education digital libraries that allow students to view digital specimens, research databases, electronic copies of field notes, and other resources used by scientists in their daily endeavors. These initiatives are enhanced with lesson plans, glossaries, chat rooms, and additional facilities that foster interactive learning.

Digital libraries of this nature classify and provide access to objects via *topical labeling* and *taxonomic systems* found in the physical library environment. Although these classificatory systems provide a logical architecture for organizing objects in the tangible environment, they may present unforeseen navigation and access challenges in the digital world given its more abstract quality. This consideration may be particularly true for user groups that have not reached a certain level of cognitive maturity. The hypothesis posited here is rooted in Piaget's theory of cognitive development and applies primarily children in the *concrete operational* stage, or earlier *stages* [1]. Further support for this hypothesis is found with the difficulties

M. Agosti and C. Thanos (Eds.): ECDL 2002, LNCS 2458, pp. 560-567, 2002.

children experience when searching online catalogs—a more abstract exercise compared to browsing the physical library bookshelf [2, 3].

Although the web is becoming a central tool for educational initiatives, little is known about how classificatory systems developed for the physical world transfer into the digital libraries. If digital libraries are to engage students in scientific learning, designers need to understand students' abilities to cognitively process and navigate classificatory structures in the digital environment. The research presented here considers this topic by having middle school students engage in classification task and answer a survey after exposure to the University of North Carolina's Plant Information Center (PIC) [hereafter referred to as PIC].

2 Classification Environments

Classification, the grouping and labeling of like objects, relies on terminological (verbal) and notational (e.g. letters, numbers, and/or punctuation) systems. These systems range from informal word lists to highly structured schemas, such as thesauri and taxonomies, constructed according to formal rules (e.g., International Standards Organization (IS0) standards).

Physical libraries classify objects via *broad categories* (subject, genre, and format) and *formal classification schemas* (Dewey Decimal Classification (DDC)). A top classificatory level is provided by signage or labels, which give an immediate orientation and create a sensory connection to a physical collection. For example, signs may identify collection subjects (e.g., "History" and "Science"), genres (e.g., "Fiction" and "Non-Fiction"), and formats (e.g., "Books," "Videos," and "Sound recordings"). Formalized schemas arrange collection objects at the secondary level. We can anticipate that sixth grade students have a certain comfort level navigating the physical library because labeling provides a visual map, there is a tangible connection to the collection, and the majority of students in this age group are familiar with the environment having experienced it since early primary education. Projects, such as Dewey Memory and Dewey Lotto Cards, aimed at promoting the use of the library's Dewey Decimal Classification scheme, implemented in the Christchurch City Libraries, New Zealand help support this assertion [7].

Digital libraries often emulate the classificatory systems used in physical libraries. Topical labeling is found in site maps, navigation bars, and hot-lists (lists of hyperlinks), making digital libraries more concrete at the top level, and formalized schemas are often applied at the secondary level. An example is Science Net, which organizes educational resources by discipline (e.g., Chemistry, Zoology, Paleontology, Astronomy, Physics and Geology) at the top level and then uses the DDC for organization of resources under these topics (http://sciencenet.tpl.toronto.on.ca/).

Scientific classification, a topic important to the research at hand, is used to facilitate genus/species identification. Exposure to the scientific classification's basic framework (e.g., Kingdom, Phylum, Class, Order, Family, Genus, and Species) is incorporated into school curricula in the United States during the latter part of primary education (fourth through sixth or seventh grade). Greater use of scientific taxonomies is found in sixth and seventh grade, when students create a leaf-book (a compilation identifying local foliage) or study part of animal's life-cycle (i.e., observing the incubation, hatching, and early development of a chicken). Given the above, it makes sense that scientific taxonomies are considered a source for organizing science educational digital libraries. An example is found with the Global Awareness Project, which includes a species index for endangered animals and is constructed in part by students (http://library.thinkquest.org/2551/species.html).

UNC's Plant Information Center (PIC) is a digital library, (http://www.ibiblio.org/pic/) connecting students to primary scientific resources used by botanists for plant identification. Broad topical categories (Figure 1) and scientific classification (Figure 2) found in the physical world are used to organize specimens and other collection resources. We sought to determine if sixth grade students could successfully navigate PIC and apply these schemas when engaged in plant identification. We question students' comprehension of classificatory systems in the physical world and their ability to understand the applications of these systems in the digital library. We are particularly interested in students in early stages of cognitive development who are learning about scientific classification.

Fig. 1. PIC Site Map – Example of Broad Topical Categories

3 Classification and Cognitive Development

Jean Piaget's *stages of cognitive development* [1], one of the most influential theories in this area, includes four stages of development: The Sensorimotor stage (children from birth to two years old), Pre-operational stage (two to six years olds), Concrete Operational stage (seven to twelve years old), and Formal Operational stage (twelve to eighteen years old). Of interest to PIC designers is the ability of children to move from concrete to abstract environments, particularly children about to transfer from Piaget's concrete operational stage to the formal operational stage and who are learning about scientific classification. In the concrete operational stage, children's thinking is limited to objects that are present, and they have difficulty solving abstract or hypothetical problems. Children in the *formal operational stage* are able to generalize, think more abstractly, hypothesize, and perceive analogies; they use metaphors, sarcasm, and other complex language forms to explain their thinking. Researchers need to consider students' cognitive abilities and theories such as Piaget's, as educational initiatives incorporate web technologies and build digital libraries for e-learning. This is particularly necessary for scientific libraries that adopt classificatory methods from the physical world and, at the same time, introduce scientific classification.

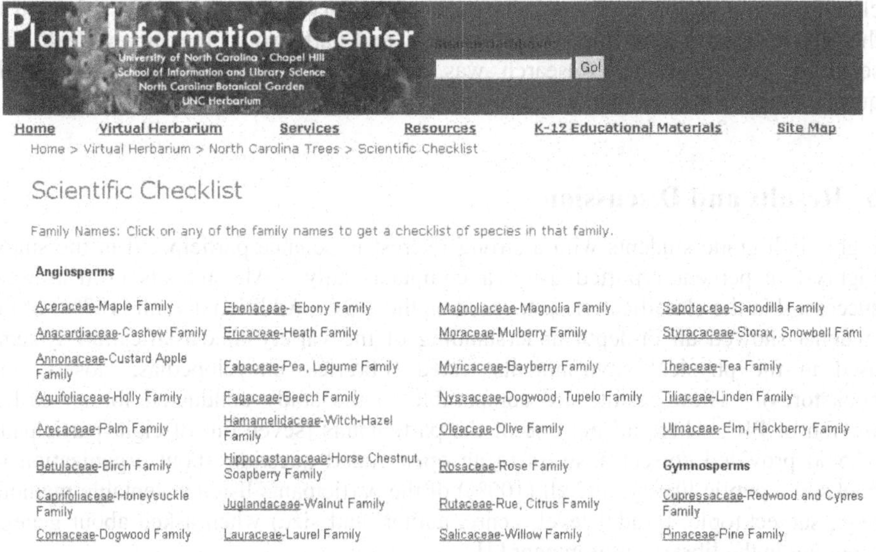

Fig. 2. PIC Scientific Checklist – Example of Scientific Classification

4 Research Objective

This research explored student's understanding of classification in the *physical* and *digital library* and student comprehension of *scientific classification.* Three questions guided this examination:

1. Do sixth grade students understand object categorization in the physical library?
2. Do they understand object categorization in the digital library environment?
3. Do these students understand scientific classification sufficiently to use PIC?

5 Methodology

The methodology included a classification task and a survey, which were implemented after a plant identification exercise. These methods were selected in order to balance the exploration of students' comprehension of classification practices and their ability to navigate a digital library. Participants were sixth grade students, all age 11 or 12, who had been introduced to the fundamentals of scientific classification in the fifth grade. Through their current education (sixth grade science class) they had at least five hours of scientific classification lessons and three additional hours focusing specifically on botanical taxonomy. The study was conducted in a computer laboratory at McDougle Middle School, Carrboro, North Carolina. The classification task required students to assign DDC top-level classification notation to objects. Part one of the survey focused on classification in the physical and digital library environment, and part two of the survey dealt with scientific classification. Research was also supported by a participant profile questionnaire, a post-examination questionnaire, and direct observation by proctors.

6 Results and Discussion

Eight sixth grade students with a strong interest in science participated in the study. Eighty-five percent reported using a computer daily. All students (100%) were successful in the classification task based on the DDC. Additionally, all (100%) of the students showed an in-depth understanding of the variety of classification systems used in the physical environments tested (libraries, encyclopedias, closets, and bookstores). These results are comparable to the study conducted for an earlier version of PIC, where all but one of the participants (seven out of eight participant, 87.5%) provided correct answers to an open ended question about organization of books in a public library, and all (100%) of the participants listed acceptable methods (e.g., subject/topic, [grade] level, genre, author, and size) when asked about general grouping in the library environment [4].

Students were asked a series of questions about how objects were groups in selected physical environments, such as: "How are materials arranged in a bookstore?" On average, students identified 2.5 categorization methods in the physical library with an average of 95.0% of the answers being specific and correct. Example of correct answers were that library items are grouped by "genre/type," "subject/topic," "author" "type," "format," and "size." Conversely, the results showed only a superficial understanding of PIC's classificatory structures, identifying an average of 1.13 grouping practices, with 44.4% of the answers being specific and correct (e.g., by "subject/topic" and "type") and the remaining answers being vague with responses, such as, "by purpose," "by what people want to find out," and "by what you would usually come to the website for." The vague answers given suggest that students have difficulty in transferring classification knowledge to the digital environment as a limitation in PIC's design.

Table 1. Classification Systems Identified in the Physical and Digital Library Environment

environ.	average no. of systems identified	% specific answers (correct)	% vague answers
Physical	2.5	95.0	5.0
PIC	1.13	44.4	55.6

Answers to a series of analogy questions addressing scientific classification showed students had good comprehension of the basic relationship between genus and species, although their responses were weak when answering questions requiring cognitive processing about the application of this knowledge. For example, all students asserted that Latin names were important, but they were unable to state correctly why they are important. Responses included, "so everybody can pronounce the word," "so kids can give Latin names," "to give the name for a project or homework." The inability of students to perceive the value of a naming system for grouping raises questions, especially given that this was a fundamental part of their instruction in this area. In this venue, students did not demonstrate a *big picture* understanding of scientific taxonomy the way they perceived the use of DDC or broad topical grouping for resources in the physical library.

Students also lacked a strong understanding for the application of scientific classification when asked how scientists worked with a taxonomy. Here, only three of the eight (37.5%) students recognized that scientific classification was useful for designing plant and animal identification charts, and again only three of eight students (37.5%) found scientific classification useful for global communication among the scientific community. While the results show that almost half of the students had good comprehension in both cases, we had anticipated that a greater majority would have provided sufficient answers. Students' comprehension-gap in this area was further evidenced by their inability to adequately explain the specifics of the genus species relationship (general to specific). Overall, students exhibited knowledge of scientific classification on the surface level, but were not able to apply this knowledge in answering cognitively difficult questions. These results are similar to those found in the examination with the earlier version of PIC [4], where student understanding of scientific classification in the digital library were less definitive than the questions pertaining to the physical library classification. In the earlier study, three of the eight students (37.5%) incorrectly selected word-pairs that best expressed a genus/species relationship. These results and the findings from the research presented here help to raise questions about students' conceptual understanding of classification in general and superordinate and subordinate relationships expressed through hierarchies.

7 Implications for Digital Libraries

Students in Piaget's concrete operational stage, or transferring to his formal operational stages (around the age of twelve), seem to understand the role of classification in the physical library environment, although they appear to have difficulties comprehending this application in the digital library. These difficulties are made more evident when working with scientific taxonomies, which are introduced to students at this age and being incorporated into science education digital libraries.

These findings have may have implications for the design of educational digital libraries that are looking for intuitive ways to organize their systems, particularly libraries that want to excite interest in the sciences. We found that children in Piaget's concrete operational stage understand classification better in tangible environments and advocate that digital libraries emulate the organization of physical libraries for this age group. Some methods for achieving this could include obvious age-appropriate icons, highlighted sitemaps and navigation bars, and graphics (e.g., maps or virtual bookshelves) providing a sense of physical proximity. Additionally, we suggest grouping by topical unambiguous terms similar to "genre" and "subject" and the use of the top-level nodes from formal classificatory systems [5]. The fact that fifty-percent of the students stated that the sitemap and images were the most useful features navigating the PIC, lends support to these considerations.

Our results also verify that students in Piaget's *concrete operational stage* have difficulty comprehending scientific classification applications. Given that web technology is increasingly used to introduce scientific subjects, including classification to students, we recommend that designers consider incorporating the features advocated above (e.g., icons, etc.). These features could ease learning anxieties in the sciences and could play a significant role in encouraging students, including female and minority students, to major in the sciences [6]. If designers keep in mind the importance of concrete physical representations for children in this stage, science education digital libraries could play a more prominent role in teaching about problem solving and scientific discovery. Moreover, these libraries could be seen as tools to facilitate cognitive development and learning about classification is a useful manner

8 Conclusions and Future Research

This study found that sixth grade students, likely in Piaget's concrete operational stage, or transferring to his formal operational stages, understand physical library classification applications, but are less sure about digital library classificatory structures. These observed difficulties became more evident when working with scientific classification. The results impact PIC's effectiveness. We are incorporating above recommended changes and also creating an introduction to PIC's use of scientific taxonomies for organizing resources.

Classification, the grouping of like objects, is a daily activity for people in many disciplines. Young children learn about classification primarily with cognitive exercises requiring them to select the objects that are similar or dissimilar. Due to the infancy of digital libraries, we are just beginning to examine the relationship between cognitive development and the ability of students to understand classification in the digital world. The results of this study are consistent with an earlier study [4] and supported by previous online catalog research [2, 3], although they are limited to the sample of eight students and PIC's design. More in-depth and task oriented research is needed in a variety of digital libraries and with a larger population of students transferring from the *concrete operational* to the *formal operational stage*. Research in this area might also consider questions associated with digital library use of newly formed classificatory structures instead of traditional schemas [8]. PIC researchers plan to conduct a larger study with more users. The design of future digital libraries that aim to introduce scientific topics to primary and middle school children can be informed by research on this topic.

Acknowledgments. The PIC team would like to acknowledge the Institute of Museum and Library Services' (IMLS) support of this project, Sara Breese, Project Coordinator for facilitating the study, SILS student proctors, and Anne Bauers for assisting with the data analysis.

References

1. Piaget, J., and Inhelder, B. (1969). *The psychology of the child*. New York: Basic Books.
2. Borgman, C.L., Hirsh, Sandra G. and Walter, Virginia A. Children's Searching Behavior on Browsing and Keyword Online Catalogs : The Science Library Catalog Project. *Journal of the American Society for Information Science* 46(9), 1995, 663-684.
3. Solomon, P. Children's Information Retrieval Behavior: A Case Analysis of an OPAC. *Journal of the American Society for Information Science* 44(5), 1993, 245-264.
4. Greenberg, J. and James, M. L. ([2001]). An Examination of Student Comprehension of Classificatory Systems in an Educational Science Digital Library. Unpublished paper
5. Brown, M.E. By Any Other Name: Accounting for Failure in the Naming of Subject Categories. *Library and Information Science Research* 17(4), 1995, 347-385.
6. Fort, D.C. Science shy, science savvy, science smart. *Phi Delta Kappan* 74(9), 1993, 674-683.
7. McMillan, D. (2001). Taking up the challenge: how can public libraries help develop information literate children? Australasian Public Libraries and Information Services, 14 (1): 4-12.
8. Hudon, M. (2001). Structuration du savoir et organisation des collections dans les repertoires du Web. Bulletin des Bibliotheques de France, 46 (1): 57-62

Designing Protocols in Support of Digital Library Componentization

Hussein Suleman and Edward A. Fox

Department of Computer Science, Virginia Tech, Blacksburg, VA, USA
{hussein,fox}@vt.edu
http://www.dlib.vt.edu/

Abstract. Reusability always has been a controversial topic in Digital Library (DL) design. While componentization has gained momentum in software engineering in general, there has not been broad DL standardization in component interfaces. Recently, the Open Archives Initiative (OAI) has begun to address this by creating a standard protocol for accessing metadata archives. We propose that the philosophy and approach adopted by the OAI can be extended easily to support inter-component protocols. In particular, we propose building DLs by connecting small components that communicate through a family of lightweight protocols, using XML as the data interchange mechanism. In order to test the feasibility of this, a set of protocols was designed based on the work of the OAI. Components adhering to these protocols were implemented and integrated into production and research DLs. The performance of these components was analyzed from the perspective of execution speed, network traffic, and data consistency. On the whole, this work has shown promise in the approach of applying the fundamental concepts of the OAI protocol to the task of DL component design and implementation.

1 Background and Motivation

As computers across the globe become part of the ever-expanding Internet, the communities of users and providers of information both grow. The providers of information contribute to increasing the body of information available to users, while the users, knowing this information exists, desire focused and instantaneous access to relevant information. The need to carefully manage collections of information contributed to the emergence of digital libraries (DLs), while the need to merge together collections to serve the needs of users has prompted the development of interoperability standards.

Special attention recently has been focused on the latter issue of interoperability with the emergence of the Open Archives Initiative (OAI) and its Protocol for Metadata Harvesting (PMH) [24]. The former issue of designing digital libraries to manage information has not received as much attention from the perspective of standardization. We propose in this paper that the philosophy and basic technical approach of the OAI can be applied to the design and construction of standardized components within digital libraries. Examples of such components include search engines, browsing services, annotation tools, peer review systems, and recommendation systems. When connected together in a loosely coupled network to

M. Agosti and C. Thanos (Eds.): ECDL 2002, LNCS 2458, pp. 568-582, 2002.

store data and provide services, such a collection of components constitutes an Open Digital Library (ODL), with many advantages over conventional DL architectures, notably: simplicity, reusability, and flexibility [22]. An example of such an ODL architecture is illustrated in Figure 1.

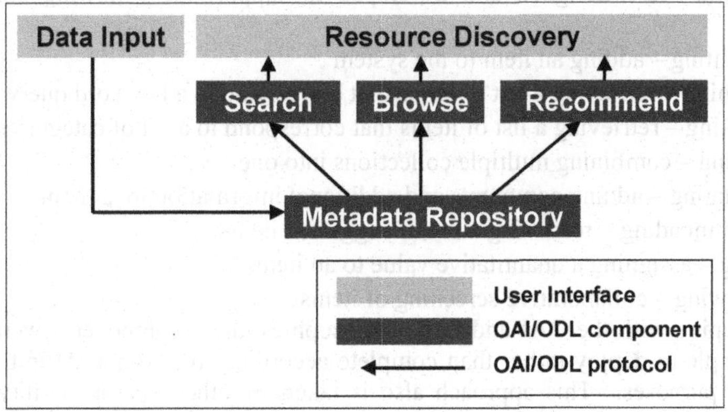

Fig. 1. Example ODL network of components

In keeping with current practices in software engineering, it long has been argued that DLs may benefit from software models based on object-oriented technology in general and componentization in particular [9]. Any such approach relies on an underlying component framework or set of application programming interfaces that are well defined and commonly known. Prior efforts have looked at various such mechanisms for inter-component communication.

Dienst [11] is a protocol (and software package) that used HTTP, and eventually XML, to provide for inter-component communication. Members of the Networked Computer Science Technical Reference Library [13] used earlier versions of Dienst for many years as the basis of their DL architecture and interoperability solution. (Dienst was one of the projects that served as a precursor to the current OAI-PMH.) The FEDORA project [17] further developed the Dienst repository architecture by defining abstract interfaces to structured digital objects, initially implemented over a CORBA communications medium.

The University of Michigan Digital Library Project [2] built DLs as collections of autonomous agents, with protocol-level negotiation to perform tasks collaboratively. The Stanford InfoBus project [1] wrapped its components into objects, with remote method invocation for communication.

All of these component models are built upon popular syntactic layers, such as HTTP and CORBA, and define additional semantics where necessary. This need for a common communications mechanism also is a driving force behind interoperability protocols such as the OAI-PMH, which we investigated as the basis for an alternative glue to bind together components in a DL.

2 Components and Requirements

One of our aims was to define a set of simple components that could be composed into production DL systems with minimal effort. To illustrate proof-of-concept, components were designed and developed to support the following common DL tasks:

- Submitting – adding an item to the system
- Searching – retrieving a list of items that correspond to a keyword query
- Browsing – retrieving a list of items that correspond to a set of categories
- Merging – combining multiple collections into one
- Annotating – adding comments and additional information to an item
- Recommending – retrieving a list of suggested items
- Rating – assigning a quantitative value to an item
- Reviewing – collaborative screening of items

In keeping with the OAI and ODL philosophies, these components were designed to be simple to deploy rather than complete according to a formal definition of their intended purposes. This approach also is taken by other interoperability protocols such as SDLIP [16], which wraps search systems with a common syntactic layer. However, SDLIP addresses only searching, which is just one aspect of the multitude of available services in modern DLs.

Each of the listed components needs to have a well-defined interface to communicate with other components. Table 1 lists gross requirements of some of the components in terms of their interfaces with other components.

Table 1. List of requirements for some ODL components

Component	Requirements
Search	Retrieve a list of items that match the supplied query. Add items to the search engine indices.
Browse	Retrieve a list of items that match a given set of criteria. Add items to the classification scheme.
Rating	Add a numerical rating for an item. Retrieve the numerical ratings, averages, and associated information for an item.
Annotate	Add an annotation to an item. Retrieve a list of annotations for an item.

The similarities in requirements suggest that a simpler model could be developed to factor out common features and incorporate those into a lower-level layer. The most basic operations needed for such a layer are the abilities to submit, retrieve, and delete items from a component or archive, as defined by Kahn and Wilensky [10] in their Repository Access Protocol. The ability to retrieve items is already provided by the OAI Protocol for Metadata Harvesting, so the approach taken was to first analyze this protocol and determine what needed to be modified or added in order to support the full range of functions needed for the identified DL components.

3 The OAI Protocol for Metadata Harvesting

The development of the OAI-PMH was a direct response to the need for simple interoperability standards [12], and this simplicity has led to adoption of the standard by many existing and new archives.

The OAI-PMH, commonly referred to as the OAI protocol, is a client-server protocol that is used to transfer XML-encoded records over an HTTP transport layer, with mechanisms to facilitate periodic updating. Table 2 lists the 6 service requests of this protocol that can be issued to obtain archive- or record-level metadata.

Table 2. OAI-PMH service requests and expected responses

Service Request	Expected Response
Identify	Description of archive: standards and protocols implemented
ListMetadataFormats	List of supported metadata formats
ListSets	List of archive sets and subsets
ListIdentifiers	List of record identifiers, optionally corresponding to a specified set and/or date range
GetRecord	Single metadata record corresponding to a specified identifier and in a specified metadata format
ListRecords	List of metadata records corresponding to a specified metadata format and, optionally, a set and/or date range

Archives that function as data providers implement the server end of this protocol and respond to these service requests, while those which wish to import or harvest data from data providers implement the client logic. These two pieces fit together to support simple metadata-transfer interoperability between archives.

4 Extensibility of the OAI Protocol

The OAI protocol is specifically aimed at the transfer of metadata among network-accessible devices. The mission of the OAI does not extend to supporting fine-grained inter-component interaction so the protocol was not designed with this in mind. However, since many of the requirements for such component protocols are already met by the OAI-PMH, it is possible and desirable to design new protocols based on the OAI-PMH, but with different purposes and somewhat different semantics. In keeping with this philosophy of reuse, we have looked into the development of new protocols as extensions of the OAI-PMH for inter-component communication.

The OAI-PMH already defines a specialized set of simple semantics for data access. Building on these semantics has the potential for greater impact on system developers because the baseline OAI-PMH semantics are becoming increasingly well known in the DL community [14].

In order to design DL component interaction protocols based on the OAI-PMH it was first necessary to analyze the features that made this feasible or infeasible. Table 3 lists protocol features that were identified as supporting extension, those that need to be added to support extension, and those that inhibit extension. This list of features applies only to v1.1 of the OAI-PMH - later versions such as v2.0 address some of these. Further discussion of these features can be found in [23].

Table 3. Features of OAI protocol that affect extensibility

Supporting	Missing	Inhibiting
1 Set organization 2 GetRecord access 3 Metadata containers 4 Identification containers	5 Response-level containers 6 Submission	7 Harvesting granularity 8 DC requirement

Taking these into account, we propose a new protocol [23] to act as the underlying layer for component interaction protocols. This new protocol, the Extended OAI-PMH (XOAI-PMH), is an extension to v1.1 of the OAI-PMH, to exploit its inherent extensibility and attempt to overcome the stated limitations. XOAI-PMH involves four general syntax changes and one service request addition to OAI-PMH - a PutRecord analogue to the GetRecord request. XOAI-PMH is thus a different protocol from OAI-PMH, with a different purpose and different semantics. We do not propose XOAI-PMH as a replacement for OAI-PMH, but rather as an independent protocol for inter-component communication.

5 Open Digital Libraries

This new protocol fulfils the role of a baseline Repository Access Protocol, as defined by Kahn and Wilensky [10], in each component of the DL. More specific semantics then can be layered upon this to support the differing individual requirements of each component as discussed earlier. Ultimately, the components can be integrated into a configurable Open Digital Library of loosely connected and independent data and service providers, such as is shown in Figure 1.

Individual protocols were defined, as specialized versions of the XOAI-PMH, to meet the requirements of each component. Brief summaries of some of these specialized protocols follow.

5.1 The ODL-Search Protocol

Queries are encapsulated in *ListRecords* and *ListIdentifiers* service requests, with the list of keywords encoded into the set parameter along with the query language and bounds for the range of results to be returned. An example of such a query is:

```
...verb=ListIdentifiers&set=odlsearch1/computer
science/1/10
```

In order to acquire records to be indexed, the component may harvest records using OAI-PMH or XOAI-PMH.

5.2 The ODL-Browse Protocol

Just as in ODL-Search, *ListRecords* and *ListIdentifiers* are used to obtain lists of records, with the set parameter encoding the categories and sort order. An example of a query is:

```
...verb=ListIdentifiers&set=odlbrowse1/type(Computer)sort
(Year)/11/20
```

ListSets returns a list of all categories that may be used in browsing queries.

A Browse component also may harvest records using OAI-PMH or XOAI-PMH.

5.3 The ODL-Rate Protocol

PutRecord is used to add a rating for an item in the form of a metadata record encapsulating the numerical rating and the item identifier. An example of this record is:

```
<odl_rating>
   <subject>oai:People:a@b.com </subject>
   <object>oai:VTETD:12345</object>
   <rating>12</rating>
</odl_rating>
```

"subject" identifies the person submitting the rating while "object" identifies the item being rated.

Thereafter, *GetRecord* may be used to retrieve the individual ratings or an average value by specifying the "odl_rating_average" metadataPrefix for an item. An example of the metadata returned is:

```
<odl_rating_average>
   <average>12</average>
   <count>1</count>
</odl_rating_average>
```

When retrieving individual ratings, the set parameter is used to specify the item for which to return records.

5.4 The ODL-Annotate Protocol

PutRecord is used to add arbitrary annotations to the component, with the identifier of the item being annotated supplied as the set parameter (where that item could itself be a prior annotation). *ListRecords* and *ListIdentifiers* then list all annotations for an item in reverse date order, with proper ordering maintained by the component – the set parameter is used to specify the item for which the "set of annotations" is requested as well as the range of entries to return. An example of such a request is:

…verb=ListIdentifiers&set=21/25/oai:VTETD:12345

In this case, the subset of annotations, starting at the 21st entry and ending at the 25th entry, is returned for the item identified by "oai:VTETD:12345".

Additional information about the item is provided using "about" containers for each record.

6 ODL Experimental Applications

In order to test the feasibility of the proposed componentized architecture for DLs using real world scenarios, a suite of components was implemented to support basic DL services.

6.1 Methodology

Components were implemented in accordance with the following protocols:

- ODL-Union, to merge together data from multiple OAI-compliant sources
- ODL-Filter, to filter OAI sources for illegal characters and non-unique identifiers
- ODL-Search, to index words in the metadata and permit search operations
- ODL-Browse, to sort and categorize data and permit browse operations
- ODL-Recent, to keep track of recently added items
- ODL-Annotate, to attach comments to an item
- ODL-Review, to keep track of peer-review workflow
- ODL-Submit, to accept submissions of items

The Union, Search, Browse, Filter, and Recent components were integrated into a simple user interface for the NDLTD system as shown in Figures 2 and 3, using metadata corresponding to Electronic Theses and Dissertations [21]. Figures 4 and 5 similarly display the user interface and architecture of the Browse component that was incorporated into the legacy DL system of the Computer Science Teaching Center (CSTC) [6].

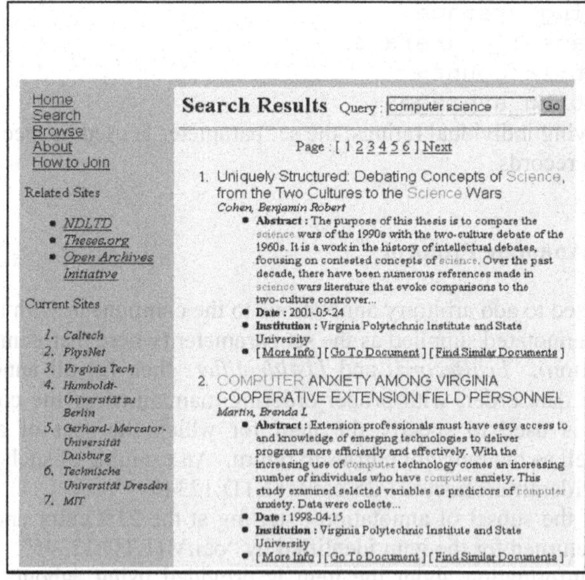

Fig. 2. User interface of NDLTD ODL

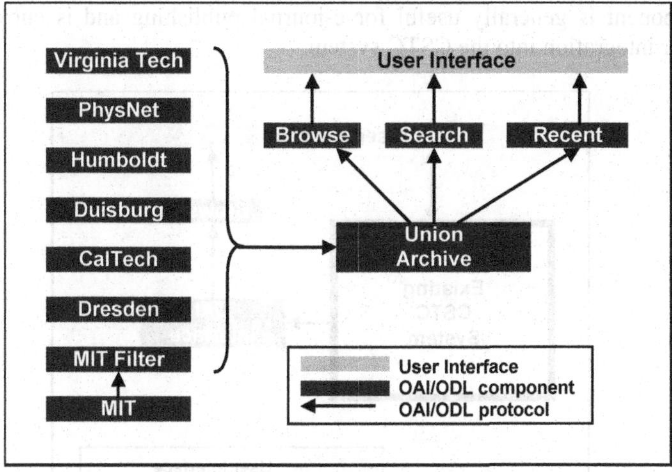

Fig. 3. Architecture of the NDLTD ODL

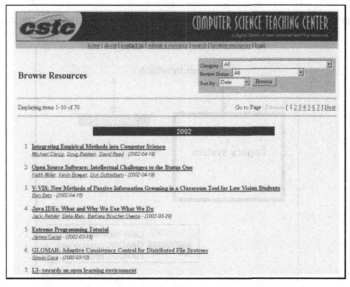

Fig. 4. User interface for the browsing function of CSTC

For early testing, these prototype components were all derived from the original OAI protocol rather than the XOAI protocol, to allow for the use of existing testing and validation tools like the Repository Explorer [20]. Thus, using response-level containers, such information was embedded into other unused fields in the responses. Later tests involving the Annotate and Review components were fully conformant with the respective protocols. Figure 6 is an architectural overview of a general-purpose threaded discussion board based on the ODL-Annotate protocol. Figure 7 illustrates the back-end component architecture of a peer-review system originally under development for the ACM Journal of Educational Resources in Computing.

This component is generally useful for e-journal publishing and is currently being adapted for integration into the CSTC system.

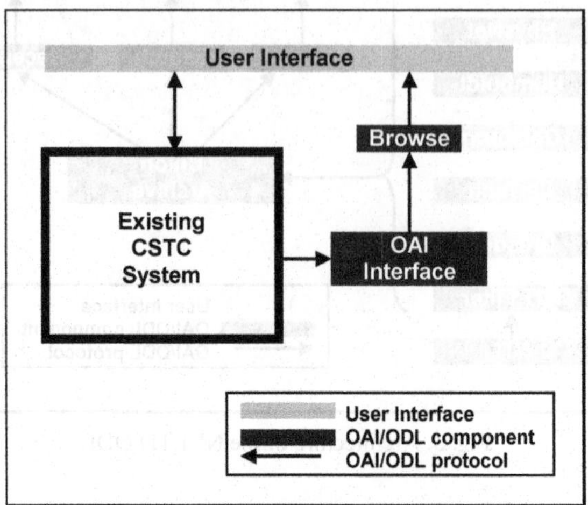

Fig. 5. Architecture of the CSTC system, incorporating Browse ODL component

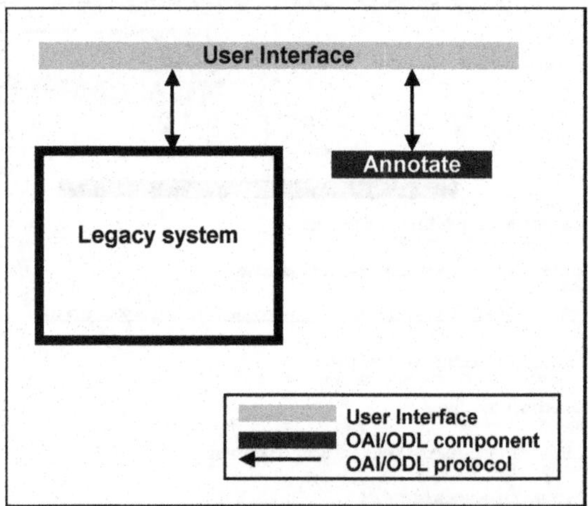

Fig. 6. ODL architecture of annotation system

6.2 Component Composition

The sequence of interactions corresponding to a typical use of a Search component is illustrated in Figure 8. The simplified ODL network consists of a source of data in the form of an OAI-compliant archive and a Search component. The user interface layer is made up of a client's Web browser and the Web server, with scripts to generate HTML pages and forward requests to the ODL network.

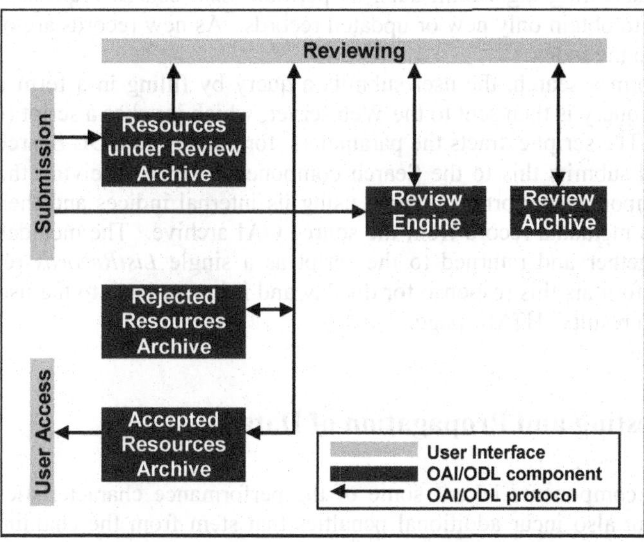

Fig. 7. ODL architecture of peer review system

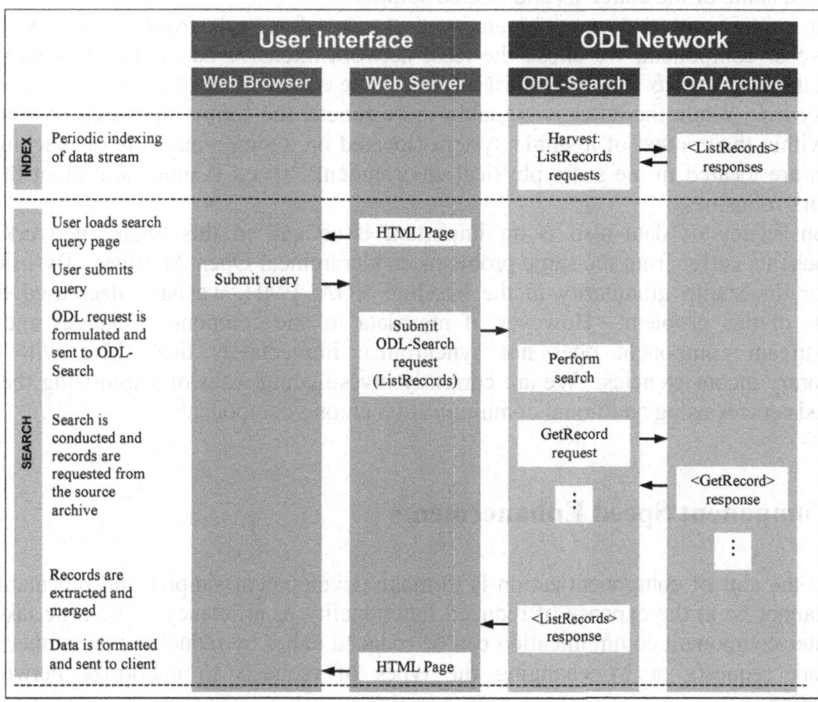

Fig. 8. Interface and component interaction during indexing and search operations

There are two functions performed: incremental indexing of the data and searching. In the former case, the Search component harvests data from the source archive using a typical harvesting algorithm, such as periodic *ListRecords* requests with the date range used to obtain only new or updated records. As new records are observed, they are added to the index.

To perform a search, the user submits a query by filling in a form on an HTML page. This query is then sent to the Web server, which invokes a script (or handler) to process it. The script extracts the parameters, formulates an ODL-Search *ListRecords* request and submits this to the Search component. Upon receiving the request, the Search component performs a search using its internal indices and then proceeds to obtain each metadata record from the source OAI archive. The metadata records are merged together and returned to the script as a single *ListRecords* response. The script then formats this response for display and it is sent back to the user in the form of a "search results" HTML page.

7 Harvesting and Propagation of Data

Interacting components inherit some of the performance characteristics of the OAI protocol, but also incur additional penalties that stem from the chaining together of components where each behaves asynchronously and, perhaps, remotely. We explored some of the concerns and related solutions.

For components that required an input stream of records from an OAI/XOAI archive or component, we chose the least network-intensive harvesting algorithm - using the *ListRecords* service request instead of the combination of *ListIdentifiers* and *GetRecord*. While the latter is arguably more robust, the former approach is faster, and within the context of a single system (located on a single machine or machines which are located in the same physical environment), speed is more important than network robustness.

Consistency of data also is an important issue and in this regard networked components suffer from the same problems as hierarchical Open Archives. By using a finer timestamp granularity in the baseline XOAI-PMH, we have decreased the effects of this problem. However, if metadata in one component changes and a downstream component does not synchronize immediately then there will be temporary inconsistencies. We are currently investigating ways of minimizing these inconsistencies using additional communication among components.

8 Component Speed Enhancements

While the aim of componentization is to make development simpler and repeatable, this cannot be at the expense of reduced functionality or efficiency. The time taken for inter-component communication can be reduced either by reducing the number of network requests or by changing the types of requests to maximize network utilization.

Various approaches were investigated to increase speed without sacrificing the advantages of a componentized system. The most successful and promising solutions found to maximize network utilization and minimize the processing delay normally associated with executing Web applications are discussed below.

8.1 Caching

Using caching at various levels within the experimental systems resulted in speed improvements. For example, the Browse component cached the results from the Union component, thus minimizing the number of recurring requests. Secondly, the user interface cached the responses to most requests; thus speeding up the process of browsing through a list of returned items. Together, these had a noticeable effect on system performance. One problem that manifested itself was that of stale data in a cache. It is still being investigated – there are ways to force a refresh from the Web browser to propagate to the server's scripts, but this apparently only works for Netscape browsers and works differently in each version.

8.2 FastCGI

FastCGI [4] is an add-on kit that provides persistent script capabilities to a Web server, independently of the programming language. Scripts need to be modified slightly by encapsulating them in a simple loop but this is relatively minor and for some components it was possible to create both regular and FastCGI versions without much change. FastCGI provides an add-on server module that loads a script on demand and keeps it persistent, with support for dynamic reloading and dynamic load balancing. This was tested for some components. There were additional security problems that needed to be resolved since FastCGI enforced a higher level of security than regular scripts, but better programming discipline and security is good for component development, so this can be seen as another advantage.

8.3 SpeedyCGI

Without modification to the Web server, it is possible for a component to stay resident in memory and be glued into the Web server whenever necessary by a much smaller program. This is the approach taken by the SpeedyCGI toolkit [19], which improves performance without any modification of the source code. Unlike the other approaches, this toolkit only worked with the Perl language, but the technique is generally applicable to any development environment.

8.4 Batch Requests

At a protocol level it is possible to reduce the number of requests by combining responses. In the ODL-Review protocol, the reviewable items visible to an editor are listed using *GetRecord* – the response is an XML container that contains within it many individual records. Similarly, the ODL-Union protocol may be extended in the future to support requesting multiple records with a single *ListRecords* request that specifies a combined list of identifiers encoded within a single set parameter.

9 Future Work and Conclusions

9.1 Development and Refinement of Component Libraries and Protocols

We have developed sample protocol designs for many existing digital library use cases, including searching, browsing, threaded discussions, peer review, recommendation, and rating systems. These and additional components will be integrated into existing and new DL systems to test for reusability and portability.

This set of designs will be re-evaluated in light of recent developments in the OAI-PMH. Some of the issues that currently need to be addressed by the XOAI protocol may be irrelevant if they are incorporated into a future OAI protocol, as we have suggested by way of our involvement in the OAI technical and steering committees. In addition, we will attempt to integrate our work with emerging standards in web-based services such as SOAP [3] and WSDL [15], which are expected to provide a general syntactic layer for high-level application protocols.

Our prototyping work has demonstrated some feasible component designs. These will be extended to other components, with additional generality introduced wherever possible. Further work will be done on separating instances of components from configuration information – ultimately allowing for the possibility of a suite of components servicing multiple DLs, and visual composition of components.

The VIDI protocol [25] for connecting visualization components to digital libraries is being independently developed to co-exist with and build upon ODL components.

9.2 Component Testing and Validation

Testing of the OAI protocol is largely supported by the Repository Explorer [20], which we developed specifically for the purposes of validation of requests and responses and standardization of implementations.

This software will be extended to support the additional functionality of the ODL protocols by building in support for the XOAI protocol. This tool would then support the development of components using the ODL protocols. Particular support for individual ODL protocols is also an option if the software can be specialized to test for more specific semantics based on specifications.

9.3 Evaluation

Further evaluation of the feasibility of building Digital Libraries as networks of extended Open Archives will be carried out in terms of their equivalence to monolithic systems, extensibility of components, and usability of the component model. Performance evaluation is an ongoing process, and further work is being done on:

- Communications and protocol overhead incurred by OAI/XOAI/ODL protocols.
- Stability of the communications protocols relative to the datestamp granularities – evaluation of the trade-off between duplication of records and the possibility of missing records.

- Speed of the ODL networks compared with monolithic systems.
- Storage required for components and the effects of data duplication.
- Consistency among various copies of data stored on different nodes.
- Harvesting algorithms and their efficiencies in terms of speed and network utilization.

9.4 Conclusions

It is hoped that the ongoing results of this work will change the way people build digital libraries, so they can utilize simple and reusable component models based on already established standards. In particular, we hope our work will help lead to "ODL-in-a-box" solutions that can be tailored to classes of applications, such as the National STEM Digital Library (www.nsdl.nsf.gov). Unlike other "DL-in-a-box" solutions like Eprints [8] and Repository-in-a-Box [18], ODL-based systems will be trivially extensible.

Building upon this foundation of extensibility, it then will be possible to work on providing more interesting services to users, thus bridging the wide gap between current research and production systems, and ultimately making information more accessible to people.

Acknowledgements. Thanks are given for the support of NSF through its grants: IIS-9986089, IIS-0002935, IIS-0080748, IIS-0086227, DUE-0121679, DUE-0121741, and DUE-0136690.

References

1. Baldonado, M., Chang, C. K., Gravano, L., and Paepcke, A. The Stanford Digital Library Metadata Architecture, in International Journal on Digital Libraries 1, 2 (1997), 108-121. Available http://www-diglib.stanford.edu/cgi-bin/get/SIDL-WP-1996-0051.
2. Birmingham, W. P. An Agent-Based Architecture for Digital Libraries, in D-Lib Magazine 1, 1 (July 1995). Available http://www.dlib.org/dlib/July95/07birmingham.html.
3. Box, D., Ehnebuske, D., Kakivaya, G., Layman, A., Mendelsohn, N., Nielsen, H. F., Thatte, S., and Winer, D. Simple Object Access Protocol (SOAP) v1.1, W3C Technical Note, (8 May 2000). Available http://www.w3.org/TR/SOAP/
4. Brown, M. R. FastCGI – A High-Performance Gateway Interface, position paper at "Programming the Web - a search for APIs" workshop, Fifth International World Wide Web Conference, (Paris, France, 6 May 1996). Available http://www.fastcgi.com/devkit/doc/www5-api-workshop.html
5. Clark, J. (editor) XSL Transformations Version 1.0, W3C Recommendation, (November 1999). Available http://www.w3.org/TR/xslt
6. Computer Science Teaching Center; www.cstc.org/. Accessed 26 June 2002
7. Dublin Core Metadata Initiative. Dublin Core Metadata Element Set Version 1.1: Reference Description, 1997. Available http://www.dublincore.org/documents/dces/.
8. EPrints; http://www.eprints.org/. Accessed 26 June 2002

9. Gladney, H., Ahmed, Z., Ashany, R., Belkin, N. J., Fox, E. A., and Zemankova, M. Digital Library: Gross Structure and Requirements (Report from a Workshop), IBM Almaden Research Center, Research Report RJ9840, May 1994. Available http://www.ifla.org.sg/documents/libraries/net/rj9840.pdf
10. Kahn, R., and Wilensky, R. A Framework for Distributed Digital Object Services, CNRI, 1995. Available http://www.cnri.reston.va.us/k-w.html.
11. Lagoze., C., and Davis, J. R. Dienst – An Architecture for Distributed Document Libraries, in Commun. ACM 38, 4 (April 1995), 47.
12. Lagoze, C., and Van de Sompel, H. The Open Archives Initiative: Building a low-barrier interoperability framework, in Proceedings of JCDL 2001 (Roanoke VA, June 2001), ACM Press, 54-62.
13. Leiner, B. M. The NCSTRL Approach to Open Architecture, in D-Lib Magazine 4, 11 (December 1998). Available http://www.dlib.org/dlib/december98/leiner/12leiner.html
14. Nichols, Bill. Open Meta Tools, in BYTE Magazine, 25 February 2002. Available http://www.byte.com/documents/s=7023/byt1014229948533/0225_nicholls.html
15. Ogbuji, U. Using WSDL in SOAP Applications, IBM developerWorks, (November 2000). Available http://www-106.ibm.com/developerworks/webservices/library/ws-soap/index.html
16. Paepcke, A., Brandriff, R., Janee, G., Larson, R., Ludaescher, B., Melnik, S., and Raghavan S. Search Middleware and the Simple Digital Library Interoperability Protocol, in D-Lib Magazine 6, 3 (March 2000). Available http://www.dlib.org/dlib/march00/paepcke/03paepcke.html
17. Payette, S., and Lagoze, C. Flexible and Extensible Digital Object and Repository Architecture, in Proceedings of Second European Conference on Research and Advanced Technology for Digital Libraries (Heraklion, Crete, Greece, September 21-23 1998), Springer, 1998, (Lecture notes in computer science; Vol. 1513).
18. Repository-in-a-Box; http://www.nhse.org/RIB/. Accessed 26 June 2002
19. SpeedyCGI; http://daemoninc.com/speedycgi/. Accessed 26 June 2002
20. Suleman, H. Enforcing Interoperability with the Open Archives Initiative Repository Explorer, in Proceedings of JCDL 2001, (Roanoke, VA, June 2001), ACM Press, 63-64.
21. Suleman, H., Atkins, A., Gonçalves, M. A., France, R. K., Fox, E. A., Chachra, V., Crowder, M., and Young, J. Networked Digital Library of Theses and Dissertations: Bridging the Gaps for Global Access - Part 1: Mission and Progress, and Part 2: Services and Research, in D-Lib Magazine 7, 9 (September 2001). Available http://www.dlib.org/dlib/september01/suleman/09suleman-pt1.html and http://www.dlib.org/dlib/september01/suleman/09suleman-pt2.html.
22. Suleman, H., and Fox, E. A. A Framework for Building Open Digital Libraries, in D-Lib Magazine 7, 12 (December 2001). Available http://www.dlib.org/dlib/december01/suleman/12suleman.html.
23. Suleman, H., and Fox, E. A. Beyond Harvesting: Digital Library Components as OAI Extensions, Technical Report, Department of Computer Science, Virginia Tech (January 2001).
24. Van de Sompel, H., and Lagoze, C. The Open Archives Initiative Protocol for Metadata Harvesting. Open Archives Initiative, 2001. Available http://www.openarchives.org/OAI_protocol/openarchivesprotocol.html.
25. Wang, Jun. VIDI: A Lightweight Protocol Between Visualization Tools and Digital Libraries, Master's Thesis, Virginia Tech (May 2002).

Exploring Small Screen Digital Library Access with the Greenstone Digital Library

George Buchanan[1], Matt Jones[2], and Gary Marsden[3]

[1]Interaction Design Centre, Middlesex University
g.buchanan@mdx.ac.uk
[2]Department of Computer Science, Waikato University
mattj@cs.waikato.ac.nz
[3]Department of Computer Science, University of Cape Town
gaz@cs.uct.ac.za

Abstract. In recent years, the use of small screen devices has multiplied rapidly. This paper covers a number of different issues which arise when digital libraries are used in combination with such displays. Known limitations of small screens are presented to the Digital Library community. Two evaluations of pilot small-screen DL systems are presented, with some unexpected cultural and socio-technical concerns which arose. The pilot systems also demonstrate the delivery of small-screen access using an existing popular DL system.

1 Introduction

The usual tool for interacting with digital libraries is a generic web browser on a standard desktop display. However, there are many circumstances where this norm is not going to hold. Many uses of small-screen devices as access tools to DLs are emerging. For instance, handheld computers, such as Palm and Pocket-PC devices, are increasingly being used for casual browsing alongside extended work co-ordination tasks by knowledge workers – typically, frequent users of digital libraries and web-published information. Secondly, the desk-based stereotype of the information worker is both historically biased and under attack from changing work practices. For example, in many sciences key work is performed out of doors, in areas where broadband network access or physically large displays are impracticable, and mains power supplies an expensive luxury. Thirdly, in much of the world, particularly where population and/or wealth is sparse, the absence of current fixed infrastructures for services such as power and communications, is leading to a leapfrog to wireless-based technologies.

These differing pictures of the use and users impact all forms of information services, from executive information systems in businesses to open, public, digital libraries. It is unsurprising, therefore, that the combination of small screen technology and digital libraries is of increasing significance; for instance, Cathy Marshall and Christine Ruotolo have recently presented a paper on small-screen reading at JCDL 2002 [20], and other mobile use of DLs was observed in [19].

M. Agosti and C. Thanos (Eds.): ECDL 2002, LNCS 2458, pp. 583-596, 2002.

This paper presents two separate pilot small-screen DL systems implemented on Greenstone. We include the evaluation of a novel presentation of search results, and a brief evaluation of the provision of DL access through small displays using the WAP protocol, which has different limitations to HTML-based access.

Our findings are not only of interest in the context of small screens – cultural and technical expectations of users significantly impacted the outcome of our evaluations.

2 Background and Overview

The New Zealand Digital Library project's main work has been on the open-source Greenstone Digital Library software [29]. Greenstone's adoption in a wide variety of organisations has lead to an exposure to a wide variety of uses. Recent related DL projects include information resources for field workers for Non-Governmental Organisations in isolated areas; and in Cape Town, South Africa, one of the authors has observed the widespread adoption of handheld devices by students - offering an opportunity for providing information more pervasively than with desktop-based access. Circumstances such as this have alerted us to the need to support small-screen devices.

As well as being involved in digital library research, we have also studied the issues of small-screen web use [2, 7, 8], particularly the improvement of browsing between documents. In the context of small-screen DL access, as in our earlier work, there is a need to separate the different factors involved in wireless and/or palmtop systems. Our interest is focussed upon the peculiarities of small screens alone. The wide variation of factors such as network communications (wireless, wired or none), input devices (pen, keyboard, keypad, touch-pad etc.) and form factor (handheld or embedded) cannot be successfully confounded with display size if generalisable understanding is required.

Our earlier research [15] demonstrates that techniques which give benefits to users of small screens can also benefit users of normal, desktop-sized displays. Therefore, discovering small-screen access techniques for digital libraries may result in novel and effective means of accessing digital libraries generally, which particularly benefit those working with less display capacity.

3 Small Screen Usability

With the recent growth in popularity of a variety of small-screen consumer devices, increasing attention has been given to the challenges of providing effective interaction through small displays. However, it would be inaccurate to believe that small screens are a recent novelty – they have long been used in Automatic Telling Machines at banks, visitor information systems at museums and controlling machine tools. Unsurprisingly, related research dates back to these earlier uses.

The recent mushrooming of mobile phone usage has rather clouded matters by synonymising „small screen" with handheld consumer technologies and very small displays.

It is worth clarifying what size of display we intend when we say „small screen". There are two primary types: micro-displays, more synonymous with mobile phones and containing only perhaps 80 letters in approximately 5 lines of text; and small-displays, common with Pocket-PC, Palm etc. handheld computers, containing approximately 500 or more characters in up to twenty lines of text depending on the screen orientation and text size. Compared to the capacity of the average desktop display, typically 7 to 12 thousand characters, either represents a significant loss of display capacity. Our recent work [4] indicates that some of the problems expected of micro-displays is not misplaced; however, we and others have demonstrated that small displays can be used with less penalty in terms of effectiveness (task time and success rate) than expected [7,8].

3.1 Reading on the Small Screen

A primary form, some may say the principal form, of activity in a digital library is the reading of documents. Studies of the reading of texts using small screens date back to their earliest uses. In various studies, including [9, 10, 23], researchers tested the reading rate and comprehension performance of users using various screen sizes and proportions (covering both small- and micro- displays). Consistently, researchers found no difference in comprehension rates across screen sizes [9]. The number of displayed lines of text little affected reading speed, with smaller displays reducing performance by 15% [24]. The only point at which the effectiveness of users dropped significantly was when the number of lines of text displayed was very small (4 lines of text or fewer), and particularly when only one line of text appeared. Line width had a bigger impact – a 25% drop in reading rate observed when the display was reduced to 1/3rd [10] – but, again, the speed of reading remained substantially similar to that on desktop-sized displays.

3.2 Access: Searching and Browsing

A second key component in digital libraries is the access to documents. This is traditionally achieved through two methods: firstly, the discovery of documents using a query; and secondly through the browsing of an organised hierarchy or list, such as topic or author indexes.

To take the latter first, the activity of browsing across and within documents on small displays has also been assessed. Swierenga [27] tested the performance of users choosing commands from a hierarchical list of selections, again with differing screen topologies. When small and large screens were compared, users achieved similar accuracy and speed on each display type.

However, menu and hypertext navigation are not the same. We wondered what the impact of screen size would be on hypertext browsing. We tested the difference when browsing a hypertext system with index, and discovered that task completion times and outcomes were poorer on small screens than on conventional desktop displays [14].

In response to this, we developed an outline-style interaction technique in which the topic tree could be expanded or contracted interactively by the user, before a final document selection was made. On small screens, the overall task completion times fell by 35% and success rates rose [15]. However, there were identifiable performance issues surrounding the structure of the hierarchy – large, 'flat' structures proving poorer than deeper, more balanced ones.

The study of interactive querying on small screens is, unlike the question of reading and browsing, considerably less researched. Some work has been done on adapting desktop visualisation methods (e.g. [26]) to small displays [12], and certain systems have been evaluated in isolation [7]. However, comparative studies of search tools are unavailable.

3.3 Summary

From existing studies of reading, we can be assured that the use of small screens does not mean per se that reading becomes ineffective. However, as Marshall and Ruotolo's recent studies [20] find, screen size may impact the purpose and form of reading done by users – small displays for casual, opportunistic reading, larger displays for more intensive study.

Our knowledge of information seeking on small displays is more varied: browsing on PDA-sized displays is covered, and the results are encouraging, though the use of very small displays requires further study. In the case of search, current scientific understanding is poorly developed.

In this paper, we will present an experiment to assess different presentation methods on small displays, and the outcome of initial studies of browsing and searching on micro-displays, widening the scope of available data.

4 Experimental Systems

In order to gain grounded data on small-screen use in DLs, we have developed two pilot systems built upon the open-source Greenstone DL software:

1) Providing outline-based searching on small screens §4.1
2) Browsing and Searching using WAP devices §4.2

These systems highlight distinct, yet complementary, aspects of small-screen use and usability. In creating them, we have observed some difficulties which may impact on the use of categories and outline presentations in DLs, both on small screens and generally.

The first system evaluates the use of category hierarchies and outliner interaction, successfully used in browsing, in the context of search and highlights some interesting learning effects.

The second implements a general DL system in a context more restricted than the internet, and unveils some cultural difficulties with classification and hierarchies.

4.1 LibTwig – An Outliner-Style DL Browse and Search Tool

LibTwig is a Greenstone-based DL implementation of our WebTwig browsing tool [15]. LibTwig, and an updated WebTwig, have been created to start to systematically evaluate a number of different alternative interaction styles for search tasks on small screens.

The interaction method for browsing is the same, outliner, style as WebTwig: the user browses over a hierarchical index, and can expand a category to reveal its component documents and sub-categories, or close it to leave just it's own title visible. Within a category, documents are listed in Greenstone's default, alphabetic, ordering. LibTwig also supports searching, with results given in one of two presentations: a reduced outline hierarchy containing only items and branches which match the search; or alternatively a traditional ranked list. In the case of the outline mode, the ordering of documents within categories is the same, alphabetical, order as when browsing.

If you refer to figure 1, the outline presentation, with categories partly (left) and fully (centre) expanded, can be compared to the ranked list display (right), with documents ranked by relevance, the most relevant at the top.

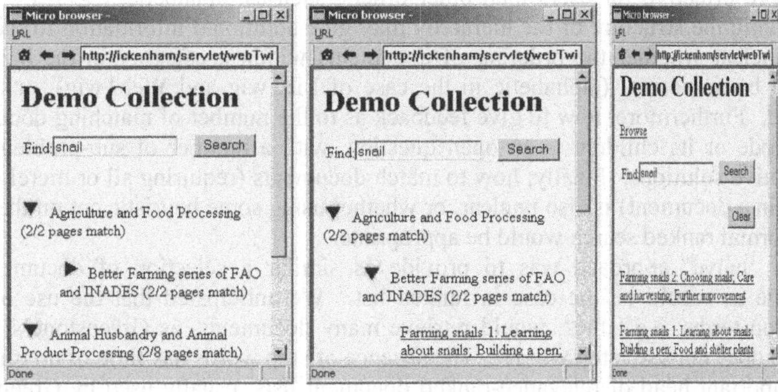

Fig. 1. LibTwig in use on the Greenstone Demo Collection. Left – Outline search; Centre – Outline search with category expanded and a document link visible; Right – Ranked List. The browser window is fixed to Pocket-PC display capacity.

Our initial study of patterns of information seeking by users of small-display devices [14], demonstrated that interactive search was the initial information seeking method for 80% of users – twice the rate on desktop displays. Thus, search is particularly important on the small-screen [4].

The use of an outline-style presentation for browsing tasks significantly benefited those using small displays, reducing task completion times and increasing success rates [15]. These benefits also occurred in a smaller degree when using desktop displays. Later alternative implementations of outline browsing on small screens, e.g. by Buyukkokten [6], have demonstrated similar results.

Given the benefits of an outline access method for browsing tasks, it is reasonable to hypothesise that such a presentation may also benefit interacting with search results. The Cluster hypothesis [23] predicts that most „real" matches for a search will be in a common classifier, so a corollary is that matches not in that category are probably less relevant. Therefore, the thematic division of results by subject category can improve the effective selectivity of the document review task [25].

With LibTwig, we have carried out a pilot study to evaluate the relative merits of a naïvely implemented version of the outline presentation of search results compared to the traditional ranked-list. Experimental systems which use some form of the outline search presentation exist. Some have been presented at DL conferences (e.g. [21]). However, usability evaluations of these have not been widely available.

Design and Implementation

LibTwig communicates with Greenstone through Greenstone's internal CORBA protocol [1], and utilises Greenstone's search facility. Greenstone is entirely a 'full text' digital library, and does not use 'stop words'. This affected our implementation decisions, as we shall see.

There are a number of alternative implementations of the outline search presentation. A significant problem which could be expected may be the loss of relevance information through the loss of ranking. It is well proven that ranked lists are more effective for users than other orders, such as alphabetic, e.g. [2]. Whilst preserving the structure of the hierarchy may give additional information to the user, it is unclear whether the ordering of documents within a category in the hierarchy should be as normal (alphabetic in the case of LibTwig and WebTwig), or ranked instead. Furthermore, how to give feedback as to the number of matching documents in a node or its children is an open question, with a number of sub-problems and alternative solutions. Finally, how to match documents (requiring all or merely some terms in a document) is also unclear, or whether using some heuristic cut on the score of a normal ranked search would be appropriate.

Our 'naïve' approach was to provide as similar a selection of documents as possible as would be the case in ranked list. We anticipated that the use of very common terms, e.g. „the", would retrieve many documents, as Greenstone's search engine does not use 'stop words'. The absence of stop words has little or no effect on the important head of relevance-ranked document lists, usually used by Greenstone, and so normally the lack of stop words has no effect. However, in the case of the 'outline' mode of presentation, relevance ranking is not used, and thus the negative effects of high retrieval would not be palliated. Therefore, to remedy this, search results were refined with a 'cut' on documents with extremely low scores, effectively reintroducing a basic level of 'stop word' provision.

The total number of matching documents within a category was given beside its name in the hierarchy. Documents were presented in the default, alphabetic, order, rather than ranked within each category by relevance score. Whilst the combined effect of these decisions was expected to be sub-optimal, the intent was to secure data towards the lower bound of performance when compared to ranked search.

Method

A panel of 12 subjects was recruited to perform an initial evaluation. All the subjects were regular library users, using a physical library once a month or more. Similarly, all were computer-literate, either owned or regularly used a mobile phone, and had some degree of experience of using the Web. A range of levels of web experience and library use were recruited. Ages ranged from 19 to 47, and the subjects were a mixture of students and staff in the department of Computing Science, Middlesex University. The material to be searched was selected as being of interest or potential interest, all subjects either studying of teaching the theme of the material (human-computer interaction); again, a range of expertise was recruited. Subjects were screened in advance to ensure a balance of subject expertise across sets of questions.

The collections used were built by end-users, not by expert librarians. Greenstone is in widespread use and many collections are not created by professional indexers. It is possible that using professionally indexed material would suggest benefits which were more related to the expertise of the librarian than the subject of our focus: the access method itself.

Subjects were given an initial training, using both the search presentations, and were then permitted an open-ended familiarisation period with each presentation style. Pre- and post- experiment questionnaires were taken.

A fixed panel of 10 questions was answered by each subject, five with each interface, and with the combination of question and interface balanced across subjects. The order of questions was also randomised to reduce any ordering effect. As with our previous experiments, some questions were more directive, others open ended. All questions had a set of appropriate target documents selected by a subject expert, of which the subjects were unaware. Subjects were invited to select appropriate documents, and had an open-ended time period to complete each question. The subject could choose to move onto another question at any time, though they could not later return to a question. Subjects were asked to give their opinion as to their degree of success on each question. Timings were taken of their performance, as was the number of target documents which they viewed, using a bespoke browser based on Internet Explorer which we have used in previous published experiments.

Results

Our first comparisons were of the time performance of users on each result presentation. Given the small sample size, and the pilot purpose of our study, results are generally indicative rather than inferential, and are seldom statistically significant.

Overall average times were within 10% of each other. Considering only those cases where the subject believed that they had succeeded, average times are virtually inseparable. As we have found previously, failure cases took significantly longer than successful tasks [17].

Table 1. Time comparisons for Ranked List and Outline presentations

	Presentation Mode	
Question Set	Ranked List	Outline
All questions	201	220
Answered questions	170	168
Failed questions	380	306

The small sample size and natural variation in timings between subjects and presentations does not account for the lack of statistical significance, however. Differences between two apparent sets of users contributed substantially to this, and identifying these two groups assists in identifying problems in the outline presentation.

Differing User Behaviours

Early in our analysis, a significant affect was observed from the frequency of web use rather than the length of web experience. Refer to Figure 2 below.

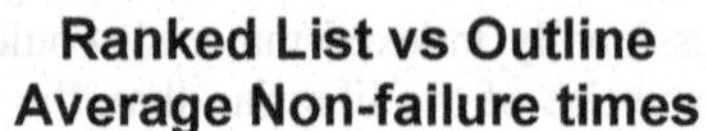

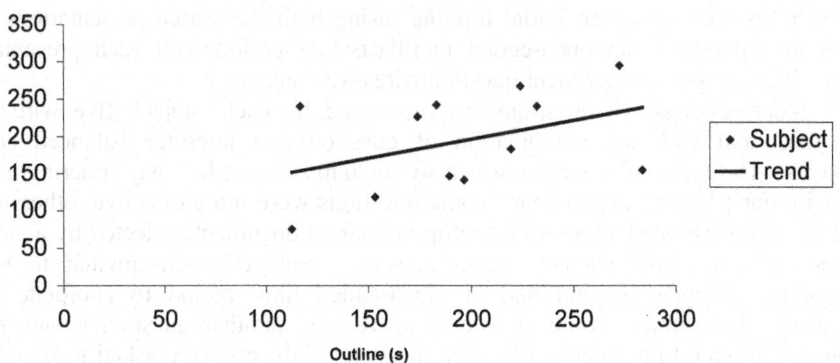

Fig. 2. Ranked List versus Outline time performance – successful and uncertain outcomes.

The average overall trend is plotted as a line – those who took longer with one method, also took longer with another. Six users, below the line, performed much better with ranked list than outline presentation – they all used the web for 10 or more hours per week (self-reported). Those above the line had comparable times in each mode, but average web use was 5 hours/week. The length of web experience was, however, similar – averaging four years (given the self-reporting here, further accuracy is misleading).

The intensive web users averaged 170 secs/question in ranked list mode. Their superior performance in this mode is perhaps unsurprising, as they may be more experienced with the presentation. However, they also experienced fewer failures – just four over all modes and questions. In outline mode, their task times were close to the non-intensive users, averaging 233 secs/question. Whilst completing the post-test questionnaire, three intensive users reported confusion over the difference between the two modes. Even permitting these users to use the tools again after the experiment did not clarify their understanding of the new outline presentation. When asked which presentation they preferred, most of the intensive users selected ranked list mode (4 versus 1, plus 1 abstention).

The non-intensive web users were slower in ranked list mode than outline mode – 244s against 218 secs/question. Furthermore, when successful in the outline presentation, they were faster than the intensive users – taking 188 seconds on average against 255 seconds for successful intensive users. Failures were much more common – 19 in all (nearly 33%) and the better speed achieved in outline mode was bought at a cost – 13 failures occurring in that presentation, twice as many as in ranked list mode. However, inspection of search terms used by the subjects illustrated that these users were much more prone to using stop words or very common words, resulting in larger sets of matching documents. As we shall see, common terms prove a problem even for the intensive users.

In the post-test questionnaire, four of the non-intensive group reported that the outline mode helped them find documents and that they got a „better picture" of the collection organisation and found related documents. The non-intensive web users unanimously preferred outline mode, though three reported problems understanding category headings.

Across these two groups, rates of reformulation (1.4 searches/question) and page viewing (2.8 documents/question) were virtually identical. Excluding the higher use of very common words by the non-intensive user group, query terms were also broadly similar. Commonplace words little affected the ordering of documents in ranked list mode. So, behavioural artefacts did not reflect differences in ranked list performance – perhaps indicating that intensive users took better advantage of the presentation.

General Presentation Differences

Considering the two presentations, failure rates differed from seven (12%) in ranked list mode to sixteen (27%) in outline mode. However, five failures in outline mode occurred on one question (two subjects being intensive users, and three non-intensive) – only one, intensive, user managed to successfully answer the question. All users used „web" or „website" in this search, on a collection about web usability, so these terms were poor distinguishers. In ranked list mode, common words had a minimal affect on the ordering of the top documents, and it is notable that of those using ranked list mode, all (three each of the intensive and non-intensive groups) successfully answered the question. On this one question in outline mode, 90% of documents matched, and one large category had over 200 matches. This poor selectivity degraded the task to browsing.

For every other question the rate of success varied by only one subject between the presentations. Overall, though significance can be gained on the failure rate at the 5% level, removing the outlier also results in a loss of significance, so the global measure cannot be unreservedly trusted.

In the post-test questionnaire, six subjects identified the (alphabetic) ordering of titles in Outline method as a problem, and asked for the documents within a category to be „sorted". Four subjects reported problems with (original author) document titles.

Evaluation

Given the naïve implementation of Outline mode, we expected it to be considerably poorer than ranked list mode. The widespread use of the ranked list presentation also meant that any novel method would be disadvantaged at first comparison, and a brief training was unlikely to counterbalance this. However, overall the outline presentation compared well, particularly for the non-intensive web users, with whom it was popular.

Clearly the current design can be improved – ranking within categories when searching as suggested by the subjects – and focussing attention on fewer, more relevant documents. The good success rate of experienced users with outline mode showed that outline mode need not impede successful searching.

In the case of the problem question noted above, normally modestly selective words („web" and „website") were common in the context of the collection being searched. This clearly impacted intensive users (half of all their failures occurring on this one question). Our non-intensive users, using more common terms generally, no doubt suffered their higher failure rate in outline mode as a consequence of the same underlying problem.

Thus, improved precision should improve performance of the outline mode for all groups.

However, in the problem question, the hierarchical structure of the collection was also a problem – one category, in which a number of the best matches occurred, had two hundred documents in it (excluding sub-categories). We have previously observed a drop in performance of the use of hierarchies in browsing tasks when such broad, flat structures occur [15], so that the same phenomenon reappearing in browsing must clearly also be a factor. Though in this case, an improved search method would have reduced the number of items in that category considerably, this may not always be the case. Thus, using Dumais and Chen's approach of only displaying the top five hits (or some other reduced selection) initially in a category, and permitting the user to request to see all the matches, may provide improved performance [8].

Previous experimental work with outline-style presentation of search results has given variable outcomes; for instance Chen and Dumais [8] report an improvement when compared to ranked list displays, whereas the evaluation of the use of clustering systems for accessing search results, e.g. [13], is much less encouraging. In the case of Dumais and Chen's study, the subjects in that case are described as „intermediate" users – and their profile is similar to our subjects whose web use was moderate. Dumais and Chen's system also contains features, such as ranking by relevance within each category, which may well improve on our current performance.

The benefit of topical browsing noted by four of our subjects echoes similar comments by users in a study of a system for clustering search results by Hearst [13].

Thus, there is clearly reason to develop the outline presentation further so that a more certain and precise comparison of an improved method can made with ranked list results. Comparative studies using standard desktop-sized displays also need to be undertaken.

Key questions surround the intensive web users. Clearly, their existing skills did not translate well to the outline method, and the clear confusion of half of this group is perplexing. Can their lack of comprehension be improved? If not, then will performance with the outline mode be permanently affected? If such effects are emerging, there are significant impacts on the future direction of information seeking research – alternative presentations finding adoption harder.

4.2 DL Access via WAP

To work, an outliner based interface into a digital library obviously requires understanding of both libraries and hierarchical document structures. Our research in South Africa has shown that this understanding may not be taken for granted.

Providing people in developing countries with information is difficult – books are relatively expensive and distribution is problematic. However, many of these nations have highly developed cellular networks – e.g. 22% of South Africa's population have a cellular handset, yet only 11% have sufficiently high wages to pay income tax [18]. Within SA, we therefore undertook a study to see if we could provide DL access using WAP technology.

A second challenging issue is the general lack of library experience in South Africa. Studies of other groups in which library exposure is low, such as the Maori of New Zealand [11], observe negative impacts on DL usability.

The system used the same outline-style access as described in the section on LibTwig above. Nodes in the hierarchy could be expanded and contracted just as in an outliner. Indentation was used to emphasise the tree structure visually. The hierarchies of the library and documents were used as one continuous hierarchy, so within a category, expanding a document would list its chapters, expanding a chapter would give its sections, etc., until actual body text was revealed.

The system's usability was assessed through a series of evaluations involving typical end-users as study subjects with handheld (small- rather than micro-display) devices. See Fig. 3. below for an overall impression of the system in use.

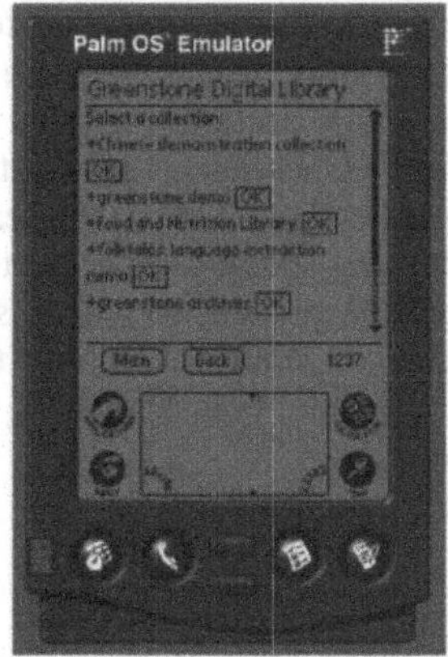

Fig.3. Greenstone's WAP interface in use through a Palm-OS Wireless Simulator – used here for image clarity.

As expected, there were some trivial usability problems which would be expected on almost any WAP-based system. One particular difficulty was users not identifying when scrolling was possible. As result, often only the first part of a longer document would be read. When questioned about why they had not scrolled, subjects reported being unaware that any more information was available. In part this appeared to be due to the small size of the scroll bars presented by WAP systems; the level of visibility is too low, more or less eliminating feedback to the user. However, this also correlates to difficulties observed when subjects were using large-screen devices with a variety of DL systems [3] – even subjects with extensive web and application experience repeatedly failed to scroll down, and repeatedly failed to observe that scrolling was possible. It would seem that a key component of DL usability, particularly on smaller screen devices, is the requirement for the browser to better support reader awareness that scrolling is possible.

On a more profound level, subjects also seemed to struggle with the concept of hierarchical access, contrary to our previous experience of the use of the outline-browsing method of access. The concept of a strict hierarchy seems alien to some cultures as shown by further studies wherein our target user group were unable to draw simple hierarchies such as a family tree [28]. This echoes findings of cultural difficulties in DLs amongst the Maori [11].

Besides the problems in understanding general hierarchical organisations, we conducted a further set of studies with the full Greenstone system on a desktop computer to see if there were problems unique to Greenstone.

Again, browsing was a problem, there appeared to be problems with even basic metaphors and structures such as indexes, chapters, sections. . Many of our subjects had never been to a library before attending university and the distinction between sections and chapters was lost on them. Consequently, they were confused by the behaviour of the interface as sometimes clicking on an icon (e.g.) chapter would give them text to read, and at other times (e.g. collection) would give them more icons.

Finally, when clicking on a heading that contained only body text, users clearly expected the hierarchy to disappear, and the content text only to appear, an expectation perhaps related to their experience on web sites.

This same phenomenon occurred in a slightly different form when searching. An individual result of a search, partially due to Greenstone's full text search facility alluded to earlier, could be anything from an entire document (many individual sections matching), down to a single section (no other matches occurring in another section of the same document). Clicking on a result could result in a variety of responses, from a list of chapter headings (where the result is an entire document), to body text (the result was a section). Again, users expected body text only.

Clearly, there are significant questions as to which issues here are related to small screens, or are particularly acute on small screens, or those which are, on the other hand, cultural issues. Overall, there was surprising symmetry between usability issues on the small and large screens.

Further results of this work are reported in [16].

5 Conclusion and Future Work

In implementing and evaluating these two tools, some common themes have emerged, particularly in regard to the use of hierarchies and outliners. Outliner interactions have provably improved small-screen browsing, and are candidate forms of search access too. However, cultural incomprehensibility and (in the context of searching) learned expectations, may limit or eliminate the benefits of hierarchies.

In the case of WAP access, work first needs to be done to address the cultural issues uncovered first before re-evaluation at Cape Town, whilst the existing system is evaluated in a context where users are more familiar with library metaphors.

The outline presentation of search needs improvements which should make comparison to ranked presentations clearer. Knowledge of the possible training effects of web use can now better inform our experimental methods. The impact of hierarchical search result presentation on desktop displays also needs pursuing, within its own merits and as a comparison against small-screen use. However, the strong preconceptions of search held by advanced users, and their strongly developed skills with ranked list presentation, may result in the outline presentation being less effective for them.

References

1. Bainbridge, D., Buchanan, G., McPherson, J., Jones, S., Mahoui, A., Witten, I. : Greenstone as a Platform for Distributed Digital Library Publications. Proc. European Conference on Digital Libraries, 137–148. Springer-Verlag (2001).
2. Belkin, N.J. et al. Using relevance feedback and ranking in interactive searching. In Harman, D. (ed.) TREC-4 Proceedings of Fourth Text Retrieval Conference. Washington, D.C., 181-209 (1996).
3. Blandford, A., Stelmaszewska, H., Bryan-Kinns, N.: Use of multiple digital libraries: a case study. JCDL 2001: 179-188
4. Buchanan G. & Jones, M. (2000). Search interfaces for handheld mobile devices. Poster proceedings 9th International Conference on the World Wide Web.
5. Buchanan, G., Farrant, S., Jones, M., Thimbleby, H., Marsden, G., Pazzani, M.J.: Improving mobile internet usability. WWW 2001:673-680
6. Buyukkokten, O., Garcia-Molina, H., Paepcke, A. & Winograd, T. (2000). Power browser: efficient Web browsing for PDAs. Proc. ACM CHI 2000, pp 430 – 437.
7. Buyukkokten, O., Garcia-Molina, H. & Paepcke, A., Focused web searching with PDAs. Proc. of WWW 9 (2000). pp213-230.
8. Chen, H., Dumais, S.T.: Bringing order to the Web: automatically categorizing search results. Proc. Of ACM CHI 2000: pp 145-152.
9. Dillon, A., Richardson, J. and McKnight, C. (1990). The effect of display size and text splitting on reading lengthy text from the screen, Behaviour and Information Technology, 9(3):215–227.
10. Duchnicky, R. L. and Kolers, P. A., (1983). Readability of text scrolled on visual display terminals as a function of window size, Human Factors, 25:683–692.
11. Duncker, E., Cross-cultural Usability of the Library Metaphor, Joint Conference on Digital Libraries 2002, in press.
12. Dunlop, M. D. & Davidson, N. (2000) Visual information seeking on palmtop devices. Vol. II Proc. BCS HCI 2000, 19-20.
13. Hearst, M. A. and Pedersen J. O. Reexamining the Cluster Hypothesis: Scatter/Gather on Retrieval Results. Proc. 19th ACM SIGIR Conference on Research and Development in Information Retrieval. 1996. 76-84
14. Jones, M, Marsden, G., Mohd-Nasir, N, Boone, K, & Buchanan, G. (1999) Improving web interaction in small screen displays. Proceedings of Web 8 conference, 51–59
15. Jones, M, Mohd-Nasir, N & Buchanan, G (1999). Evaluation of WebTwig — a site outliner for handheld Web access. International Symposium on Handheld and Ubiquitous Computing, Karlsrhue, Germany. Gellerson, H-W (Ed.), Lecture Notes in Computer Science 1707:343–345, Springer-Verlag.
16. Jones, M., Buchanan, G., Thimbleby, H., Sorting out Searching on Small Screen Devices, Conference on Mobile HCI, Sept. 2002, In press.
17. Marsden, G., Cherry, R. & Hafele, A. Small Screen Access to Digital Libraries. 2nd South African Conference on Human-Computer Interaction (CHI-SA2001). South Africa. (Electronic proceedings).
18. Marsden, G.: Subverting Technology: Meeting User Needs in a Developing Economy, Social Issues Column, SIGCHI Bulletin, March/April 2002, pp 8.
19. Marshall, C.C., Price, M.N., Golovchinsky, G., and Schilit, B.N. (1999) Introducing a digital library reading appliance into a reading group. Proc. ACM DL'99 (Berkeley, CA, August 11-14), pp. 77-84.
20. Marshall, C.C. and Ruotolo, C. Reading-in-the-Small: a study of reading on small form factor devices. To appear in Proceedings of the Joint IEEE and ACM Conference on Digital Libraries (JCDL02), Portland, Oregon, July 14-18, 2002.
21. Palmer, C.R., et al,: Hierarchical Document Clustering of Digital Library Retrieval Results, Proceedings of the Joint Conference on Digital Libraries, 2001, p.451.

22. Paynter, G.W., Witten, I.H., Cunningham, S.J. and Buchanan, G. (2000): Scalable browsing for large collections: a case study. Proc Fifth ACM Conference on Digital Libraries, San Antonio, TX, pp. 215—223.
23. C.J. van Rijsbergen: Information Retrieval. Butterworths, London, second edition, 1979.
24. Shneiderman, B.,: User Interface Design and Evaluation for an Electronic Encyclopaedia: In Salvendy, G. (Ed.), Cognitive Engineering in the Design of Human-Computer Interaction and Expert Systems, Elsevier Science, 1987, pp 207-223.
25. Shneiderman, B., Byrd, D. & Croft, B (1998). Sorting out searching. Communications of the ACM, 41(4):95–98.
26. Shneiderman, B., Feldman, D., Rose, A., and Grau, X.F. Visualizing Digital Library Search Results with Categorical and Hierarchical Axes. in Proceedings of Digital Libraries 2000 (San Antonio TX, June 2000), ACM, 57-65.
27. Swierenga, S. J. (1990) Menuing and scrolling as alternative information access techniques for computer systems: interfacing with the user, Proc. Human Factors Society, 34th Annual Meeting, Vol. 1:356–359.
28. Walton, M., Marsden, G., Vukovic, V.: Visual Literacy as Challenge to the Internationalisation of Interfaces: A Study of South African Student web users, ACM CHI 2002 Extended Abstracts pp350-351
29. Witten, I. H., Nevill-Manning, C.G., McNab, R., & Cunningham, S.J.: (1998) A public digital library based on full-text retrieval: collections and experience, Communications of the ACM, 41(4). 71–75.

Daffodil: An Integrated Desktop for Supporting High-Level Search Activities in Federated Digital Libraries*

Norbert Fuhr[1], Claus-Peter Klas[1], André Schaefer[2], and Peter Mutschke[2]

[1] University of Dortmund
{fuhr,klas}@ls6.cs.uni-dortmund.de
[2] Social Science Information Centre, Bonn
{schaefer,mutschke}@bonn.iz-soz.de

Abstract. DAFFODIL is a digital library system targeting at *strategic support* during the information search process. For the user, mainly high-level search functions, so-called stratagems, implement this strategic support, which provide functionality beyond today's digital libraries. Through the tight integration of stratagems and with the federation of heterogeneous digital libraries, DAFFODIL reaches a high synergy effect for information and services. These effects provide high-quality metadata for the searcher through an intuitively controllable user interface. The visualisation of stratagems is based on a strictly object-oriented tool-based model. This paper presents the graphical user interface with a particular view on the integration of stratagems to enable *strategic support*.

1 Introduction

Today's digital library (DL) systems offer a large variety of functions for accessing their content. However, most of these systems are restricted to a single database, whereas federated DL systems provide only minimum searching and browsing capabilities. The high-level structure of the set of functions offered is either missing or more system-oriented. Finally, the interaction style of these systems is rather restricted (i.e. by using forms and menus only). Most of them do not support direct manipulation operations (like e.g. Drag&Drop), which would make the interaction more effective. In order to overcome these deficiencies, we have developed the DAFFODIL[1] system which provides solutions to the three problems mentioned above.

DAFFODIL is a federated DL system that offers a rich set of functions across a heterogeneous set of DLs (see [1] for a description of the architecture). The current prototype integrates 10 DLs in the area of computer science. Since different DLs may contain various pieces of information about the same publications, the federation yields important synergies for the user.

---

* Funded by the German Science Foundation (DFG) as part of the research initiative "Distributed Processing and Delivery of Digital Documents".

[1] **D**istributed **A**gents **f**or User-**F**riendly Access **o**f **Di**gital **L**ibraries

M. Agosti and C. Thanos (Eds.): ECDL 2002, LNCS 2458, pp. 597–612, 2002.

For structuring the functionality, we employ the concept of high-level search activities for strategic support as proposed by Bates [2]. Based on empirical studies of the information seeking behaviour of experienced library users, Bates distinguishes four levels of search activities. Whereas typical information systems only support low-level search functions (so-called moves), Bates introduced three additional levels of strategic search functions:

- A *tactic* is one or a handful of moves made to further a search. For example, breaking down a complex information need into subproblems, broadening or narrowing a query are tactics applied frequently.
- A *stratagem* is a complex set of actions (comprising different moves and/or tactics) exercised on a single domain (e. g. citation database, tables of contents of journals). Examples for stratagems are subject search (searching for all documents referring to this subject), citation search (find all documents citing / cited by a given article) or journal run (browse through issues or complete volumes of a relevant journal).
- A *strategy* comprises a complete plan for satisfying an information need. Thus, it typically consists of more than one stratagem (e. g. perform a subject search, browse through relevant journals and then find the documents cited by the most important articles).

Strategic support during the information search process is the fundamental concept implemented within DAFFODIL. High-level search functions, based on the stratagem level, implement this strategic support for the user and provide functionality beyond today's digital libraries. To our knowledge, DAFFODIL is the first implementation of Bates' ideas.

For visualising the strategic support, we use an object-oriented tool-based model with direct manipulation. On the desktop, the set of available stratagems is represented as a set of tools. A tool can be invoked in several ways, e. g. by dragging a DL object onto it.

The design of DAFFODIL offers a wide range of synergies, starting from the information sources up to the visualisation, whereby an optimal, strategy-supported information search process is presented to the user. Furthermore, the synergies are extended through a tight integration of stratagems, e. g. by using Drag&Drop mechanisms or links to external information sources.

In the remainder of this paper, we describe the user interface, along with the main features of the DAFFODIL desktop. Furthermore, we give a survey over the set of stratagems currently available, by describing typical use cases. We present two evaluations, performed during the DAFFODIL project, before related work is discussed in section 4. The paper ends with a conclusion and outlook.

2 Daffodil Integrated Desktop Design

In this section we describe the DAFFODIL desktop, the conceptual design model and the tools we integrated into the workplace.

2.1 High-Level Search Activities

The DAFFODIL architecture is structured according to the levels of search activities named above. Each agent fulfills a function at a certain level and can invoke functions on its own or lower levels.

1. On the *move* level, *wrappers* connect to various DLs or services like thesauri or spell-checkers. The heterogeneity problem is addressed, by mapping the external data into a homogeneous XML metadata format.
2. The *tactic* level provides simple strategic actions by combining appropriate moves. For example, co-author search performs a search for all publications of an author and extracts the co-authors; in parallel, the corresponding function of HOMEPAGE-SEARCH[2] is employed, and then the results of the two steps are merged.
3. *Stratagems* provide domain specific depth-search-functionality, by applying tactics to a set of similar items, like e. g. journals (*journal run*). The available stratagems are fully described in section 2.4.

Strategies are not supported by DAFFODIL automatically, yet. Instead the user is enabled to work much more strategy-oriented, by applying the high level functions of the *stratagems* and *tactics.* To offer these services in a user-friendly way, we needed to fulfill the following requirements:

- integrate distributed services and software agents in a consistent manner,
- provide tool chains to enable users to combine different services,
- ensure a flexible work flow,
- hide complexity.

For addressing these issues, we used the WOB[3] model, which is described below. Section 2.3 outlines DAFFODIL's user interface tools. Section 2.4 discusses how central stratagems are provided by its desktop.

2.2 The WOB Model

The *WOB* model for user interface design is based on the tool metaphor [3]. It attempts to solve the inherent contradictions in the interface design process — like that between flexible dialog control and conversational prompting — using a set of co-ordinated ergonomic techniques. It tries to fill the conceptual gap between interface style guides[4] and generic international standards[5]. The general software ergonomic principles of the *WOB* model are:

[2] `http://hpsearch.uni-trier.de/`

[3] German acronym for "object oriented directly manipulative graphical user interface based on the tool metaphor"

[4] like the Java Look and Feel Guidelines [4]

[5] like e. g. ISO 13407: "Human-centred design processes for interactive systems"

- *Strict Object Orientation and Interpretability of Tools*
  Strongly related functionality of the system is encapsulated in tools that are displayed as icons (not as menus). The tools open *views*, which are 'normal' dialog windows. Due to well-defined *dialog guidelines*, the chain of views a user is working on can be interpreted as a set of forms to be filled. In contrast, experienced users will prefer the tool view, which enables them to perform tasks more quickly; however, this view is cognitively more complex, and it is not required for interpretation.
  The user can manipulate objects on the surface in a direct manipulative manner. It is essential that consistency is guaranteed for the direction of the manipulation. Thus, the model requires object-on-object interaction style with a clear direction and semantics. The generally recommended interaction style is as follows: To apply a function on an item, the latter has to be dragged to a *tool*.
- *Dynamic Adaptivity*
  The interface adapts its layout and content always to the actual state and context. This is mostly used for a reduction of complexity in non-trivial domains, like browsing simultaneously in several relevant hierarchies at once. For example, the user may set the relevant context by choosing a classification entry; when activating the journal catalogue as the next step, the journals are filtered according to the valid classification context, to reduce complexity.
- *Context Sensitive Permeability*
  When known information is reusable in other contexts, it will automatically be reused.
- *Dialog Guidelines*
  The views of the tools are functionally connected e. g. by means of action buttons, hypertext links or rules which are triggered by plan recognition. A tool can also open its view proactively if the user needs its function in a given situation.
- *Intelligent Components*
  Tools and controls in the interface have access to context and state, in order to decide, if their function is valuable for the user. If applicable, they shall interact pro-actively with the user or the shared environment (the desktop), respectively.

Two principles of the model are information system-specific:

- *Status Display with Edit Mode*
  The system shall always display a paraphrase of the current state for the user. It can be shown as a natural or formal language string or even by using some visual formalism (like a table). The most obvious use case is query formulation. With a form-based interface some aspects (e. g. boolean operators) are always hidden. Thus, DAFFODIL also displays the paraphrase (i.e. the formal query) in order to prevent the user from forgetting parts of his/her query (re-)formulation. It enables easy access to all aspects of the systems state, e. g. for iterative query formulation. Novice users can learn

details from the paraphrase they would otherwise have to guess. They also can see if the system interprets their input in the way they expect it to.
- *Iterative Retrieval and Query Transformation*
Initial query formulations tend to be inadequate for the user's intentions, due to uncertainty or unconscious goals in the search process. Therefore applications shall simplify iterative query formulation for the user. This can be achieved e. g. by summarising the query when displaying results. Furthermore, methods for automatic transformation have to be provided, in order to address the 'zero result' problem and to allow for the handling of semantic or syntactical heterogeneity of underlying data sources.

In accordance with the *Dialog Guidelines* principle, a particular feature of DAFFODIL's interface is *Multi-Level-Hypertext* [5] interaction that allows for switching the level of information, e. g. from a document to the journal or to the authors institution or homepage. External links are provided for giving strategic support when DAFFODIL's services supply no results. In these cases, queries for external search engines like Google[6] or HPSearch[7] are generated dynamically and executed from within DAFFODIL. This results in an external browser being invoked, where interaction may continue.

2.3 Daffodil's Tools

DAFFODIL's high-level search activities, as outlined above, have been designed in close accordance with the *WOB* model as a range of tools that are integrated into a common workspace environment. The goal of DAFFODIL's desktop is to provide an environment to allow for retrieval, search and browse tasks, as well as collation, organisation and reuse of the retrieved information in a user-friendly way.

When the user first sees the desktop, the most frequently used tool is open. The default setting opens the search tool, but this setting is user-specific and will be made a personal choice or part of the user's profile. The user has free choice which tool to use first. It is possible to start browsing journals before using the search tool to commit a fielded search. Typical desktop states can be seen in Figures 1 to 3.

The tools built so far include:

- *Search tool*, to specify the search domain, set filters and compose queries. The queries are broadcasted to a set of distributed information services (via agents and wrappers). Integrated result lists are displayed for navigation and detail inspection.
- *Reference Browser*, which can be invoked by dropping document items on it. Citation indexes (like e. g. NEC ResearchIndex) are consulted to find references to and from the given item.

[6] http://www.google.de
[7] http://hpsearch.uni-trier.de

- *Classification Browser*, to allow hierarchical topic-driven access to the information space. It enables browsing of classification schemes like e. g. the ACM Computing Classification System.
- *Thesaurus Browser*, to transform search terms to broader or narrower terms. Subject-specific or Web-based thesauri, like e. g. *WordNet*[8], are used for finding related terms. Items can be used via Drag&Drop to another tool.
- *Author Network Browser*, to compute and browse co-author networks for a list of given authors. The list can be either typed or given by dropping a document item on the tool.
- *Journal Browser*, to search for a journal title and browse many journal directories, often with direct access to meta-data or the full-text of articles.
- *Conference Browser*, to search for a conference title and browse conference proceedings. The full-texts are directly accessible from within the tool, provided they are available in any of the DLs connected.
- *Personal Library* which stores DL objects in personal or group folders, along with the possibility of enabling awareness for these items.

This list is not comprehensive. However, the desktop has been designed to be easily extensible such that further tools and services can be added in the future. Due to limitation of resources, we implemented the most popular functionality so far. The focus of DAFFODIL lies on the integration of services (tools) and high-level functionality as described in the following section. This integration supports free choice of the search strategy and helps to provide the right functionality at the right time. Note that all tools can be used as starting points for search activities.

2.4 Stratagems on the Desktop

A major focus of DAFFODIL is to provide the user with high-level search services, called *stratagems* (sec. 2.1). Stratagems in DAFFODIL provide a segmentation of functionality (e.g. functions useful for searching and browsing journal articles). They provide depth searches, which are frequently needed and empirically observed in information seeking behaviour (e. g. [6,7]), and exhaustively exploit the data structures of a single domain.

For the interface, we put particular emphasis on the fact that browsing and searching stratagems can be combined in a natural way. Furthermore, domain-specific properties are preserved which otherwise would have been abstracted due to heterogeneity and integration needs. In the following, we show how major stratagems of DAFFODIL can be used at its desktop.

The interactions between the DAFFODIL tools are based upon the observation that users frequently tend to initiate their strategic work with a generic or vague initial query; for this purpose, they use standard search methods, e. g. by *subject search* or *area scan*. The initial result set produced this way is usually not satisfactory.

[8] `http://www.cogsci.princeton.edu/~wn/`

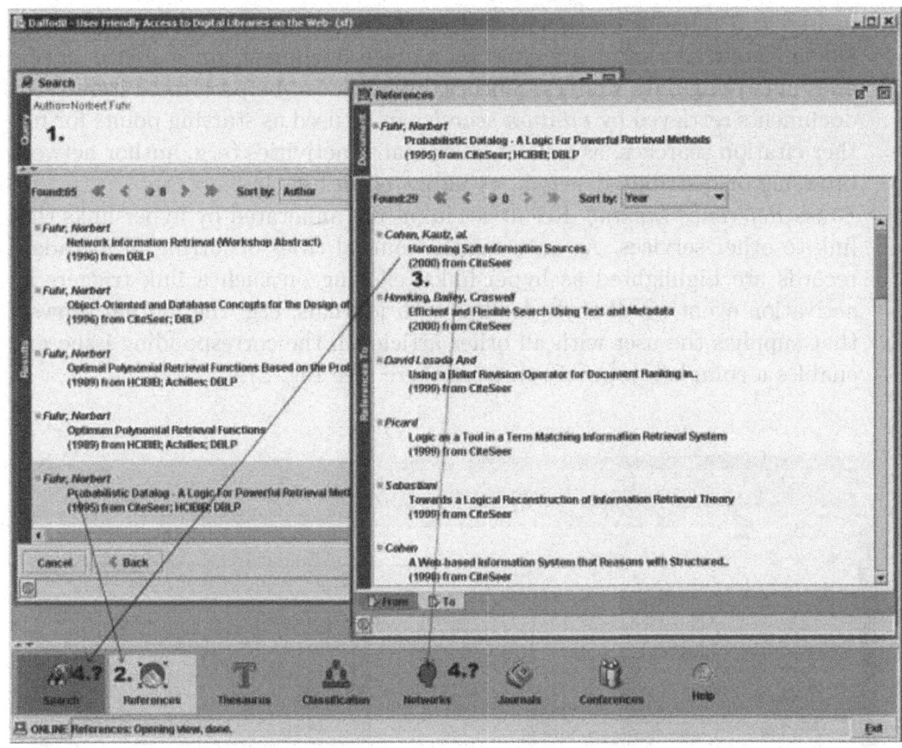

Fig. 1. Using the Citation Search for Known Item Instantiation strategies.

In Figure 1, the user started with a simple fielded search, giving a known author's name. Seeing the results he chose one entry and dragged it to the citation browse tool. He is presented the citing and cited documents, sourced from a citation index. From here he has again the free choice to continue iteratively inside the citation tool, formulate a new fielded query with the search tool, or compute a coauthors network for the authors in one of the documents. The choice is illustrated by the question mark in the Figure. Transition between the tools can be done by a drag and drop action. Accepting tools signal their acceptance by showing a green border on *drag-over.* In future the system may be enabled to give active help regarding the most promising choice for the next step. The system will learn about the most promising path by individual observation of chosen paths and the yielded results.

So at any point in the work flow, users may want to to initiate further searches on the basis of the current result. For this, two scenarios are provided by DAFFODIL:

– *Citation Search.* A typical example is to invoke a KNOWN ITEM INSTANTIATION strategy [8]: An interesting item was recognised to be relevant, and is being dropped on another tool to bring up further results. As illustrated in Fig. 1, a relevant document is dragged to the tool for citation tracking. Documents that cite or are cited by a given document are searched in several underlying data sources. Since stratagems can be performed iteratively, documents retrieved by *citation search* can be used as starting points for further citation searches, as well as other search activities (e. g. author network browsing or distributed search, as indicated in Fig. 1).

– *Cross Reference Linking.* Result set items are annotated by hyper-links that link to other services. As an example, journal titles occurring in metadata records are highlighted as hyper-links; clicking on such a link triggers an activation event to all tools dealing with journals, e. g. the journal browser that supplies the user with all other articles in the corresponding issue and enables a complete journal run from there (see Fig. 2).

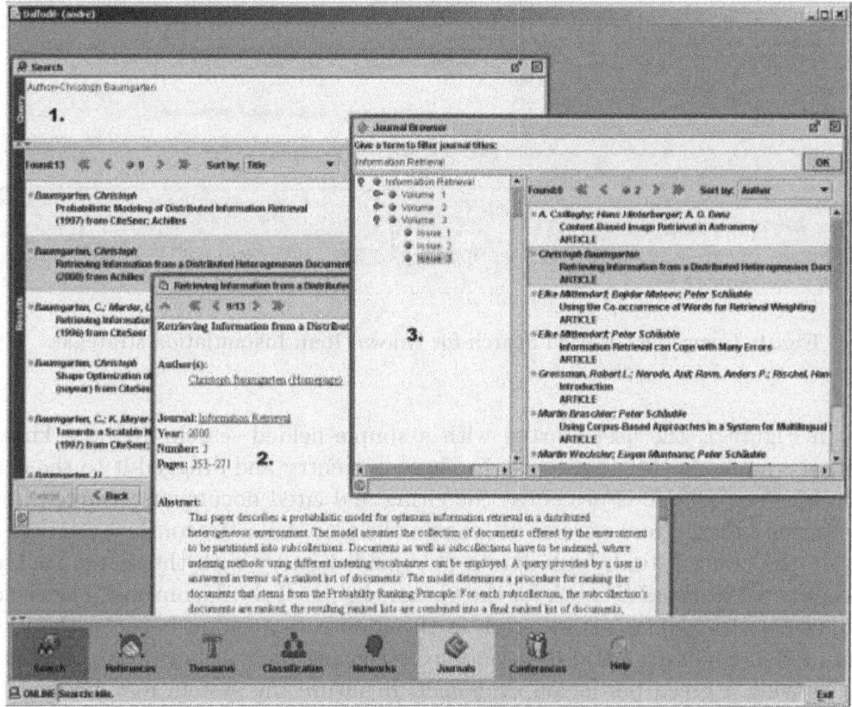

Fig. 2. Browsing for journal articles, following a link from an items detail view.

– *Author network based stratagems*, which are discussed in more detail in [9], address the interaction among the actors of scientific work and their strategic position in scientific collaboration networks. The central scenarios provided by DAFFODIL's interface are:

(1) *Author network browse:* When a user detects relevant documents in a result set, s/he can drop their authors onto the author network browser to

explore their collaboration network. The tool computes the co–author network of these authors and displays a list of authors in the structural neighbourhood of the starting authors, where relationships among the authors are represented as hyper-links. This allows the user to find further relevant documents of co–authors, resp. co–co–authors, whose documents have not been found before e. g. because of a mismatch of indexing and search terms. Since the list is ranked by the author's centrality in the network, the user may also find authors who are more central than the starting authors and can take them for further search activities.
(2) *Ranking a Document Result Set Using Author Centrality:* A specific problem of DAFFODIL is that most of the underlying services provide no ranking of the documents found due to the user's information needs. Thus, a given result set is re–ranked by descending centrality of the authors in co–author networks that are propagated on the basis of the documents in the result set.

The quality of the ranked document sets was evaluated by a small retrieval test, which was conducted for ten queries on the basis of the German social science database SOLIS[9]. Each of the ten result sets was re-ranked by both *closeness*[10] and *betweenness*[11] centrality in co-author networks that were derived from the specific result set. For precision after the top 20 documents, this method produced a value of 0.58 on average. In contrast, average precision at 20 documents for the standard output of SOLIS was 0.28. This result demonstrates the strengths of ranking document sets by author centrality in co–author networks. Central authors seem to provide more relevant documents because of their key position in the network.

As a first step towards *personalisation*, we have integrated a personal library in the desktop, which supports individuals as well as groups (see Fig. 3). This tool allows for storing DL objects — documents, authors, journals, conferences as well as query formulations — in folders (via the standard Drag&Drop interaction). For any of these objects, alerting (awareness) can be activated; in this case, the user will be informed when the system has new information concerning this object (e. g. new publications by an author, a new issue of a journal, new references to a document, new answers to a query). So alerting is similar to an SDI service, but its invocation is very simple. For group folders, awareness will highlight objects which have been added, modified or annotated by other users.

[9] `http://www.social-science-gesis.de/en/information/SOLIS`.
SOLIS was chosen because of availability of qualified relevance judgements.

[10] *Closeness* relates to the number of shortest paths of an actor to all other vertices in the graph. This stresses the level of an actor's efficiency in scientific communication and collaboration networks

[11] *Betweenness* centrality focuses on the ratio of shortest paths an actor lies on. It indicates an actor's degree of control or influence of communication and collaboration processes.

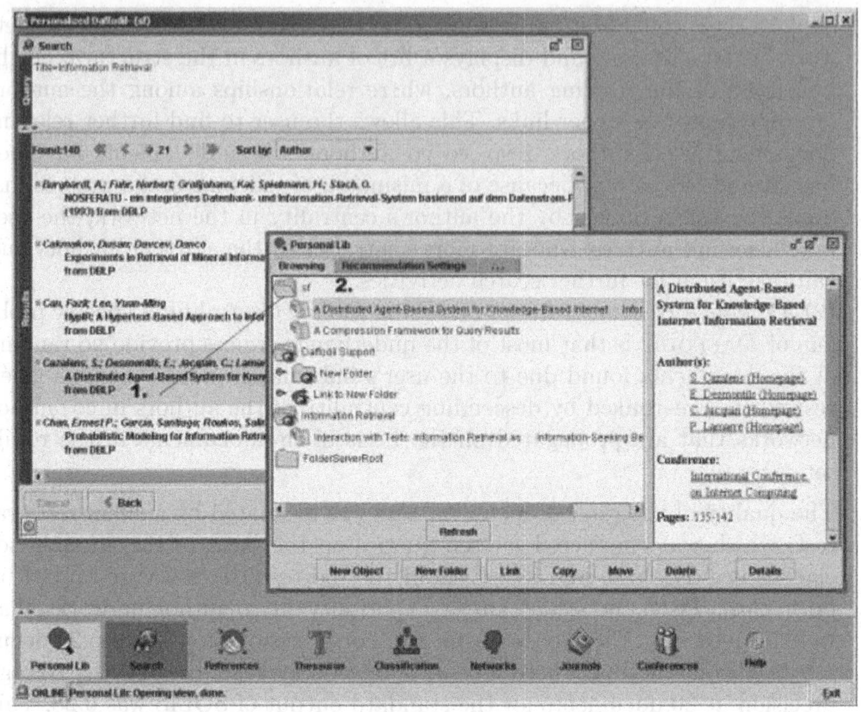

Fig. 3. Moving a document to the personal library

3 Evaluation

Two kinds of evaluation have been conducted during the project: A *heuristic evaluation* of the user interface and *questionnaire interviews* regarding system functionality. The results are described in the following.

After the first design and implementation phase, as soon as the SEARCH TOOL and the AUTHOR NETWORK TOOL were fairly stable, the interface was tested according to the *heuristic evaluation* method, as proposed by Nielsen [10]. Eight persons[12] explored the interface, while the experimenter took notes. Each problem reported by the participants was categorised according to a given list of usability heuristics.[13] The task was to search with the search tool and to apply the known item instantiation scenario, by using the AUTHOR NETWORK TOOL. This study produced the following findings:

a) *Irritations due to long waiting times*
While it was clear to the participants that a distributed search takes longer than a single search (besides waiting for the last response, re-integration and duplicate-elimination tasks in the middle layer took additional time), they

[12] A group of 5 computer science students and two academic assistants.

[13] e. g. `http://www.useit.com/papers/heuristic/heuristic_list.html`

became nervous after about 90 seconds and often interrupted the process. The need for a more transparent system state was expressed. The redesign addressed this need by cutting waiting time according to a user-defined option. The result list then contains only the documents retrieved so far. Profiling for the different wrappers will be used for dynamic adaption of filter settings in future. When a shorter maximum waiting time is specified, only those data sources are selected which are likely to respond within this time span.

b) *Interpretability of error cases*
Empty result sets posed a problem. It was unclear why the result set remains empty, as the middle layer was an additional possible source of problems. An agenda or log where one could look for possible explanations was requested. Visualisation of error states and counts for parts of the query or single data sources are needed to ease the interpretation.

c) *Acquaintance with new concepts*
The idea of using a high level tool, like the author network browser, was new to the participants. They needed time to explore the possibilities and asked for help regarding the interpretation of the results. However, when they learned how to use the tool, they expressed delight. The concept was quickly generalised and applied to the other browsers, which unfortunately had not been finished at that time. Using the rest of the GUI as mock–up, the participants followed the *tool-chain-idea* quite naturally, by applying intermediary results via drag and drop exchange or by following links.

d) *Author-networks: Computational effort and cut-off depth*
The cut-off depth of coauthor network computation had to be given by the users. It was not easy to decide, how to set this option. When choosing low values, computation was quick, but important authors were missing. Therefore the further development of a *main path analysis*, as described in [9] has been chosen to improve the situation: Instead of cutting the search at a given depth, local maxima for centrality values are computed and a hill climbing algorithm proceeds to the nearest local maxima from the starting point. This method reduces computing times while it allows to step much deeper into the social structure such that central authors who are located above a low cut-off point can be found.

After the second design phase, 14 computer science master students and six research assistants filled out a questionnaire after using DAFFODIL. The questionnaire was about ease of installation and usability of the prototype. It consisted of four parts: First, they were asked about their acquaintance with digital libraries. The second part concerned the installation of DAFFODIL via Webstart[14], an Internet installation tool for Java applications. For the third part participants had to perform small tasks with each tool. The last part was a complex task, with the intention to combine several tools in a strategic way. The goal was to find an overview article about "spatial data structures for multimedia data". Other

[14] http://java.sun.com

information sources like the DBLP database and Google should be used and compared to DAFFODIL.

The results of the questionnaire are as follows:

a) *Library usage:* Usually, the participants were acquainted with the OPAC[15] of the local library and general web search engines like Google. Digital libraries, like DBLP[16] were only known to the research assistants, but usually not to the students.
b) *Installation:* The installation with WebStart on the operating systems Solaris, Windows and Linux was straight forward and caused no further problems.
c) *Tool testing:* 85% of all participants were able to answer the questions. The others complained about problems like faulty German umlaut handling in the AUTHOR NETWORK TOOL. The problem of semantic identity of author names was discussed, as the service was sometimes not able to detect a person as unique due to differences in abbreviations and spelling.
d) *Complex task:* Only 50% of the participants found relevant articles. This was mainly due to insufficient query formulation and wrong keywords. In comparison, Google or DBLP appeared to provide an easier search, but resulted in less precise and very large result sets; so the identification of relevant documents in the result list was much harder.

One major problem was caused by the heterogeneity of query languages, where no correct translation was possible in some cases; post-processing of results will be a method for resolving this issue. Also, semantic heterogeneity caused unsatisfactory results (e. g. searching for a category of the classification scheme currently is supported by a single DL only); integration of appropriate transfer modules (like the ones described in [11]) could solve this problem. Missing functions and tools were requested, like a language translator, printing of results and a better help system (tool-tips). A personal library, which was not present at the time, was requested, to store results for later work. Also, additional pro-active integration of the tools was demanded, e. g. to combine the search tool with the thesaurus or a spell checker, if the query led to an empty answer. Nearly all participants said that, if a document is found, the quality of the detail view is very good.

The test results have been the basis for many improvements to the GUI. Most of the issues not explicitly named here are of technical nature. Thus, the tests helped substantially to improve stability and performance of the system.

4 Related Work

Several areas contributing to the digital library and agent-based information retrieval field are connected with DAFFODIL. In this section we give an overview on related work for integration of DL systems, agent based information retrieval and usability issues related to agent–user interaction.

[15] Online Public Access Catalog

[16] Digital Bibliography & Library Project: `http://dblp.uni-trier.de`

Integrated Digital Library Systems: The *Stanford Info-Bus*[17] is an early approach for integrating digital library catalogues and web sources into a federated system. With *DLITE* [12] it has an interface with several interesting design choices. It supports the search process and result (re-)presentation. Direct Manipulation is the main interaction style.

The *SketchTrieve* interface [13] enables the user to extract parts of information items. The collected items can be kept on a clipboard-like desktop for reuse in future work. Strategic support or high level services have not been integrated.

The new portal of the *ACM digital library*[18] offers an indexed collection with static links for searching, classification browsing, journal and conference browsing; however, searching on a subset of the collection selected by browsing is not directly supported. A personalised bookshelf and awareness on queries and group folders are also offered. However, DAFFODIL extends these features to federated information sources and guides the user with tools for query reformulation. Also the personalisation in DAFFODIL is based on all objects, not only queries.

The *Digital Work Environment* (DWE) [14] organises and facilitates various information sources in a tree-based interface to guide the staff and students through predefined tasks, like an exam paper preparation. Although tasks are similar to strategies, they are implemented in DWE as fixed schedules, allowing for no variations.

The *Ariadne* framework handles inconsistency between web sources, to enable information extraction, and to support wrapper re-induction for adapting to changes in dynamic sources [15].

Agent based information retrieval: The idea to employ agents for information retrieval tasks has a long history. Common approaches are WebBots or Spiders which collect information on the back end side, respective mediators and assistants on the front-end side. An example for the latest autonomous agent approach to support web searching is *InfoSpiders* [16]. Services like NECs *ResearchIndex* [17]also employ robots to search for publications and to automatically index them for building high level services, like citation tracking. The agents in *Margin Notes* [18] tries to recommend related information while traversing web pages.

Agent–User usability issues: Agents have been proposed as a means to reduce work and information overload [19]. Critics mentioned, that mediating agents reduce user control [20] and lead to lower predictability of user interfaces. However, current consensus is, that agents can provide helpful service, when acting in cooperation with the user within a common environment (for a discussion see [21]). The *Letitia* system offers helpful agents to support navigation in complicated hyper media spaces [22]. Agent based *just in time information retrieval*, is an unobtrusive interaction style [23], which is needed, as required by [24]; the latter paper also points out that trustworthiness of agents is a problem for users. *User autonomy* is crucial for work success and user satisfaction [25].

[17] For an overview refer to `http://www-diglib.stanford.edu/diglib`

[18] `http://portal.acm.org`

5 Conclusion and Outlook

In this paper we have presented the research and implementation state of the DAFFODIL user-interface along with evaluation results. The current version integrates search and browse of federated digital libraries within a graphical user interface, based on the WOB model. The tight integration of stratagems through the graphical tools enables efficient information searching with high-quality results. The key concept of *strategic support*, as proposed by Bates, is realized from the agent-framework up to the GUI. The prototype is freely accessible at `http://www.daffodil.de`.

In contrast to federal DLs based on standard protocols like e. g. Z39.50, DAFFODIL is able to integrate any DL that is accessible on the Internet. However, due to frequent changes of Web-based interfaces, continuous maintenance is required to keep the wrappers up-to-date.

Currently, we are working on the integration of intelligent components that help to further a search. A recommender–agent will analyse the result set and identify frequently occurring objects like e. g. conferences or journals. These objects will be offered to the user as links to the corresponding dedicated browsers. On link activation an optimised journal or conference run will give a specific relevance-driven view on the collections in question.

The personal library component implements personalisation and group support. Thus, we are following Paepcke's [26] vision of supporting the whole information search process consisting of the phases *Discover – Retrieve – Collate – Interpret – Re-Present*. Furthermore, the personal library will form the basis for implementing advanced features like pro-activeness and adaptivity. With pro-active agents, the system will be able to fill the personal library with more relevant data over time. Awareness-based services act upon insertion of new entries: When an entry is added, pro-active agents will become active and apply stratagems with the new entry as input, to add related items automatically (e. g. recommended readings). For pro-active search, the user can explicitly specify a depth search criterion, like the name of a known author, a topic of interest or a temporal range. Then an agent will search through all available journals and conferences (i.e. collections) for these criteria and return a list of matching articles, as well as branches of browsing trees, which contain data for the criteria. The agent will be able to monitor changes in the domain and notify the user about them. Then the user will only have to decide about acceptance or rejection of items on the recommendation list, rather than explicitly searching for them.

References

1. Fuhr, N., Gövert, N., Klas, C.P.: An agent-based architecture for supporting high-level search activities in federated digital libraries. In: Proceedings 3rd International Conference of Asian Digital Library, Taejon, Korea, KAIST (2000) 247–254
2. Bates, M.J.: Where should the person stop and the information search interface start? Information Processing and Management **26** (1990) 575–591

3. Krause, J.: Das WOB-Modell. In: Vages Information Retrieval und graphische Benutzeroberflächen: Beispiel Werkstoffinformation. Konstanz: Universitätsverlag, Konstanz (1997) 59–88
4. Sun Microsystems, Inc.: Java Look and Feel Design Guidelines. Addison Wesley Longman, Inc. (1999)
5. Fuhr, N.: Information retrieval in digitalen bibliotheken. In: 21. DGI-Online-Tagung – Aufbruch ins Wissensmanagement., Frankfurt (1999)
6. Baldonado, M.Q.W.: Interfaces for information exploration: Seeing the forest (1998)
7. Ellis, D.: Modeling the information-seeking patterns of academic researchers: a grounded theory approach. Library Quaterly **63** (1993) 469–486
8. Chen, H., Dhar, V.: Cognitive Process as a Basis for Intelligent Retrieval Systems Design. Information Processing and Management (1991) 405–432
9. Mutschke, P.: Enhancing information retrieval in federated bibliographic data sources using author network based stratagems. In Constantopoulos, P., Sölvberg, I.T., eds.: Reserach and Advanced Technology for Digital Libraries: 5th European Conference, ECDL 2001, Darmstadt, Germany, September 4-9, 2001; Proceedings. Lecture Notes in Computer Science; 2163. Springer, Berlin (2001) 287–299
10. Nielsen, J.: How to conduct a heuristic evaluation (1998)
11. Hellweg, H., Krause, J., Mandl, T., Marx, J., Müller, M.N., Mutschke, P., Strötgen, R.: Treatment of Semantic Heterogeneity in Information Retrieval. IZ-Arbeitsbericht; Nr. 23. IZ Sozialwissenschaften, Bonn (2001)
12. Cousins, S., Paepke, A., Winograd, T., Bier, E., Pier, K.: The digital library integrated task environment(dlite). In: 2nd ACM International Conference on Digital Libraries. (1997) 142–151
13. Hendry, D.G., Harper, D.J.: An informal information - seeking environment. Journal Of The American Society For Information Science **48** (1997) 1036–1048
14. Meyyappan, N., Al-Hawamdeh, S., Foo, S.: Digital work environment (dwe): Using tasks to organize digital resources. In Constantopoulos, P., Slvberg, I.T., eds.: Reserach and Advanced Technology for Digital Libraries: 5th European Conference, ECDL 2001, Darmstadt, Germany, September 4-9, 2001; Proceedings. Lecture Notes in Computer Science; 2163, Berlin, Springer (2001) 239–250
15. Knoblock, C.A., Minton, S.: The ariadne approach to web-based information integration. IEEE Intelligent Systems **13** (1998)
16. Menczer, F., Monge, A.: Scalable web search by adaptive online agents: An infospiders case study. In Klusch, M., ed.: Intelligent Information Agents. Springer (1999)
17. Lawrence, S., Giles, C.L., Bollacker, K.: Digital libraries and Autonomous Citation Indexing. IEEE Computer **32** (1999) 67–71
18. Rhodes, B.J.: Margin notes: building a contextually aware associative memory. In: Proceedings of the 5th international conference on Intelligent user interfaces, ACM Press (2000) 219–224
19. Maes, P.: Agents that reduce work and information overload. Communications of the ACM **37** (1994) 30–40
20. Shneiderman, B.: Direct manipulation for comprehensible, predictable and controllable user interfaces. In: 1997 international conference on Intelligent user interfaces, Orlando, FL United States (1997) 33–39
21. Shneiderman, B., Maes, P.: Direct manipulation vs interface agents. ACM Interactions (1997) 42–61
22. Lieberman, H.: Personal assistants for the web: An mit perspective. In Klusch, M., ed.: Intelligent Information Agents. Springer (1999)

23. Rhodes, B.J., Maes, P.: Just-in-time information retrieval agents. IBM Systems Journal **39** (2000) 685–??
24. Norman, D.: How might people interact with agents. Communications of the ACM **37** (1994) 68–71
25. Friedman, B., Nissenbaum, H.: Software agents and user autonomy. In Johnson, W.L., Hayes-Roth, B., eds.: Proceedings of the 1st International Conference on Autonomous Agents, Marina del Rey, CA USA, ACM Press (1997) 466–469
26. Paepcke, A.: Digital libraries: Searching is not enough. D-Lib Magazine **May 1996** (1996)

Using Human Language Technology for Automatic Annotation and Indexing of Digital Library Content

Kalina Bontcheva, Diana Maynard, Hamish Cunningham, and Horacio Saggion

Dept of Computer Science, University of Sheffield,
211 Portobello St, Sheffield, UK S1 4DP
{kalina,diana,hamish,saggion}@dcs.shef.ac.uk

Abstract. In this paper we show how we used robust human language technology, such as our domain-independent and customisable named entity recogniser, for automatic content annotation and indexing in two digital library applications. Each of these applications posed a unique challenge: one required adapting the language processing components to the non-standard written conventions of 18th century English, while the other presented the challenge of processing material in multiple modalities. This reusable technology could also form the basis for the creation of computational tools for the study of cultural heritage languages, such as Ancient Greek and Latin.

1 Introduction

As digital libraries grow in size and coverage, so does the need for automatic content annotation and indexing. Recent advances in human language technologies like named entity recognition, information extraction, and summarisation have made it possible to create automatically metadata (e.g., extract authors, titles) and document summaries, as well as annotate and index documents with information about persons, locations, dates, etc. These advances have been seen both in the quality of the results and in the robustness of the software solutions available. An increased acceptance of the importance of engineering to the successful application of HLT has led to more predictable systems that can realistically be technology providers for Digital Library systems (which have high reusability and portability requirements). In the digital library context, especially cultural digital libraries (e.g., [8]), language technology can offer new ways of accessing the collections (e.g., through indexes of events), as well as lower the costs of annotating documents with metadata and other relevant information. While fully-automatic solutions might not be always possible or practical, HLT can frequently be used to bootstrap these laborious tasks.

In this paper we show how we used such technologies for automatic content annotation and indexing in two digital library applications: eighteenth century court trials (OldBaileyIE) and a multilingual and multimodal collection on the Euro2000 football tournament (MUMIS). Each of these applications posed a

M. Agosti and C. Thanos (Eds.): ECDL 2002, LNCS 2458, pp. 613–625, 2002.

unique challenge: the court trials required adapting the language processing components to the non-standard written conventions of 18th century English, while the football collection presented the challenge of indexing material in multiple modalities - video, audio, semi-structured documents, and free text (newspaper reports). In the OldBailey application, the digitised content had to be annotated with various kinds of information, some of which was done automatically with minimum adaptation of our general-purpose named entity recogniser, while the rest was performed manually by human annotators. In MUMIS, the purpose was to construct automatically an index of all entities and events, which would then allow users to search the collection in novel ways, e.g., queries like "show me all goals by David Beckham in Euro2000".

In both cases, we used as a basis our robust and customisable named entity recogniser, which comes as part of ANNIE- A Nearly New Information Extraction system, distributed with the GATE language technology architecture and development environment [1] [10,13]. In OldBaileyIE we also used the graphical environment of GATE, which allows manual annotation verification and correction to be carried out on the processed texts. In MUMIS, we used a full-blown information extraction system, which contained the named entity recogniser as one of its components. This was needed because the application needed to index more complex data, than just entities.

2 Domain-Independent Named Entity Recognition

There is an increasing need for robust and general purpose tools capable of automatically annotating named entities in large volumes of text. The goal is to offer good performance without any tuning for the particular domain and/or text type and at the same time, to design the modules for easy customisation, if the user decides to do so. In response to this challenge, we developed a domain-independent Named Entity (NE) recognition system. It is capable of annotating entities such as persons, organisations (e.g., companies, government bodies), locations, dates, percents, money amounts, addresses.

Most Information Extraction (IE) systems, e.g. [7,1,9] are designed to extract fixed types of information from documents in a specific language and domain. To increase suitability for end-user applications, IE systems need to be easily customisable to new domains [17]. Driven by the MUC competitions (e.g. [18,19]), work on IE, and in particular on named entity recognition (NE), has largely focused on narrow subdomains, such as newswires about terrorist attacks (MUC-3 and MUC-4), and reports on air vehicle launches (MUC-7). In many applications, however, the type of document and domain may be unknown, or a system may be required which will process different types of documents without the need for tuning.

[1] GATE and ANNIE are available freely for download from `http://gate.ac.uk`. A demo of the named entity recogniser is available online at `http://gate.ac.uk/annie/index.jsp`.

Many existing IE systems have been successfully tuned to new domains and applications - either manually or semi-automatically – but there have been few advances in tackling the problem of making a single system robust enough to forego this need. The adaptation of existing systems to new domains is hindered by both ontology and rule bottlenecks. A substantial amount of knowledge is needed, and its acquisition and application are non-trivial tasks.

For systems to deal successfully with unknown or multiple types of source material, they must not only be able to cope with changes of domain, but also with changes of genre. By this we mean different forms of media (e.g. emails, transcribed spoken text, written text, web pages, output of OCR recognition), text type (e.g. reports, letters, books, lists), and structure (e.g. layout options). The genre of a text may therefore be influenced by a number of factors, such as author, intended audience and degree of formality. For example, less formal texts may not follow standard capitalisation, punctuation or even spelling formats. Our NE system aims to identify the parameters relevant to the creation of a name recognition system robust across these types of variability [13].

Using pattern matching for NE recognition requires the development of patterns over multi-faceted structures that consider many different token properties (e.g orthography, morphology, part of speech information etc.). Traditional pattern-matching languages such as PERL get "hopelessly long-winded and error prone" [5], when used for such complex tasks. Therefore, attribute-value notations are normally used, that allow for conditions to refer to token attributes arising from multiple analysis levels. Examples of such systems include the NEA (Named Entity Analysis) rule-based system developed within the FACILE and CONCERTO projects [6,4,15], and CPSL (Common Pattern Specification Language) [2], from which the JAPE language was developed.

The named entity recognition modules are easily customisable, because they are based on GATE's open architecture and consist of manually created sets of pattern-matching rules that can easily be extended to add new entity types, or modified for new domains. The rule patterns are based on information produced by earlier modules, which are responsible for segmenting the text into words (**tokenisation**) and sentences (**sentence splitting**), assignment of part-of-speech information to words (**POS tagging**), and annotations of specific named entity indicators (e.g., 'Ltd.', 'Mr.') (**gazetteer lists**). For example, the following rule specifies that one or more words, starting with an uppercase letter, followed by a company designator, should be annotated as an organisation.

```
Rule: OrgXKey (
  ({Token.kind == word, Token.orth == upperInitial})+
  {Lookup.type == cdg}
) :orgName -->
  :orgName.Organization
```

The Lookup annotations are created by the gazetteer lookup module, which assigns pre-specified types to the given lists of strings (e.g., a company designator list, person title list). These can be edited within GATE's visual environment as

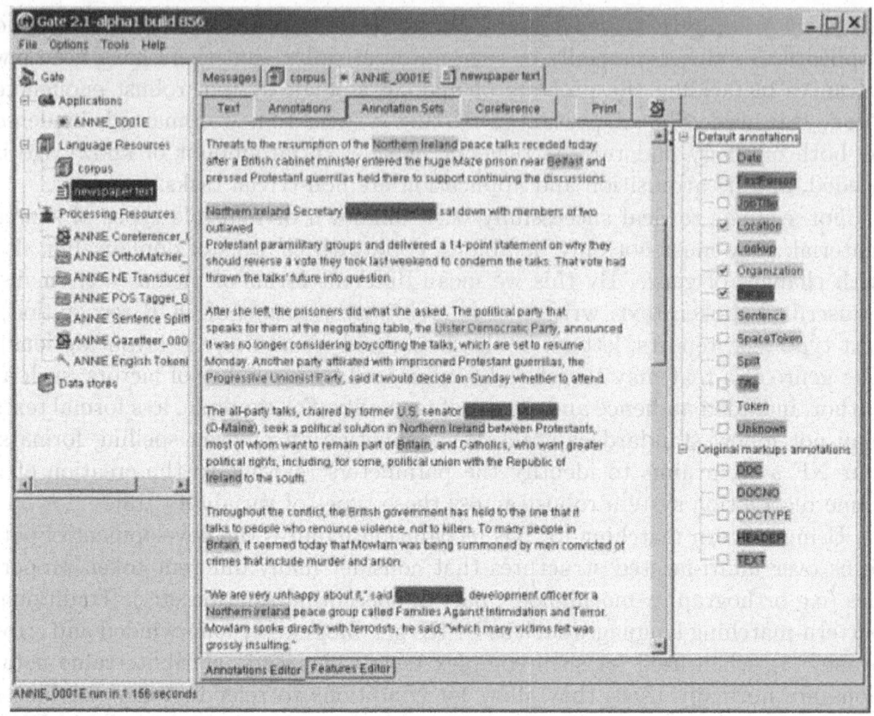

Fig. 1. Named Entities recognised by ANNIE

part of the customisation process. Modifying these lists is an easy task and was successfully carried out by non-expert users.

Rule writing requires some knowledge of the JAPE pattern-matching language [11] and ANNIE annotations. The pattern-matching language is based on regular expressions over the annotations; when a sequence of annotations is matched by the left-hand side pattern, then the right-hand side defines the type of annotation to be added (Organization in the example case above).

Our experiences with different systems and users indicate that writing rules to extract useful data from text is not conceptually difficult and can be learnt after some training. GATE's graphical environment allows visual inspection of the annotations and their features, which makes rule writing easier. Also, the types, attributes and values of the annotations produced by each module (e.g., tokeniser, part-of-speech tagger) are documented in GATE's User Guide [11].

The application for which the NE task is designed clearly has an impact on the development of Named Entity Recognition grammars. It can involve considerable effort simply to adapt a grammar to a new domain or task, particulary if different entity types are needed, or if the same entities have different structures and syntactic behaviour in their new context. However, adding rules for new entity types and changing some other rules for the needs of a new domain or text type/genre, is less effort and time consumming than building everything from scratch. This has been the focus of the MUSE system [14,13], and the default IE system (ANNIE) developed within GATE, which use general-purpose grammars as a basis for developing application-specific ones.

Though the general-purpose grammars in these systems have been developed with reusability in mind, they have originated from specific NE recognition applications. There is always some subset of a purpose-built NE recognition grammar set, that is application independent; this part can be used as a basis for creating a new grammar set for a new application, no matter how different one application is from another. This set of "core" rules corresponds to the named entities (person, organisation, location names) and fixed data structures (date, time and monetary expressions), traditionally identified by any NE recognition system, which are largely domain independent.

Other rule-based NE recognition systems such as Proteus [12] and FASTUS [3] do not seem to have this flexibility of design, and therefore are much harder to adapt to new domains and applications. Current performance of the NE recognition system is around 90-95% Precision and Recall, which is similar to other current systems.

In the following section we will discuss how the named-entity recogniser was easily adapted to deal with the different capitalisation and language conventions of 18*th* century English.

3 OldBailey – Semi-automatic Annotation of a 18*th* Century English Collection

The application required the following entity types to be recognised: Person, Location, Occupation and Status.

3.1 Adapting the Technology

There were two main ways in which the technology needed to be adapted. First, the application required some new entity types to be identified, and some modifications to the existing guidelines for annotation (for example, there was a new entity type "social status"). Second, the resources needed to be modified to take into account differences caused by the language used and the text type, such as different spelling, capitalisation, punctuation, and some noisy input.

First, new gazetteer lists had to be added for status information (e.g. "wife", "spinster", "Lord", "Governor"), since this entity type is not recognised in the default gazetteer.

Second, because the texts dealt with some very specific locations in London, such as "Addington Basin", "Aldermanbury Postern", "Cripplegate", additions had to be made to the lists of locations, and in particular, to the location keywords. For example, words such as "Fink", "Chain", "Ax", "Key", "Workhouse", "Rents" etc. would not normally be associated with locations, but these were commonly used in the 18*th* century (e.g. "Bennet Fink". We also needed to recognise facilities such as pubs as Locations, so new lists had to be added to take these into consideration.

As far as people's names were concerned, fewer changes needed to be made, but one particular feature of the reporting style was that many first names were abbreviated, e.g. "Benj." for "Benjamin", "Edw." for "Edward", etc. New entries had to be made in the gazetteer lists for people's first names to take this into account.

Although we already had a list of occupations, many additions had to be made to this, because there were some typical occupations of the 18*th* century which are rare these days, such as "Black-shoe-boy", "axle tree maker", "bottled porter dealer".

Finally, we had to deal with orthographic variations, since the punctuation, spelling and capitalisation were very inconsistent. For example, many proper nouns were spelt both with initial capital letters and without, and sometimes a hyphen was followed by a capital and sometimes by a lowercase letter. For example, "Bread Street" was also found in the text as "Bread-Street", "Bread-street" and "Bread street". These non-standard written conventions were dealt with both in the gazetteer lists (e.g. by adding variations of words with and without capital letters) and also in the grammar rules (for example, by looking for strings ending in particular patterns such as "-maker", "-draper", "-keeper", "-broker", with and without capital letters and hyphens.

Changing the gazetteer lists also meant making some changes to the grammar rules to accommodate these. For example, new rules had to be written for the new entity type "status", and further rules had to be written to solve conflicts with existing entity types. For example, "Baker" could be either an occupation or a person's name, so rules had to be written incorporating contextual information in order to disambiguate the entities.

Below we show an example of a typical rule added to the grammar to take account of the new gazetteer lists, which creates an annotation of type "Occupation". The rule matches a pattern consisting of any kind of word (recognised by the tokeniser), followed by one of the entries in the gazetteer list for job_keys (words which typically indicate jobs, such as "-seller"). It then annotates this pattern with the entity type "Occupation", and gives it a feature "rule" with value "OccupationKey". The rule feature is simply used for debugging purposes, so it is clear which particular rule has fired to create the annotation. This rule would annotate a string such as "book-seller" or "potato-merchant".

```
Rule: OccupationKey
Priority: 50
(
 {Token.kind == word}
 {Lookup.type == job_key}
):jobtitle
-->
:jobtitle.Occupation =
   {rule = "OccupationKey"}
```

Most of the adaptation to the system lay in updating the gazetteer lists and checking for conflicts between the new rules and lists, and existing ones. This latter was mainly carried out by running the system on test texts and correcting errors where they arose. The total adaptation time for the grammars and gazetteer lists (by an experienced system developer) was approximately one person-week. Further minor changes to the system were then made by the non-expert system users from the Sheffield University's Humanities Research Institute, who are creating the digital collection.

3.2 The Annotation Correction Environment

Automatic named entity annotation systems are typically capable of capturing between 85% and 95% of the entities in the texts (although these numbers are sometimes closer to 100% for entities like dates and money amounts). Nevertheless, in certain applications, as was the case with the Old Bailey collection, it is important to have all entities annotated correctly. This process involves two tasks: deleting wrong annotations and adding new annotations for the entities that have been missed. Still, because the named entity recogniser has already annotated at least 85% of all entities, this task is much less time-consuming than fully manual annotation.

Our users from the Humanities Institute used the visual annotation environment that comes with the GATE system. This environment makes the annotation process as simple and quick as possible and yet allows the flexibility to add new annotation types.

Wrong annotations are detected by the annotator visually, by inspecting the highlighted text strings; the GATE environment uses different colours for the different types of annotations (see Figure 2). To delete a wrong annotation, the user right-clicks on the highlighted text and selects the type of annotation they want deleted (there could be more than one annotations of different kinds associated with the same string). For example, in Figure 2, the system wrongly recognised '15 Foot Wall' as a location, because of a space in the digitised text, which changed the original phrase ‘15 Foot Wallnut Plank' to become ‘15 Foot Wall nut Plank'[2]. GATE also offers a facility to delete all occurences of wrong annotations, when they refer to the same entity. For example, if the House has wrongly been identified as a location, all occurrences of this entity in the text can be viewed and deleted by pressing the Delete key, when the entity is selected in the Coreference data panel on the right (see Figure 3). In this way, the user removes all occurrences with one action, rather than having to delete all these annotations individually.

New annotations are added by selecting the text with the mouse (e.g., "William Mills") and then clicking on the desired annotation type (e.g., Person), which is shown in the list of types on the right-hand-side (see Figure 2).

[2] In 18*th* century English nouns were frequently capitalised. This example also demonstrates that the digitised content contained noisy data, such as underscores, spaces, etc.

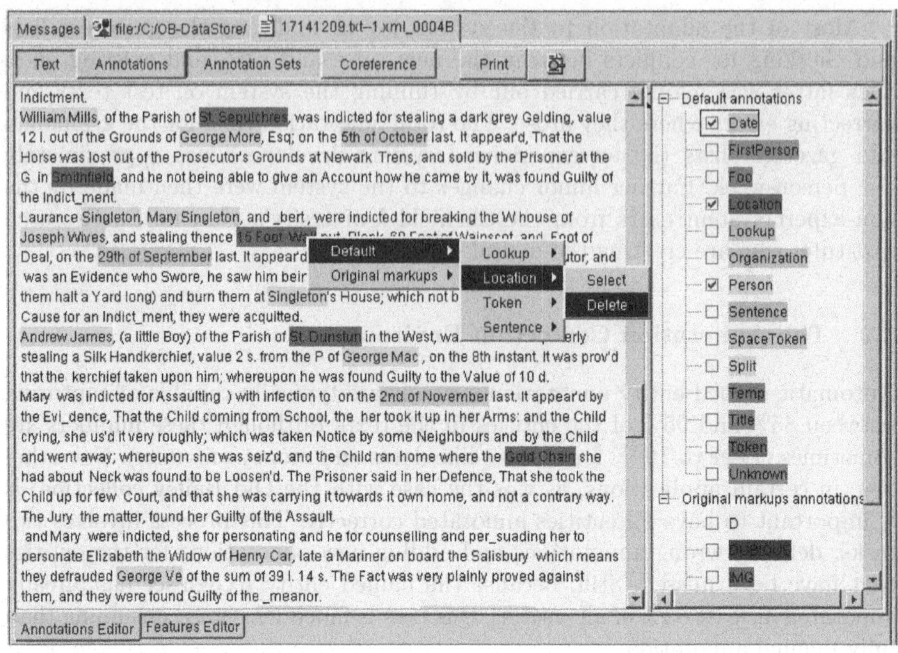

Fig. 2. An Old Bailey example text from 1714

The annotation environment comes as standard with a number of pre-defined annotation types (e.g., Person, Organization). New types can be defined and made available in the annotation environment by specifying them in the XML Schema language supported by W3C. For example, the schema for defining an Occupation annotation type looks like:

```
// Occupation schema
<?xml version="1.0"?>
<schema
xmlns="http://www.w3.org/2000/10/XMLSchema">
 <!-- XSchema deffinition for Occupation-->
  <element name="Occupation">
 </element>
</schema>
```

New schemas need to be created once for each application and shared by all users who do the actual annotation. Typically the schemas are created by the software support personnel, then they automatically appear in the visual environment, so users only need to be trained to use them.

The GATE visual annotation environment can also be used independently from the language processing tools. It offers the advantage of making the annotation process independent from the particular document format used, e.g., XML.

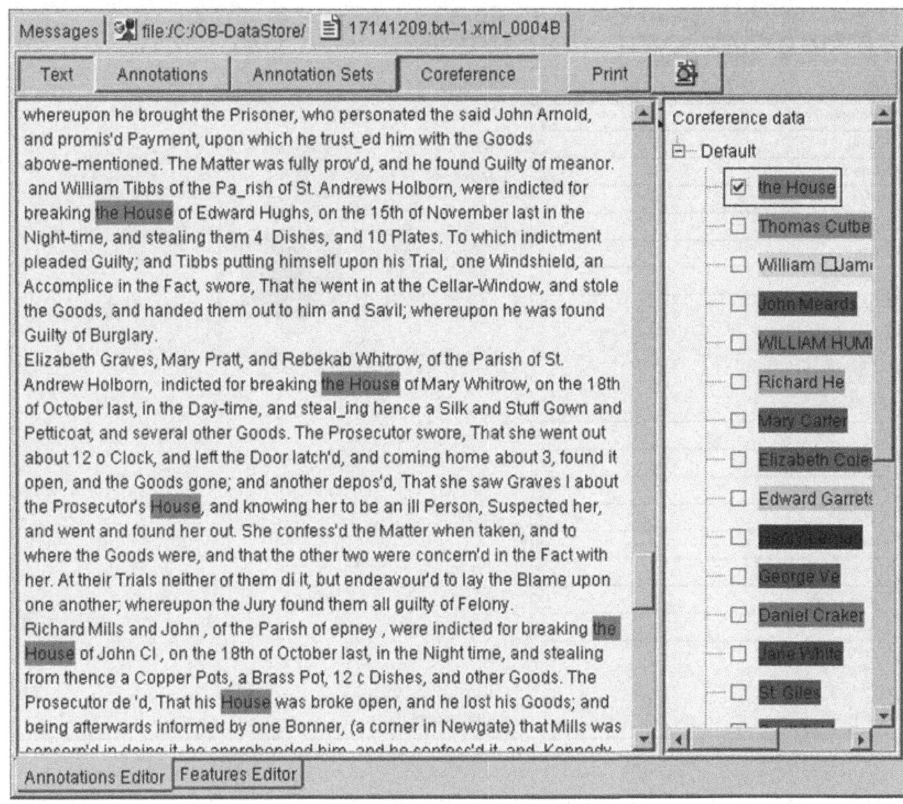

Fig. 3. Viewing and deleting all annotations for an entity

Our experience with users from the humanities has shown that they find the annotation task easier when it involves selecting text and associating types in a visual environment, than when it requires writing XML markup. The colour coding scheme which associates different types of annotations with different colours makes it easier for users to find and correct the annotations. Once the annotation process is completed, the user only needs to save the document, which automatically inserts the newly added markup in the appropriate format (e.g., HTML, XML).

4 MUMIS – Indexing and Search in Multiple Media

The MUMIS (MUltiMedia Indexing and Searching environment) system uses Information Extraction (IE) components developed within GATE to produce formal annotations about essential events in football video programme mate-

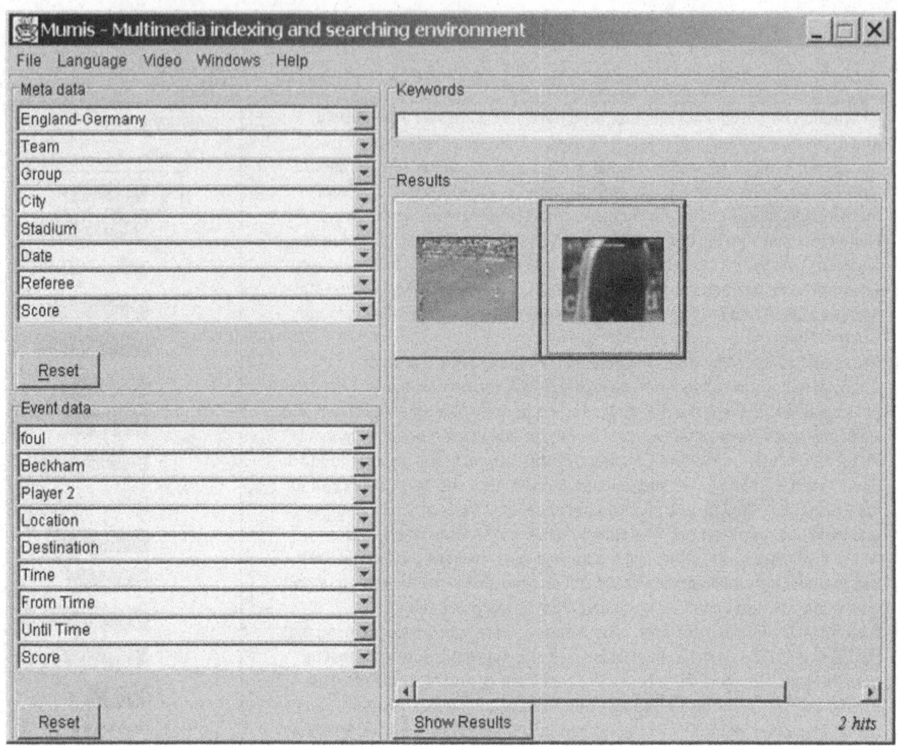

Fig. 4. The MUMIS interface

rial.[3] The textual sources used for this project are taken from reports of the Euro2000 Championships: semi-structured ticker reports that give a minute by minute objective account of the match; match reports that also give a full account of the match but may be subjective; and comments that give general information such as player profiles. These reports are drawn from a variety of online media sources (BBC-online, Press Association, The Guardian, etc.). The video material was indexed by running the IE system on the output of an automatic speech recognition system. Information about the same event in multiple sources is merged into a common index, which also contains references to the video material, thus allowing direct access to the relevant part of the video.

The indexing task in this particular application is focused on the entities and the events that occur in this domain, i.e., the aim is to enable users to access only the relevant parts of the documents, which show a particular entity and/or event of interest. Therefore, such information is collected for each document, regardless of its modality, and used to create an index of all entities and

[3] `http://mumis.vda.nl/`, funded by the EC's 5th Framework HLT programme under grant number IST-1999-10651. Project partners: Universities of Twente, Nijmegen and Sheffield, Esteam AB, VDA Ltd., DFKI.

events that have occurred in the collection (e.g., red cards, goals). This kind of "conceptual" indexing is complementary to the more general indexing problem in digital libraries, where documents are typically indexed for access by author, title, etc. One of the issues here is to determine whether or not a name has been used to refer to the same entity in two different documents. For example, Cambridge in one document might refer to Cambridge in England, while in the other document it might refer to Cambridge, Massachusetts. These issues have already been recognised in previous digital library research, not only in research on human language technology, e.g., [8].

The indexed multimedia information is accessed via a menu-based user interface (in Dutch, English, and German) (see Figure 4) which allows users to query the indexed information and play video fragments matching the query (e.g., "all fouls on Beckham").

The domain-independent named entity recogniser was extended to recognise domain-specific entities such as teams, players, and referee. Our philosophy of clean separation between linguistic data and the algorithms that process it resulted in a substantial saving of effort, since only new domain-specific data (i.e., names and grammar rules) had to be created, while the algorithms using them remained unchanged. Further details on the adaptation process and on the use of information extraction for multimedia indexing and search can found in [16].

5 Conclusion

In this paper we presented briefly the domain-independent portable named entity recogniser developed as part of the ANNIE Information Extraction system. ANNIE is intended to be useable in many different applications, on many different kinds of text and for many different purposes. Here we showed how it can be applied for annotating (semi)-automatically digital library content and also for indexing such content by entities and events. The system was built for portability and offers a comprehensive support for documents in many different formats, from badly-spelled lower case email messages to structured XML or HTML pages to newswires. It is capable of dealing with noisy data and processing of large data volumes (for further details on that see [10]). Finally, ANNIE is also capable of processing and visualising multilingual documents, based on Unicode [20], which makes it particularly suitable for digital library applications which need to deal with content in languages other than English. For example, it could be a basis for creation of computational tools for the study of cultural heritage languages, such as Ancient Greek and Latin.

The GATE visual environment was designed originally to help researchers develop HLT applications and manual annotation facilities were needed as they form an important part of the application-building process, i.e., the performance evaluation. However, our experience with the OldBailey project has shown that this environment could be used in the future as part of a tool specifically aimed at digital libraries, which support the end user with the annotation task. In the future, we hope to be able to undertake such research in collaboration with interested digital library researchers.

References

1. D. Appelt. An Introduction to Information Extraction. *Artificial Intelligence Communications*, 12(3):161–172, 1999.
2. D.E. Appelt. The Common Pattern Specification Language. Technical report, SRI International, Artificial Intelligence Center, 1996.
3. E. R. Appelt, J.R. Hobbs, J. Bear, D. Israel, M. Kameyama, A. Kehler, D. Martin, K. Myers, and M. Tyson. SRI International FASTUS System: MUC-6 Test Results and Analysis. In *Proceedings of the Sixth Message Understunding Conference* (MUC-6). Morgan Kaufmann, California, 1995.
4. W. Black and F. Rinaldi. Facile pre-processor 3.0 - a user guide. Technical report, Department of Language Engineering, UMIST, 2000.
5. W. Black, F. Rinaldi, and D. Mowatt. Facile: Description of the named entity System used for muc-7. In *Proceedings of the 7th MUC*, 1998.
6. F. Ciravegna, A. Lavelli, N. Maria, J. Matiasek, L. Gilardoni, S. Mazza, M. Ferraro, W. Black, F. Rinaldi, and D. Mowatt. Facile: Classifying texts integrating Pattern matching and information extraction. In *Proceedings of the 16th International Joint Conference on Artificial Intelligence (IJCA I99)*, 1999.
7. J. Cowie and W. Lehnert. Information Extraction. *Communications of the ACM*, 39(1):80–91, 1996.
8. Gregory Crane, Robert F. Chavez, Anne Mahoney, Thomas L. Milbank, Jeffrey A. Rydberg-Cox, David A. Smith, and Clifford E. Wulfman. Drudgery and deep thought. *Communications of the ACM*, 44(5):34–40, 2001.
9. H. Cunningham. Information Extraction: a User Guide (revised Version). Research Memorandum CS-99-07, Department of Computer Science, University of Sheffield, May 1999.
10. H. Cunningham, D. Maynard, K. Bontcheva and V. Tablan. GATE: A framework and graphical development environment for robust NLP tools and applications. In *Proceedings of the 40th Anniversary Meeting of the Association for Computational Linguistics*, 2002.
11. H. Cunningham, D. Maynard, K. Bontcheva, V. Tablan, and C. Ursu. *The GATE User Guide*. `http://gate.ac.uk/`, 2002.
12. R. Grishman. Information Extractionr Techniques and Challenges. In *Information Extraction: a Multidisciplinary Approach to an Emerging Information Technology*, Springer 1997.
13. D. Maynard, V. Tablan, H. Cunningham? C. Ursu, H. Saggion, K. Bontcheva, and Y. Wilks. Architectural elements of language engineering robustness. *Journal of Natural Language Engineering – Special Issue on Robust Methods in Analysis of Natural Language Data*, 2002. forthcoming.
14. D. Maynard, V. Tablan, C. Ursu, H. Cunningham, and Y. Wilks. Named Entity Recognition from Diverse Text Types. In *Recent Advances in Natura1 Language Processing 2001 Conference*, Tzigov Chark, Bulgaria, 2001.
15. J. McNaught, W. Black, F. Rinaldi, E. Bertino, A. Brasher, D. Deavin, B. Catania, D. Silvestri, B. Armani, A. Persidis, G. Semerano, F. Esposito, V. Candela, G.P. Zarri, and L. Gilardoni. Integrated document and knowledge management for the knowledge-based enterprise. In *Proceedings of the 3rd International Conference on the practical application of Knowledge Management.* The paractical application company, 2000.

16. H. Saggion, H. Cunningham, D. Maynard, K. Bontcheva, O. Hamza, C. Ursu, and Y. Wilks. Extracting Information for Automatic Indexing of Multimedia Material. In *3rd International Conference on Language Resources and Evaluation (LREC 2002)*, pages 669–676, Las Palmas, Gran Canaria, Spain, 2002.
17. S. Soderland. Learning to extract text-based Information from the world wide web. *Proceedings of Third International Conference on Knowledge Discovery and Data Mining (KDD-9Y)*, 1997.
18. Beth Sundheim, editor. *Proceedings of the Sixth Message Understanding Conference (MUC-6)*, Columbia, MD, 1995. ARPA, Morgan Kaufmann.
19. Beth Sundheim, editor. *Proceedings of the Seventh Message Understanding Conference (MUC-7)*. ARPA, Morgan Kaufmann, 1998.
20. V. Tablan, C. Ursu, K. Bontcheva, H. Cunningham, D. Maynard, 0. Hamza, Tony McEnery, Paul Baker, and Mark Leisher. A unicode-based environment for creation and use of language resources. In *Proceedings of 3rd Language Resources and Evaluation Conference*, 2002.

Cultural Heritage Digital Libraries: Needs and Components

Gregory Crane

Perseus Project
Tufts University
Medford MA 02155 USA
gcrane@tufts.edu

Abstract. This paper describes preliminary conclusions from a long-term study of cultural heritage digital collections. First, those features most important to cultural heritage digital libraries are described. Second, we list those components that have proven most useful in boot-strapping new collections.

1 Introduction

This paper reports preliminary conclusions from the first three years of a five year project to develop a digital library for the humanities NSF IIS 9817484; [1-5].[1] We have established a set of testbed collections to complement substantial Greco-Roman materials that have been under development since 1987. We now have in place testbeds on early modern English, the history of mechanics, the history and topography of London, slavery and the US Civil War, and various collections on US History from the Library of Congress. These collections include multiple languages, spaces of various scales, and diverse classes of objects. Our goal was to create an unwieldy set of heterogeneous, in some ways incommensurable, collections that appealed to wide-spread, complex audiences with disparate, often competing interests. In so doing, we intended to pose issues of scalability and personalization that would have remained hidden had we explored the needs of a single area or audience. In the following two years, our research will focus on the interaction between front-end transactions and back-end structures, studying the differing strengths of the collections at our disposal and the varying needs of our audiences. This paper presents some preliminary conclusions and hypotheses about the needs and possibilities facing cultural heritage digital libraries [6, 7]. While our work considers representations of space, in two and three dimensions, and at various scales[8], from individual sites to global, and of objects such as art works or scientific instruments

[1] Primary funding for this work comes from the US Digital Library Initiative, Phase II: http://www.dli2nsf.gov. A substantial portion of the support from our work came from the National Endowment for the Humanities (http://www.neh.gov). International Digital Library grants from the NSF and *Deutsches Forschungsgemeinschaft* (DFG: http://dfg.de) and from the NSF and the EU have also contributed substantially to our recent work.

M. Agosti and C. Thanos (Eds.): ECDL 2002, LNCS 2458, pp. 626-637, 2002.

[9], this paper will concentrate on textual materials and the possibilities and challenges posed by human language technologies.

We are particularly interested in identifying the needs, present and potential, similar and dissimilar, of various communities within the humanities. We began our work three years ago by studying issues that different areas within the humanities did or did not share: students of the ancient world, for example, work intensively on relatively small, very fragmentary data sets in complex languages (e.g., Latin, classical Greek, Sumerian, Sanskrit); students of modern industrial cultures, by contrast, have extraordinarily detailed records and sources. Those working with pre-modern, typically sparse materials spend much of their time extrapolating from imperfect sources, while those working with recent and often vast data sources have a greater need to filter and visualize their data. Extrapolation and reduction are, of course, complementary processes and play a role in all research. The richness of information available about London, however, challenged us to develop visualization tools for space and time that we would not have otherwise pursued but that have proven powerful also for the Greco-Roman collection.

Many issues confront digital libraries in a variety of areas and, indeed, our growing interactions with the NSF National Science Digital Library (http://www.nsdl.nsf.gov) suggest to us that the interests of humanists, social scientists and natural scientists are converging. Although the emphases may differ, all the recommendations from the June 2001 Delos Digital Library brainstorming session in San Cassiano [8], for example, are relevant to cultural heritage collections. Reading support systems that help students read Greek and Latin texts have, for example, provided the foundation for services that support interdisciplinary researchers and undergraduates as they shift from textbook culture to real scientific literature. Such services, however, raise issues about how we encode data and structure the architecture of our DL environment. Administrative guidelines complicate the role of humanists in a National Science Digital Library funded by the National Science Foundation. Nevertheless, humanists can play a vital role by bringing distinct perspectives that may complicate short-term goals but lay the foundation for a system that is in the long run more robust, general, and sustainable.

The paper has two main parts. In the first, we outline a set of overall issues that are, in aggregate, particularly important to cultural heritage collections. The second section describes what elements we have found to be useful in boot-strapping cultural heritage collections.

2 Characteristics of the Humanities

This paper reports preliminary conclusions from the first three years of a five year project to develop a digital library for the humanities NSF IIS 9817484; [1-5] .[2] We

[2] Primary funding for this work comes from the US Digital Library Initiative, Phase II: http://www.dli2nsf.gov. A substantial portion of the support from our work came from the

have established a set of testbed collections to complement substantial Greco-Roman materials that have been under development since 1987. We now have in place testbeds on early modern English, the history of mechanics, the history and topography of London, slavery and the US Civil War, and various collections on US History from the Library of Congress. These collections include multiple languages, spaces of various scales, and diverse classes of objects. Our goal was to create an unwieldy set of heterogeneous, in some ways incommensurable, collections that appealed to wide-spread, complex audiences with disparate, often competing interests. In so doing, we intended to pose issues of scalability and personalization that would have remained hidden had we explored the needs of a single area or audience. In the following two years, our research will focus on the interaction between front-end transactions and backend structures, studying the differing strengths of the collections at our disposal and the varying needs of our audiences. This paper presents some preliminary conclusions and hypotheses about the needs and possibilities facing cultural heritage digital libraries [6, 7]. While our work considers representations of space, in two and three dimensions, and at various scales[8], from individual sites to global, and of objects such as art works or scientific instruments [9], this paper will concentrate on textual materials and the possibilities and challenges posed by human language technologies.

We are particularly interested in identifying the needs, present and potential, similar and dissimilar, of various communities within the humanities. We began our work three years ago by studying issues that different areas within the humanities did or did not share: students of the ancient world, for example, work intensively on relatively small, very fragmentary data sets in complex languages (e.g., Latin, classical Greek, Sumerian, Sanskrit); students of modern industrial cultures, by contrast, have extraordinarily detailed records and sources. Those working with pre-modern, typically sparse materials spend much of their time extrapolating from imperfect sources, while those working with recent and often vast data sources have a greater need to filter and visualize their data. Extrapolation and reduction are, of course, complementary processes and play a role in all research. The richness of information available about London, however, challenged us to develop visualization tools for space and time that we would not have otherwise pursued but that have proven powerful as for the Greco-Roman collection. Perceived initial differences of the London collection set us moving in a new direction but the results were in the end unexpectedly useful for the Greco-Roman collection.

Many issues confront digital libraries in a variety of areas and, indeed, our growing interactions with the NSF National Science Digital Library (http://www.nsdl.nsf.gov) suggests to us that the interests of humanists, social scientists and natural scientists are converging. Although the emphases may differ, all the recommendations from the June 2001 Delos Digital Library brainstorming session in San Cassiano [10], for example, are relevant to cultural heritage collections. Reading support systems that help students read Greek and Latin texts have, for example, provided the foundation for services that support interdisciplinary researchers and undergraduates as they shift

National Endowment for the Humanities (http://www.neh.gov). International Digital Library grants from the NSF and *Deutsches Forschungsgemeinschaft* (DFG: http://dfg.de) and from the NSF and the EU have also contributed substantially to our recent work.

from textbook culture to real scientific literature [on which, see below]. Such services, however, raise issues about how we encode data and structure the architecture of our DL environment. Administrative guidelines complicate the role of humanists in a National Science Digital Library funded by the National Science Foundation. Nevertheless, humanists can play a vital role by bringing distinct perspectives that may complicate short-term goals but lay the foundation for a system that is in the long run more robust, general and sustainable.

The paper has two main parts. In the first, we outline a set of overall issues that are, in aggregate, particularly important to cultural heritage collections. The second section describes what elements we have found to be useful in boot-strapping cultural heritage collections, We then advance the notion of a corpus editor — a scholar with expertise in a particular area managing a corpus whose size is too large for manual methods of editing and who must therefore rely upon automated (and thus inherently imperfect) methods [2, 11]. This paper documents some of the concrete tasks that were required to develop a new collection of nineteenth century materials on slavery and the US Civil war. This study builds on results with collections on the Greco-Roman world and on the history and topography of London.

1. <u>Historical data become more valuable over time — persistence is crucial</u>: Cultural heritage digital libraries must aggressively address the problem of digital preservation. The problem is particularly serious for complex knowledge sources such as lexica or encyclopedias. Humanists may be less able than their colleagues to retrofit gigabytes of complex materials, but humanist reference works are used for decades, if not longer.
2. <u>Access to the cultural heritage of humanity is a right, not a privilege</u>: The record of human achievement is a public good and should be accessible to every citizen. At present, private corporations have undertaken the crucial task of digitizing some critical corpora and have produced intellectual gated communities. These electronic resources, tightly controlled and often priced in such a way as to guarantee a limited audience, restrict fundamental source materials to the same academic elites that had access to scarce print resources. A socio-economic infrastructure has thus begun to arise that imposes on the digital world limitations of print. We need economic models that do not replicate practices that isolate cultural heritage from the community as a whole. Governmental approaches are, however, also problematic, since governments may feel an obligation, explicit or not, to control their national image and impose restrictions on information.
3. <u>Cultural heritage digital libraries must serve the needs of diverse audiences</u>: Access to information is necessary but not sufficient. Customization is a rapidly growing field of inquiry. The system should adapt to the needs of its users, providing them with the information that they need to interpret new documents or topics, reducing, insofar as possible, the friction of their movement through a digital library (e.g.,[12]). There are limits to this — as Euclid reportedly rebuked the first Ptolemy with the statement that there is „no Royal Road to geometry,"[3] some concepts are simply difficult. Nevertheless, a humanities digital library has a social

---

[3] Reported by Proclus in his description of Euclid: see http://ww.perseus.tufts.edu/cgi-bin/ptext?doc=Perseus:text:1999.01.0086&query=head%3D%232&word=Euclid.

obligation to support the development of complex skills, by a wide audience, over a long period of time.

4. The *documents within* cultural heritage digital libraries must serve the needs of diverse audiences: Humanists cannot simply rely upon elaborate technologies to enhance their contributions to society as a whole. The Internet already reaches a huge audience and could within a very near future saturate the households of the advanced countries. The Perseus Digital Library Website has, for example, emerged as a major distribution channel within classics and now disseminates up to 9,000,000 pages of data per month to an audience far beyond traditional academia. Humanists — especially those who participate in scholarly debates that span decades or more — must think carefully about how they will respond to this vast new and expanding audience. We need to ponder both the way in which we write and the questions that we pursue. Maintaining the status quo and dismissing this new audience is itself a strong, if problematic, response.
5. The library is a laboratory where reading is a primary exercise: To some extent, this is a superset of the customization problem. A great deal of DL research addresses the cataloguing problem. A digital library is a structured space that manages a large number of objects. The user searches through the DL to find objects of interest, but, once these have been found, many systems simply hand control over to the object and the user calls up a PDF viewer etc. Humanists often study texts, images and spaces in extremely close detail. Thus, the numbered citation schemes of computer science publications — which direct readers to a document as a whole — reflect a much less general attitude to textual reference: humanists are trained to cite precise pages and, when dealing with canonical documents, often cite individual lines or words. In this environment, the granularity is much finer and users need support with words and phrases as well as with documents as a whole. The implications are, however, profound for the scale and design of humanities DLs: when each word becomes a complex multidimensional object, density of data increases by several orders of magnitude. Cultural heritage materials raise challenges that go beyond those described in the literature about citation harvesting and linking from recent scientific publications [13,14].
6. Digital objects and their components must be freely reusable: Simple access to information is not sufficient. We need complex documents that include and provide distinct visualizations of components from many sources, e.g. details from high-resolution images, clips of time-based media, tabular or graphic visualizations of data sets, quotations from larger works, and links from each inclusion to the source.
7. Standards/best practices must be descriptive rather than prescriptive: New publication series can impose guidelines on the form and structure of documents. The variations of historical sources can provide crucial information. We thus need to preserve, rather than eliminate, vagaries of spelling in early modern texts since these variations can provide important data about the compositional history of a given text [6, 15] (e.g., compositors often provided the actual spelling and uses of „do“ vs „doe,“ for example, can help determine who is responsible for what. section of Shakespeare's First Folio. The need for prescriptive rather than descriptive encoding demands a consequently far more complex encoding scheme and software infrastructure. This requirement generates a need in turn for specialized viewers, which can, for example, filter and display very precise

differences between editions. While the underlying ideas are similar to the well-known problem of versioning source code, a cultural heritage versioning system requires substantially more precision of reference and semantics: editors within the *New Variorum Shakespeare* series, for example, formally distinguish between „substantive“ and „semi-substantive“ changes to the text [16]. A versioning system must be able to manage a wide variety of such classes.

3 Building Cultural Heritage Collections

When planning for Perseus first began in 1985, we wanted to create a critical mass of information about the classical Greek world. While the *Thesaurus Linguae Graecae* [17] had already created a digital library of classical Greek source texts, we wanted to create an environment that contained every category of information about the Greek world: not only Greek source texts, but aligned translations, grammars, lexica, encyclopedias, reference articles, as well as maps, plans, pictures of places and art objects, catalogues, narrative discussions of art and archaeology., etc. Very little existed and we needed to create a self-standing, heterogeneous environment with which to experiment. We had a full-time photographer who took original images in dozens of museums across North America and Europe because few photo archives had the detailed, consistent photographic coverage that videodiscs, with room for 54,000 still color images on a side, could deliver. We digitized texts, drafted plans, commissioned articles, and addressed in-house as many tasks as we could. The results were satisfactory. Our goals were to create a corpus that was (1) large enough to support useful tasks of various kinds and (2) not tied to any one system. In the mid 1990s, we were able, with minimal effort, to migrate the Perseus DL from a *Hypercard* delivery environment to the Web and are prepared to shift data collected since the 1980s to new systems in the future. The Greco-Roman materials in Perseus remain popular, accounting for roughly 85% of the 26,000,000 pages that we served from February through April of 2002.

The rise of the Web and, more recently, of the *Open Archives Initiative* (http://www.openarchives.org/) has radically changed the information environment. If we were beginning Perseus now, we would clearly not pursue the same strategies that we adopted in the 1980s. Nevertheless, the independent work that we did many years ago continues to prove immensely useful. In part, this reflects the fact that we have control over a number of digital objects on which we can, within some limits, freely experiment. Third parties are often understandably unenthusiastic about others modifying their carefully designed data-structures.

Collection Overview: We had the resources when first developing the Greek collection in Perseus to commission from the ancient historian Thomas Martin a new book-length overview of Greek history and culture. Professor Martin produced a work that also appeared in print form [18]. The electronic version, however, was designed as a hypertext, with many cross-references complementing a clear hierarchical structure. More importantly, the electronic overview contained thousands of links to primary materials on which interpretive statements were based. Where the print version was designed for the isolated reading typical of a book aimed at a broad market, the electronic edition was designed to guide readers to the primary sources. Furthermore, while many of the links were deterministic (they pointed to particular passage or objects), some were dynamic queries: e.g., „search for women and slaves in the Greek collection.“ The results of these dynamic queries are different now from what they were when the *Overview* was first published on the Web and will continue to change, as the Greco-Roman collection evolves.

The *Greek Historical Overview* has been the most popular single work in the Perseus Digital Library. The *Overview* represented a broad synthesis of the field of Hellenic studies and drew upon the full experience of a senior faculty member. It thus constituted a major investment of time, money and support, but the results have more than justified the costs. We have created more modest introductions to other Perseus collections, but the Greek overview remains a key element and a potentially important case study in electronic publication. Not only does it contribute to the collection, but increased exposure of the web publication and the links binding text to sources have increased the audience that it has reached and the intellectual contribution which this work has been able to make. Nor have sales of the print version suffered (despite early concerns by the publisher).

Images: Digital cameras now allow novices to produce images that are useful in many contexts and institutions have begun using new technology to document their collections. The OAI is well suited to disseminating images and we are already harvesting metadata records of images that complement our collections. We no longer, for example, maintain a full-time staff photographer in Perseus nor do we see the need to provide the sorts of encyclopedic coverage that we attempted for the original Greek Perseus.

Nevertheless, the photography that we commissioned in the first ten years of the project remains a core resource. The image quality and, more importantly, the coverage are consistent: these photographs were taken to support digital publication and we assumed that we would be able to publish as many images of an object as we saw fit. In photographing Greek vases, we shot overviews from multiple angles and close-ups of individual scenes, figures and significant details — for some particularly complex vases, we shot almost two hundred individual views. The aggregate photographic coverage provides an immense amount of information and raises interesting opportunities for data-fusion techniques to stitch the disparate views into a single massive database.

Narrative texts: In this context, we define narrative texts as documents with relatively simple typographic/organizational structures (e.g., chapters/sections) that lend themselves to OCR and rapid tagging. Many thousands of public domain literary texts are now freely available, often from multiple sources, on the Web. Third party texts are, however, problematic. The quality of data entry is uneven. The bibliographic source may not be listed and even such basic citation schemes as page breaks may be lacking. Even when texts that are well edited and encoded in SGML/XML, the publicly available Web version may be informationally diluted HTML and servers may (like the Perseus Digital Library) only provide subsets of a text at a time. While third party sources are promising, they do not always remove the need to (re)digitize large local collections.

In developing our collection on London, we have chosen to enter a small number of canonical works available from other sites (e.g., Dickens' *Little Dorrit*) for experimental purposes but will rely on third parties for broader coverage. It remains to be seen how important canonical citation schemes are for most narrative texts associated with the London corpus.

2D and 3D models: While this paper focus on language issues, any mature digital library must develop a strategy to integrate 2D and 3D spatial data with textual and other materials: digital libraries provide a space in which user can theoretically move back and forth between virtual spaces, textual sources and quantitative data. Thus, users moving through a virtual London or Republican Rome should be able to ask questions such as „what is the architectural style of this building?" Such integration is hard to achieve, however, if models are developed in isolation and only with a view to generating imagery. We have long created vector based 2D models of archaeological sites and have in the past several years begun developing 3D models as well. While the technical tools for 3D modeling are well established, the scholarly conventions for vector models are still very much in flux. Where industrial developers may focus on photorealistic modeling, academics need an environment in which to critique and analyze models. A scholarly system should be able to provide the „state plan" (e.g., our evidence, whether archaeological excavations or contemporary observations of a historical space), multiple reconstructions along with the evidence on which those reconstructions are based, and details about individual elements of a space (e.g., point to a „Corinthian column" and locate similar Corinthian columns from other models). Such functionality requires data structures and labeling that are not typical of most professional drafting. The energy that we put into digital photography has now, in effect, shifted to modeling.

On the other hand, we are developing models of historical spaces as examples and case studies, designed to educate ourselves and to provide insights to others on how such data might function as part of an integrated digital library.

Geospatial data: Geospatial data have been crucial to our work from the beginning, but we have always relied upon third party gazetteers (such as the *Getty Thesaurus of Geographic Names* and the newly released gazetteer from the Alexandria Project) for our base data to which we have added supplementary information. We have accomplished a substantial amount by combining large third party datasets with modest human data collection, but the improved accuracy of GPS data and the ubiquitous availability of handheld GPS units open up immense new possibilities for collaborative collection of point data. We do not have in place the collaborative infrastructure needed so that the archaeologists who fan out across ancient sites all over the world each year can relay GIS data to a central repository. Such an infrastructure is a major desideratum for cultural heritage collections. We are moving in that direction, as are other efforts such as the *Electronic Cultural Atlas Project* at Berkeley (www.ecai.org).

Lexica: In 1987, we digitized a Greek lexicon before we had digitized any Greek texts — a prioritization that proved extremely useful and which we continue to follow. At present, we are digitizing two dictionaries of classical Arabic to spear-head a movement towards an Arabic collection.

Starting with a dictionary can seem problematic. Dictionaries tend to be large (the major Greek [19] and Latin [20] lexica were 35 megabytes each), to have complex formats that do not quite capture the logical structure of the entries, and to defy efficient OCR (although promising work is going on at the University of Maryland on OCR and analysis of dictionaries:[21]). Dictionaries are thus far more expensive than source texts, since they may need to be hand keyed, with surcharges for unfamiliar writing systems such as Greek or Arabic. Converting a 35 megabyte print lexicon to a useful electronic resource that can drive a morphological analyzer may cost as much as a double keyed 200 megabyte library of source texts. Lexicographers aside, most see dictionaries as a means to read other materials. Beginning a digital collection in a new language by lavishing time and money on a lexicon is thus not an obvious decision.

Nevertheless, the dictionary is a crucial starting point precisely because it is expensive, difficult and powerful. Our on-line dictionaries have provided a foundation for many subsequent services and add value to every text linked to the system. We mine the dictionaries for their morphological information, use these data to drive a morphological analyzer, and then provide dictionary look-up and lexically based search services. In English this would be equivalent to (1) being able to click on „were“ and calling up the entry for „to be,“ along with information about the form „were“ and (2) searching for „to be“ and retrieving „were.“ In highly inflected languages such as Greek, Latin, and Arabic, morphological analysis can be extremely complex but the resulting services correspondingly important. Anecdotal reports suggest that students read Greek and Latin twice as fast using the dictionary links in the Perseus environment as when working with print — whether or not those figures are accurate, the perceived increase in throughput has attracted substantial use. The benefits of more powerful searching are harder to quantify but substantial.

Grammars: We have entered grammars for Greek and Latin. In theory, these grammars may provide data-sources to support syntactic and semantic analysis of Greek and Latin. Where we have mined the morphological data from the lexica, the syntactic and semantic information remains embedded in the texts and we have not been able to generate linguistically based services from these resources. These grammars do, however, contain thousands of precise citations of source texts. We convert these citations to bi-directional links, so that those reading a given text can see when a grammar comments on a particular passage. Although the grammars are, in their present form, cumbersome to browse, the bi-directional links generate substantial usage and have made them popular resources within the collection.

Encyclopedias: Dictionaries concentrate on semantics — the general meanings of words. Many texts contain references to particular people and places. We did not have access to a classical dictionary when developing Greco-Roman Perseus but we used glossed indices for key reference works to provide basic information about 7,000 mythological and historical figures. We supplemented this with roughly one hundred commissioned new articles on key authors, sites and topics. We then used simple pattern matching to attach automatic links to Perseus texts. When the reader sees a reference to Alexander, a link appears that leads to descriptions of all the Alexanders about whom we have information, including Alexander the Great. We can compare the words around the Alexander in a given text to the language in the entries on the various Alexanders to determine which Alexander is probably meant, but even without such filtering, the lookup service became immensely popular and remains the most widely used function in the Perseus Digital Library.

Other Reference Works: Not all reference works are, like encyclopedias, organized with self-contained articles under discrete keywords. The London collection contains many guides — some many volumes long — describing the city. The organization is hierarchical and topographic: e.g., one section will cover Westminster and then follow the path of a hypothetical visitor. Sometimes individual buildings will have their own self-contained entries. In other cases, bold type or some other high-lighting will indicate how the text's focus shifts from one building/place to another. Tagging strategies can thus be crucial: a few hours can suffice to determine which italics phrases are keywords and which are foreign language quotes, regular emphasis, etc. Once keywords are identified as such, they can be used to generate automatic links and to lead readers to the relevant sections. It is easier to build this into the workflow for digitization than to retrofit dozens, if not hundreds, of such documents later.

All on-line data derives its value from the technologies that mediate between the user and the bits, but many of the most promising technologies require human mediation if they are to prove useful. The final section of this paper builds on the concept of a corpus editor, which we have introduced in earlier publications [2, 11].

4 Conclusion

This document has described some of the requirements and possible components that we have found to be important to cultural heritage collections. We have stressed those features that seem to us most distinctive but we have suggested that the particular needs of cultural heritage collections only anticipate issues that other disciplines may confront as their usage of digital libraries increases. We offer one service as an example of such a convergence.

Much of this paper describes strategies to support reading. Morphological analysers link inflected forms to dictionary entries. Information extraction systems map words to particular things. The importance of language and historical context have led us to focus on services of this type at an early stage of development. We are developing a knowledge tracking system for language readers: the system keeps track of what textbooks and readings an intermediate language student has read. When the student requests a new text in the target language, the system identifies which words the student should know and which unknown words are particularly important, given their frequency in this document and the interests of the student.

In the foreign language scenario, we seek to track semantics, syntax, grammar, and references to particular people and things. Consider, though, the situation of the interdisciplinary researcher moving into a new field or the student moving from text books to real scientific literature. The same infrastructure aimed at reading support can track the technical terms that the researcher/student should already know and should learn. The infrastructure is the same — indeed, in a hierarchy of difficulty technical terms are easier to identify than encyclopedic references (e.g., „Mr. Smith," „Springfield") and much easier to identify than the particular meanings of natural language (e.g., bank as „river bank" or „money bank"). By attacking the harder foreign language problem we lay the foundation for a service that supports reading in the scientific and medical areas as well.

References

1. Smith, D.A. and G.R. Crane, *Disambiguating Geographic Names in a Historical Digital Library*. 2001, Perseus Project/Tufts University: Medford, MA. http://www.perseus.tufts.edu/cgi-bin/ptext?doc=2000.06.0012.
2. Rydberg-Cox, J.A., A. Mahoney, and G.R. Crane. *Document Quality Indicators and Corpus Editions*. in *JDCL 2001: The First ACM+IEEE Joint Conference on Digital Libraries*. 2001. Roanoke, VA, USA: ACM Press.
3. Crane, G. *The Perseus Project and the Problems of Digital Humanities*. in *Standards und Methoden der Volltextdigitalisierung*. 2001. Trier, Germany: Mainz Academy.
4. Crane, G., et al., *Drudgery and Deep Thought: Designing Digital Libraries for the Humanities*. Communications of the ACM, 2001. **44**(5).
5. Crane, G., D.A. Smith, and C. Wulfman. *Building a Hypertextual Digital Library in the Humanities: A Case Study on London*. in *JDCL 2001: The First ACM+IEEE Joint Conference on Digital Libraries*. 2001. Roanoke, VA, USA: ACM Press.
6. Furuta, R., et al. *The Cervantes Project: Steps to a Customizable and Interlinked On-Line Electronic Variorum Edition Supporting Scholarship*. in *European Conference on Digital Libraries (ECDL 2001)*. 2001. Darmstadt, Germany: Springer.
7. Brocks, H., et al. *Customizable Retrieval Functions Based on User Tasks in the Cultural Heritage Domain*. in *European Conference on Digital Libraries (ECDL 2001)*. 2001. Darmstadt, Germany: Springer.
8. Chavez, R.F. and T.L. Milbank. *London calling: GIS, VR, and the Victorian period*. in *7th International Conference on Virtual Systems and Multimedia*. 2001. Berkeley, CA.
9. Daniels, M. *Is bigger better? web delivery of high-resolution images from the Museum of Fine Arts, Boston*. in *Museums and the Web*. 2000.
10. Ioannidis, Y., B. Croft, and E. Fox, *Digital Libraries in the Future: A Grand Challenge Vision for the 6th Framework Programme*. 2001, DELOS: Network of Excellence: Pisa, Italy.
11. Crane, G. and J.A. Rydberg-Cox. *New Technology and New Roles: The Need for "Corpus Editors"*. in *The Fifth ACM Conference on Digital Libraries*. 2000. San Antonio: ACM.
12. Hong, J.-S., B.-H. Chen, and J. Hsiang. *XSL-based Content Management for Multi-presentation Digital Museum Collections*. in *European Conference on Digital Libraries (ECDL 2001)*. 2001. Darmstadt, Germany: Springer.
13. Bergmark, D. and C. Lagoze. *An Architecture for Automatic Reference Linking*. in *European Conference on Digital Libraries (ECDL 2001)*. 2001. Darmstadt, Germany: Springer.

14. Mahoui, M. and S.J. Cunningham. *Search Behavior in a Research-Oriented Digital Library*. in *European Conference on Digital Libraries (ECDL 2001)*. 2001. Darmstadt, Germany: Springer.
15. Hinman, C., *The printing and proof-reading of the first folio of Shakespeare*. 1963, Oxford,: Clarendon Press. 2 v.
16. Hosley, R., R. Knowles, and R. McGugan, *Shakespeare Variorum Handbook: A Manual of Editorial Practice*. 1971, New York: Modern Language Association of America. 143.
17. Pantelia, M., *The Thesaurus Linguae Graecae*. 2002. http://www.tlg.uci.edu/~tlg/.
18. Martin, T.R., *Ancient Greece : from prehistoric to Hellenistic times*. 1996, New Haven: Yale University Press. xiii, 252.
19. Liddell, H.G., et al., *A Greek-English lexicon*. A new rev. and augm. throughout ed. 1940, Oxford,: The Clarendon Press. xlviii, 2111.
20. Andrews, E.A., et al., *A Latin dictionary founded on Andrews' edition of Freund's Latin dictionary. Rev., enl., and in geat part rewritten*. Rev., enl. ed. 1955, Oxford,: Clarendon Press. 1 l.,xiv,2019.
21. Oard, D., *Multimodal/Multingual Tools*. 2001, DARPA ITO Sponsored Research. http://www.darpa.mil/ipto/psum2001/J293-0.html.
22. Knight, E.H., *Knight's American mechanical dictionary*. 1877, New York, Hurd and Houghton, Cambridge [Mass.]: The Riverside press. 3 v.
23. Wheatley, H.B., *London Past and Present: Its History, Associations, and Traditions*. 1891, London: John Murray.
24. Dyer, F.H., *A compendium of the war of the rebellion*. 1908, Des Moines, Iowa,: The Dyer publishing company. 1796.
25. Hirschman, L., et al. *Integrated Feasibility Experiment for Bio-Security: IFE-Bio, A TIDES Demonstration*. in *HLT2001*. 2001. San Diego, CA.
26. Association for Machine Translation in the Americas. Conference (4th : 2000 : Cuernavaca Mexico) and J.S. White, *Envisioning machine translation in the information future : 4th Conference of the Association for Machine Translation in the Americas, AMTA 2000, Cuernavaca, Mexico, October 10-14, 2000 : proceedings*. 2000, Berlin ; New York: Springer. xv, 254.
27. Peters, C., ed. *CLEF 2001: Cross-Language System Evaluation Campaign*. 2001: Darmstadt, Germany.
28. Radev, D.R., S. Blair-Goldensohn, and Z. Zhang. *Interactive, Domain-Independent Identification and Summarization of Topically Related News Articles*. in *European Conference on Digital Libraries (ECDL 2001)*. 2001. Darmstadt, Germany: Springer.
29. Wayne, C.L. *Multilingual topic detection and tracking: Successful research enabled by corpora and evaluation*. in *LREC 2000: 2nd International Conference on Language Resources and Evaluation*. 2000. Athens, Greece.
30. Voohees, E.M. *Overview of the TREC 2001 Question Answering Track*. in *TREC 2001*. 2001. Gaithersburg, MD 20899: NIST.
31. Zaslavsky, A., A. Bia, and K. Monostori. *Using Copy-Detection and Text Comparison Algorithms for Cross-Referencing Multiple Editions of Literary Works*. in *European Conference on Digital Libraries (ECDL 2001)*. 2001. Darmstadt, Germany: Springer.

Visualization of Variants in Textual Collations to Analyze the Evolution of Literary Works in the Cervantes Project

Carlos Monroy, Rajiv Kochumman, Richard Furuta, Eduardo Urbina, Eréndira Melgoza, and Arpita Goenka

TEES Center for the Study of Digital Libraries
Texas A&M University
College Station, TX 77843-3112, USA
{cmonroy, rajiv, furuta, e-urbina, ere, arpita}@csdl.tamu.edu

Abstract. As part of the Cervantes Project digital library, we are developing an Electronic Variorum Edition (EVE) of *Don Quixote de la Mancha.* Multiple editors can create an EVE with our Multi Variant Editor for Documents (MVED), which allows collation of one base text against several comparison texts to identify, link and edit all existing variants among them. In this context we are investigating the use of visualizations to depict graphically variants in order to validate the accuracy of the textual transcriptions and to understand the similarities and differences among different printings and editions. Our broader goal is to enable users to analyze the collation's results and to discover facts about the evolution of the Quixote textual history, and to provide evidence to eliminate printing and compositor's errors and thus to produce a more correct edition closer to Cervantes' original manuscript. This paper describes the visualization tool, and presents the initial results of its use.

1 Introduction

The Cervantes Project was initiated in 1995 and is hosted at the Center for the Study of Digital Libraries at Texas A&M University. As stated in [9], its main goal is to provide "a comprehensive on-line reference and research site on the life and works of Miguel de Cervantes (1547-1616), the author of the classic *Don Quixote de la Mancha.*"

The main components of the project are: the Cervantes Digital Library (CDL), which provides an electronic repository of novels, plays, and other writings in different formats and versions; the Cervantes Digital Archive of Images (CDAI), an archive of photographic images documenting Cervantes' life and time; the Cervantes International Bibliography Online (CIBO), which contains a cumulative annotated bibliography of studies, editions, and translations of Cervantes' works.

M. Agosti and C. Thanos (Eds.): ECDL 2002, LNCS 2458, pp. 638-653, 2002.

The cornerstone of literary studies is the availability of critical editions that provide scholarly annotated texts. A key aspect of this process for Cervantes scholars is the access to documentary texts accurately transcribed as well as to the early printings of his works. To this end, one of the activities of our project has been to obtain multiple microfilmed copies of all the textually significant editions of Cervantes' best-known work, *Don Quixote*. Initially, the novel was published in two parts. The first edition (the *princeps*) of part one was published in Madrid in 1605. The *princeps* of part two dates from 1615, again published in Madrid. We have already obtained over thirty copies of the nine key early editions—indeed we believe that our collection is the most comprehensive ever put together—and our acquisition efforts are continuing. For example, only approximately 18 copies of the 1605 *princeps* are believe to have survived, and of these only 12 are currently accessible to scholars for digitizing and electronic editing. We have acquired already microfilms of 8 copies of the *princeps* of both parts. The work reported in this paper uses 6 of the first part *princeps* copies; the 2 remaining were acquired more recently and are still being incorporated. Additionally we report here on work using the first part princeps and copies of five additional of the significant early editions published between 1605 and 1637.

We seek to make this corpus easily-available to the Cervantes scholar. Until now, even the best of editions are based on limited knowledge of and access to textual sources, and even more limited forms of collation of such sources. Furthermore, traditionally, access to source materials has been through "filtered" sources, such as critical editions, often offering only a modernized eclectic text, and thus reflecting conjectural choices and preferences of the editors. Financial considerations associated with print have restricted the ability to include original source material. Given the current digital environment, we seek to create an *Electronic Variorum Edition* (EVE) of the *Don Quixote*, providing both the complete scholarly apparatus associated with a critical edition, but also access to the original sources in facsimile and transcribed formats. Towards that end, we have implemented tools for building, accessing, and viewing EVEs. One of the central tools, the MVED, described earlier in [8], provides the means for editing and creating an EVE.

The collation module of the MVED (Multi Variant Editor for Documents) enables an editor to collate a base text against a set of comparison texts. The output of this process is a hyperlinked set of variants, which in turn can be edited and/or annotated to provide further information and construct the critical apparatus To assist the editor in this process, we sought to find a method to highlight anomalies and discover textual patterns in the collation as basis for investigating the nature of the variants as authorial, compositorial or printing errors, and as points of departure to establish textual correlations and editorial filiation. Furthermore, we recognize a practical need in our project to validate the accuracy of the transcriptions of the texts, since those are created manually from an electronic template.

Previously, we have described briefly [11] our use of visualizations to depict the variants, and its utility in presenting anomalies that require further investigation. In this paper, we report further on our application of visualizations in detecting patterns of interest within collections of copies or editions of a text. Our earlier visualization tool presented its information as a static display. Beginning with the representations developed for static display, we have extended the visualizations to permit interactive exploration of the relationships depicted. In implementation, we have achieved this purpose by representing the information space in ItLv, a tool originally intended for presentation of timeline-based information spaces.

ItLv (Interactive TimeLine Viewer) [13] is based on earlier work in our Center by Kumar [12] regarding the use of interactive timeline viewers in representing relationships among items in an information space. Kumar investigated manipulations of the timeline representation and presentation to allow the flexible display of the attributes of a collection's information, as well as the synthesis of new attributes. Kumar noted that any attribute with ordered values could be mapped to the x or y axis of the display, and it is this observation that we use as the basis for our current visualization. ItLv represents a re-implementation and expansion of Kumar's prototype, allowing stable use of larger datasets. ItLv incorporates features and options such as searching, filtering, splitting, superimposing, and highlighting, to enable users to manipulate the results of the collation flexibly. As we will see in later sections, in our visualization we map copies/editions to the y axis and offset from the beginning of the text to the x axis. Initially, one could think that the editons should be placed on the x axis since they evolved over time; however, we extended the metaphor of the timeline in such a way that the "events" that take place in this space are the variants among the texts. A variant is positioned according to its starting point (i.e., offset from the beginning). Attributes of the variance (e.g., its length) are reflected in the visual appearance of its corresponding marker.

We are currently using the ItLv visualizations to accomplish two goals; 1) to refine the results of the collation, identifying false variants or errors in the textual transcriptions, and 2) using the refined collations to analyze the results and make targeted inferences, validating or invalidating hypotheses, and advancing interpretions about the similarities and differences among the texts. This process can lead to further discoveries such as patterns across the texts, which in turn could serve as indicators of the presence of several compositors working on different sections of the text and their individual tendencies regarding the introduction of textual variants. Therefore, the visualization provides a higher level of abstraction of the relationships among different copies of the text. In this paper, we describe the interactive options of ItLv and report the results of its use in refining the results of textual collation, as well in discovering facts about the nature of the texts themselves, and the relationships among them, to carry forward with a high degree of authority and confidence the needed editorial emendations.

2 Digital Libraries and Visualization Tools

Presently there are several initiatives and projects dedicated to the creation and use of digital libraries about ancient manuscripts, books, maps, and a variety of artifacts. The idea is not only to provide an online repository, but also to help scholars to perform analyses about the relationships among the components of the collections in the hope of understanding facts, data, and information in their historical and cultural contexts, and then to make those discoveries available to a wider audience. The Perseus Digital Library is one such example. Hosted at Tufts University, the Perseus Project [4] conceived as an evolving digital library in the humanities, was initially focused on the classical Greek world. However, it has evolved to include other topical areas in the humanities.

More focused on the analysis of textual history and variants, the Canterbury Tales Project [18] provides a computer-based repository of the transcriptions of all manuscripts and early editions of the *Canterbury Tales*. The manuscripts are then compared to generate a collection of agreements and disagreements, a process called collation. The results of the collation are used as input for computerized tools that help in reconstructing the history of the text. Finally, the materials and results of the analyses are published electronically. However, due to the fact that every word is categorized grammatically, the Canterbury Tales Project goes beyond being a collation-only project, making it interesting for areas such as; history of the language, dialects, and orthographic and morphological change.

In the process of analyzing patterns, similarities, and differences in large collection of texts, scholars often face challenges in visualizing different abstractions and datasets of those collections. Therefore, visualization tools have an important role as means to reduce the complexity of such analyses. The Compus visualization system [6] is an example of a visualization tool that depicts information about the structure of ancient textual manuscripts. Compus enables users to analyze the structure of a collection of texts by depicting TEI-enabled texts components relative to their position in the text, the tool also supports dynamic queries and structural transformations.

Visualizing elements in textual transcriptions can be accomplished in different ways based on the nature of the data and the needs of the users. LifeLines [14] illustrate the use of a visualization tool for personal histories applied to medical and court records, professional histories and other types of biographical records. In fact, regarding the benefits of the tool, they conclude, "[LifeLines] provide a complete visualization environment offering overview, zooming, filtering and details on demand. Color coding, filtering and dynamic highlighting unveiled relationships between events that may otherwise be difficult to see in paper records."

Finally, the power of visualizations using point representations in two-dimensional spaces for representing information collections and their relationships were pioneered in StarFields [1]. Ahlberg and Shneiderman focus particularly on the relevance of these displays in visual information seeking; discovery of the important attributes of large information spaces through browsing.

3 Visualizations in the Cervantes Project

3.1 Visualizations for Validating the Results of the Collation

Once the collation has generated the index of variants and prior to beginning the analysis of patterns and differences among them, it is necessary to validate the results of the collation process. The traditional approach involves the manual re-collation of the transcriptions against the digitized images in order to determine which variants are real and which are not. Obviously this constitutes a very cumbersome and time consuming process, especially for a collation with a high number of variants. Another approach is to use a graphical representation of the results of the collation, and to focus on patterns that seem unexpected or anomalous.

As an example, figure 1 shows the result of collating six copies of the *Quixote* 1605 *princeps*. One of the copies of the *princeps* is defined to be the "base", and is not represented directly in the display. The rows of the display show the result of comparing the "base" to each of the copies, in turn. The display shows the first chapter which contains four pages, delimited by the vertical bars in the visualization. Ideally, one would expect that all six copies would be the same and that any differences would flag errors. As it turns out, this is not the case for this edition. Following Knowles' early textual studies and partial collations of several copies of the *princeps*, Casasayas [3] believes that of the approximately 18 known copies, no two are completely alike. Some differences are likely due to changes made during the print run, but some may result from deliberate attempts at deception in later times [10]. Our examination of the visualization pointed out examples of transcription errors (due to unclear patches in the original microfilms), one "unexpected" action taken by the collation algorithm (represented by the unusually long length of one of the variances), and differences of the form identified by others previously (including those in the first two pages). See [11] for further explanation of this display.

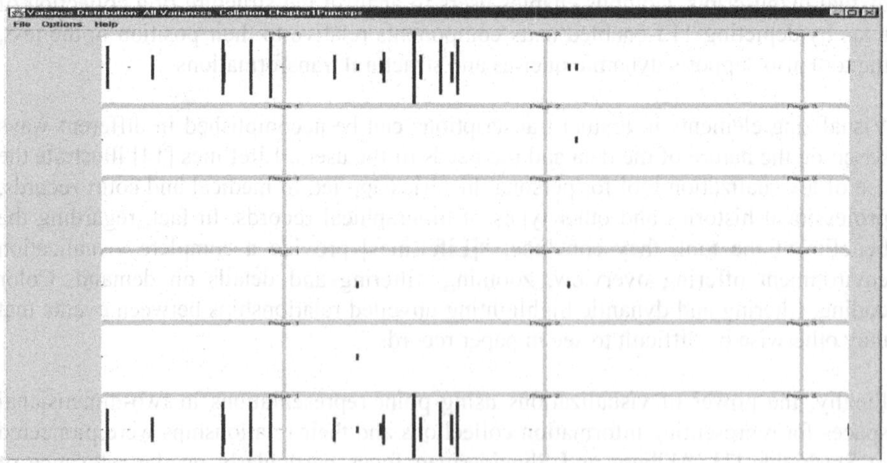

Fig. 1. Depicting variants in six copies of chapter one of the princeps

Our static visualization only depicted the results in the screen, but did not provide further information such as the content of the variant, its length in characters, and the offset in the text; nor does allow interaction. Switching to the ItLv allowed us to provide a more interactive visualization. In figure 2, variants between five editions of *Don Quixote* and the *princeps*, which is the base text in this case, are shown. The five editions are depicted in the Y-axis, the offset in the text is depicted in the X-axis, and the vertical bars represent page divisions in the *princeps*, as in the previous example. As would be expected, many more variances have been identified in this collection, since the different editions were printed in separate locations between 1605 and 1637 (more detail will be given later). In this display, the mouse cursor has been positioned over one of the variances. A pop-up window is displayed which contains information about the variant, such as its content, its offset in the text, its length, and the image of original text. This is connected to the axes by blue lines, one horizontal and the other vertical, which show the context of a variant. All variants with some similarities are displayed in a different color, in this case, are those containing the same string, possibly as a substring. In this particular case the variant is between the word "que" and its abbreviation q̃ , which we encode in our transcriptions as " <q>".

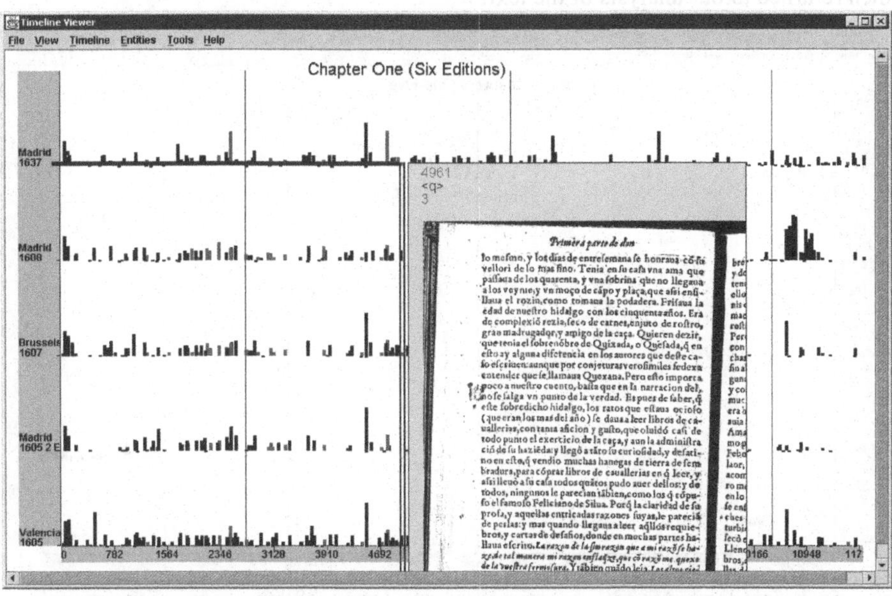

Fig. 2. The timeline viewer depicting variants among six editions of *Don Quixote*

3.2 Visualizing the Results of Collating Several Copies of One Edition

Figure 3 shows the results of collating the first five chapters of the six copies of the Quixote 1605 *princeps*. In this figure, as before, the Y-axis from bottom to top corresponds to copies one to five respectively. The X-axis from left to right corresponds to the offset in the text. Unlike the earlier example, the vertical lines here depict the beginning of each chapter.

As before, a relatively small number of variants have been identified; this is not a surprise since copies of the same edition are presumably identical. Three uncommon patterns stand out. The first is a high number of variants in chapter one of copy five– these are the rectangles depicted on the top leftmost part of figure 3. Second are a high number of variants in chapter five of copy two– these are the rectangles depicted at the bottom rightmost part of figure 3. And third is a variant containing 49 characters in chapter three of copy one, the large rectangle depicted at the center bottom in figure 3.

After reviewing the original images and the textual transcriptions we determined that the first pattern represented true variants such as capitalization, missing punctuations, abbreviations, and accentual differences. The second pattern in chapter five of the second copy was a problem in the conversion of the text because the text editor we used did not encode accented letters or special characters correctly. The third pattern was a miscalculation due to transcription of page numbering and did not represent a true variance. We noted that variances two and three required correction to the textual transcriptions and requested that the transcribers make the corrections. We then returned to our analysis of the text.

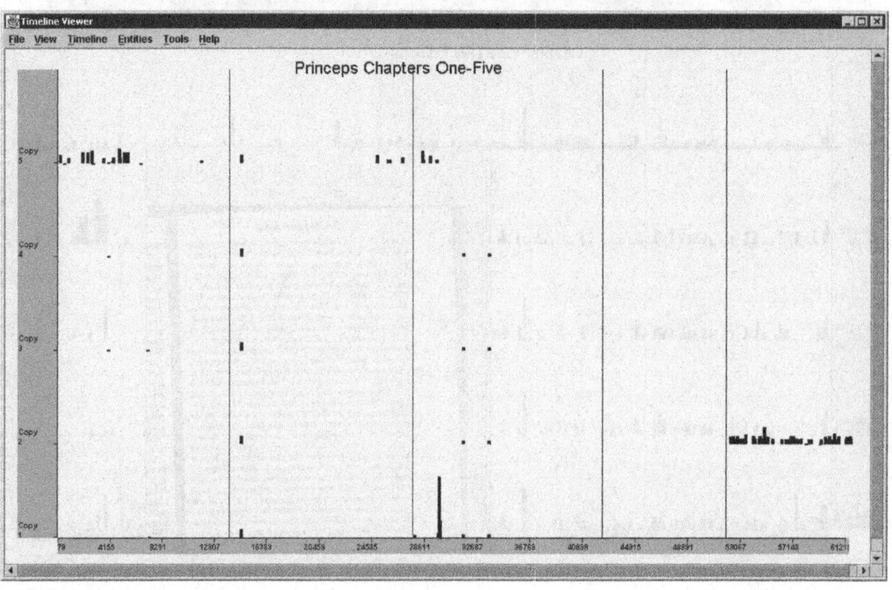

Fig. 3. Results of the collation of chapters one through five of five copies of Don Quixote's 1605 princeps before filtering false variants and transcription errors

Having determined that the variances in groups two and three were not significant to our analysis, we specified that ItLv should suppress their display. Figure 4 depicts the results of the collation after removing those variants. Note that the cluster of false variants in chapter five of copy two and the long variant in chapter three of copy one, have been removed. Further analysis could then be carried out, suggesting, for example, that copy 5 was "aberrant" in some fashion, and consequently would not be a good choice for base text when we subsequently compared multiple editions.

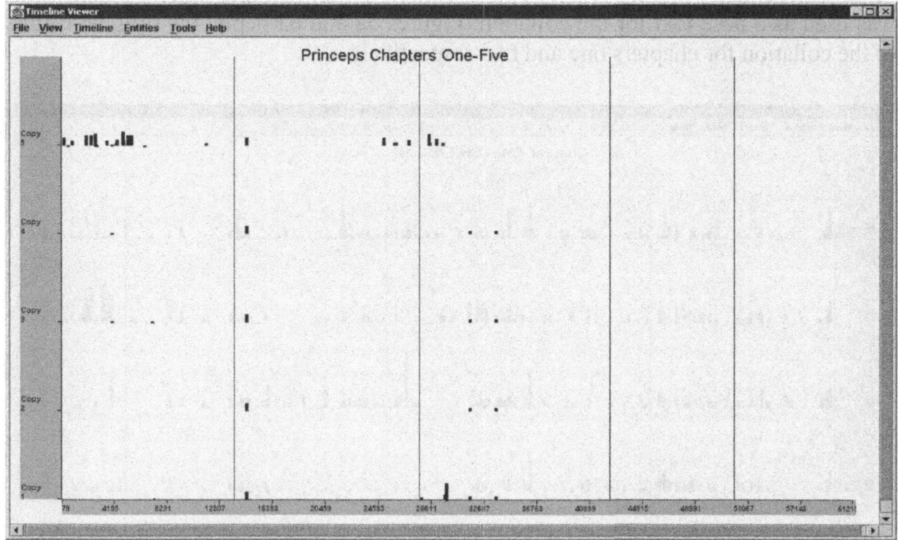

Fig. 4. Results of the collation of chapters one through five of five copies of Don Quixote's edition of Madrid 1605 called the Princeps after filtering false variants and transcription errors

In the analysis of copies of the same edition, the visualization tool can be used to detect "states" produced, as defined by Carter, [2] "When alterations, corrections, additions or excisions are effected in a book during the manufacture, so that copies exhibiting variations go on sale. These variants copies are conveniently classified as belonging to different 'states' of the edition." We believe this kind of analysis could be extremely useful for determining the existence of states of a given edition with a high degree of authority and confidence, particularly when more copies become available in the future.

3.3 Visualizations for Detecting Patterns

After false variants are detected and removed, the resulting dataset constitutes a more reliable source for textual analysis. For instance, regarding the evolution of a literary work, it is crucial to analyze the results of the variants to discover transmission and composition patterns that may show evidence regarding what happened to a given text and when. Moreover, a more ambitious goal would be to recreate the original manuscript or at least an idealized, as intended by Cervantes. This corresponds to a stated goal of the Canterbury Tales project [18]: "Our first aim is as old as textual scholarship: we want to find out, as nearly as we can, what Chaucer actually wrote."

The second case analyzed compares the results of collating chapters one and two of six editions of the first part of *Don Quixote*. Figures 5 and 6 depict the results of the collation; the Y-axis from bottom to top corresponds to five of the editions in the following order, Valencia 1605, Madrid 1605 (Second Edition), Brussels 1607, Madrid 1608, and Madrid 1637. The sixth edition is the *princeps*, Madrid 1605, which was used as a base text for the collation. Figures 5a and 6a depict the original results of the collation for chapters one and two respectively.

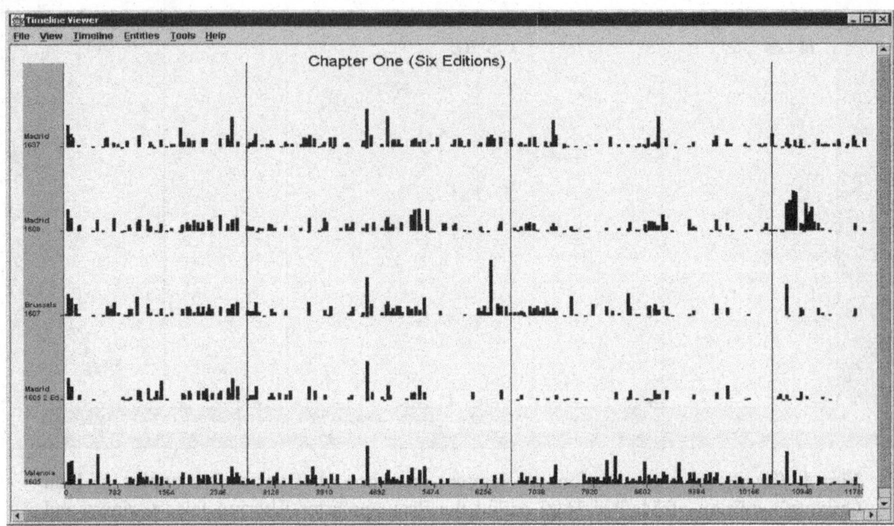

Fig. 5a. Results of the collation of chapter one before applying the filter

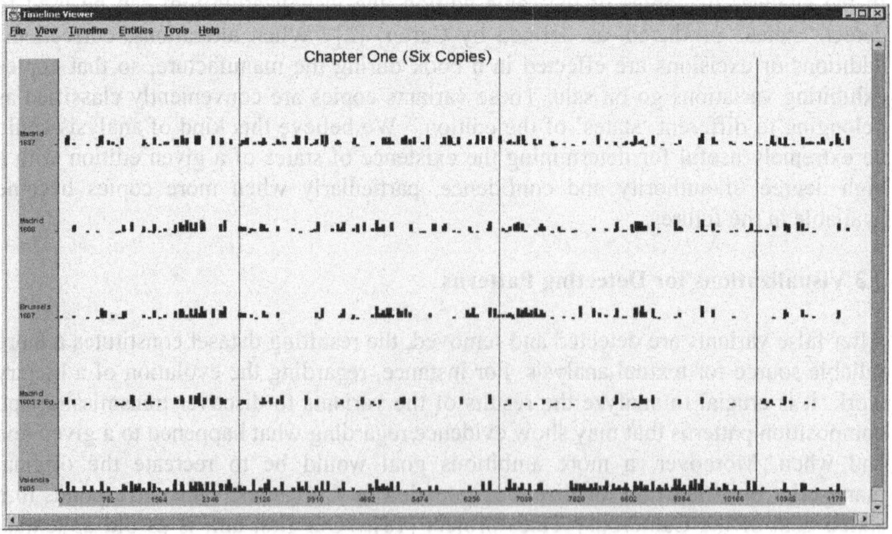

Fig. 5b. Results of the collation of chapter one after applying the filter

After reviewing the results, we found that several of the variants of length greater than ten characters were due to errors in the collation process rather than true variants. Therefore, these false variants need to be removed, otherwise the user can make false conclusions. Removing false variants as a previous step in the analysis of the collation can be done in two different ways. The first way is by modifying the textual transcriptions, rerunning the collation process, and finally displaying the results in the timeline viewer. A better and more efficient approach is having a mechanism to remove false variants directly in the visualization tool without generating the collation again; this is accomplished with the ItLv filtering option. Figures 5b and 6b depict the result of the collation for chapters one and two respectively after applying the filtering option.

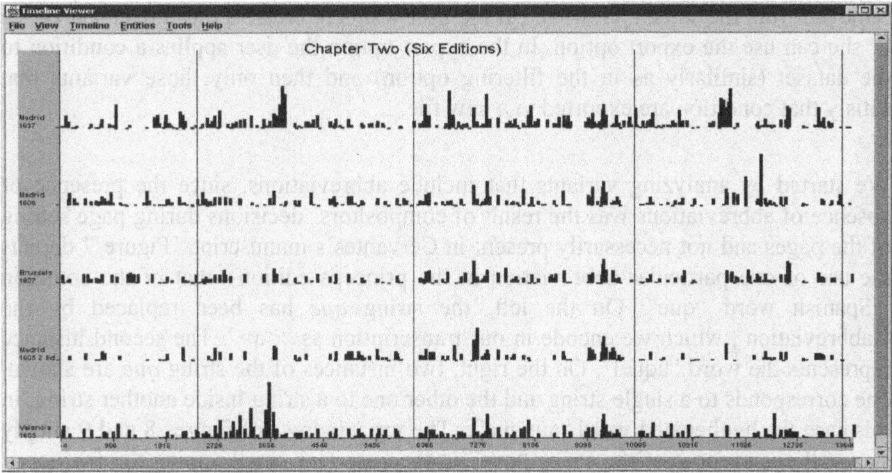

Fig. 6a. Results of the collation of chapter two before applying the filter

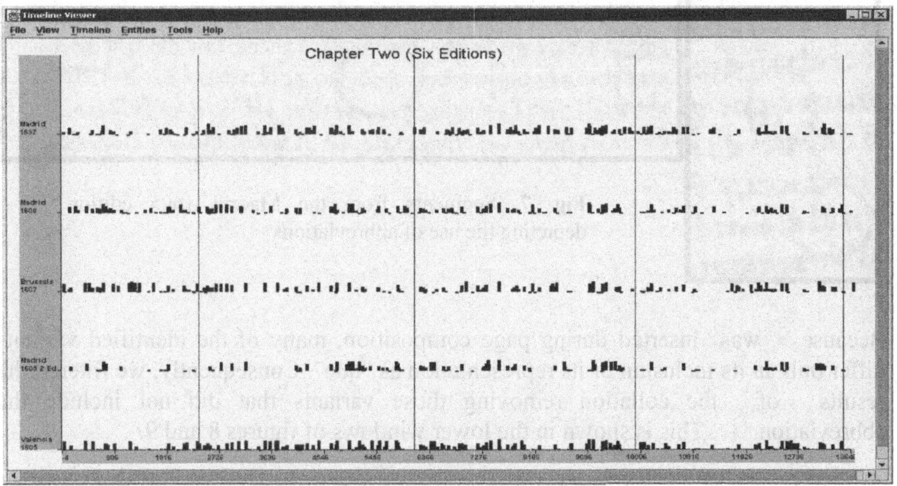

Fig. 6b. Results of the collation of chapter two after applying the filter

The filter option is constrained-based; therefore the user is presented with all the attributes of the variants, as well with the following conditions: a) equal, b) not equal, c) less than, d) greater than, e) less or equal to, f) greater or equal to, and g) containing. The last condition enables users to filter the dataset based on a substring, e.g. the user wants to filter those variants containing the string "que". Once the filter has been applied, only those variants that satisfy the condition will be depicted. The filtering option can be applied again to this subset of variants, using either the same or a different attribute and condition. And this process can be applied again and again. The filter can also be removed, this will restore the original dataset.

The filtering process do not remove false variants from the data source, they are only removed from the screen. However, if the user wants to create a clean data source, he or she can use the export option. In the export option the user applies a condition to the dataset (similarly as in the filtering option) and then only those variants that satisfy that condition are exported to a new file.

We started by analyzing variants that include abbreviations, since the presence or absence of abbreviations was the result of compositors' decisions during page setting of the pages and not necessarily present in Cervantes's manuscript. Figure 7 depicts the use of one particular abbreviation in the princeps edition—that of the common Spanish word "que". On the left, the string *que* has been replaced by the q̃abbreviation , which we encode in our transcription as "<q>". The second instance represents the word "aquel". On the right, two instances of the string *que* are shown, one corresponds to a single string and the other one to a string inside another string, in this case the hyphenated word "aunque". The top windows of figures 8 and 9 simply show all occurrences of the string "que" in the base text, emphasizing the frequency with which the word is found in chapters one and two respectively.

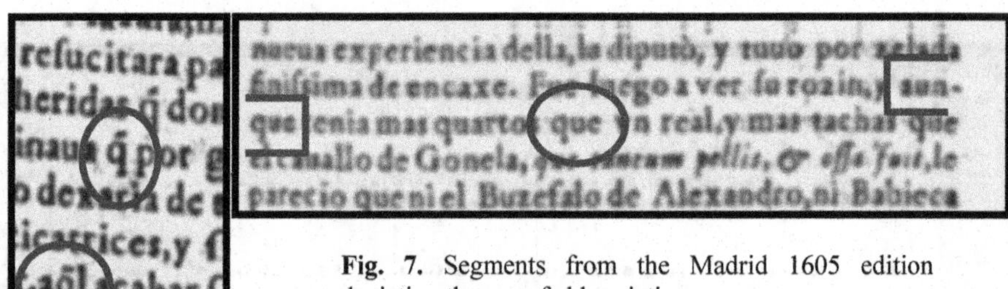

Fig. 7. Segments from the Madrid 1605 edition depicting the use of abbreviations

Because q̃ was inserted during page composition, many of the identified variants differ only in its inclusion or its representation as "que". Consequently, we filtered the results of the collation removing those variants that did not include the abbreviation q̃ . This is shown in the lower windows of figures 8 and 9.

For chapter one, with the exception of two variants at the end of page four and none in page three, we found that most variants appear from the second half of page one up to the end of page two. Initially we thought that those variants would be replacing all the "que" strings in the base text, therefore, we depicted all the ocurrences of the string "que" in the base text (window at the top of figure 8). But since the string "que" appears regularly across the q̃ whole chapter, we can therefore raise the hypothesis that the pattern of the abbreviation as a compositorial variant could reflect the preference of an individual compositor in charge of those sections of the book in the Madrid 1605 edition. Significantly, that abbreviation was passed on to the next editions as we can see a similar pattern from bottom to top (window at the bottom of figure 8).

For chapter two, variants were more scattered. However, with the exception of two variants in page one and one more in the second half of page two, most of the variants are concentrated on the first half of page three and across page four (window at the bottom of figure 9). Ocurrences of the string "que" in the base text are depicted in the window at the top of figure 9. In this case, it is more difficult to conclude about the intervention of compositors in certain parts of the text.

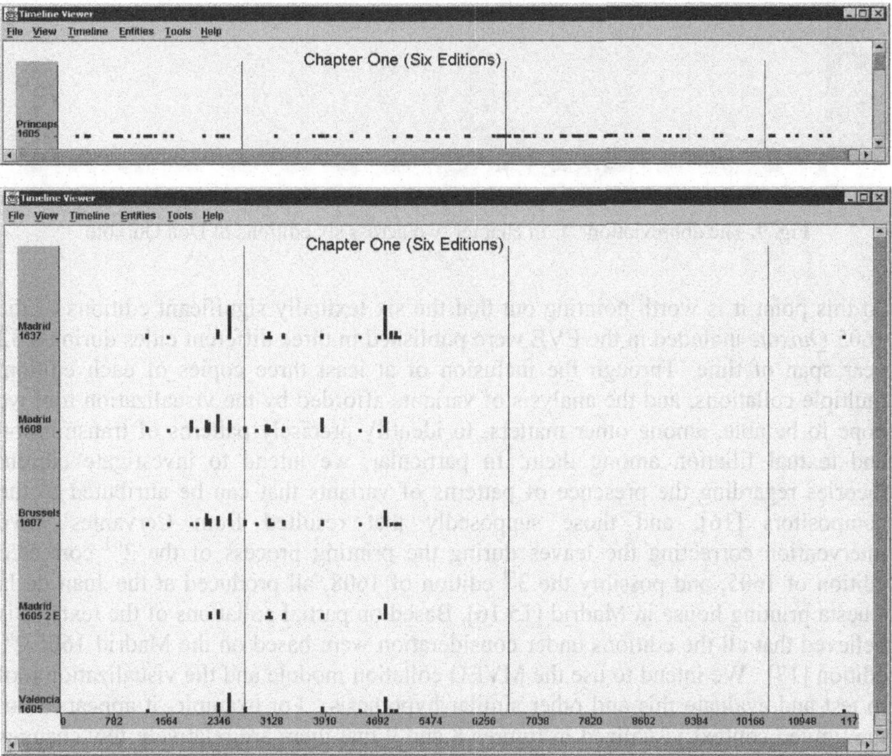

Fig. 8. The abbreviation q̃ in chapter one across six editions of Don Quixote

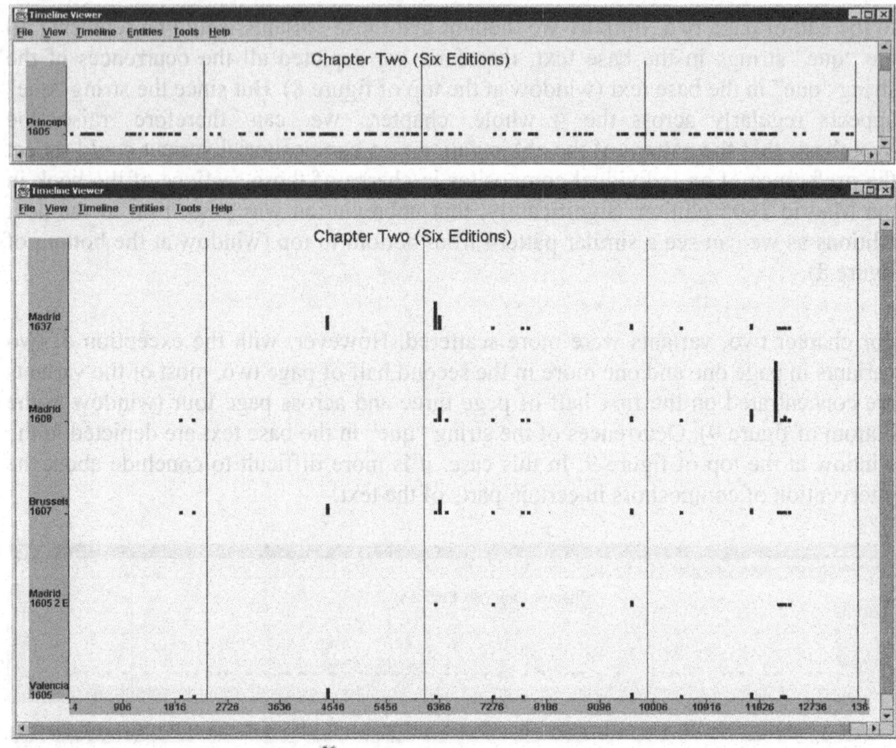

Fig. 9. The abbreviation q̃ in chapter two across six editions of Don Quixote

At this point it is worth pointing out that the six textually significant editions of the 1605 *Quixote* included in the EVE were published in three different cities during a 32 year span of time. Through the inclusion of at least three copies of each edition, multiple collations, and the analysis of variants afforded by the visualization tool we hope to be able, among other matters, to identify precisely patterns of transmission and textual filiation among them. In particular, we intend to investigate current theories regarding the presence of patterns of variants that can be attributed to the compositors [16], and those supposedly that resulted from Cervantes' own intervention correcting the leaves during the printing process of the 2nd corrected edition of 1605, and possibly the 3rd edition of 1608, all produced at the Juan de la Cuesta printing house in Madrid [15,16]. Based on partial collations of the texts, it is believed that all the editions under consideration were based on the Madrid 1605 2nd edition [17]. We intend to use the MVED collation module and the visualization tool to test and evaluate this and other similar hypothesis. For example, it appears from the limited context visualized in figures 8 and 9 that there are relatively few changes between the Madrid 1605 *princeps* and the Madrid 1605 second edition (the next to bottom row in the lower windows). This is consistent with the knowledge that both editions were produced at the same printing house. In contrast, more differences are shown between the *princeps* and the 1605 Valencia edition (the top row in the figures). Continuing this analysis across larger segments of the corpus and with selection of different editions to serve as base text for collations may provide further evidence about the relationships.

4 Conclusions and Future Work

ItLv more than an improvement with respect to state of the art visualization systems, is a tool that exploits visualization to allow the exploration of variants among different versions of texts. ItLv takes the concepts of previous visualization systems and tailors it to enable the exploration of similarities and differences among several texts, by means of its flexibility and functionality.

Despite the limited number of existing copies of the *princeps* available for digitization and textual analysis, the sample editions and chapters included in the EVE at this time in which we have tested the ItLv visualization tool shows its usefulness for validating the results of textual collation and the reliability of the transcriptions, and its functionality as a heuristic device to help to understand the relationships, similarities, and differences among different editions and/or copies of the same edition of the *Quixote.*

Nevertheless, our testing also indicates the need to further refine and expand its capabilities. For instance, in the current implementation, there is no provision to keep track of the filters that have been applied to the dataset in any given session. We think that a useful feature would be for ItLv to record the filter conditions as rules, allowing users to recreate that session and make comparisons between the application of a series or combination of filters.

As of now the collation module of the MVED generates a set of linked variants; the process of categorizing those variants is done separately during the editing process by the MVED. We believe that the interactive features of ItLv will increase the editor's ability to analyze differences and similarities among the texts, and that this will be further enhanced by including the variance categorizations identified during editing (e.g., authorial, compositorial or typographical errors) into the set of attributes available for visualization.

By graphically encoding variant attributes such as puntuation, abbreviation, typographical and spelling errors, as well as lexical changes; ItLv can support ortographical, morphological, typographical, and lexical analysis of the texts. This can be accomplished by using the filtering option, since each of the categories of variants can be isolated and visualized separately.

Edition attributes such as formal divisions in parts or chapters, presence of extratextual materials, annotations, and illustratations, can also be encoded as a separate data set. Superimposing the edition attributes on the variants dataset, we expect that will expand scholar's perspective and understanding of context in variant analysis.

Finally, we believe that ItLv can be used to better understand the textual history of a literary works such as the *Quixote* by identifying, connecting and visualizing relationships among the different components of an edition such as illustrations, extra textual materials, variants and notes, along a period of time. Therefore, it will contribute significantly in the preparation of a critical variorum edition tracing the evolution of the contributions of a particular editor or commentator, as well as in the comparative study of intertextual borrowings and influences.

Acknowledgements. This material is based upon work supported by the National Science Foundation under Grant no. IIS-0081420. Support for this work was also provided in part by the Interdisciplinary Research Initiative Program, administered by the Office of the Vice President for Research, Texas A&M University.

References

[1] Ahlberg, C., and Shneiderman, B., "Visual information seeking: tight coupling of dynamic query filters with Starfield displays", Conference proceedings on Human factors in computing systems: celebrating interdependence, Boston, MA, 1994, pp. 313-317.

[2] Carter, J., "ABC for Book Collectors." 7th edition. Oak Knoll Press, 1995.

[3] Casasayas, J. M., "Ensayo de una guía de bibliografía cervantina," Tomo V. Mallorca, 1995.

[4] Crane, G., "The Perseus Project and beyond: How building a digital library challenges the humanities and technology", *D-Lib Magazine*, January 1998.

[5] Crane, G., Smith, D., Wulfman, C., "Building a Hypertextual Digital Library in the Humanities: A Case Study on London.". Proceedings of the first ACM/IEEE-CS joint Conference on Digital Libraries, Pittsburgh, Pennsylvania, May 1998, pp. 426-434.

[6] Fekete, J., Dufournaud, N., "Compus: Visualization and Analysis of Structured Documents for Understanding Social Life in the 16th Century", Proceedings of the fifth ACM Conference on Digital Libraries, San Antonio, Texas, 2000.

[7] Flores, R. M., "The Compositors of the First and Second Madrid Editions of Don Quixote Part I." London: Modern Humanities Research Association, 1975.

[8] Furuta, R., Kalasapur, S., Kochumman, R., Urbina, E., Vivancos-Pérez, R., "The Cervantes Project: Steps to a Customizable and Interlinked On-line Electronic Variorum Edition Supporting Scholarship", Research and Advanced Technology for Digital Libraries: 5th European Conference, ECDL 2001, Darmstadt, Germany, September 2001, pp. 71-82.

[9] Furuta, R., Hu, S., Kalasapur, S., Kochumman, R, Urbina, E., Vivancos-Pérez, R., "Towards an Electronic Variorum Edition of Don Quixote", Proceedings of the first ACM/IEEE-CS joint conference on Digital Libraries, Roanoke, Virginia, 2001, pp. 444-445.

[10] Knowles, E. B., Jr., "Notes on the Madrid, 1605, editions of Don Quijote." *Hispanic Review* 14 (1946): 47-58.

[11] Kochumman, R., Monroy, C., Furuta, R., Goenka, A., Urbina, E., and Melgoza, E., "Towards an Electronic Variorum Edition of Cervantes' Don Quixote: Visualizations that support preparation.", to appear in the ACM Joint Conference on Digital Libraries, Portland Oregon, July 2002.

[12] Kumar, V., Furuta, R., Allen, R., "Metadata Visualization for Digital Libraries: Interactive Timeline Editing and Review", in Proceedings of the third ACM conference on Digital Libraries, Pittsburgh, Pennsylvania, May 1998, pp. 126-123.

[13] Monroy, C., "Augmenting Cognition through Information Visualization Using a Timeline Viewer," Masters of Computer Science Project Report, Department of Computer Science, Texas A&M University, 2002.

[14] Plaisant, C., Milash, B., Rose, A., Widoff, S., Shneiderman, B. "LifeLines: visualizing personal histories", in Proceedings of CHI'96, Vancouver, BC, Canada, April 14-18, 1996, pp. 221-227.

[15] Rico, F., "Historia del texto." *Don Quijote de la Mancha*. Barcelona: Instituto Cervantes-Crítica, 1998.

[16] Rico, F., "El 'original' del *Quijote*: del borrador a la imprenta," *Quimera* 173 (Oct 1998): 8-11.

[17] Urbina, E., Furuta, R., Goenka, A., Kochumman, R. , Melgoza, E., Monroy, C. "Texto, contextos e hipertexto: la crítica textual en la era digital y la *Edición electrónica variorum del* Quijote-*IV Centenario*." To appear in *Quaderni di Letterature Iberiche e Iberoameicane*, Issue #27, Dipartimento di Scienze del Linguaggio e delle Letterature Comparate dell'Università degli Studi di Milano, 2002.

[18] "The Canterbury Tales Project", De Montfort University, Leicester, England. http://www.cta.dmu.ac.uk/projects/ctp/index.html. Accessed on May 25, 2002.

Alinari Online: Access Quality through a Cultural Photographic Heritage Site

Andrea de Polo and Sam Minelli

Fratelli Alinari Photo Archives,
Largo Alinari 15, 50123 Florence, Italy
{andrea, sam}@alinari.it
http://www.alinari.com

Abstract. The unique heritage of the Alinari collections gives life to one of the biggest international centers of photographic and iconographic documentation with over 3.5 million vintage images from the 19the and 20the century from all over the world.
Today Alinari is a modern reality operating in the wider field of image and communication: a brand name which guarantees an age-old fund of experience combined with state-of-the-art technological skills. A good example of this sinergy is given in the REGNET project, which aims to set up a functional network of service centres in Europe which provides IT-services dedicated to Cultural Heritage organisations and will be an enabler of eBusiness activities for CH organizations. Multi media industries enabling the production of electronic publications will be integrated. It will provide access and use of digital data (scientific and cultural) as well as of physical goods as provided by museum shops.

Alinari represents an irreplaceable landmark for preserving, cataloguing, making known and handing down, through photography, Italian and European history, society, art and culture. The unique heritage of the Alinari collections gives life to one of the biggest international centers of photographic and iconographic documentation with over 3.5 million vintage images from the 19the and 20the century from all over the world.
Alinari main focus on EC projects has been: Watermarking and IP rights, cultural heritage matters, content provider, high speed communication, security and user authentication, ecommerce solution, data compression, picture retrieval/pattern recognition and wavelet compression/edge detection.
Alinari is currently in the process to provide the historical archive, on-line, through the „Alinari On Line" project. The aims of the demo is to show how is done the catalogue, restore, digitize and retrieve on-line process, through a powerful but easy to use English-Italian database.
The images are first acquired in digital form using a high end flat bed Creo EverSmart Supreme scanner. The state-of-the-art scanner is capable of scanning images up to 8000 dpi, with a dynamic range of 4.3 all over the plate (technology X-Y). Than the images are optimized and color correct on a separate workstation. Last but not least, the RGB files are embedded with the ICC ColorSync profiles in order to provide the best color gamut according to the proper final usage. A first corpus of 145.000 images are already online, and by the end of year 2003, 250.000 will be available for

M. Agosti and C. Thanos (Eds.): ECDL 2002, LNCS 2458, pp. 654-655, 2002.

consultation and professional usage. All images are watermarked using Digimarc technology.

The four players within the network are the content providers, the service centre operators, the system developers and end users. The content providers (museums, libraries, archives etc.) provide access (via wired and wireless communication) to their digital contents, services and products and offer them to their clients (B2C). In return they can use the REGNET facilities for multimedia productions and data base management, or cooperate with other REGNET partners during the creation of data bases, generation of multimedia products or creation of a virtual exhibition (B2B). The service centre operators will generate income by providing the technical infrastructure (software/hardware) to content providers and other partners within the REGNET network. They offer additional IT-services and consultancies. And the system developers are selling the REGNET system to other cultural service centres and content providers. For the end user the system offer easy and wide access to cultural heritage data information and the purchase of CH related goods and services at one point, with stress on the production of personalized goods (e.g. CDROM) and services.

ALINARI has strategic partnerships with several leading companies including:
Telecom Italy, Nikon Italy, CREO, Digimarc, IPM-NET, Apple Italy, HP Italy, IBM Italy, IPIX, etc…

An Access Control System for Digital Libraries and the Web: The *MaX* Prototype Demonstration*

Elisa Bertino[1], Elena Ferrari[2], and Andrea Perego[1]

[1] Dipartimento di Scienze dell'Informazione, Università degli Studi di Milano,
Via Comelico 39/41, 20135 Milano, Italy
{bertino,perego}@dsi.unimi.it

[2] Dip. di Sc. Chimiche, Fisiche e Matematiche, Università degli Studi dell'Insubria,
Via Valleggio 11, 22100 Como, Italy
elena.ferrari@uninsubria.it

1 Overview

The goal of this demonstration is to present the main features of *MaX*, a system enforcing access control to Web documents. This system has been developed at the Dipartimento di Scienze dell'Informazione of the University of Milano in the framework of the European project EUFORBIA, and implements the *Milano Model*, an access control mechanism conceived for Digital Library (DL) and Web environments.

The Milano Model supports a flexible specification of access control policies based on the qualifications and characteristics of users (including positive and negative policies) rather than just on specific users. In fact, to better take into account user profiles in the formulation of access control policies, the Milano Model associates each user with one or more *credentials*. A credential is a set of properties concerning a user that are relevant for security purposes. To make the task of credential specification easier, credentials with similar structures are grouped into *credential-types*, organised into a *credential-type hierarchy*. Thus, access control policies can be given either explicitly to users, by specifying their identifiers, or implicitly by imposing a set of conditions that the credentials must satisfy. Moreover, access control to DL objects is based not only on object IDs but also on objects content. Content-based access control is supported according to two different and orthogonal strategies: a) by pre-processing the objects using a document management mechanism which is capable of extracting concepts from documents and eventually organising them into a hierarchy; b) by using the labelling mechanism provided by the PICS (Platform for Internet Content Selection) W3C standard. Thus, content-based access control policies can apply to all the objects containing either a particular combination of concepts or a particular combination of PICS ratings. Finally, the Milano Model supports both *browsing* and *authoring privileges*, with various subtypes within each privilege

* The work is partially supported by the European Community under the EUFORBIA project (`http://www.saferinternet.org/filtering/euforbia.asp`).

M. Agosti and C. Thanos (Eds.): ECDL 2002, LNCS 2458, pp. 656–657, 2002.

type. Additionally, we provide support for the specification of negative as well as positive policies.

The first reference application domain of the Milano Model was the Global Legal Information Network (GLIN), a project originally undertaken by the United States Law Library of Congress. However, the Milano Model has been designed to be general enough to be suitable for the protection of other domains as well. Thanks to that characteristic, we have applied the Milano Model to a domain similar to DLs access control, that is, the *filtering* of Web documents, in the context of the European project EUFORBIA, whose main goal is to contribute to the development and use of new generations of Internet filtering systems, more powerful and flexible than the existing ones, and easier to adapt to the cultural, political or religious differences. This aim is attained by associating with Web documents *conceptual annotations* – that is, 'neutral' descriptions of Web documents content – expressed by the NKRL (Narrative Knowledge Representation Language) formal language, and using an ontology, referred to as *EUFORBIA Conceptual Hierarchy*. In this framework, the Milano Model has been used to develop an access control prototype system, referred to as Ma$\mathcal{X}$, which provides a user management model suitable for both individual and institutional users, and enforces content-based access control to Web documents. In particular, Ma$\mathcal{X}$ implements the EUFORBIA Conceptual Hierarchy and makes use of the EUFORBIA conceptual annotations for the evaluation of objects content, mantaining nevertheless the compatibility with the PICS standard.

2 System Description and Demonstration

Ma$\mathcal{X}$ is a Java-based system, built on top of the Oracle DBMS, and it is structured into three main components: 1) the *Access Control Module*, which intercepts each access request submitted by a user and verifies whether an access request can be granted or not according to the access control policies specified by the System Administrator (SA); 2) the *Database*, which stores all the needed security information; 3) the *Web Interface*, for performing user authentication and for the management of the access control system. Ma$\mathcal{X}$ works as a proxy server, and can be used both in a LAN context (installing it on a server of the local network) and by home users (by configuring the Internet connection to use as a proxy a remote server running Ma$\mathcal{X}$).

The Ma$\mathcal{X}$ demonstration is organised according to two phases. Firstly, we show a) how the SA can configure the access control system building a credential-type hierarchy suited for his/her needs and specifying credential attributes relevant for access control; b) how the SA can insert users data and specify access control policies with respect to both specific users, credential-types and constraints on credential attributes. We use as domain an institutional user, in particular a high school whose SA has to specify different access control policies with respect to students, teachers and administrative staff. Secondly, we demonstrate the behaviour of the prototype system with respect to access requests submitted by different users for Web documents with different content.

Human Language Technology for Automatic Annotation and Indexing of Digital Library Content

Kalina Bontcheva and Hamish Cunningham

Department of Computer Science, University of Sheffield
211 Portobello St, Sheffield, UK S1 4DP
{kalina,hamish}@dcs.shef.ac.uk

Abstract. This demo will present a set of domain-independent and customisable Human Language Technology (HLT) tools and the way they were applied for annotating 18*th* century OldBailey proceedings and indexing multimedia content. This demo accompanies the paper with the same title.

1 Overview

Each of these digital library applications posed a unique challenge: the court trials required adapting the language processing components to the non-standard written conventions of 18th century English, while the football collection presented the challenge of indexing material in multiple modalities - video, audio, semi-structured documents, and free text (newspaper reports). In both cases, we used as a basis our robust and customisable named entity recogniser, which comes as part of ANNIE - A Nearly New Information Extraction system (freely available as part of the GATE system: `http://gate.ac.uk`). In OldBaileyIE we also used the graphical environment of GATE, which allows humans to verify and correct the automatically annotated documents.

First we will demonstrate the set of language technology tools and how they can be used to annotate named entities in documents (e.g., person names, organisations, locations, dates, money amounts, percents). These tools are freely available for research and commercial use and are also made customisable, so they can be adapted to new domains and applications.

Next we will demonstrate the automatic annotation of the 18th century OldBailey texts and present the visual environment used for annotation error correction. We will also demonstrate how this environment can be used for manual annotation, independent of the language technology tools.

Finally we will demonstrate how multimedia content can be indexed and searched using human language technology. The demonstrator is in the football domain, where video and textual sources about matches are indexed and can be accessed via a user-friendly interface.

These tools are capable of supporting multiple languages through Unicode. For further details papers from the GATE publications page:
`http://gate.ac.uk/gate/doc/papers.html`.

M. Agosti and C. Thanos (Eds.): ECDL 2002, LNCS 2458, p. 658, 2002.

The IntraText Digital Library: XML-Driven Online Library Based on High Accessibility, Lexical Hypertextualization and Scholarly Accuracy in Philological / Textual Notations

Nicola Mastidoro

Eulogos S.p.A., Progetto IntraText, Via Cimone 59,
00141 Roma, Italy
n.mastidoro@eulogos.net
http://www.intratext.com

The IntraText Digital Library born in 1999. At June 2002 it offers over 3000 full-text books and collections in 36 languages; the readers (over 5000 subscribed the News) access over 1 million pages per month. Six interface languages are available.

The core of the project is a XML-driven Digital Library Framework offering high accessibility and scholarly quality in text representation: multi-level footnotes, philological notations, distinction between the lexicon of the author and that of other sources in concordance, hyphenation, sorting, etc. It is based on a scalable, low-cost architecture intended to manage (with workflow control) publishing and archiving books and collections by local or remote users and serving thousands of readers.

ETML, a very accurate text-to-XML translation metalanguage, has been defined. It simplifies the text-to-XML process, provides tools for philological notations and gives automatic tools to create hypertexualized collections of archived works, e.g. *opera omnia.* ETML allows non-technically-skilled people to produce XML simply using any text-editor and e-mail, dramatically reducing times in manual processing: it takes about 30 minutes to produce an XML Bible from a Word file using ETML.

The main publishing method for the library is lexical hypertextualization on highly accessible HTML pages, both on-line and on CD. Words (all or selected from a custom list) are linked to the concordance, concordance is itself linked to the text trough full references. Lists (frequency, alphabetical) and statistics are also available.

Other publishing formats (MS Reader, XML TEI, etc.) will be available within the Library. Dublin Core metadata are about to be activated.

Readers' behaviour has been monitored for three years. Interesting data have been collected and used to improve the Library's features. Non-linear reading via lexical hypertextualization is the main activity for most readers.

In the future of the IntraText project are lemmatization and IntraText Plus. Lemmatization will be improved to provide more effective search tools. IntraText Plus is scholarly-oriented interface for high-end browsing and searching on texts and collections, giving a tree representation of search process. It will allow users to customize the interface, dynamically define the textual units for Boolean operators, define subsets of the library as search areas, search by lemmata. Prototypes are available.

M. Agosti and C. Thanos (Eds.): ECDL 2002, LNCS 2458, p. 659, 2002.

The Meta Project – Automated Digitisation of Books and Journals

Günter Mühlberger and Birgit Stehno

University of Innsbruck, Innrain 52, 6020 Innsbruck
{Guenter.Muehlberger, Birgit.Stehno}@uibk.ac.at
http://meta-e.uibk.ac.at/

The digitisation of printed materials such as books and journals is still a complicated and expensive process that requires a patchwork of software programs for the single conversation steps. Many libraries therefore shrink from venturing digitisation activities. To improve and simplify digitisation by highly automating the conversion process is the prominent aim of METAe – a project co-funded by the European Commission within the 5th Framework, IST-Programme. The consortium of the METAe-project is made up of a number of leading libraries, university departments and digitisation companies from all over Europe, including the University of Innsbruck (Austria), i323 (Austria), CCS Compact Computer Systeme (Germany), Abbyy Europe/MitCom (Germany), the University of Florence (Italy), and the Scuola Normale Superiore of Pisa (Italy).

The automation of the digitisation process is be realized by the METADATA-engine, a comprehensive and extensible software-package which provides individually configurable functions for organising the whole workflow of the conversion process including scanning or batch import of image files, image pre-processing, etc.

The most innovative aspect of the METADATA-engine is a generic rules database which allows the automated zoning, extraction and labelling of structural elements such as headlines, paragraphs, caption lines, footnotes and page numbers. In addition to that, the engine understands the structural hierarchy of documents, i.e. the arrangement of logical elements into volumes, issues, contributions, chapters, sub-chapters, paragraphs, etc. The intelligent conversion layer comes complete with a graphical interface for correction, and with an OCR engine – also for old font types like the German "Fraktur" – in the background. The extracted and labelled data are assembled in an XML output file formed according to the METS guidelines. This standard allows libraries to integrate the converted material with a minimum of effort into their digital library web sites or document management systems and provides a good basis for further digital preservation strategies.

An initial prototype of the software-package is now available and first tests show encouraging results. During summer 2002 a pilot installation will be set up at the University Library Innsbruck. Further tests and evaluations will be carried out in autumn 2002 by the five European libraries making part of the project – the Bibliothèque Nationale de France, the National Library of Norway, the Biblioteca Statale A. Baldini, the University Library Graz and the Virtual Library Miguel de Cervantes.

M. Agosti and C. Thanos (Eds.): ECDL 2002, LNCS 2458, p. 660, 2002.

COVAX: A Contemporary Culture Virtual Archive in XML

Luciana Bordoni

ENEA/UDA/Advisor, Via Anguillarese 301, Roma
bordoni@casaccia.enea.it

Abstract. The objectives of the EU-funded COVAX project are:

- to build a web service for search and retrieval of contemporary European cultural documents from memory institutions.
- to make existing library, archive and museum document descriptions accessible over the Internet.
- to assist memory institutions to provide access to their collections, regardless of document type or collection size.
- to implement standards and achieve interoperability between retrieval systems operating in the cultural heritage area.

Partners in the project include technology developers and providers (public research organizations and private companies) and content owners (memory institutions). The content owners have collections of varying type and size, catalogued using a variety of library, museum and archiving systems. The project is assessing ways to improve access to these collections by converting samples of existing data into a limited set of common structured formats, each of which can be expressed using XML (eXtensible Markup Language).

According to the philosophy adopted by the project, future catalogs for libraries, museums and archives will be stored in a variety of XML formats instead of proprietary formats, or formats such as MARC which have not gained wide acceptance outside of their development context. Since much material is already described in machine-readable form, the project worked on developing tools to convert such descriptions to XML and to integrate them with native XML data in order to build user-friendly websites and data archives.

A comprehensive set of documents for the implementation of the prototype was selected. It contains a wide variety of documents, descriptions, formats and databases: standard and non-standard bibliographic records (including five different MARC formats), and four different structures for archive and museum finding aids and information in six different languages (Catalan, Italian, English, German, Spanish, Swedish).

COVAX partners have implemented two different database models: ad hoc XML databases, or existing non-XML repositories. In the latter case, information is retrieved from the original database and transformed into XML format before presenting it to users. To summarize, COVAX is not only incorporating XML as a basic standard but also integrating other standards, and adapting them to XML.

COVAX partners have implemented XML repositories using two software packages, Tamino from Software AG, a COVAX technical partner and TeXtML from IXIAsoft. Sites have been established in London, Rome, Salzburg, Graz and Madrid.

M. Agosti and C. Thanos (Eds.): ECDL 2002, LNCS 2458, pp. 661-662, 2002.

COVAX will test the benefits of XML to encode and process cultural heritage information, explore the feasibility of converting existing cultural heritage descriptions into XML encoded information, adapt cultural information systems to user requirements and contribute to the extension of standards for presentation and dissemination of cultural heritage.

Author Index

Lecture Notes in Computer Science

For information about Vols. 1–2380 please contact your bookseller or Springer-Verlag

Vol. 2382: A. Halevy, A. Gal (Eds.), Next Generation Information Technologies and Systems. Proceedings, 2002. VIII, 169 pages. 2002.

Vol. 2383: M.S. Lew, N. Sebe, J.P. Eakins (Eds.), Image and Video Retrieval. Proceedings, 2002. XII, 388 pages. 2002.

Vol. 2384: L. Batten, J. Seberry (Eds.), Information Security and Privacy. Proceedings, 2002. XII, 514 pages. 2002.

Vol. 2385: J. Calmet, B. Benhamou, O. Caprotti, L. Henocque, V. Sorge (Eds.), Artificial Intelligence, Automated Reasoning, and Symbolic Computation. Proceedings, 2002. XI, 343 pages. 2002. (Subseries LNAI).

Vol. 2386: E.A. Boiten, B. Möller (Eds.), Mathematics of Program Construction. Proceedings, 2002. X, 263 pages. 2002.

Vol. 2387: O.H. Ibarra, L. Zhang (Eds.), Computing and Combinatorics. Proceedings, 2002. XIII, 606 pages. 2002.

Vol. 2388: S.-W. Lee, A. Verri (Eds.), Pattern Recognition with Support Vector Machines. Proceedings, 2002. XI, 420 pages. 2002.

Vol. 2389: E. Ranchhod, N.J. Mamede (Eds.), Advances in Natural Language Processing. Proceedings, 2002. XII, 275 pages. 2002. (Subseries LNAI).

Vol. 2390: D. Blostein, Y.-B. Kwon (Eds.), Graphics Recognition. Proceedings, 2001. XI, 367 pages. 2002.

Vol. 2391: L.-H. Eriksson, P.A. Lindsay (Eds.), FME 2002: Formal Methods – Getting IT Right. Proceedings, 2002. XI, 625 pages. 2002.

Vol. 2392: A. Voronkov (Ed.), Automated Deduction – CADE-18. Proceedings, 2002. XII, 534 pages. 2002. (Subseries LNAI).

Vol. 2393: U. Priss, D. Corbett, G. Angelova (Eds.), Conceptual Structures: Integration and Interfaces. Proceedings, 2002. XI, 397 pages. 2002. (Subseries LNAI).

Vol. 2394: P. Perner (Ed.), Advances in Data Mining. VII, 109 pages. 2002. (Subseries LNAI).

Vol. 2395: G. Barthe, P. Dybjer, L. Pinto, J. Saraiva (Eds.), Applied Semantics. IX, 537 pages. 2002.

Vol. 2396: T. Caelli, A. Amin, R.P.W. Duin, M. Kamel, D. de Ridder (Eds.), Structural, Syntactic, and Statistical Pattern Recognition. Proceedings, 2002. XVI, 863 pages. 2002.

Vol. 2397: G. Grahne, G. Ghelli (Eds.), Database Programming Languages. Proceedings, 2001. X, 343 pages. 2002.

Vol. 2398: K. Miesenberger, J. Klaus, W. Zagler (Eds.), Computers Helping People with Special Needs. Proceedings, 2002. XXII, 794 pages. 2002.

Vol. 2399: H. Hermanns, R. Segala (Eds.), Process Algebra and Probabilistic Methods. Proceedings, 2002. X, 215 pages. 2002.

Vol. 2400: B. Monien, R. Feldmann (Eds.), Euro-Par 2002 – Parallel Processing. Proceedings, 2002. XXIX, 993 pages. 2002.

Vol. 2401: P.J. Stuckey (Ed.), Logic Programming. Proceedings, 2002. XI, 486 pages. 2002.

Vol. 2402: W. Chang (Ed.), Advanced Internet Services and Applications. Proceedings, 2002. XI, 307 pages. 2002.

Vol. 2403: Mark d'Inverno, M. Luck, M. Fisher, C. Preist (Eds.), Foundations and Applications of Multi-Agent Systems. Proceedings, 1996-2000. X, 261 pages. 2002. (Subseries LNAI).

Vol. 2404: E. Brinksma, K.G. Larsen (Eds.), Computer Aided Verification. Proceedings, 2002. XIII, 626 pages. 2002.

Vol. 2405: B. Eaglestone, S. North, A. Poulovassilis (Eds.), Advances in Databases. Proceedings, 2002. XII, 199 pages. 2002.

Vol. 2406: C. Peters, M. Braschler, J. Gonzalo, M. Kluck (Eds.), Evaluation of Cross-Language Information Retrieval Systems. Proceedings, 2001. X, 601 pages. 2002.

Vol. 2407: A.C. Kakas, F. Sadri (Eds.), Computational Logic: Logic Programming and Beyond. Part I. XII, 678 pages. 2002. (Subseries LNAI).

Vol. 2408: A.C. Kakas, F. Sadri (Eds.), Computational Logic: Logic Programming and Beyond. Part II. XII, 628 pages. 2002. (Subseries LNAI).

Vol. 2409: D.M. Mount, C. Stein (Eds.), Algorithm Engineering and Experiments. Proceedings, 2002. VIII, 207 pages. 2002.

Vol. 2410: V.A. Carreño, C.A. Muñoz, S. Tahar (Eds.), Theorem Proving in Higher Order Logics. Proceedings, 2002. X, 349 pages. 2002.

Vol. 2412: H. Yin, N. Allinson, R. Freeman, J. Keane, S. Hubbard (Eds.), Intelligent Data Engineering and Automated Learning – IDEAL 2002. Proceedings, 2002. XV, 597 pages. 2002.

Vol. 2413: K. Kuwabara, J. Lee (Eds.), Intelligent Agents and Multi-Agent Systems. Proceedings, 2002. X, 221 pages. 2002. (Subseries LNAI).

Vol. 2414: F. Mattern, M. Naghshineh (Eds.), Pervasive Computing. Proceedings, 2002. XI, 298 pages. 2002.

Vol. 2415: J.R. Dorronsoro (Ed.), Artificial Neural Networks – ICANN 2002. Proceedings, 2002. XXVIII, 1382 pages. 2002.

Vol. 2416: S. Craw, A. Preece (Eds.), Advances in Case-Based Reasoning. Proceedings, 2002. XII, 656 pages. 2002. (Subseries LNAI).

Vol. 2417: M. Ishizuka, A. Sattar (Eds.), PRICAI 2002: Trends in Artificial Intelligence. Proceedings, 2002. XX, 623 pages. 2002. (Subseries LNAI).

Vol. 2418: D. Wells, L. Williams (Eds.), Extreme Programming and Agile Methods – XP/Agile Universe 2002. Proceedings, 2002. XII, 292 pages. 2002.

Vol. 2419: X. Meng, J. Su, Y. Wang (Eds.), Advances in Web-Age Information Management. Proceedings, 2002. XV, 446 pages. 2002.

Vol. 2420: K. Diks, W. Rytter (Eds.), Mathematical Foundations of Computer Science 2002. Proceedings, 2002. XII, 652 pages. 2002.

Vol. 2421: L. Brim, P. Jančar, M. Křetínský, A. Kučera (Eds.), CONCUR 2002 – Concurrency Theory. Proceedings, 2002. XII, 611 pages. 2002.

Vol. 2422: H. Kirchner, Ch. Ringeissen (Eds.), Algebraic Methodology and Software Technology. Proceedings, 2002. XI, 503 pages. 2002.

Vol. 2423: D. Lopresti, J. Hu, R. Kashi (Eds.), Document Analysis Systems V. Proceedings, 2002. XIII, 570 pages. 2002.

Vol. 2425: Z. Bellahsène, D. Patel, C. Rolland (Eds.), Object-Oriented Information Systems. Proceedings, 2002. XIII, 550 pages. 2002.

Vol. 2426: J.-M. Bruel, Z. Bellahsène (Eds.), Advances in Object-Oriented Information Systems. Procedings, 2002. IX, 314 pages. 2002.

Vol. 2430: T. Elomaa, H. Mannila, H. Toivonen (Eds.), Machine Learning: ECML 2002. Proceedings, 2002. XIII, 532 pages. 2002. (Subseries LNAI).

Vol. 2431: T. Elomaa, H. Mannila, H. Toivonen (Eds.), Principles of Data Mining and Knowledge Discovery. Proceedings, 2002. XIV, 514 pages. 2002. (Subseries LNAI).

Vol. 2432: R. Bergmann, Experience Management. XXI, 393 pages. 2002. (Subseries LNAI).

Vol. 2434: S. Anderson, S. Bologna, M. Felici (Eds.), Computer Safety, Reliability and Security. Proceedings, 2002. XX, 347 pages. 2002.

Vol. 2435: Y. Manolopoulos, P. Návrat (Eds.), Advances in Databases and Information Systems. Proceedings, 2002. XIII, 415 pages. 2002.

Vol. 2436: J. Fong, C.T. Cheung, H.V. Leong, Q. Li (Eds.), Advances in Web-Based Learning. Proceedings, 2002. XIII, 434 pages. 2002.

Vol. 2438: M. Glesner, P. Zipf, M. Renovell (Eds.), Field-Programmable Logic and Applications. Proceedings, 2002. XXII, 1187 pages. 2002.

Vol. 2439: J.J. Merelo Guervós, P. Adamidis, H.-G. Beyer, J.-L. Fernández-Villacañas, H.-P. Schwefel (Eds.), Parallel Problem Solving from Nature – PPSN VII. Proceedings, 2002. XXII, 947 pages. 2002.

Vol. 2440: J.M. Haake, J.A. Pino (Eds.), Groupware: Design, Implementation and Use. Proceedings, 2002. XII, 285 pages. 2002.

Vol. 2442: M. Yung (Ed.), Advances in Cryptology – CRYPTO 2002. Proceedings, 2002. XIV, 627 pages. 2002.

Vol. 2443: D. Scott (Ed.), Artificial Intelligence: Methodology, Systems, and Applications. Proceedings, 2002. X, 279 pages. 2002. (Subseries LNAI).

Vol. 2444: A. Buchmann, F. Casati, L. Fiege, M.-C. Hsu, M.-C. Shan (Eds.), Technologies for E-Services. Proceedings, 2002. X, 171 pages. 2002.

Vol. 2445: C. Anagnostopoulou, M. Ferrand, A. Smaill (Eds.), Music and Artificial Intelligence. Proceedings, 2002. VIII, 207 pages. 2002. (Subseries LNAI).

Vol. 2446: M. Klusch, S. Ossowski, O. Shehory (Eds.), Cooperative Information Agents VI. Proceedings, 2002. XI, 321 pages. 2002. (Subseries LNAI).

Vol. 2447: D.J. Hand, N.M. Adams, R.J. Bolton (Eds.), Pattern Detection and Discovery. Proceedings, 2002. XII, 227 pages. 2002. (Subseries LNAI).

Vol. 2448: P. Sojka, I. Kopeček, K. Pala (Eds.), Text, Speech and Dialogue. Proceedings, 2002. XII, 481 pages. 2002. (Subseries LNAI).

Vol. 2449: L. Van Gool (Ed.), Pattern Recognotion. Proceedings, 2002. XVI, 628 pages. 2002.

Vol. 2451: B. Hochet, A.J. Acosta, M.J. Bellido (Eds.), Integrated Circuit Design. Proceedings, 2002. XVI, 496 pages. 2002.

Vol. 2452: R. Guigó, D. Gusfield (Eds.), Algorithms in Bioinformatics. Proceedings, 2002. X, 554 pages. 2002.

Vol. 2453: A. Hameurlain, R. Cicchetti, R. Traunmüller (Eds.), Database and Expert Systems Applications. Proceedings, 2002. XVIII, 951 pages. 2002.

Vol. 2454: Y. Kambayashi, W. Winiwarter, M. Arikawa (Eds.), Data Warehousing and Knowledge Discovery. Proceedings, 2002. XIII, 339 pages. 2002.

Vol. 2455: K. Bauknecht, A M. Tjoa, G. Quirchmayr (Eds.), E-Commerce and Web Technologies. Proceedings, 2002. XIV, 414 pages. 2002.

Vol. 2456: R. Traunmüller, K. Lenk (Eds.), Electronic Government. Proceedings, 2002. XIII, 486 pages. 2002.

Vol. 2458: M. Agosti, C. Thanos (Eds.), Research and Advanced Technology for Digital Libraries. Proceedings, 2002. XVI, 664 pages. 2002.

Vol. 2462: K. Jansen, S. Leonardi, V. Vazirani (Eds.), Approximation Algorithms for Combinatorial Optimization. Proceedings, 2002. VIII, 271 pages. 2002.

Vol. 2463: M. Dorigo, G. Di Caro, M. Sampels (Eds.), Ant Algorithms. Proceedings, 2002. XIII, 305 pages. 2002.

Vol. 2464: M. O'Neill, R.F.E. Sutcliffe, C. Ryan, M. Eaton, N. Griffith (Eds.), Artificial Intelligence and Cognitive Science. Proceedings, 2002. XI, 247 pages. 2002. (Subseries LNAI).

Vol. 2469: W. Damm, E.-R. Olderog (Eds.), Formal Techniques in Real-Time and Fault-Tolerant Systems. Proceedings, 2002. X, 455 pages. 2002.

Vol. 2470: P. Van Hentenryck (Ed.), Principles and Practice of Constraint Programming – CP 2002. Proceedings, 2002. XVI, 794 pages. 2002.

Vol. 2479: M. Jarke, J. Koehler, G. Lakemeyer (Eds.), KI 2002: Advances in Artificial Intelligence. Proceedings, 2002. XIII, 327 pages. (Subseries LNAI).

Vol. 2483: J.D.P. Rolim, S. Vadhan (Eds.), Randomization and Approximation Techniques in Computer Science. Proceedings, 2002. VIII, 275 pages. 2002.